Mobil
Travel Guide

Coastal Southeast

2006

Georgia

North Carolina

South Carolina

ExxonMobil
Travel Publications

Acknowledgements

We gratefully acknowledge the help of our representatives for their efficient and perceptive inspections of the lodging and dining establishments listed; the establishments' proprietors for their cooperation in showing their facilities and providing information about them; and the many users of previous editions who have taken the time to share their experiences. Mobil Travel Guide is also grateful to all the talented writers who contributed entries to this book.

www.mobiltravelguide.com

Front cover photo: Cape Hatteras Lighthouse, North Carolina

ISBN: 0-7627-3921-5

Manufactured in the United States of America.

10 9 8 7 6 5 4 3 2 1

Contents

MAP SYMBOLS

TRANSPORTATION

CONTROLLED ACCESS HIGHWAYS

Freeway
Tollway
Under Construction
Interchange and Exit Number

OTHER HIGHWAYS

Primary Highway
Secondary Highway
Divided Highway
Other Paved Road
Unpaved Road
Check conditions locally

HIGHWAY MARKERS

Interstate Route
U.S. Route
State or Provincial Route
County or Other Route
Trans-Canada Highway
Canadian Provincial Autoroute
Mexican Federal Route

OTHER SYMBOLS

Distances along Major Highways
Miles in U.S.; kilometers in Canada and Mexico
Tunnel; Pass
Auto Ferry; Passenger Ferry

RECREATION

National Park
National Forest; National Grassland
Other Large Park or Recreation Area
Small State Park
with and without Camping
Military Lands
Indian Reservation
Trail
Ski Area
Point of Interest

CITIES AND TOWNS

National Capital
State or Provincial Capital
Cities, Towns, and Populated Places
Type size indicates relative importance
Urban Area
State and province maps only
Large Incorporated Cities
City maps only

OTHER MAP FEATURES

Time Zone Boundary
+ Mt. Olympus 7,965 Mountain Peak; Elevation
in Feet
Perennial; Intermittent River

ATLANTA, GA & VICINITY

Distances in chart are in miles.
To convert miles to kilometers,
multiply the distance in miles
by 1.609.

Example:
New York, NY to Boston, MA
= 215 miles @ 346 kilometers
(215 x 1.609)

	ALBUQUERQUE, NM
ATLANTA, GA	1490
BALTIMORE, MD	1902
BILLINGS, MT	991
BIRMINGHAM, AL	1274
BISMARCK, ND	1333
BOISE, ID	966
BOSTON, MA	2240
BUFFALO, NY	1808
BURLINGTON, VT	2178
CHARLESTON, SC	1793
CHARLESTON, WV	1568
CHARLOTTE, NC	1649
CHEYENNE, WY	538
CHICAGO, IL	1352
CINCINNATI, OH	1619
CLEVELAND, OH	1619
DALLAS, TX	754
DENVER, CO	438
DES MOINES, IA	1091
DETROIT, MI	1608
EL PASO, TX	263
HOUSTON, TX	994
INDIANAPOLIS, IN	1298
JACKSON, MS	1157
KANSAS CITY, MO	894
LAS VEGAS, NV	576
LITTLE ROCK, AR	900
LOS ANGELES, CA	806
LOUISVILLE, KY	1320
MEMPHIS, TN	1033
MIAMI, FL	2155
MILWAUKEE, WI	1426
MINNEAPOLIS, MN	1339
MONTRÉAL, QC	2172
NASHVILLE, TN	1248
NEW ORLEANS, LA	1276
NEW YORK, NY	2015
OKLAHOMA CITY, OK	546
OMAHA, NE	973
ORLANDO, FL	1954
PHILADELPHIA, PA	1954
PHOENIX, AZ	466
PITTSBURGH, PA	1670
PORTLAND, ME	2338
PORTLAND, OR	1395
RAPID CITY, SD	841
RENO, NV	1876
RICHMOND, VA	1876
ST. LOUIS, MO	1051
SALT LAKE CITY, UT	624
SAN ANTONIO, TX	818
SAN DIEGO, CA	825
SAN FRANCISCO, CA	1111
SEATTLE, WA	1463
TAMPA, FL	1949
TORONTO, ON	1841
VANCOUVER, BC	1597
WASHINGTON, DC	1896
WICHITA, KS	707

(Full mileage matrix — numeric distance values between all listed city pairs — appears in the chart and is not fully transcribed here.)

Welcome

Dear Traveler,

Since its inception in 1958, Mobil Travel Guide has served as a trusted advisor to auto travelers in search of value in lodging, dining, and destinations. Now in its 48th year, the Mobil Travel Guide is the hallmark of our ExxonMobil family of travel publications, and we're proud to offer an array of products and services from our Mobil, Exxon, and Esso brands in North America to facilitate life on the road.

Whether you're looking for business or pleasure venues, our nationwide network of independent, professional evaluators offers their expertise on thousands of travel options, allowing you to plan a quick family getaway, a full-service business meeting, or an unforgettable Mobil Five-Star celebration.

Your feedback is important to us as we strive to improve our product offerings and better meet today's travel needs. Whether you travel once a week or once a year, please take the time to contact us at www.mobiltravelguide.com. We hope to hear from you soon.

Best wishes for safe and enjoyable travels.

Lee R. Raymond
Chairman and CEO
Exxon Mobil Corporation

A Word to Our Readers

Travelers are on the roads in great numbers these days. They're exploring the country on day trips, weekend getaways, business trips, and extended family vacations, visiting major cities and small towns along the way. Because time is precious and the travel industry is ever-changing, having accurate, reliable travel information at your fingertips is critical. Mobil Travel Guide has been providing invaluable insight to travelers for more than 45 years, and we are committed to continuing this service well into the future.

The Mobil Corporation (known as Exxon Mobil Corporation since a 1999 merger) began producing the Mobil Travel Guide books in 1958, following the introduction of the US interstate highway system in 1956. The first edition covered only five Southwestern states. Since then, our books have become the premier travel guides in North America, covering all 50 states and Canada.

Since its founding, Mobil Travel Guide has served as an advocate for travelers seeking knowledge about hotels, restaurants, and places to visit. Based on an objective process, we make recommendations to our customers that we believe will enhance the quality and value of their travel experiences. Our trusted Mobil One- to Five-Star rating system is the oldest and most respected lodging and restaurant inspection and rating program in North America. Most hoteliers, restaurateurs, and industry observers favorably regard the rigor of our inspection program and understand the prestige and benefits that come with receiving a Mobil Star rating.

The Mobil Travel Guide process of rating each establishment includes:

- Unannounced facility inspections
- Incognito service evaluations for Mobil Four-Star and Mobil Five-Star properties
- A review of unsolicited comments from the general public
- Senior management oversight

For each property, more than 450 attributes, including cleanliness, physical facilities, and employee attitude and courtesy, are measured and evaluated to produce a mathematically derived score, which is then blended with the other elements to form an overall score. These quantifiable scores allow comparative analysis among properties and form the basis that we use to assign our Mobil One- to Five-Star ratings.

This process focuses largely on guest expectations, guest experience, and consistency of service, not just physical facilities and amenities. It is fundamentally a relative rating system that rewards those properties that continually strive for and achieve excellence each year. Indeed, the very best properties are consistently raising the bar for those that wish to compete with them. These properties proactively respond to consumers' needs even in today's uncertain times.

Only facilities that meet Mobil Travel Guide's standards earn the privilege of being listed in the guide. Deteriorating, poorly managed establishments are deleted. A Mobil Travel Guide listing constitutes a positive quality recommendation; every listing is an accolade, a recognition of achievement. Our Mobil One- to Five-Star rating system highlights its level of service. Extensive in-house research is constantly underway to determine new additions to our lists.

- The Mobil Five-Star Award indicates that a property is one of the very best in the country and consistently provides gracious and courteous service, superlative quality in its facility, and a unique ambience. The lodgings and restaurants at the Mobil Five-Star level consistently and proactively respond to consumers' needs and continue their commitment to excellence, doing so with grace and perseverance.

- Also highly regarded is the Mobil Four-Star Award, which honors properties for outstanding achievement in overall facility and for providing very strong service levels in all areas. These award winners provide a distinctive experience for the ever-demanding and sophisticated consumer.

○ The Mobil Three-Star Award recognizes an excellent property that provides full services and amenities. This category ranges from exceptional hotels with limited services to elegant restaurants with a less-formal atmosphere.

○ A Mobil Two-Star property is a clean and comfortable establishment that has expanded amenities or a distinctive environment. A Mobil Two-Star property is an excellent place to stay or dine.

○ A Mobil One-Star property is limited in its amenities and services but focuses on providing a value experience while meeting travelers' expectations. The property can be expected to be clean, comfortable, and convenient.

Allow us to emphasize that we do not charge establishments for inclusion in our guides. We have no relationship with any of the businesses and attractions we list and act only as a consumer advocate. In essence, we do the investigative legwork so that you won't have to.

Keep in mind, too, that the hospitality business is ever-changing. Restaurants and lodgings—particularly small chains and stand-alone establishments—change management or even go out of business with surprising quickness. Although we make every effort to double-check information during our annual updates, we nevertheless recommend that you call ahead to make sure the place you've selected is still open and offers all the amenities you're looking for. We've provided phone numbers; when available, we also list fax numbers and Web site addresses.

We hope that your travels are enjoyable and relaxing and that our books help you get the most out of every trip you take. If any aspect of your accommodation, dining, or sightseeing experience motivates you to comment, please drop us a line. We depend a great deal on our readers' remarks, so you can be assured that we will read your comments and assimilate them into our research. General comments about our books are also welcome. You can write to us at Mobil Travel Guide, 7373 N Cicero Ave, Lincolnwood, IL 60712 or send an e-mail to info@mobiltravelguide.com.

Take your Mobil Travel Guide books along on every trip you take. We're confident that you'll be pleased with their convenience, ease of use, and breadth of dependable coverage.

Happy travels!

How to Use This Book

The Mobil Travel Guide Regional Travel Planners are designed for ease of use. Each state has its own chapter, beginning with a general introduction that provides a geographical and historical orientation to the state and gives basic statewide tourist information, from climate to calendar highlights to seatbelt laws. The remainder of each chapter is devoted to travel destinations within the state—mainly cities and towns, but also national parks and tourist areas—which, like the states, are arranged in alphabetical order.

The following sections explain the wealth of information you'll find about those travel destinations: information about the area, things to see and do there, and where to stay and eat.

Maps and Map Coordinates

At the front of this book in the full-color section, we have provided state maps as well as maps of selected larger cities to help you find your way around once you leave the highway. You'll find a key to the map symbols on the Contents page at the beginning of the map section.

Next to most cities and towns throughout the book, you'll find a set of map coordinates, such as C-2. These coordinates reference the maps at the front of this book and help you find the location you're looking for quickly and easily.

Destination Information

Because many travel destinations are close to other cities and towns where travelers might find additional attractions, accommodations, and restaurants, we've included cross-references to those cities and towns when it makes sense to do so. We also list addresses, phone numbers, and Web sites for travel information resources—usually the local chamber of commerce or office of tourism—as well as pertinent statistics and, in many cases, a brief introduction to the area.

Information about airports, ground transportation, and suburbs is included for large cities.

Driving Tours and Walking Tours

The driving tours that we include for many states are usually day trips that make for interesting side excursions, although they can be longer. They offer you a way to get off the beaten path and visit an area that travelers often overlook. These trips frequently cover areas of natural beauty or historical significance.

Each walking tour focuses on a particularly interesting area of a city or town. Again, these tours can provide a break from everyday tourist attractions. The tours often include places to stop for meals or snacks.

What to See and Do

Mobil Travel Guide offers information about nearly 20,000 museums, art galleries, amusement parks, historic sites, national and state parks, ski areas, and many other types of attractions. A white star on a black background ★ signals that the attraction is a must-see—one of the best in the area. Because municipal parks, public tennis courts, swimming pools, and small educational institutions are common to most towns, they generally are not mentioned.

Following an attraction's description, you'll find the months, days, and, in some cases, hours of operation; the address/directions, telephone number, and Web site (if there is one); and the admission price category. The following are the ranges we use for admission fees, based on one adult:

- ✪ **FREE**
- ✪ **$** = Up to $5
- ✪ **$$** = $5.01-$10
- ✪ **$$$** = $10.01-$15
- ✪ **$$$$** = Over $15

Special Events

Special events are either annual events that last only a short time, such as festivals and fairs, or longer, seasonal events such as horse racing, theater, and summer concerts. Our Special Events listings also include infrequently occurring occasions that mark certain dates or events, such as a centennial or other commemorative celebration.

Side Trips

We recognize that your travels don't always end where state lines fall, so we've included some side trips that fall outside the states covered in this book but that travelers frequently visit when they're in the region. Nearby national parks, major cities, and other prime tourist draws fall into this category. You'll find side trips for a particular state at the end of that state's section.

Listings

Lodgings, spas, and restaurants are usually listed under the city or town in which they're located. Make sure to check the related cities and towns that appear right beneath a city's heading for additional options, especially if you're traveling to a major metropolitan area that includes many suburbs. If a property is located in a town that doesn't have its own heading, the listing appears under the town nearest it, with the address and town given immediately after the establishment's name. In large cities, lodgings located within 5 miles of major commercial airports may be listed under a separate "Airport Area" heading that follows the city section.

LODGINGS

Travelers have different wants and needs when it comes to accommodations. To help you pinpoint properties that meet your particular needs, Mobil Travel Guide classifies each lodging by type according to the following characteristics.

Mobil Rated Lodgings

- **Limited-Service Hotel.** A limited-service hotel is traditionally a Mobil One-Star or Mobil Two-Star property. At a Mobil One-Star hotel, guests can expect to find a clean, comfortable property that commonly serves a complimentary continental breakfast. A Mobil Two-Star hotel is also clean and comfortable but has expanded amenities, such as a full-service restaurant, business

center, and fitness center. These services may have limited staffing and/or restricted hours of use.

- **Full-Service Hotel.** A full-service hotel traditionally enjoys a Mobil Three-Star, Mobil Four-Star, or Mobil Five-Star rating. Guests can expect these hotels to offer at least one full-service restaurant in addition to amenities such as valet parking, luggage assistance, 24-hour room service, concierge service, laundry and/or dry-cleaning services, and turndown service.

- **Full-Service Resort.** A resort is traditionally a full-service hotel that is geared toward recreation and represents a vacation and holiday destination. A resort's guest rooms are typically furnished to accommodate longer stays. The property may offer a full-service spa, golf, tennis, and fitness facilities or other leisure activities. Resorts are expected to offer a full-service restaurant and expanded amenities, such as luggage assistance, room service, meal plans, concierge service, and turndown service.

- **Full-Service Inn.** An inn is traditionally a Mobil Three-Star, Mobil Four-Star, or Mobil Five-Star property. Inns are similar to bed-and-breakfasts (see below) but offer a wider range of services, most significantly a full-service restaurant that serves at least breakfast and dinner.

Specialty Lodgings

Mobil Travel Guide recognizes the unique and individualized nature of many different types of lodging establishments, including bed-and-breakfasts, limited-service inns, and guest ranches. For that reason, we have chosen to place our stamp of approval on the properties that fall into these two categories in lieu of applying our traditional Mobil Star ratings.

- **B&B/Limited-Service Inn.** A bed-and-breakfast (B&B) or limited-service inn is traditionally an owner-occupied home or residence found in a residential area or vacation destination. It may be a structure of historic significance. Rooms are often individually decorated, but telephones, televisions, and private bathrooms may not be available in every room. A B&B typically serves only breakfast to its overnight guests, which is included in the room rate. Cocktails and refreshments may be served in the late afternoon or evening.

○ **Guest Ranch.** A guest ranch is traditionally a rustic, Western-themed property that specializes in stays of three or more days. Horseback riding is often a feature, with stables and trails found on the property. Facilities can range from clean, comfortable establishments to more luxurious facilities.

Mobil Star Rating Definitions for Lodgings

○ ★ ★ ★ ★ ★ : A Mobil Five-Star lodging provides consistently superlative service in an exceptionally distinctive luxury environment, with expanded services. Attention to detail is evident throughout the hotel, resort, or inn, from bed linens to staff uniforms.

○ ★ ★ ★ ★ : A Mobil Four-Star lodging provides a luxury experience with expanded amenities in a distinctive environment. Services may include, but are not limited to, automatic turndown service, 24-hour room service, and valet parking.

○ ★ ★ ★ : A Mobil Three-Star lodging is well appointed, with a full-service restaurant and expanded amenities, such as a fitness center, golf course, tennis courts, 24-hour room service, and optional turndown service.

○ ★ ★ : A Mobil Two-Star lodging is considered a clean, comfortable, and reliable establishment that has expanded amenities, such as a full-service restaurant on the premises.

○ ★ : A Mobil One-Star lodging is a limited-service hotel, motel, or inn that is considered a clean, comfortable, and reliable establishment.

Information Found in the Lodging Listings

Each lodging listing gives the name, address/location (when no street address is available), neighborhood and/or directions from downtown (in major cities), phone number(s), fax number, total number of guest rooms, and seasons open (if not year-round). Also included are details on business, luxury, recreational, and dining facilities at the property or nearby. A key to the symbols at the end of each listing can be found on the page following the "A Word to Our Readers" section.

For every property, we also provide pricing information. Because lodging rates change frequently, we list a pricing category rather than specific prices. The pricing categories break down as follows:

○ **$** = Up to $150

○ **$$** = $151-$250

○ **$$$** = $251-$350

○ **$$$$** = $351 and up

All prices quoted are in effect at the time of publication; however, prices cannot be guaranteed. In some locations, short-term price variations may exist because of special events, holidays, or seasonality. Certain resorts have complicated rate structures that vary with the time of year; always confirm rates when making your plans.

Because most lodgings offer the following features and services, information about them does not appear in the listings:

○ Year-round operation

○ Bathroom with tub and/or shower in each room

○ Cable television in each room

○ In-room telephones

○ Cots and cribs available

○ Daily maid service

○ Elevators

○ Major credit cards accepted

Although we recommend every lodging we list in this book, a few stand out—they offer noteworthy amenities or stand above the others in their category in terms of quality, value, or historical significance. To draw your attention to these special spots, we've included the magnifying glass icon to the left of the listing, as you see here.

SPAS

Mobil Travel Guide is pleased to announce its newest category: hotel and resort spas. Until now, hotel and resort spas have not been formally rated or inspected by any organization. Every spa selected for inclusion in this book underwent a rigorous inspection process similar to the one Mobil Travel Guide has been applying to lodgings and restaurants for more than four decades. After spending a year and a half researching more than 300 spas and performing exhaustive incognito inspections of more than 200 properties, we narrowed our list to the 48 best spas in the United States and Canada.

Mobil Travel Guide's spa ratings are based on objective evaluations of more than 450 attributes. Approximately half of these criteria assess basic expectations, such as staff courtesy, the technical proficiency and skill of the employees, and whether the facility is maintained properly and hygienically. Several standards address issues that impact a guest's physical comfort and convenience, as well as the staff's ability to impart a sense of personalized service and anticipate clients' needs. Additional criteria measure the spa's ability to create a completely calming ambience.

The Mobil Star ratings focus on much more than the facilities available at a spa and the treatments it offers. Each Mobil Star rating is a cumulative score achieved from multiple inspections that reflects the spa management's attention to detail and commitment to consumers' needs.

Mobil Star Rating Definitions for Spas

✪ ★ ★ ★ ★ ★ : A Mobil Five-Star spa provides consistently superlative service in an exceptionally distinctive luxury environment with extensive amenities. The staff at a Mobil Five-Star spa provides extraordinary service above and beyond the traditional spa experience, allowing guests to achieve the highest level of relaxation and pampering. A Mobil Five-Star spa offers an extensive array of treatments, often incorporating international themes and products. Attention to detail is evident throughout the spa, from arrival to departure.

✪ ★ ★ ★ ★ : A Mobil Four-Star spa provides a luxurious experience with expanded amenities in an elegant and serene environment. Throughout the spa facility, guests experience personalized service. Amenities might include, but are not limited to, single-sex relaxation rooms where guests wait for their treatments, plunge pools and whirlpools in both men's and women's locker rooms, and an array of treatments, including at a minimum a selection of massages, body therapies, facials, and a variety of salon services.

✪ ★ ★ ★ : A Mobil Three-Star spa is physically well appointed and has a full complement of staff to ensure that guests' needs are met. It has some expanded amenities, such as, but not limited to, a well-equipped fitness center, separate men's and women's locker rooms, a sauna or steam room, and a designated relaxation area. It also offers a menu of services that at a minimum includes massages, facial treatments, and at least one other type of body treatment, such as scrubs or wraps.

RESTAURANTS

All Mobil Star rated dining establishments listed in this book have a full kitchen and offer seating at tables; most offer table service.

Mobil Star Rating Definitions for Restaurants

✪ ★ ★ ★ ★ ★ : A Mobil Five-Star restaurant offers one of few flawless dining experiences in the country. These establishments consistently provide their guests with exceptional food, superlative service, elegant décor, and exquisite presentations of each detail surrounding a meal.

✪ ★ ★ ★ ★ : A Mobil Four-Star restaurant provides professional service, distinctive presentations, and wonderful food.

✪ ★ ★ ★ : A Mobil Three-Star restaurant has good food, warm and skillful service, and enjoyable décor.

✪ ★ ★ : A Mobil Two-Star restaurant serves fresh food in a clean setting with efficient service. Value is considered in this category, as is family friendliness.

✪ ★ : A Mobil One-Star restaurant provides a distinctive experience through culinary specialty, local flair, or individual atmosphere.

Information Found in the Restaurant Listings

Each restaurant listing gives the cuisine type, street address (or directions if no address is available), phone and fax numbers, Web site (if available), meals served, days of operation (if not open daily year-round), and pricing category. Information about appropriate attire is provided, although it's always a good idea to call ahead and ask if you're unsure; the meaning of "casual" or "business casual" varies widely in different parts of the country. We also indicate whether the restaurant has a bar, whether a children's menu is offered, and whether outdoor seating is available. If reservations are recommended, we note that fact in the listing. When valet parking is available, it is noted in the description. In many cases, self-parking is available at the restaurant or nearby.

Because menu prices can fluctuate, we list a pricing category rather than specific prices. The pricing categories are defined as follows, per diner, and assume that you order an appetizer or dessert, an entrée, and one drink:

- ✪ **$** = $15 and under

- ✪ **$$** = $16-$35

- ✪ **$$$** = $36-$85

- ✪ **$$$$** = $86 and up

Again, all prices quoted are in effect at the time of publication, but prices cannot be guaranteed.

Although we recommend every restaurant we list in this book, a few stand out—they offer noteworthy local specialties or stand above the others in their category in terms of quality, value, or experience. To draw your attention to these special spots, we've included the magnifying glass icon to the left of the listing, as you see here.

SPECIAL INFORMATION FOR TRAVELERS WITH DISABILITIES

The Mobil Travel Guide 🔲 symbol indicates that an establishment is not at least partially accessible to people with mobility problems. When the 🔲 symbol follows a listing, the establishment is not equipped with facilities to accommodate people using wheelchairs or crutches or otherwise needing easy access to doorways and rest rooms. Travelers with severe mobility problems or with hearing or visual impairments may or may not find the facilities they need. Always phone ahead to make sure that an establishment can meet your needs.

AMERICA'S BYWAYS™

Mobil Travel Guide is pleased to announce a new partnership with the National Scenic Byways Program. Under this program, the US Secretary of Transportation recognizes certain roads as National Scenic Byways or All-American Roads based on their archaeological, cultural, historic, natural, recreational, and scenic qualities. To be designated a National Scenic Byway, a road must possess at least one of these six intrinsic qualities. To receive an All-American Road designation, a road must possess multiple intrinsic qualities that are nationally significant and contain one-of-a-kind features that do not exist elsewhere. The road or highway also must be considered a destination unto itself.

America's Byways are a great way to explore the country. From the mighty Mississippi to the towering Rockies to the Historic National Road, these routes take you past America's most treasured scenery and enable you to get in touch with America's past, present, and future. Bringing together all the nationally designated Byways in the Coastal Southeast, this bonus section of the book is a handy reference whether you're planning to hop in the car tomorrow or you're simply looking for inspiration for future trips. Look for it at the end of the front section, before page 1.

Understanding the Symbols

What to See and Do

★ = One of the top attractions in the area

$ = Up to $5

$$ = $5.01 to $10

$$$ = $10.01 to $15

$$$$ = Over $15

Lodgings

$ = Up to $150

$$ = $151 to $250

$$$ = $251 to $350

$$$$ = Over $350

Restaurants

$ = Up to $15

$$ = $16 to $35

$$$ = $36 to $85

$$$$ = Over $85

Lodging Star Definitions

★★★★★ A Mobil Five-Star lodging establishment provides consistently superlative service in an exceptionally distinctive luxury environment with expanded services. Attention to detail is evident throughout the hotel/resort/inn from the bed linens to the staff uniforms.

★★★★ A Mobil Four-Star lodging establishment is a hotel/resort/inn that provides a luxury experience with expanded amenities in a distinctive environment. Services may include, but are not limited to, automatic turndown service, 24-hour room service, and valet parking.

★★★ A Mobil Three-Star lodging establishment is a hotel/resort/inn that is well appointed, with a full-service restaurant and expanded amenities, such as, but not limited to, a fitness center, golf course, tennis courts, 24-hour room service, and optional turndown service.

★★ A Mobil Two-Star lodging establishment is a hotel/resort/inn that is considered a clean, comfortable, and reliable establishment, but also has expanded amenities, such as a full-service restaurant on the premises.

★ A Mobil One-Star lodging establishment is a limited-service hotel or inn that is considered a clean, comfortable, and reliable establishment.

Restaurant Star Definitions

★★★★★ A Mobil Five-Star restaurant is one of few flawless dining experiences in the country. These restaurants consistently provide their guests with exceptional food, superlative service, elegant décor, and exquisite presentations of each detail surrounding the meal.

★★★★ A Mobil Four-Star restaurant provides professional service, distinctive presentations, and wonderful food.

★★★ A Mobil Three-Star restaurant has good food, warm and skillful service, and enjoyable décor.

★★ A Mobil Two-Star restaurant serves fresh food in a clean setting with efficient service. Value is considered in this category, as is family friendliness.

★ A Mobil One-Star restaurant provides a distinctive experience through culinary specialty, local flair, or individual atmosphere.

Symbols at End of Listings

🔏 Facilities for people with disabilities not available

🔺 Pets allowed

🎿 Ski in/ski out access

⛳ Golf on premises

🎾 Tennis court(s) on premises

🏊 Indoor or outdoor pool

🏋 Fitness room

✈ Major commercial airport within 5 miles

🚶 Business center

Making the Most of Your Trip

A few hardy souls might look back with fondness on a trip during which the car broke down, leaving them stranded for three days, or a vacation that cost twice what it was supposed to. For most travelers, though, the best trips are those that are safe, smooth, and within budget. To help you make your trip the best it can be, we've assembled a few tips and resources.

Saving Money

ON LODGING

Many hotels and motels offer discounts—for senior citizens, business travelers, families, you name it. It never hurts to ask—politely, that is. Sometimes, especially in the late afternoon, desk clerks are instructed to fill beds, and you might be offered a lower rate or a nicer room to entice you to stay. Simply ask the reservation agent for the best rate available. Also, make sure to try both the toll-free number and the local number. You may be able to get a lower rate from one than from the other.

Timing your trip right can cut your lodging costs as well. Look for bargains on stays over multiple nights, in the off-season, and on weekdays or weekends, depending on the location. Many hotels in major metropolitan areas, for example, have special weekend packages that offer leisure travelers considerable savings on rooms; they may include breakfast, cocktails, and/or dinner discounts.

Another way to save money is to choose accommodations that give you more than just a standard room. Rooms with kitchen facilities enable you to cook some meals yourself, reducing your restaurant costs. A suite might save money for two couples traveling together. Even hotel luxury levels can provide good value, as many include breakfast or cocktails in the price of a room.

State and city taxes, as well as special room taxes, can increase your room rate by as much as 25 percent per day. We are unable to include information about taxes in our listings, but we strongly urge you to ask about taxes when making reservations so that you understand the total cost of your lodgings before you book them.

Watch out for telephone-usage charges that hotels frequently impose on long-distance, credit-card, and other calls. Before phoning from your room, read the information given to you at check-in, and then be sure to review your bill carefully when checking out. You won't be expected to pay for charges that the hotel didn't spell out. Consider using your cell phone if you have one; or, if public telephones are available in the hotel lobby, your cost savings may outweigh the inconvenience of using them.

Here are some additional ways to save on lodgings:

- Stay in B&B accommodations. They're generally less expensive than standard hotel rooms, and the complimentary breakfast cuts down on food costs.

- If you're traveling with children, find lodgings at which kids stay free.

- When visiting a major city, stay just outside the city limits; these rooms are usually less expensive than those in downtown locations.

- Consider visiting national parks during the low season, when prices of lodgings near the parks drop by 25 percent or more.

- When calling a hotel, ask whether it is running any special promotions or if any discounts are available; many times reservationists are told not to volunteer these deals unless they're specifically asked about them.

- Check for hotel packages; some offer nightly rates that include a rental car or discounts on major attractions.

ON DINING

There are several ways to get a less expensive meal at an expensive restaurant. Early-bird dinners are popular in many parts of the country and offer considerable savings. If you're interested in visiting a Mobil Four- or Five-Star establishment, consider going at lunchtime. Although the prices are probably still relatively high at midday, they may be half of those at dinner, and you'll experience the same ambience, service, and cuisine.

ON ENTERTAINMENT

Although many national parks, monuments, seashores, historic sites, and recreation areas may be used free of charge, others charge an entrance fee and/or a usage fee for special services and facilities. If you plan to make several visits to national recreation areas, consider one of the following money-saving programs offered by the National Park Service:

○ **National Parks Pass.** This annual pass is good for entrance to any national park that charges an entrance fee. If the park charges a per-vehicle fee, the pass holder and any accompanying passengers in a private noncommercial vehicle may enter. If the park charges a per-person fee, the pass applies to the holder's spouse, children, and parents as well as the holder. It is valid for entrance fees only; it does not cover parking, camping, or other fees. You can purchase a National Parks Pass in person at any national park where an entrance fee is charged; by mail from the National Park Foundation, PO Box 34108, Washington, DC 20043-4108; by calling toll-free 888/467-2757; or at www.nationalparks .org. The cost is $50.

○ **Golden Eagle Sticker.** When affixed to a National Parks Pass, this hologram sticker, available to people who are between 17 and 61 years of age, extends coverage to sites managed by the US Fish and Wildlife Service, the US Forest Service, and the Bureau of Land Management. It is good until the National Parks Pass to which it is affixed expires and does not cover usage fees. You can purchase one at the National Park Service, the Fish and Wildlife Service, or the Bureau of Land Management fee stations. The cost is $15.

○ **Golden Age Passport.** Available to citizens and permanent US residents 62 and older, this passport is a lifetime entrance permit to fee-charging national recreation areas. The fee exemption extends to those accompanying the permit holder in a private noncommercial vehicle or, in the case of walk-in facilities, to the holder's spouse and children. The passport also entitles the holder to a 50 percent discount on federal usage fees charged in park areas, but not on concessions. Golden Age Passports must be obtained in person and are available at most National Park Service units that charge an entrance fee. The applicant must show proof of age, such as a driver's license or birth certificate (Medicare cards are not acceptable proof). The cost is $10.

○ **Golden Access Passport.** Issued to citizens and permanent US residents who are physically disabled or visually impaired, this passport is a free lifetime entrance permit to fee-charging national recreation areas. The fee exemption extends to those accompanying the permit holder in a private noncommercial vehicle or, in the case of walk-in facilities, to the holder's spouse and children. The passport also entitles the holder to a 50 percent discount on usage fees charged in park areas, but not on concessions. Golden Access Passports must be obtained in person and are available at most National Park Service units that charge an entrance fee. Proof of eligibility to receive federal benefits (under programs such as Disability Retirement, Compensation for Military Service-Connected Disability, and the Coal Mine Safety and Health Act) is required, or an affidavit must be signed attesting to eligibility.

A money-saving move in several large cities is to purchase a **CityPass.** If you plan to visit several museums and other major attractions, CityPass is a terrific option because it gets you into several sites for one substantially reduced price. Currently, CityPass is available in Boston, Chicago, Hollywood, New York, Philadelphia, San Francisco, Seattle, southern California (which includes Disneyland, SeaWorld, and the San Diego Zoo), and Toronto. For more information or to buy one, call toll-free 888/330-5008 or visit www. citypass.net. You can also buy a CityPass from any participating CityPass attraction.

Here are some additional ways to save on entertainment and shopping:

○ Check with your hotel's concierge for various coupons and special offers; they often have two-for-one tickets for area attractions and coupons for discounts at area stores and restaurants.

○ Purchase same-day concert or theater tickets for half-price through the local cheap-tickets outlet, such as TKTS in New York or Hot Tix in Chicago.

- Visit museums on their free or "by donation" days, when you can pay what you wish rather than a specific admission fee.

ON TRANSPORTATION

Transportation is a big part of any vacation budget. Here are some ways to reduce your costs:

- If you're renting a car, shop early over the Internet; you can book a car during the low season for less, even if you'll be using it in the high season.

- Rental car discounts are often available if you rent for one week or longer and reserve in advance.

- Get the best gas mileage out of your vehicle by making sure that it's properly tuned up and keeping your tires properly inflated.

- Travel at moderate speeds on the open road; higher speeds require more gasoline.

- Fill the tank before you return your rental car; rental companies charge to refill the tank and do so at prices of up to 50 percent more than at local gas stations.

- Make a checklist of travel essentials and purchase them before you leave; don't get stuck buying expensive sunscreen at your hotel or overpriced film at the airport.

FOR SENIOR CITIZENS

Always call ahead to ask if a discount is being offered, and be sure to carry proof of age. Additional information for mature travelers is available from the American Association of Retired Persons (AARP), 601 E St NW, Washington, DC 20049; phone 202/434-2277; www.aarp.org.

Tipping

Tips are expressions of appreciation for good service. However, you are never obligated to tip if you receive poor service.

IN HOTELS

- Door attendants usually get $1 for hailing a cab.

- Bell staff expect $2 per bag.

- Concierges are tipped according to the service they perform. Tipping is not mandatory when you've asked for suggestions on sightseeing or restaurants or for help in making dining reservations. However, a tip of $5 is appropriate when a concierge books you a table at a restaurant known to be difficult to get into. For obtaining theater or sporting event tickets, $5 to $10 is expected.

- Maids should be tipped $1 to $2 per day. Hand your tip directly to the maid, or leave it with a note saying that the money has been left expressly for the maid.

IN RESTAURANTS

Before tipping, carefully review your check for any gratuity or service charge that is already included in your bill. If you're in doubt, ask your server.

- Coffee shop and counter service waitstaff usually receive 15 percent of the bill, before sales tax.

- In full-service restaurants, tip 18 percent of the bill, before sales tax.

- In fine restaurants, where gratuities are shared among a larger staff, 18 to 20 percent is appropriate.

- In most cases, the maitre d' is tipped only if the service has been extraordinary, and only on the way out. At upscale properties in major metropolitan areas, $20 is the minimum.

- If there is a wine steward, tip $20 for exemplary service and beyond, or more if the wine was decanted or the bottle was very expensive.

- Tip $1 to $2 per coat at the coat check.

AT AIRPORTS

Curbside luggage handlers expect $1 per bag. Car-rental shuttle drivers who help with your luggage appreciate a $1 or $2 tip.

Staying Safe

The best way to deal with emergencies is to avoid them in the first place. However, unforeseen situations do happen, so you should be prepared for them.

IN YOUR CAR

Before you head out on a road trip, make sure that your car has been serviced and is in good working order. Change the oil, check the battery and belts, make sure that your windshield washer fluid is full and your tires are properly inflated (which can also improve your gas mileage). Other inspections recommended by the vehicle's manufacturer should also be made.

Next, be sure you have the tools and equipment needed to deal with a routine breakdown:

- Jack
- Spare tire
- Lug wrench
- Repair kit
- Emergency tools
- Jumper cables
- Spare fan belt
- Fuses
- Flares and/or reflectors
- Flashlight
- First-aid kit
- In winter, a windshield scraper and snow shovel

Many emergency supplies are sold in special packages that include the essentials you need to stay safe in the event of a breakdown.

Also bring all appropriate and up-to-date documentation—licenses, registration, and insurance cards—and know what your insurance covers. Bring an extra set of keys, too, just in case.

En route, always buckle up! In most states, wearing a seatbelt is required by law.

If your car does break down, do the following:

- Get out of traffic as soon as possible—pull well off the road.
- Raise the hood and turn on your emergency flashers or tie a white cloth to the roadside door handle or antenna.
- Stay in your car.
- Use flares or reflectors to keep your vehicle from being hit.

IN YOUR HOTEL

Chances are slim that you will encounter a hotel or motel fire, but you can protect yourself by doing the following:

- Once you've checked in, make sure that the smoke detector in your room is working properly.
- Find the property's fire safety instructions, usually posted on the inside of the room door.
- Locate the fire extinguishers and at least two fire exits.
- Never use an elevator in a fire.

For personal security, use the peephole in your room door and make sure that anyone claiming to be a hotel employee can show proper identification. Call the front desk if you feel threatened at any time.

PROTECTING AGAINST THEFT

To guard against theft wherever you go:

- Don't bring anything of more value than you need.
- If you do bring valuables, leave them at your hotel rather than in your car.
- If you bring something very expensive, lock it in a safe. Many hotels put one in each room; others will store your valuables in the hotel's safe.
- Don't carry more money than you need. Use traveler's checks and credit cards or visit cash machines to withdraw more cash when you run out.

For Travelers with Disabilities

To get the kind of service you need and have a right to expect, don't hesitate when making a reservation to question the management about the availability of accessible rooms, parking, entrances, restaurants, lounges, or any other facilities that are important to you, and confirm what is meant by "accessible."

The Mobil Travel Guide ▣ symbol indicates establishments that are not at least partially accessible to people with special mobility needs (people using wheelchairs or crutches or otherwise needing easy access to buildings and rooms). Further information about these criteria can be found in the earlier section "How to Use This Book."

A thorough listing of published material for travelers with disabilities is available from the Disability Bookshop, Twin Peaks Press, Box 129, Vancouver, WA 98666; phone 360/694-2462; disabilitybookshop.virtualave.net. Another reliable organization is the Society for Accessible Travel & Hospitality (SATH), 347 Fifth Ave, Suite 610, New York, NY 10016; phone 212/447-7284; www.sath.org.

Important Toll-Free Numbers and Online Information

Hotels

Adams Mark 800/444-2326
www.adamsmark.com

AmericInn 800/634-3444
www.americinn.com

AmeriHost Inn 800/434-5800
www.amerihostinn.com

Amerisuites 800/833-1516
www.amerisuites.com

Baymont Inns 877/229-6667
www.baymontinns.com

Best Inns & Suites 800/237-8466
www.bestinn.com

Best Value Inn 888/315-2378
www.bestvalueinn.com

Best Western 800/780-7234
www.bestwestern.com

Budget Host Inn 800/283-4678
www.budgethost.com

Candlewood Suites 888/226-3539
www.candlewoodsuites.com

Clarion Hotels 800/252-7466
www.choicehotels.com

Comfort Inns and Suites 800/252-7466
www.comfortinn.com

Country Hearth Inns 800/848-5767
www.countryhearth.com

Country Inns & Suites 800/456-4000
www.countryinns.com

Courtyard by Marriott 800/321-2211
www.courtyard.com

Cross Country Inns (KY and OH) 800/621-1429
www.crosscountryinns.com

Crowne Plaza Hotels and Resorts 800/227-6963
www.crowneplaza.com

Days Inn 800/544-8313
www.daysinn.com

Delta Hotels 800/268-1133
www.deltahotels.com

Destination Hotels & Resorts 800/434-7347
www.destinationhotels.com

Doubletree Hotels 800/222-8733
www.doubletree.com

Drury Inn 800/378-7946
www.druryinn.com

Econolodge 800/553-2666
www.econolodge.com

Embassy Suites 800/362-2779
www.embassysuites.com

ExelInns of America 800/367-3935
www.exelinns.com

Extended StayAmerica 800/398-7829
www.extendedstayhotels.com

Fairfield Inn by Marriott 800/228-2800
www.fairfieldinn.com

Fairmont Hotels 800/441-1414
www.fairmont.com

Four Points by Sheraton 888/625-5144
www.fourpoints.com

Four Seasons 800/819-5053
www.fourseasons.com

Hampton Inn 800/426-7866
www.hamptoninn.com

Hard Rock Hotels, Resorts, and Casinos 800/473-7625
www.hardrock.com

Harrah's Entertainment 800/427-7247
www.harrahs.com

Hawthorn Suites 800/527-1133
www.hawthorn.com

Hilton Hotels and Resorts (US) 800/774-1500
www.hilton.com

Holiday Inn Express 800/465-4329
www.hiexpress.com

Holiday Inn Hotels and Resorts 800/465-4329
www.holiday-inn.com

Homestead Studio Suites 888/782-9473
www.homesteadhotels.com

Homewood Suites 800/225-5466
www.homewoodsuites.com

Howard Johnson 800/406-1411
www.hojo.com

Hyatt 800/633-7313
www.hyatt.com

Inns of America 800/826-0778
www.innsofamerica.com

InterContinental 888/567-8725
www.intercontinental.com

Joie de Vivre 800/738-7477
www.jdvhospitality.com

Kimpton Hotels 888/546-7866
www.kimptongroup.com

Knights Inn 800/843-5644
www.knightsinn.com

La Quinta 800/531-5900
www.laquinta.com

Le Meridien 800/543-4300
www.lemeridien.com

Leading Hotels of the World 800/223-6800
www.lhw.com

Loews Hotels 800/235-6397
www.loewshotels.com

MainStay Suites 800/660-6246
www.mainstaysuites.com

Mandarin Oriental 800/526-6566
www.mandarin-oriental.com

Marriott Hotels, Resorts, and Suites 800/228-9290
www.marriott.com

Microtel Inns & Suites 800/771-7171
www.microtelinn.com

Millennium & Copthorne Hotels 866/866-8086
www.millenniumhotels.com

Motel 6 . . . . 800/466-8356
www.motel6.com

Omni Hotels 800/843-6664
www.omnihotels.com

Pan Pacific Hotels and Resorts 800/327-8585
www.panpac.com

Park Inn & Park Plaza 888/201-1801
www.parkinn.com

The Peninsula Group . . . . Contact individual hotel
www.peninsula.com

Preferred Hotels & Resorts Worldwide 800/323-7500
www.preferredhotels.com

Quality Inn 800/228-5151
www.qualityinn.com

Radisson Hotels 800/333-3333
www.radisson.com

Raffles International Hotels and Resorts . . . 800/637-9477
www.raffles.com

Ramada Plazas, Limiteds, and Inns 800/272-6232
www.ramada.com

Red Lion Inns 800/733-5466
www.redlion.com

Red Roof Inns 800/733-7663
www.redroof.com

Regent International 800/545-4000
www.regenthotels.com

Relais & Chateaux 800/735-2478
www.relaischateaux.com

Renaissance Hotels 888/236-2427
www.renaissancehotels.com

Residence Inn 800/331-3131
www.residenceinn.com

Ritz-Carlton 800/241-3333
www.ritzcarlton.com

RockResorts 888/367-7625
www.rockresorts.com

Rodeway Inn 800/228-2000
www.rodeway.com

Rosewood Hotels & Resorts 888/767-3966
www.rosewoodhotels.com

Select Inn 800/641-1000
www.selectinn.com

Sheraton 888/625-5144
www.sheraton.com

Shilo Inns 800/222-2244
www.shiloinns.com

Shoney's Inn 800/552-4667
www.shoneysinn.com

Signature/Jameson Inns 800/822-5252
www.jamesoninns.com

Sleep Inn 877/424-6423
www.sleepinn.com

Small Luxury Hotels of the World 800/525-4800
www.slh.com

Sofitel 800/763-4835
www.sofitel.com

SpringHill Suites 888/236-2427
www.springhillsuites.com

St. Regis Luxury Collection 888/625-5144
www.stregis.com

Staybridge Suites 800/238-8000
www.staybridge.com

Summerfield Suites by Wyndham 800/833-4353
www.summerfieldsuites.com

Summit International 800/457-4000
www.summithotels.com

Super 8 Motels 800/800-8000
www.super8.com

The Sutton Place Hotels 866/378-8866
www.suttonplace.com

Swissôtel 800/637-9477
www.swissotel.com

TownePlace Suites 888/236-2427
www.towneplace.com

Travelodge 800/578-7878
www.travelodge.com

Vagabond Inns 800/522-1555
www.vagabondinns.com

W Hotels 888/625-5144
www.whotels.com

Wellesley Inn and Suites 800/444-8888
www.wellesleyinnandsuites.com

WestCoast Hotels 800/325-4000
www.westcoasthotels.com

Westin Hotels & Resorts 800/937-8461
www.westin.com

Wingate Inns. 800/228-1000
www.wingateinns.com
Woodfin Suite Hotels. 800/966-3346
www.woodfinsuitehotels.com
WorldHotels 800/223-5652
www.worldhotels.com
Wyndham Hotels & Resorts 800/996-3426
www.wyndham.com

Airlines

Air Canada. 888/247-2262
www.aircanada.ca
AirTran. 800/247-8726
www.airtran.com
Alaska Airlines 800/252-7522
www.alaskaair.com
American Airlines. 800/433-7300
www.aa.com
America West. 800/235-9292
www.americawest.com
ATA. 800/435-9282
www.ata.com
Continental Airlines. 800/523-3273
www.continental.com
Delta Air Lines 800/221-1212
www.delta.com
Frontier Airlines 800/432-1359
www.frontierairlines.com
Hawaiian Airways 800/367-5320
www.hawaiianair.com
Jet Blue Airlines 800/538-2583
www.jetblue.com
Midwest Express 800/452-2022
www.midwestexpress.com

Northwest Airlines. 800/225-2525
www.nwa.com
Southwest Airlines. 800/435-9792
www.southwest.com
Spirit Airlines 800/772-7117
www.spiritair.com
United Airlines 800/241-6522
www.united.com
US Airways 800/428-4322
www.usairways.com

Car Rentals

Advantage. 800/777-5500
www.arac.com
Alamo. 800/327-9633
www.goalamo.com
Avis 800/831-2847
www.avis.com
Budget 800/527-0700
www.budget.com
Dollar 800/800-4000
www.dollarcar.com
Enterprise 800/325-8007
www.enterprise.com
Hertz 800/654-3131
www.hertz.com
National. 800/227-7368
www.nationalcar.com
Payless 800/729-5377
www.paylesscarrental.com
Rent-A-Wreck.com 800/535-1391
www.rent-a-wreck.com
Thrifty 800/847-4389
www.thrifty.com

Meet The Stars

Mobil Travel Guide 2006 *Five-Star* Award Winners

CALIFORNIA
Lodgings
The Beverly Hills Hotel, *Beverly Hills*
Chateau du Sureau, *Oakhurst*
Four Seasons Hotel San Francisco,
  San Francisco
Hotel Bel-Air, *Los Angeles*
The Peninsula Beverly Hills, *Beverly Hills*
Raffles L'Ermitage Beverly Hills, *Beverly Hills*
The Ritz-Carlton, San Francisco, *San Francisco*

Restaurants
Bastide, *Los Angeles*
The Dining Room, *San Francisco*
The French Laundry, *Yountville*
Gary Danko, *San Francisco*

COLORADO
Lodgings
The Broadmoor, *Colorado Springs*
The Little Nell, *Aspen*

CONNECTICUT
Lodging
The Mayflower Inn, *Washington*

DISTRICT OF COLUMBIA
Lodging
Four Seasons Hotel Washington, DC
  Washington

FLORIDA
Lodgings
Four Seasons Resort Palm Beach, *Palm Beach*
The Ritz-Carlton Naples, *Naples*
The Ritz-Carlton, Palm Beach, *Manalapan*

GEORGIA
Lodgings
Four Seasons Hotel Atlanta, *Atlanta*
The Lodge at Sea Island Golf Club,
  St. Simons Island

Restaurants
The Dining Room, *Atlanta*
Seeger's, *Atlanta*

HAWAII
Lodging
Four Seasons Resort Maui at Wailea, *Wailea,
  Maui*

ILLINOIS
Lodgings
Four Seasons Hotel Chicago, *Chicago*
The Peninsula Chicago, *Chicago*
The Ritz-Carlton, A Four Seasons Hotel, *Chicago*

Restaurant
Charlie Trotter's, *Chicago*

MAINE
Restaurant
The White Barn Inn, *Kennebunkport*

MASSACHUSETTS
Lodgings
Blantyre, *Lenox*
Four Seasons Hotel Boston, *Boston*

NEW YORK
Lodgings
Four Seasons, Hotel New York, *New York*
The Point, *Saranac Lake*
The Ritz-Carlton New York, Central Park,
  New York
The St. Regis, *New York*

Restaurants
Alain Ducasse, *New York*
Jean Georges, *New York*
Masa, *New York*
per se, *New York*

NORTH CAROLINA
Lodging
The Fearrington House Country Inn, *Pittsboro*

PENNSYLVANIA
Restaurant
Le Bec-Fin, *Philadelphia*

SOUTH CAROLINA
Lodging
Woodlands Resort & Inn, *Summerville*

Restaurant
Dining Room at the Woodlands, *Summerville*

TEXAS
Lodging
The Mansion on Turtle Creek, *Dallas*

VERMONT
Lodging
Twin Farms, *Barnard*

VIRGINIA
Lodgings
The Inn at Little Washington, *Washington*
The Jefferson Hotel, *Richmond*

Restaurant
The Inn at Little Washington, *Washington*

Mobil Travel Guide has been rating establishments with its Mobil One- to Five-Star system since 1958. Each establishment awarded the Mobil Five-Star rating is one of the best in the country. Detailed information on each award winner can be found in the corresponding regional edition listed on the back cover of this book.

Four- and Five-Star Establishments in Coastal Southeast

Georgia

★ ★ ★ ★ ★ Lodgings
Four Seasons Hotel Atlanta, *Atlanta*
The Lodge at Sea Island Golf Club, *St. Simons Island*

★ ★ ★ ★ Lodgings
The Ritz-Carlton, Buckhead, *Atlanta*
The Ritz-Carlton Lodge, Reynolds Plantation,
   Greensboro

★ ★ ★ ★ Spa
The Ritz-Carlton Spa, The Ritz-Carlton Lodge,
Reynolds Plantation,
   Greensboro

★ ★ ★ ★ ★ Restaurants
The Dining Room, *Atlanta*
Seeger's, *Atlanta*

★ ★ ★ ★ Restaurants
Bacchanalia, *Atlanta*
Park 75 at the Four Seasons, *Atlanta*

North Carolina

★ ★ ★ ★ ★ Lodging
The Fearrington House Country Inn, *Pittsboro*

★ ★ ★ ★ Lodgings
The Carolina Hotel, *Pinehurst*
Inn on Biltmore Estate, *Asheville*
Richmond Hill Inn, *Asheville*

★ ★ ★ ★ Spa
The Spa at Pinehurst, The Carolina at Pinehurst,
   Pinehurst

★ ★ ★ ★ Restaurants
Carolina CrossRoads, *Chapel Hill*
The Fearrington House Restaurant, *Pittsboro*

South Carolina

★ ★ ★ ★ ★ Lodging
Woodlands Resort & Inn, *Summerville*

★ ★ ★ ★ Lodgings
Charleston Place, *Charleston*
The Inn at Palmetto Bluff, *Hilton Head Island*
The Sanctuary at Kiawah Island, *Kiawah Island*

★ ★ ★ ★ ★ Restaurant
The Dining Room at the Woodlands, *Summerville*

★ ★ ★ ★ Restaurants
Charleston Grill, *Charleston*
Peninsula Grill, *Charleston*

America's Byways™ are a distinctive collection of American roads, their stories, and treasured places. They are roads to the heart and soul of America. In this section, you'll find the nationally designated Byway in North Carolina.

Blue Ridge Parkway

NORTH CAROLINA

The Blue Ridge Parkway is a scenic drive that crests the southern Appalachian Mountains and takes you through a myriad of natural, cultural, and recreational places. Many people drive the Blue Ridge Parkway for its natural botanical qualities. The shrubs and flowers that blossom throughout the spring and summer are a defining feature of the parkway, and in the fall, leaves burst into colors of red, yellow, and orange. And where there is lush vegetation, there is also abundant wildlife. The diverse history and culture of the southern Appalachians are described at many overlooks and facilities along the parkway.

QUICK FACTS

Length: 241 miles.

Time to Allow: 2 to 3 days.

Best Time to Drive: June through October. Visitor Centers and recreational facilities are open from May through October. High season includes July 4 and Labor Day weekends and the month of October (fall foliage).

Byway Travel Information: Byway local Web site: www.nps.gov/blri.

Special Considerations: Avoid traveling the parkway during periods of fog, snow, and ice. Bring a lightweight jacket for cool nights from spring through fall. Service stations are limited, but access points along the parkway allow for refueling in nearby communities. Also, watch for deer-crossing signs.

Restrictions: The parkway is open year-round, unless weather conditions (snow, ice, and windstorms) cause portions of the roadway to be closed. Speed is limited to 45 mph on the parkway. Swimming is not allowed in parkway lakes and ponds.

Bicycle/Pedestrian Facilities: The parkway was designed as a scenic leisure road for motorists; when bicycling, be prepared for significant distances between developed areas and services that vary by season.

The Byway Story

The Blue Ridge Parkway tells archaeological, cultural, historical, natural, recreational, and scenic stories that make it a unique and treasured Byway.

ARCHAEOLOGICAL

The story of the Blue Ridge Parkway is told partially through remnants of early Native Americans, mountain men, miners, and road builders of the Great Depression. Man and the area surrounding the Blue Ridge Parkway have been closely intertwined, and the artifacts and old buildings they leave behind provide information on the inhabitants that have lived in this area.

You find many signs of Native American culture and influence along the Blue Ridge Parkway, including those of the Cherokee. They have left behind artifacts and changes in the landscape as evidence of their lives here. Many of the fields still visible at the base of the mountains date back centuries to ancient Native American agricultural methods of burning and deadening the trees and underbrush to provide needed grazing and crop land. Mountain and river names along the parkway also reflect the Native American influence. In North Carolina, the parkway enters the Qualla Reservation at milepost 457.7 and features an informational display on the reservation at the Lickstone Parking Overlook (milepost 458.9). Evidence of European settlements and homesteads are also found all along the parkway.

CULTURAL

Along the Blue Ridge Parkway, evidence of the local cultures are found in communities, museums, and shops. The cultures of the past are in abandoned cabins and structures left behind. Old family cemeteries, springhouses, and other indications of Appalachian habitation are scattered up and down the motor road, just waiting to be discovered. Mountain handicrafts are one of the most popular attractions along the Byway, and traditional crafts and music still thrive in the Blue Ridge Mountains along with more contemporary styles. Along the parkway in North Carolina are several places to view and purchase locally made items. The Folk Art Center in Asheville offers the most impressive collection of crafts on the Byway.

HISTORICAL

The parkway was conceived as a link between the Shenandoah National Park in Virginia and the Great Smoky Mountains National Park in North Carolina and Tennessee, and that vision came to fruition in 1935. The idea to build the parkway resulted from a combination of many factors, the primary one being the need to create jobs for trained engineers, architects, and landscape designers who had been left unemployed by the Great Depression, and for the thousands of mountain families already verging on poverty. In addition, recent openings of two popular eastern parks, the Great Smoky Mountains National Park and the Shenandoah National Park, were already attracting tourists to the naturally beautiful but financially poor area. The increasing availability of the automobile brought about a new generation of motoring vacations.

World War II halted construction, but road-building resumed soon after the war ended. By 1968, the only task left was the completion of a 7-mile stretch around North Carolina's Grandfather Mountain. In order to preserve the fragile environment on the steep slopes of the mountain, the Linn Cove Viaduct, a 1,200-foot suspended section of the parkway, was designed and built. Considered an engineering marvel, it represents one of the most successful fusions of road and landscape on the parkway. The Blue Ridge Parkway was officially dedicated on September 11, 1987, 52 years after the ground-breaking.

NATURAL

The creation of the Blue Ridge Mountains, perhaps hundreds of millions of years in the geologic past,

was both violent and dramatic. Today, you can witness the flip-side to the mountain-building story—the mountain's gradual destruction. The slow, steady forces of wind, water, and chemical decomposition have reduced the Blue Ridge from Sierra-like proportions to the low profile of the world's oldest mountain range.

Diversity is the key word when understanding the ecology of the Appalachian Mountains. Park biologists have identified 1,250 kinds of vascular plants, 25 of which are rare or endangered. Four rare or endangered animals have also been identified on parkway lands. The reasons for this wide diversity are numerous. Elevation is a key factor, with parkway lands as low as 650 feet above sea level and as high as 6,047 feet above sea level. The parkway is also oriented on a north-south axis, with its two ends far apart. Combining these two factors, the parkway contains habitat as diverse as one may find when traveling from Georgia to Newfoundland, Canada.

Beginning at the parkway's lowest elevations and climbing up to its highest, you notice numerous transitions among a variety of forest types. Interspersed among these various forest types are small, unique habitats, like mountain bogs and heath balds. Many species of animals find their niche in these small pockets of habitat. Bog turtles and Gray's lily thrive in mountain bogs. Sheltered, wet coves are excellent for finding a variety of salamanders, some of which are unique to the southern Appalachians. A hemlock cove is an excellent place to find populations of red squirrel. Black-capped chickadees replace the Carolina chickadees as you climb up toward the spruce-fir forest. And of course, the Blue Ridge Mountains are also home to mountain lions, eagles, and even bears. For birding enthusiasts, the parkway offers a never-ending supply of beautiful birds, from the American bittern to the whippoorwill.

RECREATIONAL

The very nature of the Blue Ridge Parkway allows for outstanding recreational opportunities. You may choose to camp along the parkway in order to prolong your stay and make the most of all the area has to offer. Trails around the parkway let you hike into the inner regions of the Appalachian Mountains. If you're a bicyclist, you can enjoy the mountainous terrain and scenery. Anglers find a haven in the many streams and rivers that flow near the Byway. Nearby state parks and national forests have developed swimming areas perfect for a refreshing dip amid the forest-covered mountains. Rushing rivers create a playground for rafters and kayakers.

Festivals and events are often occurring in local towns and communities, from sports to outdoor adventure to drama to folk art.

SCENIC

The parkway combines awesome natural beauty with the pioneer history of gristmills, weathered cabins, and split-rail fences to create the country's most popular national park. It encompasses a world of mountain forests, wildlife, and wildflowers thousands of feet above a patchwork of villages, fields, and farms.

Share the Blue Ridge magic by stopping at overlooks and campgrounds, picnic spots and mountain trails. Leave yourself time to explore the historic, hospitable towns along the way, where you'll find food and lodging, fuel and supplies, and lots of fun and good times. From the first explosion of colorful wildflowers in the spring to the refreshing coolness of summer to the fall extravaganza in red and gold to the stark beauty of snow-covered peaks in winter, each season provides you with a completely different Blue Ridge Parkway.

Wildlife is also a delight to see along the parkway. When the sun is high, groundhogs sit erect and chipmunks and squirrels chitter and chatter. At night, skunks, bobcats, foxes, opossums, and raccoons may be seen along the roadsides. Whitetail deer and black bears are present but seldom seen. Look for them in the early morning or evening. More than 100 bird species can be seen during the spring migration season as well. Because of the seasonal changes for both wildlife and vegetation, the Blue Ridge Parkway offers new sights year-round.

Highlights

The North Carolina section of the Blue Ridge Parkway begins at the state line at milepost 216.9 near Cumberland Knob. The following points of interest are the primary sights along the Byway. A few sites located just off the Byway, which are highly popular, are listed as well. Most services are available from May through October.

○ **Milepost 217.5—Cumberland Knob,** at 2,885 feet, is a delightful spot to walk through fields and woodlands.

○ **Milepost 238.5—Brinegar Cabin** was built by Martin Brinegar about 1880 and lived in until the 1930s. The original cabin is still standing.

○ **Milepost 258.6—Northwest Trading Post** is sponsored by the Northwest Development Association to keep alive the old crafts within North Carolina's 11 northwestern counties.

○ **Milepost 272—E. B. Jeffress Park** has a self-guiding trail to the Cascades and another trail to the old cabin and church.

- **Milepost 292 to 295—Moses H. Cone Memorial Park** has 25 miles of carriage roads, ideal for hiking and horseback riding. Flat Top Manor houses the Parkway Craft Center.

- **Milepost 304.4—Linn Cove Viaduct,** a highlight of the parkway and a design and engineering marvel, skirts the side of Grandfather Mountain.

- **Milepost 316.3—Linville Falls** roars through a dramatic, rugged gorge. Take trails to overlooks.

- **Milepost 331—Museum of North Carolina Minerals** has an interpretive display of the state's mineral wealth.

- **Milepost 355.4—Mount Mitchell State Park,** reached via Highway 128, has a picnic area, a lookout tower, and the highest point east of the Mississippi River.

- **Milepost 382—Folk Art Center** offers sales and exhibits of traditional and contemporary crafts of the Appalachian Region. Interpretive programs, gallery, and library.

- **Biltmore Estate** is located 4 miles from the Highway 25-North exit near Asheville. George Vanderbilt's impressive 250-room mansion and grounds landscaped by the celebrated landscape architect Frederick Law Olmstead, designer of Central Park.

- **Milepost 408.6—Mount Pisgah** was once part of the Biltmore Estate. The estate became home of the first US forestry school and is the nucleus of the Pisgah National Forest.

- **Milepost 422.4—Devil's Courthouse** is a rugged exposed mountaintop rich in Cherokee legends. A walk to the bare rock summit yields a spectacular view of the Pisgah National Forest.

- **Milepost 431—Richland Balsam's** self-guiding trail takes you through a remnant spruce-fire forest. It's the highest point on the parkway at 6,047 feet.

- **Milepost 451.2—Waterrock Knob** provides a panorama of the Great Smokies, as well as a trail, exhibits, and comfort station.

Georgia

Georgia, beloved for its antebellum gentility and then devastated by General William Tecumseh Sherman's march to the sea, is now a vibrant, busy state typifying the economic growth of the New South. Founded with philanthropic and military aims, the only colony where rum and slavery were forbidden, the state nevertheless had the dubious honor of accepting the last shipment of slaves to this country. It boasts Savannah, one of the oldest planned cities in the United States, and Atlanta, one of the newest of the South's great cities, rebuilt atop Civil War ashes.

The Georgia Colony was founded by James Oglethorpe on behalf of a private group of English trustees and was named for King George II of England. Georgia's barrier islands not only sheltered the fledgling colony, they provided a bulwark on the Spanish Main for English forts to oppose Spanish Florida and helped end the centuries-old struggle for domination among Spanish, French, and English along the South Atlantic Coast.

Today a year-round vacation mecca, the Golden Isles were at times Native American hunting lands, vast sea island plantations, fishing communities isolated after the Civil War, and rich men's private preserves. The Colony trustees brought English artisans to found strong colonies at Savannah, Brunswick, and Darien, where Scottish Highlanders introduced golf to the New World. The Cherokee made early peace with Oglethorpe and remained within the state to set up the Republic of the Cherokee Nation a century later. Gradually, however, all Native American lands of both Creek and Cherokee were ceded; the Cherokees were banished and their lands, including the capital, distributed by lottery.

Population: 8,186,453

Area: 59,441 square miles

Elevation: 0-4,784 feet

Peak: Brasstown Bald Mountain (between Towns and Union counties)

Entered Union: Fourth of original 13 states (January 1, 1788)

Capital: Atlanta

Motto: Wisdom, Justice, and Moderation

Flower: Cherokee Rose

Bird: Brown Thrasher

Tree: Live Oak

Fair: October in Macon

Time Zone: Eastern

Web Site: www.georgia.org

Fun Fact: Georgia is the nation's largest producer of peanuts, pecans, and peaches.

From their settlements at Savannah, Brunswick, and the coastal islands, Georgia colonists followed the rivers (many of them flowing north) to found inland ports such as Augusta. Colonial boundaries were extended to the Mississippi River by the state of Georgia, but the unfortunate manipulations of land speculators in the legislature deeded all of Mississippi, Alabama, Tennessee, and more for sale as the Yazoo Tract for 1 1/2 cents an acre. Though repudiated by a subsequent legislature and declared unconstitutional by the Supreme Court, the lands were gone forever, and Georgia no longer extended from the Mississippi to the sea. It is, however, still the largest state east of the Mississippi.

Georgia's lot in the Civil War was a harsh one from the time Sherman opened his campaign in Georgia on May 4, 1864, until he achieved the Union objective of splitting the South from the Mississippi to the sea. Reconstruction ushered in the reign of carpetbaggers and a long, slow recovery.

Calendar Highlights

FEBRUARY

Georgia Heritage Festival *(Savannah). Contact the Historic Savannah Foundation, phone 912/233-7787.* Walking tours, open house at historic sites, crafts show, waterfront festival, parade, concerts, Georgia Day.

MARCH

Augusta Invitational Rowing Regatta *(Augusta). Augusta Riverfront Marina.*

Auto racing *(Atlanta). Atlanta Motor Speedway. Phone 770/946-4211.* NASCAR Winston Cup, Busch Grand National, IMSA, and ARCA events.

Cherry Blossom Festival *(Macon). Phone 770/860-4188.* Historic tours, concerts, fireworks, hot air balloons, sporting events, and parade.

APRIL

Masters Golf Tournament *(Augusta). Augusta National Golf Course. Phone 706/667-6700.*

Spring Tour of Homes *(Athens). Contact Fire Hall #2, phone 706/353-1801 or 706/353-1820.* Held by Athens-Clarke Heritage Foundation.

MAY

Seafood Festival *(Savannah). Contact the Savannah Waterfront Association, phone 912/234-0295.* Waterfront. Restaurants offer samples; entertainment, arts and crafts.

SEPTEMBER

Georgia State Fair *(Macon). Central City Park. Phone 478/746-7184.* Grandstand shows, midway, exhibit buildings.

US 10K Classic and Family Sports Festival *(Marietta). Phone 770/432-0100.*

DECEMBER

Christmas in Savannah *(Savannah). Phone toll-free 800/444-2427.* Monthlong celebration includes tours of houses, historical presentations, parades, music, caroling, and cultural events.

Georgia boasts many firsts: the *Savannah,* the first steamship to cross the ocean (1819); America's first nuclear-powered merchant ship, the *Savannah* (1959); the first big American gold strike (1828); the cotton gin, invented by Eli Whitney (1793); and the first use of ether as an anesthetic (1842), by Georgia doctor Crawford Long.

Georgia produces peanuts, pecans, cotton, peaches, wood pulp, and paper products. Near Atlanta, a number of national manufacturing and commercial concerns contribute to a diversified economy. Georgia marble is prized the world over.

Georgia boasts many wonders, from its Blue Ridge vacation lands in the north—where Brasstown Bald Mountain rises 4,784 feet—to the deep "trembling earth" of the ancient and mysterious Okefenokee Swamp bordering Florida. Stone Mountain, a giant hunk of rock that rises from the plain near Atlanta,

is the world's largest granite exposure. The coastal Golden Isles, set off by the mysterious Marshes of Glynn, support moss-festooned oaks that grow down to the white sand beaches. Visitors still pan for gold in the country's oldest gold mining town, Dahlonega, and find semiprecious stones in the Blue Ridge.

Historical attractions are everywhere, from the world's largest brick fort near Savannah to the late President Franklin D. Roosevelt's "Little White House" at Warm Springs. There is the infamous Confederate prison at Andersonville and the still-lavish splendor of the cottage colony of 60 millionaires of the Jekyll Island Club, now a state-owned resort. The battlefield marking Sherman's campaign before Atlanta and the giant ceremonial mounds of indigenous Native Americans are equally important national shrines.

Tourism is one of Georgia's primary industries. The state's visitor information centers, which are staffed year-round, offer brochures and computerized information to travelers on major highways.

When to Go/Climate

Short winters and mild temperatures are the rule in Georgia. Summers are hot and humid in the southern part of the state; winters can be cold and can include snowfall in the northern regions.

AVERAGE HIGH/LOW TEMPERATURES (° F)

Atlanta

Jan 50/32	**May** 80/59	**Sept** 82/64
Feb 55/35	**June** 86/66	**Oct** 73/52
Mar 64/43	**July** 88/70	**Nov** 63/43
Apr 73/50	**Aug** 87/69	**Dec** 54/35

Savannah

Jan 60/38	**May** 84/63	**Sept** 85/68
Feb 62/41	**June** 89/69	**Oct** 78/57
Mar 70/48	**July** 91/72	**Nov** 70/48
Apr 78/55	**Aug** 90/72	**Dec** 62/41

Parks and Recreation

Water-related activities, hiking, riding, various other sports, picnicking, and visitor centers, as well as camping and rental cottages, are available in many of Georgia's state parks. Most parks welcome campers, and there are many comfort stations with hot showers, electric outlets, and laundry. All parks have trailer dump stations, with the exception of Providence Canyon. Camping is limited to two weeks at any one park. Reservations may be made up to 11 months in advance. Parks are open year-round from 7 am-10 pm.

Georgia park vacationers may enjoy cottages at several state parks. These provide complete house-keeping facilities—kitchens with electric ranges and refrigerators, living rooms, one- to three-bedrooms (linens provided), porches, outdoor grills, and picnic tables. They are air-conditioned in summer and heated in winter.

Cottages are available at Amicalola Falls, Black Rock Mountain, Cloudland Canyon, Crooked River, Elijah Clark, Florence Marina, Fort Mountain, Franklin D. Roosevelt, Georgia Veterans Memorial, Hard Labor Creek, Hart, Indian Springs, John Tanner, Little Ocmulgee, Magnolia Springs, Mistletoe, Red Top Mountain, Seminole, Stephen C. Foster, Tugaloo, Unicoi, Vogel, and Will-A-Way (in Fort Yargo) parks. Phone toll-free 800/864-7275. Cottage reservations can be made up to 11 months in advance; there is a two-day minimum stay at cottages.

Pets are allowed in state parks only if kept on a leash not longer than 6 feet and accompanied by owner at all times. No pets are allowed in cottages, site buildings, or swimming areas. Fees are subject to change.

Detailed information on state parks may be obtained from the Department of Natural Resources, State Parks and Historic Sites, 205 Butler St SE, Suite 1352, Atlanta 30334; phone 404/656-2770.

FISHING AND HUNTING

Georgia's range of fresh and saltwater fishing rivals any other state in variety. There are 26 major reservoirs totaling more than 400,000 acres, and 10 major river systems traverse the state, with thousands of miles of clear, cold-water trout streams and smaller, warm-water streams. Approximately 60,000 small lakes and ponds add to the freshwater total. Some 200 species of freshwater fish are found, 40 of which are considered desirable by game anglers, including largemouth, shoal, striped bass, crappie, and channel catfish. Mountain streams in northern Georgia are a natural source of trout. Fishing in black-water swamp areas in southern Georgia is just as famous for lunker bass and big bream. Coastal waters are good for mackerel, redfish, speckled trout, and giant tarpon; no license is required.

A state fishing license is required for all freshwater fishing; nonresident: season, $24; seven-day permit, $7; one-day permit, $3.50; trout stamp (required to fish in trout waters or to keep trout caught): season, $13. Fees subject to change. For further information on saltwater fishing, contact the Department of Natural Resources, Coastal Resources Division, 1

Conservation Way, Brunswick 31520-8600; phone 912/264-7218. For further information on freshwater fishing, contact the Department of Natural Resources, Wildlife Resources Division, 2123 Hwy 278SE, Social Circle, 30279; phone 770/918-6418.

There is hunting from the Blue Ridge in northern Georgia to the piney woods of the south. Nonresident: season, $59; seven-day, $25; one-day, $5.50; big game (deer, wild turkey), $118. Preserve license, $12; bow hunting permit, $25. Wildlife Management Area stamp, $73. Waterfowl stamp, $5.50 (federal stamp also required). Fees are subject to change. For seasons, bag limits, and other details contact the Department of Natural Resources, Wildlife Resources Division, 2111 Hwy 278SE, Social Circle 30279; phone 770/918-6416.

Driving Information

Safety belts are mandatory for all persons in the front seat of a vehicle and all minors anywhere in a vehicle; ages 3 and 4 may use a regulation safety belt; age 2 and under must use an approved safety seat. For further information, phone 404/657-9300.

GEORGIA'S BLUE RIDGE FOOTHILLS

Less than two hours north of downtown Atlanta, the Blue Ridge Mountains offer a scenic landscape for leisurely driving and sightseeing. The deeper mountains are largely protected within the Chattahoochee National Forest, while the foothills are full of quaint country towns. A 200-mile-loop trip takes drivers to some of the more celebrated destinations, with a wide range of attractions for children and families. From Atlanta, head north on Highway 400 (a toll road) and drive about 50 miles toward Dahlonega; Highway 19 leads you the rest of the way into town.

Named from the Cherokee word *talonega* (yellow), Dahlonega (dah-LON-ah-ga) was the site of the nation's first gold rush in the 1830s. In 1838, the federal government built a branch of the US Mint in Dahlonega, stamping the town's name on $6 million worth of gold coins before the operation was shut down at the onset of the Civil War. The story is told at the Dahlonega Gold Museum (phone 706/864-2257), housed within the old courthouse building in the center of the town square. This is the oldest building in northern Georgia. In the surrounding square, you'll find a colorful assortment of shops, restaurants, cafés, and an old-fashioned general store that sells penny candy. Stop by the visitor center for local maps and guides, including information about gold mine tours right outside of town. Before taking a tour, try your hand at the small (but fruitful!) gold-panning station beside the visitor center. On the south side of the square, the landmark Smith House (84 S Chestatee St; phone 706/864-2348 or toll-free 800/852-9577), which reportedly was built above a gold mine, has been serving all-you-can-eat family-style Southern meals for more than 80 years; they also offer overnight lodging.

From Dahlonega, follow Highway 19 north to Highway 129 east for about 25 miles to Cleveland. Cleveland found its way onto the national map in the 1970s as the birthplace of Cabbage Patch dolls, which still "grow" here in a "hospital" outside of town. Tours offer visitors the chance to witness the dolls being pulled from a cabbage patch twinkling with Christmas lights.

For more family fun, proceed to Helen by heading north on Highway 75. Helen was just a modest mountain town until local promoters were inspired to remake it as a Bavarian village. The villagers took to wearing dirndls and lederhosen, serving bratwurst and Heineken, observing Oktoberfest, and filling the air with accordion music. A museum in the castle on Main Street (phone 706/878-3140) tells the full story. A scenic stretch of the Chattahoochee River cuts through the busy tourist town, and local outfitters shuttle people upstream for leisurely float trips back down.

Return south on Highway 75 and turn east at the old Indian mound onto Highway 17, which rolls through a quieter stretch of the scenic foothills to Clarkesville. A small village here holds antique shops and a couple of cafés. Clarkesville is only 2 miles from the Highway 441/365 expressway that leads south back to Atlanta. Continuing south, the highway merges into I-985 around Gainesville for a speedy return to the city.
(Approximately 200 miles)

INTERSTATE HIGHWAY SYSTEM

The following alphabetical listing of Georgia towns in this book shows that these cities are within 10 miles of the indicated interstate highways. Check a highway map for the nearest exit.

Highway Number	Cities/Towns within 10 Miles
Interstate 16	Dublin, Macon, Savannah.
Interstate 20	Atlanta, Augusta, Carrollton, Madison.
Interstate 75	Adel, Atlanta, Calhoun, Cartersville, Cordele, Dalton, Forsyth, Macon, Marietta, Perry, Tifton, Valdosta.
Interstate 85	Atlanta, Buford, Commerce, La Grange, Norcross.
Interstate 95	Brunswick, Darien, Jekyll Island, Savannah, St. Simons Island.

Additional Visitor Information

For visitor information, including brochures and other materials, contact the Department of Industry, Trade, and Tourism, PO Box 1776, Atlanta 30301-1776; phone 404/656-3590 or toll-free 800/847-4842. Visitor centers are located in Augusta, Columbus, Kingsland, Lavonia, Plains, Ringgold, Savannah, Sylvania, Tallapoosa, Valdosta, and West Point. Information is available 8:30 am-5:30 pm.

Adel (E-3)

See also Tifton, Valdosta

Population 5,307
Elevation 240 ft
Area Code 229
Zip 31620
Information Adel-Cook County Chamber of Commerce, 100 S Hutchinson Ave, PO Box 461; phone 229/896-2281
Web Site www.adelga.net

What to See and Do

Reed Bingham State Park. *542 Reed Bingham Rd, Adel (31620). 6 miles W off Hwy 37. Phone 229/896-3551. www.gastateparks.org/info/reedbing/.* Less than 6 miles from busy I-75, this park includes a 375-acre lake that provides opportunities for fishing (bass, crappie, catfish, and bream), boating (three ramps), and water-skiing. You'll also find the Coastal Plain and Gopher Tortoise nature trails and a huge population of black and turkey vultures, which come here to roost in winter. Best viewing is in the morning or late afternoon. Picnicking, camping, playground. For more information, contact the Park Office, Rte 2, Box 394B-1. (Daily 7 am-10 pm)

Limited-Service Hotels

★ ★ **DAYS INN.** *1200 W 4th St, Adel (30121). Phone 229/896-4574; toll-free 800/329-7466; fax 229/896-4575. www.daysinn.com.* 78 rooms, 2 story. Pets accepted, some restrictions; fee. Check-out 11 am. Restaurant. Outdoor pool. **$**
🐾🏊

★ **SUPER 8.** *1103 W 4th St; I-75 exit 10, Adel (31620). Phone 229/896-2244; toll-free 800/446-4656; fax 229/896-2245. www.super8.com.* 69 rooms, 2 story. Pets accepted, some restrictions; fee. Check-out noon. Outdoor pool. **$**
🐾🏊

Albany (E-2)

See also Americus, Cordele

Founded 1836
Population 76,939
Elevation 208 ft
Area Code 229
Information Convention and Visitors Bureau, 225 W Broad Ave, 31701; phone 229/434-8700
Web Site www.albanyga.com

Albany lies in a semitropical setting of oaks and pines located in the Plantation Trace region of the state. Colonel Nelson Tift, a Connecticut Yankee, led a party up the Flint River from Apalachicola, Florida, and constructed the first log buildings in Albany. Settlers followed when the Native Americans were moved to western lands. Paper-shell pecans grown in surrounding Dougherty County have made this the "pecan capital of the world." Surrounded by numerous plantations, the area is also well known for quail hunting.

What to See and Do

Albany Museum of Art. *311 Meadowlark Dr, Albany (31707). Phone 229/439-8400. www.albanymuseum.com.* This small museum holds an average of 15 permanent and changing exhibits of works by national and regional artists. The collection of sub-Saharan African art is particularly strong. (Tues-Fri 10 am-5 pm, Sat-Sun noon-5 pm; closed holidays) **$**

Lake Chehaw. *Lee County on Philema Rd, Albany. 2 miles NE off Hwy 91.* At the confluence of the Kinchafoonee and Muckalee creeks and the Flint River. Water-skiing, fishing, and boating.

The Parks at Chehaw. *105 Chehaw Park Rd, Albany (31701). 2 1/2 miles NE on Hwy 91. Phone 229/430-5275. www.parksatchehaw.org.* This 800-acre park invites visitors to commune with nature. The creeks, streams, and cypress swamps are home to all sorts of wildlife, including deer, beavers, tortoises, alligators, and all sorts of birds, and the nature trails throughout the park allow visitors to see the animals up close. An old-style locomotive takes visitors on a 20-minute train ride through a restored area. Also here are a BMX track, a children's play park, and a wild animal park designed by famed naturalist Jim Fowler. Housing 40 animals in natural habitats, the park has the only cheetah population in Georgia. Kids love the petting zoo; there's also an amphitheater where special programs and demonstrations are held. Tent and RV camping (dump station), picnicking. (Daily 9 am-5 pm; closed Jan 1, Thanksgiving, Dec 25) **$$**

Thronateeska Heritage Center. *100 W Roosevelt Ave, Albany (31701). Phone 229/432-6955. www.heritagecenter.org.* This complex of former railroad buildings houses exhibits as well as a hands-on Science Discovery Center for children. Also here is the Wetherbee Planetarium. (Thurs-Sat noon-4 pm; closed holidays) **$$**

Special Event

Fall on the Flint Festival. Entertainment, parade, exhibits, athletic contests. Last weekend in Sept.

Limited-Service Hotels

★ **COMFORT SUITES.** *1400 Dawson Rd, Albany (31707). Phone 229/888-3939; toll-free 800/228-5150; fax 229/435-4431. www.choicehotels.com.* 62 rooms, 2 story. Complimentary continental breakfast. Check-out noon. Airport transportation available. **$**

★ **HAMPTON INN.** *806 N Westover Blvd, Albany (31707). Phone 912/883-3300; toll-free 800/426-7866; fax 912/435-4092. www.hamptoninn.com.* 82 rooms, 2 story. Complimentary continental breakfast. Check-out noon. Outdoor pool. **$**

★ ★ **QUALITY INN.** *1500 Dawson Rd, Albany (31706). Phone 229/435-7721; toll-free 888/462-7721; fax 229/439-9386. www.merryacres.com.* 108 rooms. Complimentary continental breakfast. Check-out noon. Restaurant, bar. Fitness room. Outdoor pool, children's pool. **$**

★ **RAMADA INN.** *2505 N Slappey Blvd, Albany (31701). Phone 229/883-3211; toll-free 800/272-6232; fax 229/439-2806. www.ramada-albany.com.* 158 rooms, 2 story. Pets accepted; fee. Check-out noon. Restaurant, bar. Outdoor pool, children's pool. Airport transportation available. **$**

★ **REGENCY INN.** *911 E Oglethorpe Expy, Albany (31705). Phone 229/883-1650; fax 229/883-1163.* 151 rooms, 4 story. Complimentary full breakfast. Check-out noon. Outdoor pool. Airport transportation available. **$**

Alpharetta (B-2)

Population 34,854
Web Site alpharetta.ga.us

Full-Service Hotel

★ ★ ★ **MARRIOTT ALPHARETTA.** *5750 Windward Pkwy, Alpharetta (30005). Phone 770/754-9600; toll-free 800/228-9290; fax 770/754-9629. www.marriott.com.* 318 rooms, 8 story. Check-in 3 pm, check-out noon. High-speed Internet access, wireless Internet access. Restaurant, bar. Fitness room. Indoor pool, outdoor pool, whirlpool. Airport transportation available. Business center. **$$**

Restaurants

★ **CAMEAUX LOUISIANA.** *9925 Haynes Bridge Rd, Alpharetta (30022). Phone 770/442-2524; fax 770/442-8644. www.cameaux.com.* Cajun menu. Lunch, dinner. Closed Jan 1, Dec 25. Bar. Children's menu. **$$**

★ ★ **RAY'S KILLER CREEK CHOP HOUSE.**
1700 Mansell Rd, Alpharetta (30004). Phone 770/649-0064; fax 770/649-1391. www.raysrestaurants.com.
Seafood, steak menu. Dinner. Closed holidays. Bar. Children's menu. Valet parking. Outdoor seating. **$$$**

★ ★ **VINNY'S ON WINDWARD.** *5355 Windward Pkwy, Alpharetta (30004). Phone 770/772-4644; fax 770/772-4244. www.knowwheretogogh.com.* Italian menu. Lunch, dinner. Bar. Children's menu. Casual attire. Reservations recommended. Valet parking. Outdoor seating. **$$**

Americus (D-2)

See also Albany, Andersonville, Cordele, Lumpkin

Founded 1832
Population 17,013
Area Code 229
Zip 31709
Information Americus-Sumter County Chamber of Commerce, Tourism Division, 400 Lamar St, Box 724; phone 229/924-2646 or toll-free 888/278-6837
Web Site www.americus-online.com

Americus is at the center of an area once known as the "granary of the Creek nations," so called because Native Americans favored this area for the cultivation of maize. The town was named, it is said, either for Americus Vespucius or for the settlers themselves, who were referred to as "merry cusses" because of their happy-go-lucky ways. The town flourished in the 1890s. Many Victorian and Gothic Revival buildings remain from that period.

Today, peanuts, corn, cotton, small grain, and pecans are grown, and bauxite and kaolin are mined in the area. Americus is also a manufacturing center, producing lumber commodities, metal lighting equipment, heating products, and textiles. The town's livestock sales are second in volume in the state. Plains, nine miles west via Hwy 280, is the hometown of the 39th president, Jimmy Carter.

What to See and Do

Americus Historic Driving Tour. *Phone 229/928-6059 (Tourism Council).* Tour features 38 houses of various architectural styles, including Victorian, Greek Revival, and Classical Revival.

Georgia Southwestern College. *800 Wheatley St, Americus (31709). 2 miles E of junction Hwys 19, 280.* (1906) (2,600 students) Campus (187 acres) with lake. Also here is

> **Carter Display.** *800 Wheatley St, Americus (31709).* Focusing on former President Jimmy Carter and First Lady Rosalynn Carter; photographs, memorabilia; located in James Earl Carter Library. (Daily; closed school breaks, holidays) **FREE**

⭐ **Jimmy Carter National Historic Site.** *300 N Bond St, Plains (31780). 10 miles W on Hwy 280. Phone 229/824-4104. www.nps.gov/jica.* The visitor center is located in Plains High School, where Jimmy and Rosalynn Carter attended grammar and high school. The school now functions as a museum, with an orientation film, campaign memorabilia, and exhibits on Carter's life and career. Also here is the Plains Depot Museum, the oldest building in town (1888), which served as Carter's campaign headquarters in 1976. (Daily 9 am-5 pm; closed Jan 1, Thanksgiving, Dec 25) **FREE**

Limited-Service Hotel

★ ★ **WINDSOR HOTEL.** *125 W Lamar St, Americus (31709). Phone 229/924-1555; toll-free 888/297-9567. www.windsor-americus.com.* Built right before the turn of the century, this wonderful country escape has beautiful architecture and design and is located near local antique shops and shopping. Guests will appreciate the rich history that is evident here. Period-style rooms with 12-foot ceilings and ceiling fans. 53 rooms, 3 story. Check-out noon. Restaurant, bar. **$**

Specialty Lodging

The following lodging establishment is approved by Mobil Travel Guide, but due to its unique and individualized nature has not been given a traditional Mobil Star rating. Included in this listing you may find bed-and-breakfasts, limited-service inns, guest ranches, and other unique hotel properties.

1906 PATHWAY INN BED & BREAKFAST. *501 S Lee St, Americus (31709). Phone 229/928-2078; toll-free 800/889-1466. www.1906pathwayinn.com.* For a small-town getaway, this English colonial bed-and-breakfast offers guests relaxation, Southern style. The Old South charm here is warm and inviting. 5 rooms, 2 story. Pets accepted, some restrictions; fee. Complimentary full breakfast. Check-in 4 pm, check-out 11 am. **$**

Restaurant

★ ★ ★ **GRAND DINING ROOM.** *125 W Lamar St, Americus (31709). Phone 229/924-1555. www.windsor-americus.com.* Located in the Windsor Hotel (see), this restaurant offers traditional Southern favorites along with cuisine from different regions of the country. Charming Victorian settings complete the elegant and intimate dining experience. American menu. Breakfast, lunch, dinner. Bar. **$$**

Andersonville (D-2)

See also Americus, Cordele, Perry

Population 331
Elevation 390 ft
Area Code 229
Zip 31711
Web Site www.maconcountyga.org

What to See and Do

Andersonville National Historic Site. *Hwy 49 N, Andersonville. Phone 229/924-0343. www.nps.gov/ande.* Camp Sumter, a Confederate military prison, was built in early 1864 on a 26-acre tract by soldiers and slaves requisitioned from nearby plantations. The lofty pines that grew in the sandy soil were cut and used to form a stockade. Built to accommodate 10,000 men, the prison at one time held as many as 33,000. Overcrowding, inadequate food, insufficient medicines, and a breakdown of the prisoner exchange system resulted in a high death rate. The site is now a memorial to all prisoners of war throughout history. Included on the grounds are escape tunnels and wells dug by prisoners, Confederate earthworks, three reconstructed sections of stockade wall, and state monuments. (Daily 8 am-5 pm) **FREE** Here are

Andersonville National Cemetery. *US Hwy 49 N, Andersonville. 1/2 miles N of prison site.* Graves of more than 17,000 Union soldiers and veterans of US military are in striking contrast to the landscaped grounds. The initial interments were Union soldiers who died in the prison camp. Dedicated as a national cemetery on August 17, 1865.

National Prisoner of War Museum. *Andersonville National Historic Site, Hwy 49 N, Andersonville. www.nps.gov/ande.* Exhibits, interpretive programs, and interactive videos depict the role of military prisoners in the nation's history. (Daily 8:30 am-5 pm; closed Jan 1, Thanksgiving, Dec 25) **FREE**

Providence Spring. The spring, which bubbled up from the ground after a heavy rain, was said to be in answer to the prisoners' prayers during the summer of 1864.

Civil War Village of Andersonville. *114 Church St, Andersonville. Phone 229/924-2558.* Restored village from the days of the Civil War. Welcome center, pioneer farm, museum (fee), antique shops. (Daily; closed Dec 25) **$$**

Special Event

Andersonville Historic Fair. *114 Church St, Andersonville. Phone 229/924-2558.* Civil War reenactments, old time craftsmen, antique dealers; RV campsites. Contact Andersonville Historic Fair, PO Box 6; phone 229/924-2558. Memorial Day weekend and the first weekend in Oct.

Athens (B-3)

See also Commerce, Madison, Washington, Winder

Founded 1801
Population 45,734
Elevation 775 ft
Area Code 706
Information Convention and Visitors Bureau, 300 N Thomas St, 30601; phone toll-free 800/653-0603; or Athens Welcome Center, 280 E Dougherty St, 30601; phone 706/353-1820
Web Site www.visitathensga.com

Georgia's "Classic City" is the site of the University of Georgia, chartered in 1785. Diversified industry produces nonwoven fabrics, textiles, clocks, electronic components, precision parts, chemicals, and animal feed. Lyman Hall, a signer of the Declaration of Independence, proposed the University, and Abraham Baldwin, the acknowledged founding father, wrote the charter. Although allotted 10,000 acres by the legislature in 1784, it was another 17 years before Josiah Meigs, Baldwin's successor and first official president, erected a few log buildings, called it Franklin College, and held classes under the tolerant eyes of curious Cherokees.

Athens was incorporated in 1806. Its setting on a hill beside the Oconee River is enhanced by towering oaks and elms, white-blossomed magnolias, old-fashioned boxwood gardens, and many well-preserved and still-occupied antebellum houses.

What to See and Do

Double-barreled cannon. *College and Hancock aves, Athens. City Hall lawn.* (1863) A unique Civil War weapon cast at Athens's foundry. Believed to be the only double-barreled cannon in the world.

Historic houses. *Phone 706/353-1870.* For tour information, contact Athens Welcome Center in Church-Waddel-Brumby House (see) or contact the Athens Convention and Visitors Bureau.

Church-Waddel-Brumby House. *280 E Dougherty St, Athens. Phone 706/353-1820.* (Circa 1820) Restored Federal-style house thought to be the oldest residence in Athens. Houses Athens Welcome Center, which has information on self-guided tours of other historic houses and buildings (Mon-Sat, Sun afternoons). **FREE**

Founders Memorial Garden. *325 S Lumpkin St, Athens. On University of Georgia campus. Phone 706/542-1365.* Memorial to founders of Ladies' Garden Club of Athens, the first garden club in the United States.

Other historic houses. Includes Ross Crane House (Sigma Alpha Epsilon fraternity) (1842), 247 Pulaski St; Lucy Cobb Institute (1858), 200 N Milledge Ave; Joseph Henry Lumpkin House (1841), 248 Prince Ave; Old Franklin Hotel (1845), 480 E Broad St; Governor Wilson Lumpkin House (1842), South campus, University of Georgia. University of Georgia, N campus, also has numerous pre-1860 buildings.

Taylor-Grady House. *634 Prince Ave, Athens. Phone 706/549-8688.* (1839) Restored Greek Revival mansion surrounded by 13 columns said to symbolize 13 original states; period furniture. (Mon-Thurs; closed holidays) **$$**

University president's house. *570 Prince Ave, Athens.* (Circa 1855) Greek Revival mansion surrounded on three sides by massive Corinthian columns. Extensive gardens and picket fences complement classic design. Private residence.

Sandy Creek Nature Center. *205 Old Commerce Rd, Athens. 1/2 mile N of Athens bypass, off Hwy 441. Phone 706/613-3615.* Approximately 200 acres of woods, fields, and marshland; includes a live animal exhibit, a 180-year-old cabin, nature trails. (Tues-Sat; closed Thanksgiving, Dec 25) **FREE** Also here is

ENSAT Center. *205 Old Commerce Rd, Athens (30607). Phone 706/613-3615.* Model of sustainable "green" architecture with ecological exhibits. (Tues-Sat) **FREE**

Sandy Creek Park. *400 Bob Holman Rd, Athens (30607). N on Hwy 441. Phone 706/613-3631.* Swimming (beach), fishing, boating; hiking, tennis, basketball, picnicking, playgrounds, primitive camping. Walkways. (Tues-Sun) **$**

Tree That Owns Itself. *Dearing and Finley sts, Athens (30601).* White oak, descendant of original tree, stands on a plot deeded to it.

University of Georgia. *College Station and River rds, Athens. Phone 706/542-3000.* (1785) (32,000 students) Consisting of 14 schools and colleges, the main campus extends more than 2 miles south from the Arch (1858), College Ave, and Broad St. Nearby are farms managed by the College of Agriculture, a forestry preserve, and University Research Park. Historic buildings include Demosthenian Hall (1824); chapel (1832), housing an oil painting (17 by 23 1/2 feet) of the interior of St. Peter's Basilica; Old College (1806), oldest building, designed after Connecticut Hall at Yale; Waddel Hall (1821); and Phi Kappa Hall (1834). Also on campus are

Butts-Mehre Heritage Museum. *1 Selig Cir, Athens. Third and fourth floors of Butts-Mehre Heritage Hall, Lumpkin St and Pinecrest Dr. Phone 706/542-9036.* Exhibits, videos, and trophy cases display Georgia sports memorabilia. (Mon-Fri, Sat afternoons) **FREE**

Georgia Museum of Art. *90 Carlton St, Athens (30602). Phone 706/542-4662.* Contains more than 8,000 pieces, including Eva Underhill Holbrook Collection; traveling and special exhibits. (Tues-Sun; closed holidays, week of Dec 25) **FREE**

State Botanical Garden. *2450 S Milledge Ave, Athens. Phone 706/542-1244.* Approximately 300 acres with natural trails, wildlife, and special collections. Gardens (daily); conservatory/visitors center (daily); Callaway Building (Mon-Fri). **FREE**

Special Events

Crackerland Tennis Tournament. *Dan Magill Tennis Complex, University of Georgia, Athens.* Juniors, late July-early Aug. Seniors, mid-Aug.

Marigold Festival. *125 N Church St, Athens. Hwy 78 to Cherokee Rd, in Winterville. Phone 706/742-8006.*

Arts, crafts, antiques, parades, and other events. Phone 706/742-8006. Late June.

North Georgia Folk Festival. *Sandy Creek Park, 293 Hoyt St, Athens (30601). Phone 706/208-0985. www.uga.edu/folkdance/folkfest.htm.* This annual music festival showcases several different types of music that have roots in the region. Genres include bluegrass, gospel, and more. Early Oct. **$$**

Spring Tour of Homes. *489 Prince Ave, Athens. Phone 706/353-1801 or 706/353-1820.* Celebration of Athens architecture held by the Athens-Clarke Heritage Foundation. Last weekend in Apr.

Limited-Service Hotels

★ **BEST WESTERN COLONIAL INN.** *170 N Milledge Ave, Athens (30601). Phone 706/546-7311; toll-free 800/592-9401; fax 706/546-7959. www.bestwestern.com.* 70 rooms, 2 story. Pets accepted; fee. Complimentary continental breakfast. Check-in 2 pm, check-out 11 am. Outdoor pool. **$**
🐾 🏊

★ ★ **HOLIDAY INN.** *197 E Broad St, Athens (30603). Phone 706/549-4433; toll-free 800/862-8436; fax 706/548-3031. www.holiday-inn.com.* Adjacent to University of Georgia. 306 rooms, 6 story. Check-in 3 pm, check-out noon. Restaurant, bar. Indoor pool, whirlpool. Airport transportation available. Business center. **$**
🏊 🏃

★ **HOLIDAY INN EXPRESS.** *513 W Broad St, Athens (30601). Phone 706/546-8122; toll-free 800/465-4329; fax 706/546-1722. www.holiday-inn.com.* 160 rooms, 5 story. Pets accepted, some restrictions; fee. Check-in 3 pm, check-out 11 am. Fitness room. Outdoor pool. **$**
🐾 🏃 🏊

Specialty Lodging

The following lodging establishment is approved by Mobil Travel Guide, but due to its unique and individualized nature has not been given a traditional Mobil Star rating. Included in this listing you may find bed-and-breakfasts, limited-service inns, guest ranches, and other unique hotel properties.

RIVENDELL BED AND BREAKFAST. *3581 S Barnett Shoals Rd, Watkinsville (30677). Phone 706/769-4522; fax 706/769-4393.* 5 rooms, 2 story. Children

over 10 years only. Complimentary full breakfast. Check-in 5-8 pm, check-out 11 am. **$**
🗔

Restaurants

★ ★ **HARRY BISSETT'S NEW ORLEANS CAFE.** *279 E Broad St, Athens (30601). Phone 706/353-7065; fax 706/549-7802. www.harrybissetts.net.* A popular hangout for local University of Georgia students, this old bank building on the main street of downtown Athens has retained the tin ceilings and brickwork of its original 1860s structure. Fresh seafood is flown in every day, and the barbecued shrimp is a favorite here. Cajun/Creole menu. Lunch, dinner, brunch. Closed Dec 25. Bar. Casual attire. Outdoor seating. **$$**
🗔

★ **VARSITY.** *1000 W Broad St, Athens (30601). Phone 706/548-6325.* Hamburgers, hot dogs. Breakfast, lunch, dinner. Outdoor seating. **$**

Atlanta (B-2)

See also Atlanta Hartsfield Airport Area, Buford, Cartersville, Marietta, Norcross, Roswell, Winder

Founded 1837
Population 416,474
Elevation 1,050 ft
Area Code 404
Information Convention and Visitors Bureau, 233 Peachtree St NE, Suite 2000, 30303; phone 404/521-6600 or toll-free 800/285-2682
Web Site www.atlanta.net
Suburbs Marietta, Norcross. (See individual alphabetical listings.)

When Atlanta was just 27 years old, 90 percent of its houses and buildings were razed by Union armies after a 117-day siege. Rebuilt by railroads in the 20th century, the city gives an overall impression of modernism.

Standing Peachtree, a Creek settlement, occupied Atlanta's site until 1813. Lieutenant George R. Gilmer led 22 recruits to build a fort here because of difficulties among the Creek and Cherokee. This became the first white settlement and grew into an important trading post.

Martin Luther King Jr. Historic District

"Free at last, free at last, thank God Almighty we are free at last."
- Reverend Martin Luther King Jr. (1929-1968)

East of downtown Atlanta is a small neighborhood named Sweet Auburn. Established in the late 19th century, the neighborhood was once known as "the richest Negro street in the world." Martin Luther King Jr. was born in Sweet Auburn on January 15, 1929. Since his death and entombment here, much of the neighborhood has been declared a National Historic District.

The best way to approach the district from downtown Atlanta is to start at the central Five Points MARTA station. Go north on Peachtree Street, the city's main artery, to pick up Auburn Avenue on the far side of the small brown-bagger's Woodruff Park. Follow Auburn Street east to the King Center, about a mile. On the way you will pass many landmarks that shed light on the community. The modern Auburn Avenue Research Library (101 Auburn) maintains a special collection on African-American history and heritage. The APEX Museum (135 Auburn) has an exhibit on the development of the neighborhood, including a short video, along with displays of African art. The Southern Christian Leadership Conference continues to work for social change out of its offices in the Prince Hall Masonic Building (332 Auburn Ave). The Ebenezer Baptist Church (407 Auburn) is the heart of the community. This 1922 sanctuary where Dr. King,

his father, and his grandfather preached grew so popular with visitors that the congregation needed to build a much larger sanctuary across the street and now maintains the original 750-seat building for special services. Adjacent to the small sanctuary is the King Center for Nonviolent Social Change (449 Auburn), where the crypt of Martin Luther King Jr. remains set behind an eternal flame in a reflecting pond in the plaza, visible 24 hours a day. The Center, founded by Dr. King's widow, Coretta Scott King, and now directed by his son Dexter King, maintains exhibits displaying personal effects and mementos, including exhibits on Mahatma Gandhi, who inspired King's dedication to nonviolence. Across the street at the Martin Luther King Jr. Historic Site visitor center (450 Auburn), the National Park Service has displays about the Nobel Peace Prize winner and screens a 30-minute film with historical footage from the Civil Rights era. The National Park Service also leads guided walking tours of the district.

Martin Luther King Jr. was born in an upstairs bedroom in a two-story Victorian house at 501 Auburn Avenue. His father, Reverend Martin Luther King, and mother, the former Alberta Williams, had been married in the house three years earlier, and all three of their children where born here. The nine-room Queen Anne-style house has been restored and furnished to reflect the time when "M. L." (as he was known) was growing up.

After Georgia's secession from the Union on January 19, 1861, the city became a manufacturing, storage, supply, and transportation center for the Confederate forces. This made Atlanta the target and last real barrier on General William Tecumseh Sherman's "March to the Sea." Although Atlanta had quartered 60,000 Confederate wounded, it was untouched by actual battle until Sherman began the fierce fighting of the Atlanta Campaign on May 7, 1864, with the engagement at Tunnel Hill, just over the Tennessee line. Despairing of capturing the city by battle, Sherman undertook a siege.

Guns were brought in, and Atlanta civilians got a foretaste of 20th-century warfare as the population

and defenders alike were subjected to continuous bombardment by the Union's heaviest artillery. People took refuge in cellars, trenches, and dugouts. Those who could escaped southward by wagon, foot, or train until Union forces seized the railroad 20 miles south at Jonesboro on September 1. General Hood evacuated Atlanta that same night, and the mayor surrendered the city the next day, September 2. Although the terms of surrender promised protection of life and property, Sherman ordered the city evacuated. All but 400 of the 3,600 houses and commercial buildings were destroyed in the subsequent burning.

Many citizens had returned to the city by January of 1865. By June, steps had been taken to reorganize business and repair wrecked railroad facilities. In 1866, Atlanta was made federal headquarters for area reconstruction. During the Reconstruction Convention of 1867-1868 called by General John Pope in Atlanta, the city offered facilities for the state government if it should be chosen the capital. The convention accepted this proposition, and Atlanta became the capital on April 20, 1868.

Atlanta's recovery and expansion as a rail center was begun by 1872, when two more railroads met here. Today, hundreds of manufacturers produce a wide variety of commodities.

Metropolitan Atlanta's population of 2.8 million is as devoted to cultural activities (such as its famed Alliance Theatre) as it is to its many golf courses and its major sports teams. Today Peachtree Street considers itself the South's main street and is more Fifth Avenue than Scarlett O'Hara's beloved lane. Skyscrapers, museums, luxury shops, and hotels rub shoulders along this concourse where Coca-Cola was first served; there are few peach blossoms left.

There are 29 colleges and universities in Atlanta. Georgia Institute of Technology, home of "a rambling wreck from Georgia Tech and a hell of an engineer," is one of the nation's top technological institutes. Other schools include Georgia State, Emory, and Oglethorpe universities. Atlanta University Center is an affiliation of six institutions of higher learning: Atlanta University, Spelman, Morehouse, Clark, and Morris Brown colleges, and the Interdenominational Theological Center.

Additional Visitor Information

For additional accommodations, see ATLANTA HARTSFIELD AIRPORT AREA, which follows ATLANTA.

For information, contact the Convention and Visitors Bureau, 233 Peachtree St NE, Suite 2000, 30303; phone 404/222-6688. Welcome centers are located at Underground Atlanta, Peachtree Center Mall, Lenox Square Mall, and Atlanta Hartsfield Airport.

Public Transportation

Buses and subway trains (MARTA); phone 404/848-4711; www.itsmarta.com.

Atlanta Fun Fact

• Coca-Cola was invented by Dr. John S. Pemberton in May 1886. It was first sold at a soda fountain at Jacob's Pharmacy in Atlanta by Willis Venable.

What to See and Do

A. G. Rhodes Memorial Hall. *1516 Peachtree St NW, Atlanta (30309). Phone 404/885-7800. www.georgia trust.org/rhodes.html.* (1903) An outstanding example of Victorian Romanesque architecture. The Georgia Trust offices are housed here; the first floor is a museum. (Mon-Fri 11 am-4 pm, Sun noon-3 pm; closed holidays) **$**

Atlanta Botanical Garden. *1345 Piedmont Ave, Atlanta (30309). Phone 404/876-5859. www.atlantabotanical garden.org.* Features 15 acres of outdoor gardens: Japanese, rose, perennial, and others. The Fuqua Conservatory has tropical, desert, and rare plants from around the world; there's also a special exhibit area for carnivorous plants. (Apr-Sept: Tues-Sun 9 am-7 pm, Oct-Mar: Tues-Sun 9 am-5 pm; closed Jan 1, Dec 25) **$$$**

Atlanta Braves (MLB). *Turner Field, 775 Hank Aaron Dr, Atlanta (30302). Phone 404/522-7630. www.atlantabraves.com.* Professional baseball team.

Atlanta Cyclorama. *Grant Park, 800 Cherokee Ave SE, Atlanta (30315). Phone 404/658-7625.* This theater in the round tells the story of the 1864 Battle for Atlanta as the studio revolves around a massive painting and diorama completed in 1885. (Daily 9 am-4:30 pm) **$$**

Atlanta Falcons (NFL). *Georgia Dome, 1 Georgia Dome Dr, Atlanta. Phone 770/965-3115. www.atlantafalcons.com.* Professional football team.

Atlanta Hawks (NBA). *Philips Arena, 1 Philips Dr, Atlanta (30303). Phone 404/827-3865. www.hawks.com.* Professional basketball team.

Atlanta History Center. *130 W Paces Ferry Rd, Atlanta (30305). Phone 404/814-4000. www.atlantahistory center.com.* The center consists of five major structures and 33 acres of woodlands and gardens. (Mon-Sat 10 am-5:30 pm, Sun noon-5:30 pm; closed holidays) **$$$** On-site are

Atlanta History Museum. *130 W Paces Ferry Rd, Atlanta (30305). www.atlantahistorycenter.com.* Historical exhibits relating to Atlanta, the Civil War, Southern folk life, and African Americans. (Mon-Sat 10 am-5:50 pm, Sun noon-5:30 pm; closed holidays)

McElreath Hall. *130 W Paces Ferry Rd, Atlanta (30305).* Research library, archives, and Cherokee Garden Library with gardening and horticulture research collection (Mon-Fri; closed holidays). Special events.

Swan House. *130 W Paces Ferry Rd, Atlanta (30305).* (1928) A classically styled mansion preserved as an example of early 20th-century architecture and decorative arts. Mansion is part of spacious landscaped grounds that includes terraces with cascading fountains, formal boxwood garden, and Victorian playhouse. On premises is the Philip Trammell Shutze Collection of Decorative Arts. (Daily; closed holidays) Guided tours.

Tullie Smith Farm. *130 W Paces Ferry Rd, Atlanta (30305).* Guided tours of 1840 plantation-style farmhouse, herb gardens, pioneer log cabin, and other outbuildings; craft demonstrations.

Atlanta Thrashers (NHL). *Philips Arena, 1 Philips Dr, Atlanta (30303). Phone 404/827-5300. www.atlanta thrashers.com.* Professional hockey team.

Centennial Olympic Park. *265 Luckie St NW, Atlanta (30303). Bounded by Marietta Ave, Techwood Dr, and Baker St. www.centennialpark.com.* This 21-acre park was constructed for the 1996 Summer Olympics and serves as Atlanta's downtown centerpiece. It features the Fountain of Rings (where water shoots up in the shape of Olympic rings), an amphitheater and Great Lawn for festivals and concerts, a visitor center, and a memorial to the two people killed in the bombing here during the Games. (Daily 7 am-11 pm)

CNN Studio Tour. *1 CNN Ctr, Atlanta (30348). At Centennial Park Dr and Marietta St. Phone 404/827-2300; toll-free 877/426-6868. www.atlantanation.com/cnntour.html.* Tour the studio, view a re-creation of the main control room, visit an interactive exhibit of top news stories, or learn the secrets of map-pointing only TV weather forecasters know. (45-minute tours leave every 20 minutes; reservations recommended; no children under 4 years permitted). (Daily 9 am-5 pm; closed Easter, Thanksgiving, Dec 25) **$$**

Fernbank Museum of Natural History. *767 Clifton Rd NE, Atlanta (30307). Phone 404/929-6300. www.fernbank .edu.* This monumental four-story modern museum houses exhibits on the Earth's formation, the dinosaur era, the first European settlers in North America, and more. An IMAX theater shows nature-themed films on its giant screen and hosts "Martinis & IMAX" every Friday night. (Mon-Sat 10 am-5 pm, Sun noon-5 pm; closed Thanksgiving, Dec 25) **$$$**

Fernbank Science Center. *156 Heaton Park Dr NE, Atlanta (30307). Phone 678/874-7102. www.fernbank.edu.* The center includes an exhibit hall, an observatory, a planetarium ($), and a science library; the grounds also contain a 65-acre forest area with marked trails. (Mon-Wed 8:30 am-5 pm, Thurs-Fri 8:30 am-10 pm, Sat 10 am-5 pm, Sun 1-5 pm; closed holidays) **FREE**

Fort McPherson. *Lee St, Atlanta. Hwy 29, approximately 3 miles SW via I-75 and Lakewood Frwy. Phone 404/464-0486. www.mcpherson.army.mil.* A military reservation since May 4, 1889. Historical tours (Mon-Fri, by appointment). **FREE**

Fox Theatre. *660 Peachtree St NE, Atlanta (30308). Phone 404/881-2100. www.foxtheatre.org.* (1929) The "Fabulous Fox," one of the most lavish movie theaters in the world, was conceived as a Shriners' temple with a more than 4,000-seat auditorium. Guests in the theater sit in an Arabian courtyard under an azure-painted sky with hundreds of 11-watt bulbs fixed in crystals, twinkling like stars. With 3,622 pipes, the colossal organ is the second-largest theater organ in the United States. The theater also features the world's largest Moller organ console and three elaborate ballrooms. The restored theater's ornate architecture combines exotic Moorish and Egyptian details. Hosts performances of the Atlanta Ballet, Broadway shows, a summer film festival, a full spectrum of concerts, theatrical events, trade shows, and conventions. Tours (Mon, Wed-Thurs 10 am; Sat 10 am and 11 am). **$$**

Georgia State Farmers' Market. *16 Forest Pkwy, Forest Park (30297). 10 miles S on I-75. agr.state.ga.us/html/atlanta_farmers_market.html.* Owned and operated by the state and covering 146 acres, this is one of the largest farmers' markets of its kind in the Southeast. (Tues-Sat; closed Dec 25) **FREE**

Jimmy Carter Library and Museum. *441 Freedom Pkwy, Atlanta (30307). Phone 404/331-0296. www.jimmy carterlibrary.org.* This museum has exhibits on life in the White House, major events during the Carter administration, and the life of President Carter. It includes a full-scale replica of the Oval Office. (Museum: Mon-Sat 9 am-4:45 pm, Sun noon-4:45 pm; library: Mon-Fri 8:30 am-4:30 pm; closed Jan 1, Thanksgiving, Dec 25) **$$**

Margaret Mitchell House. *990 Peachtree St NE, Atlanta (30309). At 10th St. Phone 404/249-7015. www.gwtw.org.* Home of the famous Atlanta native, author of *Gone with the Wind,* written here in a cramped basement apartment. The museum displays a portrait of Scarlett O'Hara from the movie; the original door from Tara, Scarlett's home; and a great collection of movie posters. Hour-long guided tours. (Daily 9:30 am-5:30 pm; closed Jan 1, Thanksgiving, Dec 24-25) **$$$**

⭐ **Martin Luther King Jr. National Historic Site.** *450 Auburn Ave, Atlanta. Phone 404/331-5190. www.nps.gov/malu.* A two-block area in memory of the famed leader of the Civil Rights movement and winner of the Nobel Peace Prize. Features include the Freedom Hall Complex, Chapel of All Faiths, King Library and Archives, and the reflecting pool; films and slides on Dr. King's life and work may be viewed in the screening room (fee). The National Park Service operates an information center. Guided tours of King's boyhood home are conducted by park rangers. (Daily 9 am-5 pm, until 6 pm Memorial Day weekend-Labor Day; closed Jan 1, Thanksgiving, Dec 25) **FREE** At the site are

   Ebenezer Baptist Church. *450 Auburn Ave NE, Atlanta (30312). Phone 404/688-7263. www.nps.gov/malu.* Dr. King was co-pastor at Ebenezer from 1960-1968. Next door to the church is his gravesite with an eternal flame. (Mon-Sat 9 am-5 pm, Sun 1-5 pm) **DONATION**

   King Birthplace. *501 Auburn Ave, Atlanta. Phone 404/331-3920.* **FREE**

Parks. Atlanta parks offer dogwood blooms in spring and varied recreational facilities, including golf, swimming, and picnic areas.

   Chastain Memorial Park. *135 W Wieuca Rd, Atlanta (30327). Between Powers Ferry Rd and Lake Forrest Dr. www.gpconservancy.org.* Swimming, tennis, golf, picnicking, amphitheater. Fees for various activities.

   Grant Park. *800 Cherokee Ave SE, Atlanta (30315).* Many miles of walks and roads; visible traces of breastworks built for defense of Atlanta; cyclorama depicting the Battle of Atlanta; Atlanta

Zoo with a variety of species. Swimming, tennis, picnicking, park (daily). Zoo (daily; closed Jan 1, Thanksgiving, Dec 25).

   Piedmont Park. *Piedmont Ave NE and 14th St, Atlanta. Off Monroe Dr on Park Dr. Phone 404/875-7275. www.piedmontpark.org.* Swimming (fee), lake; tennis (fee); picnicking.

Robert W. Woodruff Arts Center. *1280 Peachtree St NE, Atlanta. www.woodruffcenter.org/wac.* Largest arts complex in the Southeast. Headquarters of Atlanta College of Art and

   Alliance Theatre Company. *1280 Peachtree St NE, Atlanta (30309). At the Woodruff Arts Center. Phone 404/733-5000. www.alliancetheatre.org.* This regional theater company presents six mainstage productions, three studio theater productions, and two children's theater productions annually. (Sept-May)

   High Museum of Art. *1280 Peachtree St NE, Atlanta. Phone 404/733-4444. www.high.org.* African sculpture; European, American, and contemporary painting and sculpture; decorative art; photography. Rotating exhibits. (Tues-Sat 10 am-5 pm, Sun from noon; closed holidays) **$$**

   Symphony Hall. *1280 Peachtree St, Atlanta (30309). Phone 404/733-5000. www.atlantasymphony.org.* The largest auditorium in the Arts Center. It's the permanent home of the Atlanta Symphony Orchestra, Chorus, and Youth Orchestra; performances (Sept-May and mid-June-mid-Aug).

Six Flags Over Georgia. *7561 Six Flags Pkwy, Austell (30168). 12 miles W of downtown via I-20, exit 47 Six Flags Pkwy, just beyond Atlanta city limits. Phone 770/948-9290. www.sixflags.com/parks/overgeorgia.* A family theme park featuring Georgia's history under the flags of England, France, Spain, the Confederacy, Georgia, and the United States. More than 100 rides, shows, and attractions, including the Georgia Cyclone roller coaster, modeled after Coney Island's famous Cyclone; the Ninja roller coaster with five upside-down turns; water rides; children's activities; and live shows. (Mid-May-early Sept: daily; early Mar-mid-May and early Sept-Oct: weekends only) **$$$$**

State Capitol. *1 Capitol Sq, Atlanta. Phone 404/656-2844. www.cr.nps.gov/nr/travel/atlanta/geo.htm. (1884-1889)* The dome, topped with native gold, is 237 feet high. Inside are historical flags, statues, and portraits.

Tours 10 am, 11 am, 1 pm, and 2 pm. (Mon-Fri 8 am-5:30 pm) **FREE** On the fourth floor is

Georgia Capitol Museum. *431 State Capitol, Atlanta (30334). Phone 404/651-6996. www.sos.state.ga.us/museum/default.htm.* Exhibits of wildlife, snakes, fish, rocks, minerals, and fossils. Dioramas of Georgia industry (Mon-Fri 8 am-5:30 pm) **FREE**

⭐ **Stone Mountain Park.** *Hwy 78 E, Stone Mountian (30087). 19 miles E on Hwy 78. Phone 770/498-5690. www.stonemountainpark.com.* This 3,200-acre park surrounds the world's largest granite monolith, which rises 825 feet from the plain. A monument to the Confederacy, the deep relief carving on the mountain's face depicts three figures: General Robert E. Lee, General "Stonewall" Jackson, and Confederate President Jefferson Davis. It was first undertaken by Gutzon Borglum after World War I, continued by Augustus Lukeman, and completed by Walker Hancock. The top of the mountain is accessible by foot or cable car (fee). Surrounding the sculpture are Memorial Hall, a Civil War museum with commentary in seven languages about the mountain and its carving; an antebellum plantation featuring 19 buildings restored and furnished with 18th- and 19th-century heirlooms, formal and kitchen gardens, cookhouse, slave quarters, country store, and other outbuildings; Antique Auto and Music Museum housing cars dating to 1899 and an antique mechanical music collection; riverboat *Scarlett O'Hara,* providing scenic trips around a 363-acre lake; scenic railroad with full-size replicas of Civil War trains that make a 5-mile trip around the base of the mountain. Also, a laser show is projected onto the north face of the mountain in 50-minute productions (mid-May-Labor Day: nightly; Apr-mid-May and after Labor Day-Oct: Sat) and a 732-bell carillon plays concerts (Wed-Sun). In addition, the park has 10 miles of nature trails where wild and domestic animals live on 20 wooded acres; beach with bathhouse, fishing, boat rentals; tennis courts, 36-hole golf course, miniature golf, ice skating, picnicking, snack bars, three restaurants, inn, and campground with tent and trailer sites (hook-ups, dump station). (Daily 6 am-midnight; attractions open at 10 am; closed Dec 25) **$$$$**

Theater of the Stars. *660 Peachtree Street NE, Atlanta. Phone 404/252-8960. www.theaterofthestars.com.* Nine Broadway musicals with professional casts, most staged at the Fox Theatre (see). Late June-early Nov.

⭐ **Underground Atlanta.** *50 Upper Alabama St SW # 7, Atlanta (30303). Bounded by Wall, Central, Peachtree sts and Martin Luther King, Jr. Dr. Phone 404/523-2311. www.underground-atlanta.com.* A "festival marketplace" featuring shops, pushcart peddlers, restaurants and nightclubs, street entertainers, and various attractions. The six-block area was created in the 1920s when several viaducts were built over existing streets at second-story level to move traffic above multiple rail crossings. Merchants moved their shops to the second floors, relegating the first floors to oblivion for nearly half a century. Today's visitors descend onto the cobblestone streets of a Victorian city in perpetual night. On lower Alabama Street, the shops are housed in the original, once-forgotten storefronts. Underground Atlanta was first "discovered" in the late 1960s and flourished as a center of nightlife before being closed down in 1981 due to a combination of crime and subway construction. The "rediscovered" Underground combines the original below-ground streets with above-ground plazas, promenades, fountains, more shops and restaurants, and a 138-foot light tower. (Shopping Mon-Sat 10 am-9 pm, Sun 11 am-6 pm; open later in summer; restaurant and club hours may vary; closed Dec 25) Highlighted here is

The World of Coca-Cola. *55 Martin Luther King Jr. Dr SW, Atlanta (30303). Between Central Ave and Washington St, S of the New Georgia Railroad Depot. Phone 404/676-5151. www.woccatlanta.com.* A square block of interactive displays and exhibits trace history of Coca-Cola from its introduction in 1886 at Jacob's Pharmacy Soda Fountain on Atlanta's Peachtree St to present; world's largest collection of Coca-Cola memorabilia; movies; old-fashioned soda fountain. (Sept-May: Mon-Sat 9 am-5 pm, Sun 11 am-5 pm; June-Aug: Mon-Sat 9 am-6 pm, Sun 11 am-5 pm; closed holidays) **$$**

William Breman Jewish Heritage Museum. *1440 Spring St NW, Atlanta (30309). Phone 404/873-1661. www.thebreman.org.* The largest Jewish heritage museum in the Southeast houses a Holocaust gallery and heritage gallery, which tells the story of Atlanta's Jewish community from the first German immigrants in 1845. (Sun-Fri) **$$**

Wren's Nest. *1050 Ralph D. Abernathy Blvd SW, Atlanta. Phone 404/753-7735.* Eccentric Victorian house of Joel Chandler Harris, journalist and transcriber of "Uncle Remus" stories. Original family furnishings, books, photographs. Ongoing restoration. (Tues-Sun; closed holidays) Group tours (25+) Tues-Sat (reservations required); individual tours Tues, Thurs, Sat. **$$$**

Yellow River Game Ranch. *4525 Hwy 78, Lilburn. Approximately 17 miles E. Phone 770/972-6643. www. yellowrivergameranch.com.* A 24-acre animal preserve on the Yellow River where more than 600 animals roam free in a natural wooded area. Visitors can pet, feed, and photograph the animals. Some of the animals at the park include deer, bears, cougars, and buffalo. (Daily; closed Jan 1, Thanksgiving, Dec 24-25)

Zoo Atlanta. *Grant Park, 800 Cherokee Ave SE, Atlanta (30315). Phone 404/624-5600. www.zooatlanta.org.* Features natural habitat settings and is known for its primate center, aviary, and representative Southeastern habitats exhibits. The giant panda exhibit is a major draw as well. (Daily 9:30 am-4:30 pm; closed Jan 1, Thanksgiving, Dec 25) **$$$$**

Special Events

Atlanta Dogwood Festival. *20 Executive Park Dr NE #2019, Atlanta. Phone 404/329-0501. www.dogwood.org.* This springtime festival in celebration of the blooming of Atlanta's dogwood trees features an artist market, a Frisbee dog contest, a Kids Village full of activities, and live music. Early Apr.

Atlanta Motor Speedway. *1500 Hwy 19-41, Hampton. S on I-75, exit 77, and then approximately 15 miles S on Hwy 19/41. Phone 770/946-4211. www.atlantamotor speedway.com.* NASCAR Winston Cup, Busch Grand National, IMSA, and ARCA auto racing events.

Atlanta Steeplechase. *Kingston Downs, Cumming. At Seven Branches Farm. Phone 404/237-7436. www. atlantasteeplechase.org.* Gates open at 9 am; post time 1:30 pm. Second Sat in Apr.

Georgia Renaissance Festival. *6905 Virlyn B. Smith, Atlanta. Approximately 20 miles S on I-85, exit 12. Phone 770/964-8575. www.garenfest.com.* Hundreds of costumed characters, authentic crafts, games, and food in a re-created 16th-century English village. Seven weekends, mid-Apr-early June.

US 10K Classic and Family Festival. *Cobb Pkwy and Akers Mill Rd SE, Atlanta (30303). Phone 770/432-0100. www.us10k.org.* The US 10K Classic raises money for children's charities and is host to several different race categories: running, walking, wheelchair racing, in-line skating, and cycling. There is also plenty to do for individuals and families not racing including a pre-race pizza and pasta dinner, celebrity autograph sessions, a children's activity area, and finish line celebration. Labor Day weekend.

Limited-Service Hotels

★ **DAYS INN.** *6840 Shannon Pkwy, Union City (30291). Phone 770/306-6067; toll-free 800/964-3777; fax 770/306-6062. www.daysinn.com.* 90 rooms, 2 story. Pets accepted; fee. Complimentary continental breakfast. Check-in 2 pm, check-out 11 am. Outdoor pool. **$**

★★**EMBASSY SUITES BUCKHEAD.** *3285 Peachtree Rd NE, Atlanta (30305). Phone 404/261-7733; toll-free 800/362-2779; fax 404/261-6857. www.embassysuites.com.* This atrium-style hotel accommodates guests looking to stay in the prestigious Bucktown neighborhood. The spacious guest suites feature kitchenettes, hair dryers, and irons. 317 rooms, 16 story, all suites. Complimentary full breakfast. Check-in 3 pm, check-out noon. Restaurant, bar. Fitness room. Indoor pool, outdoor pool, whirlpool. Airport transportation available. **$$**

★ ★ **EMBASSY SUITES HOTEL ATLANTA-AT CENTENNIAL OLYMPIC PARK.** *267 Marietta St, Atlanta (30313). Phone 404/223-2300; toll-free 800/362-2779; fax 404/223-0925. www.embassysuites.com.* This hotel occupies a prime spot across from Centennial Olympic Park. At night, sit on the balcony and watch the dazzling light display at the Olympic Rings Fountain. Suites offer large bedrooms and living rooms with comfortable couches. 321 rooms, all suites. Complimentary full breakfast. Check-in 3 pm, check-out noon. High-speed Internet access. Restaurant, bar. Fitness room. Outdoor pool, whirlpool. Business center. **$**

★ ★ **EMORY INN.** *1641 Clifton Rd, Atlanta (30329). Phone 404/712-6000; toll-free 800/933-6679; fax 404/712-6701. www.emoryconferencecenter.com.* Located at Emory University and just minutes from downtown Atlanta and Buckhead, this hotel features spacious country French-style guest rooms, a garden courtyard with pool and whirlpool, and a café. It can be tricky to find—look for the sign for the conference center, which is down the hill from the inn. Guests can enjoy nearby shopping, sporting events, and theaters. 105 rooms, 2 story. Check-in 3 pm, check-out noon. Restaurant. Outdoor pool, whirlpool. Business center. **$**

★ ★ ★ **GEORGIA TECH HOTEL AND CONFERENCE CENTER.** *800 Spring St NW, Atlanta (30308). Phone 404/347-9440; toll-free 800/706-2899; fax 404/347-9088. www.gatechhotel.com.* This hotel in Midtown offers state-of-the-art conveniences to a clientele of mostly business travelers. From T-1 Internet lines to flat-screen televisions, the urban-style guest rooms are as contemporary as they are easy on the eye. This hotel is a great choice if you're planning a group meeting or conference, as the facilities for these types of gatherings are top-notch. 252 rooms. Check-in 3 pm, check-out noon. High-speed Internet access, wireless Internet access. Restaurant, two bars. Fitness room. Indoor pool, whirlpool. Airport transportation available. Business center. **$**

★ **HAMPTON INN.** *3398 Piedmont Rd NE, Atlanta (30305). Phone 404/233-5656; toll-free 888/537-1091; fax 404/237-4688. www.hamptoninn.com.* 154 rooms, 6 story. Complimentary continental breakfast. Check-in 3 pm, check-out noon. Outdoor pool. **$**

★ **HOLIDAY INN EXPRESS.** *505 Pharr Rd, Atlanta (30305). Phone 404/262-7880; toll-free 800/465-4329; fax 404/262-3734. www.hiexpress.com.* Located in the fashionable Buckhead district, this hotel is great for extended stays and families. With a fully stocked kitchen and separate living area in each suite, guests will feel like they never left home. 87 rooms, 3 story, all suites. Complimentary continental breakfast. Check-in 3 pm, check-out 11 am. Fitness room. Outdoor pool, whirlpool. **$**

Full-Service Hotels

★ ★ ★ **ATLANTA MARRIOTT MARQUIS.** *265 NE Peachtree Center Ave, Atlanta (30303). Phone 404/521-0000; toll-free 800/228-9290; fax 404/586-6299. www.marriott.com.* This polished convention hotel tickles and awes guests with its 50-story atrium and exciting and unlimited view of the city. Guests will delight in the elegantly appointed guest rooms and 120,000 square feet of meeting space. Pleasures also can be found with the first-class comforts this hotel has to offer. 1,675 rooms, 50 story. Check-in 4 pm, check-out noon. Restaurant, bar. Fitness room. Indoor pool, outdoor pool, whirlpool. Business center. **$$**

★ ★ ★ **CROWNE PLAZA.** *3377 Peachtree Rd, Atlanta (30326). Phone 404/264-1111; fax 404/233-7061. www.crowneplaza.com.* Set in the prestigious Buckhead section of the city, this newly renovated hotel with boutique-style décor is conveniently close to shopping, dining, and nightlife on Atlanta's renowned Peachtree Street. Unwind after a day of exploring the city in the outdoor pool or fitness room or enjoy dinner at the hotel's Mediterranean restaurant. A MARTA Rail Station is adjacent to the hotel, and attractions such Six Flags over Georgia and the CNN Center are also nearby. 291 rooms, 11 story. Check-in 4 pm, check-out noon. Restaurant, bar. Fitness room. Outdoor pool. **$**

★ ★ ★ ★ ★ **FOUR SEASONS HOTEL ATLANTA.** *75 14th St, Atlanta (30309). Phone 404/881-9898; toll-free 800/332-3442; fax 404/873-4692. www.fourseasons.com.* The Four Seasons Hotel is Atlanta's premier address. This Neoclassical granite tower reigns over Midtown, where world-class culture, flourishing businesses, and enticing stores line the streets. Well-suited for both business and leisure travelers, this hotel offers its guests the finest accommodations and flawless, intuitive service. Neutral tones and polished woods set a relaxed elegance in the rooms and suites, while striking views of downtown or midtown Atlanta inspire occupants. Visitors swoon over the luxurious amenities, from plush furnishings to sensational beds, and in-room massage and spa therapies ensure pure relaxation. The state-of-the-art fitness center is complete with an indoor pool and sun terrace, perfect for exercise or repose. Park 75's fresh approach to American cuisine earns praise from locals and hotel guests alike, and its ficus-lined terrace is a pleasing alternative. 244 rooms, 19 story. Pets accepted, some restrictions. Check-in 3 pm, check-out noon. High-speed Internet access. Restaurant, bar. Fitness room. Indoor pool, whirlpool. Business center. **$$$**

★ ★ ★ **GRAND HYATT ATLANTA.** *3300 Peachtree Rd NE, Atlanta (30305). Phone 404/365-8100; toll-free 800/233-1234; fax 404/233-5686. www.atlanta.hyatt.com.* Perched in the heart of Buckhead, Atlanta's well-known fashionable district, this elegant hotel offers impeccable service and handsomely appointed accommodations. 438 rooms, 25 story. Pets accepted, some restrictions; fee. Check-in 3 pm, check-out noon. Restaurant, bar. Fitness room, spa. Outdoor pool. Business center. **$$**

★ ★ ★ **HILTON ATLANTA AND TOWERS.**
255 Courtland St NE, Atlanta (30303). Phone 404/659-2000; toll-free 800/445-8667; fax 404/221-6368. www.hilton.com. From the fitness center, jogging track, and basketball and tennis courts to the pool and billiard room, this hotel is guaranteed to restore the senses. 1,224 rooms, 30 story. Check-in 3 pm, check-out 11 am. Restaurant, bar. Fitness room. Outdoor pool. Tennis. Business center. **$**

★ ★ ★ **HOTEL INDIGO ATLANTA.** *683 Peachtree St NE, Atlanta (30308). Phone 404/874-9200; fax 404/873-4245. www.hotelindigo.com.* 140 rooms. Pets accepted. Check-in 3 pm, check-out noon. Restaurant, bar. **$$**

★ ★ ★ **HYATT REGENCY ATLANTA.** *265 Peachtree St NE, Atlanta (30303). Phone 404/577-1234; toll-free 800/233-1234; fax 404/588-4137. www.hyatt.com.* Located in the hustle and bustle of downtown, this 23-story atrium hotel successfully combines the convenience of a downtown hotel with superb accommodations and first-class amenities. Minutes away are the Atlanta Market Center, Georgia Dome, Underground Atlanta, and Centennial Olympic Park. 1,260 rooms, 23 story. Check-in 3 pm, check-out noon. Restaurant, bar. Fitness room. Outdoor pool. Business center. **$$**

★ ★ ★ **JW MARRIOTT HOTEL LENOX ATLANTA.** *3300 Lenox Rd NE, Atlanta (30326). Phone 404/262-3344; toll-free 800/228-9290; fax 404/262-8689. www.marriott.com.* The JW Marriott Hotel Lenox treats its visitors to a privileged address in the heart of Atlanta's fashionable Buckhead neighborhood. This sleek hotel is an obvious choice for business and leisure travelers with its excellent amenities, fine service, and stylish setting. Its location adjacent to the premium shops of Lenox Mall makes it a hit with shopaholics, and many of the city's major attractions are just a short distance away. Business travelers appreciate the little extras here, from the full-service business center with secretarial services to the high-speed Internet access in all rooms. A fitness center and indoor pool attract those who like to fit in a workout on the road, while a restaurant, coffee shop, lounge, and room service cater to appetites at all hours. 375 rooms, 25 story. Check-in 4 pm, check-out noon. High-speed Internet access. Restaurant, bar. Fitness room. Indoor pool, whirlpool. Business center. **$**

★ ★ ★ **INTERCONTINENTAL BUCKHEAD.**
3315 Peachtree Rd, Atlanta (30326). Phone 404/946-9000; fax 404/946-9001. 422 rooms. Pets accepted, some restrictions; fee. Check-in 4 pm, check-out noon. Restaurant, bar. Fitness room. Outdoor pool. **$$**

★ ★ ★ **OMNI HOTEL AT CNN CENTER.** *100 CNN Center NW, Atlanta (30303). Phone 404/659-0000; toll-free 800/843-6664; fax 404/525-5050. www.omnihotels.com.* Located in downtown Atlanta and conveniently connected to the CNN Center and the Georgia World Congress Center, this well-appointed hotel offers guests spacious rooms, flawless service, and an attention to detail to ensure guests' standards are met and surpassed. Take a stroll through Centennial Olympic Park located across the street or enjoy the 50,000-square-foot, state-of-the-art Turner Athletic Club. 1067 rooms, 15 story. Pets accepted, some restrictions; fee. Check-in 3 pm, check-out noon. Restaurant, bar. Fitness room. Airport transportation available. Business center. **$$**

★ ★ ★ **THE RITZ-CARLTON, ATLANTA.** *181 Peachtree St NE, Atlanta (30303). Phone 404/659-0400; toll-free 800/241-3333; fax 404/688-0400. www.ritzcarlton.com.* The Ritz-Carlton is the shining star of downtown Atlanta. This cosmopolitan hotel enjoys a prime location in the heart of the city, making it convenient to businesses, government offices, and sporting arenas. The guest accommodations are handsomely appointed with traditional furnishings, fabrics, and artwork. Bay windows draw attention to striking views of the city skyline. Many suites have kitchenettes, and some even feature baby grand pianos. Twice-daily housekeeping and the Ritz-Carlton's signature Technology Butler Service pamper guests. Diners develop a soft spot for the clubby atmosphere of the Atlanta Grill, with its sophisticated updates on Southern cooking. 444 rooms, 25 story. Pets accepted, some restrictions; fee. Check-in 3 pm, check-out noon. High-speed Internet access. Restaurant, two bars. Children's activity center. Fitness room. Airport transportation available. Business center. **$$**

★ ★ ★ **THE RITZ-CARLTON, BUCKHEAD.**
3434 Peachtree Rd NE, Atlanta (30326). Phone 404/237-2700; toll-free 800/241-3333; fax 404/239-0078. www.ritzcarlton.com. The Ritz-Carton Buckhead is unquestionably the grande dame of Atlanta. This gracious hotel, nestled in the fashionable uptown

neighborhood, has long been the favorite of the social set. Southern grace and Ritz-Carlton standards blend here, resulting in a warm and luxurious experience. The guest rooms enchant with European furnishings, antiques, and sublime amenities. Bay windows showcase lovely views of the wooded locale or the downtown skyline. Attentive and exceptional service ensures that all guests are cosseted. The fitness center appeals to athletic-minded visitors, and the indoor pool with sundeck adds a relaxing touch. Afternoon tea in the Lobby Lounge is a Georgia tradition, especially after a day of perusing the area's world-famous stores, and The Café is a popular gathering place to enjoy casual fare. The pièce-de-résistance, however, is The Dining Room (see), where award-winning French cuisine infused with Asian flavors delights the senses. 553 rooms, 22 story. Pets accepted, some restrictions; fee. Check-in 3 pm, check-out noon. High-speed Internet access. Restaurant, bar. Fitness room, spa. Indoor pool, whirlpool. Airport transportation available. Business center. **$$$**

★ ★ ★ **SHERATON ATLANTA HOTEL.** *165 Courtland St, Atlanta (30303). Phone 404/659-6500; toll-free 800/325-3535; fax 404/524-1259. www.sheraton.com.* With all its dining options and other conveniences, this hotel is a home-away-from-home for business and leisure travelers alike. 765 rooms, 12 story. Pets accepted, some restrictions. Check-in 3 pm, check-out noon. Three restaurants, bar. Fitness room. Indoor pool, outdoor pool, whirlpool. Business center. **$**

★ ★ ★ **W ATLANTA AT PERIMETER CENTER.** *111 Perimeter Ctr W, Atlanta (30346). Phone 770/396-6800; toll-free 800/683-6100; fax 770/399-5514. www.whotels.com.* Located in the Perimeter Center Office Complex and conveniently within walking distance to numerous restaurants, cinemas, and all the delights of downtown Atlanta. This refreshing hotel offers guests unsurpassed sophisticated elegance combined with a twist of all the comforts of home. From the signature pillow-top beds and divine linens to the exquisitely appointed guest rooms, this hotel makes for a truly memorable stay. 275 rooms, 12 story. Pets accepted; fee. Check-in 3 pm, check-out noon. Restaurant, bar. Fitness room. Outdoor pool, whirlpool. **$$**

★ ★ ★ **THE WESTIN BUCKHEAD ATLANTA.** *3391 Peachtree Rd NE, Atlanta (30326). Phone 404/365-0065; toll-free 800/253-1397; fax 404/365-8787. www.westin.com.* Located in the elegant and scenic Buckhead area and adjacent to Lenox Square Mall, this graceful 22-story hotel is a landmark and a delight to stay in. All of the guest rooms are spacious and handsomely appointed with Biedermeier-style furnishings. The fitness center is state-of-the-art and the lap pool sparkling and inviting. Nearby attractions include Zoo Atlanta, the Fernbank-Musuem of Natural History, and the Jimmy Carter Presidential Center. Just 15 minutes away is the birthplace of Dr. Martin Luther King Jr. 377 rooms, 22 story. Pets accepted, some restrictions. Check-in 3 pm, check-out noon. Restaurant, bar. Fitness room. Indoor pool. Business center. **$**

★ ★ ★ **THE WESTIN PEACHTREE PLAZA.** *210 Peachtree St NW, Atlanta (30303). Phone 404/659-1400; toll-free 800/937-8461; fax 404/589-7424. www.westin.com.* As if the superb service, relaxing ambience, and spacious guest rooms with views of downtown weren't enough, this hotel surpasses others by offering special touches such as the "heavenly bed." Guests can dine at any of the three delectable restaurants, enjoy a workout in the health club and fitness center, or just relax at the indoor or outdoor pool. 1,068 rooms, 73 story. Pets accepted, some restrictions. Check-in 3 pm, check-out noon. Three restaurants, bars. Fitness room, spa. Indoor pool, outdoor pool. Business center. **$$**

★ ★ ★ **WYNDHAM ATLANTA DOWNTOWN HOTEL.** *160 Spring St NW, Atlanta (30303). Phone 404/688-8600; toll-free 877/999-3223; fax 404/524-5543. www.wyndham.com.* Ideal for business travelers who also look to enjoy a bit of the city, this contemporary hotel with intimate yet open spaces offers ample meeting space, a friendly staff and a location that affords guests the opportunity to savor all that Atlanta has to see and do. 312 rooms, 9 story. Check-in 3 pm, check-out noon. Restaurant, bar. Fitness room. Outdoor pool. Airport transportation available. Business center. **$**

★ ★ ★ **WYNDHAM PEACHTREE CONFERENCE CENTER HOTEL.** *2443 Hwy 54 W, Peachtree City (30269). Phone 770/487-2000; fax 770/487-5190. www.wyndham.com.* 250 rooms, 4 story.

Check-in 3 pm, check-out 11 am. High-speed Internet access, wireless Internet access. Two restaurants, bar. Fitness room, fitness classes available. Indoor pool, outdoor pool, whirlpool. Tennis. Airport transportation available. Business center. **$**

Specialty Lodgings

The following lodging establishments are approved by Mobil Travel Guide, but due to their unique and individualized nature have not been given a traditional Mobil Star rating. Included in this listing you may find bed-and-breakfasts, limited-service inns, guest ranches, and other unique hotel properties.

ANSLEY INN. *253 15th St, Atlanta (30309). Phone 404/872-9000; toll-free 800/446-5416; fax 404/892-2318. www.ansleyinn.com.* A turn-of-the-century English Tudor house built in 1907, the Ansley Inn provides the comforts of home in the heart of Midtown. Set on a quiet, tree-lined street, it is within walking distance of the High Museum of Art, the Margaret Mitchell House, and the Atlanta Botanical Gardens. Large fireplaces; crystal chandeliers; and Chippendale, Queen Anne, and Empire furnishings pay homage to the period, while four-poster beds and Oriental rugs create a warm ambience in the guest rooms. 21 rooms, 3 story. Complimentary full breakfast. Check-in 3 pm, check-out 11 am. **$$**

GASLIGHT INN BED & BREAKFAST. *1001 St. Charles Ave NE, Atlanta (30306). Phone 404/875-1001; fax 404/876-1001. www.gaslightinn.com.* Located in the Virginia Highlands area, with easy access to MARTA, the freeway, and plentiful shopping and dining, this popular bed-and-breakfast is full of warmth. The proprietor knows it well, having used it as a private residence until turning it into a bed-and-breakfast. Gaslights and private alcoves characterize this early-1900s home, where guests can enjoy meals in the flower garden or on the front porch. 8 rooms, 2 story. Complimentary continental breakfast. Check-in 3-6 pm, check-out noon. **$**

KING-KEITH HOUSE BED & BREAKFAST. *889 Edgewood Ave NE, Atlanta (30307). Phone 404/688-7330; toll-free 800/728-3879; fax 404/584-8408. www.kingkeith.com.* 6 rooms, 3 story. Check-in 3 pm, check-out 11 am. **$**

LAUREL HILL BED & BREAKFAST. *1992 McLendon St, Atlanta (30307). Phone 404/377-3217; fax 404/377-0756. www.laurelhillbandb.com.* 6 rooms. Pets accepted; fee. No children allowed. Complimentary full breakfast. Check-in 3-6 pm, check-out 11 am. Wireless Internet access. **$**

SERENBE BED & BREAKFAST. *10950 Hutcheson Ferry Rd, Palmetto (30268). Phone 770/463-2610; fax 770/463-4472. www.serenbe.com.* A cheerful place to bring the kids, this inn, built in 1901, is located on a farm where guests can feed the animals, go on a hayride, or have a marshmallow roast. Guests can enjoy canoe rides and the majestic waterfalls. 7 rooms, 2 story. Complimentary full breakfast. Check-in 3 pm, check-out 11 am. Outdoor pool, whirlpool. **$**

SHELLMONT INN. *Piedmont and 6th sts, Atlanta (30308). Phone 404/872-9290; fax 404/872-5379. www.shellmont.com.* Located in midtown Atlanta's theater and cultural district, this beautifully restored Victorian masterpiece is filled with antiques, Oriental rugs, Tiffany windows, and artwork. Guests here will enjoy an intimate setting. 6 rooms, 2 story. Children under 12 in carriage house only. Complimentary full breakfast. Check-in 3 pm, check-out 11 am. **$$**

SUGAR MAGNOLIA. *804 Edgewood Ave NE, Atlanta (30307). Phone 404/222-0226; fax 404/681-1067. www.sugarmagnoliabb.com.* Nestled in Atlanta's historic Inman Park neighborhood, this elegant Victorian bed-and-breakfast was built in 1892. With six fireplaces, a grand staircase, and beveled windows, the beauty of the architecture is immense. Guest suites are cozy and inviting with period furnishing. 4 rooms, 2 story. Complimentary continental breakfast. Check-in 1 pm, check-out 11 am. Business center. **$**

Restaurants

★ ★ **THE ABBEY.** *163 Ponce de Leon Ave NE, Atlanta (30308). Phone 404/876-8831; fax 404/876-8832. www.theabbeyrestaurant.com.* Costumed servers. American menu. Dinner. Closed holidays. Bar. Casual attire. Valet parking. **$$$**

★ ★ **ANTHONY'S.** *3109 Piedmont Rd NE, Atlanta (30305). Phone 404/262-7379; fax 404/261-6009.*

www.anthonysfinedining.com. This restaurant is set back from the road on a wooded lot in a plantation home that dates from 1797. The main dining room has seven working fireplaces. The menu has some classics, like veal Anthony (scallopine stuffed with lobster) and pumpkin seed- and coriander-crusted grouper. American menu. Dinner. Closed Sun; holidays; Dec 25-29. Business casual attire. Reservations recommended. Valet parking. **$$$**

★ ★ ★ **ARIA.** *490 E Paces Ferry Rd, Atlanta (30305). Phone 404/233-7673; fax 404/262-5208. www.aria-atl.com.* This cozy space in the Buckhead neighborhood has been transformed into a shrine of industrial chic. Leather walls and metal curtains are all part of the scheme to lure diners in for chef Gerry Klaskala's Southern-inspired, American cuisine. American menu. Dinner. Closed Sun; holidays. Bar. Business casual attire. Reservations recommended. Valet parking. Outdoor seating. **$$$**

★ ★ ★ **ATLANTA FISH MARKET.** *265 Pharr Rd, Atlanta (30305). Phone 404/262-3165; fax 404/240-6656. www.buckheadrestaurants.com.* Slightly tucked away from the bustle of the Buckhead section, this large, family-friendly seafood restaurant is a favorite among locals. The restaurant, features several airy, comfortable dining rooms and menus printed twice daily to ensure that entrees are fresher than fresh. Seafood menu. Lunch, dinner. Closed Thanksgiving, Dec 25. Bar. Children's menu. Casual attire. **$$**

★ ★ ★ **AU PIED DE COCHON.** *3315 Peachtree Rd, Atlanta (30326). Phone 404/946-9070; fax 404/946-9001.* French bistro menu. Breakfast, lunch, dinner, late-night. Bar. Children's menu. Reservations recommended. Outdoor seating. **$$**

★ ★ **BABETTE'S CAFE.** *573 N Highland Ave, Atlanta (30307). Phone 404/523-9121; fax 404/523-9121. www.babettescafe.com.* French menu. Dinner. Closed Mon; holidays. Bar. Children's menu. Casual attire. **$$**

★ ★ ★ ★ **BACCHANALIA.** *1198 Howell Mill Rd, Suite 100, Atlanta (30318). Phone 404/365-0410; fax 404/365-8020.* Bacchanalia feels like it just tumbled out of New York City's or London's SoHo. Set in a rehabilitated factory complex, this urban dining room has an edgy, sleek, industrial-chic feel to it. The dramatic vaulted ceiling of the dining room boasts a long, low-lit, sexy bar and a glass-enclosed kitchen and is framed by exposed brick-trimmed factory windows. The vibrant seasonal menu changes daily and offers carefully composed upscale American fare that focuses on organic and small-farm produce. Plates are presented with little fuss but lots of flavor and enthusiasm. The wine list, selected by the chef, includes a thoughtful collection of food-friendly half-bottle choices. American menu. Lunch, dinner. Closed Sun; holidays; Dec 25-Jan 1, week of July 4. Bar. Casual attire. Outdoor seating. **$$$$**

★ **BASIL'S MEDITERRANEAN CAFE.** *2985 Grandview Ave, Atlanta (30305). Phone 404/233-9755; fax 404/233-8042. www.basilsinbuckhead.com.* The attraction of this quaint Buckhead cottage-turned-café is twofold: first, the atmosphere is that of a laid-back elegance that's hard to find in the hustle and bustle of downtown Atlanta. The other draw is the fact that, in contrast to some places that call themselves Mediterranean when in fact they serve nouveau Italian or Greek food, the food here really is Mediterranean. Influences for the menu are drawn from Spain, Italy, Greece, and Turkey, while the service remains friendly and familiar. Try the "mesa" appetizer, loaded up with stuffed grape leaves, tabouleh, and house-made hummus and babaghanouj, or the Greek shrimp sautéed with white wine and feta cheese. Mediterranean menu. Lunch, dinner. Closed holidays. Bar. Casual attire. Reservations recommended. Outdoor seating. **$$**

★ ★ ★ **BRASSERIE LE COZE.** *3393 Peachtree Rd, Atlanta (30326). Phone 404/266-1440; fax 404/266-1436.* Bastille Day dinners are served every year in celebration of the French holiday at this chic but charming authentic Parisian establishment. French menu. Lunch, dinner. Closed Sun; Thanksgiving, Dec 25. Bar. Casual attire. Outdoor seating. **$$**

★ ★ ★ **THE CAFE.** *3434 Peachtree Rd NE, Atlanta (30326). Phone 404/237-2700; toll-free 800/241-3333; fax 404/239-0078. www.ritzcarlton.com.* Chef Robert Guillou takes cues from his native Provence for the menu in this all-day restaurant of the Ritz-Carlton Buckhead hotel. Sunday brunch is a particular treat. International menu. Breakfast, lunch, dinner, late-night, Sun brunch. Bar. Children's menu. Casual attire. Valet parking. Outdoor seating. **$$$**

★ ★ ★ **CANOE.** *4199 Paces Ferry Rd NW, Atlanta (30339). Phone 770/432-2663; fax 770/433-2542. www.canoeatl.com.* Situated on the banks of the Chattahoochee River amidst rambling gardens, this casual but sophisticated restaurant serves a delicious American cuisine prepared by chef Gary Mennie. The eclectic menu ranges from barbecued duck springrolls to seared Carolina trout. American menu. Lunch, dinner, Sun brunch. Bar. Casual attire. Valet parking. Outdoor seating. **$$$**

★ ★ **CARBO'S CAFE.** *3717 Roswell Rd, Atlanta (30342). Phone 404/231-4162; fax 404/237-6826. www.carbos-cafe.com.* This fine dining restaurant was established in 1980 and continues to satisfy diners with its elegant service and sophisticated menu. Specialties include terrine of foie gras; she-crab soup; Dover sole; and large, tender, and juicy veal chops. American menu. Dinner. Closed Sun-Tues; holidays. Bar. Valet parking. **$$$**

★ ★ ★ **CHOPS.** *70 W Paces Ferry Rd, Atlanta (30305). Phone 404/262-2675; fax 404/240-6645. www.buckheadrestaurants.com.* Two restaurants in one: upstairs is a clubby steakhouse where power diners chomp on delicious prime aged beef; downstairs is the Lobster Bar where romantic diners sit in white stuccco grottos and savor delicate seafood creations. Steak menu. Lunch, dinner. Closed holidays. Bar. Casual attire. Valet parking. **$$$**

★ ★ ★ **CITY GRILL.** *50 Hurt Plz, Ste 200, Atlanta (30303). Phone 404/524-2489; fax 404/529-9474. www.citygrillatlanta.com.* This restaurant features regional American cuisine in an elegant clublike environment set in a renovated historic building. It is an elegant establishment with great views, a good choice for intimate dinners. American menu. Lunch, dinner. Closed Sun; holidays. Bar. Children's menu. Business casual attire. Reservations recommended. Valet parking. **$$$**

★ **THE COLONNADE.** *1879 Cheshire Bridge Rd, Atlanta (30324). Phone 404/874-5642.* Southern menu. Lunch, dinner. Closed Dec 24-25. Bar. **$**

★ **COWTIPPERS.** *1600 Piedmont Ave, Atlanta (30324). Phone 404/874-3751; fax 404/875-1666. www.cowtippersatlanta.com.* With a rustic cowboy theme, this steakhouse features an expansive menu with beef and fish specialties. Imaginative details are found throughout the restaurant, including tables painted in cowhide patterns, tin ceilings above the bar, and open-beam ceilings in the dining area. Steak menu. Lunch, dinner. Bar. Children's menu. Casual attire. Outdoor seating. **$$**

★ ★ **DAILEY'S.** *17 International Blvd, Atlanta (30303). Phone 404/681-3303; fax 404/681-6643. www.daileysrestaurant.com.* Beyond the restored warehouse exterior of this restaurant, patrons enter through a villa-style hallway into one of Atlanta's favorite special-occasion gathering spots. The downstairs features

an intimate jazz and cigar bar with leather couches, while the large, spacious dining room upstairs features imaginative American fare and impeccable service. American menu. Lunch, dinner. Closed holidays. Bar. Casual attire. **$$**

★ ★ **DANTE'S DOWN THE HATCH.** *3380 Peachtree Rd NE, Atlanta (30326). Phone 404/266-1600; fax 404/266-2229. www.dantesdownthehatch.com.* Surrounding diners with an eclectic mix of nautical décor, this fondue restaurant houses antiques and a ship built inside the dining room. Cabin-style booths and a pond with turtles and alligators add to the experience. Fondue menu. Dinner. Closed Jan 1, Dec 25. Bar. Casual attire. **$$$**

★ ★ ★ ★ **THE DINING ROOM.** *3434 Peachtree Rd NE, Atlanta (30326). Phone 404/237-2700; toll-free 800/241-3333; fax 404/239-0078. www.ritzcarlton.com.* If you're looking for a luxurious spot for fine, divine dining in posh Buckhead, head over to The Ritz-Carlton (see) and beg for a table at The Dining Room, the hotel's magnificent venue for sophisticated fare. The room is opulent, decorated ornately in European style. Deep, tufted banquettes are cloaked in plush Victorian green silk, the walls are decorated with muted sage-toned chinoisserie fabric, and Frette linens top spacious tables. Vintage wall sconces give the room a soft glow, and grand oil paintings add an old-world elegance. The menu is an exercise in pleasure and wonder. Not a note is off as the chef employs subtle Asian touches to accent stunning regional ingredients. After dessert and a spectacular cheese course, it's time for petit fours, which arrive in a mobile cart in numbers. Loosen your belt. This is luxury at its finest, served to perfection. French, Japanese menu. Dinner. Closed Sun-Mon; holidays. Jacket required. Reservations recommended. Valet parking. **$$$$**

★ ★ **DISH.** *870 N Highland Ave NE, Atlanta (30306). Phone 404/897-3463; fax 404/874-2886.* American menu. Dinner. Closed holidays. Bar. Former filling station (1939). Outdoor seating. **$$**

★ **DUSTY'S BARBECUE.** *1815 Briarcliff Rd NE, Atlanta (30329). Phone 404/320-6264; fax 404/320-1343. www.dustys.com.* Located near Emory University, this popular spot is decorated with all manner of pig paraphernalia, but the draw is the tangy barbecue. Ask for the "sizzling sauce" if you want a more fiery experience. Locals rave about the blackberry cobbler. Barbecue menu. Lunch, dinner. Children's menu. Casual attire. Outdoor seating. **$**

★ ★ **FIRE OF BRAZIL CHURRASCARIA.** *118 Perimeter Center W, Atlanta (30346). Phone 770/551-4367; fax 770/551-9652. www.fireofbrazil.com.* This unique Brazilian steakhouse is perfect for diners who are looking for a totally new experience. The main focus here is grilled meats—beef, pork, lamb, chicken, and sausage—which are brought to each table and carved to the guest's liking, and accompanied by a huge 150-item buffet. Brazilian menu. Lunch, dinner. Bar. Children's menu. Casual attire. **$$$**

★ ★ ★ **THE FOOD STUDIO.** *887 W Marietta St, Studio K 102, Atlanta (30318). Phone 404/815-6677; fax 404/815-1178. www.thefoodstudio.com.* Inside a century-old renovated factory building lies this tucked-away oasis of eclectic dining. With dishes such as seared sea scallops with edamame succotash and smoked tomato vinaigrette, and an organic heirloom tomato salad with grilled cornbread and lemon mayonnaise, this restaurant celebrates the wide array of regional flavors found across America. The dining room is located in the upstairs loft of the building, with soft, dim lighting and crisp white-on-white tablecloths, while the downstairs area is designed for takeout diners. American menu. Dinner. Closed holidays. Bar. Casual attire. Valet parking. Outdoor seating. **$$$**

★ ★ **FRITTI.** *309 N Highland Ave, Atlanta (30307). Phone 404/880-9559; fax 404/880-0462. www.fritti restaurant.com.* Traditional brick-oven pizza is the specialty here. Located a few blocks from the Virginia-Highland section of the city, this upscale eatery is a great place to stop for lunch or dinner after a stroll through the neighborhood. Pizza menu. Lunch, dinner. Closed Sun. Bar. Children's menu. Casual attire. Outdoor seating. **$$**

★ **GEORGIA GRILLE.** *2290 Peachtree Rd, Atlanta (30309). Phone 404/352-3517; fax 404/8419964. www.georgiagrille.com.* Serving Southwestern fare in a friendly environment since 1990, this restaurant was named for and inspired by the art of Georgia O'Keeffe. Small oil paintings are featured throughout the dining room, as are hand-painted tables and an antique cake cooler. Southwestern menu. Dinner. Closed Mon; Thanksgiving, Dec 25. Bar. Casual attire. **$$**

★ ★ **HARVEST RESTAURANT.** *853 N Highland Ave NE, Atlanta (30306). Phone 404/876-8244; fax 404/876-1844. www.harvestrestaurant.net.* A vaulted ceiling on the second floor complements a fireplace and bar. American menu. Lunch, dinner. Closed Labor Day, Thanksgiving, Dec 25. Bar. Casual attire. Valet parking. Outdoor seating. **$$$**

★ **HAVELI.** *225 Spring St, Atlanta (30303). Phone 404/522-4545; fax 404/522-4526.* Indian menu. Dinner. Closed Dec 25. Bar. Casual attire. **$$**

★ ★ **HORSERADISH GRILL.** *4320 Powers Ferry Rd, Atlanta (30342). Phone 404/255-7277; fax 404/847-0603. www.horseradishgrill.com.* For classic Southern food with a modern twist, Atlanta's oldest continuously operating restaurant has kept locals coming back again and again for years. Originally a country inn, the restaurant gets its herbs fresh from an outdoor patch and specializes in variations on old favorites, such as the rosemary-grilled lamb chop with dijon-mint jelly glaze and fried green tomatoes with melted goat cheese and spicy pecans. Southern menu. Lunch, dinner, Sun brunch. Closed Jan 1, Dec 25. Bar. Children's menu. Casual attire. Outdoor seating. **$$**

★ ★ **HSU'S GOURMET CHINESE.** *192 Peachtree Center Ave, Atlanta (30303). Phone 404/659-2788; fax 404/577-3456. www.hsus.com.* This informal Chinese restaurant is located downtown. Korean-born chef Charlie Shan specializes in Hong Kong and Szechwan cuisine. Succulent Peking duck can be ordered without any advance warning; the whole fish and spicy noodles are superb. Chinese menu. Lunch, dinner. Closed July 4, Thanksgiving, Dec 25. Bar. Casual attire. Reservations recommended. **$$**

★ ★ **IMPERIAL FEZ.** *2285 Peachtree Rd NE, Atlanta (30309). Phone 404/351-0870; fax 404/351-1272. www.imperialfez.com.* Belly dancers move to Moroccan music while customers sit at low tables with silk-cushioned seating and enjoy the exotic but traditional food under tented ceilings. Moroccan menu. Dinner. Bar. Children's menu. Casual attire. Valet parking. **$$$**

★ ★ ★ **JOEL.** *3290 Northside Pkwy, Atlanta (30327). Phone 404/233-3500; fax 404/467-9450. www.joelrestaurant.com.* International/Fusion menu. Lunch, dinner. Closed Sun. Bar. Casual attire. Reservations recommended. Valet parking. **$$$**

★ ★ ★ **KYMA.** *3085 Piedmont Rd, Atlanta (30305). Phone 404/262-0702; fax 404/841-9924. www.buckhead restaurants.com.* True to its name, the atmosphere at Kyma, meaning "wave" in Greek, brings to mind the crisp, clean seascape colors of the Greek Islands—deep blue and pure white. Enjoy a glass of wine and appetizers on the year-round patio, and then head inside to sit under the unique painted constellations that adorn the ceilings. The restaurant specializes in classic Greek dishes, especially fresh seafood, and be sure to take a look at the wall mosaic in the entry—a unique piece of traditional Greek art made from bits of broken plates. Greek menu. Dinner. Closed Sun. Bar. Casual attire. Outdoor seating. **$$**

★ ★ ★ **LA GROTTA.** *2637 Peachtree Rd NE, Atlanta (30305). Phone 404/231-1368; fax 404/231-1274. www.la-grotta.com.* There are two outposts of this upscale Italian restaurant (this one in Buckhead and a sister in Dunwoody). The professional service and tempting menu cannot be beat. Homemade pastas (such as goat cheese ravioli) and tempting entrées (such as grilled salmon) are sure to satisfy. More exotic items like snails and octopus are also available. Italian menu. Dinner. Closed Sun; holidays; last week in June-first week in July. Bar. Jacket required. Reservations recommended. Valet parking. Outdoor seating. **$$$**

★ ★ **LOMBARDI'S.** *94 Pryor St, Atlanta (30303). Phone 404/522-6568; fax 404/577-4457.* Set in the same location in Underground Atlanta for more than 15 years, tourists and government employees tend to dominate the clientele here, since the proximity to both downtown attractions and government buildings is convenient. The menu is comprised of traditional Italian dishes with modern flair, as well as an array of desserts, all made in-house. Italian menu. Lunch, dinner. Bar. Casual attire. **$$**

★ **MARY MAC'S TEA ROOM.** *224 Ponce de Leon Ave NE, Atlanta (30308). Phone 404/876-1800; fax 404/881-6003. www.marymacs.com.* An informal neighborhood café first opened in 1945, Mary Mac's offers traditional "meat and three" meals and super-sweet iced tea. Southern/Soul menu. Lunch, dinner. Bar. Children's menu. Casual attire. **$$**

★ ★ ★ **MCKENDRICK'S.** *4505 Ashford Dunwoody Ave, Atlanta (30346). Phone 770/512-8888; fax 770/379-1470. www.mckendricks.com.* Guests will enjoy the appetizers and cuisine at this dark, clubby steakhouse, a veritable institution. Large martinis add to the enjoyment. Steak menu. Lunch, dinner. Closed holidays. Bar. Casual attire. Valet parking. **$$$**

★ **MCKINNON'S LOUISIANE.** *3209 Maple Dr, Atlanta (30305). Phone 404/237-1313; fax 404/237-2026. www.mckinnons.com.* Fresh seafood is the big draw at this Buckhead location, where meals are served in the casual Grill Room or a more formal dining room. Cajun/Creole menu. Dinner. Closed

holidays. Bar. Children's menu. Business casual attire. Reservations recommended. **$$**

★ ★ **NAKATO JAPANESE RESTAURANT.** *1776 Cheshire Bridge Rd NE, Atlanta (30324). Phone 404/873-6582; fax 404/874-7897. www.nakato restaurant.com.* Traditional sushi forms the basis for a meal at this understated Japanese restaurant in the Cheshire Bridge section of town. Beautiful flower arrangements decorate the dining room, and the service is attentive and friendly. Japanese menu. Dinner. Bar. Children's menu. Casual attire. Valet parking. **$$**

★ ★ **NAVA.** *3060 Peachtree Rd, Atlanta (30305). Phone 404/240-1984; fax 404/240-1831. www.buckhead restaurants.com.* The captivating and dramatic décor complements the food, full of bold flavors; vibrant colors; and exotic textures. Southwestern menu. Lunch, dinner. Bar. Children's menu. Business casual attire. Reservations recommended. Valet parking. Outdoor seating. **$$**

★ ★ **NICKIEMOTO'S.** *990 Piedmont Ave, Atlanta (30309). Phone 404/253-2010; fax 404/253-2014.* Pan-Asian menu. Lunch, dinner, late-night. Closed Dec 25. Bar. Casual attire. Reservations recommended. Outdoor seating. **$$**

★ ★ ★ **NIKOLAI'S ROOF.** *255 Courtland St NE, Atlanta (30303). Phone 404/221-6362; fax 404/221-6811. www.nikolaisroof.com.* Located atop the downtown Hilton, this French-Russian restaurant serves a stunning view along with its chilled vodka and Russian classics like borscht and piroshkis. The setting and service are formal. International/Fusion menu. Dinner. Closed Sun-Mon. Bar. Business casual attire. Reservations recommended. Valet parking. **$$$$**

★ **NINO'S ITALIAN RESTAURANT.** *1931 Cheshire Bridge Rd NE, Atlanta (30324). Phone 404/874-6505; fax 404/874-3596. www.ninosatlanta.com.* Italian menu. Dinner. Closed Jan 1, July 4, Dec 25. Bar. Casual attire. Reservations recommended. Outdoor seating. **$$**

★ ★ ★ **PANO'S & PAUL'S.** *1232 W Paces Ferry Rd, Atlanta (30327). Phone 404/261-3662; fax 404/261-4512. www.buckheadrestaurants.com.* The dining room of this upscale Atlanta institution has an Art Deco touch. Locals say this restaurant defines fine dining for the area. Chef Peter Kaiser's American menu includes the famous fried lobster tail and other contemporary specialties. An extensive wine list and friendly service complete the experience. Continental, seafood menu. Dinner. Closed Sun; holidays. Bar. Casual attire. **$$$**

★ ★ ★ ★ **PARK 75 AT THE FOUR SEASONS.** *75 14th St NE, Atlanta (30309). Phone 404/253-3840; toll-free 800/332-3442; fax 404/253-3935. www.fourseasons.com.* Located in the Four Seasons Hotel, Atlanta (see), Park 75 is a bright and airy restaurant, a classic choice for tranquil and comfortable fine dining. The serene, pale-yellow dining room is warmed by iron candelabras, custom lighting, and oversized watercolor murals, while the ficus tree-lined terrace takes its calm from the open air. Although the dining room is soft and soothing, the food is bright and bold. The cross-cultural American menu lives by the seasons, offering a wonderful selection of the finest local vegetables, meats, and fish, sparked to life with classic techniques and a jolt of original style. The signature Park 75 surf and turf, for example, twists the classic by combining butter-braised Maine lobster with milk-fed veal filet and foie gras. A well-conceived wine list is mostly American, although it also offers many boutique and international selections. For a special treat, reserve the chef's table and enjoy an eight-course menu with wines to match. American menu. Breakfast, lunch, dinner, Sun brunch. Bar. Children's menu. Business casual attire. Reservations recommended. **$$$**

★ ★ **PETITE AUBERGE.** *2935 N Druid Hill Rd, Atlanta (30329). Phone 404/634-6268; fax 404/636-3306. www.petiteauberge.com.* Offering old-world European charm and classic continental-style haute cuisine, the staff of European chefs prepare dishes in the classical philosophy of French cooking. French menu. Lunch, dinner. Closed Sun; holidays. Bar. Children's menu. Casual attire. **$$**

★ ★ **PHILIPPE'S BISTRO.** *10 Kings Cir, Atlanta (30305). Phone 404/231-4113; fax 404/231-4710. www.philippesbistro.com.* Award-winning Belgian chef-owner Philippe Haddad has made this restaurant one of the Buckhead neighborhood's most popular dinner destinations. The menu offers specialties from Haddad's native country alongside more familiar, yet innovative, upscale fare. Brunch is also a special treat here, offering, of course, authentic Belgian waffles, as well as other tantalizing dishes. Belgian menu. Dinner, brunch. Closed Mon. Children's menu. Casual attire. Outdoor seating. **$$$**

★ **PITTYPAT'S PORCH.** *25 International Blvd, Atlanta (30303). Phone 404/525-8228; fax 404/524-0471.* Southern menu. Dinner. Bar. Children's menu. Casual attire. Reservations recommended. **$$**

★ ★ **PLEASANT PEASANT.** *555 Peachtree St, Atlanta (30308). Phone 404/874-3223; fax 404/897-2051. www.thepeasantrestaurants.com.* In an old building, slightly off the beaten path of Peachtree Street, this restaurant is a local favorite for relaxed dining. It specializies in unique dishes such as lobster sliders and pecan-crusted salmon. American menu. Lunch, dinner, brunch. Closed Thanksgiving, Dec 25. Bar. Children's menu. Casual attire. Outdoor seating. **$$**

★ ★ **PRICCI.** *500 Pharr Rd, Atlanta (30305). Phone 404/237-2941; toll-free 877/282-4323; fax 404/261-0058. www.buckheadrestaurants.com.* There's a certain glitz to this see-and-be-seen upscale Italian restaurant, another member of the Buckhead Group. Among the menu highlights are the pastas and any entrée with veal. The wine list has an extensive selection of regional Italian labels. Italian menu. Lunch, dinner. Closed holidays. Bar. Business casual attire. Valet parking. **$$**

★ ★ ★ **PRIME.** *3393 Peachtree Rd NE, Atlanta (30326). Phone 404/812-0555; fax 404/812-0225. www.heretoserverestaurants.com.* This restaurant redefines the term surf and turf by including sushi as part of the surf portion. Floor-to-ceiling windows, an open kitchen, and its location in the upscale Lenox Square Mall make it an exciting alternative to the traditional steakhouse. Steak, sushi menu. Lunch, dinner. Closed holidays. Bar. Children's menu. Casual attire. Valet parking. **$$**

★ ★ **RAY'S ON THE RIVER.** *6700 Powers Ferry Rd, Atlanta (30339). Phone 770/955-1187; fax 770/612-2465.* Just from looking at the menu of this river-view restaurant, it's clear that this place is serious about seafood. Selections of steak, chicken, and pork are also available. Seafood menu. Lunch, dinner, Sun brunch. Closed Dec 25. Bar. Children's menu. Casual attire. Outdoor seating. **$$**

★ ★ ★ **RESTAURANT EUGENE.** *2277 Peachtree Rd, Atlanta (30309). Phone 404/355-0321; fax 404/355-0322.* American menu. Dinner. Closed Sun. Bar. Children's menu. Reservations recommended. Valet parking. **$$**

★ ★ ★ **THE RIVER ROOM.** *4403 Northside Pkwy, Atlanta (30327). Phone 404/233-5455; fax 404/233-3073. www.riverroom.com.* If you only have time to experience a handful of restaurants in Atlanta, this popular favorite should be one of them. Like sitting outside so you can people-watch as you dine? Done—there's a spacious fountainside patio that looks out onto a very charming, European-looking square. Jazz fan? Come on a Friday night to the tavern lounge and listen to some of the city's best musicians. Self-proclaimed food connoisseur? The menu here is extensive yet unpretentious, with Southern-infused choices such as feta-stuffed free range chicken served with couscous and chili-fried onion rings, and baked lobster with a cornbread stuffing. American menu. Lunch, dinner, Sun brunch. Bar. Children's menu. Casual attire. Outdoor seating. **$$**

★ **ROCK BOTTOM.** *3242 Peachtree Rd, Atlanta (30305). Phone 404/264-0253; fax 404/264-9109.* If you've been running around Buckhead for half the day and need to recharge with food, drink, and a little relaxation, this is the place. Flop into a cushy booth, order up one of their specialty brews, and peruse their menu chock-full of options, including pizza, pasta, salads, sandwiches, and more. American menu. Lunch, dinner. Closed Thanksgiving, Dec 25. Bar. Children's menu. Casual attire. Outdoor seating. **$$**

★ ★ ★ **RUTH'S CHRIS STEAK HOUSE.** *5788 Roswell Rd, Atlanta (30328). Phone 404/255-0035; toll-free 800/544-0808; fax 404/255-3111. www.ruths chrisatlanta.com.* Prime aged beef, generous side dishes, professional service, and all of the other features that have made this one of the nation's most successful steakhouse chains are all present at this Atlanta outpost. Steak menu. Dinner. Closed July 4, Dec 25. Bar. Casual attire. Valet parking. **$$$**

★ ★ ★ ★ ★ **SEEGER'S.** *111 W Paces Ferry Rd, Atlanta (30305). Phone 404/846-9779; fax 404/846-9217. www.seegers.com.* Giving Atlanta locals a taste of culinary excitement, Seeger's is a deliciously indulgent and comfortably adventurous place to dine. You'll feel swept away the second you enter the 1938 whitewashed brick cottage and take a seat in Seeger's bright and airy dining room, furnished with contemporary style and modest grace. Well-spaced tables are set with Riedel crystal and Bernardaud china; smooth damask linens and fresh flowers in precious glass bud vases dress the tabletops. Brocade-pattered upholstered chairs; soft leather banquettes; antique French armoires; cherry-wood paneled walls; and glowing, teardrop-shaped lighting add warmth to the stylish space. The impeccably prepared nouvelle French menu changes daily and showcases both the pristine ingredients of the season and the wellspring of talent and dedication in the kitchen. Presentations are exciting and entertaining, making incredible use of garnishes and unique presentation pieces. Chef

Seeger's exceptional prowess in the kitchen glows brightly in each course, from bread through dessert. The wine selections are incredibly diverse and will match any ingredient the chef may be featuring on an evening. Throughout the meal, the staff is consistently smooth and complimentary, applying a degree of Southern charm and warmth to each interaction. Seeger's is a sublime experience that will call you back to Atlanta, if only for dinner. Dinner. Closed Sun; Jan 1, Thanksgiving, Dec 25. Bar. Business casual attire, jacket required. Reservations recommended. Outdoor seating. **$$$$**

★ ★ **SOHO CAFE.** *4300 Paces Ferry Rd, Ste 107, Atlanta (30339). Phone 770/801-0069; fax 770/801-0093. www.sohoatlanta.com.* Eclectic menu. Lunch, dinner. Closed Sun; holidays. Bar. Outdoor seating. **$$**

★ ★ ★ **SOTTO SOTTO.** *313 N Highland Ave, Atlanta (30307). Phone 404/523-6678; fax 404/880-0462. www.sottosottorestaurant.com.* Located right next door to its sister restaurant, Fritti (see), this dining spot is consistently rated one of the best Italian restaurants in Atlanta. The dishes here prove that simplicity is the best way to highlight the best ingredients. Diners can see and smell the magic happening in the open kitchen, which is also visible from the street outside. Italian menu. Dinner. Closed Sun. Bar. Casual attire. Outdoor seating. **$$**

★ ★ **SOUTH CITY KITCHEN.** *1144 Crescent Ave, Atlanta (30309). Phone 404/873-7358; fax 404/873-0317. www.southcitykitchen.com.* Southern menu. Lunch, dinner, Sun brunch. Bar. Business casual attire. Reservations recommended. Outdoor seating. **$$**
🅱

★ **SUNDOWN CAFE.** *2165 Cheshire Bridge Rd, Atlanta (30324). Phone 404/321-1118. www.sundowncafe.com.* Southwestern menu. Lunch, dinner. Closed Sun; holidays. Bar. Casual attire. **$$**

★ **THAI CHILI.** *2169 Briarcliff Rd NE, Atlanta (30329). Phone 404/315-6750; fax 404/315-9367. www.thaichilicuisine.com.* Thai menu. Lunch, dinner. Closed Dec 25. Casual attire. **$**

★ **TOULOUSE.** *2293 Peachtree Rd NE, Atlanta (30309). Phone 404/351-9533; fax 404/351-2299. www.toulouserestaurant.com.* Locals rave about the awesome wine list here, and with more than 60 wines by the glass, as well as occasional wine tastings, it's no wonder. As you enter the restaurant, you'll be hit by the aroma of all things tasty coming from the wood-burning oven in the open kitchen, and although the atmosphere is that of a laid-back bistro, the menu is anything but dull. Make sure you check out their seasonal menu, which in the past has included intriguing options like strawberry soup and seared flounder with andouille sausage. French bistro menu. Dinner. Closed Jan 1, Dec 25. Bar. Casual attire. Reservations recommended. Outdoor seating. **$$**

★ **THE VARSITY.** *61 North Ave, Atlanta (30308). Phone 404/881-1706; fax 404/881-0273. www.thevarsity .com.* The Varsity has been serving Atlanta its famous chilidogs, onion rings, and fried apple pies since 1928. Servers shout orders like Naked Dog, Walk the Dog, Jo-Ree, and Bag of Rags while avoiding collisions with each other in almost choreographed confusion. It's a show all to itself. American menu. Breakfast, lunch, dinner. Outdoor seating. **$**

★ ★ ★ **VENI VIDI VICI.** *41 14th St, Atlanta (30309). Phone 404/875-8424; fax 404/875-6533. www.buckheadrestaurants.com.* The first Buckhead Group restaurant outside of Buckhead, this upscale midtown trattoria serves some of the best Italian food in town. The menu is organized into small antipasti, perfect for tasting many different things; homemade pastas; and entrées. Italian menu. Lunch, dinner. Bar. Business casual attire. Reservations recommended. Valet parking. Outdoor seating. **$$$**

★ ★ ★ **VILLA CHRISTINA.** *4000 Summit Blvd, Atlanta (30319). Phone 404/303-0133; fax 404/303-0118. www.villachristina.com.* Italian menu. Lunch, dinner. Closed Sun; holidays. Bar. Casual attire. Valet parking. Outdoor seating. **$$**

★ ★ **THE VININGS INN.** *3011 Paces Mill Rd, Atlanta (30339). Phone 770/438-2282; fax 770/438-0653. www.viningsinn.com.* Featuring a range of dining areas, including the Sunroom, Bear Room, and the Attic Bar, this restaurant is great for anything from drinks and appetizers, to a romantic dinner for two, to a large family gathering. Originally a residence from the 1850s, the restaurant has become a destination for an upscale yet relaxed dining experience. American menu. Lunch, dinner. Bar. Casual attire. Outdoor seating. **$$$**

★ **ZOCALO.** *187 10th St, Atlanta (30309). Phone 404/249-7576; fax 404/876-3047.* Famous for its margaritas and selection of more than 100 types of tequila, this Mexican hot spot is located just a block from Peachtree. Colorful painted tables and chairs, antique signs and pictures, and old-fashioned chandeliers give the dining area a desert saloon feel, while roll-down windows let in refreshing breezes. Mexican menu. Lunch, dinner, Sun brunch. Closed holidays. Children's menu. Casual attire. Outdoor seating. **$$**

Atlanta Hartsfield Airport Area (B-2)

See also Atlanta

Information Phone 404/530-7300 or toll-free 800/897-1910.
Web Site www.atlanta-airport.com.
Lost and Found Phone 404/530-2100, ext. 100
Weather Phone 770/486-8834
Cash machines Concourse A
Airlines Aeromexico, Air Canada, Air France, Air Jamaica, AirTran Airways, American Airlines, American West, ASA, British Airways, ComAir, Continental, Corporate, Delta, Frontier Airlines, Hooters Air, jetBlue Airways, Korean Air, Lufthansa, Midwest Airlines, Northwest, South African Airways, United, USAir.

Limited-Service Hotel

★ ★ **COURTYARD BY MARRIOTT.** *2050 Sullivan Rd, College Park (30337). Phone 770/997-2220; toll-free 800/321-2221; fax 770/994-9743. www.marriott.com.* 144 rooms, 3 story. Check-in 3 pm, check-out noon. High-speed Internet access. Restaurant, bar. Fitness room. Indoor pool, whirlpool. Airport transportation available. Business center. **$**

Full-Service Hotel

★ ★ ★ **HILTON ATLANTA AIRPORT AND TOWERS.** *1031 Virginia Ave, Atlanta (30354). Phone 404/767-9000; toll-free 800/411-8065; fax 404/768-0185. www.atlantaairport.hilton.com.* This hotel is conveniently located near the airport as well as near many of Atlanta's attractions like the zoo, Stone Mountain, and Six Flags. Guests will enjoy the complimentary 24-hour transportation to the airport and MARTA station, as well as the Olympus Gym, pools, Jacuzzi, and 24-hour room service. 504 rooms, 17 story. Pets accepted; fee. Check-in 3 pm, check-out noon. Restaurant, bar. Fitness room. Indoor pool, outdoor pool, whirlpool. Tennis. Business center. **$$**

Augusta (B-4)

Founded 1736
Population 44,639
Elevation 414 ft
Area Code 706
Information Metropolitan Convention and Visitors Bureau, 1450 Greene St, Suite 110, 30901; phone 706/823-6600 or toll-free 800/726-0243.
Web Site www.augustaga.org

Augusta was the second town marked off for settlement by General James E. Oglethorpe. Today it is as famed for golf as for its red Georgia clay bricks. The city has been a military outpost and upriver trading town, the leading 18th-century tobacco center, a river shipping point for cotton, the powder works for the Confederacy, an industrial center for the New South, and a winter resort.

During the Revolution, the town changed hands several times, but Fort Augusta, renamed Fort Cornwallis by its British captors, was finally surrendered to "Lighthorse Harry" Lee's Continentals on June 5, 1781.

The Civil War played havoc with many of the wealthy families who had contributed to the Confederate cause. To help revive their depleted bank accounts, some Summerville residents opened their houses to paying guests. Attracted by Augusta's mild winter climate, northern visitors began an annual migration in increasing numbers, and by the turn of the 20th century, Augusta had become a popular winter resort. Many wealthy northerners built winter residences here in the 1920s. Golf courses and country clubs added to the lure. The Masters Tournament attracts the interest of golfers worldwide.

Augusta's many firsts include the state's first medical academy (chartered 1828); the first and oldest newspaper in the South to be published continuously, the *Augusta Chronicle* (1785); the first steamboat to be launched in southern waters (1790), invented and built by William Longstreet; and the experimental site for one of Eli Whitney's early cotton gins.

Augusta lies at the head of navigation on the Savannah River. Its importance as a cotton market, and a producer of cotton textiles, kaolin tiles, and brick has been enhanced by diversified manufacturing, processing of cottonseed, farm products, and fertilizers. Fort Gordon, an army base southwest of the city, also contributes to the area's economy. With the Medical College of Georgia, Augusta is a leading medical center in the Southeast.

What to See and Do

Augusta Museum of History. *560 Reynolds St, Augusta (30901). Phone 706/722-8454. www.augustamuseum .org.* (1802) Historical collections. (Tues-Sat 10 am-5 pm, Sun 1-5 pm; closed holidays) **$$**

Augusta State University. *2500 Walton Way, Augusta. Between Katharine St and Arsenal Ave. Phone 706/737-1444.* (1925) (5,000 students) Site of Augusta Arsenal (1826-1955), of which portions are preserved.

Confederate Powder Works Chimney. *1717 Goodrich St, Augusta.* A memorial honoring war dead, this brick chimney is all that remains of what was once the second-largest powder factory in the world.

Cotton Exchange. *32 8th St, Augusta (30901). Phone 706/823-6600.* Handsome brick building, built in 1886, now houses visitor center. (Daily) **FREE**

Gertrude Herbert Institute of Art. *506 Telfair St, Augusta. Phone 706/722-5495.* Old Ware's Folly Mansion (1818) houses changing exhibits; works by local artists. (Tues-Fri; closed holidays) **DONATION**

Harris House. *1822 Broad St, Augusta. Phone 706/724-0436.* (Circa 1795) House of Ezekiel Harris, tobacco merchant. Period furnishings. Tours (Sat afternoons or by appointment) **$**

Meadow Garden. *1320 Independence Dr, Augusta. Phone 706/724-4174.* House (1791-1804) of George Walton, signer of the Declaration of Independence. Period furnishings. Guided tours (Mon-Fri; also Sat by appointment). **$$**

Morris Museum of Art. *1 10th St, Augusta (30901). Phone 706/724-7501. www.themorris.org.* This museum houses a collection of paintings by Southern artists depicting landscapes, portraits, and Civil War scenes; it also has small folk-art collection. Free admission Sun. (Tues-Sat 10 am-5 pm, Sun noon-5 pm) **$**

National Science Center's Fort Discovery. *1 7th St, Augusta. Phone 706/821-0200; toll-free 800/325-5445. www.nationalsciencecenter.org.* An innovative hands-on science, communications, and technology center with 250 interactive exhibits; high-tech theater; KidScape for children ages 3-7. Also here are a Teacher

Resource Center, traveling exhibits, and a science store. (Mon-Sat 10 am-5 pm, Sun noon-5 pm; closed holidays) **$$**

Riverwalk. Augusta's high Savannah River levee has been lavishly restored as a promenade for strollers, skaters, and cyclists, linking the city's major attractions.

St. Paul's Episcopal Church. *605 Reynolds St, Augusta (30901). Phone 706/724-2485. www.saintpauls.org.* (1750) A granite Celtic cross in the churchyard marks the site of a fort and the spot where Augusta began, established by James Oglethorpe in 1736 in honor of Princess Augusta. Oglethorpe Park, a recreational area on the Savannah River, is located behind the church; picnicking.

Special Events

Augusta Invitational Rowing Regatta. *Augusta Riverfront Marina., Augusta.* Mid-late July.

Augusta Opera. *1301 Greene St, Augusta (30901). Phone 706/826-4710. www.augustaopera.com.* In addition to several opera performances, the Augusta Opera also provides several community outreach programs to further promote this art form. Mid-Sept-mid-May. **$$$$**

Augusta Symphony Orchestra. *Sacred Heart Cultural Center, 1301 Greene St, Suite 200, Augusta (30901). Phone 706/826-4705; fax 706/826-4735. www.augustasymphony.org.* The Augusta Symphony's season is always packed full with concerts and events designed to please all types of audiences. Choose from traditional orchestra concerts, pops performances featuring world famous guest artists, and smaller and more intimate chamber concerts. The Symphony also sponsors community outreach programs intended to attract both children and adult participation. Mid-Sept-mid-May.

Masters Golf Tournament. *Augusta National Golf Course, 2604 Washington Rd, Augusta. Phone 706/667-6000. www.masters.org.* The Masters is one of four major golfing tournaments held each year. It is held every year at Augusta National Golf Club. In addition to a cash award, the winner is presented with the famous green sportcoat, highly coveted among professional golfers. First full week in Apr.

Limited-Service Hotels

★ ★ **AUGUSTA TOWERS HOTEL AND CONVENTION CENTER.** *2651 Perimeter Pkwy, Augusta (30909). Phone 706/855-8100; fax 706/860-1720.* The serene and airy atrium lobby is filled with towering palm trees and beautifully lush plants. Relax in the elegantly appointed guest rooms. Enjoy extra amenities like the indoor and outdoor pools, sauna, whirlpool, and fitness center. 179 rooms. Pets accepted; fee. Check-in 3 pm, check-out noon. Restaurant, bar. Fitness room. Indoor pool, outdoor pool, whirlpool. Airport transportation available. **$$$**
🐾 🏃 🌊

★ ★ **COURTYARD BY MARRIOTT.** *1045 Stevens Creek Rd, Augusta (30907). Phone 706/737-3737; toll-free 800/321-2211; fax 706/738-7851. www.courtyard.com.* Located on Augusta's north side, this hotel designed for business travelers features a business center, and large desks and high-speed Internet access in each room. After a busy day, head to the distinguished Augusta National Golf Club nearby, or relax in the outdoor pool or whirlpool. 130 rooms, 2 story. Check-in 3 pm, check-out noon. High-speed Internet access. Fitness room. Outdoor pool, whirlpool. Business center. **$**
🏃 🌊 🏃

★ ★ **RADISSON RIVERFRONT HOTEL AUGUSTA.** *2 10th St, Augusta (33870). Phone 706/722-8900; toll-free 800/333-3333; fax 706/823-6513. www.radisson.com.* Offering Southern charm along with warm hospitality and outstanding accommodations, this hotel promises a very comfortable and relaxing stay. Elegantly appointed guest rooms are spacious and well equipped with everything from workstations to makeup mirrors and offer views of the beautiful Savannah River, downtown Augusta, and the scenic Riverwalk. The hotel's superb location allows guests to be just minutes from restaurants, antique shops, art galleries, and museums. 237 rooms, 11 story. Pets accepted, some restrictions. Check-out noon. Restaurant, bar. Fitness room. Outdoor pool. **$**
🐾 🏃 🌊

Specialty Lodgings

The following lodging establishments are approved by Mobil Travel Guide, but due to their unique and individualized nature have not been given a traditional Mobil Star rating. Included in this listing you may find bed-and-breakfasts, limited-service inns, guest ranches, and other unique hotel properties.

1810 WEST INN. *254 N Seymour Dr, Thomson, (30824). Phone 706/595-3156; toll-free 800/515-1810; fax 706/595-3155. www.1810westinn.com.* Restored farmhouse (1810); antiques. 11 rooms, 2 story. Children over 12 years only. Complimentary continental breakfast. Check-in 3 pm, check-out noon. **$**
Ⓓ

AZALEA INN. *312 Greene St, Augusta (30901). Phone 706/724-3454; toll-free 877/292-5324; fax 706/724-1033. www.theazaleainn.com.* This enchanting bed-and-breakfast is perfect for a romantic getaway. Located near Augusta's Riverwalk, antiques shops, and brick-lined plazas. 21 rooms, 3 story. Complimentary continental breakfast. Check-in 3-6 pm, check-out 11 am. **$**

ROSEMARY HALL & LOOKAWAY HALL. *804 Carolina Avenue, North Augusta (29841). Phone 803/278-6222; toll-free 800/531-5578; fax 803/278-4877. www.augustainns.com.* This historic inn combines two restored Greek Revival homes, one that dates from 1898 and the other from 1902. Located just 1 1/2 miles from downtown Augusta, the inn is situated around natural gardens, and the rooms are filled with antique furnishings. 23 rooms, 2 story. Children over 12 years only. Complimentary full breakfast. Check-in 3 pm, check-out 11 am. **$**

Restaurants

★ ★ **CALVERTS.** *475 Highland Ave, Augusta (30909). Phone 706/738-4514; fax 706/312-2121.* Established in 1977, this restaurant in the Surrey Center maintains its position on the top of local favorites. American menu. Dinner. Closed Sun. Bar. Children's menu. Business casual attire. Reservations recommended. **$$$**

★ ★ ★ **LA MAISON RESTAURANT & VERITAS WINE & TAPAS.** *404 Telfair St, Augusta (30901). Phone 706/722-4805; fax 706/722-1753. www.lamaisontelfair.com.* This fine dining restaurant in a Southern Revival home is the epitome of Southern hospitality. In between preparing his game specialties (such as lamb, buffalo, pheasant, and quail), the chef makes sure to stop by every table to say hello. International menu. Dinner. Closed Sun. Bar. Business casual attire. Reservations recommended. Outdoor seating. **$$**

Bainbridge (E-2)

See also Tallahassee, Thomasville

Founded 1829
Population 11,722
Elevation 135 ft
Area Code 229
Zip 31717
Information Bainbridge-Decatur County Chamber of Commerce, PO Box 755, 31718; phone 229/246-4774 or toll-free 800/243-4774
Web Site www.bainbridgega.com

On the banks of 37,500-acre Lake Seminole, Bainbridge is Georgia's first inland port. It is a town of giant water oaks and live oaks on the Flint River. Andrew Jackson's troops built an earthworks defense (Fort Hughes) near the present town during the Indian Wars (1817-1821). The town was later named in honor of William Bainbridge, commander of the frigate *Constitution*. The forests were so rich in this area that Bainbridge was known as the wealthiest town in the state when fortunes were made in lumbering in the early 20th century.

What to See and Do

Earl May Boat Basin and Park. *Bainbridge. W Shotwell St at bypass. Phone 229/246-4774.* This 600-acre park on Lake Seminole has exhibits of turn-of-the-century steam engines and locomotives. Beach swimming; boating (ramps). Volleyball court; playing fields. Camping (hookups). Visitor center (Mon-Fri; closed holidays).

Seminole State Park. *7870 State Park Dr, Donalsonville (39845). 23 miles W on Hwy 253. Phone 229/861-3137. www.gastateparks.org.* Lake Seminole, shallow by Georgia standards, holds a greater number of fish species than any other lake in the state. Swimming beach, boating, water-skiing, fishing; miniature golf, picnicking, concession; camping, cottages. (Daily 7 am-10 pm) **$**

Special Events

Decatur County Fall Festival and Fair. Carnival, rides, exhibits, livestock show. Mid-Oct.

Riverside Arts Festival. *119 W Water St, Bainbridge.* Arts festival featuring a different state each year. First week in May.

Limited-Service Hotels

★★ **CHARTER HOUSE INN.** *1401 Tallahassee Hwy, Bainbridge (31717). Phone 229/246-8550; toll-free 800/768-8550; fax 229/246-0260. www.thecharter houseinn.com.* 124 rooms, 2 story. Check-out noon. Restaurant, bar. Outdoor pool. **$**
🖹 🛋

★ **SUPER 8.** *751 W Shotwell St, Bainbridge (31717). Phone 229/246-0015; toll-free 800/800-8000; fax 229/246-0015. www.super8.com.* 53 rooms, 2 story. Complimentary continental breakfast. Check-out 11 am. Outdoor pool, whirlpool. **$**
🛋

Blakely (E-1)

See also Dothan

Founded 1826
Population 5,696
Elevation 275 ft
Area Code 229
Zip 31723
Information Chamber of Commerce, 52 Court Sq, PO Box 189; phone 229/723-3741
Web Site www.blakelyearlychamber.com

Named for US Navy Captain Johnston Blakeley, a hero of the War of 1812, this is an important peanut producing area.

What to See and Do

Coheelee Creek Covered Bridge. *Old River Rd, 9 miles SW via Hwy 62.* This 96-foot-long bridge is the southernmost standing covered bridge in the United States, built in 1891.

Courthouse Square. On the grounds stands what may be the world's only monument honoring the peanut. And the South's last remaining wooden Confederate flagpole, erected in 1861.

Kolomoki Mounds State Historic Park. *205 Indian Mounds Rd, Blakely (39823). 6 miles N off Hwy 27. Phone 229/724-2150. www.gastateparks.org.* Native American mounds, temple mound, and some excavation indicate a settlement here between AD 800 and AD 1200. Swimming pool, fishing, boating (ramps, dock) on Kolomoki Lake; miniature golf, hiking trails, picnicking, camping. For more information, contact the Superintendent, Rte 1, Box 114. (Daily 7 am-10 pm) In the park is

Indian Museum. Exhibits explain artifacts and civilization of Kolomoki, Weeden Island, and Swift Creek cultures. Entry into excavated burial mound. Video presentation (fee). (Tues-Sat; closed Jan 1, Thanksgiving, Dec 25) **$**

Full-Service Inn

★★★ **TARRER INN.** *155 S Cuthbert St, Colquitt (39837). Phone 229/758-2888; toll-free 888/282-7737; fax 229/758-2825.* Recently restored to its natural and timeless beauty, this charming bed-and-breakfast takes guests back to an era of grand style. Guest rooms are exquisitely decorated with beautiful antiques, and there are three fine dining rooms for ultimate dining pleasure. 12 rooms, 3 story. Complimentary full breakfast. Check-in 3 pm, check-out 11 am. Restaurant. **$**

Restaurant

★ **OUR PLACE.** *310 S Main St, Blakely (39823). Phone 229/723-8880.* American menu. Breakfast, lunch, dinner. Closed holidays. Children's menu. **$$**
🖹

Braselton

Web Site www.braselton.net

Restaurant

★★ **CHATEAU ELAN'S LE CLOS.** *100 Tour De France, Braselton (30517). Phone 678/425-0900; fax 678/425-6000. www.chateauelan.com.* French menu. Dinner. Closed Sun-Tues. Reservations recommended. **$$$**

Brunswick (E-5)

See also Darien, Jekyll Island, Sea Island, St. Simons Island

Settled 1771
Population 15,600
Elevation 10 ft
Area Code 912
Information Brunswick-Golden Isles Visitors Bureau, 4 Glynn Ave, 31520; phone 912/265-0620 or toll-free 800/933-2627
Web Site www.brunswick-georgia.com

Brunswick, on the southern third of Georgia's sea-coast, separated from the Golden Isles by the Marshes of Glynn and the Intracoastal Waterway, was laid out in 1771 by the Colonial Council of the Royal Province of Georgia. Named to honor George II of the House of Brunswick (Hanover), it later became the seat of Glynn County, named in honor of John Glynn, member of the British Parliament and sympathizer with the colonists' struggle for independence.

Gateway to St. Simons Island, Jekyll Island, and Sea Island (see all), Brunswick is also a manufacturing and seafood processing town. Among its principal products are pulp, paper, lumber machinery, lumber products, and processed seafood. Its harbor is a full oceangoing seaport, as well as a home port to coastal fishing and shrimping fleets. Brunswick is known as one of the shrimp capitals of the world. Its natural beauty is enhanced by plantings of palms and flowering shrubs along main avenues, contrasting with moss-covered ancient oaks in spacious parks.

What to See and Do

James Oglethorpe Monument. *Queens Sq, Brunswick. E side of Newcastle St.* Honors the founder of Georgia.

Lover's Oak. *Albany and Prince sts, Brunswick.* Giant oak said to be more than 900 years old; the trunk, at a point 3 feet above ground, measures 13 feet in diameter.

Marshes of Glynn. Marshes separate Brunswick from St. Simons Island, Sea Island, Little St. Simons Island, and Jekyll Island (see all). Traversed by causeways connecting with Hwy 17, the vast saltwater marshes are bisected by several rivers and the Intracoastal Waterway. Of them Sidney Lanier wrote "Oh, like to the greatness of God is the greatness within the range of the marshes, the liberal marshes of Glynn." Marshes of Glynn Overlook Park has picnic facilities, view of marshes.

Mary Miller Doll Museum. *209-211 Gloucester St, Brunswick. Phone 912/267-7569.* Collection of 4,000 dolls, dollhouses, miniatures, boats, and toys; exhibit subjects includes antique dolls, foreign dolls, and modern doll artists. (Mon-Fri; closed holidays) **$$**

Limited-Service Hotels

★ ★ **BEST WESTERN BRUNSWICK INN.** *5323 New Jesup Hwy, exit 36 B, Brunswick (31523). Phone 912/264-0144; fax 912/262-0992. www.bestwestern.com.* 145 rooms, 2 story. Pets accepted. Complimentary continental breakfast. Check-in noon, check-out 11 am. Restaurant. Outdoor pool. **$**

★ **EMBASSY SUITES.** *500 Mall Blvd, Brunswick (31525). Phone 912/264-6100; toll-free 800/432-3229; fax 912/267-1615. www.embassysuites.com.* The Southern ambience and convenient location of this property will make it perfect for all guests. The property is attached to the Glynn Place Mall and features complimentary full breakfast, an outdoor pool, exercise room, and meeting facilities. 130 rooms, 5 story, all suites. Pets accepted, some restrictions; fee. Complimentary continental breakfast. Check-in 3 pm, check-out noon. Airport transportation available. **$$**

★ **JAMESON INN.** *661 Scranton Rd, Brunswick (31520). Phone 912/267-0800; toll-free 800/526-3766; fax 912/265-1922. www.jamesoninns.com.* 62 rooms, 2 story. Pets accepted. Complimentary continental breakfast. Check-in 3 pm, check-out 11 am. Fitness room. Outdoor pool. **$**

★ **QUALITY INN.** *125 Venture Dr, Brunswick (31525). Phone 912/265-4600; toll-free 888/394-8495; fax 912/265-8268. www.qualityinn.com.* 83 rooms, 2 story. Complimentary continental breakfast. Check-in 2 pm, check-out 11 am. Outdoor pool. **$**

Restaurants

★ **CAPTAIN JOE'S.** *5296 New Jesup Hwy (Hwy 341), Brunswick (31523). Phone 912/264-8771; fax 912/265-6759.* Seafood, steak menu. Lunch, dinner. Closed Thanksgiving, Dec 24-25. Children's menu. Casual attire. **$$**

★ ★ **MATTEO'S ITALIAN RESTAURANT.** *5323 New Jesup Hwy (Hwy 341), Brunswick (31523). Phone 912/267-0248.* Italian, pizza menu. Lunch, dinner. Closed Sun; holidays. Children's menu. Casual attire. **$**

★ **NEW CHINA.** *3202 Glynn Ave (Hwy 17), Brunswick (31520). Phone 912/265-6722.* Chinese menu. Lunch, dinner. Closed Thanksgiving, Dec 25. Casual attire. **$**

Buford (B-2)

See also Atlanta, Gainesville, Norcross

Population 10,668
Elevation 1,187 ft
Area Code 770
Zip 30518
Information Gwinnett Convention and Visitors Bureau, 6500 Sugarloaf Pkwy, Suite 200, Duluth 30097; phone 770/623-3600
Web Site www.gcvb.org

What to See and Do

Chateau Elan Winery and Resort. *100 Rue Charlemagne, Braselton (30517). 11 1/2 miles NW on I-85, exit 126. Phone 678/425-0900; toll-free 800/233-9463. www.chateauelanatlanta.com.* Winery tours and tastings begin Mon-Sat at 11 am, Sun at noon; closed Dec 25. Two 18-hole public golf courses ($$$$); golf academy. Equestrian center, tennis center, 7 miles of bike trails. Restaurants, hotel (see FULL-SERVICE RESORTS). **FREE**

Lake Lanier Islands. *4400 SW 27th Ave, Buford. N of town. Phone 770/932-7200.* A 1,200-acre, year-round resort. Swimming, water-skiing, beach, and water park with wave pool, ten water slides, and other attractions, fishing, boating (ramps, rentals); horseback riding, two 18-hole golf courses, tennis, picnicking, two hotels, resort (see), cottages, tent and trailer camping (hookups). Special events are held May-Oct. Fees for some activities. Contact 6950 Holiday Rd, Lake Lanier Islands, 30518.

Limited-Service Hotel

★ **DAYS INN.** *4267 Buford Dr, Buford (30180). Phone 770/932-0111; fax 770/945-3261.* 40 rooms, 2 story. Check-out 11 am. **$**

Full-Service Resorts

○ ★ ★ ★ **CHATEAU ELAN WINERY AND RESORT.** *100 Rue Charlemagne, Braselton (30517). Phone 678/425-0900; fax 678/425-6000.* Escape to the French countryside without ever leaving Georgia's Southern hospitality behind when visiting the Château Élan Winery and Resort. Just 40 minutes north of Atlanta, this delightful resort feels a continent away from the big city's hustle and bustle with its charming manor house and lush vineyards. Winemaking is a source of great pride here, and the eight restaurants perfectly complement the property's excellent product. European influences are discovered throughout the resort, from the classic styling of the elegant accommodations to the tranquil spa. Guests fill their days with a wide variety of activities; golf is a favored pursuit, with three courses and an academy, and the equestrian center is considered one of the state's best. 310 rooms, 5 story. Check-in 3 pm, check-out noon. Restaurant, bar. Children's activity center. Fitness room. Two indoor pools, two outdoor pools, whirlpools. Golf, 63 holes. Tennis. Airport transportation available. Business center. **$$**

★ ★ ★ **EMERALD POINTE RESORT.** *7000 Holiday Rd, Buford (30518). Phone 770/945-8787; toll-free 800/768-5253; fax 770/932-5471. www.lake lanierislands.com.* Best known for its championship golf course, here guests will find a fun-filled experience. Set on a hillside surrounded by hardwood trees and Lake Sidney Lanier, the islandlike setting has swimming, boating, and more. This is a favorite Southern retreat. 224 rooms, 4 story. Check-in 3 pm, check-out noon. Restaurant, bar. Children's activity center. Fitness room. Beach. Outdoor pool, children's pool, whirlpool. Golf. Business center. **$**

★ ★ ★ **RENAISSANCE PINEISLE RESORT AND GOLF CLUB.** *9000 Holiday Rd, Buford (30518). Phone 770/945-8921; toll-free 800/372-7409; fax 770/945-0351. www.renaissancehotels.com.* Sparkling waters and grand forests are the setting at this beautiful resort overlooking Lake Lanier. With championship golf, tennis, seven tempting restaurants, and 22,000 square feet of meeting space, guests can enjoy all there is to offer. 250 rooms, 5 story. Check-in 3 pm, check-out noon. Restaurant, bar. Children's activity center. Fitness room. Beach. Indoor pool, outdoor pool, whirlpool. Golf. Tennis. Business center. **$**

Full-Service Inn

★ ★ ★ **WHITWORTH INN.** *6593 McEver Rd, Flowery Branch (30542). Phone 770/967-2386; fax 770/967-2649. www.whitworthinn.com.* Bask in the tranquility of this beautifully landscaped bed and breakfast located 40 miles north of Atlanta. Guests will enjoy the country setting of this quiet, intimate hideaway and leave relaxed and renewed. 10 rooms, 3 story. Complimentary full breakfast. Check-in 3 pm, check-out 11 am. **$**

Restaurant

★ ★ **BREEZES.** *9000 Holiday Rd, Buford, (30518). Phone 770/945-8921; fax 770/945-1024. www.pineisle.com.* This casual restaurant serves satisfying American food. In season, an all-you-can-eat lobster boil is served on Friday nights. American menu. Breakfast, lunch, dinner, Sun brunch. Bar. Valet parking. **$$**

Calhoun (A-1)

See also Chatsworth, Dalton, Rome

Population 10,667
Elevation 715 ft
Area Code 706
Zip 30701
Information Gordon County Chamber of Commerce, 300 S Wall St; phone 706/625-3200 or toll-free 800/887-3811
Web Site www.cityofcalhoun-ga.com

Once called Oothcaloga, "place of the beaver dams," the name was changed in 1850 to honor John Caldwell Calhoun, Secretary of State to President John Tyler. Although the town was directly in the path of General Sherman's 1864 "March to the Sea," Calhoun was not destroyed. Now, Calhoun is the seat of Gordon County and center of a dairy, beef cattle, and poultry raising area. The town has a major carpet industry and several major manufacturing companies that provide a wide range of products.

What to See and Do

New Echota State Historic Site. *1211 Chatsworth Hwy NE, Calhoun (30701). 1/2 mile E of I-75, exit 317, on Hwy 225. Phone 706/624-1321. www.gastateparks.org.* Tavern (1805), an 1830s log store, and a museum orientation center. Citizens of Calhoun bought the 200-acre site in the early 1950s and donated it to the state. After establishing a government in 1817, the legislature of the Cherokee Indian Nation in 1825 established a capital surrounding the site of their Council House. The written form of the Cherokee language, created by the brilliant Sequoyah, had been developed by 1821, and the print shop was built in 1827. The first issue of the Cherokee newspaper, the *Cherokee Phoenix,* was printed in this shop in 1828 in both Cherokee and English; the paper continued publication until 1834. Samuel A. Worcester, a most able missionary, arrived from Boston in 1827 and built a house, which is the only original building still standing. The Vann Tavern, built by Cherokees at another location, was moved to the park as part of the restoration. The Cherokee Nation had a legislative hall, a supreme court house, a mission, and several other buildings at New Echota. At the height of Cherokee prosperity, gold was found in Cherokee territory, which then included parts of Georgia, North Carolina, Alabama, and Tennessee. In 1835, after a long legal battle, the Cherokees were forced to sell their territory and move to Oklahoma. In the winter of 1838-1839, the Cherokees were driven to their new location over the "Trail of Tears," one-fourth of them dying en route. Many hid out in the Great Smoky Mountains; their descendants now form the Eastern Cherokees. The buildings of the restored New Echota are furnished authentically and are a dramatic reconstruction of a remarkable episode in Native American history. (Tues-Sat 9 am-5 pm, Sun 2-5:30 pm; closed Jan 1, Thanksgiving, Dec 25) **$**

Resaca Confederate Cemetery. *5 miles N on I-75, Resaca exit (320).* Site of the Civil War battle that opened the way to Atlanta for General Sherman. Civil War markers and cemetery on the Civil War Discovery Trail. (Daily) **FREE**

Limited-Service Hotels

★ **JAMESON INN.** *189 Jameson St SE, Calhoun (30701). Phone 706/629-8133; toll-free 800/526-3766; fax 706/629-7985. www.jamesoninns.com.* This Colonial-style inn prides itself on service, comfort, and affordability. Guests suites are large with a separate sitting area. It's also located near local parks and lakes. 59 rooms, 2 story. Complimentary continental breakfast. Check-out 11 am. Fitness room. Outdoor pool. **$**
🏋 🏊

★ ★ **QUALITY INN.** *915 Hwy 53 E SE, Calhoun (30701). Phone 706/629-9501; toll-free 800/225-4686; fax 706/629-9501. www.qualityinn.com.* 100 rooms, 2 story. Pets accepted, some restrictions; fee. Complimentary continental breakfast. Check-out 11 am. Restaurant, bar. Fitness room. Outdoor pool. **$**
🍴 🏋 🏊

Full-Service Hotel

★ ★ ★ **BARNSLEY GARDENS.** *597 Barnsley Gardens Rd, Calhoun (30103). Phone 770/773-7480; fax 770/773-1779. www.slh.com/barnsley.* 70 rooms, 1 story. Pets accepted; fee. Check-out noon. Restaurant, bar. Fitness room. Indoor pool, outdoor pool, whirlpool. Airport transportation available. Business center. **$$**

🅓 ❧ ⅄ ⇌ ⋀

Restaurant

★ **PENGS PAVILLION.** *1120 S Wall St, Calhoun (30701). Phone 706/629-1453.* Chinese menu. Lunch, dinner. Closed Sun; holidays. **$**

Carrollton (B-1)

Population 19,843
Elevation 1,116 ft
Area Code 770
Zip 30117
Information Carroll County Chamber of Commerce, 200 Northside Dr; phone 770/832-2446
Web Site www.carroll-ga.org

Carrollton was named in honor of Charles Carroll, one of the signers of the Declaration of Independence. The town serves as a regional retail, service, manufacturing, and health care center for several counties in western Georgia and eastern Alabama. Carrollton is home to Southwire, one of the nation's largest privately owned rod and cable manufacturing companies. The world's largest tape and record manufacturing plant, owned by Sony, is located here as well.

What to See and Do

John Tanner State Park. *354 Tanner Beach Rd, Carrollton. 6 miles W off Hwy 16. Phone 770/830-2222.* Two lakes offer the longest beach in the state park system. Swimming, fishing, boating (rentals); picnicking, camping, motel.

State University of West Georgia. *1600 Maple St, Carrollton (30118).* (1933) (7,500 students) A unit of the state university system. On campus are the John F. Kennedy Memorial Chapel and

> **Thomas Bonner House.** *1600 Maple St, Carrollton (30118). Phone 770/836-6464.* (Circa 1840) Restored plantation house, campus information center. (Mon-Fri; closed holidays, school breaks)

Limited-Service Hotel

★ **COMFORT INN.** *128 Hwy 61 Connector, Villa Rica (30180). Phone 770/459-8000; toll-free 800/228-*

5150; fax 770/459-8413. www.comfortinn.com. 64 rooms, 2 story. Complimentary continental breakfast. Check-out 11 am. Outdoor pool. **$**

⇌

Restaurant

★ **MAPLE STREET MANSION.** *401 Maple St, Carrollton (30117). Phone 770/834-2657; fax 770/834-3812. www.maplestreetmansion.com.* This turn-of-the-century mansion has been turned into a charming restaurant and banquet site. Some Carrollton residents insist the house is haunted by several spirits. American menu. Lunch, dinner. Closed Sun-Mon; Jan 1, Dec 24-25. Bar. **$$**

Cartersville (B-1)

See also Atlanta, Marietta, Rome

Founded 1832
Population 15,925
Elevation 787 ft
Area Code 770
Zip 30120
Information Cartersville/Bartow County Convention and Visitors Bureau, PO Box 200397; phone 770/387-1357 or toll-free 800/733-2280
Web Site www.notatlanta.org

Cartersville is in the center of an area rich in minerals. Its economy is based on textile manufacturing, plastics, the quarrying of limestone, and the mining of ocher, barite, and manganese. An Anheuser-Busch brewery also contributes to the economy.

What to See and Do

Allatoona Lake. *513 Allatoona Dam Rd SE, Cartersville. Headquarters is 3 miles N on I-75, exit 125, then E on Hwy 20, then 4 miles S on Spur 20. Phone 770/382-4700.* (US Army Corps of Engineers) Swimming, water-skiing, fishing, boating (ramps); hiking trails, overlook, picnicking, camping (fee). Contact Park Ranger, PO Box 487.

Etowah Indian Mounds Historic Site and Archaeological Area. *3 miles S, off Hwys 113, 61. Phone 770/387-3747.* The most impressive of more than 100 settlements in the Etowah Valley, this village was occupied from AD 1000-1500. It was the home of several thousand people of a relatively advanced culture. Six earthen pyramids grouped around two public squares, the largest of which occupies several acres, served as funeral mounds, bases for temples, and the residences of the chiefs. Museum displays artifacts from the excavations; crafts, foods, way of life of the Etowah; painted white marble mortuary. (Tues-Sun; closed Jan 1, Thanksgiving, Dec 25) **$$**

Red Top Mountain State Lodge Park. *50 Lodge Rd SE, Cartersville. 2 miles E of I-75, exit 285. Phone 770/975-0055.* Swimming, water-skiing, boating (ramps, dock, marina); trails, miniature golf, picnicking, concession. Restaurant. Lodge. Camping, cottages.

William Weinman Mineral Museum. *51 Mineral Museum Dr, Cartersville. I-75 exit 293. Phone 770/386-0576.* Displays of cut gemstones, minerals, and rocks from Georgia and around the world; mine tunnel with waterfall. (Tues-Sun; closed holidays) **$$**

Limited-Service Hotels

★ **COMFORT INN.** *28 SR 20 Spur SE, Cartersville (30121). Phone 770/387-1800; toll-free 800/228-5150; fax 678/535-0007. www.comfortinn.com.* 60 rooms, 2 story. Complimentary continental breakfast. Check-out 11 am. Outdoor pool. **$**

★ **DAYS INN.** *5618 Hwy 20 SE, Cartersville (30121). Phone 770/382-1824; toll-free 800/329-7466; fax 770/606-9312. www.daysinn.com.* 52 rooms, 2 story. Complimentary continental breakfast. Check-out noon. Outdoor pool. **$**

★ ★ **HOLIDAY INN.** *2336 Hwy 411 NE, Cartersville (30184). Phone 770/386-0830; toll-free 800/465-4329; fax 770/386-0867. www.holiday-inn.com.* 144 rooms, 2 story. Pets accepted. Check-out noon. Restaurant, bar. Outdoor pool, whirlpool. **$**

Restaurant

★ **MORRELL'S.** *I-75 and Hwy 20, Cartersville (30131). Phone 770/382-1222.* American menu. Breakfast, lunch, dinner. Closed Thanksgiving, Dec 25. Children's menu. **$**

Chatsworth (A-1)

See also Calhoun, Dalton; also see Chattanooga, TN

Population 3,531

Elevation 750 ft
Area Code 706
Zip 30705
Information Chatsworth-Murray County Chamber of Commerce, 126 N Third Ave; phone 706/695-6060
Web Site www.northga.net/murray

Murray County has a strong carpet industry. Almost a third of the land is forest and mountains. Opportunities for fishing, hunting, camping, backpacking, and mountain biking abound in the surrounding Cohutta Wilderness and woodlands. A Ranger District office of the Chattahoochee National Forest is located in Chatsworth. Talcum, a mineral that most people know only as a comfort to the skin, was once mined here in large quantities.

What to See and Do

Carters Lake. *181 Fort Mountain Park Rd, Chatsworth. 15 miles S, off Hwy 411. Phone 706/334-2248.* Swimming, fishing, boating (ramps); hiking trails, overlooks, camping (mid-Apr-late Oct; fee). Contact Resource Manager's office at dam site.

Fort Mountain State Park. *181 Fort Mountain Park Rd, Chatsworth. 7 miles E via Hwy 52. Phone 706/695-2621.* A mountain park with ruins of a prehistoric stone wall; observation tower. Swimming, fishing, paddleboats (rentals); self-guided nature trail, picnicking, cabins, camping. Standard hours, fees.

Vann House State Historic Site. *82 Hwy 225 N, Spring Place. 3 miles W on Hwy 52-A at junction Hwy 225. Phone 706/695-2598.* (1804) This brick house was the showplace of the Cherokee Nation. James Vann was half Scottish, half Cherokee. His chief contribution to the tribe was his help in establishing the nearby Moravian Mission for the education of the young Cherokees. The three-story house, with foot-thick brick walls, is modified Georgian in style; partly furnished. (Tues-Sun; closed Jan 1, Thanksgiving, Dec 25) **$$**

Special Event

Appalachian Wagon Train. *1 mile E via Hwy 76. Phone 706/695-7122.* Horse and mule shows, trail rides, square dancing, parade. Late June-early July.

Limited-Service Hotel

★ ★ **COHUTTA LODGE & CONFERENCE CENTER.** *500 Cochise Trail, Chatsworth*

(30705). Phone 706/695-9601; fax 706/695-0913. www.cohuttalodge.com. 61 rooms, 3 story. Check-out 11 am. Restaurant. Indoor pool. Tennis. **$**

Restaurant

★ **COHUTTA DINING ROOM.** *500 Cochise Trail, Chatsworth (30705). Phone 706/695-9601; fax 706/695-0913. www.cohuttalodge.com.* American menu. Breakfast, lunch, dinner. **$$**

Chickamauga and Chattanooga National Military Park (A-1)

See also Dalton

Web Site www.nps.gov/chch

9 miles S of Chattanooga, TN on Hwy 27.

Established in 1890, this is the oldest and largest national military park in the United States. The two-day battle fought at Chickamauga was one of the Civil War's fiercest, with 36,000 casualties, and was the greatest success of Confederate armies in the West. However, the inability of General Braxton Bragg to follow up the success of September 19 and 20, 1863, and his defeat two months later on Missionary Ridge at Chattanooga, Tennessee, meant the loss of a strategic railway center and opened the gateway to a Union advance into the Deep South.

General Bragg had evacuated Chattanooga on September 9, to maintain rail communications southward after Union Commander Rosecrans had abruptly crossed the Tennessee River southwest of the city. However, with the arrival of reinforcements from Lee's army in the east giving him a numerical advantage, Bragg turned back north to surprise Rosecrans' scattered forces. On September 18, the two armies stumbled into each other on the west bank of Chickamauga Creek.

By the morning of September 19, Union troops attacked and were driven back in heavy fighting.

Confederate troops broke the Union line the morning of the 20th, sweeping the entire right wing and part of the center from the field. Union troops on the left, with the aid of reserve corps and all under the command of General George H. Thomas, took up new positions on Snodgrass Hill, holding up under terrific assaults by Confederates until the Union Army was able to retreat in good order to Chattanooga. Thomas earned the nickname "Rock of Chickamauga."

Highway 27 extends more than 3 miles through the 5,400-acre Chickamauga Battlefield, where the battle has been commemorated by markers, monuments, tablets, and artillery pieces. Woods and fields are kept as close as possible to the way they were in wartime, and some old buildings lend added atmosphere.

Chickamauga Battlefield is but one of 17 areas forming the National Military Park. Other major areas (all in Tennessee) are Point Park on Lookout Mountain, the Reservations on Missionary Ridge, Signal Point on Signal Mountain, and Orchard Knob in Chattanooga—totaling nearly 3,000 acres.

The Chickamauga visitor center, on Highway 27 at the north entrance to the battlefield, is the logical starting point for auto tours. The center has the Fuller Collection of American Military Shoulder Arms, consisting of 355 weapons, as well as a 26-minute multimedia program (fee) describing the Battle of Chickamauga. Visitor center (daily; closed Dec 25). Park (daily). The National Park Service also offers guided tours, walks, evening programs, and musket/cannon firing demonstrations (June-August). For further information, contact PO Box 2128, Fort Oglethorpe 30742; phone 706/866-9241.

Clayton (A-3)

See also Hiawassee, Toccoa

Population 2,019
Elevation 1,925 ft
Area Code 706
Zip 30525
Information Rabun County Chamber of Commerce, Box 750; phone 706/782-4812; a Rabun County Welcome Center is located on Hwy 441 N; phone 706/782-5113 or 706/782-4812
Web Site co.clayton.ga.us

Located in the mountainous and forested northeast corner of Georgia, Clayton offers visitors a wide variety of activities, including hiking, mountain climbing, camping, boating, fishing, hunting, skiing, and whitewater rafting. A ranger district office of the Chattahoochee National Forest (see DAHLONEGA) is located in Clayton.

What to See and Do

Chattooga Wild and Scenic River. *8 miles SE via Hwy 76.* Originating in the mountains of North Carolina, the Chattooga tumbles southward 57 miles to its terminus, Lake Tugaloo, between Georgia and South Carolina. Designated a Wild and Scenic River by Congress in 1974, the Chattooga is one of the few remaining free-flowing streams in the Southeast. The scenery along the river is spectacular, with gorges, waterfalls, and unusual rock formations.

Foxfire Museum and Center. *2737 Hwy 441, Clayton. In Mountain City. Phone 706/746-5828.* Located in replica of log cabin, the museum contains artifacts and crafts of early Appalachian life, including the inner workings of an old gristmill. (Mon-Sat; closed holidays) **$$**

Raft trips. Southeastern Expeditions. *50 Executive Park S, Suite 5016, Atlanta (30329). Phone 404/329-0433; toll-free 800/868-7238.* Whitewater raft trips on the Chattooga River in northeast Georgia. Full-day tours. (Mar-Oct) **$$$$**

Special Event

Homemakers' Harvest Festival. *7 miles N on Hwy, 23, 441 in Dillard.* Mountain arts and crafts. Fri-Sat in Oct.

Columbus (D-1)

See also Lumpkin, Pine Mountain

Founded 1827
Population 185,781
Elevation 250 ft
Area Code 706
Information Tourist Division, Convention and Visitors Bureau, 1000 Bay Ave, PO Box 2768, 31901; phone 706/322-1613 or toll-free 800/999-1613; or the Georgia Welcome Center, 1751 Williams Rd; 24-hour visitor information hotline; phone 706/322-3181
Web Site www.visitcolumbusga.com

Power from the falls of the Chattahoochee River feeds the industries of this dynamic city. With a 9-foot-deep navigable channel to the Gulf of Mexico, it is at the head of navigation on the Chattahoochee. Originally a settlement of the Creek Indians, the site was chosen as a border stronghold by Governor Forsyth in 1828. The city reached a peak of frenzied manufacturing and commerce between 1861 and 1864, when it supplied the Confederate Army with shoes, caps, swords, and pistols.

The Columbus Iron Works (1853) supplied Columbus and the surrounding area with cast-iron products, farming equipment, steam engines, and industrial and building supplies. It was a major supplier of cannons for the Confederate States during the Civil War. Reconstruction created havoc for a time, but by 1874 Columbus's industries were more numerous and varied than before the war: from 1880 to 1920 a commercial ice-making machine was produced in the town, and by the beginning of World War II, Columbus was a great iron-working center and the second-largest producer of cotton in the South.

Much of the original city plan of 1827 is still evident, with streets 99- to 164-feet wide flanked by magnificent trees. Dogwood and wisteria add color in the spring. The atmosphere is exemplified by the brick-lined streets and gaslights in the 28-block historic district and by the Victorian gardens, gazebos, and open-air amphitheaters on the Chattahoochee Promenade along the banks of the river.

What to See and Do

Columbus Convention and Trade Center. *801 Front Ave, Columbus. Phone 706/327-4522.* Converted from the historic Columbus Iron Works. Exhibit space, banquet facilities, outdoor amphitheater.

The Columbus Museum. *1251 Wynnton Rd, Columbus. Phone 706/649-0713.* Features Chattahoochee Legacy, a regional history gallery with re-created period settings; fine and decorative arts galleries; and Transformations, a youth-oriented participatory gallery. (Tues-Sun; closed holidays) **FREE**

Fort Benning. *I-185, S of Atlanta, Columbus (31905). Phone 706/545-2958.* Largest infantry post in the United States, established during World War I, the fort was named for Confederate General Henry L. Benning of Columbus. Infantry school; demonstrations of

Airborne 5000 at jump tower (Mon mornings). **FREE** Here is

> **National Infantry Museum.** *Bldg 396, Baltzell Ave, Fort Benning (31905). Phone 706/545-2958.* Exhibits of US infantry weapons, uniforms, equipment from the Revolutionary War to the Gulf War; experimental and developmental weapons; collection of foreign weapons and equipment. (Daily; closed holidays) **FREE**

Port Columbus Civil War Naval Museum Center. *1002 Victory Dr, Columbus. Phone 706/327-9798.* Salvaged remains of Confederate gunboats *Jackson* and *Chattahoochee;* relics, ship models, uniforms, paintings, and other exhibits on Confederate naval operations. (Daily; closed Dec 25) **$$**

Springer Opera House. *103 10th St, Columbus. At 1st Ave. Phone 706/327-3688 (box office).* (1871) Restored Victorian theater in which many famous performers have appeared, including Shakespearean actor Edwin Booth; museum. Guided tours.

Special Event

Riverfest Weekend. *708 Broadway, Columbus (31901). At the riverfront. Phone 706/324-7417. www.columbus riverfest.com.* Riverfest Weekend features two main entertainment areas: the Folklife Village with a juried arts and crafts show, folk art, Native American exhibits, and living history demonstrations and the Salisbury Fair with a food court, live entertainment, antique cars, and a carnival. Late Apr.

Limited-Service Hotels

★ **BEST WESTERN COLUMBUS.** *3443 B Macon Rd, Columbus (31907). Phone 706/568-3300; toll-free 800/780-7234; fax 706/563-2388. www.bestwestern.com.* 66 rooms, 3 story. Complimentary continental breakfast. Check-out noon. Fitness room. Outdoor pool. **$**

★ ★ **FOUR POINTS BY SHERATON.** *5351 Sidney Simons Blvd, Columbus (31904). Phone 706/327-6868; fax 706/327-0041. www.starwood.com.* 178 rooms, 5 story. Check-out noon. Restaurant, bar. Outdoor pool, whirlpool. Airport transportation available. **$**

★ **LA QUINTA INN.** *3201 Macon Rd, Columbus (31906). Phone 706/568-1740; toll-free 800/687-6667; fax 706/569-7434. www.laquinta.com.* 122 rooms, 2 story. Pets accepted. Complimentary continental breakfast. Check-out noon. Outdoor pool. **$**

Full-Service Hotel

★ ★ ★ **WYNDHAM.** *800 Front Ave, Columbus (31901). Phone 706/324-1800; toll-free 800/996-3426; fax 706/327-8042. www.wyndham.com.* Situated among the scenic downtown historical business district, this hotel caters to corporate travelers and families alike. Leave the worrying behind because this hotel offers the ultimate in services and makes for a welcoming retreat. Relax and enjoy the warm and friendly service, spacious guest rooms, and outdoor pool. Step outside and enjoy, within walking distance, a stroll along the Chattahoochee River and Riverwalk. 177 rooms, 6 story. Check-out noon. Restaurant, bar. Outdoor pool. Airport transportation available. **$**

Restaurants

★ ★ ★ **BLUDAU'S GOETCHIUS HOUSE.** *405 Broadway, Columbus (31901). Phone 706/324-4863; fax 706/324-0438.* This classic Southern restaurant is situated in a restored antebellum mansion overlooking the river. A special Chateaubriand is the favorite entrée. Mint juleps are served in the speakeasy downstairs. American menu. Dinner. Closed Sun. Bar. Outdoor seating. **$$**

★ **COUNTRY'S NORTH.** *6298 Veterans Pkwy, Columbus (31909). Phone 706/660-1415; fax 706/660-1616. www.countrysbarbcue.com.* American menu. Lunch, dinner. Closed holidays. Children's menu. Outdoor seating. **$**

★ ★ **OLD MILL TOWNE.** *2955 Warm Springs Rd, Columbus (31909). Phone 706/321-9500; fax 706/321-1010.* American menu. Lunch, dinner. Closed Thanksgiving, Dec 25. Bar. Children's menu. Outdoor seating. **$$**

Commerce (B-3)

See also Athens, Gainesville, Toccoa

Population 5,292
Elevation 931 ft
Area Code 706
Zip 30529
Web Site www.commercega.org

What to See and Do

Crawford W. Long Medical Museum. *28 College St, Commerce. 10 miles SW via Hwy 15, on College St in Jefferson or 5 miles S on I-85, exit 50.* Phone 706/367-5307. Museum contains diorama of Dr. Long's first use of ether as an anesthetic in surgery, an enormous breakthrough in medicine. Also here are documents, artifacts, and history of anesthesia exhibit. Entrance is in Jackson County Historical Society building, which has other exhibits on local history. A third building has an 1840s doctor's office, an apothecary shop, a 19th-century general store exhibit, and an herb garden. (Tues-Sat; closed holidays) **DONATION**

Limited-Service Hotel

★ **HOWARD JOHNSON.** *148 Eisenhower Dr, Commerce (30529).* Phone 706/335-5581; fax 706/335-7889. www.hojo.com. 120 rooms, 2 story. Pets accepted; fee. Complimentary continental breakfast. Check-out noon. Outdoor pool, children's pool. **$**

Cordele (D-2)

See also Albany, Americus, Andersonville, Perry

Founded 1888
Population 11,608
Elevation 319 ft
Area Code 229
Zip 31015
Information Cordele-Crisp Tourism Commission, 302 E 16th Ave, PO Box 158; phone 229/273-3526
Web Site www.cordele-crisp-chamber.com

Watermelons, sweet potatoes, soybeans, pecans, cotton, peanuts, corn, and cantaloupes are produced in Crisp County, of which Cordele is the seat. The local state farmers' market sells more watermelons than any other market in the state; Cordele residents thus refer to their city as the "Watermelon Capital of the World." Garment making and the manufacture of enormous baling presses for scrap metals, agricultural implements, air conditioners, foundry products, mobile homes, livestock feed, fiberglass items, steel fittings, and several other industries are locally important.

What to See and Do

Georgia Veterans Memorial State Park. *2459-A Hwy 280 W, Cordele. 9 miles W via Hwy 280.* Phone 229/276-2371. Swimming pool, water-skiing, fishing, boating; golf, picnicking, concession, camping, cabins. Museum; model airplane field with historic aircraft.

Special Event

Watermelon Festival. Parade; watermelon-eating, seed-spitting, and largest watermelon contests; fishing rodeo; Miss Heart of Georgia contest; arts and crafts; entertainment. Early-mid-July.

Limited-Service Hotel

★ **COMFORT INN.** *1601 16th Ave E, Cordele (31015).* Phone 229/273-2371; toll-free 800/228-5150; fax 229/273-8351. www.comfortinn.com. 59 rooms, 2 story. Complimentary continental breakfast. Check-out 11 am. Outdoor pool. **$**

Restaurants

★ ★ **DAPHNE LODGE.** *US 280 W, Cordele (31015).* Phone 229/273-2596. American menu. Dinner. Closed Sun-Mon; holidays. **$$**

★ **OLDE INN.** *2536 Hwy 280 W, Cordele (31015).* Phone 229/273-1229. Late 1800s building with original fireplace. American menu. Dinner. Closed Sun-Mon; July 4, Thanksgiving, Dec 25. Children's menu. **$$**

Cumberland Island (E-5)

See also Brunswick, Jekyll Island, St. Simons Island

Web site www.nps.gov/cuis

What to See and Do

Cumberland Island National Seashore. *Off the coast, NE of St. Marys. Phone 912/882-4335. www.nps.gov/cuis.* Cumberland Island National Seashore, off the coast of Georgia, is an island 16 miles long and 1 1/2 to 3 miles wide. It is accessible by passenger tour boat, which operates year-round. Mainland departures are from St. Marys (fee); reservations by phone are necessary.

A visit to the island is a walking experience, and there are no restaurants or shops. The island's western side is fringed with salt marsh, and white sand beaches face the Atlantic Ocean. The interior is forested primarily by live oak; interspersed are freshwater marshes and sloughs. Activities include viewing the scenery and wildlife, swimming, and exploring historical areas led by a ranger. Native Americans, Spanish, and English have all lived on the island; most structures date from the pre-Civil War plantation era, though there are turn-of-the-century buildings built by the Thomas Carnegie family. Camping (daily); reservations by phone necessary. Ferry (mid-Mar-Sept, daily; winter, Mon, Thurs-Sun; closed Dec 25) For further information, contact the Superintendent, PO Box 806, St. Marys 31558.

Full-Service Inn

★ ★ ★ **THE GREYFIELD INN.** *Cumberland Island. Mailing address: 8 Second St, Fernandina Beach, FL (32035). Phone 904/261-6408. www.greyfieldinn.com.* To truly get away from it all, escape to the historic Greyfield Inn, built in 1900. Accessible by private ferry from Fernandina Beach, Florida, this inn is a tranquil place to enjoy Cumberland Island's natural beauty and abundant wildlife, including wild horses and many species of birds. The mansion's veranda comes complete with rocking chairs for whiling away the afternoon, while elegant cuisine is offered in the inn's candlelit dining room in the evenings. Furnished with family heirlooms and antiques, the guest rooms and suites vary widely; note that not all have private baths. Room rates include breakfast, picnic lunch, gourmet dinner (jacket required, so pack appropriately), and snacks throughout the day, as well as unlimited use of the inn's sporting, fishing, and beach equipment. A two-night minimum stay is required. 17 rooms, 4 story. Children over 6 years only. Check-out noon. Restaurant, bar. Fitness room. **$$$$**

🖐

Dahlonega (A-2)

See also Gainesville

Settled 1833
Population 3,638
Elevation 1,454 ft
Area Code 706
Zip 30533
Information Dahlonega-Lumpkin County Chamber of Commerce, 13 S Park St; phone 706/864-3711
Web Site www.dahlonega.org

Gold fever struck this area in 1828, 20 years before the Sutter's Mill discovery in California. Dahlonega, derived from the Cherokee word for the color yellow, yielded so much ore that the federal government established a local mint which produced $6,115,569 in gold coins from 1838 to 1861. Dahlonega is the seat of Lumpkin County, where tourism, manufacturing, higher education, and agribusiness are the major sources of employment. A US Forest Service Visitor Center is located in Dahlonega.

What to See and Do

Amicalola Falls State Park. *418 Amicalola Falls Lodge Rd, Dawsonville (30534). 20 miles W off Hwy 52. Phone 706/265-8888.* Highest waterfall in the eastern US (729 feet). Trout fishing, hiking trails, picnicking, concession, restaurant, camping, cabins, lodge.

Chattahoochee National Forest. *1755 Cleveland Hwy, Dahlonega. Phone 770/297-3000. www.fs.fed.us/conf.* This vast forest (748,608 acres) includes Georgia's Blue Ridge Mountains toward the north, which have elevations ranging from 1,000 to nearly 5,000 feet. Because the forest ranges from the Piedmont to mountainous areas, the Chattahoochee has a diversity of trees and wildlife. There are 25 developed camping areas, 24 picnicking areas, ten wilderness areas, and six swimming beaches. For the Chattahoochee-Oconee National Forest Recreation Area directory, contact the US Forest Service, 508 Oak St NW, Gainesville, 30501. In the forest are

Anna Ruby Falls. *Off Hwy 356, 6 miles N of Helen.* Approximately 1,570 acres surrounding a double waterfall, with drops of 50 and 153 feet. This scenic area is enhanced by laurel, wild azaleas, dogwood, and rhododendron. Visitor center. **$**

Appalachian National Scenic Trail. *799 Washington St, Dahlonega (25425). Phone 304/535-6331.* Thirteen lean-tos are maintained along the 76 miles marked southern portion of the trail. Following the crest of the Blue Ridge divide, the trail begins outside Dahlonega and continues for more than 2,000 miles to Mount Katahdin, Maine.

Track Rock Gap. *1881 Hwy 515, Dahlonega (30514). Off Hwy 76, 8 miles SW of Young Harris.* Well-preserved rock carvings of ancient Indian origin; figures resemble animal and bird tracks, crosses, circles, and human footprints.

Consolidated Gold Mines. *185 Consolidated Gold Mine Rd, Dahlonega. At junction GA 52, US 19 and GA 9. Phone 706/864-8473.* Underground mine tour (35-40 minutes) through tunnel network; displays of original equipment used. Instructors available for gold panning. (Daily; closed Thanksgiving, Dec 25) **$$$**

Crisson's Gold Mine. *2736 Morrison Moore Pkwy E, Dahlonega. 2 1/2 miles N via US 19 to end of Wimpy Mill Rd, then 1 mile E. Phone 706/864-6363.* Gold and gem panning; indoor panning (winter). Demonstration of working stamp mill, more than 100 years old. Gift shop. (Daily; closed Dec 25) **$$**

Dahlonega Courthouse Gold Museum State Historic Site. *1 Public Sq, Dahlonega. In old Lumpkin County Courthouse (1836). Phone 706/864-2257.* Exhibits on first major gold rush; display of gold coins minted in Dahlonega. Film shown every half hour. (Daily; closed Jan 1, Thanksgiving, Dec 25) **$$**

Lake Winfield Scott. *1881 Hwy 515, Dahlonega. 15 miles N on Hwy 19, 129, then 4 miles SW on Hwy 180. Phone 706/745-6928.* A US Forest Service -Recreation Area with an 18-acre lake in the Blue Ridge Mountains. Swimming, bathhouse, fishing; picnicking, campsites (fee). (May-Oct) For more information, contact the Ranger District Office, Box 9, Blairsville, 30512.

North Georgia College and State University. *Hwy 60, College Cir, Dahlonega (30597). Phone 706/864-1800.* (1873) (4,000 students) Part of the state university system, North Georgia College's administration building, Price Memorial, was built on the foundation of the old US Branch Mint; unique gold steeple. Liberal arts and military college.

Vogel State Park. *7485 Vogel State Park Rd, Blairsville (30512). 25 miles N of Dahlonega, 11 miles S of Blairsville on Hwy 19/129. Phone 706/745-2628.* Rugged area in the heart of north Georgia's mountains. At the foot of Blood and Slaughter Mountains, 22-acre Lake Trahlyta has swimming, bathhouse, fishing, paddleboats; picnicking, grills, playground, camping, 35 furnished cabins. **$**

Special Events

Gold Panning Competition. Consolidated gold mine. Third weekend in Apr.

Gold Rush Days. *Phone 706/864-3711; toll-free 800/231-5543. www.dahlonega.org.* A celebration remembering the gold rush of 1828, Gold Rush Days draws visitors to the mountains to view more than 300 related exhibits and participate in family activities. Third weekend in Oct.

Limited-Service Hotel

★ **SUPER 8.** *20 Mountain Dr SW; Hwy 60 S, Dahlonega (38305). Phone 706/864-4343; toll-free 800/800-8000; fax 706/864-4343. www.super8.com.* 60 rooms, 2 story. Check-out noon. Outdoor pool. **$**
🏊

Full-Service Resort

★ ★ **FORREST HILLS MOUNTAIN RESORT.** *135 Forrest Hills Dr, Dahlonega (30533). Phone 706/864-6456; toll-free 800/654-6313; fax 706/864-0757. www.foresths.com.* Surrounded by north Georgia mountain forest. 30 rooms. Check-in 3 pm, check-out 11 am. Restaurant. Outdoor pool. Tennis. Business center. **$**
🏊 🎿 🚶

Specialty Lodging

The following lodging establishment is approved by Mobil Travel Guide, but due to its unique and individualized nature has not been given a traditional Mobil Star rating. Included in this listing you may find bed-and-breakfasts, limited-service inns, guest ranches, and other unique hotel properties.

THE SMITH HOUSE. *84 S Chestatee St, Dahlonega (30533). Phone 706/867-7000; toll-free 800/852-9577; fax 706/864-7564. www.smithhouse.com.* 16 rooms, 2 story. Complimentary continental breakfast. Check-in until 10 pm, check-out 11 am. Restaurant. Outdoor pool. **$**
🏊

Restaurant

★ ★ **SMITH HOUSE.** *84 S Chestatee St, Dahlonega (30533). Phone 706/867-7000; fax 706/864-7564. www.smithhouse.com.* Southern menu. Lunch, dinner. Closed Mon. **$**

Dalton (A-1)

See also Calhoun, Chatsworth, Chickamauga and Chattanooga National Military Park

Founded 1837
Population 27,912
Elevation 759 ft
Area Code 706
Information Convention and Visitors Bureau, 2211 Dug Gap Battle Rd, PO Box 2046, 30722-2046; phone 706/272-7676 or toll-free 800/331-3258
Web Site www.daltoncvb.com

Once a part of the Cherokee Nation, Dalton was involved in fierce battles and skirmishes in the Civil War as Union forces advanced on Atlanta. Today, Dalton has more than 100 carpet outlets and manufactures a large portion of the world's carpets. Dalton also produces other tufted textiles, chemicals, latex, thread, and yarn.

What to See and Do

Crown Garden and Archives. *715 Chattanooga Ave, Dalton. 2 miles N via I-75 and Hwy 41, Walnut Ave exit. Phone 706/278-0217.* Headquarters of the Whitfield-Murray Historical Society. Genealogical library; changing exhibits include Civil War items; permanent exhibit on the history of bedspread tufting in the area. (Tues-Fri; closed holidays) **DONATION**

Special Event

Prater's Mill Country Fair. *452 Varnell School St, Dalton. 10 miles NE on Hwy 2. Phone 706/272-7676.* Food, late 1800s entertainment; canoeing on Coahulla Creek, pony rides, exhibits; Three-story gristmill in operation. Mother's Day weekend and Columbus Day weekend.

Limited-Service Hotels

★ ★ **BEST WESTERN INN OF DALTON.** *2106 Chattanooga Rd, Dalton (30720). Phone 706/226-5022; toll-free 800/780-7234; fax 706/226-5022.*

www.bestwestern.com. 99 rooms, 2 story. Pets accepted; fee. Check-out noon. Restaurant, bar. Outdoor pool. **$**
🐾 🏊

★ ★ **HOLIDAY INN.** *515 Holiday Dr, Dalton (30720). Phone 706/278-0500; toll-free 800/753-6510; fax 706/278-7082. www.holiday-inn.com.* 199 rooms, 2 story. Pets accepted; fee. Check-out noon. Restaurant, bar. Fitness room. Outdoor pool, children's pool. **$**
🐾 🏋 🏊

Restaurant

★ ★ **DALTON DEPOT.** *110 Depot St, Dalton (30720). Phone 706/226-3160; fax 706/275-9721.* American menu. Lunch, dinner. Closed Sun; holidays. Bar. Children's menu. **$$**

Darien (E-5)

See also Brunswick, Jekyll Island, Sea Island, St. Simons Island

Founded 1736
Population 1,719
Elevation 20 ft
Area Code 912
Zip 31305
Information McIntosh Chamber of Commerce, 105 Fort King Georgia Dr, PO Box 1497; phone 912/437-6684
Web Site www.mcintoshcounty.com

James Oglethorpe recruited Scottish Highlanders to protect Georgia's frontier on the Altamaha River in 1736. Calling their town Darien, they guarded Savannah from Spanish and native attack and carved out large plantations from the south Georgia wilderness. After 1800, Darien thrived as a great timber port until the early 20th century. Today, shrimp boats dock in the river over which Darien Scots once kept watch.

What to See and Do

Fort King George State Historic Site. *14 George Dr, Darien (31305). 1 1/2 miles E of Hwy 17 on Fort King George Dr. Phone 912/437-4770.* (1721) South Carolina scouts built this fort near an abandoned Native American village and Spanish mission to block Spanish and French expansion into Georgia, thereby establishing the foundation for the later English Colony of Georgia. The fort and its blockhouse have been entirely reconstructed to original form. The museum interprets the periods of Native American, Spanish, and British occupations; the settlement of Darien; and Georgia's timber industry. (Tues-Sat 9 am-5 pm, Sun 2-5:30 pm; closed Jan 1, Thanksgiving, Dec 25) **$**

Hofwyl-Broadfield Plantation State Historic Site. *5556 Hwy 17 N, Brunswick (31525). 6 miles S on Hwy 17. Phone 912/264-7333.* (1807) The evolution of this working rice plantation (1807-1973) is depicted through tours of the 1851 plantation house, museum, and trails. Tours (Tues-Sun; closed Jan 1, Thanksgiving, Dec 25). **$**

Special Event

Blessing of the Fleet Festival. *At Darien Bridge. Phone 912/437-6684. www.mcintoshcounty.com.* Elaborately decorated boats parade down the river as clerics of several denominations stand on the bridge and bless them as they pass. While the Sunday morning boat parade is the highlight of the weekend, activities begin the Friday before with a street parade, fish fry, and art festival. Weekend in Mar, Apr, or May.

Doraville

Restaurants

★ **SEOUL GARDEN.** *5938 Buford Hwy, Doraville (30340). Phone 770/452-0123; fax 770/452-7735.* Korean menu. Lunch, dinner. **$$**

★ **YEN JING CHINESE RESTAURANT.** *5302 Buford Hwy A-6, Doraville (30340). Phone 770/454-6688; fax 770/458-4747.* Chinese menu. Lunch, dinner. **$**

Douglas (E-3)

Founded 1858
Population 10,639
Elevation 259 ft
Area Code 912
Zip 31533
Information Chamber of Commerce, 211 S Gaskin Ave, PO Box 2470, 31534; phone 912/384-1873
Web Site www.douglasga.org

The town's central location between Interstates 75 and 95 has helped Douglas develop into a leading trade

and distribution center for the southeast. A number of *Fortune* 500 companies operate within Coffee County.

What to See and Do

General Coffee State Park. *46 John Coffee Rd, Nicholls (31554). 6 miles E on Hwy 32. Phone 912/384-7082.* A 1,510-acre park on the Seventeen-Mile River in Coffee County. Swimming pool, fishing; nature trails, picnicking, playgrounds, camping, lodging.

Limited-Service Hotel

★ ★ **HOLIDAY INN.** *1750 S Peterson Ave, Douglas (31533). Phone 912/384-9100; toll-free 800/465-4329. www.holiday-inn.com.* 100 rooms, 2 story. Pets accepted; fee. Check-out noon. Restaurant, bar. Outdoor pool. Airport transportation available. **$**

Dublin (B-2)

Population 15,857
Elevation 228 ft
Area Code 478
Information Dublin-Laurens County Chamber of Commerce, 1200 Bellevue Ave, PO Box 818, 31040; phone 478/272-5546
Web Site www.dublin-georgia.com

The seat of Laurens County, Dublin sits on land once occupied by Creek Indians. Area industries manufacture a wide range of goods, including textiles, carpeting, missile control systems, and computer components. The first aluminum extrusion plant in the United States is located here. Agricultural products include soybeans, wheat, grain, peanuts, corn, cotton, and tobacco.

What to See and Do

Dublin-Laurens Museum. *311 Academy Ave, Dublin. Bellevue and Academy at Church. Phone 478/272-9242.* Local history museum featuring Native American artifacts, art, textiles, and relics from early settlers. (Tues-Fri; closed Jan 1, Thanksgiving, Dec 25) **FREE**

Fish Trap Cut. *Oconee River, Hwy 19.* Believed to have been built between 1000 BC and AD 1500, this large rectangular mound, smaller round mound, and canal may have been used as an aboriginal fish trap.

Historic buildings. Greek Revival and Victorian houses can be found along Bellevue Avenue.

Special Event

St. Patrick's Festival. Includes parade, ball, contests, golf tournaments, arts and crafts show, square dancing, and entertainment. Mar.

Limited-Service Hotel

★ **HOLIDAY INN EXPRESS.** *2192 Hwy 441 S, Dublin (31040). Phone 478/272-7862; toll-free 800/ 465-4329; fax 478/272-1077. www.holiday-inn.com.* 124 rooms, 2 story. Pets accepted, some restrictions. Complimentary full breakfast. Check-out noon. Restaurant, bar. Fitness room. Outdoor pool. Airport transportation available. **$**

🔒 🏃 🏊

Eatonton (C-3)

See also Madison, Milledgeville

Population 6,764
Area Code 706
Zip 31024
Information Eatonton-Putnam Chamber of Commerce, 105 Sumter St, PO Box 4088; phone 706/485-7701 or 706/485-4875
Web Site www.eatonton.com

In the early 19th century, large tracts of land in this area were acquired and put under cultivation; by the mid-1800s, the town of Eatonton had become a center of planter culture, that archetypal romantic concept of cotton fields, mansions, wealth, and Southern grace. Joel Chandler Harris was born in Eatonton in 1848. He successfully immortalized the traditional ways of the Old South by creating the character "Uncle Remus" to retell the "Br'er Rabbit" and "Br'er Fox" folk tales heard on the plantation.

Eatonton is also the hometown of Alice Walker, author of *The Color Purple,* an acclaimed depiction of the South of a different time. Eatonton, the seat of Putnam County, is known as the largest dairy producer in the state.

What to See and Do

Alice Walker: A Driving Tour. *105 Sumter St, Eatonton. Phone 706/485-7701.* Driving tour past the author's

birthplace, church, and house where she grew up. Contact the Chamber of Commerce for brochure and information.

Lake Oconee. *125 Wallace Dam Rd, Eatonton (31024). Lawrence Shoals Recreation Area. Off Hwy 16 (see MADISON). Lake Sinclair. S on Hwy 441 (see MILLEDGEVILLE). Phone 706/485-8704.* Both are Georgia Power Company projects created by the impoundment of the Oconee River.

Rock Eagle Effigy. *350 Rock Eagle Rd, Eatonton (31024). 7 miles N on Hwy 441, located in Rock Eagle 4-H Center. Phone 706/484-2800.* This 8-foot-high mound of milky white quartz is shaped like a great prone bird, wings spread, head turned eastward, 102 feet from head to tail and 120 feet wingtip to wingtip. Archaeologists estimate the monument is more than 5,000 years old and was probably used by Native Americans for religious ceremonies. It may be viewed from an observation tower. **FREE**

Uncle Remus Museum. *214 S Oak St, Eatonton. 3 blocks S of courthouse on Hwy 441 in Turner Park. Phone 706/485-6856.* Log cabin made from two original slave cabins. Reconstruction of cabin fireplace; shadow boxes with illustrations of 12 tales; mementos of era, first editions; diorama of old plantation; other relics. (June-Aug: daily; rest of year: Wed-Mon) **$**

Special Event

Putnam County Dairy Festival. Parade, dairy and farming-related contests, arts and crafts fair, entertainment. First Sat in June.

Forsyth (C-2)

See also Macon

Population 3,776
Elevation 705 ft
Area Code 478
Zip 31029
Information Forsyth-Monroe County Chamber of Commerce, 267 Tift College Dr, PO Box 811; phone 478/994-9239

What to See and Do

Jarrell Plantation State Historic Site. *711 Jarrell Plantation Rd, Forsyth (31046). 18 miles E of I-75 exit 185 on Hwy 18 E, then N on Jarrell Plantation Rd. Phone 478/986-5172. www.gastateparks.org/info/jarrell.* This authentic plantation has 20 historic buildings dating from 1847 to 1940, including a plain-style plantation house, sawmill, gristmill, and blacksmith shop. Farm animals; seasonal demonstrations. (Tues-Sat 9 am-5 pm, Sun 2-5:30 pm; closed Jan 1, Thanksgiving, Dec 25) **$**

The Whistle Stop Cafe. *443 McCrackin St, Juliette. I-75, exit 186, then 8 miles E to Juliette. Phone 478/992-8886.* Town of Juliette, GA was where the movie *Fried Green Tomatoes* was filmed. Café and other stores along Mc-Crackin St. Café (Mon-Sat and Sun afternoons).

Limited-Service Hotels

★ **BEST WESTERN HILLTOP INN.** *951 Hwy 42 N, Forsyth (31029). Phone 478/994-9260; toll-free 800/780-7234; fax 478/994-1280. www.bestwestern.com.* 120 rooms, 2 story. Check-out noon. Outdoor pool, children's pool. **$**
🅳 🛏

★ ★ **HOLIDAY INN.** *480 Holiday Cir, Forsyth (31029). Phone 478/994-5691; toll-free 800/465-4329; fax 478/994-3254. www.holiday-inn.com.* 120 rooms, 2 story. Pets accepted, some restrictions; fee. Check-out noon. Restaurant, bar. Fitness room. Outdoor pool, children's pool. Business center. Chapel on premises. **$**
🍴 🏋 🛏 🚶

Restaurant

★ **WHISTLE STOP CAFE.** *443 McCrackin St, Juliette (31046). Phone 478/992-8886.* Film site of *Fried Green Tomatoes.* Breakfast, lunch. Closed holidays. **$**

Fort Frederica National Monument (E-5)

See also Brunswick, Jekyll Island, Sea Island, St. Simons Island

Web Site www.nps.com/fofr

12 miles NE of Brunswick via St. Simons/Sea Island Causeway toll.

Fort Frederica marked the southern boundary of British Colonial North America. It was carefully planned by the trustees in London in 1736 and included the town of Frederica, named after Frederick, Prince of Wales.

Having picked the site of the fort on a bluff commanding the Frederica River, General James Oglethorpe returned to England and helped select families to build and settle it. Forty-four men and 72 women and children landed at St. Simons Island on March 16, 1736. In 1738, a regiment of 650 British soldiers arrived. The fort was then strengthened with "tabby" (a kind of cement made of lime, oyster shells, sand, and water), and the whole town was enclosed with earth and timber works from 10 to 13 feet high that included towers and a moat.

Oglethorpe used Fort Frederica as a command post for his invasion of Florida. He built other forts on St. Simons and other islands and attacked Spanish outposts to the south. In July 1742, Spaniards launched an attack on Fort Frederica, but Oglethorpe repulsed this with an ambush at Bloody Marsh, ending Spanish attempts to gain control of Georgia.

Frederica flourished as a military town until after the peace of 1748. With the withdrawal of the regiment the following year, the shopkeepers and tradesmen at Frederica had to move elsewhere. The town did not long survive these losses. Archaeological excavations have exposed some of it, and stabilization work has been done by the National Park Service. Outdoor exhibits make it easy to visualize the town as it was, and the visitor center has exhibits, touch computers, and a film dealing with its life and history. Self-guided audio tour (fee). (Daily; closed Dec 25) Contact the Superintendent, Rte 9, Box 286-C, St. Simons Island, 31522; phone 912/638-3639. Golden Age Passport (see MAKING THE MOST OF YOUR TRIP). Entrance per vehicle **$**

Fort McAllister Historic Park (D-5)

See also Savannah

Web Site gastateparks.org/info/ftmcallister

25 miles S of Savannah, via Hwy 144 from I-95 or Hwy 17, 10 miles E of Richmond Hill off Hwy 17.

This Confederate fort built for the defense of Savannah stands on the left bank of the Great Ogeechee River, commanding the river's mouth. Fort McAllister's fall on December 13, 1864, marked the end of Sherman's march to the sea, opening communications between the Union Army and the fleet and rendering further defense of Savannah hopeless.

Prior to this, McAllister had proved that its type of massive earthwork fortifications could stand up against the heaviest naval ordnance. It protected the blockade-running ship *Nashville* from pursuit by Union gunboats in July and November 1862. It successfully resisted the attacks of *Monitor*-type ironclads of the Union Navy in 1863. The USS *Montauk* shelled the fort with the heaviest shells ever fired by a naval vessel against a shore work up to that time. The fort sustained only one casualty. There were huge holes in its parapets, but the damage was minor. Its gun emplacements were separated by large "traverses," several used to house powder magazines. The fort that seemed to be "carved out of solid earth" was termed "a truly formidable work" by a Union naval officer in 1864. General Sherman called the capture of the fort and overpowering its garrison "the handsomest thing I have seen in this war." Union losses were 24 killed, 110 wounded (mostly by mines outside the fort); the Confederate garrison of 230 men had 70 casualties—16 killed and 54 wounded—in the 15-minute battle.

The earthworks have been restored to approximate conditions of 1863-1864. A museum containing mementos of the *Nashville* and the fort was completed in 1963 and opened on the centennial of the great bombardment. (Tues-Sat, also Sun afternoon; closed Thanksgiving, Dec 25; fee) Fort McAllister has a campground and day-use facilities (fee); boating (ramps, dock). Contact the Superintendent, 3894 Fort McAllister Rd, Richmond Hill, 31324; phone 912/727-2339.

Fort Pulaski National Monument (D-5)

See also Savannah

Web Site www.nps.gov/fopu

15 miles E of Savannah off Hwy 800.

A unit of the Department of the Interior's National Park Service, Fort Pulaski National Monument was established by President Coolidge in 1924. The site, named in honor of Revolutionary war hero Casimir Pulaski, commemorates an international turning point in the history of fortification and artillery. It was here on April 11, 1862, that newly developed rifled cannons easily overtook a masonry fortification. After centuries of use throughout the world, both masonry forts and smooth-bore cannons were obsolete.

Most visitors begin the tour at the visitor center, which contains a small museum, an information desk, and a bookstore featuring more than 300 items on the Civil War and other site-related and regional subjects.

Restored to its mid-19th-century appearance, the fort contains several rooms, or casemates, depicting garrison life during its Confederate (1861-1862) and Union (1862-1875) occupations. This exhibit includes an officer's quarters and mess, medical dispensary, chapel, quartermaster's office, supply room, and enlisted men's quarters. Other displays include several examples of smooth-bore and rifled artillery and carriages. While self-guided tours are available year-round, ranger-conducted programs and demonstrations are presented daily in the summer.

There are three major trails in the monument. The nature trail is a 1/4 mile paved loop through several historic sites. The picnic trail is a 1/2-mile paved trail from the visitor center to the picnic and recreation area, which borders the vast salt marshes and forested hammocks of the Savannah River estuary. The third trail follows the historic dike originally surveyed by Robert E. Lee. A walk on any segment of the trail provides excellent opportunities to see a wide variety of plants and wildlife, as well as scenic views of the fort.

Fishing, boating, and other water-related activities are offered at the park. The north channel shoreline and the bridge approaches at the south channel are the best fishing locations. A boat ramp and fishing dock just off Hwy 80 at Lazaretto Creek provide more opportunities for fishing. All facilities are open daily except Dec 25. For more information, phone 912/786-5787.

Gainesville (A-2)

See also Buford, Commerce, Dahlonega, Toccoa

Population 25,578
Elevation 1,249 ft
Area Code 770
Information Gainesville/Hall County Convention and Visitors Bureau, 830 Green St, 30501; phone 770/536-5209
Web Site www.gainesville.org

On the shore of 38,000-acre Lake Sidney Lanier, Gainesville is a poultry producing and marketing center with a variety of industries. It is also the headquarters for the Chattahoochee National Forest (see DAHLONEGA). Contact the Forest Supervisor, US Forest Service, 508 Oak St, 30501; phone 770/536-0541.

What to See and Do

Brenau University. *1 Centennial Cir, Gainesville. Phone 770/534-6299.* (1878) (2,000 students) Liberal arts residential college for women with coed evening and weekend programs; off-campus, graduate, and undergraduate divisions. On campus is Brenau Academy, a four-year preparatory high school for girls. Pearce Auditorium (1897) has fine acoustics, stained-glass windows, and ceiling frescoes. Trustee Library has displays of American art.

Green Street Historical District. A broad street with Victorian and Classical Revival houses dating from the late 19th and early 20th centuries. Here is

> **Green Street Station.** *311 Green St SE, Gainesville. Phone 770/536-0889.* Home of Georgia Mountains Historical and Cultural Trust. Houses historical and arts and crafts exhibits of northeast Georgia, as well as the Mark Trail Memorial Exhibit. (Tues-Fri; closed holidays) **$**

Lake Lanier Islands. *6950 Holiday Rd, Gainesville (30518). W edge of town.* (see BUFORD).

North Geogia Premium Outlets. *800 Hwy 400 S, Dawsonville (30534). Off Hwy 400, 23 miles NE on Hwy 53. Phone 706/216-3609. www.premiumoutlets.com.* An outlet mall with about 140 stores, including Coach, Crate & Barrel, and Hugo Boss. (Mon-Sat 10 am-9 pm, Sun noon-6 pm)

Special Event

Road Atlanta. *5300 Winder Hwy, Gainesville. 8 miles S via Hwy 53. Phone 770/967-6143.* Sports car and motorcycle racing. Also street-driving and road-racing training programs. Mar-Nov.

Limited-Service Hotels

★ ★ **BEST WESTERN LANIER CENTRE.** *400 E Butler Pkwy, Gainesville (30501). Phone 770/531-0907; toll-free 800/782-8966; fax 770/531-0788. www.bestwestern.com.* 122 rooms, 4 story. Check-out noon. Restaurant, bar. Fitness room. Outdoor pool. **$**
🏃 🏊

★ ★ **QUALITY INN & SUITES.** *726 Jesse Jewell Pkwy, Gainesville (30504). Phone 770/536-4451; toll-free 800/228-5151; fax 770/538-2880. www.choicehotels.com.* 132 rooms, 3 story. Pets accepted, some restrictions. Check-out noon. Restaurant, bar. Outdoor pool. **$**
🐾 🏊

Specialty Lodging

The following lodging establishment is approved by Mobil Travel Guide, but due to its unique and individualized nature has not been given a traditional Mobil Star rating. Included in this listing you may find bed-and-breakfasts, limited-service inns, guest ranches, and other unique hotel properties.

DUNLAP HOUSE BED & BREAKFAST. *635 Green St NE, Gainesville (30501). Phone 770/536-0200; toll-free 800/276-2935; fax 770/503-7857. www.dunlaphouse.com.* Built in 1910, this captivating bed-and-breakfast warms guests with Old South hospitality. Located on historic Green Street, guest suites are designed for ultimate comfort. 9 rooms, 2 story. Complimentary full breakfast. Check-in 3 pm, check-out 11 am. **$**

Restaurants

★ **POOR RICHARD'S.** *1702 Park Hill Dr, Gainesville (30501). Phone 770/532-0499.* Steak menu.

Dinner. Closed Sun; holidays. Bar. Children's menu. **$$**

★ ★ ★ **RUDOLPH'S.** *700 Green St, Gainesville (30501). Phone 770/534-2226; fax 770/536-8261.* Located on the city's most historic street, this American restaurant offers pleasing renditions of traditional preparations of filet mignon, veal, and seafood. American menu. Dinner, Sun brunch. Closed Sun; holidays. Bar. Children's menu. **$$$**

Golden Isles (E-5)

See also Brunswick, Jekyll Island, Sea Island, St. Simons Island

Web Site www.bgivb.com

2744 Hwy 17 S, Brunswick (31523).

Four barrier subtropical islands off Georgia's coast at Brunswick. Best known of the group are Sea Island (see), St. Simons Island (see), and Jekyll Island (see), all of which may be reached by road. Others are Cumberland, Little St. Simons Island, Ossabaw, St. Catherine's, and Sapelo, reachable only by water.

Native Americans hunted on these islands for giant turtles, waterfowl, deer, and other animals. Spaniards established a chain of missions, which existed for about a century, the largest on St. Simons. The French made halfhearted efforts to settle on the islands. James Oglethorpe built Fort Frederica (see) on St. Simons in 1736 and later defeated Spanish forces attempting to recapture the island.

Now the Golden Isles are resort areas, offering beautiful scenery, swimming, a wide variety of sports facilities, and accommodations.

Greensboro (B-3)

Population 3,238
Web Site www.greeneccoc.org

Full-Service Resort

★ ★ ★ ★ **THE RITZ-CARLTON LODGE, REYNOLDS PLANTATION.** *1 Lake Oconee Trail, Greensboro (30642). Phone 706/467-0600; fax 706/467-7124. www.ritzcarlton.com.* The Ritz-Carlton Lodge has one of the most enviable resort locations in the South. Just over an hour from Atlanta, this sprawling resort on the 8,000-acre Reynolds Plantation overlooks the sparkling water of Lake Oconee, Georgia's second-largest lake. While imparting first-class service and modern-day conveniences, this fantastic resort mimics the grand style of the Great Camps that populated the Adirondacks during the early 20th century. Like a wealthy relative's lake home, The Ritz-Carlton Lodge welcomes you with its gracious style and magnificent setting. You can fill your days with endless activities, and the lake provides a wealth of opportunities from fishing and boating to swimming and water-skiing. Golf is a major attraction here, and with 81 holes designed by legends like Jack Nicklaus, Rees Jones, Tom Fazio, and Bob Cupp, it is no wonder. The Gun Club entertains with its skeet and trap shooting, five-stand shooting pavilion, and sporting clay course. After an active day, retire to one of the exceedingly comfortable guest rooms. Dominated by a rich blend of American and European design principles, the accommodations are sophisticated without pretension and welcome the entire family. 251 rooms. Check-in 3 pm, check-out noon. High-speed Internet access. Restaurant, bar. Children's activity center. Fitness room, spa. Indoor pool, outdoor pool, children's pool, whirlpool. Golf, 81 holes. Business center. **$$$**

Spa

★ ★ ★ ★ **THE SPA AT THE RITZ-CARLTON LODGE, REYNOLDS PLANTATION.** *1 Lake Oconee Trail, Greensboro (30642). Phone 706/467-0600; toll-free 800/241-3333. www.ritzcarlton.com.* The 26,000-square-foot spa is the shining star at Reynolds Plantation. The facility is superbly designed with the spa visitor in mind. Private spaces that inspire reflection and relaxation can be found throughout, from the outdoor terraces with lake views to the indoor pool with lounges and a towering stone fireplace. This dynamic facility pays tribute to the Creek Indians, the first inhabitants of the Lake Oconee area. Everything from the architecture to the philosophy and the treatments reflects the spa's dedication to Native American healing traditions. The seasonally inspired body buffs and polishes pay special attention to the skin's varying needs throughout the year. The winter body buff tackles dry skin with its blend of evening primrose, eucalyptus, and rosewood, while the summer body glow uses lemongrass, grapefruit seed, and sassafras root to achieve a healthy skin tone. Thistle and Peru balsam are used in the spring scrub, while the fall's sweet orange, patchouli, pumpkin seeds, and sea salt help soothe sun-exposed skin and awaken the senses. Wood, fire, earth, metal, and water are each represented by a different type of clay in the five-element body wrap that concludes with a luxurious bath; select the clay that best suits your needs. The Oconee mud wrap uses indigenous mud along with wild yam, elderberry, juniper, and sage to hydrate skin. The resort's wellness center caters to health and sports enthusiasts with its advanced cardiovascular equipment, indoor lap pool, health screenings, and consultations with counselors who will design an exercise program to help you achieve higher levels of fitness.

Hamilton

Web Site www.harris-county.com/hamiltonga

Restaurant

★ ★ ★ **OAK TREE VICTORIAN RESTAURANT.**
Hwy 27, Hamilton (31811). Phone 706/628-4218; fax 706/628-5478. www.victoriangrill.com. Owned by Joyce and Robert Cusic, this restaurant highlights French and Italian specialties. The Victorian setting makes for an elegant dining experience. French menu. Dinner. Closed Sun; holidays. **$$**

Helen (A-2)

See also Toccoa

Population 430
Elevation 1,446 ft
Area Code 706
Zip 30545
Information Helen/White County Convention and Visitors Bureau, 726 Brucken St, PO Box 730; phone 706/878-2181 or toll-free 800/858-8027
Web Site www.helenga.org

The natural setting of the mountains and the Chattahoochee River helped create the atmosphere for this logging town, transformed into a charming alpine village. Helen was reborn in 1969 when the citizens, with the help of a local artist, decided to improve the town's appearance.

The result is the relaxed atmosphere of a small Bavarian town. Quaint cobblestone streets, gift shops with an international flavor, crafters, restaurants, and festivals—a bit of the Old World in the heart of the mountains of northeast Georgia.

What to See and Do

Anna Ruby Falls. *In Chattahoochee National Forest.* (see DAHLONEGA).

Babyland General Hospital. *73 W Underwood St, Cleveland. 9 miles SW via GA 75 N, on US 129. Phone 706/865-2171.* Authentic turn-of-the-century hospital, home of the original "Cabbage Patch Kids"—soft-sculptured "babies" created by artist Xavier Roberts. (Daily; closed holidays) **FREE**

Nacoochee Indian Mound. *1 mile SE on Hwy 17.* Located in former center of the Cherokee Nation.

Richard B. Russell Scenic Highway. *5 miles N of Helen.* Highway winds around mountainsides, offering spectacular scenic views.

Stovall Covered Bridge over Chickamauga Creek. *7 miles E on Hwy 255.* The smallest covered bridge in Georgia.

Unicoi State Park. *1788 Hwy 356 N, Helen. 2 miles NE on Hwy 356. Phone 706/878-2201.* A 1,081-acre park adjacent to Anna Ruby Falls. Swimming beach, fishing, paddleboat (rentals), canoeing (rentals); nature and hiking trails, picnicking, camping, cottages, lodge/conference center, restaurant, craft shop. Programs on natural resources, folk culture. Contact Director of Sales, PO Box 849.

Special Events

Fasching Karnival. German Mardi Gras. Jan-Feb.

Helen to the Atlantic Balloon Race & Festival. *Hwy 75, Helen (30545). Phone 706/878-2271 (Helendorf Inn). www.helenballoon.com.* The weekend begins with a Friday morning liftoff for about 25 balloons participating in the Helen to the Atlantic race, which ends anywhere along I-95. After those balloons take off, several more stay in Helen for local flights or special activities—visitors can help with inflation, be a part of a chase crew, or even take a tethered balloon ride. First weekend in June.

Oktoberfest. *726 Brucken Strasse, Helen.* German music and beer festival; one of the longest running Oktoberfests in the country. Sept-Oct.

Volksmarch. *1074 Edelweiss Strasse, Helen.* Bavarian walk in the forest. Third weekend in Apr.

Limited-Service Hotels

★ ★ **CASTLE INN.** *8590 Main St, Helen (30545).*

Phone 706/878-3140; toll-free 877/878-3140; fax 706/878-2470. 12 rooms, 2 story. Check-out 11 am. Restaurant. **$**

★ **COMFORT INN.** *101 Edelweiss Strasse, Helen (30545). Phone 706/878-8000; toll-free 800/443-6488; fax 706/878-1231. www.comfortinn.com.* 60 rooms, 2 story. Complimentary continental breakfast. Check-out 11 am. Outdoor pool. **$**

★ ★ **UNICOI LODGE AND CONFERENCE CENTER.** *Hwy 356, Helen (30545). Phone 706/878-2201; toll-free 800/573-9659; fax 706/878-1897. www.unicoilodge.com.* 100 rooms, 3 story. Check-out 11 am. Restaurant. Tennis. Access to all facilities of state park. **$**

Specialty Lodging

The following lodging establishment is approved by Mobil Travel Guide, but due to its unique and individualized nature has not been given a traditional Mobil Star rating. Included in this listing you may find bed-and-breakfasts, limited-service inns, guest ranches, and other unique hotel properties.

BURNS-SUTTON HOUSE INN. *855 Washington St, Clarkesville (30523). Phone 706/754-5565; fax 706/754-9698.* Built in 1901; Victorian style and décor. 7 rooms, 3 story. Complimentary full breakfast. Restaurant. **$**

Restaurant

★ ★ **HOFBRAUHAUS.** *1 Main St, Helen (30545). Phone 706/878-2248; fax 706/878-1202. www.hofbrausinn.com.* German menu. Dinner. Closed Dec 25. Bar. Children's menu. **$$**

Hiawassee (A-2)

See also Clayton

Population 808
Elevation 1,980 ft
Area Code 706
Zip 30546
Web Site www.mountaintopga.com

A picturesque mountain town in the heart of Georgia's "Little Switzerland," Hiawassee is on Lake Chatuge, surrounded by Chattahoochee National Forest (see DAHLONEGA). Its backdrop is a range of the Blue Ridge Mountains topped by Brasstown Bald Mountain, Georgia's highest peak. Rock hunting, including hunting for the highly prized amethyst crystal, is a favorite activity in surrounding Towns County. Mountaineers of northern Georgia gather from 26 surrounding counties to participate in a fair, the rule of which is "everybody can bring something."

What to See and Do

Brasstown Bald Mountain-Visitor Information Center. *2941 St Hwy 180, Hiawassee (30546). S on Hwy 17, 75, then W on Hwy 180, then N on Hwy 180 spur. Phone 706/896-2556.* At 4,784 feet, this is Georgia's highest peak. Observation deck affords a view of four states. Visitor center has interpretive programs presented in mountain-top theater and exhibit hall. Parking/shuttle fee. (June-Oct, daily; late Apr-May, weekends only, weather permitting) **FREE**

Lake Chatuge. *Hwy 76 W, Hiawassee (30546). W edge of town. Phone 706/896-2835.* This approximately 7,000-acre TVA lake provides opportunities for fishing, boating, and camping.

Special Events

Georgia Mountain Fair. *Hwy 76 W, Hiawassee (30546). Phone 706/896-4191.* Individual accomplishment and "friendlier living" is the theme of this gathering of mountain farm people; arts and crafts, farm produce, flowers, minerals, Native American relics; board splitting, soap and hominy making, quilting; general store, still, farm museum, midway, music hall; entertainment, parade. Camping, beach, and tennis courts at Georgia Mountain Fairgrounds and Towns County Recreation Park. Twelve days in early Aug.

Georgia Mountain Fall Festival. *Fairgrounds, Hwy 76 W, Hiawassee (30546). Phone 706/896-4191.* Ten days in mid-Oct.

Full-Service Resort

★ ★ ★ **BRASSTOWN VALLEY RESORT.** *6321 Hwy 76, Young Harris (30582). Phone 706/379-9900; toll-free 800/201-3205; fax 706/379-9999. www.brasstownvalley.com.* Guests get lost in the views from this mountain lodge as they take in the beautiful Blue Ridge Mountain countryside. This resort offers a rustic feel with many modern touches and with plenty to see and do. 102 rooms, 5 story. Check-in 4 pm, check-out noon. Restaurant, bar. Children's activity center. Fitness room. Indoor/outdoor pool, whirlpool. Golf. Tennis. Business center. **$**

🏋 🛥 🍴 🏌 🚶

Indian Springs State Park (C-2)

Web Site gastateparks.org/info/indspr

5 miles S of Jackson on Hwy 42.

Called "the oldest state park in the United States," this was originally a gathering place for Creek Native Americans, who valued sulphur springs for curative powers. General William McIntosh, a Creek, headed the encampment in this area in 1800. In 1821, McIntosh signed a treaty ceding most of the Creek lands between the Flint and Ocmulgee rivers and north to the Chattahoochee. In 1825, he relinquished the rest of the Creek land in Georgia. The state disposed of all Native American lands except 10 acres called Indian Springs Reserve. Butts County citizens bought an adjoining 513 acres, donating it to the state for a park with a mineral spring, a 105-acre lake, and a museum (summer only). Swimming beach, fishing, boating (rentals); nature trails, picnicking, camping, cottages. Standard hours, fees. Contact Superintendent, 678 Lake Clark Rd, Flovilla 30216; phone 770/504-2277.

Jekyll Island (E-5)

See also Brunswick, Darien, Golden Isles, Sea Island, St. Simons Island

Population 1,500
Elevation 5 ft
Area Code 912
Information Jekyll Island Convention and Visitors Bureau, PO Box 13186, 31527; phone 912/635-3636 or toll-free 800/841-6586
Web Site www.jekyllisland.com

Connected to the mainland by a causeway, Jekyll Island, the smallest of Georgia's coastal islands (see GOLDEN ISLES) with 5,600 acres of highlands and 10,000 acres of marshland, was favored by Native Americans for hunting and fishing. Spanish missionaries arrived in the late 16th and early 17th centuries

and established a mission. In 1734, during an expedition southward, General James Oglethorpe passed by the island and named it for his friend and financial supporter, Sir Joseph Jekyll. Later, William Horton, one of Oglethorpe's officers, established a plantation on the island.

Horton's land grant passed to several owners before the island was sold to Christophe du Bignon, a Frenchman who was escaping the French Revolution. It remained in the du Bignon family as a plantation for almost a century. In 1858, the slave ship *Wanderer* arrived at the island and unloaded the last major cargo of slaves to land in the United States. In 1886, John Eugene du Bignon sold the island to a group of wealthy businessmen from the northeast, who formed the Jekyll Island Club.

Club members who wintered at Jekyll in exclusive privacy from early January to early April included J. P. Morgan, William Rockefeller, Edwin Gould, Joseph Pulitzer, and R. T. Crane Jr. Some built fabulous "cottages," many of which are still standing. But by World War II, the club had been abandoned for economic and social reasons, and in 1947, the island was sold to the state. The Jekyll Island Authority was created to conserve beaches and manage the island while maintaining it as a year-round resort.

What to See and Do

Horton House. *NW side of the island.* Ruins of former house (1742) of William Horton, sent from St. Simons as captain by General James Oglethorpe. On Jekyll, he established an outpost and plantation. Horton became major of all British forces at Fort Frederica after Oglethorpe's return to England. This house was later occupied by the du Bignon family as part of their plantation.

Jekyll Island Club Historic District. *901 Jekyll Island Causeway, Jekyll Island (31527).* Once one of the nation's most exclusive resorts, this restored district is a memorable example of turn-of-the-century wealth. Exhibition buildings and shops are open daily (closed Jan 1, Dec 25). Tours are available (daily, fee; tickets, information at the visitor center, the former Jekyll Island Club stables) for Mistletoe Cottage (1900), Indian Mound (or Rockefeller) Cottage (1892), du Bignon Cottage (1884), and the Faith Chapel (1904). Period rooms and changing exhibits can be viewed in several houses.

Public facilities. Beachfront bathhouses, pier fishing, charter boats for offshore and inlet fishing, sightseeing cruises, nature center; bicycle trails, rentals, golf, driving range, miniature golf, 13 clay tennis courts, pro shop. Picnicking on E shore; shopping center. Camping at N end. Some fees.

Summer Waves. *210 S Riverview Dr, Jekyll Island. Phone 912/635-2074.* Water park (11 acres) featuring wave pool, enclosed speed slide, serpentine slides, tubing river, children's pool; picnicking, concessions. (Late May-early Sept, daily) **$$$$**

Special Event

Beach Music Festival. *901 Jekyll Pkwy, Jekyll Island.* Music groups perform all afternoon on the famous beach. Late Aug.

Limited-Service Hotel

★ ★ **HOLIDAY INN.** *200 S Beachview Dr, Jekyll Island (31527). Phone 912/635-3311; toll-free 800/ 753-5955; fax 912/635-3919. www.holiday-inn.com.* 198 rooms, 4 story. Pets accepted; fee. Check-in 4 pm, check-out 11 am. Restaurant, bar. Fitness room. Beach. Outdoor pool, children's pool. **$**

Full-Service Resort

★ ★ ★ **JEKYLL ISLAND CLUB HOTEL.** *371 Riverview Dr, Jekyll Island (31527). Phone 912/635-2600; toll-free 800/535-9547; fax 912/635-2818. www.jekyllclub.com.* Once a popular and exclusive retreat for the nation's wealthy elite, this gorgeous hotel on Georgia's historic Jekyll Island will leave guests feeling pampered and entertained. With golf, fishing, water sports, shopping, and more, it's simply a piece of heaven on earth. 157 rooms, 4 story. Check-in 4 pm, check-out noon. Restaurant, bar. Children's activity center. Beach. Outdoor pool. Golf. Tennis. Airport transportation available. **$$**

Restaurants

★ ★ **BLACKBEARD'S.** *200 N Beachview Dr, Jekyll Island (31527). Phone 912/635-3522; fax 912/635-4106.* American menu. Lunch, dinner. Closed Dec 25. Bar. Children's menu. Casual attire. Outdoor seating. **$$**

★ ★ ★ **GRAND DINING ROOM.** *371 Riverview Dr, Jekyll Island (31527). Phone 912/635-2600; fax*

912/635-2818. www.jekyllclub.com. The formal dining room of this historic resort is as grand as its name suggest. A dramatic colonnade leads to a large fireplace, lined by plushly upholstered chairs. The low-country cooking features local fish and seafood. American menu. Breakfast, lunch, dinner, Sun brunch. Children's menu. Jacket required (dinner). Reservations recommended. Valet parking. **$$$**

★ **LATITUDE 31.** *1 Pier Rd, Jekyll Island (31527). Phone 912/635-3800.* American menu. Lunch, dinner. Closed Mon; holidays. Bar. Children's menu. Casual attire. Outdoor seating. **$$**

★ **ZACHRY'S SEAFOOD.** *44 Beachview Dr, Jekyll Island (31527). Phone 912/635-3128; fax 912/635-9889.* Seafood menu. Dinner. Closed Dec 25, Children's menu. Casual attire. **$$**

Kennesaw Mountain National Battlefield Park (B-2)

See also Atlanta, Marietta

Web Site www.nps.gov/kemo

Approximately 3 miles NW of Marietta off Hwy 41 or I-75, exit 116.

At Kennesaw Mountain in June of 1864, General William Tecumseh Sherman executed the last of a series of flanking maneuvers that were started 100 miles to the north on May 7. The Battle of Kennesaw Mountain stalled but did not halt General Sherman's invasion of Georgia. Kennesaw Mountain National Battlefield Park commemorates the 1864 Atlanta campaign.

In a series of flanking maneuvers and minor battles in May and June, Sherman's 100,000-man Union Army forced the 65,000-man Confederate Army, under the command of General Joseph E. Johnston, back from Dalton to the vicinity of Kennesaw Mountain 20 miles north of Atlanta. On June 19, Johnston took position and dug in, anchoring his right flank on the steep mountain slopes and extending his left flank several miles to the south. He trusted that strong fortifications and rugged terrain would make up for the disparity in numbers.

The Confederates abandoned their positions after a heavy day's fighting and occupied strong points between Kennesaw and Lost mountains. Sherman first tried to march around to an area just south of the Confederate position, but Johnston shifted 11,000 troops to counter the maneuver. In fierce fighting at Kolb's Farm on June 22, Confederate attacks were repulsed, but Sherman was temporarily stymied.

Although the Confederate entrenchments seemed strong, Sherman suspected that they were weakly held. A sharp frontal attack, he decided, might break through and destroy Johnston's entire army. On the morning of June 27, after a heavy artillery bombardment, Sherman struck the Confederate line at two places simultaneously. At Pigeon Hill, 5,500 attackers were quickly driven under cover by sheets of Southern bullets. Two miles to the south, 8,000 Union infantrymen stormed up Cheatham Hill and for a few minutes engaged the Confederates in hand-to-hand combat on top of their earthworks. Casualties were so severe that the location was nicknamed "Dead Angle." By noon, both attacks had failed. Sherman had lost 3,000 men, Johnston only 500.

Sherman reverted to his flanking strategy, and on July 2, the Confederates withdrew, eventually to Atlanta. The siege and fall of Atlanta soon followed. Sherman then began his devastating "March to the Sea."

The visitor center, on Hwy 41 and Stilesboro Road, north of Kennesaw Mountain, has exhibits, an audio-visual program, and information (daily; closed Dec 25). A road leads to the top of Kennesaw Mountain (daily: Mon-Fri, drive or walk; Sat-Sun, bus leaves every half hour, Feb-Nov, or walk—no driving). (The Cheatham Hill area, in the south-central section of the park, has the same hours as the Kennesaw Mountain road; closed Dec 25).

Park (daily; closed Dec 25). Self-guided tours. For additional information, contact Park Ranger, 900 Kennesaw Mountain Dr, Kennesaw 30152-4854; phone 770/427-4686. **FREE**

La Grange (C-1)

See also Pine Mountain

Settled 1828
Population 25,998
Elevation 772 ft
Area Code 706
Zip 30240
Information La Grange-Troup County Chamber of Commerce, 111 Bull St, Box 636, 30241-0636; phone 706/884-8671
Web Site www.lagrangechamber.com

La Grange is said to be the only town in the Confederacy that organized its own female military company. Legend has it that La Grange was so loyal to the Confederacy that every man marched off to battle. A women's home guard was named for Nancy Hart, Revolutionary heroine. When the defenseless city was about to be invaded by Wilson's Raiders, the Nancy Harts marched out to the fray. The Union colonel, named La Grange, was so affected by this female defense that he marched on without burning the city.

What to See and Do

Bellevue. *204 Ben Hill St, La Grange. Phone 706/884-1832.* (1852-1853) Greek Revival house of US senator Benjamin Harvey Hill; period furnishings. (Tues-Sat; closed holidays) **$$**

Chattahoochee Valley Art Museum. *112 Hines St, La Grange. Phone 706/882-3267.* Art museum housed in remodeled 1800s jail. Changing exhibits by local, national, and international artists. (Tues-Sat; closed holidays) **FREE**

West Point Lake. *500 Resource Management Dr, La Grange (31833). W on Hwy 109. Phone 706/645-2937.* Approximately 26,000 acres with 525 miles of shoreline. Swimming, fishing, boating; hunting, camping (fee).

Limited-Service Hotel

★ **BEST WESTERN LAFAYETTE GARDEN INN.** *1513 Lafayette Pkwy, La Grange (30241). Phone 706/884-6175; fax 706/884-1106. www.lafayettegardeninn.com.* 143 rooms, 2 story. Check-out noon. Fitness room. Outdoor pool. **$**
🐾 🖼️

Lookout Mountain

Web Site www.lookoutmtnattractions.com

Specialty Lodging

The following lodging establishment is approved by Mobil Travel Guide, but due to its unique and individualized nature has not been given a traditional Mobil Star rating. Included in this listing you may find bed-and-breakfasts, limited-service inns, guest ranches, and other unique hotel properties.

CHANTICLEER INN. *1300 Mockingbird Ln, Lookout Mountain (30750). Phone 706/820-2015; fax 706/820-7976. www.stayatchanticleer.com.* 17 rooms. Complimentary continental breakfast. Check-out 11 am. High-speed Internet access. Outdoor pool. **$**

Lumpkin (D-1)

See also Americus, Columbus

Population 1,250
Elevation 593 ft
Area Code 229
Zip 31815

What to See and Do

Lake Walter F. George. *Approximately 18 miles W via Hwy 39C, or approximately 30 miles SW via Hwy 27. Phone 229/768-2516.* This 45,000-acre lake, stretching south along the border of Georgia and Alabama, was created by the damming of the Chattahoochee River. Fishing is good for bass, bream, crappie, and catfish, and the lake's 640-mile shoreline provides countless hidden coves and inlets. Various state parks are situated on the lake's border, including

Florence Marina State Park. *Phone 229/838-4244.* More than 140 acres at the northern end of Lake Walter F. George. Swimming pool, fishing, boating, johnboat rentals (fee); 18-hole miniature golf (fee), tennis, camping, cottages. Contact Manager, Rte 1, Box 36, Omaha, 31821.

Providence Canyon State Conservation Park. *Rte 39 C, Lumpkin. 7 miles W via Hwy 39C. Phone 229/838-6202.* Georgia's "Little Grand Canyon" has spectacular erosion gullies up to 150 feet deep. Hiking, picnicking,

interpretive center (daily). Contact Superintendent, Rte 1, Box 158.

Westville. *Martin Luther King Blvd, Lumpkin. Phone 229/838-6310.* Living history village featuring buildings (circa 1850); decorative arts and work skills of early Georgia. Demonstrations by craftsworkers include quilting, weaving, candlemaking, potterymaking, blacksmithing, and basket weaving; syrup making in season. (Tues-Sun; closed Jan 1, Thanksgiving, Dec 25; also early Jan) **$$$**

Special Event

Westville events. *Phone 229/838-6310.* Westville has many varied events throughout the year. Of special interest are the Spring Festival (early Apr), the May Day celebration (early May), Independence Day (July 4), "Fair of 1850" (late Oct-early Nov), and a variety of Christmas activities (Dec).

Macon (C-3)

See also Forsyth, Milledgeville, Ocmulgee National Monument, Perry

Founded 1823
Population 97,255
Elevation 325 ft
Area Code 478
Information Macon-Bibb County Convention and Visitors Bureau, Terminal Station, 200 Cherry St, PO Box 6354, 31208; phone 478/743-3401 or toll-free 800/768-3401
Web Site www.maconga.org

Macon began as a trading post. It served as a fort and rallying point for troops in the War of 1812; later it became a river landing for shipping to the seacoast by oar-propelled flat-bottom boats; then Macon became a major regional cotton market. Having launched *The Pioneer*, a forerunner of all Southern river steamers, Macon was not content to remain just a port. In 1838, a railroad linked Macon with Forsyth; five years later it was connected by rail to Savannah. In 1848, a third line, the Southwestern, connected Macon with the fertile southwest section of the state. The town had become a major railroad center.

Macon's role in the Civil War was to manufacture and distribute quartermaster supplies and ordnance. Harnesses, small weapons, cannons, and shots were produced, and the city harbored $1.5 million in

Confederate gold. In 1864, refugees poured in from devastated northern Georgia. In July and November, Union forces were twice repulsed. The city finally surrendered to Wilson's Raiders in April 1865.

Sidney Lanier was born and lived here, practicing law before turning to poetry. Macon is also the hometown of rock 'n' roll singer Little Richard and soul singer Otis Redding.

What to See and Do

Around Town Tours of Historic Macon. *935 High St, Macon. Phone 478/743-3851.* Operated by the Middle Georgia Historical Society. Guides available (fee) for private tours of city or bus tours.

City Hall. *700 Poplar St, Macon. Phone 478/751-7170.* (1836) Main entrance of Classical Revival building is flanked by panels depicting history of Macon area. Building was state capitol November 18, 1864-March 11, 1865, during the last session of the Georgia General Assembly under the Confederate States of America. Tours. (Mon-Fri; closed holidays) **FREE**

Georgia Music Hall of Fame. *200 Martin Luther King Jr. Blvd, Macon. Phone 478/750-8555; toll-free 888/427-6257.* Georgia's musical heritage is explored through different exhibits such as the Soda Fountain playing songs of the 1950s, the Jazz Club, Gospel Chapel, and Rhythm & Blues Revue. Videos can be selected for viewing in the Gretsch Theater. (Daily; closed holidays) **$$$**

Georgia Sports Hall of Fame. *301 Cherry St, Macon (31201). Phone 478/752-1585. www.gshf.org.* Built to resemble a classic ballpark, the Hall houses exhibits on Georgia's famous athletes and professional and college teams. (Daily) **$$**

Grand Opera House. *651 Mulberry St, Macon. Phone 478/301-5470.* Originally the Academy of Music (1884), theater was restored in 1970.

Hay House. *934 Georgia Ave, Macon. Phone 478/742-8155.* (1855-1859) An Italian Renaissance Revival villa with 24 rooms; elaborate ornamental plaster, woodwork, stained glass; ornate period furnishings, and objets d'art. (Daily; closed holidays) **$$$**

Lake Tobesofkee. *6600 Moseley Dixon Rd, Macon. 3 miles W via I-475, exit Hwy 74. Phone 478/474-8770.* A 1,750-acre lake and a 650-acre park. Swimming, water-skiing, fishing, boating (launch); nature trails, tennis, picnicking, camping (hook-ups). (Daily)

Macon Historic District. *Downtown, Macon.* District comprises nearly all of old Macon; 48 buildings and houses have been cited for architectural excellence and listed on National Register of Historic Places; an additional 575 structures have been noted for architectural significance. Walking and driving tours noted on Heritage Tour Markers. For tour maps, contact the Convention and Visitors Bureau.

Macon Museum of Arts and Sciences & Mark Smith Planetarium. *4182 Forsyth Rd, Macon. Phone 478/477-3232.* Three galleries with permanent and changing art and science exhibits; displays of live amphibians, birds, reptiles, and small mammals; nature trails; observatory. Planetarium shows. (Daily; closed Jan 1, Dec 25) **$$**

Mercer University. *1400 Coleman Ave, Macon. Phone 478/301-2715.* (1833) (6,100 students) Founded as Mercer Institute in Penfield, moved to Macon in 1871. Liberal arts, business, law, engineering, and medicine are offered at Macon campus; also campus in Atlanta.

Old Cannonball House & Macon-Confederate Museum. *856 Mulberry St, Macon. Phone 478/745-5982.* (1853) Greek Revival house struck by Union cannonball in 1864. Museum contains Civil War relics and Macon historical items. (Mon-Sat; closed Jan 1, Thanksgiving, Dec 25) **$$**

Sidney's Tours of Historic Macon. *200 Cherry St, Macon. Phone 478/743-3401; toll-free 800/768-3401.* Operated by the Macon-Bibb County Convention and Visitors Bureau. Examples of Greek Revival architecture, Victorian cottages, Italianate mansions, antebellum houses; statues, monuments, other landmarks left standing by General Sherman on his "March to the Sea." (Mon-Sat; no tours holidays) **$$$$**

Sidney Lanier Cottage. *935 High St, Macon. Phone 478/743-3851.* (1840) Gothic Revival house was birthplace of the nationally known poet; period furnishings. Headquarters of Middle Georgia Historical Society. (Mon-Fri and Sat mornings; closed holidays) **$$**

Tubman African-American Museum. *340 Walnut St, Macon. Phone 478/743-8544.* Features African American art, African artifacts, and traveling exhibits on the history and culture of African American people. Resource center, workshops, and tours (by appointment). (Daily; closed holidays) **$$**

Wesleyan College. *4760 Forsyth Rd, Macon. On Hwy 41. Phone 478/477-1110.* (1836) (700 women) This four-year liberal arts college was chartered to grant degrees to women. Campus tours by appointment.

Special Events

Cherry Blossom Festival. *794 Cherry St, Macon.* Historic tours, concerts, fireworks, hot air balloons, sporting events, parade. Mid Mar.

Georgia State Fair. *Central City Park, 1 Riverside Dr, Macon. Phone 478/746-7184.* Entertainment stages, midway, exhibit buildings. Late Sept.

Limited-Service Hotels

★ ★ **BEST WESTERN RIVERSIDE INN.** *2400 Riverside Dr, Macon (31204). Phone 478/743-6311; toll-free 888/454-4565; fax 478/743-9420. www.bestwestern.com.* 122 rooms, 2 story. Check-out noon. Restaurant, bar. Outdoor pool. **$**

★ **HOLIDAY INN EXPRESS.** *2720 Riverside Dr, Macon (31204). Phone 478/743-1482; toll-free 800/465-4329; fax 478/745-3967. www.holiday-inn.com.* 93 rooms, 6 story. Pets accepted; fee. Complimentary continental breakfast. Check-out noon. Outdoor pool. **$**

Full-Service Hotel

★ ★ ★ **CROWNE PLAZA.** *108 1st St, Macon (31201). Phone 478/746-1461; toll-free 800/227-6963; fax 478/738-2460. www.crowneplaza.com.* Located in the heart of historic downtown, this elegant hotel welcomes guests with gracious accommodations and first-class leisure activities. From the outdoor pool with sauna and sundeck, to the nightclub that entices guests to dance the night away, this hotel offers an oasis of comfort. 298 rooms, 16 story. Check-out noon. Restaurant, bar. Fitness room. Outdoor pool. Airport transportation available. **$**

Madison (B-3)

See also Athens, Eatonton

Population 3,636
Elevation 667 ft
Area Code 706
Zip 30650

Information Welcome Center, 115 E Jefferson, PO Box 826; phone 706/342-4454 or toll-free 800/709-7406
Web Site www.madisonga.org

General Sherman spared Madison on his Civil War "March to the Sea." The result is a contemporary city with a wealth of well-preserved antebellum and Victorian residences. Several movies have been filmed in the town to take advantage of the 19th-century atmosphere.

What to See and Do

Lake Oconee. *125 Wallace Dam Rd, Madison (31024). E on I-20. Phone 706/485-8704.* This lake, approximately 19,000 acres with 374 miles of shoreline, was created by the impoundment of the Oconee River. Around the lake, visitors can beach, swim, fish, boat (marinas), picnic, and camp.

Madison-Morgan Cultural Center. *434 S Main St, Madison. Phone 706/342-4743.* Romanesque Revival school building (1895) with art galleries, restored schoolroom, museum of local history, original auditorium, and ongoing schedule of performances. (Tues-Sun; closed holidays) **$$**

Special Events

Holiday Tour of Homes. Historic private homes. First weekend in Dec.

Spring Tour of Homes. Historic houses, scenic gardens, period furnishings, and antiques. Apr-May.

Limited-Service Hotel

★ **HOLIDAY INN EXPRESS.** *10111 Alcovy Rd, Covington (30014). Phone 770/787-4900; toll-free 800/788-1390; fax 770/385-9805. www.holiday-inn.com.* 50 rooms, 2 story. Pets accepted; fee. Complimentary continental breakfast. Check-out noon. Fitness room. Outdoor pool. **$**

Specialty Lodgings

The following lodging establishments are approved by Mobil Travel Guide, but due to their unique and individualized nature have not been given a traditional Mobil Star rating. Included in this listing you may find bed-and-breakfasts, limited-service inns, guest ranches, and other unique hotel properties.

BRADY INN BED AND BREAKFAST. *250 N 2nd St, Madison (30650). Phone 706/342-4400. www.bradyinn.com.* Restored Victorian cottage in historic downtown. 7 rooms. Complimentary full breakfast. Check-in 6 pm, check-out noon. **$**

BURNETT PLACE. *317 Old Post Rd, Madison (30650). Phone 706/342-4034. www.burnettplace.com.* Federal-style house (circa 1830) typical of the Piedmont region. 3 rooms, 2 story. Complimentary full breakfast. Check-in 3 pm, check-out 11 am. **$**

Marietta (B-2)

See also Atlanta, Cartersville, Norcross

Founded 1834
Population 58,748
Elevation 1,128 ft
Area Code 770
Information Cobb County Convention and Visitors Bureau, One Galleria Pkwy, Atlanta, 30339; phone toll-free 800/451-3480
Web Site www.cobbcvb.com

What to See and Do

White Water. *250 Cobb Pkwy N, Marietta (30062). Phone 770/424-9283.* Water theme park with 40 rides; body flumes, rapids ride, wave pool, float. (Memorial Day-Labor Day: daily; May: weekends) **$$$$** Adjacent is

> **American Adventures.** *250 Cobb Pkwy N, Marietta (30062). Phone 770/424-6683.* Children's amusement park with over a dozen rides. (Daily; closed holidays) Fee for various activities. **$$$$**

Limited-Service Hotels

★ **HAMPTON INN.** *455 Franklin Rd SE, Marietta (30067). Phone 770/425-9977; toll-free 800/426-7866; fax 770/427-2545. www.hamptoninnmarietta.com.* 139 rooms, 4 story. Complimentary full breakfast. Check-in 3 pm, check-out noon. High-speed Internet access, wireless Internet access. Fitness room. Outdoor pool, children's pool. **$**

★ ★ **HOLIDAY INN.** *2265 Kingston Ct SE, Marietta (30067). Phone 770/952-7581; toll-free 800/465-4329; fax 770/952-1301. www.holiday-inn.com.* 193 rooms, 7 story. Check-in 3 pm, check-out noon. High-speed Internet access, wireless Internet access. Restaurant, bar. Fitness room. Outdoor pool. Airport transportation available. **$**

★ **LA QUINTA INN.** *2170 Delk Rd SE, Marietta (30067). Phone 770/951-0026; toll-free 800/531-5900; fax 770/952-5372. www.lq.com.* 130 rooms, 3 story. Pets accepted. Complimentary continental breakfast. Check-in 3 pm, check-out noon. Outdoor pool. **$**

Full-Service Hotels

★ ★ ★ **HYATT REGENCY SUITES PERIMETER NORTHWEST ATLANTA.** *2999 Windy Hill Rd, Marietta (30067). Phone 770/956-1234; toll-free 800/233-1234; fax 770/956-9479. www.atlanta suites.hyatt.com.* Located just 15 minutes from downtown Atlanta, this property offers a fitness center, an outdoor pool, an indoor whirlpool, and a sundeck. 202 rooms, 7 story. Pets accepted, some restrictions; fee. Check-in 3 pm, check-out noon. High-speed Internet access, wireless Internet access. Restaurant, bar. Fitness room. Outdoor pool, whirlpool. Airport transportation available. Business center. **$$**

★ ★ ★ **MARIETTA CONFERENCE CENTER AND RESORT.** *500 Powder Springs St, Marietta (30064). Phone 770/427-2500; toll-free 888/685-2500; fax 678/819-3224. www.mariettaresort.com.* Come enjoy the history of beautiful Marietta while relaxing in luxury suites, dining on delectable cuisine, and enjoying all of the first class-amenities this hotel offers. Overlooking a championship golf course, this resort turns business into pleasure and makes pleasure a way of life. This hotel is a delight to both the business and leisure traveler. 199 rooms, 6 story. Check-in 3 pm, check-out noon. High-speed Internet access, wireless Internet access. Two restaurants, bar. Fitness room. Outdoor pool, whirlpool. Golf, 18 holes. Tennis. Airport transportation available. Business center. **$$**

Specialty Lodging

The following lodging establishment is approved by Mobil Travel Guide, but due to its unique and individualized nature has not been given a traditional Mobil Star rating. Included in this listing you may find bed-and-breakfasts, limited-service inns, guest ranches, and other unique hotel properties.

THE WHITLOCK. *57 Whitlock Ave, Marietta (30064). Phone 770/428-1495; fax 770/919-9620. www.whitlockinn.com.* Just north of Atlanta, this fully restored Victoria mansion with distinctively different guest rooms provides all the charm one would expect in the South. Guests can enjoy antique shopping and carriage rides as they embrace Southern hospitality. 5 rooms, 2 story. Children over 12 years only. Complimentary continental breakfast. Check-in 3 pm, check-out 11 am. **$**
🅳

Restaurants

★ ★ **GRAZIE A BISTRO.** *1000 Whitlock Ave NW, Marietta (30064). Phone 770/499-8585; fax 770/499-8585. www.grazieabistro.com.* With live piano and jazz five days a week, side dishes and appetizers built for two to share, and sophisticated villalike surroundings, including a fireplace, it's clear that this bistro is great for a romantic night out. And as if the atmosphere wasn't enough, you might want to make a return trip just to get a better taste of the extensive, diverse menu. Italian menu. Lunch, dinner, Sun brunch. Bar. Children's menu. Casual attire. Reservations recommended. Outdoor seating. **$$$**

★ **LA STRADA.** *2930 Johnson Ferry Rd NE, Marietta (30067). Phone 770/640-7008. www.lastradainc.com.* Don't be surprised if you're the only non-local dining at this neighborhood restaurant, where returning customers can't stay away from the soft-shell crab and tiramisu. Italian menu. Dinner. Bar. Children's menu. Casual attire. **$$**

★ **SHILLING'S ON THE SQUARE.** *19 N Park Sq NE, Marietta (30060). Phone 770/428-9520; fax 770/428-9918. www.shillingsonthesquare.com.* This old-fashioned building actually houses two restaurants in one: downstairs, diners will find a casual atmosphere with an equally casual menu including sandwiches and salads, while upstairs lies a more formal dining area. The restaurant enjoys many loyal customers because of this versatility—accommodating many types of groups and occasions—as well as the varied American menu. American menu. Lunch, dinner, Sun brunch. Closed Jan 1, Thanksgiving, Dec 25. Bar. Casual attire. **$**

Milledgeville (C-3)

See also Eatonton, Macon

Founded 1803
Population 18,757
Elevation 335 ft
Area Code 478
Zip 31061
Information Convention and Visitors Bureau, 200 W Hancock St; phone 478/452-4687 or toll-free 800/653-1804
Web Site www.milledgevillecvb.com

Milledgeville was laid out to be the state capital and served in that capacity from 1804 to 1868. When the state records were transferred to Milledgeville from Louisville in 1807, wagons were escorted by troops of cavalry from Washington, DC.

Milledgeville's houses typify the development of Southern architecture. The earliest structures had small stoops; houses of the next period had two porches, one above the other; with the third period, the two-story columns became Greek porticos, the second story, a balcony. Later, porches became broad, multicolumned verandas, extending across the front and even around to the sides and back of the house.

What to See and Do

Georgia College. *231 W Hancock St, Milledgeville. Phone 478/453-5350.* (1889) (5,500 students) Occupies one of four 20-acre plots "reserved for public use" when the city was laid out. The Museum and Archives of Georgia Education is located on campus. Also on campus is

Old Governor's Mansion. *120 S Clark St, Milledgeville. Phone 478/453-4545.* Greek Revival residence of Georgia governors from 1839 to 1868. Guided tours. (Tues-Sat, also Sun afternoons; closed holidays, Thanksgiving weekend, week of Dec 25) **$$**

Historic Guided Trolley Tour. *200 W Hancock, Milledgeville.* Includes stops at St. Stephens Episcopal Church and Stetson-Sanford House. Tour departs from the Convention and Visitors Bureau Office. The office also has information on walking tours. Trolley tour (Tues-Fri mornings, Sat afternoons). **$$$**

Lake Sinclair. *3069 N Columbia St, Milledgeville. N on Hwy 441, Hwy 24. Phone 478/452-1605.* This

15,330-acre lake with 417 miles of shoreline was created by the impoundment of the Oconee River. It offers fishing, boating (marinas), and camping.

Limited-Service Hotel

★ **DAYS INN.** *2551 N Columbia St, Milledgeville (31061). Phone 478/453-8471; toll-free 800/329-7466; fax 478/453-8482. www.daysinn.com.* 100 rooms, 2 story. Complimentary continental breakfast. Check-out 11 am. Fitness room. Outdoor pool, children's pool, whirlpool. Tennis. **$**

Norcross (B-2)

See also Atlanta, Buford, Marietta, Winder

Population 8,410
Elevation 1,057 ft
Area Code 770
Information City of Norcross, 65 Lawrenceville St, 30071; phone 770/448-2122
Web Site www.gcvb.org

Norcross, a suburb of Atlanta, is approximately 20 miles northeast of the city. Citizens have preserved many old residences; there is a 112-acre historic district here with a restored downtown square.

Special Event

BellSouth Golf Classic. *Tournament Players Club at Sugarloaf, 2595 Sugarloaf Club Dr, Duluth (30097). Phone 770/436-2643. www.bellsouthclassic.com.* Jack Nicklaus, Phil Mickelson, and Tiger Woods are just three of the famous faces who have participated in—and won—The BellSouth Classic, a PGA event. More than 125,000 fans attend the tournament each year, as the course has several mounds for easy viewing, making it ideal for spectators. Late Mar-early Apr.

Limited-Service Hotels

★ **COMFORT INN AND SUITES.** *5985 Oakbrook Pkwy, Norcross (30093). Phone 770/662-8175; toll-free 800/252-7466; fax 770/840-1183. www.choicehotels.com.* 115 rooms, 3 story. Pets accepted; fee. Complimentary continental breakfast. Check-in 3 pm, check-out 11 am. Outdoor pool, whirlpool. **$**

★ **HOMEWOOD SUITES.** *10775 Davis Dr, Alpharetta (30004). Phone 770/998-1622; toll-free 800/225-5466; fax 770/998-7834. www.homewoodsuites.com.* 112 rooms, 6 story, all suites. Pets accepted; fee. Complimentary full breakfast. Check-in 3 pm, check-out noon. High-speed Internet access, wireless Internet access. Fitness room. Outdoor pool. Business center. **$**

★ **CLUBHOUSE INN.** *5945 Oakbrook Pkwy, Norcross (30093). Phone 770/368-9400; fax 770/441-9396.* 247 rooms, 3 story. Pets accepted, some restrictions; fee. Complimentary full breakfast. Check-in 3 pm, check-out 11 am. Outdoor pool, whirlpool. **$**

Full-Service Hotels

★ ★ ★ **HILTON ATLANTA NORTHEAST.** *5993 Peachtree Industrial Blvd, Norcross (30092). Phone 770/447-4747; toll-free 800/445-8667; fax 678/533-2888. www.hilton.com.* This hotel ensures that even the most discerning guest will find pleasure in being offered a relaxing stay amid spacious and recently designed guest rooms, as well as a warm and friendly staff catering to a guest's every desire. 272 rooms, 10 story. Pets accepted, some restrictions; fee. Check-in 3 pm, check-out noon. High-speed Internet access, wireless Internet access. Restaurant, bar. Fitness room. Indoor pool, outdoor pool, whirlpool. Airport transportation available. Business center. **$**

★ ★ **HOLIDAY INN.** *6050 Peachtree Industrial Blvd, Norcross (30071). Phone 770/448-4400; fax 770/840-8008. www.hisatlanta.com.* 244 rooms, 8 story. Check-in 3 pm, check-out noon. High-speed Internet access, wireless Internet access. Restaurant, bar. Fitness room. Indoor pool, outdoor pool, whirlpool. Business center. **$**

★ ★ ★ **MARRIOTT ATLANTA GWINNETT PLACE.** *1775 Pleasant Hill Rd, Duluth (30096). Phone 770/923-1775; toll-free 800/228-9290; fax 770/923-0017. www.marriott.com/atlgp.* Located on 11 landscaped acres in the heart of Gwinnett County in the northeastern suburb of Atlanta, this hotel offers a very relaxing stay. Enjoy the spacious guest rooms, indoor and outdoor pool, whirlpool, and health club, or relax in the Buttons Lounge offering live entertainment on the weekends. 426 rooms, 17 story. Check-in 4 pm, check-out noon. High-speed Internet access, wireless Internet access. Two restaurants, two bars. Fitness room. Indoor pool, outdoor pool, whirlpool. Business center. **$$**

★ ★ ★ **MARRIOTT ATLANTA NORCROSS-PEACHTREE CORNERS.** *475 Technology Pkwy, Norcross (30092). Phone 770/263-8558; toll-free 800/228-9290; fax 770/263-0766. www.marriott.com.* Located in Technology Park, this well-appointed 218-room hotel is a business traveler's delight. With a well-equipped business center and 4,000 square feet of meeting space, the hotel and its staff ensure that every meeting is a success. 222 rooms, 6 story. Check-in 3 pm, check-out 11 am. High-speed Internet access, wireless Internet access. Restaurant, bar. Fitness room. Indoor pool, whirlpool. Business center. **$**

Restaurants

★ ★ **DOMINICK'S.** *95 S Peachtree St, Norcross (30071). Phone 770/449-1611; fax 770/449-0096. www.dominickslittleitaly.com.* Italian menu. Lunch, dinner. Closed Sun; Dec 25. Bar. Children's menu. **$$**

★ ★ ★ **HI LIFE.** *3380 Holcomb Bridge Rd, Norcross (30092). Phone 770/409-0101; fax 770/409-1160. www.atlantahilife.com.* This American restaurant has a sleek, modern design. The creative food is fresh and flavorful; of particular note is a four-course lobster tasting menu. American menu. Lunch, dinner. Closed Sun; Jan 1, Thanksgiving, Dec 25. Bar. Children's menu. Business casual attire. Reservations recommended. Outdoor seating. **$$**

★ ★ **SIA'S RESTAURANT.** *10305 Medlock Bridge Rd, Duluth (30097). Phone 770/497-9727; fax 770/497-1131. www.siasrestaurant.com.* Asian menu. Lunch, dinner. Closed Sun. Bar. Reservations recommended. **$$$**

★ **ZAPATA.** *5975 Peachtree Pkwy, Norcross (30092). Phone 770/248-0052.* Serving traditional Mexican food and featuring live music on Fridays and Saturdays, this colorfully decorated restaurant offers friendly service and more moderate portions—perfect for diners who want to try a few new things. Mexican menu. Lunch, dinner. Bar. Casual attire. **$**

Ocmulgee National Monument (C-3)

See also Macon

Web Site www.nps.gov/ocmu
2 miles E of Macon on Hwy 80, Alt 129.

Ocmulgee, the most scientifically excavated of the South's major Native American sites, shows evidence of 12,000 years of settlement, including six successive occupations from at least 10,000 BC to 1825. The major remains consist of nine ceremonial mounds, a funeral mound, and a restored ceremonial earth lodge of the early Mississippian Period (AD 900 to 1100).

Exhibits and dioramas in the museum depict this sequence: Paleo-Indian Period, from more than 12,000 years ago, when Ice Age hunters trailing mammoth and other now-extinct game arrived using stone-tipped spears. During the Archaic Period, after the Ice Age ended, hunter-gathering people hunted small game and supplemented their diet with mussels, fish, seeds, berries, and nuts. They made polished stone tools and camped along the streams. By 2000 BC, crude pottery was fashioned. During the Woodland Period (beginning 1000 BC), some plants were cultivated, villages were larger, and mounds were being built. Pottery was stamped with elaborate designs carved into wooden paddles. The Early Mississippian Period began about AD 900, when invaders brought cultivated corn, beans, squash, and tobacco to the Macon Plateau. They built a large town with burial and temple mounds and circular, earth-covered council chambers. This ceremonial center declined around AD 1100. Late Mississippian Period villagers of the Lamar Culture combined elements of the Mississippian and older Woodland ways of life. They may have been direct ancestors of the historic Creek who lived here when Europeans first settled Georgia. The Creek soon became involved in the struggle between France, Spain, and England for possession of the New World.

Exhibits and dioramas in the museum show the Native American from earliest origins to his removal to Oklahoma in the early 1800s. Great Temple Mound, more than 40 feet high, is the largest in the park. An audio program is conducted in the restored earthlodge, which was the Mississippian council chamber. (Daily; closed Jan 1, Dec 25) For information, contact the Superintendent, 1207 Emery Hwy, Macon, 31217; phone 912/752-8257.

Okefenokee Swamp (E-4)

See also Waycross

Web Site www.okefenokee.com

Information Refuge Manager, Rte 2, Box 3330, Folkston 31537; phone 912/496-7836.

One of the largest preserved freshwater wetlands in the United States, the Okefenokee Swamp encompasses more than 700 square miles, stretching an average of 25 miles in width and 35 miles in length. The swamp's southern border is beyond the Florida line. Called "land of trembling earth" by Native Americans, its lakes of dark brown water, lush with moss-draped cypress, are headwaters for the Suwannee and St. Marys rivers. The swamp embraces vast marshes, termed "prairies," which comprise 60,000 acres.

What to See and Do

Okefenokee National Wildlife Refuge. *11 miles SW Folkston, Okefenokee Swamp (31537). Phone 912/496-7836.* Occupies more than 90 percent of the swamp region and harbors bears, deer, bobcats, alligators, and aquatic birds. Naturalists have discovered many rare plants on the swamp floor, which has been described as "the most beautiful and fantastic landscape in the world." The cypress stand mile after mile, their dense formations broken by watery "prairies" or covered by deposits of peat on the swamp's floor ranging to 15 feet in thickness. It is possible to cause small trees and shrubs to shake by stamping on the "trembling earth"; these trees take root in the crust of peat beds and never reach the solid bottom. Such forests are interspersed with varied swamp vegetation. The bay, one of the swamp's most distinctive trees, blooms from May to October, producing a white flower in contrast to its rich evergreen foliage. Aquatic flowers, such as yellow spatterdock and white water lily, blend with pickerelweed, golden-club, and swamp iris in the spring. The swamp is also the home of the sandhill crane and round-tailed muskrat. (Hours vary with season) **$$**

Okefenokee Swamp Park. *5700 Okefenokee Swamp Park Rd, Okefenokee Swamp. Phone 912/283-0583.* This park, located on Cowhouse Island, has serpentarium and reptile shows. Guided boat tours (fee); canoe rentals. Cypress boardwalk into swamp to 90-foot-high observation tower. Picnicking. Interpretive centers. (Daily) No overnight facilities. Camping available at nearby Laura S. Walker State Park (see WAYCROSS). **$$$$**

Stephen C. Foster State Park. *Hwy 177, Fargo. Phone 912/637-5274.* Park offers access to Billy's Lake, Minnie's Lake, and Big Water (daily during daylight hours without a guide). Fishing, boating (rentals, basin, dock, ramp), canoeing (rentals), sightseeing boat tours; nature trails, picnicking, concession, camping, cabins. Museum. Standard hours, fees.

Suwannee Canal Recreation Area. *11 miles SW of Folkston, Okefenokee Swamp (31537). Phone 912/496-7836.* Area provides entry to the Chesser, Grand, Mizell, and Chase prairies, where small lakes and "gator holes" offer some of the nation's finest birdwatching. Area also has restored swamp homestead and guided swamp tours. Boating (ramp, boat, and motor rentals), canoeing, guided boat tours; nature trails, boardwalk (3/4 mile) with observation tower. Picnicking. Visitor center. (Daily; closed Dec 25) Fees for some activities.

Wilderness canoeing. *Phone 912/496-3331.* There are seven overnight stops and trips available from two to five days (three-day limit Mar-Apr); wooden platforms for campsites. Mar-May and Oct-early Nov are most popular times. Buy advance reservations (two months) and special permit from the refuge manager. **$$$**

Perry (D-2)

See also Andersonville, Cordele, Macon

Population 9,602
Elevation 337 ft
Area Code 478
Zip 31069
Information Perry Area Convention and Visitors Bureau, 101 General Courtney Hodges Blvd, PO Box 1619; phone 478/988-8000
Web Site www.perryga.com

The blooming wildflowers and trees during March and April have made Perry a favorite stopover place for spring motorists. The town is full of stately houses and historical churches. Perry is known as the "Crossroads of Georgia" because of its location near the geographic center of the state.

What to See and Do

⭐ **The Andersonville Trail.** *A 75-mile loop drive from Perry to Cordele (see).* Along the drive are American Camellia Society gardens, two state parks, antebellum houses, and Andersonville National Historic Site. Contact the Convention and Visitors Bureau for information.

Massee Lane Gardens. *100 Massee Ln, Perry. 14 miles W on Hwy 127 to Marshallville, then 3 miles N on Hwy 49.* Phone 478/967-2722. Camellia garden (10 acres) reaches height of bloom between November and March; large greenhouse, Japanese garden, rose garden. Colonial-style headquarters contains more than 300 sculptures of Boehm and other porcelains, other items. Headquarters include the Annabelle Lundy Fetterman Educational Museum, exhibition hall (rare books, porcelain); auditorium with presentation on history of gardens, gift shop. (Mar-June: Tues-Sun; Feb: daily). **$$**

Special Events

Mossy Creek Barnyard Festival. *Deep Piney Woods, N on I-75, exit 142, 3 miles E.* Phone 478/922-8265. Semi-annual event with craftsmen, artists, entertainment, and demonstrations. Third weekend in Apr and third weekend in Oct.

Old-Fashioned Christmas at the Crossroads. Community Christmas tree, parade, candlelight service. Dec.

Limited-Service Hotels

⭐ **COMFORT INN.** *1602 Sam Nunn Blvd, Perry (31069).* Phone 478/987-7710; toll-free 800/642-7710; fax 478/988-2624. www.comfortinn.com. 102 rooms, 2 story. Complimentary continental breakfast. Check-out 11 am. Fitness room. Indoor pool, whirlpool. **$**
🏋 🛳

⭐⭐ **HOLIDAY INN.** *200 Valley Dr, Perry (31069).* Phone 478/987-3313; toll-free 800/808-8804; fax 478/988-8269. www.holiday-inn.com. 203 rooms, 2 story. Restaurant, bar. Fitness room. Outdoor pool. **$**
🏋 🛳

⭐⭐ **NEW PERRY HOTEL.** *800 Main St, Perry (31069).* Phone 478/987-1000; toll-free 800/877-3779; fax 478/987-4866. www.newperryhotel.com. 43

rooms, 3 story. Pets accepted; fee. Check-out noon. Restaurant. Outdoor pool. **$**
🅿 🐾 🛳

Specialty Lodging

The following lodging establishment is approved by Mobil Travel Guide, but due to its unique and individualized nature has not been given a traditional Mobil Star rating. Included in this listing you may find bed-and-breakfasts, limited-service inns, guest ranches, and other unique hotel properties.

THE EVANS-CANTRELL HOUSE B & B. *300 College St, Fort Valley (31030).* Phone 478/825-0611; fax 478/822-9925. 4 rooms, 2 story. Children over 10 years only. Complimentary full breakfast. Check-in 3 pm, check-out 11 am. **$**
🅿

Pine Mountain (C-1)

See also Columbus, La Grange

Population 1,141
Elevation 860 ft
Area Code 706
Zip 31822
Web Site www.pinemountain.org

What to See and Do

Franklin D. Roosevelt State Park. *2970 Hwy 190, Pine Mountain (Harris County). 5 miles SE off jct Hwy 27, Hwy 190.* Phone 706/663-4858. One of the largest parks in the state system, it has many historic buildings and King's Gap Indian trail. Swimming pool, fishing; hiking, bridle and nature trails, picnicking, camping, cottages.

⭐ **The Gardens at Callaway.** *Hwy 27 and Hwy 18, Pine Mountain.* This distinctive public garden and resort, consisting of 14,000 acres of gardens, woodlands, lakes, recreation areas, and wildlife, was conceived by prominent textile industrialist Cason J. Callaway to be "the finest garden on earth since Adam was a boy." Originally the family's weekend vacation spot in the 1930s, Callaway and his wife, Virginia, expanded the area and opened it to the public in 1952. Today Callaway is home to more than 100 varieties of butterflies, 230 varieties of birds, 400 varieties of fruits and vegetables, and thousands of species of plantlife, including the rare plunifolia azalea, indigenous to the area. The complex offers swimming, boating, and other water recreation around 13 lakes, including 175-acre Mountain Creek Lake and the white sand beach of Robin Lake; 23 miles of roads and paths for hiking or jogging, 63 holes of golf (a 9-hole and three 18-hole courses), 10 lighted tennis courts, 2 indoor racquetball courts, 10 miles of bike trails, skeet and trapshooting ranges, fishing, fly-fishing, picnicking, country store, cottages, villas, and inn (see FULL-SERVICE RESORT), restaurants, and 5,000-foot paved and lighted runway and terminal. Also on the garden grounds are

Cecil B. Day Butterfly Center. *Hwy 27 and Hwy 18, Pine Mountain.* An 8,000-square-foot, glass-enclosed conservatory housing up to 1,000 free-flying butterflies, as well as ground pheasants, exotic plants, and waterfalls.

Ida Cason Callaway Memorial Chapel. *Hwy 27 and Hwy 18, Pine Mountain.* Phone 706/663-2281. A woodland chapel patterned after rural wayside chapels of the 16th and 17th centuries; organ concerts year-round. Pioneer log cabin is an authentic 18th-century structure in which life of early Georgia settlers is demonstrated. **$$$$**

John A. Sibley Horticultural Center. *Hwy 27 and Hwy 18, Pine Mountain.* Five acres displaying unique collections of exotic and native plants, seasonal flower beds, and lush green lawns; also sculpture garden and 22-foot waterfall.

Mr. Cason's Vegetable Garden. *Hwy 27 and Hwy 18, Pine Mountain.* Vegetable garden (7 1/2 acres) that produces hundreds of varieties of fruits, vegetables, and herbs; setting for the *Victory Garden South* television show.

★ **Little White House Historic Site.** *401 Little White House Rd, Warm Springs. Approximately 15 miles E on Hwy 18 and Hwy 194, then 1/2 mile S on Hwy 85 W.* Phone 706/655-5870. Cottage in which President Franklin D. Roosevelt died on Apr 12, 1945, is preserved as it was on the day he died. On display is original furniture, memorabilia, and the portrait on which Elizabeth Shoumatoff was working when the president was stricken with a massive cerebral hemorrhage. A film about Roosevelt's life at Warm Springs and in Georgia is shown at the F. D. Roosevelt Museum and Theater. Picnic area, snack bar. (Daily; closed Jan 1, Thanksgiving, Dec 25) **$$**

Full-Service Resort

★ ★ ★ **MOUNTAIN CREEK INN AT CALLAWAY GARDENS.** *Hwy 27, Pine Mountain (31822). Phone 706/663-2281; toll-free 800/225-5292; fax 706/663-5090. www.callawaygardens.com.* Offering plenty of outdoor recreational treats, including tennis and a championship golf course, this 14,000-acre property provides a perfect venue to relax, have fun, and play your cares away. A butterfly conservatory is also on-site. 349 rooms, 3 story. Check-in 4 pm, check-out noon. Restaurant, bar. Children's activity center. Fitness room. Beach. Indoor pool, outdoor pool, children's pool. Golf. Tennis. Airport transportation available. Business center. **$**

Restaurant

★ ★ **BULLOCH HOUSE.** *Hwy 41S, Warm Springs (31830). Phone 706/655-9068.* House built in 1892; original floors and fireplaces. Southern menu. Lunch, dinner. Closed holidays. Children's menu. Outdoor seating. **$**

Rome (B-1)

See also Calhoun, Cartersville

Founded 1834
Population 34,980
Elevation 605 ft
Area Code 706
Zip 30161
Information Greater Rome Convention and Visitors Bureau, 402 Civic Center Hill, PO Box 5823, 30162-5823; phone 706/295-5576; or toll-free 800/444-1834
Web Site www.romegeorgia.com

According to legend, five men, seven hills, three rivers, a spring, and a hat were the equation that led to the founding of Rome, Georgia. The seven hills suggested that "Rome" be one of the names drawn from the hat by the five founders, two of whom had discovered the site at the junction of three rivers.

Nobles' Foundry Lathe, one of the few that produced Confederate cannons, is on display on Civic Center Hill and is a reminder of Sherman's occupation. Rome fell despite the frantic ride of Georgia's Paul Revere, a mail carrier named John E. Wisdom, who rode 67 miles by horse from Gadsden, Alabama, in 11 hours to warn "the Yankees are coming."

What to See and Do

Berry College. *2277 Martha Berry Blvd, Mt. Berry (30149). On Hwy 27. Phone 706/291-1883.* (1902) (1,800 students) Campus, forest preserves, and 100 buildings comprise more than 26,000 acres, one of the largest campuses in the world. Old overshot waterwheel is one of the largest in the world. Close to campus is

Oak Hill and the Martha Berry Museum. *2277 Martha Berry Hwy, Mt. Berry (30149). Veterans Memorial Hwy and Hwy 27. Phone 706/291-1883.* Antebellum plantation house of Martha Berry, founder of Berry College. Manicured lawns, formal gardens, and nature trails. Museum is located on grounds of Oak Hill and serves as reception center for visitors. (Mon-Sat, Sun afternoons) **$$**

Capitoline Wolf Statue. *In front of City Hall.* Replica of the famous statue of Romulus and Remus in Rome, Italy. Presented by that city as a gift to Rome, Georgia in 1929.

Chieftains Museum. *501 Riverside Pkwy, Rome. N off Hwy 27. Phone 706/291-9494.* Eighteenth-century house of prominent Cherokee leader Major Ridge; artifacts with emphasis on Cherokee history. (Tues-Sat; closed holidays) **$$**

The Old Town Clock (1871) and Clocktower Museum. *601 Broad St, Rome. Phone 706/236-4416.* Surmounting 104-foot-high water tower of brick and superstructure of cypress wood, clock face is 9 feet in diameter. Bronze striking bell is 32 inches high, 40 inches in diameter at rim. Tower was built to hold the city's water supply and is located atop one of Rome's seven hills. Now, the water tank houses a museum with artifacts from Rome's history. (Apr-Nov, weekends; also by appointment)

Special Event

Heritage Holidays. River rides, parade, tours, wagon train, music. Third weekend in Oct.

Limited-Service Hotels

★ **DAYS INN.** *840 Turner McCall Blvd, Rome (30161). Phone 706/295-0400; toll-free 800/329-7466; www.daysinn.com.* 107 rooms, 5 story. Complimentary continental breakfast. Check-out 11 am. Outdoor pool. **$**
⛴

★ ★ **HOLIDAY INN.** *20 Hwy 411 E, Rome (30161). Phone 706/295-1100; toll-free 800/465-4329; fax 706/291-7128. www.holiday-inn.com.* 200 rooms, 2 story. Pets accepted; fee. Check-out noon. Restaurant, bar. Fitness room. Indoor, outdoor pool, whirlpool. Business center. **$**
🐾 🏋 ⛴ 🚶

Roswell (B-2)

See also Atlanta

Web Site cvb.roswell.ga.us

Limited-Service Hotel

★ ★ **HOLIDAY INN.** *1075 Holcomb Bridge Rd, Roswell (30076). Phone 770/992-9600; fax 770/993-6539.* 174 rooms, 7 story. Pets accepted; fee. Check-in 3 pm, check-out noon. High-speed Internet access, wireless Internet access. Restaurant, bar. Fitness room. Outdoor pool. **$**
🅿 🐾 🏋 ⛴

Restaurants

★ ★ ★ **DICK & HARRY'S.** *1570 Holcomb Bridge Rd, Roswell (30076). Phone 770/641-8757; fax 770/641-8884. www.dickandharrys.com.* American menu. Lunch, dinner. Closed Sun; holidays. Bar. Children's menu. Casual attire. Valet parking. Outdoor seating. **$$**

★ ★ **LICKSKILLET FARM.** *1380 Old Roswell Rd, Roswell (30077). Phone 770/475-6484; fax 770/343-9982. www.lickskilletfarm.com.* This quaint restaurant in an old country house is located in a northern suburb of Atlanta. The portions are generous and the food is rich. American menu. Lunch, dinner, brunch. Closed Mon; Dec 24-25. Bar. Outdoor seating. **$$$**

★ **SUBURB-A-NIGHT PIZZA.** *1090 Alpharetta St, Roswell (30075). Phone 770/594-8765.* Pizza. Dinner, late-night. Closed Mon-Tues; holidays. Bar. **$$**

★ ★ ★ **VAN GOGH'S.** *70 W Crossville Rd, Roswell (30075). Phone 770/993-1156; fax 770/643-0854.* This out-of-the-way restaurant offers a surprisingly lovely dining experience. The food is eclectic American, while the setting is all old-Southern charm. The combination makes for a fun time. American menu. Lunch, dinner. Closed holidays. Bar. Children's menu. Valet parking. **$$$**

Savannah (C-5)

See also Fort McAllister Historic Park, Fort Pulaski National Monument, Tybee Island

Founded 1733
Population 131,510
Elevation 42 ft
Area Code 912
Information Savannah Area Convention and Visitors Bureau, 101 E Bay St, 31401, 31402; phone 912/944-0455 or toll-free 877/728-2662
Web Site www.savcvb.com

Savannah has a wealth of history and architecture that few American cities can match. Even fewer have managed to preserve the same air of colonial grace and charm. The city's many rich, green parks are blooming legacies of the brilliance of its founder, General James E. Oglethorpe, who landed at Yamacraw Bluff with 120 settlers on February 12, 1733. His plan for the colony was to make the "inner city" spacious, beautiful, and all that a city should be. Bull Street, named for Colonel William Bull, one of Oglethorpe's aides, stretches south from the high bluffs overlooking the Savannah River and is punctuated by five handsome squares and Forsyth Park.

Savannah then changed its outer garb of wood palisades to a gray "Savannah brick" fort surmounting the bluff. By Revolutionary times wharves served ocean trade, and sailors caroused in seamen's inns. The town had its liberty pole and a patriots' battalion when news of Lexington came. The Declaration of Independence led to Savannah's designation as capital of the new state. By December, however, the British had retaken the city with 2,000 troops, and the royal governor, who had fled earlier, returned. An attempt by American troops to recapture Savannah failed, and more than 1,000 Americans and 700 Frenchmen were killed. General "Mad Anthony" Wayne's forces finally drove the British from Savannah in 1782.

In 1795, tobacco culture and Eli Whitney's cotton gin brought prosperity back to Savannah. Meanwhile, the city's growth followed the orderly pattern laid out by Colonel Bull. By the first decade of the new century, Classical Revival or Regency architecture had superseded Georgian Colonial. Savannah, with new forts protecting the estuary and strengthening Fort Wayne on the bluff, fared better during the War of 1812.

Afterward, architect William Jay and master builder Isaiah Davenport added splendid mansions that fronted palm-lined squares. The steamboat *Enterprise* plied upriver from here to Augusta in 1816; three years later, on May 22, 1819, the SS *Savannah* set sail from Savannah for Liverpool to be the first steamer to cross the Atlantic. Savannah had become the leading market and shipping point for cotton, naval stores, and tobacco, and prosperity increased until the Civil War.

Throughout the war, Savannah tried to hold its own. Fort Pulaski (see), which the Confederates took control of even before Secession, was retaken by a Union artillery assault on April 11, 1862, and became a Union military prison. Despite repeated Union naval battering, the Confederates held Fort McAllister (see) until Sherman's "March to the Sea" on December 13, 1864. Although Confederate troops resisted for three days after Sherman demanded Savannah's surrender, Union forces eventually occupied the city, and Confederates were forced to escape to Hutchison Island.

Reconstruction was painful, but 20 years later cotton was king again. Surrounding pine forests produced lumber and resins; the Cotton and Naval Stores Exchange was launched in 1882 while financiers and brokers strode the streets with confidence. By the 20th century, Savannah turned to manufacturing. With more than 200 industries by World War II, the city's prosperity has been measured by the activity of its port, which included shipbuilding booms during both world wars. Extensive developments by the Georgia Port Authority in the past decade have contributed to the city's commercial, industrial, and shipping growth.

Today more than 1,400 historically and architecturally significant buildings have been restored in Savannah's historic district, making it one of the largest urban historic landmark districts in the country. Another area, the Victorian district south of the historic district, offers some of the best examples of post-Civil War Victorian architecture in the country. The city that launched the Girl Scouts of America also plays host to modern Girl Scouts who visit the shrine of founder Juliette Gordon Low.

Additional Visitor Information

Visitor information is also available from the Savannah Area Convention and Visitors Bureau, PO Box 1628, 31402-1628; phone 912/644-6401 or toll-free 877-728-2662.

The Savannah Visitors Center, 301 Martin Luther King Jr. Blvd, is open daily, providing information on area attractions (including a free visitors guide with translations in French, German, Spanish, and Japanese). All guided bus tours depart from the center on a regular basis.

What to See and Do

Andrew Low House. *329 Abercorn St, Savannah. Phone 912/233-6854.* (Circa 1848) Built for Andrew Low, this was later the residence of Juliette Gordon Low, founder of Girl Scouts of America. Period furnishings. (Mon-Wed, Fri-Sun; closed holidays; also mid-late Dec) **$$**

Christ Episcopal Church. *18 Abercorn St, Savannah. Johnson Sq between E St. Julian and E Congress sts. Phone 912/232-4131.* (1838) The mother church of Georgia, the congregation dates from 1733. Among early rectors were John Wesley and George Whitfield. The present church is the third building erected on this site. (Tues and Fri, limited hours)

City Hall. *Bull and Bay sts, Savannah.* (1905) A gold dome tops the four-story neoclassic facade of this building, which replaced the original 1799 structure. A tablet outside commemorates sailing of the SS *Savannah;* a model is displayed in the Council Chamber. Another tablet is dedicated to the *John Randolph,* the first iron-sided vessel launched in American waters (1834). (Mon-Fri) **FREE**

Colonial Park Cemetery. *E Oglethorpe Ave and Abercorn St, Savannah.* (1753) This was the colony's first and only burial ground for many years; Button Gwinnett, a signer of the Declaration of Independence, is buried in cemetery, as are other distinguished Georgians. Closed since 1853, it has been a city park since 1896.

Congregation Mickve Israel. *20 E Gordon St, Savannah. E side of Monterey Sq. Phone 912/233-1547.* Only Gothic-style synagogue in United States contains Torah scroll brought to America by congregation founders, Portuguese and German Jews who came to Savannah in 1733. Synagogue museum has portraits, religious objects, documents, letters from Presidents Washington, Jefferson, Madison. Guided tours (Mon-Fri). **FREE**

Davenport House. *324 E State St, Savannah. Phone 912/236-8097.* (1815-1820) Built by master builder Isaiah Davenport, this is one of the finest examples of Federal architecture in Savannah. Saved from demoli-

tion in 1955 by the Historic Savannah Foundation, it is now restored and furnished with period antiques. Gardens. (Daily; closed holidays) **$$$**

Factors Walk. *W and E Bay sts, Savannah. Between Bull and E Broad sts.* Named by cotton factors of the 19th century, this row of business houses "on the Bay" is accessible by a network of iron bridgeways over cobblestone ramps.

Georgia Historical Society. *501 Whitaker St, Savannah (31410). Phone 912/651-2128.* Research library and archives for Savannah and Georgia history and genealogy. (Tues-Sat) **FREE**

Gray Line bus tours. *215 W Boundary St, Savannah. Phone 912/234-8687. www.grayline.com.* Contact 1115 Louisville Rd, 31415.

Green-Meldrim House. *14 W Macon St, Savannah (31410). Phone 912/233-3845.* Antebellum house used by General Sherman during occupation of Savannah (1864-1865) is now Parish House of St. John's Church. Tours. (Tues and Thurs-Sat; closed holidays, occasionally for parish activities, also the last two weeks before Easter) **$$**

Historic Savannah Waterfront Area. *John P. Rousakis Riverfront Plz, Savannah.* Restoration of the riverfront bluff to preserve and stabilize the historic waterfront, including a nine-block brick concourse of parks, studios, museums, shops, restaurants, and pubs.

Juliette Gordon Low Birthplace. *10 E Ogelthorpe Ave Savannah. Phone 912/233-4501.* (1818-1821) Resto Regency town house was birthplace, in 1860, of th founder of Girl Scouts of the USA. Many origina Gordon family pieces. Garden restored to Victo period. (Mon-Tues, Thurs-Sun; closed holiday

Laurel Grove Cemetery (South). *37th and O Savannah.* Possibly the oldest black cemete in use; both antebellum slave and free bla Buried here is Andrew Bryan (1716-181 Baptist preacher.

Owens-Thomas House. *124 Abercorn Phone 912/233-9743.* (1816-1819) / furnished Regency-style house de Jay. Lafayette was an overnight g garden is designed and planted closed holidays, also Jan) **$$**

Savannah History Museum. *Jr. Blvd, Savannah. Adjacer Center. Phone 912/238-17*

road shed was renovated to house historical orientation center. Mural in lobby chronicles major events in Savannah's 250-year history. (Daily; closed Jan 1, Thanksgiving, Dec 25). **$$** Here are

Auxiliary Theater. *112 Bryan Ctr, Savannah (90848).* Special audiovisual presentations.

Exhibit Hall. Artifacts, antiques, and memorabilia from Savannah's past; pre-colonial Native American artifacts, Revolutionary and Civil war uniforms and weapons; 1890 *Baldwin* locomotive; replica of the SS *Savannah,* first steamboat to cross the Atlantic.

Main Theater. Orientation film provides an overview of the history of Savannah from 1733 to present as seen through the eyes of General James E. Oglethorpe.

Savannah National Wildlife Refuge. *N via Hwy 17 or Hwy 17 A, across the Savannah River in South Carolina.*

Ships of the Sea Maritime Museum. *41 Martin Luther King Jr. Blvd, Savannah. Phone 912/232-1511.* Ship models, figureheads; scrimshaw, sea artifacts; ship's carpenter shop. (Tues-Sun; closed holidays) **$$**

Telfair Museum of Art. *121 Barnard St, Savannah. Phone 912/232-1177.* Regency mansion (1818) is one of three surviving buildings in Savannah by William Jay, English architect. Period rooms with family furnishings, silverware, porcelains; Octagon Room. Telfair is the oldest public art museum in the Southeast, with a permanent collection of 18th-, 19th-, and 20th-century American and European paintings and sculpture; prints, silver, decorative arts. Concerts, lectures; tours. (Daily; closed holidays) **$$**

Touring Savannah. *250 Martin Luther King Jr. Blvd, Savannah. Old Savannah Tours. Phone 912/234-8128.* Various guided bus tours of historic landmark district and other areas. Tours depart from the visitor center (ADDITIONAL VISITOR INFORMATION) and downtown hotels and inns. (Daily; closed St. Patrick's, Thanksgiving, Dec 25)

's Garden Site. *E Broad St, Savannah.* Original 10-acre experimental garden modeled in 1733 on Chelsea Gardens in London by colonists to produce silk, wine, and drugs. Peach ed in garden were responsible for Georgia's try. Fort Wayne occupied the site in 1762. ry importance until the Revolution, the d for General "Mad Anthony" Wayne. y the British (1779), the Ameri-

cans rebuilt it during the War of 1812. The massive buttressed brick walls later served as the foundation for a municipal gas company building. The Pirates' House (1734), former inn for visiting seamen, has been restored and is a restaurant; Robert Louis Stevenson referred to the inn in *Treasure Island.*

US Customs House. *Bull and E Bay sts, Savannah.* (1850) Erected on the site of the colony's first public building. The granite columns' carved capitals were modeled from tobacco leaves. Tablet on Bull St marks the site where John Wesley preached his first Savannah sermon; tablet on Bay St marks the site of Oglethorpe's headquarters.

Wormsloe State Historic Site. *7601 Skidaway Rd, Savannah (31406). Phone 912/353-3023.* Remains of early fortified 18th-century tabby house. (Tabby is a kind of cement made from lime, oyster shells, sand, and water.) Visitor center exhibits outline history of site and of Noble Jones family, owners for more than 200 years. (Tues-Sun) **$**

Special Events

Georgia Heritage Festival. Walking tours, open house at historic sites, crafts show, waterfront festival, parade, concerts, Georgia Day. Late Jan-mid-Feb.

Great Atlantic Seafood Festival. *404 E Bay St, Savannah. Waterfront. Phone 912/234-0295.* Restaurants sell samples; entertainment, arts and crafts. Contact Savannah Waterfront Association. First weekend in May.

N. O. G. S. Tour of Hidden Gardens of Savannah. Includes eight private walled gardens in historic Savannah, tea at Telfair Museum of Art. Late Apr.

Night in Old Savannah. *Savannah Visitors Center, Savannah. Phone 912/651-3673.* Foods of more than 25 countries; entertainment, including jazz, country, and rhythm and blues. Mid-Apr.

Savannah Scottish Games and Highland Gathering. *Old Fort Jackson, Savannah. 2 miles E via President St extension.* The clans gather for a weekend of Highland games, piping, drumming, dancing, and the traditional "Kirkin' o' th' Tartans." Second Sat in May.

Savannah Tour of Homes and Gardens. *18 Abercorn St, Savannah. Phone 912/234-8054.* Sponsored by Christ Episcopal Church with Historic Savannah Foundation. Day and candlelight tours of more than 30 private houses and gardens. Contact 18 Abercorn St, 31401. Mar.

St. Patrick's Day Parade. Rivals New York City's in size. Mar.

Limited-Service Hotels

★ ★ **COURTYARD BY MARRIOTT.** *6703 Abercorn St, Savannah (31405). Phone 912/354-7878; toll-free 800/321-2211; fax 912/354-1432. www.courtyard.com.* 144 rooms, 3 story. Check-in 3 pm, check-out noon. Restaurant, bar. Fitness room. Outdoor pool, whirlpool. **$**

★ ★ **DAYS INN.** *201 W Bay St, Savannah (31401). Phone 912/236-4440; toll-free 877/542-7666; fax 912/232-2725. www.daysinn.com.* 257 rooms, 7 story. Check-in 3 pm, check-out 11 am. Restaurant. Outdoor pool. **$**

★ **HAMPTON INN.** *201 Stephenson Ave, Savannah (31405). Phone 912/355-4100; fax 912/356-5385. www.hamptoninn.com.* 128 rooms, 2 story. Complimentary continental breakfast. Check-in 3 pm, check-out noon. Outdoor pool. **$**

★ ★ **HOLIDAY INN.** *601 E Bay St, Savannah (31401). Phone 912/238-1200; fax 912/236-2184. www.savannahhotel.com.* Located on scenic Washington Square, in the heart of the Historic District, this elegant hotel welcomes guests with a genuine hospitality and serene ambience that takes guests back to a long-forgotten era. The guest rooms have been renovated with guest comfort in mind. Offering luxurious accommodations charmingly appointed with touches of Savannah's rich history, along with a staff trained to ensure guests every comfort, this hotel makes for a truly delightful stay. 145 rooms, 3 story. Check-in 3 pm, check-out noon. Restaurant, bar. Fitness room. Outdoor pool, whirlpool. **$$$**

Full-Service Hotels

★ ★ ★ **HILTON SAVANNAH DE SOTO.** *15 E Liberty St, Savannah (31401). Phone 912/232-9000; toll-free 800/774-1500; fax 912/232-6018. www.hilton.com.* 246 rooms, 10 story. Check-in 4 pm, check-out noon. Restaurant, bar. Fitness room. Outdoor pool. Airport transportation available. Business center. **$$**

★ ★ ★ **HYATT REGENCY SAVANNAH.** *2 W Bay St, Savannah (31401). Phone 912/238-1234; fax 912/944-3678. www.hyatt.com.* Located in the heart of the historic district and perched along the exquisitely scenic waterfront of Savannah River, this hotel successfully combines superb accommodations, first-class amenities, and an attentive staff to ensure that even the most strenuous guests leave satisfied after experiencing the friendly Southern hospitality. 347 rooms, 7 story. Check-in 2 pm, check-out noon. Restaurant, bar. Fitness room. Indoor pool. Business center. **$**

★ ★ ★ **MARRIOTT SAVANNAH RIVERFRONT.** *100 General McIntosh Blvd, Savannah (31401). Phone 912/233-7722; fax 912/233-3765. www.marriott.com.* Adjacent to the world-renowned River Street and located on the historic Riverfront, this hotel makes for a truly delightful stay. Inside, guests are welcomed with attentive service and handsomely appointed accommodations. A stroll along the hotel's riverwalk will lead guests to all the delights River Street has to offer with its friendly taverns, quaint shops and succulent restaurants. 383 rooms, 8 story. Check-in 4 pm, check-out 11 am. Restaurant, bar. Fitness room. Indoor pool, outdoor pool, whirlpool. **$$**

Full-Service Resort

★ ★ ★ **THE WESTIN SAVANNAH HARBOR RESORT AND SPA.** *1 Resort Dr, Savannah (31421). Phone 912/201-2000; fax 912/201-2001. www.westin.com.* 403 rooms, 16 story. Check-in 3 pm, check-out noon. Restaurant, bar. Children's activity center. Fitness room, spa. Outdoor pool, children's pool, whirlpool. Golf. Tennis. Airport transportation available. Business center. **$$**

Full-Service Inns

★ ★ ★ **17 HUNDRED 90 INN & RESTAURANT.** *307 E President St, Savannah (31401). Phone 912/236-7122; toll-free 800/487-1790; fax 912/236-7123. www.17hundred90.com.* 14 rooms. Complimentary continental breakfast. Check-in 2 pm, check-out noon. Restaurant. **$$**

★ ★ ★ **EAST BAY INN.** *225 E Bay St, Savannah (31401). Phone 912/238-1225; toll-free 800/500-1225;*

fax 912/232-2709. www.eastbayinn.com. Just steps away from the historic waterfront, this romantic inn has many beautiful rooms filled with period furnishings and antiques. Enjoy a cheese and wine reception each evening. 28 rooms, 3 story. Pets accepted; fee. Complimentary continental breakfast. Check-in 3 pm, check-out 11 am. Restaurant. **$$**

★ ★ ★ **THE PRESIDENT'S QUARTERS INN.** *225 E President St, Savannah (31401). Phone 912/233-1600; toll-free 800/233-1776; fax 912/238-0849. www.presidentsquarters.com.* Once a place where diplomats and generals layed their heads, the President's Quarters, now opens its doors to guests. Feel like royalty relaxing in the elegantly appointed parlors, or strolling through their renowned gardens. 19 rooms, 4 story. Complimentary full breakfast. Check-in 2 pm, check-out 11 am. Restaurant. **$$**

★ ★ ★ **RIVER STREET INN.** *115 E River St, Savannah (31401). Phone 912/234-6400; fax 912/234-1478.* 86 rooms, 5 story. Check-in 4 pm, check-out noon. Restaurant, bar. **$$**

Specialty Lodgings

The following lodging establishments are approved by Mobil Travel Guide, but due to their unique and individualized nature have not been given a traditional Mobil Star rating. Included in this listing you may find bed-and-breakfasts, limited-service inns, guest ranches, and other unique hotel properties.

BALLASTONE INN & TOWNHOUSE. *14 E Oglethorpe Ave, Savannah (31401). Phone 912/236-1484; toll-free 800/822-4553; fax 912/236-4626. www.ballastone.com.* Opening as Savannah's first bed-and-breakfast, this inn sets the standard for all bed-and-breakfasts to follow. Set in this 160-year-old mansion, each spacious suite is ensured to make guests feel like they are receiving the royal treatment. 17 rooms, 4 story. Children over 16 years only. Complimentary full breakfast. Check-in 3 pm, check-out 11 am. **$$**

BED & BREAKFAST INN. *117 W Gordon St, Savannah (31401). Phone 912/238-0518; toll-free 888/238-0518; fax 912/233-2537. savannahbnb.com.* Restored 1853 Federal townhouse in the Historic District. 15 rooms, 4 story. Complimentary full breakfast. Check-in 4 pm, check-out 11 am. **$**

ELIZA THOMPSON HOUSE. *5 W Jones St, Savannah (31401). Phone 912/236-3620; toll-free 800/348-9378; fax 912/238-1920. www.elizathompsonhouse .com.* Elegantly restored and recently refurbished, each room offers quiet and comfortable surroundings. The gracious staff on hand is always ready to show off their prized inn and their beautiful city. 25 rooms, 3 story. Complimentary full breakfast. Check-in 3 pm, check-out 11 am. **$$**

FOLEY HOUSE INN. *14 W Hull St, Savannah (31401). Phone 912/232-6622; toll-free 800/647-3708; fax 912/231-1218. www.foleyinn.com.* To say the staff makes guests feel at home here is an understatement. Located in the heart of historic Savannah, this is a great choice for a romantic getaway. 18 rooms, 4 story. Complimentary full breakfast. Check-in 3 pm, check-out 11 am. **$$**

THE GASTONIAN. *220 E Gaston St, Savannah (31401). Phone 912/232-2869; toll-free 800/322-6603; fax 912/232-0710. www.gastonian.com.* 17 rooms, 4 story. Children over 12 years only. Complimentary full breakfast. Check-in 3 pm, check-out noon. Whirlpool. **$$$**

THE KEHOE HOUSE. *123 Habersham St, Savannah (31401). Phone 912/232-1020; toll-free 800/820-1020; fax 912/231-0208. www.kehoehouse.com.* Savor the many charms of Savannah at The Kehoe House. This inviting and gracious bed-and-breakfast enjoys a superior location in the heart of the Historic District overlooking Columbia Square. History buffs will relish the many treasures within walking distance from this stunning mansion listed on the National Register of Historic Places. Guests are treated to a unique experience here, where the 13 rooms are individually designed and elegantly appointed. This inn manages to celebrate its history while welcoming the present, with crystal chandeliers, antiques, and period furnishings residing alongside high- speed Internet access and multi-line telephones. The breakfasts here are extraordinary and made to order, while the afternoons invite guests to linger with a cup of tea and a plate of exceptional hors d'oeuvres. 14 rooms, 5 story. Complimentary full breakfast. Check-in 3 pm, check-out 11 am. **$$$$**

MAGNOLIA PLACE INN. *503 Whitaker St, Savannah (31401). Phone 912/236-7674; toll-free 800/238-7674; fax 912/236-1145. www.magnoliaplace inn.com.* As guests enjoy afternoon tea in the parlor at Magnolia Place, they can close their eyes and almost feel the past all around them. Classic and romantic are just two words of many used to sum up this beautiful inn. 16 rooms, 3 story. Children over 11 years only. Complimentary full breakfast. Check-in 2:30 pm, check-out 11 am. **$$**

OLDE HARBOUR INN. *508 E Factors Walk, Savannah (31401). Phone 912/234-4100; toll-free 800/553-6533; fax 912/233-5979. www.oldeharbourinn.com.* Built in 1892, originally housed the offices and warehouse of an oil company. 24 rooms, 3 story. Pets accepted; fee. Complimentary continental breakfast. Check-in 3 pm, check-out 11 am. **$$**

Restaurants

★ ★ **17 HUNDRED 90 INN & RESTAURANT.** *307 E President St, Savannah (31401). Phone 912/236-7122.* International/Fusion menu. Lunch, dinner. Bar. Casual attire. **$$$**

★ ★ ★ **45 SOUTH.** *20 E Broad St, Savannah (31401). Phone 912/233-1881; fax 912/233-5757. www.thepirateshouse.com.* American food and fine service distinguish this local favorite. Specialties include peppered rack of lamb, seared tuna, and carpaccio of beef with fried capers and shaved parmesan. American menu. Dinner. Closed Sun; holidays. Bar. Jacket required. Valet parking. **$$$**

★ ★ **BELFORD'S.** *315 W St. Julian St, Savannah (31401). Phone 912/233-2626; fax 912/233-2621.* American menu. Breakfast, lunch, dinner. Closed Thanksgiving, Dec 24-25. Bar. Children's menu. Casual attire. Reservations recommended. Outdoor seating. **$$**

★ ★ **BISTRO SAVANNAH.** *309 W Congress St, Savannah (31401). Phone 912/233-6266; fax 912/232-7957.* Seafood menu. Dinner. Closed Thanksgiving, Dec 25. Bar. Casual attire. **$$$**

★ ★ **CHART HOUSE.** *202 W Bay St, Savannah (31401). Phone 912/234-6686; fax 912/232-4872.* Covered balcony over Savannah River. Seafood, steak menu. Dinner. Bar. Children's menu. Casual attire. Outdoor seating. **$$**

★ ★ **DOWNTOWN CAFE AT MAIN.** *1 W Broughton St, Savannah (31401). Phone 912/233-8666.* American menu. Lunch, dinner. Bar. Casual attire. Reservations recommended. **$$**

★ ★ ★ **ELIZABETH ON 37TH.** *105 E 37th St, Savannah (31401). Phone 912/236-5547; fax 912/232-1095. www.elizabethon37th.com.* Opened in 1981 by chef Elizabeth Terry and her husband, Michael, this charming restaurant is a birthplace of New Southern cuisine. The interior of the 1900 Greek Revival-style mansion feels like home with brightly painted walls, antique chairs, and warm service. The fresh tastes and authenticity of the cuisine (Terry extensively researched 18th- and 19th-century Savannah cooking) draws admiration from across the country. Southern/Soul menu. Dinner. Closed holidays; the last two weeks of Aug. Casual attire. **$$$**

★ ★ **GARIBALDI'S CAFE.** *315 W Congress St, Savannah (31401). Phone 912/232-7118; fax 912/232-7957.* Former 1871 Germania firehouse in historic district. Seafood menu. Dinner. Closed Dec 25. Bar. Casual attire. **$$$**

★ **JOHNNY HARRIS.** *1651 E Victory Dr, Savannah (31404). Phone 912/354-7810; toll-free 888/547-2823; fax 912/354-6567. www.johnnyharris.com.* This restaurant is Savannah's oldest continuously operating restaurant. American menu. Lunch, dinner. Closed Sun; Jan 1, Dec 25. Bar. Children's menu. Casual attire. **$$**

★ **MOON RIVER BREWING CO.** *21 W Bay St, Savannah (31401). Phone 912/447-0943.* American menu. Lunch, dinner. Bar. Children's menu. Casual attire. **$$**

★ ★ **MRS. WILKES' DINING ROOM.** *107 W Jones St, Savannah (31401). Phone 912/232-5997.* American menu. Lunch. Closed Sat-Sun; holidays. Casual attire. **$**

★ ★ **OLDE PINK HOUSE.** *23 Abercorn St, Savannah (31412). Phone 912/232-4286; fax 912/231-1934.* This is the only restaurant in town located in a historic mansion (dating from the 18th century). The seven candlelit dining rooms are furnished with period pieces and artwork. Southern menu. Dinner. Bar. Children's menu. Casual attire. **$$**

★ ★ **RIVER HOUSE.** *125 W River St, Savannah (31401). Phone 912/234-1900; fax 912/234-7007. www.riverhouseseafood.com.* Seafood menu. Lunch, dinner. Closed Thanksgiving, Dec 25. Bar. Children's menu. Casual attire. **$$**

★ **WILLIAM'S SEAFOOD.** *8010 Tybee Rd, Tybee (31410). Phone 912/897-2219; fax 912/897-1151.* Seafood menu. Lunch, dinner. Closed Dec 25. Bar. Children's menu. Casual attire. Outdoor seating. **$$**

Sea Island (E-5)

See also Brunswick, Darien, Fort Frederica National Monument, Golden Isles, Jekyll Island, St. Simons Island

Population 750
Elevation 11 ft
Area Code 912
Zip 31561
Web Site www.seaisland.com

Full-Service Hotel

★ ★ ★ ★ ★ **THE LODGE AT SEA ISLAND GOLF CLUB.** *100 1st St, St. Simons Island (31561). Phone 912/638-3611; toll-free 866/465-3536; fax 912/638-5159. www.seaisland.com.* Generations of privileged travelers have made Sea Island their vacation destination. Marrying the romance of the Old South with the grand tradition of old-world Europe, this scenic island allows guests to time-travel to a bygone era of refinement and splendor, where round-the-clock personal butlers attend to every need and the strains of a bagpipe signal the end of the day. The Lodge's guest rooms are a delightful interpretation of a genteel manor house, with teak furnishings, wood floors graced by priceless carpets, and ample amenities. Created in the spirit of European sporting estates, this resort is a playground for the elite with plentiful country pursuits. The 70-year-old Shooting School is a source of great pride; tennis and equestrian facilities are first-rate; and avid golfers are thrilled by the three championship golf courses just steps from the Atlantic Ocean. The accommodations have private balconies if relaxing with a good book is more your style. From sensational spa treatments to exquisite meals, this resort is dedicated to excellence. 42 rooms, 3 story. Complimentary continental breakfast. Check-in 4 pm, check-out noon. High-speed Internet access. Restaurant, bar. Children's activity center. Fitness room, spa. Beach. Outdoor pool, whirlpool. Golf, 34 holes. Tennis. Business center. **$$$$**
🚇 🏃 🛳 🏌 🎿 🏊

Full-Service Resort

★ ★ ★ **THE CLOISTER.** *100 Hudson Pl, Sea Island (31561). Phone 912/638-3611; toll-free 800/732-4752; fax 912/634-3964. www.cloister.com.* The Cloister is the jewel in the crown of Sea Island's resorts. This elegant retreat is an American classic, catering to vacationing couples and families for nearly 75 years. Exclusive, though unpretentious, The Cloister feels like a private club. The accommodations are the last word in coastal elegance, where traditional furnishings are enlivened with pastel colors and lively prints. This resort is the embodiment of the sporting life, offering everything from boating, tennis, and golf to shooting, equestrian activities, and a spa. For those who need a little R and R, the resort's 5-mile stretch of sandy beach is the answer to the overscheduled day. After a long day of sunning or sporting, the four restaurants entice with sophisticated Southern cuisine, seafood, and beef. 212 rooms, 3 story. Complimentary continental breakfast. Check-in 3 pm, check-out noon. Restaurant, bar. Children's activity center. Fitness room, spa. Beach. Outdoor pool, whirlpool. Golf, 54 holes. Tennis. Airport transportation available. Business center. **$$$$**
🏃 🛳 🏌 🎿 🏊

Smyrna (B-2)

Population 40,999
Web Site www.ci.smyrna.ga.us

Restaurant

★ **OLD SOUTH BAR-B-Q.** *601 Burbank Cir, Smyrna (30080). Phone 770/435-4215.* Barbecue, Southern menu. Lunch, dinner. Closed Mon; holidays. Children's menu. **$**

St. Simons Island (E-5)

See also Brunswick, Darien, Golden Isles, Jekyll Island, Sea Island

Population 13,381
Elevation 0-30 ft
Area Code 912
Zip 31522
Information St. Simons Visitors Center, 530 B Beachview Dr, Neptune Park; phone toll-free 800/933-2627
Web Site www.gacoast.com

One of Georgia's Golden Isles (see), St. Simons Island has been under five flags: Spain, France, Britain, US, and Confederate States of America. Fragments of each culture remain.

John and Charles Wesley preached under St. Simons' oaks before a church was built at Frederica, and later Aaron Burr spent a month at Hampton's Point after killing Alexander Hamilton in a duel. St. Simons' plantations flourished and were noted for the luxurious and sporting life of planters from about 1800 to the Civil War. Cotton and slavery collapsed after Sherman's forces razed the estates. Former slave quarters remained; inhabitants turned to fishing and garden crops for subsistence as St. Simons was nearly forgotten until the 20th century.

What to See and Do

Coastal Alliance for the Arts. *319 Mallory St, St. Simons Island. Phone 912/638-8770.* Exhibitions of works by regional artists, traveling exhibits, lectures. (Mon-Sat; closed holidays) **FREE**

Gascoigne Bluff. *Where the bridge crosses the Frederica River, SW side of island.* This is a low-wooded, shell-covered bank named for Captain James Gascoigne, commander of HMS *Hawk,* which convoyed the two ships bringing settlers (1736). Great live oaks cut here were used to build first US Navy vessels, including the *Constitution* ("Old Ironsides") (1794). St. Simons Marina is open to the public.

St. Simons Island Lighthouse Museum. *101 12th St, St. Simons Island. Phone 912/638-4666.* Housed in restored 1872 lightkeeper's house; exhibits on history of St. Simons lighthouse and Golden Isles. (Daily; closed holidays) **$$** Includes

St. Simons Lighthouse. *S end of island.* The original lighthouse (1810), which was 75 feet high, was destroyed by Confederate troops in 1861 to prevent it from guiding Union invaders onto the island. The present lighthouse, 104 feet high, has been in continuous operation, except during wartime, since 1872. Visitors may climb to the top.

Special Events

Golden Isles Art Festival. *Neptune Park, 550 Beachview Dr, St. Simons Island (31522).* Juried arts and crafts exhibits, demonstrations, entertainment, food. Mid-Oct.

Homes and Gardens Tour. *Phone 912/638-3166.* Tour of houses and gardens on St. Simons Island and Sea Island. Varies each year. Mid-Mar.

Sunshine Festival. *Neptune Park, 550 Beachview Dr, St. Simons Island (31522).* Juried arts and crafts exhibits; food; fireworks on July 4. Weekend closest to July 4.

Limited-Service Hotel

★ **BEST WESTERN ISLAND INN.** *301 Main St, St. Simons Island (31522). Phone 912/638-7805; toll-free 800/673-6323; fax 912/634-4720. www.bestwestern.com.* 74 rooms, 2 story. Complimentary continental breakfast. Check-out 11 am. Outdoor pool, whirlpool. **$**
🏊

Full-Service Resorts

★ ★ ★ **KING AND PRINCE RESORT.** *201 Arnold Rd, St. Simons Island (31522). Phone 912/638-3631; toll-free 800/342-0212; fax 912/638-7699. www.kingandprince.com.* This wonderful resort is directly on the beach, and guests will find no shortage of recreation, relaxation, or enjoyment. 184 rooms, 4 story. Check-out 11 am. Restaurant, bar. Fitness room. One indoor pool, four outdoor pools, whirlpool. Golf. Tennis. Airport transportation available. **$**
🏃 🏊 ⛳ 🎾

★ ★ ★ **SEA PALMS GOLF & TENNIS RESORT.** *5445 Frederica Rd, St. Simons Island (31522). Phone 912/638-3351; toll-free 800/841-6268; fax 912/634-8031. www.seapalms.com.* Ideal for both conference retreats or personal playtimes, Sea Palms offers spacious rooms to recover from a hard day at play at several of the water sports. 155 rooms, 3 story. Check-in 4 pm, check-out 11 am. Restaurant, bar. Fitness room. Beach. Three outdoor pools. Golf. Tennis. **$**
🏃 🏊 ⛳ 🎾

Full-Service Inn

★ ★ ★ **THE LODGE ON LITTLE ST. SIMONS ISLAND.** *8th and Bruce sts, St. Simons Island (31582). Phone 912/638-7472; fax 912/634-1811. www. littlestsimonsisland.com.* 13 rooms, 2 story. Check-in 4:30 pm, check-out 10:30 am. Restaurant. Fitness room. **$$$$**
🐾 🏃 🏊

Specialty Lodging

The following lodging establishment is approved by Mobil Travel Guide, but due to its unique and individualized nature has not been given a traditional Mobil Star rating. Included in this listing you may find bed-and-breakfasts, limited-service inns, guest ranches, and other unique hotel properties.

ST. SIMONS INN BY THE LIGHTHOUSE. *609 Beachview Dr, St. Simons Island (31522). Phone 912/ 638-1101; fax 912/638-0943. www.stsimonsinn.com.* 34 rooms, 3 story. Complimentary continental breakfast. Check-in 3 pm, check-out 11 am. Outdoor pool. **$** 🛆

Restaurants

★ **BENNIE'S RED BARN.** *5514 Frederica Rd, St. Simons Island (31522). Phone 912/638-2844; fax 912/ 634-2440.* American menu. Dinner. Closed holidays. Bar. Children's menu. **$$** 🖻

★ **BROGEN'S.** *200 Pier Alley, St. Simons Island (31522). Phone 912/638-1660; fax 912/638-2047. www.brogens.com.* American menu. Lunch, dinner. Closed Sun, Oct-Apr; Jan 1, Easter, Dec 25. Bar. Outdoor seating. **$$** 🖻

★ ★ **CHELSEA.** *1226 Ocean Blvd, St. Simons Island (31522). Phone 912/638-2047.* American menu. Dinner. Bar. Children's menu. **$$**

★ ★ **J. MAC'S.** *407 Mallery St, St. Simons Island (31522). Phone 912/634-0403; fax 912/638-0814.* Seafood menu. Dinner. Closed Sun; holidays. Bar. **$**

★ **MIYABI SEAFOOD & STEAK.** *202 Retreat Village Shopping Center, St. Simons Island (31522). Phone 912/638-0885; fax 912/638-2797.* Japanese menu. Dinner. Closed Thanksgiving, Dec 25; also Super Bowl Sun. Bar. Children's menu. **$$**

★ ★ **ROONEY'S.** *2465 Demere Rd, St. Simons Island (31522). Phone 912/638-7097.* There are two options available at this island restaurant, a casual café and a more formal Garden Room restaurant. The American specialties include bourbon-glazed quail and lobster taquitos. American menu. Dinner. Closed holidays; first week in Jan. Bar. **$$$**

Statesboro (D-4)

Settled 1796
Population 22,698
Elevation 258 ft
Area Code 912
Zip 30458
Information Convention and Visitors Bureau, 322 S Main St, PO Box 1516; phone 912/489-1869
Web Site www.visit-statesboro.com

What to See and Do

Georgia Southern University. *Hwy 301 S, Statesboro (30460). Phone 912/681-5611.* (1906) (14,000 students) On campus are art department gallery (Mon-Fri; closed holidays); museum (Mon-Fri, Sun; closed holidays); planetarium (by appointment); Herty Nature Trail (daily); Center for Wildlife Education and Raptor Center (Mon-Fri, Sun; closed holidays).

Special Event

Regional Ogeechee Fair. *Fairgrounds, Hwy 67, Statesboro.* Sept-Oct.

Full-Service Inn

★ ★ ★ **HISTORIC STATESBORO INN.** *106 S Main St, Statesboro (30458). Phone 912/489-8628; toll-free 800/846-9466; fax 912/489-4785. www.statesboroinn.com.* This country inn boasts an atmosphere and surroundings unmatched in comfort and style. Rich in history, this inn also offers elegant dining featuring a menu of seasonal favorites with Southern flavors. 16 rooms, 2 story. Pets accepted. Complimentary full breakfast. Check-in 3 pm, check-out 11 am. Restaurant. **$** 🖻 🔝

Thomasville (E-2)

See also Bainbridge

Population 18,162
Elevation 285 ft
Area Code 229
Zip 31792
Information Welcome Center, 135 N Broad St, PO Box 1540, 31799; phone 229/227-7099
Web Site www.thomasvillega.com

What to See and Do

Big Oak. *Crawford and Monroe sts, Thomasville. 1 block behind Post Office and Federal Courthouse.* Giant live oak is 68 feet tall, has a limb spread of 162 feet, and a trunk circumference of 24 feet. The approximately 310-year-old tree was enrolled as a member of the National Live Oak Society in 1936.

Lapham-Patterson House State Historic Site. *626 N Dawson St, Thomasville. Phone 229/225-4004.* (1885) Restored three-story Victorian house features decorative shinglework, elaborate chinoiserie porches, fanciful gables, and cantilevered balconies; built by Chicago merchant as resort cottage. Tours on the hour. (Tues-Sun; closed Jan 1, Thanksgiving, Dec 25) **$$**

Pebble Hill Plantation. *1251 Hwy 319 S, Thomasville. 5 miles SW via Hwy 319. Phone 229/226-2344.* Historic plantation dates from 1820s; elaborate Greek Revival house furnished with art, antiques, porcelains, crystal, silver, and Native American relics belonging to Hanna family of Ohio, who rebuilt house, guest houses, stables, and garages after a fire in the 1930s. Gardens; livestock. Wagon rides; tours (Tues-Sun; closed Thanksgiving, Dec 24-25, also Sept; must be over 6 years of age). **$$$**

Thomas County Museum of History. *725 N Dawson St, Thomasville. Phone 229/226-7664.* Five buildings on the property include a log house with period furnishings; an 1877 frame house furnished in middle-class fashion of that period; an 1893 Victorian bowling alley; a garage housing historic vehicles; and a 1920s mansion, which houses the main museum. Photographs, period costumes, artifacts. (Closed holidays, also last week in Sept) **$$**

Thomasville Cultural Center. *600 E Washington St, Thomasville. Phone 229/226-0588.* A center for visual and performing arts. Facilities include art galleries with permanent and changing exhibits, children's room, and 550-seat auditorium. Concerts, musicals, children's programs, art classes, and other programs are offered. Galleries, building tours (daily, except holidays; fee). **FREE**

Special Event

Rose Festival. Parade, rose show, arts and crafts. Late Apr.

Limited-Service Hotel

★ **DAYS INN.** *3538 Hwy 84 E, Cairo (31728). Phone 229/377-4400; toll-free 800/329-7466; fax 229/377-5831. www.daysinn.com.* 34 rooms, 2 story. Check-out 11 am. Outdoor pool. **$**
⊠

Full-Service Resort

★ ★ ★ **MELHANA THE GRAND PLANTATION.** *301 Showboat Ln, Thomasville (31792). Phone 229/226-2290; toll-free 888/920-3030; fax 229/226-4585. www.melhana.com.* Built on the grounds of a historic plantation, this resort has an indoor pool, tennis courts, horseback riding, as well as a wide assortment of leisure activities. Explore the vast grounds by day and enjoy gourmet dining in the dining room each evening. 30 rooms, 2 story. Complimentary full breakfast. Check-in 3 pm, check-out noon. Restaurant, bar. Children's activity center. Fitness room. Indoor pool. Tennis. Airport transportation available. Business center. **$$**
🏋 ⊠ 🎿 🏃

Specialty Lodgings

The following lodging establishments are approved by Mobil Travel Guide, but due to their unique and individualized nature have not been given a traditional Mobil Star rating. Included in this listing you may find bed-and-breakfasts, limited-service inns, guest ranches, and other unique hotel properties.

1884 PAXTON HOUSE INN. *445 Remington Ave, Thomasville (31792). Phone 229/226-5197; fax 229/226-9903. www.1884paxtonhouseinn.com.* Stroll from this Victorian mansion and see the rich history and beauty of Thomasville. Marvel in the beauty and grace of the old inn as worries are rocked away on the spacious veranda. 4 rooms, 2 story. Children over 12 years only. Complimentary full breakfast. Check-in 3-6 pm, check-out 11 am. Indoor pool. **$$**
🅳 ⊠

SERENDIPITY COTTAGE. *339 E Jefferson St, Thomasville (31792). Phone 229/226-8111; toll-free 800/383-7377; fax 229/226-2656. www.serendipity cottage.com.* 4 rooms, 2 story. Children over 13 years only. Complimentary full breakfast. Check-in 4-6 pm, check-out 11 am. **$**

🄳

Restaurant

★ ★ **PLAZA RESTAURANT.** *217 S Broad St, Thomasville (31792). Phone 229/226-5153; fax 229/226-2458.* Greek, American menu. Breakfast, lunch, dinner. Closed holidays. Bar. Children's menu. **$$**

Tifton (E-3)

See also Adel

Population 15,060
Elevation 357 ft
Information Tifton-Tift County Chamber of Commerce, 100 Central Ave, PO Box 165, 31793; phone 229/382-6200
Web Site www.tiftontourism.com

What to See and Do

Georgia Agrirama, 19th-Century Living History Museum. *I-75 exit 20 and 8th St, Tifton. Phone 229/386-3344. www.agrirama.com.* Operating exhibits include farms and farmhouses, one-room school, gristmill, newspaper office, blacksmith shop, church, cotton gin, sawmill, turpentine still, country store, drugstore, variety works, and more from 1870 to 1910. A logging train runs year-round. Costumed interpreters. (Tues-Sat 9 am-5 pm; closed Jan 1, Thanksgiving, Dec 22-25) **$$**

Limited-Service Hotel

★ **COMFORT INN.** *1104 King Rd, Tifton (31794). Phone 229/382-4410; toll-free 800/223-5234; fax 229/382-3967. www.comfortinn.com.* 91 rooms, 2 story. Pets accepted, some restrictions; fee. Complimentary continental breakfast. Check-out 11 am. Bar. Indoor pool, whirlpool. **$**

🐾 🏊

Restaurant

★ **CHARLES SEAFOOD RESTAURANT.** *701 W 7th St (Hwy 82), Tifton (31794). Phone 229/382-9696; fax 229/387-7413.* American menu. Lunch, dinner. Closed Sun; July 4, Dec 25. **$$**

Toccoa (A-3)

See also Clayton, Commerce, Gainesville, Helen

Population 9,323
Elevation 1,017 ft
Area Code 706
Zip 30577
Information Toccoa-Stephens County Chamber of Commerce, 901 E Currahee St, PO Box 577; phone 706/886-2132
Web Site www.toccoagachamber.com

What to See and Do

Hartwell Lake. *5625 Anderson Hwy, Hartwell (30643). 6 miles E on Hwy 123 to the lake; continue approximately 21 miles E on the same road to access Twin Lakes campground, follow signs. Phone 706/376-4788.* This 56,000-acre reservoir with 962 miles of shoreline was created by a dam on the Savannah River. Swimming, water-skiing, fishing, boating (ramps, marinas); picnicking. Numerous campsites (Mar-Nov; fee) surround the lake. Reservoir (daily).

Toccoa Falls College. *Falls Rd, Toccoa Falls. NW edge of town off Hwy 17 A. Phone 706/886-6831.* (1907) (911 students) On November 6, 1977, a 40-year-old earthen dam above the college collapsed, spewing tons of water over the 186-foot Toccoa Falls and inundating the campus—one of the worst such disasters in Georgia history. There is no longer a lake or dam above the falls. Toccoa Falls is open to the public (daily; closed Dec 25). **$**

Traveler's Rest State Historic Site. *8162 Riverdale Rd, Toccoa (30577). 6 miles NE off Hwy 123. Phone 706/886-2256.* Plantation house (circa 1840) built on land granted in 1785 to Jesse Walton, a Revolutionary soldier and political leader. Two-story structure covers 6,000 square feet. Later owned and enlarged by Devereaux Jarrett, it served as a stagecoach inn and post office. Museum (Thurs-Sun; closed Jan 1, Thanksgiving, Dec 25). **$**

Limited-Service Hotel

★ **DAYS INN.** *1101 S Big A Rd, Toccoa (30577). Phone 706/886-9461; toll-free 800/329-7466; fax 706/886-0907. www.daysinn.com.* 78 rooms, 2 story. Complimentary continental breakfast. Check-out 11 am. Outdoor pool. **$**

Tybee Island (D-5)

See also Savannah

Population 3,392
Elevation 17 ft
Area Code 912
Zip 31328
Information Savannah Area Convention and Visitors Bureau, 101 E Bay St; phone toll-free 877/728-2662
Web Site www.tybeeisland.com

A popular year-round Georgia resort has evolved on this V-shaped sandbar fronting the Atlantic for nearly 4 miles and the Savannah River for more than 2 miles. The beach runs the entire length of the island; its north end is marked by old coastal defenses, a museum, and a lighthouse at the tip. Reached by a causeway from Savannah and Highway 80, the beach has a boardwalk, fishing pier, amusements, hotels, motels, and vacation cottages.

What to See and Do

Tybee Museum and Lighthouse. *30 Meddian Dr, Tybee Island. N end of island. Phone 912/786-5801.* Museum is housed in a coastal artillery battery built in 1898. Battery Garland is one of six gun emplacements that made up Fort Screven. Museum traces history of Tybee from colonial times to 1945; exhibits on Martello Tower, Civil War, Fort Screven; doll and gun collections. The lighthouse is one of the oldest active lighthouses in the United States; visitors may climb to the top for a scenic view of Tybee and historic Fort Screven. Exhibits and gift shop in 1880s lighthouse keeper's cottage. (Wed-Mon; closed holidays). **$$**

Valdosta (E-3)

See also Adel

Settled 1860
Population 43,724
Elevation 229 ft
Area Code 229
Information Chamber of Commerce, 416 N Ashley St, 31603-1964; phone 229/247-8100
Web Site www.valdostacity.com

When local citizens discovered that surveyors had left the town off the railroad right-of-way, they lost no time moving the town 4 miles east of the original community (then called Troupville). Named for Val de Aosta (Vale of Beauty), the governor's estate, Valdosta later became a rail center with seven branch lines of three systems. One of the state's most prosperous small cities, Valdosta's products include timber, tobacco, and cattle. Agriculture, tourism, Valdosta State University, and Moody Air Force Base, 12 miles to the north, also contribute to the economy. Valdosta is in the center of a large wooded area with many lakes nearby.

What to See and Do

Barber House. *416 N Ashley St, Valdosta. Phone 229/247-8100.* (1915) Restored neo-Classical house serves as offices for Valdosta-Lowndes County Chamber of Commerce; elaborate woodwork, original light fixtures and furniture. Self-guided tours. (Mon-Fri) **FREE**

Converse Dalton Ferrell House. *305 N Patterson St, Valdosta.* (1902) Neo-Classical house with wide two-story porch that wraps around front and two sides. Interior has 20-foot ceilings, 14-foot high pocket doors, golden-oak woodwork, some original light fixtures. (By appointment only) Contact the Convention and Visitors Center.

The Crescent (Valdosta Garden Center). *904 N Patterson St, Valdosta. Phone 229/244-6747.* (1898) Neoclassical house named for the dramatic two-story, crescent-shaped porch supported by 13 columns. House includes grand staircase, second-floor bathroom with gold-leaf tiles and fireplace, and ballroom on third floor. In garden are chapel and octagonal school house. (Mon-Fri; also by appointment) **DONATION**

Lowndes County Historical Society Museum. *305 W Central Ave, Valdosta. Phone 229/247-4780.* Originally a Carnegie library, now contains collection of artifacts from Civil War to present; genealogical library. (Mon-Sat; closed holidays) **FREE**

Limited-Service Hotels

★ ★ **BEST WESTERN KING OF THE ROAD.** *1403 N St. Augustine Rd, Valdosta (31602). Phone 229/244-7600; toll-free 800/780-7234; fax 229/245-1734. www.bestwestern.com.* 137 rooms, 3 story. Pets accepted, some restrictions. Complimentary continental breakfast. Check-out 11 am. Restaurant, bar. Outdoor pool. Airport transportation available. **$**

★ **COMFORT INN.** *2101 W Hill Ave, Valdosta (31601). Phone 229/242-1212; toll-free 800/228-5150; fax 229/242-2639. www.comfortinn.com.* 138 rooms, 2 story. Complimentary continental breakfast. Check-out noon. Bar. Outdoor pool. Airport transportation available. Business center. **$**

★ **HAMPTON INN.** *1705 Gornto Rd, Valdosta (31601). Phone 229/244-8800; toll-free 800/426-7866; fax 229/244-6602. www.hamptoninn.com.* 102 rooms, 2 story. Complimentary continental breakfast. Check-out noon. Outdoor pool. **$**

★ **LA QUINTA INN AND SUITES.** *1800 Club House Dr, Valdosta (31601). Phone 229/247-7755; toll-free 800/531-5900; fax 229/245-1359. www.laquinta.com.* 121 rooms, 2 story. Complimentary continental breakfast. Check-out noon. Outdoor pool, whirlpool. Business center. **$**

Restaurants

★ ★ **CHARLIE TRIPPER'S.** *4479 N Valdosta Rd, Valdosta (31602). Phone 229/247-0366; fax 229/244-5367.* American menu. Dinner. Closed Sun-Mon; holidays. Bar. **$$$**

★ **JP MULLDOONS.** *1405 Gornto Rd, Valdosta (31602). Phone 229/247-9200; fax 229/247-3377.* American menu. Dinner. Closed Sun; holidays. Bar. **$$**

★ ★ **MOM & DAD'S.** *4143 N Valdosta Rd, Valdosta (31602). Phone 229/333-0848; fax 229/247-8167.* Italian menu. Dinner. Closed Sun-Mon; holidays. Bar. Children's menu. **$$**

Washington (B-3)

See also Athens

Settled 1769
Population 4,295
Elevation 618 ft
Area Code 706
Zip 30673
Information Washington-Wilkes Chamber of Commerce, 104 Liberty St, Box 661; phone 706/678-2013
Web Site www.washingtonwilkes.com

The first city incorporated in the name of George Washington, it was the site of the Confederacy's last cabinet meeting (May 5, 1865) and the home of the South's first woman newspaper editor (Sarah Hillhouse of *The Monitor,* who printed editorials about the weather). Natives refer to this town as "Washington-Wilkes" (it is in Wilkes County) to distinguish it from the nation's capital.

Settlers first built a stockade called Heard's Fort. Elijah Clark led them in resistance to British troops, enabling patriots to hold Wilkes County when the rest of Georgia fell in 1779 (Kettle Creek Battleground). The last Confederate cabinet meeting convened in the Heard Building with President Davis and 14 officials on May 5, 1865. On June 4, Union soldiers seized $100,000 of the $500,000 in gold remaining in the Confederate Treasury. Legend persists that the rest of the gold (not recovered when Davis was captured at Irwinville) is buried in or near Washington.

What to See and Do

Alexander H. Stephens. *456 Alexander St N, Waycross. 19 miles SW on GA 47 to Crawfordville, then 1/2 mile N. Phone 706/456-2602.* In 1,190-acre park is Liberty Hall (circa 1830), restored house of A. H. Stephens, Vice President of the Confederacy; Confederate Museum (Tues-Sat, also Sun afternoons; closed Thanksgiving, Dec 25; fee). Fishing, boating, rentals; nature trails, picnicking, camping. Contact Superintendent, PO Box 283, Crawfordville, 30631.

Callaway Plantation. *2160 Lexington Rd, Washington (30673). 5 miles W on Hwy 78.* This complete working plantation complex includes a red brick Greek Revival mansion (1869); a gray frame "Federal plainstyle" house (circa 1790) with period furnishings; a hewn log kitchen (circa 1785) with utensils; and agricultural equipment. RV parking (hook-ups). (Tues-Sat 10 am-5 pm, Sun 2-5 pm; closed holidays) **$**

Courthouse Square. On square are historic markers noting last cabinet meeting of Confederacy; inscription of first land-grant record; capstone from cotton factory (1811); World War II Memorial; Hill House (circa 1784), first property owned by a woman in northeast Georgia; and a Vietnam Memorial.

Elijah Clark State Park. *2959 McCormick Hwy, Washington. 23 miles NE on Hwy 378, on the western shore of Clark Hill Lake. Phone 706/359-3458.* The park includes a log cabin museum with colonial life demonstrations, as well as opportunities for swimming beach, water-skiing, fishing, and boating (ramp). Nature trails, picnicking, camping, cottages.

J. Strom Thurmond Dam and Lake. *Lincolnton. 16 miles NE on Hwy 378 to Lincolnton, then S on Hwy 47, E on Hwy 150. Phone toll-free 800/533-3478.* Swimming, fishing, boating (ramps); hiking, picnicking, camping (year-round; fee). For more information, contact the Resource Manager's Office (E end of dam), Thurmond Lake, Rte 1, Box 12, Clarks Hill, SC, 29821.

Kettle Creek Battleground. *8 miles SW on Kettle Creek, off Hwy 44.* Marker indicates site of a decisive battle of Revolutionary War.

Robert Toombs House State Historic Site. *216 E Robert Toombs Ave, Washington. Phone 706/678-2226.* (1797) Restored residence of unreconstructed Confederate statesman and soldier. Frame Federal-era house with Greek Revival portico; period furniture, exhibits, video. Contact the Superintendent, PO Box 605. (Tues-Sat, also Sun afternoons; closed holidays) **$**

Washington-Wilkes Historical Museum. *308 E Robert Toombs Ave, Washington. Phone 706/678-2105.* Located in white frame, antebellum house (circa 1836), the museum includes period furnishings, Civil War mementos, Native American items, earthenware. (Tues-Sat, also Sun afternoons; closed Jan 1, Thanksgiving, Dec 25) **$**

Limited-Service Hotel

★ **JAMESON INN.** *115 Ann Denard Dr, Washington (30673). Phone 706/678-7925; fax 706/678-7962.* 43 rooms, 2 story. Complimentary continental breakfast. Check-out 11 am. **$**

Waycross (E-4)

See also Okefenokee Swamp

Settled 1818
Population 15,333
Elevation 135 ft
Area Code 912
Zip 31501
Information Tourism and Conference Bureau, 317 Plant Ave, 31501; phone 912/283-3742
Web Site www.okefenokeetourism.com

The name Waycross reflects the town's strategic location at the intersection of nine railroads and five highways. Situated at the edge of the Okefenokee Swamp, the town's early settlers put up blockhouses to protect themselves from local Native Americans. The production of naval stores and the marketing of furs were of prime importance before Okefenokee became a national wildlife refuge. Today the economy of Waycross is based on a diversity of industries, including timber, railroad, mobile homes, and tourism.

What to See and Do

Laura S. Walker State Park. *5653 Laura Walker Rd, Waycross. 9 miles SE via Hwy 82 and Hwy 177. Phone 912/287-4900.* Within the park is a 106-acre lake. Swimming pool, water-skiing, fishing, boating; golfing, picnicking, playground, camping.

Okefenokee Heritage Center. *1460 N Augusta Ave, Waycross. Phone 912/285-4260.* Exhibits on Okefenokee area history; art gallery with changing exhibits; social science room with exhibit on Native Americans of southern Georgia; 1912 train depot and railroad cars; turn-of-the-century print shop; nature trails; Power House building; 1840s pioneer house. (Daily; closed holidays) **$**

Southern Forest World. *1440 N Augusta Ave, Waycross. Phone 912/285-4056.* Exhibits, with audiovisual displays, detail development and history of forestry in the South; logging locomotive, 38-foot model of a loblolly pine, giant cypress tree. Nature trails. (Tues-Sat; closed holidays) **$**

Special Event

Pogofest. Parade, exhibits, barbecue. Apr.

Limited-Service Hotel

★ ★ **HOLIDAY INN.** *1725 Memorial Dr, Waycross (31501). Phone 912/283-4490; toll-free 800/465-4329; fax 912/283-4490. www.holiday-inn.com.* 148 rooms, 2 story. Pets accepted; fee. Complimentary full breakfast. Check-out noon. Restaurant, bar. Fitness room. Outdoor pool. Airport transportation available. **$**
🐾 🚶 〰️

Winder (B-2)

See also Athens, Atlanta, Norcross

Population 10,201
Elevation 984 ft
Area Code 770
Zip 30680
Information Barrow County Chamber of Commerce, 6 Porter St, PO Box 456; phone 770/867-9444
Web Site www.cityofwinder.com

What to See and Do

Fort Yargo State Park. *210 S Broad St, Winder (30680). 1 mile S via Hwy 81. Phone 770/867-3489.* The park is named for a fort of hand-hewn pine logs built during Native American uprisings in the 1790s. Swimming, beach, fishing, boating, and canoeing (rentals); nature trails, picnicking, camping. Contact Manager. At the north end is

Will-A-Way Recreation Area. *Phone 770/867-5313.* Designed to benefit disabled persons. Swimming pool, fishing, boating; nature trails, picnicking, camping area for disabled and special chairs for water access.

Limited-Service Hotel

★ **DAYS INN.** *802 N Broad St, Monroe (30656). Phone 770/267-3666; toll-free 800/329-7466; fax 770/267-7189. www.daysinn.com.* 45 rooms, 2 story. Complimentary continental breakfast. Outdoor pool. **$**
〰️

Side Trips

In just a few hours' drive from Georgia, you could be sunning yourself on Florida's famed beaches or soaking up the rich history in Birmingham and Montgomery, Alabama. In Jacksonville, Florida, you'll be treated to a modern city with a tropical flavor. Florida's capital, Tallahassee, will transport you back in time to the elegance of Southern plantation days. For that special getaway, visit Florida's Amelia Island for a round of golf or to relax on the bluff-height dunes and white, wide beaches. If you are a history buff or, more specifically, a Civil Rights history buff, a trip to Birmingham and Montgomery are a must. There you will find a plethora of information and artifacts from that era in US history.

Birmingham, AL

2 1/2 hours, 147 miles from Atlanta, GA

Founded 1871
Population 242,820
Elevation 601 ft
Area Code 205
Information Convention & Visitors Bureau, 2200 9th Ave N, 35203; phone 205/458-8000 or toll-free 800/458-8085
Web Site www.birminghamal.org

A city of great industrial strength, Birmingham once proudly called itself the "Pittsburgh of the South." Today Birmingham is equally proud of its reputation as an international medical center. Advances in medical science through research at the University of Alabama medical complex attract patients worldwide.

At the turn of the 19th century, Native Americans who painted their faces and weapons red were known by early settlers as "Red Sticks." Even when the red paint was found to be hematite iron ore, it was still considered worthless, and many years passed before Red Mountain

ore became the foundation for Birmingham's steel industry. The Confederacy's lack of iron in 1863 led to the building of a small blast furnace which produced cannonballs and rifles until Wilson's Raiders destroyed it in 1865.

Birmingham was born in 1871 when two railroads intersected. A year later, the Elyton Land Company had sold most of its 4,150 acres at fabulous prices. (It had bought the land for $25 an acre.) But in 1873, a double disaster struck. First, cholera drove hundreds from the new city; then, the nationwide financial panic nearly doomed Birmingham to extinction. Refusing to give in, Charles Linn, a former Civil War blockade runner who had opened a small bank in 1871, built a grand three-story brick bank for the huge (at that time) sum of $36,000. He then sent out 500 invitations to a "Calico Ball," as he called it, to celebrate its opening. Guests came from all over the state, women in ball gowns and men in formal dress all cut from calico. "Linn's folly" paid off—Birmingham was saved.

Today Birmingham is a modern, progressive city—one of culture as well as steel, and of education as well as the social life that began with the Calico Ball. To visitors, it offers much in recreational and sightseeing opportunities. Birmingham Green, a major renaissance of the downtown area, added walkways, plantings, benches, and the DART trolley. The Five Points South area, featuring clubs with many styles of quality entertainment, plays a major role in Birmingham's nightlife. This is indeed the heart of the New South.

Additional Visitor Information

Contact the Greater Birmingham Convention and Visitors Bureau, 2200 9th Ave N, 35203; phone 205/458-8000; or the Birmingham/Jefferson Visitor Information Center, 1201 University Blvd, 35233; phone 205/458-8001.

Public Transportation

Airport Information. Information, phone 205/599-0500; lost and found phone 205/599-0500; weather phone 205/945-7000.

Buses Birmingham/Jefferson County Transit Authority; phone 205/521-0101.

Downtown Birmingham

Birmingham, the home of the Civil Rights Institute, is an important stop on any African American history tour itinerary. While the city is most notorious for turbulence during the civil rights era, the cultural contributions of African Americans to Birmingham are less well known.

Start at the Historical Fourth Avenue Visitor Center (319 17th St N; phone 205/328-1850), where you can pick up a map or take a guided tour of the historic African American business district.

Across the street from the visitor center is the Alabama Jazz Hall of Fame, located within the historic Carver Theater (1631 Fourth Ave N; phone 205/254-2731). Exhibits cover the history of jazz and celebrate such artists as Dinah Washington, Nat King Cole, Duke Ellington, and W. C. Handy, among others. The theater also plays host to live performances. On the other side of the visitor center, the Alabama Theater (1817 Third Ave N) has been restored to its 1920s splendor and is now a cinema.

Head west along Third Avenue one block to another beloved local landmark: La Vase (328 16th St N), a restaurant that serves hearty home-style soul food. After your meal, proceed north up 16th Street three blocks to Kelly Ingram Park, the scene of civil rights clashes in the 1950s and 1960s. The inscription at its entrance reads "A Place for Revolution and Reconciliation," and the park commemorates its role in civil rights history with statues and sculptures.

The Birmingham Civil Rights Institute (520 16th St; phone 205/328-9696), across the street from the park, is the city's premiere attraction. A short film introduces the city's history, and vintage footage illustrates the Jim Crow era and the development of the civil rights movement. Exhibits emphasize the events that took place in Birmingham, including, for example, the door from the city jail cell that housed Reverend Martin Luther King Jr., the inspiration for Dr. King's famous "Letter from a Birmingham Jail." The bookshop has a good selection of African American history and heritage titles.

Cross Sixth Avenue to reach the 16th Street Baptist Church (1530 Sixth Ave N; phone 205/251-9402), which was bombed in a 1963 attack that killed four girls. The rebuilt church hosts tens of thousands of visitors each year.

What to See and Do

Alabama Sports Hall of Fame Museum. *2150 Civic Center Blvd, Birmingham (35203). Phone 205/323-6665. www.alasports.org.* Showcase for memorabilia of Alabama sports figures; sound-sensored displays; theater. (Mon-Sat 9 am-5 pm, Sun 1-5 pm; closed holidays) **$$**

Arlington Antebellum Home and Gardens. *331 Cotton Ave SW, Birmingham (35211). Phone 205/780-5656.* (Circa 1850) Birmingham's last remaining antebellum house in the Greek Revival style features a diverse collection of 19th-century decorative art. Located on a sloping hill in Elyton, the house is surrounded by oak and magnolia trees, and seasonal plantings. (Tues-Sat 10 am-4 pm, Sun 1-4 pm; closed holidays) **$**

Birmingham Botanical Gardens. *2612 Lane Park Rd, Birmingham (35223). Phone 205/414-3950. www.bbgardens.org.* Includes orchids, lilies, dogwood, wildflowers, azaleas; 26-foot floral clock, conservatory, and arboretum of rare plants, shrubs, and trees. (Daily, dawn-dusk) Restaurant on grounds. **FREE** Includes

Japanese Gardens. *2616 Lane Park Rd, Birmingham (35223). Phone 205/414-3950.* Gardens landscaped with Asian plants, waterfalls. Also here is a bonsai complex, Asian statuary, and a Zen garden. Gravel paths. (Daily)

Birmingham Civil Rights Institute. *520 16th St N, Birmingham (35203). Phone 205/328-9696; toll-free 866/328-9696. www.bcri.org.* Exhibits portray the struggle for civil rights in Birmingham and across the nation from the 1920s to the present; multimedia presentations. Free admission on Martin Luther King Jr. holiday (Tues-Sat 10 am-5 pm, Sun 1-5 pm; closed Mon and holidays) **$$**

Birmingham-Jefferson Convention Complex. *Between 9th and 11th aves, 19th and 21st sts. Phone 205/458-8400. www.bjcc.org.* The entire complex covers seven square blocks. The center contains 220,000 square feet of exhibition space; 3,000-seat concert hall; 1,100-seat theater; 18,000-seat coliseum.

Birmingham Museum of Art. *2000 8th Ave N, Birmingham (35203). Across from Linn Park. Phone 205/254-2565. www.artsbma.org.* Features collections of Renaissance, Asian, and American art, including Remington bronzes; 20th-century collection; 17th-through 19th-century American and European paintings and decorative arts. Also featured are pre-Columbian art and artifacts, Native American art, and the largest collection of Wedgwood outside of England. Changing exhibits. Multilevel sculpture garden with two reflecting pools and a waterfall. (Tues-Sat 10 am-5 pm, Sun noon-5 pm; closed holidays) **FREE**

Birmingham-Southern College. *900 Arkadelphia Rd, Birmingham (35254). Phone 205/226-4600. www.bsc.edu.* (1856) (1,500 students) A 200-acre campus on wooded rolling hills. Here is the state's first planetarium (for schedule, reservations, phone 205/226-4771; fee). Tours of campus.

Birmingham Zoo. *2630 Cahaba Rd, Birmingham (35223). Phone 205/879-0409. www.birminghamzoo .com.* Nearly 1,000 animals on display. Highlights include sea lions, Endochinese tiger, and the predator building. (Daily 9 am-5 pm; extended hours Memorial Day-Labor Day: Tues, Fri-Sat to 7 pm) **$$**

McWane Center. *1421 22nd St S, Birmingham (35234). Phone 205/714-8300. www.mcwane.org.* Natural history museum located on the slopes of Red Mountain. Extensive collection of fossils including a 14-foot mosasaur (extinct marine lizard); geologic history displays and exhibits; hands-on exhibits. Walkway carved into the face of the mountain above expressway. More than 150 million years of geologic history are exposed for 1/3 mile. Picnicking. (Sept-May: Mon-Fri 9 am-5 pm, Sat 10 am-6 pm, Sun 1-5 pm; June-Aug: Mon-Sat 10 am-6 pm, Sun 1-6 pm; closed holidays) **$**

Miles College. *5500 Myron Massey Blvd, Fairfield (35064). Phone 205/929-1000. www.miles.edu.* (1905) (1,500 students) Extensive collection of African American literature; exhibits of African art forms. Two historic landmark buildings. Tours.

Oak Mountain State Park. *200 Terrace Dr, Pelham (35124). 15 miles S on I-65, exit 246. Phone 205/620-2524. www.dcnr.state.al.us.* Peavine Falls and Gorge and two lakes sit amidst 9,940 acres of the state's most rugged mountains. Activities include swimming, fishing, boating (marina, ramp, rentals), hiking, backpacking, bridle trails, golf (18 holes; fee), tennis, picnicking (shelters, barbecue pits, fireplaces), concession, camping, cabins, and a demonstration farm. **$**

Rickwood Caverns State Park. *370 Rickwood Park Rd, Warrior (35180). 20 miles N on I-65 to exit 284 (just N of Warrior) then 4 miles W on Skyline Dr to Rickwood Rd, follow state signs. Phone 205/647-9692. dcnr.state.al.us.* This 380-acre park offers swimming pools; hiking, carpet golf, miniature train ride, picnicking, concession, gift shop, primitive and improved camping (standard fees). One-hour tours of cave with 260 million-year-old limestone formations (Memorial Day-Labor Day: daily; after Labor Day-Oct and Mar-May: weekends). Park (all year); pool (seasonal). Fee for some activities. **$**

Ruffner Mountain Nature Center. *1214 81st St S, Birmingham (35206). Phone 205/833-8264. www. ruffnermountain.org.* Contains 1,011 acres of the last undeveloped section of this area's Appalachian Mountains. Displays focus on Ruffner Mountain's biology, geology, and history. Wildlife refuge with nature trails. Special programs (fee). (Tues-Sat 9 am-5 pm, Sun 1-5 pm; closed holidays, also Dec 24) **FREE**

Samford University. *800 Lakeshore Dr, Birmingham (35229). In Shades Mountain section. Phone 205/726-2011. www.samford.edu.* (1841) (4,600 students) A 172-acre campus with brick Georgian Colonial buildings. The Samford Murals are on view in Rotunda, Dwight and Lucille Beeson Center for the Healing Arts. Science Center has conservatory of medicinal plants and planetarium with shows (Mon evenings). Beeson Divinity Hall Chapel is topped by a copper-clad dome that has a detailed ceiling mural on the interior (tours available). Tours of campus.

Sloss Furnaces National Historic Landmark. *20 32nd St N, Birmingham (35222). Phone 205/324-1911. www.slossfurnaces.com.* An industrial museum and site for concerts and downtown festivals. (Tues-Sun) **FREE**

Southern Museum of Flight/Alabama Aviation Hall of Fame. *4343 73rd St N, Birmingham (35206). Phone 205/833-8226. www.southernmuseumofflight.org.* View a full-size Wright Flyer replica, a 1912 Curtiss Pusher replica, a Fokker VII, a VariEze experimental homebuilt, two US Air Force fighter jet cockpit simulators, and flight-related memorabilia. (Tues-Sat 9:30 am-4:30 pm, Sun 1-4:30 pm) **$**

University of Alabama at Birmingham. *1400 University Blvd, Birmingham (35233). Phone 205/934-4475. www.uab.edu.* (16,500 students) On 70-square-block area on south edge of downtown. Reynolds Historical Library in the Lister Hill Library of the Health Sciences, 1700 University Blvd, six blocks W of Hwy 31 and Hwy 280, has collections of ivory anatomical mannequins, original manuscripts, and rare medical and scientific books; Alabama Museum of Health Sciences has memorabilia of Alabama doctors, surgeons, optometrists, and other medical practitioners; reproductions of doctor and dentist turn-of-the-century offices (Mon-Fri). **FREE**

Vulcan. *20th St and 19th Ave, Birmingham. On Valley Ave off Hwy 31 at top of Red Mountain in Vulcan Park. Phone 205/328-2863.* (1904) The figure of Vulcan, designed for the Louisiana Purchase Exposition in St. Louis, is one of the largest iron figures ever cast, standing 55 feet tall and weighing 60 tons. It surveys the city from a pedestal 124 feet high. Made of Birmingham iron and cast locally, Vulcan, Roman god of fire and forge, legendary inventor of smithing and metalworking, stands as a monument to the city's iron industry atop Red Mountain; and since 1939, he holds a lighted torch aloft over the city. A glass-enclosed elevator takes passengers to observation deck. Vulcan's torch shines bright red when there's been a traffic fatality in the city in the previous 24 hours. Park (daily; closed Thanksgiving, Dec 25). **$**

Special Events

City Stages. *1929 3rd Ave N, Birmingham. Phone 205/251-1272.* Billed as "Birmingham's World-Class Music Festival," City Stages features approximately 160 musical performances on 11 stages. Artists include both local and nationally known musicians (George Clinton, Al Green, and Kid Rock have been past performers). Third weekend in June.

Greater Alabama Fall Fair & Festival. *Alabama State Fairgrounds, 2331 Bessemer Rd, Birmingham (35208). Phone 205/786-8100 (Alabama State Fair Authority).* Features food, games, agricultural exhibitions, contests, livestock demonstrations, and arts and crafts vendors. Ten days in late Oct-early Nov.

International Festival. *205 20th St N, Birmingham. Phone 205/252-7652.* Each year, the Birmingham International Festival highlights the culture of a different country to promote education as well as business and trade relationships between Alabama and the selected country. A party early in the year kicks off a series of events to take place in the months to follow, which includes a trade expo, conferences, art exhibits, lectures, and a black-tie dinner. The free educational programs bring musicians, performers, and storytellers to Alabama schools, and includes a student art exhibition. Feb-May.

Limited-Service Hotels

★ **BAYMONT INN.** *513 Cahaba Park Cir, Birmingham (35242). Phone 205/995-9990; toll-free 877/229-6668; fax 205/995-0563. www.baymontinns.com.* 99 rooms, 3 story. Pets accepted. Complimentary continental breakfast. Check-out noon. **$**

★ ★ **BEST WESTERN RIME GARDEN INN & SUITES.** *5320 Beacon Dr, Birmingham (35210). Phone 205/951-1200; toll-free 888/828-1768; fax 205/951-1692. www.bestwestern.com.* 290 rooms, 3 story. Complimentary continental breakfast. Check-out noon. Restaurant, bar. Outdoor pool. Airport transportation available. **$**

★ ★ **COURTYARD BY MARRIOTT.** *500 Shades Creek Pkwy, Homewood (35209). Phone 205/879-0400; toll-free 800/321-2211; fax 205/879-6324. www.courtyard.com.* Conveniently located, this hotel is a short drive from Birmingham's airport. Great for the traveler on the go, guests should check out nearby Oak Mountain State Park or Birmingham Zoo. 140 rooms, 3 story. Check-out noon. Restaurant, bar. Fitness room. Outdoor pool, whirlpool. **$**

★ ★ **CROWNE PLAZA HOTEL BIRMINGHAM-THE REDMONT.** *2101 5th Ave, Birmingham (35203). Phone 205/324-2101; toll-free 800/227-6963; fax 205/324-0610. www.crowneplaza.com/cpbhmdowntown.* As Birmingham's oldest operating hotel, this downtown location was originally The Redmont Hotel, and has since been meticulously renovated. Guests here are in the heart of the city's business and historical district, and are within walking distance of the Civil Rights Institute, the Alabama Theater, and the Alabama Sports Hall of Fame, among many other attractions. 114 rooms, 12 story. Check-in 3 pm, check-out noon. High-speed Internet access. Restaurant, bar. Fitness room. Airport transportation available. Business center. **$**

★ ★ **EMBASSY SUITES.** *2300 Woodcrest Pl, Birmingham (35051). Phone 205/879-7400; toll-free 800/362-2779; fax 205/870-4523. www.embassy-suites .com.* This hotel is situated in Corporate Business Park, Southbridge, and is only 3 miles from the University of Alabama. Spacious suites have a full array of amenities. 243 rooms, 8 story, all suites. Complimentary full breakfast. Check-out noon. Restaurant, bar. Indoor pool, whirlpool. Airport transportation available. **$**

★ ★ **FOUR POINTS BY SHERATON BIRMINGHAM AIRPORT.** *5216 Airport Hwy, Birmingham (35212). Phone 205/591-7900; fax 205/591-6004.* 193 rooms, 4 story. Check-out noon. Restaurant, bar. Fitness room. Outdoor pool. Airport transportation available. **$**

★ **HAMPTON INN BIRMINGHAM- COLONNADE.** *3400 Colonnade Pkwy, Birmingham (35243). Phone 205/967-0002; toll-free 800/861-7168; fax 205/969-0901. www.hamptoninn.com.* With a close proximity to area attractions such as botanical gardens, bowling, a zoo, and shopping, and a staff that exemplifies traditional Southern hospitality, this conveniently located hotel also features mountain views. 133 rooms, 5 story. Pets accepted, some restrictions. Complimentary continental breakfast. Check-in 3 pm, check-out noon. High-speed Internet access. Fitness room. Outdoor pool. Business center. **$**

★ ★ **QUALITY INN ON THE LAKE.** *1548 Montgomery Hwy, Birmingham (35216). Phone 205/822-4350; toll-free 800/228-5151; fax 205/822-0350. www.qualityinn.com.* 166 rooms, 3 story. Check-out noon. Restaurant, bar. Outdoor pool, whirlpool. **$**

★ ★ **RADISSON HOTEL BIRMINGHAM.** *808 S 20th St, Birmingham (35205). Phone 205/933-9000; toll-free 800/333-3333; fax 205/933-0920. www.radisson.com.* In the heart of downtown and two blocks from the University and UAB Medical Center. It is just a short walk to the Five Points entertainment and restaurant district. 298 rooms, 14 story. Check-out noon. Restaurant, bar. Outdoor pool. Airport transportation available. **$**

Full-Service Hotels

★ ★ ★ **HILTON BIRMINGHAM PERIMETER PARK.** *8 Perimeter Park S, Birmingham (35243). Phone 205/967-2700; toll-free 800/774-1500; fax 205/972-8603. www.hilton.com.* Set in an up-and-coming business and entertainment area, this large hotel is in close proximity to the downtown area, with its cultural and corporate destinations. Among the amenities in the attractive rooms are work desks and dual-line phones. 205 rooms, 8 story. Check-in 3 pm, check-out noon. Wireless Internet access. Restaurant, bar. Fitness room. Outdoor pool. Airport transportation available. Business center. **$**

★ ★ ★ **MARRIOTT BIRMINGHAM.** *3590 Grandview Pkwy, Birmingham (35243). Phone 205/968-3775; toll-free 800/228-9290; fax 205/968-3742. www.marriott.com.* A mix of cozy and contemporary furnishings gives this hotel, just off Highway 280, an inviting and comfortable feel. Friendly staff, a huge array of amenities, and a location close to many business headquarters and entertainment options make this a prime option. 295 rooms, 7 story. Check-in 3 pm, check-out noon. High-speed Internet access, wireless Internet access. Restaurant, bar. Fitness room. Indoor pool. Business center. **$$**

★ ★ ★ **SHERATON BIRMINGHAM.** *2101 Richard Arrington Jr. Blvd N, Birmingham (35203). Phone 205/324-5000; toll-free 800/325-3535; fax 205/307-3085. www.sheraton.com.* Located in downtown Birmingham, this hotel is a short stroll on the skywalk to the convention center. Explore the zoo, art museum, and Five Points South historical district nearby. 770 rooms, 17 story. Check-in 3 pm, check-out noon. Restaurant, bar. Fitness room. Indoor pool, whirlpool. Business center. **$$**

★ ★ ★ **WYNDHAM TUTWILER HOTEL.** *2021 Park Pl N, Birmingham (35203). Phone 205/322-2100; toll-free 877/999-3223; fax 205/325-1198. www.wyndham.com.* This American classic built in the 1920s has been restored to its original grandeur and now is an elegant experience with gracious service and amenities. Nearby is the McWane Center and the Birmingham Museum of Art. 147 rooms, 8 story. Pets accepted, some restrictions; fee. Complimentary full breakfast. Check-in 3 pm, check-out noon.

High-speed Internet access. Restaurant, bar. Airport transportation available. Business center. **$$$**

★ ★ ★ **THE WYNFREY HOTEL.** *1000 Riverchase Galleria, Birmingham (35244). Phone 205/987-1600; toll-free 800/996-3739; fax 205/988-4597. www.wynfrey.com.* The Wynfrey Hotel is Birmingham's best lodging. Located just on the edge of the city, this gracious hotel combines Southern hospitality with European panache. The rooms and suites are tastefully appointed with stylish furnishings and plentiful amenities. This hotel is a favorite destination of shoppers, with special access to the city's renowned Riverchase Galleria. After a tiring day of bargain hunting, guests retire to the Spa Japonika to recharge and relax. Three restaurants and in-room dining ensure that all moods and tastes are satisfied at this sophisticated urban retreat. 329 rooms, 16 story. Check-in 4 pm, check-out 11 am. High-speed Internet access, wireless Internet access. Two restaurants, two bars. Fitness room. Outdoor pool. Airport transportation available. Business center. **$$**

Restaurants

★ **GOLDEN CITY CHINESE RESTAURANT.** *4647 Hwy 280, Birmingham (35242). Phone 205/991-3197.* Chinese menu. Lunch, dinner. Closed holidays. Bar. **$$**

★ ★ ★ **HIGHLANDS.** *2011 11th Ave S, Birmingham (35205). Phone 205/939-1400; fax 205/939-1405. www.highlandsbarandgrill.com.* This has been one of Birmingham's premiere restaurants for many years. The food has a southern emphasis, the chef's signature style. French menu. Dinner. Closed Sun, Mon; holidays. Bar. Valet parking. **$$$**

★ ★ **NIKI'S WEST.** *233 Finley Ave W, Birmingham (35204). Phone 205/252-5751; fax 205/252-8163.* Steak and seafood are on the menu, but you are welcome to go through the busy cafeteria line as well. Niki's is known for its "meat and three" options. Come hungry. American menu. Lunch, dinner. Closed Sun; holidays. **$$**

Montgomery, AL

2 hours 40 minutes, 160 miles from Atlanta, GA

Settled 1819
Population 201,568
Elevation 287 ft
Area Code 334
Information Montgomery Area Chamber of Commerce, 41 Commerce St, 36101; phone 334/834-5200
Web Site www.montgomerychamber.com

Between tall, stately columns on the portico of the state capitol, a bronze star marks the spot where Jefferson Davis was inaugurated President of the Confederate States of America on February 18, 1861. At that moment, Montgomery became the Confederacy's first capital. From this city went the telegram "Fire on Fort Sumter" that began the Civil War. Approximately 100 years later, Montgomery became embroiled in another kind of "war," the battle for civil rights.

Today, Montgomery is home to the nation's first Civil Rights Memorial. The memorial chronicles key events and lists the names of approximately 40 people who died in the struggle for racial equality from 1955 to 1968.

Montgomery is a city of considerable distinction, with many historic houses and buildings. Although Montgomery's most important business is government, it is also a livestock market and a center of manufacturing. As an educational center, it offers many cultural activities.

What to See and Do

Alabama Shakespeare Festival. *1 Festival Dr, Montgomery (36117). Phone toll-free 800/841-8273 (box office). www.asf.net.* Professional repertory company performs classic and contemporary comedy and drama. Musical performances as well. Two theaters: 750-seat Festival Stage and 225-seat Octagon. (Nov-Sept, Wed-Sun; weekend matinees) Hotel/play packages available. Inquire about facilities for the disabled and hearing impaired.

Alabama State University. *915 S Jackson St, Montgomery (36104). Phone 334/229-4100. www.alasu.edu.* (1867) (5,500 students) Authorized by the legislature in 1873 as the Lincoln Normal School, this university was moved from Marion to Montgomery in 1887. On campus are an art gallery, African American collection, and Tullibody Fine Arts Center (daily during academic year; closed holidays). Tours.

⭐ **Civil Rights Memorial.** *400 Washington Ave, Montgomery (36104). Washington Ave and Hull St at the Southern Poverty Law Center.* Designed by Vietnam Veterans Memorial artist Maya Lin.

⭐ **Dexter Avenue King Memorial Baptist Church.** *454 Dexter Ave, Montgomery (36104). Phone 334/263-3970. www.dexterkingmemorial.org.* (1877) The Reverend Dr. Martin Luther King Jr. was a pastor from 1954 to 1960; from the church he directed the Montgomery bus boycott, which sparked the modern civil rights movement. In the church is the mural and original painting "The Beginning of a Dream." Guided tours (Mon-Thurs 10 am and 2 pm), walk through (Fri 10 am), and by appointment (Sat 10:30 am-1:30 pm). Sun worship 10:30 am.

F. Scott and Zelda Fitzgerald Museum. *919 Felder Ave, Montgomery (36106). Phone 334/264-4222. www.fitzgerald-museum.org.* The famous author and his wife lived in this house from 1931 to 1932. Museum contains personal artifacts detailing the couple's public and private lives. Paintings by Zelda, letters, and photographs; 25-minute video presentation. (Wed-Fri, Sat-Sun afternoons; closed holidays) **FREE**

Fort Toulouse/Jackson Park National Historic Landmark. *2521 W Fort Toulouse Rd, Montgomery (36093). 12 miles NE, 3 miles W off Hwy 231 near Wetumpka. Phone 334/567-3002.* At the confluence of the Coosa and Tallapoosa rivers, Fort Toulouse was opened by Bienville in 1717 to establish trade in the heart of Creek territory. Abandoned in 1763, Andrew Jackson built a fort on the same site in 1814 after the Battle of Horseshoe Bend. Fort Toulouse has been reconstructed, and Fort Jackson has been partially reconstructed. This is also the site of mounds dating from approximately AD 1100. The park features a boat ramp, nature walks, picnicking, improved camping, and a museum. A living history program can be seen the third weekend of each month. Visitor center. (Daily; closed Jan 1, Dec 25) **$**

Greyhound racing. *VictoryLand Track, 8680 County Rd 40, Shorter (36075). 20 miles E via I-85, exit 22. Phone 334/269-6087. www.victoryland.com.* Clubhouse, restaurant. Over 19 years only. (Nightly; Mon-Wed, Sat-Sun afternoons; closed Thanksgiving, late Dec) **$**

Hank Williams's grave. *Hank Williams Memorial, Oakwood Cemetery, 1305 Upper Wetumpka Rd, Montgomery (36107).* Gravesite memorial to country music legend.

Huntingdon College. *1500 Fairview Ave, Montgomery (36106). 2 miles SE. Phone 334/833-4497. www.huntingdon.edu.* (1854) (700 students) Founded in Tuskegee to provide higher education for women, the liberal arts school became coeducational after World War II; 58-acre campus of woods and hills; Gothic buildings. Tours (by appointment).

Lower Commerce Street Historic District. *100 block of Commerce St, Montgomery.* Wholesale and railroad district along the Alabama River. Buildings, primarily Victorian in style, date from the 1880s to turn of the century. Riverfront tunnel to Riverfront Park dates to cotton days.

Maxwell Air Force Base. *55 S LeMay Plz, Montgomery (36112). 2 miles S, off I-65. Phone 334/953-1110. www.au.af.mil.* This has been an airfield since 1910, when Wilbur Wright began the world's first flying school on this site. Orville Wright made his first flight in Montgomery on March 26, 1910, four years before the Aviation Section of the Signal Corps was created. Maxwell Field was named on November 8, 1922, for Lieutenant William C. Maxwell of Atmore, Alabama, killed while serving with the Third Aero Squadron in the Philippines. It is now the site of Air University. Tours by appointment. (Daily; closed holidays) **FREE**

Montgomery Museum of Fine Arts. *1 Museum Dr, Montgomery (36117). Phone 334/244-5700. www.fineartsmuseum.com.* Collections of 19th- and 20th-century American art; European works on paper; regional and decorative arts. Hands-on children's exhibits. Lectures, concerts. (Tues, Fri-Sat 10 am-5 pm, Thurs to 9 pm, Sat noon-5 pm; closed holidays) **FREE**

Montgomery Zoo. *2301 Colosseum Pkwy, Montgomery (36110). Phone 334/240-4900. zoo.ci.montgomery.al.us.* Forty-acre zoo housing, mammals, birds, and reptiles in geographical groupings. (Daily 9 am-5 pm; closed Jan 1, Thanksgiving, Dec 25) **$$**

Murphy House. *22 Bibb St, Montgomery (36104). Bibb and Coosa sts. Phone 334/206-1600.* (1851) Fine example of Greek Revival architecture with fluted Corinthian columns and wrought-iron balcony is now headquarters of the Montgomery Water Works. (Mon-Fri; closed holidays)

Old Alabama Town. *301 Columbus St, Montgomery (36104). Phone 334/240-4500. www.oldalabama town.com.* Includes the Ordeman-Shaw House, an Italianate town house (circa 1850) with period furnishings; service buildings with household items; reconstructed 1840 barn; carriage house; 1820s log cabin depicting pioneer life; shotgun cottage depicting black urban life; urban church (circa 1890); country doctor's office; drugstore museum and cotton gin museum; blacksmith shop; print shop; corner grocery from the late 1890s; one-room schoolhouse; exhibition (Grange) hall. Taped driving tour of historic Montgomery also available. Films, tours, information center.(Mon-Sat 9 am-3 pm; closed holidays) **$$**

St. John's Episcopal Church. *113 Madison Ave, Montgomery (36104). At N Perry St. Phone 334/262-1937. www.stjohnsmontgomery.org.* (1855) Stained-glass windows, Gothic pipe organ, Jefferson Davis' pew. (Sun-Fri)

State Capitol. *Bainbridge and Dexter aves, Montgomery. Phone 334/242-3935.* (1851) Seat of Alabama's government for more than 100 years. Opposite the capitol are

> **Alabama Department of Archives and History.** *624 Washington Ave, Montgomery (36130). Phone 334/242-4363. archives.state.al.us.* Houses historical museum and genealogical research facilities. Artifact collections include exhibits on the 19th century, the military, and early Alabama Native Americans. Also an interactive children's gallery. (Mon-Fri 8:30 am-4:30 pm, first Sat of the month 8:30 am-4:30 pm; closed holidays) **FREE**

> **First White House of the Confederacy.** *644 Washington Ave, Montgomery (36130). Phone 334/242-1861.* (1835) This two-story, white frame house was the residence of Jefferson Davis and his family while Montgomery was the Confederate capital. Moved from its original location at Bibb and Lee streets in 1920, it is now a Confederate museum containing period furnishings, personal belongings, and paintings of the Davis family and Confederate mementos. (Mon-Fri 8 am-4:30 pm; closed holidays) **FREE**

Special Events

Alabama National Fair. *Garrett Coliseum, 1555 Federal Dr, Montgomery (36107). NE on Federal Dr. Phone 334/272-6831. www.alnationalfair.org.* This weeklong fair includes concerts, a circus, children's rides, and pig races. Oct. **$$**

Blue-Gray All-Star Classic. *Movie Gallery Stadium at Troy State University, 100 University Ave, Montgomery. www.bluegrayfootball.com.* This classic football game between North and South college senior all-stars was first played in 1939. The game was the brainchild of Champ Pickens, an Alabama football manager and promoter, but was acquired by the Montgomery Lions Club in 1955. Since then, the proceeds of each game are donated to Lions Club charities. Dec 25. **$$$$**

Jubilee City Fest. *640 S McDonough St, Montgomery (36104). Downtown. www.jubileecityfest.org.* This festival features national musical acts as well as cultural events and children's activities. Memorial Day weekend.

Southeastern Livestock Exposition and Rodeo. *Garrett Coliseum, 1555 Federal Dr, Montgomery (36107). Phone 334/265-1867.* Some of the nation's best cowboys and cowgirls compete in this PRCA event, the largest rodeo east of the Mississippi. Mid-Mar.

Limited-Service Hotels

★ **COMFORT SUITES.** *5924 Monticello Dr, Montgomery (36117). Phone 334/272-1013; fax 334/260-0425.* 49 rooms, 3 story, all suites. Complimentary continental breakfast. Check-out noon. Fitness room. Outdoor pool. **$**
🏃 🖼️

★ **FAIRFIELD INN.** *5601 Carmichael Rd, Montgomery (36117). Phone 205/270-0007; toll-free 800/228-2800; fax 205/270-0007. www.fairfieldinn.com.* 133 rooms, 3 story. Complimentary continental breakfast. Check-out noon. Outdoor pool. **$**
🖼️

★ ★ **HOLIDAY INN.** *1185 Eastern Bypass, Montgomery (36117). Phone 334/272-0370; toll-free 800/465-4329; fax 334/270-1046. www.holiday-inn.com.* 211 rooms, 2 story. Pets accepted, some restrictions; fee. Check-out noon. Restaurant, bar. Fitness room. Indoor pool, whirlpool. **$**
🔖 🏃 🖼️

★ **LA QUINTA INN.** *1280 Eastern Blvd, Montgomery (36117). Phone 334/271-1620; toll-free 800/531-5980; fax 334/244-7919. www.laquinta.com.* 130 rooms, 2 story. Pets accepted. Complimentary continental breakfast. Check-out noon. Outdoor pool. **$**
🔖 🖼️

★ **RAMADA INN.** *1355 East Blvd, Montgomery (36117). Phone 334/277-2200; toll-free 800/240-2200;*

fax 334/277-2200. www.ramada.com. 152 rooms, 2 story. Complimentary full breakfast. Check-out noon. Bar. Outdoor pool. **$**

★ ★ **RAMADA INN.** *1100 W South Blvd, Montgomery (36105). Phone 334/281-1660; toll-free 800/272-6232; fax 334/281-1667. www.ramada.com.* 150 rooms, 4 story. Pets accepted, some restrictions; fee. Check-out noon. Restaurant, bar. Outdoor pool. Airport transportation available. **$**

Specialty Lodgings

The following lodging establishments are approved by Mobil Travel Guide, but due to their unique and individualized nature have not been given a traditional Mobil Star rating. Included in this listing you may find bed-and-breakfasts, limited-service inns, guest ranches, and other unique hotel properties.

LATTICE INN. *1414 S Hull St, Montgomery (36104). Phone 334/832-9931.* Located in historic Garden District this home was built in 1906 and is furnished with antiques and family pieces. A large Southern breakfast is served each morning. 4 rooms, 2 story. **$**

RED BLUFF COTTAGE BED. *551 Clay St, Montgomery (36101). Phone 334/264-0056; toll-free 888/551-2529. www.redbluffcottage.com.* 19th century Victorian cottage located in downtown Montgomery featuring a large Southern breakfast. 6 rooms, 3 story. **$**

Restaurants

★ ★ **ALA THAI.** *1361 Federal Dr, Montgomery (36114). Phone 334/262-5830.* Authentic cuisine with an emphasis on noodle dishes in a romantic environment. Thai menu. Lunch, dinner. **$**

★ **MARTHA'S PLACE.** *458 Sayre St, Montgomery (36104). Phone 334/263-9135.* Classic soul food restaurant in a homelike setting. Famous for fried chicken. Southern/Soul menu. Breakfast, lunch. Closed Sat-Sun. **$**

★ ★ ★ **VINTAGE YEAR.** *405 Cloverdale Rd, Montgomery (36106). Phone 334/264-8463; fax 334/269-5700.* Located in Montgomery's historic Cloverdale District, this restaurant serves unique appetizers and desserts. Modern décor with intimate lighting makes it a great spot for a romantic dinner. Seafood menu. Dinner. Closed Sun-Mon; holidays. Bar. **$$**

Amelia Island, FL

2 hours 20 minutes, 130 miles from Savannah, GA

Population 7,250
Elevation 10 ft
Area Code 904
Zip 32035
Information Amelia Island Tourist Development Council, 102 Centre St, PO Box 472, Fernandina Beach 32035; phone toll-free 800/226-3542
Web Site www.ameliaisland.org

Amelia Island is separated from the mainland by the St. Mary's River on the north, the Amelia River Intracoastal Waterway on the west, and Nassau Sound on the south. Cumberland Island and the Georgia coast can be seen from the north shore.

What to See and Do

Amelia Island Plantation. *6800 First Coast Hwy, Amelia Island (32034). Phone 904/261-6161; toll-free 888/261-6161. www.aipfl.com.* Features 54 championship holes. Tom Fazio designed the par-72 Long Point course (6,775 yards); Pete Dye designed the par-72 Oak Marsh course (6,502 yards); and Bobby Weed and Pete Dye designed the par-70 Ocean Links course (6,200 yards).

Full-Service Resorts

★ ★ ★ **AMELIA ISLAND PLANTATION INN.** *6800 First Coast Hwy, Amelia Island (32035). Phone 904/277-5192; fax 904/277-5945.* This sprawling 1,300-acre resort boasts panoramic views of the Atlantic Ocean. Kids and parents will appreciate the extensive recreation program that can be tailored to individual interests. There are several restaurants that exploit the bountiful Florida produce and have stunning ocean views. 905 rooms, 6 story. Pets accepted; fee. Check-in 4 pm, check-out 11 am. High-speed Internet access, wireless Internet access. Seven restaurants, three bars. Children's activity center. Fitness room, fitness classes available, spa. Beach. 23 indoor/outdoor pools, children's pool, whirlpool. Golf, 54 holes. Tennis. Business center. **$$**

★ ★ ★ **THE RITZ-CARLTON, AMELIA ISLAND.** *4750 Amelia Island Pkwy, Amelia Island (32034). Phone 904/277-1100; toll-free 800/241-3333;*

fax 904/261-9064. www.ritzcarlton.com. The Ritz-Carlton is Amelia Island's premier resort. Nestled in the wild dunes of a barrier island off Florida's northeastern coast, this resort captures the essence of this magical place, where time seems to stand still and leisurely pursuits are the order of the day. The guest rooms, characterized by floral prints and pastel colors, share a casual elegance with occupants, and coastal or ocean views are available from all accommodations. An array of activities entices guests away from their lounge chairs, including tennis, golf, swimming, and water sports. Horseback riding is available on the beach, and the resort even has its own 19th-century replica sailing schooner for day sails. Fernandina Beach, a quaint Victoria area with specialty boutiques, is just down the road and not to be missed. The resort's six restaurants and lounges offer cures for empty stomachs with a variety of delicious specialties. 449 rooms, 8 story. Check-in 3 pm, check-out noon. Restaurant, bar. Children's activity center. Fitness room. Indoor pool, outdoor pool, whirlpool. Golf. Tennis. Airport transportation available. Business center. **$$$**

Full-Service Inns

★ ★ ★ **1857 FLORIDA HOUSE INN.** *20 S 3rd St, Amelia Island (32034). Phone 904/261-3300; toll-free 800/258-3301; fax 904/277-3831. www.floridahouseinn.com.* This gem on the National Register of Historic Places is in the heart of the Fernandina Beach Historic District and is Florida's oldest surviving hotel. Operating since 1857, this inn is only 2 miles from the Atlantic Ocean and features a wraparound veranda with rocking chairs. 17 rooms, 2 story. Pets accepted; fee. Complimentary full breakfast. Check-in 2 pm, check-out 11 am. Restaurant, bar. **$$**

★ ★ ★ **ELIZABETH POINTE LODGE.** *98 S Fletcher Ave, Amelia Island (32034). Phone 904/277-4851; toll-free 800/772-3359; fax 904/277-6500. www.elizabethpointelodge.com.* The glorious main house perched on the Amelia Island sand is 1890s "Nantucket Shingle-style" with a wraparound porch and plenty of rocking chairs. Enjoy a walk to the barrier island sand dunes. 25 rooms, 3 story. Complimentary full breakfast. Check-in 3 pm, check-out 11 am. High-speed Internet access. Restaurant. Beach. **$$**

Specialty Lodgings

The following lodging establishments are approved by Mobil Travel Guide, but due to their unique and individualized nature have not been given a traditional Mobil Star rating. Included in this listing you may find bed-and-breakfasts, limited-service inns, guest ranches, and other unique hotel properties.

AMELIA ISLAND WILLIAMS HOUSE. *103 S 9th St, Amelia Island (32034). Phone 904/277-2328; toll-free 800/414-9258; fax 904/321-1325. www.williamshouse.com.* A 149-year-old antebellum mansion houses this National Historic inn. The courtyard and English gardens are only one reason it is one of the island's most charming places to stay. 11 rooms, 2 story. Children over 12 years only. Complimentary full breakfast. Check-in 3 pm, check-out 11 am. **$$**

BAILEY HOUSE. *28 S 7th St, Fernandina Beach (32034). Phone 904/261-5390; toll-free 800/251-5390; fax 904/321-0103. www.bailey-house.com.* This Amelia Island Victorian inn was built in 1895 by Kate and Effingham Bailey and is on the National Register of Historic Places. The rooms have original woodwork, stained glass, and 19th-century antiques. 10 rooms, 2 story. Children over 8 years only. Complimentary full breakfast. Check-in 3 pm, check-out 11 am. **$**

FAIRBANKS HOUSE. *227 S 7th St, Amelia Island (32034). Phone 904/277-0500; toll-free 888/261-4888; fax 904/277-3103. www.fairbankshouse.com.* Canopy and four-poster beds, fireplaces, and other indulgent amenities are standard throughout this inn, which is just minutes from the beach and the center of the quaint, historic town. 12 rooms, 3 story. Children over 12 years only. Complimentary full breakfast. Check-in 3 pm, check-out 11 am. Outdoor pool. **$$$**

GOODBREAD HOUSE B AND B. *209 Osborne St, Saint Marys (31558). Phone 912/882-7490. www.eagnet.com/goodbread.* Built in 1872 as a hotel. 5 rooms, 2 story. Pets accepted. Complimentary full breakfast. Check-in 2 pm, check-out noon. **$**

SPENCER HOUSE INN BED & BREAKFAST. *200 Osborne St, Saint Marys (31558). Phone 912/882-1872; toll-free 888/840-1872; fax 912/882-9427. www.spencerhouseinn.com.* Built in 1872 as a hotel. 14 rooms, 3 story. Complimentary full breakfast. Check-in 3-7 pm, check-out 11 am. **$$**

Restaurants

★ ★ **BRETT'S WATERWAY CAFE.** *1 S Front St, Amelia Island (32034). Phone 904/261-2660; fax 904/ 261-2838.* Seafood, steak menu. Lunch, dinner. Closed holidays. Bar. Children's menu (dinner). **$$**

★ ★ ★ ★ **THE GRILL.** *4750 Amelia Island Pkwy, Amelia Island (32034). Phone 904/277-1100; toll-free 800/241-3333; fax 904/277-1145. www.ritzcarlton.com.* The Grill may sound like a local joint to pick up juicy, greasy burgers with golden fries and perhaps a nice, cold pint of beer, but the food here is a bit more, shall we say, refined. This grill is the flagship restaurant of the Ritz-Carlton (see) on Amelia Island, where you'll be hard-pressed to find anything resembling a burger on the restaurant's haute menu. This is not to say that you will be disappointed. Quite the opposite. You'll be treated to a stellar selection of seasonal, contemporary French fare tinged with global flavors. The tasteful, formal dining room is marked by its panoramic views of the Atlantic, a breathtaking sight. Romance is easy here, which makes a seat at a window table in the dining room a nice choice for couples who long to gaze into each other's eyes. Those past the butterflies stage will also be happy, as the room is well appointed and comfortable and makes a great choice for friends and family to gather. The wine list features about 500 selections, so there should be no issue with lack of options here. French menu. Dinner. Closed Mon. Bar. Business casual attire. Reservations recommended. Valet parking. **$$$**

★ ★ **HORIZONS.** *802 Ash St, Amelia Island (32034). Phone 904/321-2430; fax 904/321-2432.* American menu. Dinner. Closed Sun. Bar. **$$**

Jacksonville, FL

2 hours 20 minutes, 140 miles from Savannah, GA

Settled 1822
Population 735,617
Elevation 19 ft
Area Code 904
Information Jacksonville and the Beaches Convention & Visitors Bureau, 201 E Adams St, 32202; phone 904/798-9111 or toll-free 800/733-2668
Web Site www.jaxcvb.com

Jacksonville, once primarily an industrial and maritime Southern city, now has a sparkling skyline of skyscrapers; yet the city is still graced with tropical scenery, white sandy beaches, and a certain Southern flavor and heritage. The Riverwalk near the St. Johns River, Jacksonville's financial focal point, and the Jacksonville Landing, a festive marketplace with events and entertainment, are two manifestations of the city's new modern, prosperous image.

Draped around an S curve of the broad St. Johns River, Jacksonville is a major tourist and business center in Florida. The river is the hub for cruise boats and sightseeing excursions. Although 12 miles inland from the mouth of the river, Jacksonville berths freighters, ocean liners, and a fleet of shrimp boats.

Under the British flag, Jacksonville was known as Cowford, a name that persisted until the purchase of Florida by the United States, when the town was renamed for Andrew Jackson. In the peace following the Seminole War, the city emerged as a prosperous and boisterous harbor town. Jacksonville was occupied by Union troops four times during the Civil War, but emerged during the Reconstruction period as a popular winter resort.

Public Transportation

Airport. **Jacksonville International Airport.** Information phone 904/741-4902; lost and found phone 904/741-2040; weather phone 904/741-4311.

Buses Jacksonville Transportation Authority, phone 904/630-3100.

What to See and Do

Anheuser-Busch Brewery Tour. *111 Busch Dr, Jacksonville (32218). N via I-95 toward airport. Phone 904/751-8117. www.budweisertours.com.* Tours of brewery conclude in Hospitality Room for beer tasting. Guided and self-guided tours. (Mon-Sat 9 am-4 pm; closed Jan 1, Thanksgiving, Dec 25) **FREE**

The *Annabelle Lee.* *1511 Montana Ave, Jacksonville (32207). Phone 904/396-2333.* Tours on the St. Johns River aboard 300-passenger cruise ship. Lunch, dinner, and sightseeing cruises. (Fri-Sun; schedule varies rest of week; closed Dec 25)

Cummer Museum of Art & Gardens. *829 Riverside Ave, Jacksonville (32204). Phone 904/356-6857. www.cummer.org.* Contains 14 galleries and the Tudor Room from the original Cummer Mansion. The mansion's formal gardens (2 1/2 acres) were retained as setting for the gallery. Collection ranges

Downtown Jacksonville

Downtown Jacksonville, along the St. Johns River, has been developing for decades into a lively destination for shopping, dining, and culture—something for everyone in the family. Begin on the Northbank at Jacksonville Landing (2 Independent Drive off Main St), an industrial-design place to eat, shop at more than 65 outlets, or just stroll along the waterfront and learn about history from commemorative plaques. If you have kids, take them to the second floor of the complex to enjoy virtual reality games and fastfood while you drink in the view. They will also love the new Kids Kampus, an interactive park with kid-sized streetscapes, cool play toys, and splash pools near Metropolitan Park to the east. (Follow Northbank Riverwalk to Liberty Street and turn right on Bay Street to get there.) More awaits on Southbank, which you can reach via water taxi from Jacksonville Landing. Southbank Riverbank is a linear boardwalk park that leads to three museums. Stop for lunch or dinner at River City Brewing Co. (835 Museum Cir), overlooking the river with great,

exciting food and a lively atmosphere. Then head east, past Friendship Fountain and boats bobbing in the marina. The boardwalk takes you under the Main Street bridge to Jacksonville Maritime Museum (1015 Museum Cir), where you can explore Jacksonville's rich maritime past through models and photographs. Continue along the boardwalk to Jacksonville Historical Center, a small, homey museum that traces Jacksonville's colonial-era importance through to its naval role in World War II. The best of the museums, the Museum of Science and History, lies just around the corner at 1025 Museum Circle. It has hands-on exhibits for kids of every age, including a treehouse for toddlers and a cool marine mammals exhibit and aircraft carrier simulator. Upstairs, the peek at history focuses on Civil War days. If you want to see a really huge tree, walk along Riverplace Boulevard (behind the museum) to Flagler Avenue and turn right on Prudential Drive to Jessie Ball duPont Park. The park is home to Treaty Oak, which is believed to be 200 years old.

from ancient Egypt to the 20th century and features 700 pieces of early Meissen porcelain and important American paintings. Interactive exhibits. (Tues, Thurs 10 am-9 pm, Wed, Fri-Sat to 5 pm, Sun from noon; closed holidays) **$$**

Jacksonville Jaguars (NFL). *Alltel Stadium, 1 Alltel Stadium Pl, Jacksonville (32202). Phone 904/633-6000. www.jaguars.com.*

Jacksonville University. *2800 University Blvd N, Jacksonville (32211). On E bank of St. Johns River. Phone 904/744-3950. www.ju.edu.* (1934) (2,300 students) This 260-acre riverfront campus houses the library of the Jacksonville Historical Society and Charter Marine Science Center. Delius House is the restored house of British composer Frederick Delius (1862-1934) (daily, by request). Also here is

Alexander Brest Museum. *2800 University Blvd N, Jacksonville (32211). Phone 904/745-7371.* Contains large collection of European and Asian ivory; changing exhibits of painting, pottery, weaving, sculpture; collections of pre-Columbian artifacts; Steuben glass. (Mon-Fri; closed holidays) **FREE**

Jacksonville Zoological Gardens. *8605 Zoo Pkwy, Jacksonville (32218). Via Heckscher Dr, off I-95. Phone 904/757-4462. www.jaxzoo.org.* More than 700 mammals, birds, and reptiles in natural environments along the Trout River. Train ride; animal shows; restaurant. (Daily 9 am-5 pm; closed Thanksgiving, Dec 25) **$$**

Kingsley Plantation. *11676 Palmetto Ave, Jacksonville (32226). N on Hwy A1A, on Fort George Island; reached by ferry from Mayport or via Hwy 105 (Heckscher Dr). Phone 904/251-3537.* Plantation house, kitchen house, barn, and tabby slave houses reflect 19th-century life on a Sea Island cotton plantation. Ranger programs (seasonal). A National Park Service area. (Daily 9 am-5 pm; closed Dec 25) **FREE**

Little Talbot Island State Park. *12157 Heckscher Dr, Jacksonville (32226). 17 miles NE on Hwy A1A. Phone 904/251-2320. www.floridastateparks.org/ littletalbotisland.* More than 2,500 acres of wide Atlantic beaches and extensive salt marshes teem with life, including migrating birds and sea turtles. Sand dunes, forests. Swimming, surfing, fishing; picnicking, playground, camping (hook-ups, dump station). (Daily 8 am-sundown) **$**

Museum of Science and History. *1025 Museum Cir, Jacksonville (32207). Phone 904/396-7062. www.themosh.org.* Interactive exhibits on science, marine mammals, and north Florida history, including the natural and physical sciences, wildlife, Native Americans, and Civil War artifacts from battleship *Maple Leaf.* Free planetarium, science, and reptile shows. (Mon-Fri 10 am-5 pm, Sat to 6 pm, Sun 1-6 pm; closed holidays) **$$**

Special Events

Delius Festival. *Jacoby Symphony Hall, 300 W Water St, Jacksonville (32202). Phone 904/389-0587. www.jaxsymphony.org/concerts/calendar.* Event features works by the late 19th-century British-born composer who had lived in Jacksonville; performances by various musical groups; lectures; exhibits. Early Mar. **$$$$**

Gator Bowl. *Alltel Stadium, 1 Alltel Stadium Pl, Jacksonville (32202). Phone 904/798-1700. www.gatorbowl.com.* One of the major college football bowl games. Jan 1.

Great American Jazz Piano Competition. *Florida Theatre, 128 E Forsyth St, Jacksonville (32202). Phone 904/630-3690. www.coj.net.* Come and watch five of the world's best amateur jazz pianists play and compete for the chance to perform in the annual Jacksonville Jazz Festival. Apr.

Greyhound racing. Jacksonville Kennel Club. *1440 N McDuff Ave, Jacksonville (32254). Phone 904/646-0001. www.jaxkennel.com.* Nightly Mon, Wed-Sun; matinees Wed, Sat-Sun. Also at **Orange Park Kennel Club,** 445 Park Ave, in Orange Park, and **St. Johns Greyhound Park,** 6322 Racetrack Rd in Bayard.

Historic Home Tour. *2623 Herschel St, Jacksonville (32204). Phone 904/389-2449.* Tour representing work of locally prominent architects and builders between 1870 and 1930. Mid-May.

Riverside Art Festival. *2523 Herschel St, Jacksonville (32204). Phone 904/389-2449.* Juried art show in a variety of media; food, entertainment. Mid-Sept.

Limited-Service Hotels

★ **BEST INN.** *8220 Dix Ellis Trail, Jacksonville (32256). Phone 904/739-3323; toll-free 800/237-8466; fax 904/739-3323. www.bestinn.com.* 109 rooms, 2 story. Pets accepted, some restrictions; fee. Complimentary continental breakfast. Check-out noon. Outdoor pool. **$**

★ ★ **COURTYARD BY MARRIOTT.** *4600 San Pablo Rd, Jacksonville (32224). Phone 904/223-1700; toll-free 800/321-2211; fax 904/223-1026. www.courtyard.com.* This hotel is an easy drive from many of Jacksonville's attractions, including the beaches and Sawgrass. It is also adjacent to the Mayo Clinic at Jacksonville. 146 rooms, 3 story. Check-out noon. Restaurant, bar. Fitness room. Outdoor pool, whirlpool. **$**

★ ★ **DOUBLETREE HOTEL.** *4700 Salisbury Rd, Jacksonville (32256). Phone 904/281-9700; fax 904/281-1957. www.doubletree.com.* Located in the Southpoint business district, this hotel is easily accessible to downtown, Jacksonville Municipal Stadium, shopping, and nightlife, as well as Jacksonville's magnificent beaches. 167 rooms, 6 story. Check-in 3 pm, check-out 11 pm. Restaurant, bar. Fitness room. Outdoor pool, whirlpool. **$**

★ ★ **EMBASSY SUITES.** *9300 Baymeadows Rd, Jacksonville (32256). Phone 904/731-3555; toll-free 800/362-2779; fax 904/731-4972. www.embassysuites.com.* 277 rooms, 7 story, all suites. Complimentary full breakfast. Check-out noon. Restaurant, bar. Fitness room. Indoor pool, whirlpool. Business center. **$**

★ **HAMPTON INN.** *1331 Prudential Dr, Jacksonville (32077). Phone 904/396-7770; toll-free 800/426-7866; fax 904/396-8044. www.hampton-inn.com.* 118 rooms, 5 story. Complimentary continental breakfast. Check-out noon. Outdoor pool. **$**

★ ★ **HOLIDAY INN.** *9150 Baymeadows Rd, Jacksonville (32256). Phone 904/737-1700; toll-free 800/828-1191; fax 904/737-0207. www.holiday-inn.com.* Only 10 miles from downtown Jacksonville. 240 rooms, 4 story. Pets accepted. Check-out noon. Restaurant, bar. Fitness room. Outdoor pool. **$**

★ ★ **HOLIDAY INN.** *14670 Duval Rd, Jacksonville (32256). Phone 904/741-4404; toll-free 800/465-4329; fax 904/741-4907. www.holiday-inn.com.* 489 rooms, 6 story. Pets accepted. Check-out noon. Restaurant, bar. Fitness room. Indoor pool, outdoor pool. Tennis. Business center. **$**

★ **HOMEWOOD SUITES JACKSONVILLE-BAYMEADOWS.** *8737 Baymeadows Rd, Jacksonville (32256). Phone 904/733-9299; fax 904/448-5889.* 116 rooms, 3 story, all suites. Pets accepted; fee. Complimentary continental breakfast. Check-in 3 pm, check-out noon. Fitness room. Outdoor pool, whirlpool. Business center. **$**

★ ★ **RADISSON RIVERWALK HOTEL.** *1515 Prudential Dr, Jacksonville (32207). Phone 904/396-5100; toll-free 800/333-3333; fax 904/396-7154. www.radisson.com.* Set on the beautiful St. John's River, this hotel's guest rooms offer stunning riverfront views. The beaches are just a few minutes away. 322 rooms, 5 story. Check-out noon. High-speed Internet access. Restaurant, bar. Fitness room. Outdoor pool. Tennis. Business center. **$**

★ ★ **RAMADA INN MANDARIN.** *3130 Hartley Rd, Jacksonville (32257). Phone 904/268-8080; toll-free 800/393-1117; fax 904/262-8718. www.ramada-inn.com.* 152 rooms, 2 story. Pets accepted; fee. Complimentary full breakfast. Check-out noon. Restaurant, bar. Outdoor pool, children's pool. **$**

Full-Service Hotels

★ ★ ★ **HILTON JACKSONVILLE RIVERFRONT.** *1201 Riverplace Blvd, Jacksonville (32207). Phone 904/398-8800; toll-free 800/774-1500; fax 904/398-9170. www.hiltonjacksonville.com.* Located on 3.8 acres along the south bank of the St. Johns River on Riverplace Boulevard. Convenient to the Riverwalk, Prime Osborn Convention Center, Jacksonville International Airport, Jacksonville Landing, and historic San Marco. 292 rooms, 10 story. Check-out 11 am. Restaurant, bar. Fitness room. Outdoor pool, whirlpool. Airport transportation available. Business center. **$**

★ ★ ★ **OMNI JACKSONVILLE HOTEL.** *245 Water St, Jacksonville (32202). Phone 904/355-6664; toll-free 800/843-6664; fax 904/791-4812. www.omnihotels.com.* A heated rooftop pool and sundeck overlooking the St. Johns River is not to be missed during your stay at this high-rise hotel in downtown Jacksonville. 348 rooms, 16 story. Check-out noon. Restaurant, bar. Fitness room. Outdoor pool. Tennis. **$$**

Restaurants

★ **ALHAMBRA DINNER THEATRE.** *12000 Beach Blvd, Jacksonville (32246). Phone 904/641-1212; toll-free 800/668-7469; fax 904/642-3505. www.alhambradinnertheatre.com.* American menu. Dinner. Closed Mon; Jan 1, Dec 25. Bar. Reservations recommended. **$$$**

★ **CRAWDADDY'S.** *1643 Prudential Dr, Jacksonville (32207). Phone 904/396-3546; fax 904/396-5292.* On the St. John's River. Seafood menu. Lunch, dinner, brunch. Bars. Children's menu. Outdoor seating. **$$**

★ ★ **MARKER 32.** *14549 Beach Blvd, Jacksonville (32225). Phone 904/223-1534; fax 904/223-7763.* Friendly, khaki-clad service staff serve fresh fish at this casual, unassuming spot on the Intracoastal Waterway. Fresh-baked breads are offered daily alongside dishes like oysters with spinach, sun-dried tomatoes and Pecorino, or pan-fried red snapper over okra and tomatoes. Seafood menu. Dinner. Closed holidays. Bar. **$$**

★ ★ ★ **MATTHEW'S.** *2107 Hendricks Ave, Jacksonville (32207). Phone 904/396-9922; fax 904/396-5222. www.matthewsatsanmarco.com.* Guests leave Matthew's with one thought on their minds: "When can I come back and do this all over again?" It is the sort of place that, unfortunately, gets relegated to special-occasion dining, but really should be enjoyed more frequently if at all possible. You can choose to dine à la carte or treat yourself to the chef's tasting menu with either three or five courses. Either way, you won't have a problem licking your plates clean of chef/owner Matthew Medure's palate-pleasing fare. The sleek, sexy dining room, swathed in soft moss tones with terrazzo floors inlaid with bronze, was originally built as a bank in the 1920s. Chefs pirouette around the open kitchen (a granite food bar that seats four offers a front-and-center view of the action), while relaxed diners recline in luxurious comfort as dinner is served. The chef takes care to select organically grown vegetables and attempts to source most produce and meat from local boutique farms. The menu is divided among Appetizers, The Garden & Tureen (salads and soups), The Sea, and The Farm (poultry, beef, lamb, and game). Southern, Mediterranean, Asian, and Middle Eastern accents play well together on the plates. The food is thoughtful, complex, and brilliant. The wine list offers more than 420 selections, and the staff is approachable and gifted at helping with pairings. The service is the perfect balance of knowledge, efficiency, and charm. Matthew's is a distinctive and singular dining experience, and you should make every effort to fit it into your travel schedule at least once. International/Fusion menu. Dinner. Closed Sun. Jacket required. **$$$**

★ ★ ★ **MORTON'S, THE STEAKHOUSE.** *1510 Riverplace Blvd, Jacksonville (32207). Phone 904/399-3933. www.mortons.com.* Steak menu. Dinner. Bar. **$$$**

★ **PAGODA CHINESE RESTAURANT.** *8617 Baymeadows Rd, Jacksonville (32256). Phone 904/731-0880; fax 904/241-0414.* Chinese menu. Lunch, dinner. Closed Sun; Thanksgiving, Dec 25. Bar. **$**

★ **SEBASTIAN'S.** *10601 San Jose Blvd, Jacksonville (32257). Phone 904/268-4458; fax 904/268-4458.* Italian menu. Dinner. Closed Mon; holidays. Children's menu. **$$**

★ ★ ★ **STERLING'S OF AVONDALE.** *3551 St. Johns Ave, Jacksonville (32205). Phone 904/387-0700; fax 904/388-1660.* This candlelit dining room has a long-standing reputation in the Avondale shopping district. Gaze at oil paintings inside or enjoy the open-air courtyard setting. American menu. Lunch, dinner. Bar. Outdoor seating. **$$$**

Tallahassee, FL

5 1/2 hours, 274 miles from Atlanta, GA

Founded 1824
Population 150,624
Elevation 190 ft
Area Code 850
Information Tallahassee Area Convention and Visitors Bureau, 106 E Jefferson St, 32301; phone 850/413-9200 or toll-free 800/628-2866
Web Site www.co.leon.fl.us/visitors/index.htm

The capital of Florida, Tallahassee retains the grace of plantation days and the echoes of its rustic pioneer past. During the Civil War this majestic city was the only Confederate capital east of the Mississippi not captured by Union forces. The city, as well as Leon County, are now strongly oriented toward state and local government. Lumber and wood production, food production, printing, and publishing maintain its economy.

What to See and Do

Alfred B. Maclay Gardens State Park. *3540 Thomasville Rd, Tallahassee (32309). 5 1/2 miles N on Hwy 319. Phone 850/487-4556. www.floridastateparks.org.* Planted as a private estate garden; outstanding azaleas, camellias, dogwood, and others, including some rare plant species, on 308 acres; donated to the state in 1953. Museum in house has an interpretive display (Jan-Apr). No dogs. The Lake Hall Recreation area has swimming, fishing, boating; nature trails, biking, horsebacking riding, gardens, picnicking. (Daily 8 am-sunset) **$**

The Columns. *100 N Duval St, Tallahassee (32301). Phone 850/224-8116.* (1830) Moved from its original site in 1972, this three-story brick mansion once served as a bank, boarding house, doctor's office, and restaurant. Restored and furnished with antiques, it now serves as the office of the Chamber of Commerce. (Mon-Fri)

First Presbyterian Church. *110 N Adams St, Tallahassee (32301). Phone 850/222-4504. www.oldfirstchurch.org.* (1832) Florida's oldest public building in continuous use; has galleries where slaves worshiped. (Mon-Fri; closed holidays)

Florida Agricultural and Mechanical University. *M. L. King Blvd and Wahnish Way, Tallahassee (32301). Phone 850/599-3000. www.famu.edu.* (1887) (9,300 students) On campus is the Florida Black Archives, Research Center, and Museum (Mon-Fri; closed holidays).

Florida State University. *University Center B, W Tennessee and Copeland sts, Tallahassee (32304). Phone 850/644-3246. www.fsu.edu.* (1851) (35,462 students) On a 400-acre campus with everything from two supercomputers to its own collegiate circus (see SPECIAL EVENTS). Campus tours (Mon-Fri); maps at Visitor Services. On campus is

Museum of Fine Arts. *Fine Arts Building, Copeland and W Tennessee sts, Tallahassee (32304). Phone 850/644-6836.* (Sept-May: daily; rest of year: Mon-Fri; closed school holidays) **FREE**

Goodwood Museum and Gardens. *1600 Miccosukee Rd, Tallahassee (32308). Phone 850/877-4202.* 19 acres of vintage buildings and Old South lawns and gardens. (Mon-Fri 10 am-3:30 pm, Sat 10 am-2 pm) **$**

Governor's Mansion. *700 N Adams St, Tallahassee (32303). Phone 850/488-4661.* (1957) Tours during

The Capitol District

Florida's state capital boasts a gracious Southern personality and little of the metropolitan bustle associated with most state capitals. Downtown's capitol and historic districts make for a delightful stroll where government-at-work bustle is tempered by Southern good manners. Begin at Capitol Square, bordered by South Monroe, West Pensacola Street, and South Duval Street. Here the past and present juxtapose architecturally where the old Greek Revival-style capitol stands next to the sleek, modern 22-story skyscraper. Take the elevator to the top of the new capitol for a 360-degree view of Tallahassee. On a clear day, you can see all the way to Georgia! In the first floor lobby at the West Plaza entrance, grab information about touring the city, including a walking guide to downtown. Among the cluster of government buildings at the capitol's base, you'll find the Capital Cultural Center (350 S Duval St), home to the Museum of Art, which showcases permanent and traveling exhibits, and the interactive educational fun of Odyssey Science Center. West of the capitol complex a couple blocks, at the corner of South Bronough Street and West Pensacola Street, the Museum of Florida History takes you on a journey that begins in prehistoric times. Adams Street Commons, a brick-paved block between Pensacola Street and College Avenue, is lined with interesting shops and restaurants where members of Congress hang out by day, university students by night. Head north to the Chain of Parks along Park Avenue National Register Historic District. At its western end, Old City Cemetery is an example of a plantation-era segregated graveyard, where slaves were separated from the tombs of the town's plantation owners and other white population. Along the park's lovely landscaped length, several historic sites recall eras past. Among those you can visit, Knot House Museum, 301 East Park Avenue, is one of the most unusual. Known as "the House that Rhymes," the Victorian home has poems, penned by former resident Luella Knot, attached to pieces of furniture. Also open to the public within the historic district are LeMoyne Art Foundation (125 N Gadsden St), Murphy House (317 E Park Ave), David S. Walker Library (209 E Park Ave), The Columns (100 N Duval St), and St. John's Episcopal Cemetery (Call St and Martin Luther King Blvd).

regular session of legislature (Mar-May: Mon, Wed, Fri 10 am-noon; closed holidays). **FREE**

LeMoyne Art Foundation. *125 N Gadsden St, Tallahassee (32301). Phone 850/222-8800. www.lemoyne.org.* Features works by Florida and Georgia artists. (Tues-Sat 10 am-5 pm, Sun from 1 pm; closed July 4, Dec 25-Jan 1; also last week in Aug)

Mary Brogan Museum of Art and Science. *350 S Duval St, Tallahassee (32301). Phone 850/513-0700. www.thebrogan.org.* Three floors of interactive experience include the museum's permanent collection and featured traveling presentations—Dali to dinosaurs, Picasso to plants. Exhibitions change every three months and cover a diverse range of topics. For all ages; group rates available. (Mon-Sat 10 am-5 pm, Sun from 1 pm) **$$**

Museum of Florida History. *500 S Bronough St, Tallahassee (32399). At Pensacola St. Phone 850/488-1484.* Contains historical artifacts and information about Florida; changing exhibits. (Mon-Fri 9 am-4:30 pm, Sat from 10 am, Sun from noon; closed Thanksgiving, Dec 25) **FREE**

Natural Bridge Battlefield Historic State Park. *1022 Desoto Park Dr, Tallahassee (32301). 9 miles S on Hwy 363 to Woodville, then 6 miles E on Natural Bridge Rd. Phone 850/922-6007. www.floridastateparks.org.* This 8-acre monument on the St. Marks River marks the spot where a militia of Confederate forces (mostly young boys and old men) stopped Union troops, barring the way to Tallahassee. The battle, which took place on March 6, 1865, left Tallahassee as the only Confederate capital east of the Mississippi that never fell into Union hands. Picnicking. (See SPECIAL EVENTS) (Daily 8 am-sunset) **FREE**

Old Capitol Museum. *S Monroe St and Apalachee Pkwy, Tallahassee (32399). Phone 850/487-1902.* Restored to its 1902 grandeur, the building is now a museum, furnished with authentic period pieces and reproductions of original furniture. Historical exhibits; architectural tours (Sat mornings). (Mon-Fri 9 am-4:30 pm, Sat from 10 am, Sun from noon; closed Thanksgiving, Dec 25) **FREE**

San Marcos de Apalache Historic State Park. *148 Old Fort Rd, St. Marks (32355). 24 miles S via Hwy 363. Phone 850/925-6216.* This site was first visited by Panfilo de Narvaez in 1527 and Hernando de Soto in 1539; ruins of a fort (1739); museum on the site of an old federal marine hospital. Picnicking, nature trails. (Daily) **$**

St. Marks National Wildlife Refuge. *15 miles S on Hwy 363 to St. Marks, then 3 miles S on County Rd 59. Phone 850/925-6121. saintmarks.fws.gov.* A 65,000-acre refuge heavily populated with birds, deer, alligators, and waterfowl in fall and winter. Freshwater fishing, saltwater boat launching; nature and primitive walking trails, picnicking, visitor center (daily; closed holidays). Observation decks. Golden Eagle, Golden Age, Golden Access passports accepted (see MAKING THE MOST OF YOUR TRIP). (Mon-Fri 8:15 am-4:15 pm, Sat-Sun 10 am-5 pm) **$**

State Capitol. *400 S Monroe St, Tallahassee (32301). Phone 850/488-6167.* At the top of Tallahassee's second-highest hill, the modern, 22-story capitol building towers above the city; observation level on top floor. **FREE**

Tallahassee Antique Car Museum. *3550 Mahan Dr, Tallahassee (32308). Phone 850/942-0137. www.tacm.com.* More than 85 rare automobiles, the original Batmobiles, pedal cars, boat motors dating to 1908, Indian artifacts, motorcycles, cash registers, golf collections, and more. (Mon-Sat 10 am-5 pm, Sun from noon) **$$**

Tallahassee Museum of History & Natural Science. *3945 Museum Dr, Tallahassee (32310). On Lake Bradford. Phone 850/575-8684. tallahasseemuseum.org.* Fifty-two acres with restored 1880s Big Bend farm and 1854 plantation house; gristmill, schoolhouse, church; hands-on Discovery Center; natural habitat zoo with wild animals native to the area, including the endangered Florida panther; gopher nature trail. Visitor center. (See SPECIAL EVENTS) (Mon-Sat 9 am-5 pm, Sun 12:30-5 pm; closed Thanksgiving, Dec 25) **$$**

Wakulla Springs State Park. *550 Wakulla Park Dr, Wakulla Springs (32305). 14 miles S on Hwy 61 to Hwy 267. Phone 850/224-5950. www.floridastateparks.org.* Located in the heart of this 2,860-acre state park is one of the world's larger and deeper freshwater springs. Glass-bottomed boats allow visitors to see the entrance to the cavern 120 feet below the surface. Wildife observation boat tours encounter alligators, turtles, and a variety of birds. Many fossils and artifacts of prehistoric dwellers have been found by skin divers. Facilities include swimming in season; nature trails, picnic area, snack bar, dining room, lodge and conference center (see FULL-SERVICE RESORTS), gift shop. Glass-bottom boat tour and riverboat tour (daily; $$). (Daily 8 am-sundown) **$**

Special Events

Flying High Circus. *Florida State University, 502 Copeland St, Tallahassee (32304). Phone 850/644-4874. www.fsu.edu.* Approximately 80 students perform in a three-ring circus. Evening and matinee performances. First two weekends in Apr.

Natural Bridge Battle Reenactment. *Natural Bridge State Historic Site, 1022 Desoto Park Dr, Tallahassee (32301). Phone 850/922-6007.* Reenactment of the battle between Confederate and Union forces on this site. Early Mar.

North Florida Fair. *Fairgrounds, 441 Paul Russell Rd, Tallahassee (32301). Phone 850/671-8400. www.north floridafair.com.* Entertainment at the fair includes everything from bluegrass and gospel music to pig races and children's shows. The fair also recognizes one family from each participating county as the Outstanding Farm Family of the Year. Nov. **$$**

Spring Farm Days. *Tallahassee Museum of History and Natural Science, 3945 Museum Dr, Tallahassee (32310). Phone 850/576-1636. www.tallahassemuseum.org.* Focuses on spring activities on an 1880s farm; features sheep shearing. Mid-Apr.

Springtime Tallahassee. *209 E Park Ave, Tallahassee (32301). Phone 850/224-5012. www.springtime tallahassee.com.* Commemorates founding of city. Parades, concerts, art shows, tours of homes and gardens, and numerous other activities in various parts of the city. Four weeks in late Mar-early Apr.

Swamp Stomp. *Tallahassee Museum of History and Natural Science, 3945 Museum Dr, Tallahassee (32310). Phone 850/576-1636. www.tallahasseemuseum.org.* Continuous musical entertainment from bluegrass to folk and "saltwater" music. Mid-July.

Winter on the Farm. *Tallahassee Museum of History and Natural Science, 3945 Museum Dr, Tallahassee (32310). Phone 850/576-1636. www.tallahassee museum.org.* Focuses on fall activities on an 1880s farm; features syrup-making. Nov.

Limited-Service Hotels

★ **BEST WESTERN PRIDE INN & SUITES.** *2016 Apalachee Pkwy, Tallahassee (32301). Phone 850/656-6312; toll-free 800/827-7390; fax 850/942-4312. www.bestwestern.com.* 78 rooms, 2 story. Pets accepted; fee. Complimentary continental breakfast. Check-in 2 pm, check-out 11 am. Outdoor pool. Business center. **$**

★ **CABOT LODGE TALLAHASSEE NORTH MONROE.** *2735 N Monroe St, Tallahassee (32303). Phone 850/386-8880; toll-free 800/223-1964; fax 850/386-4254. www.cabotlodgenorthmonroe.com.* 160 rooms, 2 story. Complimentary continental breakfast. Check-in 2 pm, check-out noon. Outdoor pool. Business center. **$**

★★ **COURTYARD BY MARRIOTT.** *1018 Apalachee Pkwy, Tallahassee (32301). Phone 850/222-8822; toll-free 800/321-2211; fax 850/561-0354. www.courtyard.com.* 154 rooms, 2 story. Check-in 3 pm, check-out noon. High-speed Internet access. Fitness room. Outdoor pool, whirlpool. Business center. **$**

★★ **HILTON GARDEN INN TALLAHASSEE.** *3333 Thomasville Rd, Tallahassee (32308). Phone 850/385-3553; toll-free 877/782-9444; fax 850/385-4242. www.hiltongardeninn.com.* 99 rooms, 4 story. Check-in 3 pm, check-out noon. High-speed Internet access. Restaurant, bar. Fitness room. Outdoor pool, whirlpool. Business center. **$$**

★★ **RADISSON HOTEL TALLAHASSEE.** *415 N Monroe St, Tallahassee (32301). Phone 850/224-6000; toll-free 800/333-3333; fax 850/222-0335. www.radisson.com.* 119 rooms, 7 story. Check-in 3 pm, check-out 11 am. High-speed Internet access. Restaurant, bar. Fitness room. Business center. **$**

Full-Service Resort

★★ **WAKULLA SPRINGS STATE PARK & LODGE.** *550 Wakulla Park Dr, Wakulla Springs (32327). Phone 850/224-5950; fax 850/561-7282.* Atmosphere of an old Southern hotel; located in 2,900-acre state park on Wakulla Springs. 27 rooms, 2 story. Check-in 2:30 pm, check-out 11 am. Restaurant. **$**

Specialty Lodging

The following lodging establishment is approved by Mobil Travel Guide, but due to its unique and individualized nature has not been given a traditional Mobil Star rating. Included in this listing you may find bed-and-breakfasts, limited-service inns, guest ranches, and other unique hotel properties.

GOVERNOR'S INN. *209 S Adams St, Tallahassee (32301). Phone 850/681-6855; fax 850/222-3105.* Located within walking distance of the capitol building and downtown, this French country escape adds a sense of historic restoration to the Adams Street Commons. The uniquely decorated rooms in this 50-year-old pine-filled building are named after Florida governors. 40 rooms, 3 story. Complimentary continental breakfast. Check-in 3 pm, check-out noon. **$$**

Restaurants

★★ **ANDREW'S 228.** *228 S Adams St, Tallahassee (32301). Phone 850/222-3444; fax 850/222-2433. www.andrewsdowntown.com.* International/Fusion menu. Lunch, dinner. Closed Sun; Thanksgiving, Dec 25, lunch in winter. Casual attire. Reservations recommended. Valet parking. **$$**

★★ **CHEZ PIERRE.** *1215 Thomasville Rd, Tallahassee (32303). Phone 850/222-0936; fax 850/681-3507. www.chezpierre.com.* French menu. Lunch, dinner. Closed holidays. Bar. **$$**

North Carolina

North Carolina, besides being a wonderful place for a vacation, is a cross-section of America—a state of magnificent variety with three distinctive regions: the coast, the heartland, and the mountains. Its elevation ranges from sea level to 6,684 feet atop Mount Mitchell in the Black Mountain Range of the Appalachians. It has descendants of English, German, Scottish, Irish, and African immigrants. It has Quakers, Moravians, Episcopalians, and Calvinists. It produces two-thirds of our flue-cured tobacco, as well as cotton, peanuts, and vegetables on its farms. Fabrics, furniture, and many other products are made in its factories. It also has one of the finest state university systems in the nation with campuses at Chapel Hill, Raleigh, Greensboro, Charlotte, Asheville, and Wilmington.

Population: 6,628,637

Area: 48,843 square miles

Elevation: 0-6,684 feet

Peak: Mount Mitchell (Yancey County)

Entered Union: Twelfth of original 13 states (November 21, 1789)

Capital: Raleigh

Motto: To Be Rather Than to Seem

Nickname: Tar Heel State, Old North State

Flower: American Dogwood

Bird: Cardinal

Tree: Pine

Fair: October in Raleigh

Time Zone: Eastern

Web Site: www.visitnc.com

Fun Fact: North Carolina is the largest producer of sweet potatoes in the United States.

In 1585, the first English settlement was unsuccessfully started on Roanoke Island. Another attempt at settlement was made in 1587—but the colony disappeared, leaving only the crudely scratched word "CROATOAN" on a tree—perhaps referring to the Croatan Indians who may have killed the colonists or absorbed them into their own culture, leaving behind one of history's great mysteries. Here, in the Great Smoky Mountains, the Cherokees lived before the government drove them westward to Oklahoma over the Trail of Tears, on which one-third of them died. Descendants of many members of this tribe, who hid in the inaccessible rocky coves and forests, still live here. Some "mountain people," isolated, independent, still singing songs dating back to Elizabethan England, also live here. Few North Carolinians owned slaves, very few owned many, and, early on, the state accepted free blacks (in 1860 there were 30,463) as a part of the community.

Citizens take pride in being called "Tar Heels." During the Civil War, North Carolinians returning from the front were taunted by a troop from another state who had "retreated" a good deal earlier. The Carolinians declared that Jefferson Davis had decided to bring up all the tar from North Carolina to use on the heels of the other regiment to make them "stick better in the next fight." General Lee, hearing of the incident, said, "God bless the Tar Heel boys."

Individualist and democratic from the beginning, this state refused to ratify the Constitution until the Bill of Rights had been added. In 1860 its western citizens strongly supported the Union. It did not join the Confederate States of America until after Fort Sumter had been fired upon and Lincoln had called for volunteers. Its independence was then challenged, and it furnished one-fifth of the soldiers of the Southern armies even though its population was only one-ninth of the Confederacy's. Eighty-four engagements (most of them small) were fought on its soil. Jealous of its rights, North Carolina resisted the authority of Confederate Army officers from Virginia and loudly protested many of the policies of Jefferson Davis, but

Calendar Highlights

APRIL

Greater Greensboro Chrysler Classic Golf Tournament *(Greensboro). For more information, contact the Convention and Visitors Bureau, phone 336/379-1570.* Top golfers compete for more than $1.8 million on the PGA circuit.

North Carolina Azalea Festival *(Wilmington). Phone 910/794-4650.* Garden and home tours, horse show, celebrity entertainers, pageants, parade, and a street fair.

Springfest *(Charlotte).* Three-day festival in up-town offers food and live entertainment.

MAY

Artsplosure Spring and Arts Festival *(Raleigh). Moore Square and City Market. Phone 919/832-8699.* Citywide celebration of the arts. Showcase for regional dance, music, and theater performances by nationally known artists; outdoor arts and crafts show; children's activities.

Gliding Spectacular *(Nags Head, Outer Banks). Phone toll-free 877/359-8447.* Hang-gliding competition, novice through advanced. Spectacular flying and fun events.

JUNE

Rogallo Kite Festival *(Nags Head, Outer Banks). Phone toll-free 877/359-8447.* Competition for homebuilt kites; stunt kite performances, demonstrations; kite auction.

"Singing on the Mountain" *(Linville). Phone toll-free 800/468-7325.* On the slopes of Grandfther Mountain. All-day program of modern and traditional gospel music featuring top groups and nationally known speakers. Concessions or bring your own food.

JULY

Mountain Dance and Folk Festival *(Asheville). Civic Center. Phone 828/257-4530 or toll-free 800/257-1300.* Folk songs and ballads. Finest of its kind for devotees of the five-string banjo, gut-string fiddle, clogging, and smooth dancing.

SEPTEMBER

Bull Durham Blues Festival *(Durham). Historic Durham Athletic Park. Phone 919/683-1709.* Celebrates the blues with performances held at the location where *Bull Durham* was filmed.

CenterFest *(Durham). Phone 919/560-2787.* Downtown. Two-day event with more than 250 artists and craftsmen; musicians, jugglers, and clowns; continuous entertainment from three stages.

OCTOBER

Southern Highland Craft Guild Fair *(Asheville). Civic Center. Phone 828/298-7928.* More than 175 craftsmen from nine Southern states exhibit and demonstrate their skills. Folk and contemporary entertainment daily.

State Fair *(Raleigh). State Fairgrounds. Phone 919/733-2145 or 919/821-7400.*

its 125,000 men fought furiously, and 40,000 of them died for what they believed was right. For years after the Civil War, North Carolina was a poverty-stricken state, although it suffered less from the inroads of carpetbaggers than many of its neighbors did.

Today, the state seems designed for vacationers. Beautiful mountains and flowering plants, lake and ocean swimming and boating, hunting and fishing, superb golf courses, old towns, festivals, pageantry, and parks are a few of the state's many attractions.

When to Go/Climate

North Carolina has the most varied climate of any state on the East Coast. Subtropical temperatures on the coast are contrasted by a medium continental climate in the western mountain areas. Fall is hurricane season along the coast; winter in the western mountains can be snowy and cold. Fall foliage is magnificent in September and October; March and April are marked by blooming dogwood and azaleas.

THE OUTER BANKS

North Carolina has two coasts: the mainland coast, which runs along a wide expanse of tidal rivers, estuaries, and marshlands; and the Atlantic coast, which follows a series of barrier islands with shifting dunes, exotic wildlife, and live oaks misshapen by fierce winds (hurricane season runs from June through November). From Nags Head to Morehead City, a 75-mile stretch of these narrow barrier islands are protected as the Cape Hatteras National Seashore, constituting the largest stretch of undeveloped coastline on the Eastern Seaboard. A scenic drive from the Virginia state line to Morehead City takes drivers along the 200 miles of highway linking these islands.Start on Highway 168 at the Virginia border, 22 miles south of Norfolk. Highway 168 proceeds south and then merges with Highway 158 in Barco. Continue south across the Wright Memorial Bridge to the Outer Banks. Your first stop will be in Kitty Hawk, home to the Wright Brothers National Memorial (phone 919/441-7430). The memorial commemorates the first powered airplane flight, which took place on December 17, 1903, off the Highway 158 bypass south of town. Also in Kitty Hawk, a National Park Service ranger station distributes maps of the national seashore, marking places to hike, bike, and camp.Pick up the Highway 12 "Beach Road" by jogging east off the central highway to reach the popular resort of Nags Head, 6 miles south of Kitty Hawk. The most developed of the Outer Bank towns, Nags Head offers a wide range of lodging and dining choices for visitors. The beach road and bypass merge a few miles south of Nags Head at Whalebone Junction. Just east on Highway 64, a 5-mile detour takes you to the Fort Raleigh National Historic Site on Roanoke Island (phone 252/473-5772), where they tell the story of the "Lost Colony" of Roanoke, the first English settlement in North America. The colony at Roanoke was founded in 1585, but within a few years, the colonists had disappeared without a trace, creating one of our nation's greatest unsolved mysteries.South of Whalebone, Highway 12 becomes the central route south along the islands. The route leads 50 miles south past pristine beaches and old fishing villages and around Cape Hatteras. (Another visitor center is west of the cape around Buxton.) A ferry transports cars across the narrow inlet between Hatteras Island and Ocracoke Island, where the highway resumes for another 14 miles south to Ocracoke.Downtown Ocracoke makes a pleasant stop for a stroll. You'll find many fine restaurants, cafés, and inns, and bike rentals abound near the small harbor. There's a visitor center across from the ferry landing. From the dock, ferries take two different routes east across the Pamlico Sound: one ferry heads north to Swan Quarter, while the other travels south to Cedar Island. Either route is about 50 miles from Highway 17, the old Atlantic Coast Highway, which can lead you back north toward Virginia or south toward South Carolina. Reservations are recommended for either ferry route (phone toll-free 800/293-3779).

(Approximately 200 miles)

AVERAGE HIGH/LOW TEMPERATURES (° F)

Cape Hatteras National Seashore

Jan 52/37	May 74/60	Sept 81/68
Feb 53/38	June 81/68	Oct 72/58
Mar 60/44	July 85/72	Nov 65/49
Apr 67/51	Aug 85/72	Dec 57/41

Raleigh

Jan 49/29	May 79/55	Sept 81/61
Feb 53/31	June 85/64	Oct 72/48
Mar 62/39	July 88/68	Nov 63/40
Apr 72/46	Aug 87/68	Dec 53/32

Parks and Recreation

Water-related activities, hiking, riding, various other sports, picnicking, and visitor centers, as well as camping, are available in many of North Carolina's parks. Parks are open daily: June-Aug, 8 am-9 pm; Apr-May and Sept to 8 pm; Mar and Oct to 7 pm; Nov-Feb to 6 pm. Most parks have picnicking and hiking. Swimming ($3; 6-12, $2; under 3, free) and concessions open Memorial Day-Labor Day. Admission and parking free (excluding reservoirs; $4); canoe and boat rentals ($3/hour for the first hour, $1/hour thereafter); fishing. Campgrounds: open all year, limited facilities in winter; family of six for $12/day; hook-ups $5 more; primitive sites

$8/day; youth group tent camping $1/person ($8 minimum). Senior citizen discounts offered. Dogs on leash only. Campgrounds are on first come, first served basis; reservations are allowed for minimum of seven days, maximum of 14 days.

Information, including a comprehensive brochure, may be obtained from the Division of Parks and Recreation, Department of Environment, Health, and Natural Resources, 1615 MSC Raleigh 27699-1615; phone 919/733-7275 or 919/733-4181.

FISHING AND HUNTING

Nonresident fishing license: $30; daily license: $10; three-day license: $15. Nonresident six-day license: $25; basic hunting license: $40. Nonresident trapping license: $100. Waterfowl stamp (mandatory): $10.

For latest regulations, contact License Section, Wildlife Resources Commission, Archdale Building, 512 N Salisbury St, Raleigh 27604-1188, phone 919/662-4370.

Driving Information

Safety belts are mandatory for all persons in the front seat of a vehicle. Children under 6 years anywhere in a vehicle must be in an approved child passenger restraint system; ages 3-6 may use a regulation safety belt; children under 3 years must use an approved child passenger restraint system. For further information, phone 919/733-7952.

INTERSTATE HIGHWAY SYSTEM

The following alphabetical listing of North Carolina towns listed in this book shows that these cities are within 10 miles of the indicated interstate highways. Check a highway map for the nearest exit.

Highway Number	Cities/Towns within 10 Miles
Interstate 26	Asheville, Hendersonville, Tryon.
Interstate 40	Asheville, Burlington, Durham, Greensboro, Hickory, Maggie Valley, Marion, Morganton, Raleigh, Statesville, Waynesville, Wilmington, Winston-Salem.
Interstate 77	Charlotte, Cornelius, Statesville.
Interstate 85	Burlington, Charlotte, Concord, Durham, Gastonia, Greensboro, Henderson, High Point, Lexington, Salisbury.
Interstate 95	Dunn, Fayetteville, Lumberton, Roanoke Rapids, Rocky Mount, Smithfield, Wilson.

Additional Visitor Information

The North Carolina Gazetteer, by William S. Powell (University of North Carolina Press, Chapel Hill, 1968) lists more than 20,000 entries that will enable the reader to find any place in the state, as well as information about size, history, and derivation of name. The Travel and Tourism Division, 301 N Wilmington, Raleigh, 27601, phone toll-free 800/847-4862, has free travel information, including brochures.

North Carolina Welcome Center locations are I-85 N, Box 156, Norlina 27563; I-85 S, Box 830, Kings Mountain 28086; I-95 N, Box 52, Roanoke Rapids 27870; I-40, Box 809, Waynesville 28786; I-95 S, Box 518, Rowland 28383; I-26, Box 249, Columbus 28722; I-77 N, Box 1066, Dobson 27017; and I-77 S, Box 410724, Charlotte 28241-0724.

Albemarle (B-5)

See also Concord

Founded 1857
Population 15,680
Elevation 455 ft
Area Code 704
Zip 28001
Information Stanly County Chamber of Commerce, 116 E North St, PO Box 909, 28002; phone 704/982-8116

Albemarle is in the gently rolling hills of the Uwharrie Mountains, in the Piedmont section of the state. It manufactures textiles, aircraft tires, automotive parts, and aluminum.

What to See and Do

Cotton Patch Gold Mine. *740 Gurley Rd, Albemarle. 3 miles W off Hwy 740. Phone 704/463-5797.* Prospecting; concessions, picnic facilities. Camping (hookups). (Wed-Sun) **$$$**

Morrow Mountain State Park. *740 Morrow Mt Rd, Albemarle. 7 miles E off Hwy 740. Phone 704/982-4402.* Approximately 4,700 acres of hilly forested terrain, touched on two sides by Lake Tillery. Swimming pool, bathhouse, fishing, boating (rentals, launching). Natural history museum. Nature trails, hiking, riding. Picnic facilities, concessions. Camping (no hook-ups); six cabins, families only (Mar-Nov; advance reservations required).

Stanly Museum and Visitor Center. *245 E Main St, Albemarle. Phone 704/983-7316.* Originally built as a three-room log cabin in the 1850s, the Snuggs House has been enlarged and houses period artifacts. Research room. (Tues-Fri; also weekends by appointment; closed holidays) Also on lot is Marks House, town's oldest building (1850s) once used as residence/law office. **FREE**

Town Creek Indian Mound State Historic Site. *509 Town Creek Mound Rd, Albemarle. 11 miles S on Hwy 52, then 12 miles E on Hwy 731 to Town Creek Mound Rd. Phone 910/439-6802.* Reconstructed 14th-century Native American ceremonial center with stockade, temples, and mortuary. Visitor center, audiovisual shows, exhibits (Apr-Oct: daily; rest of year: Tues-Sun; closed holidays in winter). Picnic area. **FREE**

Asheboro (B-5)

See also Greensboro, High Point, Lexington

Founded 1779
Population 21,672
Elevation 844 ft
Area Code 336
Zip 27203
Information Asheboro-Randolph Chamber of Commerce, 317 E Dixie Dr, PO Box 4774; phone 336/626-2626
Web Site chamber.asheboro.com

Situated in the agriculturally and industrially rich Piedmont and the timber-covered Uwharrie Mountains, Asheboro has served as the seat of Randolph County for over a century. Planked roads, covered bridges, and the waters of the Deep and Uwharrie rivers provided the impetus for industrial development late in the 19th century. Asheboro is in the heart of North Carolina's pottery-making country.

What to See and Do

North Carolina Zoological Park. *4401 Zoo Pkwy, Asheboro (27205). 6 miles S on Hwy 159. Phone toll-free 800/488-0444. www.nczoo.org.* The nation's first natural habitat zoo. North American region exhibits span more than 200 acres; African habitats cover more than 300 acres and feature nine outdoor exhibits; Forest Aviary. (Apr-Sept: daily 9 am-5 pm; Oct-Mar: daily 9 am-4 pm; closed Dec 25) **$$**

Seagrove Area Potteries. *250 East Ave, Seagrove (27341). 10 miles S on Hwy 73/74. Phone 336/626-0364.* More than 80 artists practice traditional hand-turning of pottery. Shops. (Daily) **FREE**

Special Event

Asheboro Fall Festival. *Phone 336/629-0399.* Arts, crafts, food, parade, music, entertainment. First weekend in Oct.

Asheville (B-2)

See also Brevard, Burnsville, Hendersonville, Maggie Valley, Waynesville

Settled 1794
Population 68,889
Elevation 2,134 ft
Area Code 828
Information Convention and Visitors Bureau, 151 Haywood St, PO Box 1010, 28802-1010; phone 828/258-6101 or toll-free 800/257-1300
Web Site www.exploreasheville.com

Thomas Wolfe came from Asheville, the seat of Buncombe County, as did the expression "bunkum" (nonsense). A local congressman, when asked why he had been so evasive during a masterful oration in which he said nothing, replied, "I did it for Buncombe." Wolfe wrote often of his hill-rimmed home, shrewdly observant of the people and life of Asheville.

Asheville is a vacation headquarters in the Blue Ridge Mountains, as well as a marketing and industrial city. It is the North Carolina city closest to the Great Smoky Mountains National Park (see) and attracts many of the park's visitors with its annual mountain fetes, local handicrafts, and summer theaters. It is the headquarters for the Uwharrie National Forest, Pisgah National Forest (see BREVARD), Nantahala National Forest (see FRANKLIN), and Croatan National Forest

Angels in Asheville

Asheville, the capital of North Carolina's beautiful mountain region, is best known for the glamorous Biltmore Estate south of town. By comparison, downtown Asheville seems rather homespun. In fact, its most notorious landmark, the house where the novelist Thomas Wolfe grew up, is positively down at the heels, preserved that way to remain true to its description in Wolfe's most famous novel, *Look Homeward, Angel*, a thinly disguised portrait of Asheville.

The heart of downtown Asheville is Pack Square, at the intersection of Broadway and Patton Avenue. Around the square lie City Hall; the county courthouse; a library; and Pack Place (phone 828/257-4500), the city's education, art, and science center. Pack Place contains a variety of museums, performing arts venues, galleries, and shops. Children favor the health museum here, which features a talking transparent woman and a skeletal cyclist, as well as the mineral and gem museum. The YMI Cultural Center highlights African American history.

The southwest corner of the square bears the statue of an angel, looking homeward, marking the spot where the angel appears in Wolfe's famous story.

This was also the site of the stonecutting shop once run by Wolfe's father. Head two blocks north to Walnut Street, turn east on Walnut, then north again on Spruce to find the house where Thomas Wolfe lived from 1900 to 1920, known locally as the "Old Kentucky Home." Wolfe fans recognize the ordinary white frame house, however, as the "Dixieland" boardinghouse so vividly described in his most famous novel. The house is now officially designated the Thomas Wolfe National Historic Site (48 Spruce St, phone 828/253-8304), and the visitor center screens a film about the author's life.

Return to Broadway and head back south toward Pack Square to find Bean Street, on Broadway at College, for a cup of coffee. Go east on College a block to the T. S. Morrison Emporium (39 N Lexington), which continues to ply its trade in penny candy, toys, tools, and housewares—just as it has since it opened in 1891. For more entertainment, head back to Broadway, which turns into Biltmore Avenue south of Pack Square. Hear nationally known musicians at the Be Here Now club (5 Biltmore Ave) or take in an art flick at the Fine Arts Cinema across the street.

(see NEW BERN). The Blue Ridge Parkway brings many travelers to Asheville on their way south from the Shenandoah Valley of Virginia.

For further information about Croatan, Nantahala, Pisgah, and Uwharrie national forests, contact the US Forest Service, phone 828/257-4202.

What to See and Do

Asheville Community Theatre. *35 E Walnut St, Asheville. Phone 828/254-1320 (for schedule).* Comedies, musicals, and dramas performed throughout the year. **$$$$**

⭐ **Biltmore Estate.** *1 North Pack Sq, Asheville (28801). S on Hwy 25, three blocks N of I-40 exit 50. Phone 828/255-1700. www.biltmore.com.* The 8,000-acre country estate includes 75 acres of formal gardens, numerous varieties of azaleas and roses, and the 250-room chateau (85 rooms are open for viewing), which is the largest house ever built in the New World. George

W. Vanderbilt commissioned Richard Morris Hunt to design the house, which was begun in 1890 and finished in 1895. Materials and furnishings were brought from many parts of Europe and Asia; a private railroad was built to transport them to the site. Life here was living in the grand manner. Vanderbilt employed Gifford Pinchot, later governor of Pennsylvania and famous for forestry and conservation achievements, to manage his forests. Biltmore was the site of the first US forestry school. Much of the original estate in now part of Pisgah National Forest. Tours of the estate include gardens, conservatory, and winery facilities; tasting. Four restaurants on grounds. Guidebook (fee) is recommended. (Daily; closed Thanksgiving, Dec 25) **$$$$**

Biltmore Homespun Shops. *111 Grovewood Rd, Asheville (28804). Near Macon Ave, 2 miles NE. Phone 828/253-7651.* At the turn of the century, Mrs. George W. Vanderbilt opened a school to keep alive the skills of hand-dyeing, spinning, and hand-weaving wool into cloth. The business still has the old machinery and handlooms. An antique automobile museum and the North Carolina Homespun Museum are in an 11-acre park adjoining Grove Park Inn Resort. (Apr-Oct: daily; rest of year: Mon-Sat; closed Thanksgiving, Dec 25) **FREE**

Botanical Gardens at Asheville. *151 WT Weaver Blvd, Asheville (28804). On the campus of University of North Carolina. Phone 828/252-5190. www.ashevillebotanical gardens.org.* A 10-acre tract with thousands of flowers, trees, and shrubs native to southern Appalachia; 125-year-old "dog trot" log cabin. (Daily dawn-dusk) Visitor center, gift shop (Mar-mid-Nov daily 9:30 am-4 pm). **FREE**

Chimney Rock Park. *25 miles SE on Hwy 74, just past jct Hwys 64, 9. Phone 828/625-9611; toll-free 800/277-9611. www.chimneyrockpark.com.* The towering granite monolith Chimney Rock affords a 75-mile view; four hiking trails lead to the 404-foot Hickory Nut Falls, Moonshiner's Cave, Devil's Head balancing rock, and Nature's Showerbath. Trails, stairs, and catwalks; picnic areas, playground; nature center; observation lounge with snack bar, gift shop. 26-story elevator shaft through granite. (Daily 8:30 am-6 pm, weather permitting; closed Jan 1, Thanksgiving, Dec 25) **$$$**

Folk Art Center. *382 Blue Ridge Pkwy, Asheville. 5 miles E on US 70, then 1/2 miles N on the Blue Ridge Pkwy to Milepost 382. Phone 828/298-7928.* Home of the Southern Highland Craft Guild. Stone and timber structure; home of Blue Ridge Pkwy info center; craft exhibits, demonstrations, workshops, related programs. (Daily; closed Jan 1, Thanksgiving, Dec 25) **FREE**

Graves of Thomas Wolfe (1900-1938) and O. Henry (William Sydney Porter) (1862-1910). *Riverside Cemetery, 53 Birch St, Asheville (28801). Entrance on Birch St off Pearson Dr. Phone 828/258-8480.*

Mount Mitchell State Park. *Burnsville. 27 miles NE on Blue Ridge Pkwy, then 5 miles N on Hwy 128.* (See LITTLE SWITZERLAND)

Nantahala Outdoor Center. *1377 Hwy 19 W, Bryson City (28713). Phone toll-free 800/232-7238. www.noc.com.* Offers various trips on the Nantahala, French Broad, Ocee, Pigeon, Nolichucky, and Chattooga rivers ranging from 1 1/2 to 6 hours. **$$$$**

Pack Place Education, Arts, and Science Center. *2 S Pack Sq, Asheville (28801). Phone 828/257-4500. www.packplace.org.* This 92,000-square-foot complex features multiple museums and exhibit galleries

as well as a state-of-the-art theater. A permanent exhibit entitled "Here Is the Square" relates the history of Asheville. Restaurant (lunch only); gift shop. (Tues-Sat 10 am-5 pm, Sun 1-5 pm; closed Jan 1, Thanksgiving, Dec 24-25) Includes

Asheville Art Museum. *2 S Pack Sq, Asheville (28801). Phone 828/253-3227. www.ashevilleart.org.* Permanent collection and changing exhibits. (Tues-Sat 10 am-5 pm, Fri until 8 pm, Sun 1-5 pm) **$$**

Colburn Gem and Mineral Museum. *2 S Pack Sq, Asheville (28801). Phone 828/254-7162.* Displays of 1,000 minerals from around the world; includes information on mineral locations in the state. **$**

Diana Wortham Theatre. *2 S Pack Sq, Asheville (28801). Phone 828/257-4530.* This 500-seat theater hosts local, regional, and national companies.

The Health Adventure. *2 S Pack Sq, Asheville (28801). Phone 828/254-6373.* Extensive collection of imaginative, educational exhibits on the human body, including a talking transparent woman, a bicycle-pedaling skeleton, and an opportunity to hear the sound of your own heartbeat. Also on premises is Creative PlaySpace, a special exhibit for young children. **$**

YMI Cultural Center. *39 S Market St, Asheville (28801). Phone 828/252-4614.* Galleries featuring permanent and rotating exhibts of African American art. **$**

Thomas Wolfe Memorial. *52 N Market, Asheville. Phone 828/253-8304.* The state maintains the Wolfe boardinghouse as a literary shrine, restored and furnished to appear as it did in 1916. In Asheville it is known as the "Old Kentucky Home." In *Look Homeward, Angel* it was referred to as "Dixieland"; Asheville was "Altamont." Visitor center with exhibit. (Tues-Sat; closed holidays) **$**

Western North Carolina Nature Center. *Gashes Creek Rd, Asheville. 3 miles E on Hwy 81. Phone 828/298-5600.* Live animals, children's petting barnyard, natural history exhibits, nature trail, educational programs. (Daily) **$$**

Wolf Laurel Ski Resort. *Valley View Cir, Mars Hill. 27 miles N off Hwy 23. Phone 828/689-4111; toll-free 800/817-4111. www.skiwolflaurel.com.* Quad, double chair lifts, tow rope; patrol, school, rentals; snow making; restaurant, lodge. Longest run 3/4 mile; vertical drop 700 feet. (Mid-Dec-mid-Mar, daily) **$$$$**

Zebulon B. Vance Birthplace State Historic Site. *911 Reems Creek Rd, Weaverville (28787). 9 miles N on Hwy 19/23, exit New-Stock Rd, then 6 miles N on Reems Creek Rd. Phone 828/645-6706.* Log house (reconstructed 1961) and outbuildings on site where Civil War governor of North Carolina grew up. Honors Vance family, which was deeply involved with early history of state. Visitor center, exhibits. Picnic area. (Apr-Oct: Mon-Fri; rest of year: Tues-Fri) **FREE**

Special Events

Mountain Dance and Folk Festival. *Diana Wortham Theater, 87 Haywood St, Asheville (28801). Phone 828/257-4530.* Folk songs and ballads. Finest of its kind for devotees of the five-string banjo, gut-string fiddle, clogging, and smooth dancing.

Shakespeare in the Park. *246 Cumberland Ave, Asheville (22880). Phone 828/254-4540.* Montford Park Players. Weekends early June-late Aug.

Shindig-on-the-Green. *College and Spruce sts, Asheville. In front of City Hall. Phone 828/258-6109.* Mountain fiddling, dulcimer players, singing, square dancing. Sat evenings, July-Labor Day, except the last weekend in July.

Southern Highland Craft Guild Fair. *Civic Center, 87 Haywood St, Asheville (28801). Just off I-240. Phone 828/298-7928.* More than 175 craftsmen from nine Southern states exhibit and demonstrate their skills. Folk and contemporary entertainment daily. Mid-July and mid-Oct.

World Gee Haw Whimmy Diddle Competition. *Folk Art Center, 382 Blue Ridge Pkwy, Asheville (28805). Phone 828/298-7928.* Competitions, demonstrations, storytelling, music, dance. Third weekend in Sept.

Limited-Service Hotels

★ **AMERICAN COURT.** *85 Merrimon Ave, Asheville (28801). Phone 828/253-4427; toll-free 800/233-3582; fax 828/253-2507. www.americancourt.com.* 21 rooms. Check-in 1 pm, check-out 11 am. Outdoor pool. **$**
🅳 ⌹

★ ★ **BEST WESTERN BILTMORE.** *22 Woodfin St, Asheville (28801). Phone 828/253-1851; toll-free 888/854-6897; fax 828/252-9205. www.bestwestern.com.* 154 rooms, 5 story. Complimentary continental breakfast. Check-in 3 pm, check-out noon. Restaurant. Fitness room. Outdoor pool. **$**
🏃 ⌹

★ **COMFORT INN.** *890 Brevard Rd, Asheville (28806). Phone 828/665-4000; toll-free 800/228-5150; fax 828/665-9082. www.choicehotels.com.* 125 rooms, 5 story, all suites. Pets accepted; fee. Complimentary continental breakfast. Check-in 3 pm, check-out noon. Fitness room. Outdoor pool, whirlpool. Airport transportation available. **$**
🐾 🏃 ⌹

★ **DAYS INN.** *1445 Tunnel Rd, Asheville (28805). Phone 828/298-4000; fax 828/210-0197. www.daysinn.com.* 84 rooms, 3 story. Pets accepted, some restrictions; fee. Complimentary continental breakfast. Check-in 3 pm, check-out noon. Outdoor pool. **$**
🅳 🐾 ⌹

★ ★ **DOUBLETREE HOTEL.** *115 Hendersonville Rd, Asheville (28803). Phone 828/274-1800; fax 828/274-1802. www.biltmoreasheville.doubletree.com.* 160 rooms, 5 story. Check-in 3 pm, check-out noon. Restaurant, bar. Fitness room. Outdoor pool, whirlpool. **$**
🏃 ⌹

★ **FOREST MANOR INN.** *866 Hendersonville Rd, Asheville (28803). Phone 828/274-3531; toll-free 800/866-3531; fax 828/274-3531. www.forestmanorinn.com.* 21 rooms. Closed Jan-Mar. Complimentary continental breakfast. Check-in 3 pm, check-out 11 am. Outdoor pool. On 4 wooded acres. **$**
🅳 ⌹

Full-Service Hotels

★ ★ ★ **HAYWOOD PARK HOTEL AND PROMENADE.** *1 Battery Park Ave, Asheville (28801). Phone 704/252-2522; toll-free 800/228-2522; fax 704/253-0481. www.haywoodpark.com.* This all-suite hotel has been elegantly furnished and decorated with polished brass, warm oak, and Spanish marble. There are 33 rooms available, each with fine furnishings, a wet bar, and a bathroom that features either a garden tub or Jacuzzi. 33 rooms, 4 story. Check-in 2 pm, check-out noon. High-speed Internet access. Restaurant, bar. Fitness room. **$$**
🏃

★ ★ ★ ★ **INN ON BILTMORE ESTATE.** *1 Antler Hill Rd, Asheville (28803). Phone 828/225-1660; toll-free 866/336-1240; fax 828/225-1680. www.biltmore.com.* The Inn on Biltmore Estate provides guests with world-class accommodations in the heart of an American landmark. This gracious hotel is uniquely situated within the historic Vanderbilt Biltmore Estate, offering guests the chance to gambol the grounds that Vanderbilt and his illustrious guests once roamed. While ensconced in the resplendent accommodations, guests can easily imagine what it was like to visit this American aristocrat. Set against the backdrop of the smoky Blue Ridge Mountains, the property is rife with recreational opportunities, from carriage and horseback rides to river float trips on the French Broad River with a view of the estate. The hotel's distinguished character extends to its dining establishments. The Dining Room showcases refined regional cooking; afternoon tea is a daily tradition; and the Lobby Lounge is ideal for informal meals. 213 rooms, 7 story. Check-in 4 pm, check-out 11 am. Restaurant, bar. Fitness room. Outdoor pool, whirlpool. Airport transportation available. **$$$**

★ ★ ★ **RENAISSANCE HOTEL.** *1 Thomas Wolfe Plz, Asheville (28801). Phone 828/252-8211; fax 828/236-9616. www.renaissancehotels.com.* This property is centrally located around the area's attractions. Visitors will find plenty of shopping in the local mall, a farmers' market, and other complexes in the area. Also nearby are art galleries, a civic center, and more. 281 rooms, 12 story. Check-in 4 pm, check-out noon. High-speed Internet access. Restaurant, bar. Fitness room. Outdoor pool. Business center. **$**

Full-Service Resorts

★ ★ ★ **THE GROVE PARK INN RESORT & SPA.** *290 Macon Ave, Asheville (28804). Phone 828/252-2711; fax 828/252-6102.* Since 1913, health enthusiasts and those seeking respite from the everyday have made their way to the historic Grove Park Inn. This spectacular destination, set in the shadow of Asheville's Blue Ridge Mountains, is the ultimate year-round resort. Light-filled and spacious, the guest rooms pay homage to the Arts & Crafts aesthetic with Mission-style furnishings and decorative accents. Active-minded travelers choose from the 18-hole Donald Ross-designed golf course, a superb tennis facility, and a state-of-the-art fitness center, while relaxation-seekers head for the 40,000-square-foot, grotto-like spa. The spa, crafted out of natural rock, is a delight for the senses with cascading waterfalls and golden sunlight streaming in through the skylights. From hydro bath treatments to flotation body masques, it exceeds the expectations of its well-traveled visitors. 510 rooms, 10 story. Check-in 4 pm, check-out 11 am. Six restaurants, two bars. Children's activity center. Fitness room, spa. Indoor

pool, outdoor pool, whirlpool. Golf, 18 holes. Tennis. Business center. **$$$**

★ ★ **HOLIDAY INN.** *1 Holiday Inn Dr, Asheville (28806). Phone 828/254-3211; toll-free 800/733-3211; fax 828/254-1603. www.sunspree.com.* 272 rooms, 5 story. Pets accepted, some restrictions; fee. Check-in 3 pm, check-out 11 am. Restaurant, bar. Children's activity center. Fitness room. Outdoor pool. Golf. Tennis. **$$**

Full-Service Inn

★ ★ ★ ★ **RICHMOND HILL INN.** *87 Richmond Hill Dr, Asheville (28806). Phone 828/252-7313; toll-free 888/742-4554; fax 828/252-8726. www.richmondhillinn.com.* Visitors retreat to Richmond Hill Inn for quiet reflection and repose. Once the private home of an influential politician, this Victorian estate now welcomes guests seeking a break from quotidian concerns. The Queen Anne-style mansion and croquet cottages are magically set among 6 acres of formal gardens, meandering brooks, and a 9-foot waterfall. Tranquility is paramount here; strolling the grounds often leads to the discovery of a favorite hidden corner. Located on the upper floors of the mansion and in the cottages, the rooms and suites reflect the traditions of the late 19th century. Guests enjoy delicious country breakfasts before heading out to explore Asheville's historic treasures or traverse its great outdoors, and a lovely afternoon tea awaits their return. Gabrielle's décor is firmly rooted in the Victorian era, but the kitchen proudly embraces modern times with its sensational continental menu. 36 rooms, 3 story. Closed Jan. Complimentary full breakfast. Check-in 3 pm, check-out 11 am. Restaurant. Fitness room. **$$$**

Specialty Lodgings

The following lodging establishtments are approved by Mobil Travel Guide, but due to their unique and individualized nature have not been given a traditional Mobil Star rating. Included in this listing you may find bed-and-breakfasts, limited-service inns, guest ranches, and other unique hotel properties.

ALBEMARLE INN. *86 Edgemont Rd, Asheville (28801). Phone 828/255-0027; toll-free 800/621-7435; fax 828/236-3397. www.albemarleinn.com.* This dramatic, majestic home, with enormous white pillars and beautiful, well-manicured gardens, offers guests an elegant and luxurious experience. Rooms are thoughtfully decorated and feature 360-thread count lace sheets, Egyptian cotton towels, and clawfoot tubs. The dining area features wicker tables set with crisp white tablecloths, lillies, and floral place mats and napkins. Complimentary wine and hors d'oeuvres are served nightly on the veranda in summer and around the fireplace in winter. 11 rooms, 3 story. Children over 12 years only. Complimentary full breakfast. Check-in 3-7 pm, check-out 11 am. **$$**

APPLEWOOD MANOR INN. *62 Cumberland Cir, Asheville (28801). Phone 828/254-2244; toll-free 800/442-2197; fax 828/254-0899. www.applewoodmanor.com.* Colonial turn-of-the-century home built in 1910; antiques. 4 rooms, 2 story. Children over 12 years only. Complimentary full breakfast. Check-in 3-7 pm, check-out 11 am. **$**

THE BEAUFORT HOUSE VICTORIAN INN. *61 N Liberty St, Asheville (28801). Phone 828/254-8334; toll-free 800/261-2221. www.beauforthouse.com.* Experience Victorian afternoon tea, gourmet breakfasts, and elegant guest rooms in the former home of Charleton Heston. The mansion is surrounded by 2 acres of beautifully landscaped grounds complete with 5,000 flowers. 11 rooms, 4 story. Children over 11 years only. Complimentary full breakfast. Check-in 3-7 pm, check-out 11 am. **$**

CEDAR CREST VICTORIAN INN. *674 Biltmore Ave, Asheville (28803). Phone 828/252-1389; toll-free 800/252-0310. www.cedarcrestinn.com.* Dating from 1891, the luxurious mansion that has been transformed into this romantic inn is listed on the National Register of Historic Places. Of particular note is the ornate woodwork on the first floor and the Victorian gardens, lush with dogwood and rhododendrons. 12 rooms, 3 story. Children over 10 years only. Complimentary full breakfast. Check-in 3-10 pm, check-out 11 am. **$$**

LION AND THE ROSE. *276 Montford Ave, Asheville (28801). Phone 828/255-7673; toll-free 800/546-6988; fax 828/285-9810. www.lion-rose.com.* This elegantly restored Georgian mansion is nestled in beautifully landscaped gardens. The innkeepers' personal attention and impeccable attention to detail add to its quaint romantic feel. For those who appreciate

antiques, this inn will not disappoint. 5 rooms, 3 story. Children over 12 years only. Complimentary full breakfast. Check-in 3-8 pm, check-out 11 am. **$$**

THE OLD REYNOLDS MANSION. *100 Reynolds Heights, Asheville (28804). Phone 828/254-0496; toll-free 800/709-0496. www.oldreynoldsmansion.com.* Outdoor pool. Antebellum mansion (1855) on hill overlooking mountains, verandas. 10 rooms, 3 story. Closed Sun-Thurs, Nov-June. Complimentary full breakfast. Check-in 3-8:30 pm, check-out 11 am. **$**

OWL'S NEST. *2630 Smokey Park Hwy, Candler (28715). Phone 828/665-8325; toll-free 800/665-8868; fax 828/667-2539. www.engadineinn.com.* Located just outside of Asheville, this inn was built in 1885 and has been restored to its original Victorian grandeur. The wraparound porches and mountain views are exquisite, and dining by the fireplace is cozy and relaxing. 5 rooms, 3 story. Children over 12 years only. Complimentary full breakfast. Check-in 3-6 pm, check-out 11 am. **$**

Restaurants

★ **CAFE MAX & ROSIE'S.** *52 N Lexington Ave, Asheville (28801). Phone 828/254-5342; fax 828/281-3872.* Vegetarian menu. Lunch. Closed Sun. Children's menu. Casual attire. Outdoor seating. **$**

★ ★ ★ **FLYING FROG CAFE.** *1 Battery Park Ave, Asheville (28801). Phone 828/254-9411; fax 828/225-4858. www.flyingfrogcafe.com.* International/Fusion menu. Dinner. Closed Mon-Tues. Bar. Casual attire. **$$**

★ ★ ★ **GABRIELLE'S.** *87 Richmond Hill Dr, Asheville (28806). Phone 828/252-7313; toll-free 888/742-4554; fax 828/252-8726. www.richmondhillinn.com.* Every meal at Gabrielle's is an extraordinary dining experience. Savor the American cuisine in one of Gabrielle's two elegant dining rooms. While the formal service mirrors the elegance of a bygone era, the food combines old and new into a sumptuous culinary and visual experience. Only the finest ingredients, grown locally, are used to create the seasonally changing menu. American menu. Dinner. Closed Tues; Jan. Bar. Jacket required. Reservations recommended. Valet parking. **$$$**

★ ★ **GREENERY.** *148 Tunnel Rd, Asheville (28803). Phone 828/253-2809; fax 828/254-0645. www.greenery restaurant.net.* American menu. Dinner. Closed Jan 1. Bar. Children's menu. Casual attire. **$$**

★ ★ ★ **GROVE PARK INN RESORT.** *290 Macon Ave, Asheville (28804). Phone 828/252-2711; toll-free 800/438-5800; fax 828/252-6442. www.groveparkinn.com.* Located in the Grove Park Inn, this restaurant has sweeping views, elegant décor, and innovative classic cuisine. An extensive wine list will provide a wonderful accompaniment to any meal. International/Fusion menu. Dinner. Bar. Jacket required. Reservations recommended. Valet parking. **$$$**

★ ★ **LA PAZ.** *10 Biltmore Plz, Asheville (28803). Phone 828/277-8779; fax 828/277-1974. www.lapaz.com.* Mexican menu. Lunch, dinner. Bar. Children's menu. Casual attire. Outdoor seating. **$$**

★ ★ **THE MARKET PLACE RESTAURANT & WINE BAR.** *20 Wall St, Asheville (28801). Phone 828/252-4162; fax 828/253-3120. www.marketplace-restaurant.com.* American, French menu. Dinner. Closed Sun-Mon in Jan-Feb, Sun in Mar-Sept and Nov-Dec; holidays. Bar. Casual attire. Outdoor seating. **$$$**

★ **MAX'S CELEBRITY GRILL.** *130 College St, Asheville (28801). Phone 828/258-1162. www.maxsgrill.com.* American, Greek menu. Lunch, dinner. Closed Sun. Casual attire. Outdoor seating. **$**

Banner Elk (A-3)

See also Blowing Rock, Boone, Linville

Population 811
Elevation 3,739 ft
Area Code 828
Zip 28604
Information Chamber of Commerce, PO Box 335; phone 828/898-5605
Web Site www.banner-elk.com

What to See and Do

Grandfather Mountain. *2050 Blowing Rock Hwy, Banner Elk (28646). 3 miles N via Hwy 221.* (see LINVILLE).

Ski Beech. *1007 Beech Mountain Pkwy, Banner Elk. 3 miles N on Hwy 184. Phone 828/387-2011; toll-free 800/438-2093. www.skibeech.com.* Quad chairlift, six double chair lifts, J-bar, rope tow; patrol, school, rentals; snowmaking, ice skating; restaurant, cafeteria; nursery, shopping. Vertical drop 830 feet. Night skiing. (Mid-Nov-mid-Mar, daily) **$$$$**

Sugar Mountain. *Off Hwy 184. Phone 828/898-4521. www.skisugar.com.* Triple, four double chair lifts, three surface lifts; patrol, school, rentals, snowmaking; children's program; lodging, cafeteria; nursery. Vertical drop 1,200 feet. (Mid-Nov-mid-Mar, daily)

Limited-Service Hotel

★ ★ **HOLIDAY INN.** *Hwy 184, Banner Elk (28604). Phone 828/898-4571; toll-free 877/877-4553; fax 828/898-8437. www.holidayinnbannerelk.com.* For a quiet mountain hotel, there's an awful lot going on at this property, right on the main access road on Beech Mountain. Featuring grills and picnic tables, no additional charge for guests with pets, a heated outdoor pool, and live entertainment in the hotel's restaurant, the Manhattan Italian Chophouse, everyone can find something to enjoy here. 101 rooms, 2 story. Pets accepted. Check-in 3 pm, check-out 11 am. Restaurant, bar. Fitness room. Outdoor pool. **$**
🐾 🧍 🏊

Specialty Lodging

The following lodging establishment is approved by Mobil Travel Guide, but due to its unique and individualized nature has not been given a traditional Mobil Star rating. Included in this listing you may find bed-and-breakfasts, limited-service inns, guest ranches, and other unique hotel properties.

ARCHER'S MOUNTAIN. *2489 Beech Mountain Pkwy, Banner Elk (28604). Phone 828/898-9004; toll-free 888/827-6155; fax 828/898-9007. www.archersinn.com.* Nestled high on the side of Beech Mountain, this rustic inn features wood-burning fireplaces and porches complete with mountain views and rocking chairs. Enjoy breakfast, lunch, or dinner (or all three) at the inn's restaurant and take a break from the bustle of the world below. 15 rooms, 2 story. Complimentary full breakfast. Check-in 3 pm, check-out 11 am. Restaurant. **$**
🔒 🏊

Restaurant

★ ★ **JACKALOPE'S VIEW.** *2489 Beech Mountain Pkwy, Banner Elk (28604). Phone 828/898-9004; fax*

828/898-9007. *www.archersinn.com.* American menu. Dinner. Closed Mon; Dec 25. Bar. Casual attire. Outdoor seating. **$$$**

Beaufort (C-9)

See also Morehead City

Population 3,771
Elevation 7 ft
Area Code 252
Zip 28516
Information Crystal Coast Visitors Center, 3409 Arendell St, PO Box 1406, Morehead City 28557; phone 252/726-8148 or toll-free 800/786-6962
Web Site www.historicbeaufort.com

Beaufort, dating from the colonial era, is a seaport with more than 125 historic houses and sites.

What to See and Do

Beaufort Historic Site. *138 Turner St, Beaufort (28516). Phone 252/728-5225. www.historicbeaufort.com.* Old burying ground, 1829 restored old jail, restored houses (1767-1830), courthouse (circa 1796), apothecary shop, art gallery, and gift shop. Obtain additional information and a self-guided walking tour map from the Safrit Historical Center, 138 Turner St, PO Box 363. (Daily except Sun; closed holidays) **$$$**

Cape Lookout National Seashore. *131 Charles St, Harkers Island (28531). Phone 252/728-2250. www.nps.gov/calo.* This unit of the National Park System, on the outer banks of North Carolina, extends 55 miles south from Ocracoke Inlet and includes unspoiled barrier islands. There are no roads or bridges; access is by boat only (fee). Catch a ferry from Beaufort, Harkers Island, Davis, Atlantic, or Ocracoke (Apr-Nov). Excellent fishing and shell collecting; primitive camping; interpretive programs (seasonal). The lighthouse (1859) at Cape Lookout is still operational. Visitor center (daily 8:30 am-4:30 pm; closed Jan 1, Dec 25).

North Carolina Maritime Museum and Watercraft Center. *315 Front St, Beaufort. Phone 252/728-7317.* Natural and maritime history exhibits, field trips; special programs in maritime and coastal natural history. (Museum, daily; Watercraft Center, Tues-Sun; closed Jan 1, Thanksgiving, Dec 25) **FREE**

Special Events

Beaufort by the Sea Music Festival. Late Apr.

Old Homes Tour and Antiques Show. *138 Turner St, Beaufort (28516). Phone 919/728-5225.* Private homes and historic public buildings; Carteret County Militia; bus tours and tours of old burying ground; historical crafts. Sponsored by the Beaufort Historical Association, Inc., PO Box 1709. Last weekend in June.

Specialty Lodgings

The following lodging establishments are approved by Mobil Travel Guide, but due to their unique and individualized nature have not been given a traditional Mobil Star rating. Included in this listing you may find bed-and-breakfasts, limited-service inns, guest ranches, and other unique hotel properties.

THE CEDARS INN. *305 Front St, Beaufort (28516). Phone 252/728-7036; fax 252/728-1685. www.cedarsinn.com.* 11 rooms, 2 story. Children over 10 years only. Complimentary full breakfast. Check-in 3 pm, check-out 11 am. Restaurant. Beach. **$**
🗋

PECAN TREE INN. *116 Queen St, Beaufort (28516). Phone 252/728-6733. www.pecantree.com.* 7 rooms, 2 story. Children over 10 years only. Complimentary continental breakfast. Check-in 3 pm, check-out 11 am. Restaurant. **$**
🗋

Belhaven

Population 1,968

Specialty Lodging

The following lodging establishment is approved by Mobil Travel Guide, but due to its unique and individualized nature has not been given a traditional Mobil Star rating. Included in this listing you may find bed-and-breakfasts, limited-service inns, guest ranches, and other unique hotel properties.

RIVER FOREST MANOR. *738 E Main St, Belhaven (27810). Phone 252/943-2151; toll-free 800/346-2151; fax 252/943-6628. www.riverforestmanor.com.* 9 rooms, 2 story. Complimentary continental breakfast. Check-in 2 pm, check-out 11 am. Restaurant. Outdoor pool, whirlpool. Tennis. Airport transportation available. View of river. Golf carts available for touring town. **$**

Restaurant

★ ★ **RIVER FOREST MANOR.** *738 E Main St, Belhaven (27810). Phone 252/943-2151; fax 252/943-6628. www.riverforestmanor.com.* Southern menu. Dinner, Sun brunch. Bar. **$$**

Blowing Rock (A-3)

See also Banner Elk, Boone, Linville

Founded 1889
Population 1,418
Elevation 4,000 ft
Area Code 828
Zip 28605
Information Chamber of Commerce, PO Box 406; phone 828/295-7851 or toll-free 800/295-7851
Web Site www.blowingrock.com

On the Blue Ridge Parkway, Blowing Rock was named, based on Native American folklore, for the cliff near town where lightweight objects thrown outward are swept back to their origin by the wind. It has been a resort area for more than 100 years; a wide variety of recreational facilities and shops can be found nearby.

What to See and Do

Appalachian Ski Mountain. *940 Ski Mt Rd, Blowing Rock. 3 miles N on Hwy 321, near Blue Ridge Pkwy intersection. Phone 828/295-7828; toll-free 800/322-2373 (reservations). www.appskimtn.com.* Two quad, double chair lift, rope tow, handle-pull tow; patrol; French-Swiss Ski College, Ski-Wee children's program; equipment rentals; snowmaking; restaurant; eight runs, longest run 2,700 feet, vertical drop 400 feet. (Dec-mid-Mar; closed Dec 24 evening-Dec 25) Night skiing (all slopes lighted); half-day and twilight rates. **$$$$**

Blowing Rock. *452 Sunset Dr #1, Blowing Rock. 2 miles SE on Hwy 321. Phone 828/295-7111.* Cliff (4,000 feet) hangs over Johns River Gorge 2,000-3,000 feet below. Scenic views of Grandfather, Grandmother, Table Rock, and Hawksbill mountains. Observation deck. Gift shop. (Daily) **$$**

Julian Price Memorial Park. *Linville Rd, Blowing Rock. SW via Hwy 221 and Blue Ridge Pkwy. Phone 828/295-7591.* Boating (hand-powered only, rentals). Picnicking. Camping (trailer facilities, no hookups; June-Oct only; fee). Amphitheater; evening interpretive programs (May-Oct). Park open year-round (weather permitting). **FREE**

Moses H. Cone Memorial Park. *Linville Rd, Blowing Rock. On Blue Ridge Pkwy. Phone 828/295-7591.* Former summer estate of textile magnate. Bridle paths, two lakes, 25 miles of hiking and cross-country skiing trails. (May-Oct, daily) **FREE**

Parkway Craft Center. *667 Service Rd, Blowing Rock. Blue Ridge Pkwy mile post 294. Phone 828/295-7938.* Demonstrations of weaving, wood carving, pottery, jewelry making, other crafts. (May-Oct, daily) Handcrafted items for sale. **FREE**

Mystery Hill. *129 Mystery Hill Ln, Blowing Rock. N on Hwy 321. Phone 828/264-2792.* Educational exhibits explore science, optical illusion, and natural phenomena. Features Mystery House, Hall of Mystery, and BubbleRama. Gift shop. (Daily; closed Thanksgiving, Dec 25) **$$$**

Tweetsie Railroad. *296 Tweetsie Railroad, Blowing Rock. 4 miles N on Hwy 321. Phone 828/264-9061.* A 3-mile excursion, with mock holdup and raid, on old narrow-gauge railroad; Western town with variety show at Tweetsie Palace; country fair, petting zoo; craft village; chair lift to Mouse Mountain Picnic Area. (May-Oct, limited hours) **$$$$**

Special Event

Tour of Homes. *Phone 828/295-7851.* Fourth Fri in July.

Limited-Service Hotels

★ **ALPINE VILLAGE INN.** *297 Sunset Dr, Blowing Rock (28605). Phone 828/295-7206. www.alpine-village-inn.com.* 17 rooms. Pets accepted; fee. Check-in 2 pm, check-out 11 am. **$**

★ **BLOWING ROCK INN.** *788 N Main St, Blowing Rock (28605). Phone 828/295-7921; fax 828/295-9948. www.blowingrockinn.com.* 24 rooms. Closed mid-Dec-Mar. Check-in 2 pm, check-out 11 am. **$**

★ **CLIFF DWELLERS INN.** *116 Lakeview Terrace, Blowing Rock (28605). Phone 828/295-*

3121; toll-free 800/322-7380; fax 828/295-3121. www.cliffdwellers.com. 21 rooms, 3 story. Check-in 3 pm, check-out 11 am. View of mountains. **$**

Full-Service Resorts

★ ★ ★ CHETOLA RESORT AT BLOWING

ROCK. *N Main St, Blowing Rock (28605). Phone 828/ 295-5500; toll-free 800/243-8652; fax 828/295-5529. www.chetola.com.* This Blue Ridge Mountains retreat, bordered on one side by a national forest, leaves guests wanting for nothing. The Highlands Sports and Recreation Center, conference center, professional tennis courts, and other amenties are all located within the resort's 78-acre property. 104 rooms, 3 story. Check-in 3 pm, check-out 11 am. High-speed Internet access, wireless Internet access. Three restaurants, bar. Children's activity center. Fitness room, fitness classes available. Indoor pool, whirlpool. Tennis. Business center. **$$**

★ ★ ★ HOUND EARS CLUB. *328 Shulls Mills*

Rd, Blowing Rock (28607). Phone 828/963-4321; fax 828/963-8030. www.houndears.com. Set atop the Blue Ridge Mountains, this small, secluded resort is a relaxing respite. The golf course was designed by George Cobb, and the views are breathtaking. 28 rooms, 2 story. Check-in 3 pm, check-out 11 am. Two restaurants, three bars. Children's activity center. Fitness room, fitness classes available. Outdoor pool. Golf, 18 holes. Tennis. **$$**

Full-Service Inn

★ ★ ★ CRIPPEN'S COUNTRY INN. *239*

Sunset Dr, Blowing Rock (28605). Phone 828/295-3487; toll-free 877/295-3487; fax 828/295-0388. www.crippens.com. 8 rooms, 3 story. Children over 12 permitted. Complimentary continental breakfast. Check-in 3 pm, check-out 11 am. High-speed Internet access, wireless Internet access. Restaurant. Bar. Business center. **$**

Specialty Lodgings

The following lodging establishments are approved by Mobil Travel Guide, but due to their unique and individualized nature have not been given a traditional Mobil Star rating. Included in this listing you may find bed-and-breakfasts, limited-service inns, guest ranches, and other unique hotel properties.

INN AT RAGGED GARDENS. *203 Sunset, Blowing Rock (28605). Phone 828/295-9703. www.ragged-gardens.com.* The historic vacation village of Blowing Rock in the Appalachian high country is home to this elegant 19th-century inn. Original stone pillars and floors, period furnishings, individually decorated rooms, and a full acre of beautifully landscaped property beckon. 11 rooms, 3 story. Children over 12 years only. Complimentary full breakfast. Check-in 3-7 pm, check-out 11 am. **$$**

MAPLE LODGE. *152 Sunset Dr, Blowing Rock (28605). Phone 828/295-3331; fax 828/295-9986. www.maplelodge.net.* 11 rooms, 2 story. Closed Jan-Feb. Children over 12 years only. Complimentary full breakfast. Check-in 3-9 pm, check-out 11 am. **$$**

Restaurants

★ ★ BEST CELLAR. *Hwy 321 and Blowing Rock Rd, Blowing Rock (28605). Phone 828/295-3466; fax 828/295-4772.* American menu. Dinner. Closed Sun in May-Nov; Tues-Wed in Dec-Apr. Valet parking. **$$**

★ ★ ★ CRIPPEN'S. *239 Sunset Dr, Blowing Rock (28607). Phone 828/295-3487; fax 828/295-0388. www.crippens.com.* This spacious, cozy dining room is located in the Crippens Country Inn. American menu. Dinner. Closed Mon; holidays; also Super Bowl Sun. Bar. Children's menu. **$$$**

Boone (A-3)

See also Banner Elk, Blowing Rock, Jefferson, Linville

Settled 1772
Population 13,472
Elevation 3,266 ft
Area Code 828
Zip 28607
Information Convention and Visitors Bureau, 208 Howard St, 28607-4032; phone 828/262-3516 or toll-free 800/852-9506; or North Carolina High Country Host, 1700 Blowing Rock Rd; phone 828/264-1299 or toll-free 800/438-7500
Web Site www.visitboonenc.com

Boone, the seat of Watauga County, was named for Daniel Boone, who had a cabin and hunted here in the 1760s. This "Heart of the High Country" sprawls over a long valley, which provides a natural pass through the hills. Watauga County boasts several industrial firms providing its economic base, in addition to tourism, agriculture, and Appalachian State University. Mountain crafts are featured in a variety of craft fairs, festivals, and shops.

What to See and Do

Appalachian State University. *504 Dauphblan St, Boone (28608). Atop Blue Ridge Mountains. Phone 828/262-2000.* (1899) (13,000 students) Offers 90 undergraduate and 12 graduate majors. Dark Sky Observatory. (See also SPECIAL EVENTS) Opposite is

Appalachian Cultural Museum. *University Hall Dr, Blowing Rock (28605). Phone 828/262-3117. www.museum.appstate.edu.* This regional museum presents an overview of the Blue Ridge area. Exhibits include Native American artifacts, plus exhibit on Daniel Boone, mountain music, and the environment. (Tues-Sat 10 am-5 pm, Sun 1-5 pm) **$**

Daniel Boone Native Gardens. *651 Horn in the West Dr, Boone (28607). 1 mile E off Hwy 421, adjacent to Daniel Boone Amphitheatre. Phone 828/264-6390.* Native plants in informal setting; Squire Boone Cabin, wishing well, fern garden. (May-Sept, daily; Oct, weekends) **$**

Special Events

An Appalachian Summer. *Appalachian State University, 504 Dauphblan St, Boone (28608). Phone toll-free 800/ 841-2787.* Concerts, drama, art exhibits.

Horn in the West. *Daniel Boone Amphitheatre, Boone. 1 mile E off Hwy 421. Phone 828/264-2120.* Outdoor drama depicts Daniel Boone and settlers of the mountains during the Revolutionary War. Tues-Sun evenings. Mid-June-mid-Aug.

Limited-Service Hotels

★ **HOLIDAY INN EXPRESS.** *1855 Blowing Rock Rd, Boone (28607). Phone 828/264-2451; toll-free 800/ 465-4329; fax 828/265-3861. www.holiday-inn.com.* 138 rooms, 2 story. Complimentary continental breakfast. Check-out 11 am. Fitness room. Outdoor pool. **$**
🧍 🛌

★ ★ **QUALITY INN.** *949 Blowing Rock Rd, Boone (28607). Phone 828/262-0020; toll-free 800/903- 8209; fax 828/262-9818. www.qualityinnboone.com.* Extensive renovations have brought this large hotel to a new level in value and appeal. The mountain setting, with nearby ski access, serves as a backdrop for cozy, lodgelike furnishings and stone walls in the lobby. Other amenities include room service and a game room—perfect for relaxing after a visit to nearby Appalachian State University or a day of shopping. 134 rooms, 7 story. Complimentary continental breakfast. Check-in 3 pm, check-out 11 am. High-speed Internet access. Restaurant, bar. Fitness room. Indoor pool. Business center. **$**
🧍 🛌 🏃

Specialty Lodging

The following lodging establishment is approved by Mobil Travel Guide, but due to its unique and individualized nature has not been given a traditional Mobil Star rating. Included in this listing you may find bed-and-breakfasts, limited-service inns, guest ranches, and other unique hotel properties.

LOVILL HOUSE INN. *404 Old Bristol Rd, Boone (28607). Phone 828/264-4204; toll-free 800/849-9466. www.lovillhouseinn.com.* Captain E. F. Lovill, a Civil War hero and state senator, built this traditional farmhouse in 1875. The 11-acre, wooded property offers a charming wraparound porch with plenty of rocking chairs. 6 rooms, 2 story. Closed Mar; two weeks in Sept. Children over 12 years only. Complimentary full breakfast. Check-in 3 pm, check-out 11 am. **$$**
🅓

Restaurants

★ **DAN'L BOONE INN.** *130 Hardin St, Boone (28607). Phone 828/264-8657. www.danlbooneinn.com.* Southern menu. Breakfast, lunch, dinner. Casual attire. No credit cards accepted. **$**

★ ★ **MAKOTO.** *2124 Blowing Rock Rd, Boone (28607). Phone 828/264-7976; fax 828/262-0579. www.makotos-boone.com.* Japanese menu. Lunch, dinner. Bar. Children's menu. Casual attire. Outdoor seating. **$$**

Brevard (B-2)

See also Asheville, Hendersonville

Settled 1861
Population 6,789
Elevation 2,230 ft
Area Code 828
Zip 28712
Information Chamber of Commerce, 35 W Main St, PO Box 589; phone 828/883-3700 or toll-free 800/648-4523
Web Site www.brevardnc.com

An industrial and mountain resort center near the entrance to Pisgah National Forest, Brevard has several industries, including Sterling Diagnostic Imaging, Inc, Coats American Company, and the Ecusta division of P. H. Glatfelter.

What to See and Do

Mount Pisgah. *Blue Ridge Pkwy, Hwy 276 to within 1 mile of the summit; a trail takes visitors the rest of the way.* 5,749 feet.

Pisgah National Forest. *160A Zillicoa St, Asheville (28802). Phone 828/257-4200. www.cs.unca.edu/nfsnc.* A 499,816-acre, four-district forest. The Cradle of Forestry Visitor Center (summer, daily; fee) is at the site of the first forestry school in the United States. The forest surrounds Mount Mitchell State Park (see LITTLE SWITZERLAND), which contains the highest point in the US east of the Mississippi (6,684 feet). Linville Gorge Wilderness is 10,975 acres of precipitous cliffs and cascading falls (permit required May-Oct for overnight camping; contact the Grandfather Ranger District in MARION). Wiseman's View looks into Linville Gorge. Shining Rock Wilderness contains 18,500 acres of rugged alpine scenery. The forest shares with Cherokee National Forest in Tennessee the 6,286-foot Roan Mountain, with its purple rhododendron and stands of spruce and fir. Swimming; good fishing for trout, bass, and perch; hunting for deer, bears, and small game; miles of hiking and riding trails; picnic sites; campgrounds (fee).

Special Events

Festival of the Arts. *1000 Probart St, Brevard (28712). Phone 828/884-2011.* Music, crafts, art, sporting events. Second week in July.

Summer Festival of Music. *Brevard Music Center. Whittington-Pfhol Auditorium, 1000 Probart St, Brevard (28712). Phone 828/884-2019.* More than 50 programs presented, including symphonic, choral, chamber, recital; musical comedy and operatic performances; guest artists. Late June-early Aug. Mon-Sat evenings, Sun afternoons.

Twilight Tour on Main. *62 W Main St, Brevard (28712). Phone 828/884-3278.* Horse and buggy rides, entertainment, refreshments. First Sat in Dec.

Limited-Service Hotel

★ **HOLIDAY INN EXPRESS HOTEL & SUITES.** *1570 Asheville Hwy, Brevard (28712). Phone 828/862-8900; fax 828/862-8909. www.brevardexpress.com.* 63 rooms. Check-in 3 pm, check-out 11 am. Outdoor pool. **$**
🖼

Bryson City (B-2)

See also Cherokee, Fontana Dam, Franklin, Great Smoky Mountains National Park, Robbinsville, Waynesville

Population 1,411
Elevation 1,736 ft
Area Code 828
Zip 28713
Information Chamber of Commerce, PO Box 509-W; phone 828/488-3681 or toll-free 800/867-9246
Web Site www.greatsmokies.com

At the confluence of the Little Tennessee and Tuckasegee rivers, Bryson City is also at the entrance to Great Smoky Mountains National Park. Fontana Lake, part of the TVA system, is nearby. Industries include textiles.

What to See and Do

Great Smoky Mountains Railway. *119 Front St, Dillsboro (28725). Phone toll-free 800/872-4681. www.gsmr.com.* Half-day rail excursions to Nantahala Gorge aboard diesel or steam locomotives. One-hour layover; view whitewater sports. Special excursions throughout the year (fees and dates vary). (Mar-Nov) **$$$$**

Whitewater rafting. Rolling Thunder River Company. *10 miles W on Hwy 19 S/74 W, at Nantahala Gorge.*

Phone 828/488-2030; toll-free 800/344-5838. www.roll ingthunderriverco.com. Guided raft, canoe, and kayak trips through the Smoky Mountains; day and overnight. Reservations recommended. For information and fees, contact Box 88, Almond 28702. (Apr-Oct)

Specialty Lodgings

The following lodging establishments are approved by Mobil Travel Guide, but due to their unique and individualized nature have not been given a traditional Mobil Star rating. Included in this listing you may find bed-and-breakfasts, limited-service inns, guest ranches, and other unique hotel properties.

THE CHALET INN. *285 Lone Oak Dr, Whittier (28789). Phone 828/586-0251; toll-free 800/789-8024. www.chaletinn.com.* European ambience in the Blue Ridge Mountains. 6 rooms, 2 story. Children over 12 years only. Complimentary full breakfast. Check-in 3 pm, check-out 10:30 am. **$**

FOLKESTONE INN BED & BREAKFAST. *101 Folkestone Rd, Bryson City (28713). Phone 828/ 488-2730; toll-free 888/812-3385; fax 828/488-0722. www.folkestone.com.* Built in 1926; restored country farmhouse. 10 rooms, 3 story. Closed Jan-Mar. Pets accepted. Children over 12 years only. Complimentary full breakfast. Check-in 3 pm, check-out 11 am. **$**
🐾

Burlington (A-6)

See also Greensboro, High Point

Settled Circa 1700
Population 44,917
Elevation 656 ft
Area Code 336
Information Burlington/Alamance County Convention and Visitors Bureau, PO Drawer 519, 27216; phone 336/570-1444 or toll-free 800/637-3804
Web Site www.burlington-area-nc.org

In 1837, E. M. Holt converted his father's gristmill on Alamance Creek into a textile mill. The Alamance Mill produced the first commercially dyed plaids south of the Potomac, changing the face of the textile industry in the South.

What to See and Do

Alamance Battleground State Historic Site. *5803 S Hwy 62, Burlington (27215). 6 miles SW on Hwy 62. Phone 336/227-4785.* On May 16, 1771, a two-hour battle was fought here between the colonial militia under Royal Governor Tryon and about 2,000 rebellious "Regulators." The latter were defeated. Restored log house; visitor center, exhibits, audiovisual presentation; picnic area. (Apr-Oct: daily; rest of year: Tues-Sun; closed holidays) **FREE**

Alamance County Historical Museum. *4777 S Hwy 62, Burlington (27215). 5 miles S on Hwy 62. Phone 336/ 226-8254.* 19th-century house-museum depicts life of textile pioneer E. M. Holt. Period rooms, audiovisual presentations. Rotating exhibits feature antique clothing and toys, Native American artifacts, traditional pottery and local history pieces. Docent-guided tours. (Tues-Sat) **FREE**

Dentzel Menagerie Carousel. *S Main and Church sts, Burlington (27216). In City Park. Phone 336/222-5033.* (Circa 1910) Rare hand-carved carousel; restored. (Apr-Oct, Tues-Sun) **$**

Lake Cammack Park and Marina. *4790 Union Ridge Rd, Burlington (27217). Phone 336/421-3872.* An 800-acre city reservoir. Water-skiing, fishing, boating. Picnic area, playground. (Mon-Wed, Fri-Sun; days vary winter) **$**

Special Events

Antiques Fair. Three-day event where antiques are sold and auctioned. Mar.

The Sword of Peace Summer Outdoor Drama. *301 Drama Rd, Snow Camp (27349). 18 miles SW via I-85, Liberty 49 S exit, then Hwy 49S and Hwy 1005 to Snow Camp. Phone 910/376-6948; toll-free 800/726-5115.* Repertory outdoor theater (evenings) and summer arts festival; 150-year-old and 200-year-old buildings converted into museums, craft gallery, and cane mill. Late June-late Aug. Thurs-Sat. Contact PO Box 535, Snow Camp, 27349.

Limited-Service Hotel

★ **HAMPTON INN.** *2701 Kirkpatrick Rd, Burlington (27215). Phone 336/584-4447; fax 336/585-1300.* 116 rooms, 4 story. Complimentary continental breakfast. Check-in 3 pm, check-out noon. Fitness room. Outdoor pool, whirlpool. **$**
🏃 🏊

Burnsville (B-3)

See also Asheville, Little Switzerland

Population 1,482
Elevation 2,814 ft
Area Code 828
Zip 28714
Information Yancey County Chamber of Commerce, 106 W Main St; phone 828/682-7413 or toll-free 800/948-1632
Web Site www.yanceychamber.com

A Ranger District office of the Pisgah National Forest (see BREVARD) is located here.

Special Events

Mount Mitchell Crafts Fair. *Town Square, Burnsville.* First Fri and Sat in Aug.

Old Time Days. *Town Square, Burnsville.* Late Sept.

Specialty Lodging

The following lodging establishment is approved by Mobil Travel Guide, but due to its unique and individualized nature has not been given a traditional Mobil Star rating. Included in this listing you may find bed-and-breakfasts, limited-service inns, guest ranches, and other unique hotel properties.

NU WRAY INN. *102 Town, Burnsville (28714). Phone 828/682-2329; toll-free 800/368-9729; fax 828/682-1113. www.nuwrayinn.com.* 26 rooms, 3 story. Check-in 3 pm, check-out 11 am. Restaurant. **$**

Buxton (B-10)

See also Cape Hatteras National Seashore, Ocracoke

Population 3,250
Elevation 10 ft
Area Code 252
Zip 27920
Web Site www.outerbanks.org

This town is on Hatteras Island, part of the Outer Banks (see). It is surrounded by Cape Hatteras National Seashore (see).

Limited-Service Hotel

★ **COMFORT INN.** *Hwy 12 and Old Lighthouse Rd, Buxton (27920). Phone 252/995-6100; toll-free 800/424-6423; fax 252/995-5444. www.choicehotels.com.* 60 rooms, 2 story. Complimentary continental breakfast. Check-in 3 pm, check-out 11 am. Beach. Outdoor pool. **$**

Restaurant

★ **TIDES.** *Hwy 12, Buxton (27920). Phone 252/995-5988.* American menu. Breakfast, dinner. Closed Dec-Mar. **$$**

Cape Hatteras National Seashore (B-10)

See also Buxton, Fort Raleigh National Historic Site, Hatteras, Kill Devil Hills, Nags Head, Ocracoke

Web Site www.nps.gov/caha
Enter from Cedar Island or Swan Quarter toll ferry. Free ferry from Ocracoke Island to Hatteras Island.

This thin strand stretches for 75 miles along the Outer Banks (see), threaded between the windy, pounding Atlantic and the shallow Pamlico Sound. Nags Head (see) is the northern limit of the recreational area, which has three sections (separated by inlets): Bodie (pronounced *body*), Hatteras (largest of the barrier islands), and Ocracoke (see), the most picturesque. Bounded on three sides by the park, but separate from it, are the villages of Rodanthe, Waves, Salvo, Avon, Buxton, Frisco, Hatteras, and Ocracoke. Although the area is noted for long expanses of sand beaches, wildflowers bloom most of the year. There are also stands of yaupon (holly), loblolly pine, and live oak. Several freshwater ponds are found on Bodie, Hatteras, and Ocracoke Islands. Many migratory and nonmigratory waterfowl winter here, including gadwalls, greater snow and Canada geese, loons, grebes, and herons.

There is an information station at Whalebone Junction (Memorial Day-Labor Day, daily), south of Nags Head. Near Bodie Island Lighthouse is a bird observation platform, a nature trail, and a visitor center

(Good Friday-Columbus Day, daily) with natural history exhibits. There are also visitor centers with history exhibits at Ocracoke (same hours), Bodie Island Lighthouse (same hours), and the Cape Hatteras Lighthouse at Buxton (daily; closed Dec 25).

Sportfishing, boating, sailing, swimming (recommended only at protected beaches); picnicking and camping (fee), also waterfowl hunting in season under regulation. For further information, contact the Superintendent, Rte 1, Box 675, Manteo, 27954; or call the Hatteras Island Visitor Center, phone 252/995-4474.

Cashiers (C-2)

See also Franklin, Highlands

Population 196
Elevation 3,486 ft
Area Code 828
Zip 28717
Information Cashiers Area Chamber of Commerce, PO Box 238; phone 828/743-5191
Web Site www.cashiersnorthcarolina.com

High in the Blue Ridge Mountains, this well-known summer resort area offers scenic drives on twisting mountain roads, hiking trails, views, waterfalls, lake sports, fishing, and other recreational activities.

What to See and Do

Fairfield Sapphire Valley Ski Area. *70 Sapphire Valley Rd, Sapphire (28774). 3 miles E on Hwy 64. Phone 828/743-3441. www.skisapphire.com.* Chair lift, rope tow; patrol, school, snowmaking. Longest run 1,600 feet, vertical drop 200 feet. (Mid-Dec-mid-Mar, daily) Night skiing. Evenings, half-day rates. Other seasons: swimming, fishing, boating; hiking, horseback riding; golf, tennis; recreation center. Restaurants, inn. **$$$$**

Lake Thorpe. *5 miles N on Hwy 107.* Fishing, swimming, water-skiing. Boats may be rented at Glenville (on the lake) or launched from here.

Full-Service Resort

★ ★ ★ **HIGH HAMPTON INN AND COUNTRY CLUB.** *Hwy 107 S, Cashiers (28717). Phone 828/743-2411; toll-free 800/334-2551; fax 828/743-5991. www.highhamptoninn.com.* Nestled in the Blue Ridge Mountains, this 1,400-acre property boasts a private lake and a quiet, wooded landscape. Guests of the inn, private cottages, or colony homes stay busy with the inn's scenic golf course, six clay tennis courts, and hiking trails. 120 rooms, 3 story. Closed Dec-Apr. Pets accepted, some restrictions; fee. Check-in 3 pm, check-out 1 pm. Two restaurants, bar. Children's activity center. Fitness room. Beach. Golf, 18 holes. Tennis. Airport transportation available. Business center. **$$**

Full-Service Inn

★ ★ ★ **THE GREYSTONE.** *Greystone Ln, Lake Toxaway (28747). Phone 828/966-4700; fax 828/862-5689. www.greystoneinn.com.* The main building of this historic inn was built in 1915 and welcomed Fords and Rockefellers to the natural beauty of the picturesque lake. Restored in 1985, the inn still pampers with individually decorated rooms, a full-service spa, and outdoor recreation. 33 rooms, 3 story. Complimentary full breakfast. Check-in 3 pm, check-out noon. Restaurant. Children's activity center. Beach. Outdoor pool. Golf. Tennis. **$$$**

Specialty Lodging

The following lodging establishment is approved by Mobil Travel Guide, but due to its unique and individualized nature has not been given a traditional Mobil Star rating. Included in this listing you may find bed-and-breakfasts, limited-service inns, guest ranches, and other unique hotel properties.

INNISFREE VICTORIAN INN. *7 Lakeside Knoll, Glenville (28736). Phone 828/743-2946. www.innisfreeinn.com.* This inn and neighboring garden house is a wonderful place to visit whatever the season. The large, wraparound veranda is shaded by oak trees and faces Lake Glenville and the surrounding Blue Ridge Mountains. 10 rooms, 2 story. No children allowed. Complimentary full breakfast. Check-in 3 pm, check-out 11 am. **$$**

Chapel Hill (B-6)

See also Durham, Raleigh

Founded 1793
Population 48,715
Elevation 487 ft
Area Code 919
Information Chapel Hill-Carrboro Chamber of

Commerce, 104 S Estes Dr, PO Box 2897, 27515; phone 919/967-7075
Web Site www.carolinachamber.org

The community of Chapel Hill is centered around the University of North Carolina, the oldest state university in the United States. This school has been a leader in American education for more than 170 years and is now part of a "research triangle," together with Duke University at Durham and North Carolina State University at Raleigh. Despite heavy losses of faculty and students to the Civil War, the school remained open until the years of Reconstruction, 1870-1875. During the next decade, the university was reborn.

What to See and Do

Chapel of the Cross. *304 E Franklin St, Chapel Hill. Adjacent to Morehead Planetarium. Phone 919/929-2193.* (1842-1848) Antebellum Gothic Revival Episcopal church. (Sun-Fri)

Horace Williams House. *610 E Rosemary St, Chapel Hill. Phone 919/942-7818.* Historic house is home to the Chapel Hill Preservation Society; changing art exhibits, chamber music concerts. Guided tours. (Tues-Fri, also Sun afternoons; closed holidays and the first two weeks in Aug) **FREE**

North Carolina Botanical Garden. *15501 Old Mason Farm Rd, Chapel Hill. Phone 919/962-0522.* Approximately 600 acres; variety of trees and plants of the southeastern United States; wildflower areas, herb gardens. Nature trails. (Daily). **FREE**

University of North Carolina at Chapel Hill. *250 E Franklin St, Chapel Hill (27599). Phone 919/962-1630.* (1795) (Approximately 27,000 students) This institution, the first state university in the country, is on a 720-acre campus and has more than 200 buildings. On campus are

    Coker Arboretum. *Cameron Ave and Raleigh St, Chapel Hill (27599). Phone 919/962-0522.* Covers 5 acres. Extensive collection of ornamental plants and shrubs.

    Davie Poplar. *N of Old Well.* Ancient ivy-covered tree named for the "father of the university," William Richardson Davie; more than 200 years old.

    Kenan Stadium. *University of North Carolina at Chapel Hill, behind Bell Tower. Phone 919/962-1039.* (1927) Seats 52,000; in a wooded natural bowl.

Memorial Hall. *Cameron Ave and South Rd, Chapel Hill (27514). Opposite New West.* (1930) White columns front this structure dedicated to war dead, honored alumni, and university benefactors. James K. Polk, class of 1818, has a commemorative tablet here. He graduated first in his class and became the 11th President of the United States.

Morehead-Patterson Memorial Bell Tower. *Stadium Dr and South Rd, Chapel Hill (27514).* (1930) A 172-foot Italian Renaissance campanile; concert chimes. The 12 bells range in weight from 300 pounds to almost 2 tons. Popular tunes are rung daily.

Morehead Planetarium. *250 E Franklin St, Chapel Hill (27514). Phone 919/549-6863.* Offers indoor star-gazing, art gallery with permanent and changing exhibits, scientific exhibits; rare Zeiss instrument. Shows (daily; closed Dec 24-25). Rose garden has mammoth sundial showing time around the world. **$$**

Old East. *E of Old Well.* Oldest state university building in the country; cornerstone laid in 1793. Matched by Old West (1823). Still being used as a residence hall.

Old Well. *Cameron Ave, Chapel Hill. In the center of campus.* Long the unofficial symbol of the university, this well was the only source of water here for nearly a century. The present "Greek temple" structure dates to 1897.

Paul Green Theater. *South and Country Club rds, Chapel Hill (27514). Phone 919/962-1630.* (1978) PlayMakers Repertory Company. Named for one of the first dramatic arts students at the university. Green is known as the father of American outdoor drama. (Sept-May)

PlayMakers Theater. *Country Club and South rds, Chapel Hill (27514).* (1851) Greek Revival temple was designed as a combination library and ballroom.

South (Main) Building. *Cameron Ave and Raleigh St, Chapel Hill (27514). Opposite Old Well.* Cornerstone laid in 1798, but the building was not completed until 1814, during which time the boys lived inside the roofless walls in little huts. Future President James K. Polk lived here from 1814 to 1818.

Wilson Library. *South Rd and Stadium Dr, Chapel Hill (27514). Phone 919/962-0114.* Houses special collections. Includes North Carolina Collection

Gallery; historic rooms, texts, and artifacts. Also here is the Southern Historical Collection, featuring manuscripts, rare books, and photographs (daily).

Limited-Service Hotels

★ **BEST WESTERN UNIVERSITY INN.** *Hwy 54, Chapel Hill (27515). Phone 919/932-3000; fax 919/ 968-6513. www.bestwestern.com.* 84 rooms, 1 story. Complimentary continental breakfast. Check-in 1 pm, check-out noon. Outdoor pool. **$**

★ **HAMPTON INN.** *1740 Hwy 15/501, Chapel Hill (27514). Phone 919/968-3000; fax 919/929-0322. www.hamptoninnchapelhill.com.* 121 rooms, 2 story. Complimentary continental breakfast. Check-out noon. Outdoor pool. **$**

★ ★ **HOLIDAY INN.** *1301 N Fordham Blvd, Chapel Hill (27514). Phone 919/929-2171; fax 919/929-5736. www.holidayinnchapelhill.com.* 135 rooms, 2 story. Check-in 3 pm, check-out noon. Restaurant, bar. Fitness room. Outdoor pool. **$**

Full-Service Hotels

★ ★ ★ **THE CAROLINA INN.** *211 Pittsboro St, Chapel Hill (27516). Phone 919/933-2001; toll-free 800/ 962-8519; fax 919/918-2760. www.carolinainn.com.* Guests can enjoy the quiet village setting of Chapel Hill from this inn, which provides excellent accommodations. Located within a short distance to art galleries, museums, charming shops, and fine restaurants. 184 rooms, 3 story. Pets accepted, some restrictions; fee. Check-in 3 pm, check-out noon. Restaurant, bar. Fitness room. **$$**

★ ★ ★ **SHERATON HOTEL.** *1 Europa Dr, Chapel Hill (27514). Phone 919/968-4900; fax 919/968-3520. www.sheratonchapelhill.com.* Each room features the expected amenities. A fitness center and outdoor pool are available for visitors, and there are plenty of local attractions nearby. 168 rooms, 4 story. Check-in 3 pm, check-out noon. Restaurant, bar. Fitness room. Outdoor pool. **$**

★ ★ ★ **SIENA HOTEL.** *1505 E Franklin St, Chapel Hill (27514). Phone 919/929-4000; toll-free 800/223-7379; fax 919/968-8527. www.sienahotel.com.*

Southern hospitality and grand European styling make The Siena Hotel a favorite in Chapel Hill. This elegant hotel is a gracious home-away-from-home with its welcoming service and lavish ambience. The guest rooms and suites are tastefully appointed with fine furnishings, rich fabrics, and unique decorative objects, while modern amenities ensure the highest levels of comfort. Guest privileges at the UNC golf course and nearby fitness center and spa are extended to hotel occupants, and business travelers appreciate the many thoughtful amenities created especially for them. Dining is of special note here, where Il Palio Ristorante (see) charms visitors throughout the day with its bountiful breakfasts and delicious northern Italian-influenced lunch and dinner selections. 80 rooms, 4 story. Pets accepted, some restrictions; fee. Complimentary continental breakfast. Check-in 4 pm, check-out noon. Restaurant, bar. Airport transportation available. **$$**

Restaurants

★ **ALLEN & SON BARBEQUE.** *6203 Milhouse Rd, Chapel Hill (27514). Phone 919/942-7576.* Barbecue menu. Lunch, dinner. Closed Sun-Mon. Casual attire. Outdoor seating. **$**

★ ★ **AURORA.** *1350 Raleigh Rd, Chapel Hill (27514). Phone 919/942-2400; fax 919/929-5927. www.aurorarestaurant.com.* Italian menu. Dinner. Closed holidays. Bar. Casual attire. Reservations recommended. Valet parking. Outdoor seating. **$$**

★ ★ ★ **CAROLINA CROSSROADS.** *211 Pittsboro St, Chapel Hill (27516). Phone 919/933-2001; toll-free 800/222-8733; fax 919/918-2795. www.carolinainn.com.* Set in the historic Carolina Inn, the Carolina Crossroads restaurant is a picture-perfect example of Southern hospitality. The dining room seems primed for an elegant evening soiree, with hardwood floors, mahogany chairs, blue and white floral tapestry chairs, and dramatic fabric drapes. The menu often strikes delicious notes, with regional dishes incorporating local, seasonal ingredients prepared in a progressive American style. You'll find everything from a classic North Carolina pulled pork sandwich (a necessary food group in these parts) to more lady-like dishes like salmon with grilled acorn squash in white-wine butter sauce, part of the chef's nightly six-course tasting menu. For a chance to feel like Scarlet O'Hara, settle in for afternoon tea or cocktails at the restaurant's old-world bar, complete with cozy, tufted leather chairs and a blazing fireplace. Southern, New Age menu. Breakfast, lunch, dinner. Bar. Children's menu. Business casual attire. Reservations recommended. Valet parking. Outdoor seating. **$$$**

★ ★ ★ **IL PALIO.** *1505 E Franklin St, Chapel Hill (27514). Phone 919/929-4000; toll-free 800/223-7379; fax 919/968-8527. www.sienahotel.com.* Situated in the Siena Hotel, this restaurant offers guests a fine-dining experience. A wine steward will help in selecting the right wine for the occassion. Italian menu. Breakfast, lunch, dinner, Sun brunch. Bar. Casual attire. **$$$**

★ ★ **LA RESIDENCE.** *202 W Rosemary St, Chapel Hill (27516). Phone 919/967-2506; fax 919/967-2504.* French menu. Dinner, late-night. Closed Jan 1, Dec 24-25. Bar. Business casual attire. Reservations recommended. Outdoor seating. **$$$**

★ **SPANKY'S.** *101 E Franklin St, Chapel Hill (27514). Phone 919/967-2678; fax 919/967-6260. www.spankysrestaurant.com.* American, Bar Food. Lunch, dinner. Bar. Casual attire. **$**

★ **SQUID'S.** *1201 N Fordham Blvd, Chapel Hill (27514). Phone 919/942-8757; fax 919/942-8798. www.squidschapelhill.com.* Seafood menu. Dinner. Closed holidays. Bar. Children's menu. Casual attire. **$**

Charlotte (B-4)

See also Concord, Cornelius, Gastonia

Settled 1748
Population 540,828
Elevation 700 ft
Area Code 704
Information Convention and Visitors Bureau, 122 E Stonewall St, 28202; phone 704/334-2282 or toll-free 800/722-1994
Web Site www.charlottecvb.org

The Carolinas' largest metropolis, Charlotte grew quickly as a regional retail, financial, and distribution center and became the nation's leader in the textile industry. General Cornwallis occupied the town for a short time in 1780, but met such determined resistance that he called it a "hornet's nest," a name that has been applied with pride on the city seal and by several local groups. Gold was discovered here in 1799, and the region around Charlotte was the nation's major gold producer until the California gold rush in 1848. There was a US Mint here between 1837 and

1861. The last Confederate Cabinet meeting was held here in 1865.

Chiefly agricultural and dependent on slave labor in antebellum days, the region took eagerly to industry after Appomattox. Abundant water power for electricity from the Catawba River has been a principal reason for its rapid growth. Today, Charlotte is among the largest banking centers in the country.

Public Transportation

Airport. Information 704/359-4013; lost and found 704/359-4012.

Buses Charlotte Transit System, phone 704/336-3366

What to See and Do

Carolina Panthers (NFL). *Bank of America Stadium, 800 S Mint St, Charlotte (28202). Phone 704/358-7000. www.panthers.com.*

Charlotte Bobcats (NBA). *Charlotte Coliseum, 100 Paul Buck Blvd, Charlotte (28217). Phone 704/262-2287. www.nba.com/bobcats.* New professional basketball team.

Charlotte Coliseum. *100 Paul Buck Blvd, Charlotte. Phone 704/357-4700.* This 23,000-seat arena hosts various sport events as well as family shows and concerts.

The Charlotte Museum of History and Hezekiah Alexander Homesite. *3500 Shamrock Dr, Charlotte (28215). Phone 704/568-1774. www.charlottemuseum.org.* Includes the Hezekiah Alexander House (1774), the oldest dwelling still standing in Mecklenburg County; two-story springhouse; working log kitchen. Tours (fee). Admission free Sun. (Tues-Sat 10 am-5 pm; Sun 1-5 pm; open Mon in summer; closed holidays) **$$**

Charlotte Sting (WNBA). *Charlotte Coliseum, 100 Paul Buck Blvd, Charlotte (28217). Phone 704/357-4801. www.wnba.com/sting.* Women's professional basketball team.

Discovery Place. *301 N Tryon St, Charlotte (28202). Phone 704/372-6261; toll-free 800/935-0553. www.discoveryplace.org.* Discovery Place is a hands-on science museum that gives kids (and adults who like to play) a chance to learn about electricity, weather, rocks, minerals, and other scientific wonders. Visit the aquarium, science circus, life center, rain forest, collections gallery, and OMNIMAX theater, as well as major traveling exhibits. (Daily; closed Thanksgiving, Dec 24-25) **$$**

James K. Polk Memorial State Historic Site. *308 S Polk St, Pineville (28134). Phone 704/889-7145.* Replica of log cabin and outbuildings at the birthplace of the 11th President of the United States. Visitor center with exhibits, film. Guided tour. (Tues-Sat) **FREE**

Latta Plantation Center and Nature Preserve. *5226 Sample Rd, Huntersville (28078). 12 miles NW via I-77, exit 16B (Sunset Rd W), right at Beattie's Ford Rd, 5 miles, then left at Sample Rd. Phone 704/875-1391. www.lattaplantation.org.* A more than 1,200-acre nature preserve on Mount Island Lake. Interpretive center, Carolina Raptor Center, Audubon bird sanctuary, equestrian center (fees apply for some). Bridle paths, hiking trails, fishing, picnicking, canoe access. (Daily) **FREE** Also here are

Historic Latta Plantation. *5225 Sample Rd, Huntersville (28078). Phone 704/875-2312.* (Circa 1800) Restored Federal-style plantation house, original smokehouse; barns, farm animals; kitchen garden, cotton field. (Tues-Sun; closed holidays) **$$**

Mint Museum of Art. *2730 Randolph Rd, Charlotte (28207). Phone 704/337-2000. www.mintmuseum.org.* The first Branch of the US Mint operated in the building from 1837 to 1861 and 1867 to 1913, and in 1933 it was chartered as an art museum. Collections include European and American art from Renaissance to contemporary, fine pottery and porcelain, maps, period costumes, pre-Columbian and African artifacts, and an exhibition of coins. (Tues-Sun; closed holidays) **$$**

Mint Museum of Craft and Design. *220 N Tryon St, Charlotte. Phone 704/337-2000.* (Tues-Sun; closed holidays) **$$$**

Levine Museum of the New South. *200 E Seventh St, Charlotte (28202). Phone 704/333-1887. www.museum ofthenewsouth.org.* The museum chronicles the history of the post-Civil War South with an ever-changing series of exhibits featuring industry, ideas, people, and historical eras such as the civil rights movement. (Tues-Sat 10 am-5 pm, Sun noon-5 pm) **$$**

Nature Museum. *1658 Sterling Rd, Charlotte. Phone 704/372-6261.* Live animal room, nature trail, puppet theater, earth science hall. (Daily; closed Thanksgiving, Dec 25) **$$**

Ovens Auditorium. *2700 E Independence Blvd, Charlotte. 5 miles E on Hwy 74. Phone 704/372-3600 (for schedule).* Shows by touring Broadway companies (fall-late spring), musicals, symphony.

Paramount's Carowinds. *14523 Carowinds Blvd, Charlotte (28273). I-77, exit 90, at state line. Phone 704/588-2600; toll-free 800/888-4386. www.carowinds.com.* This 100-acre family theme park has more than 40 rides, shows, and attractions including the 12-acre water entertainment complex WaterWorks; Nickelodeon Central children's area; Drop Zone stunt tower; and rollercoasters. The 13,000-seat Paladium Amphitheater hosts special events. (June-late Aug: daily; Mar-May and Sept-Oct: weekends) **$$$$**

Spirit Square Center for the Arts and Education. *345 N College St, Charlotte. Phone 704/333-4686.* Exhibitions by well-known contemporary artists; studio art classes (fee); performances (fee).

University of North Carolina at Charlotte. *9201 University Blvd, Charlotte. NE off I-85. Phone 704/547-4286.* (1946) (15,000 students) Beautiful landscaping and blooming plants (Mar-Nov); rhododendron garden (blooms Apr-May); ornamental garden, public greenhouse with rainforest and orchid collection. Sculpture garden. Rare book room and panoramic view of campus, 10th floor of library (Mon-Fri; closed holidays). Walking tour guide and map.

Special Events

Auto racing. *Lowe's Motor Speedway, 5555 Concord Pkwy, Charlotte. Phone 704/455-3200.* Coca-Cola 600 Winston Cup stock car race (Memorial Day weekend); CUAW GM 500 (Oct); Spring AutoFair car show and flea market (mid-Apr); Fall AutoFair (mid-Sept-Oct).

Center City Fest. *129 W Trade St, Charlotte (28202).* Three-day festival in uptown. Food, live entertainment. Last weekend in Apr.

Festival in the Park. *Freedom Park, 1900 E Blvd, Charlotte (28203). Phone 704/338-1060. www.festivalin thepark.org.* Arts and crafts, entertainment. Mid-Sept.

Opera Carolina. *345 N College St, Charlotte. Phone 704/332-7177. www.operacarolina.org.* Oct-Apr.

Symphony. *201 S College St, Charlotte. Phone 704/332-6136.* Charlotte Symphony Orchestra, Inc. Performs year-round.

Theatre Charlotte. *501 Queens Rd, Charlotte. Phone 704/334-9128.* Classic and Broadway plays. Features six productions a year on alternate months beginning in Sept. Thurs-Sat evenings, Sun.

Limited-Service Hotels

★ ★ **COURTYARD BY MARRIOTT CITY CENTER.** *237 S Tryon St, Charlotte (28202). Phone 704/926-5800; fax 704/926-5801. www.courtyard.com.* 171 rooms. Outdoor pool. **$$**
🏊

★ ★ **COURTYARD BY MARRIOTT.** *333 W W. T. Harris Blvd, Charlotte (28262). Phone 704/ 549-4888; toll-free 800/321-2211; fax 704/549-4946. www.courtyard.com.* Situated near Highway 85, as well as the UNC campus, this hotel features guest laundry and high-speed Internet access in the lobby. Varied dining and shopping options are also located nearby. 152 rooms, 4 story. Check-in 3 pm, check-out noon. High-speed Internet access. Laundry services. Restaurant. Fitness room. Outdoor pool, whirlpool. **$**
🧍 🏊

★ ★ **DOUBLETREE HOTEL.** *895 W Trade St, Charlotte (28202). Phone 704/347-0070; toll-free 800/ 222-8733; fax 704/347-0267. www.doubletree.com.* This property's location makes it convenient for business travelers, as it is just blocks from the convention center, and for leisure travelers, since uptown offers shopping and dining. Guest rooms feature equipped work desks and data ports. 187 rooms, 8 story. Check-in 3 pm, check-out noon. Wireless Internet access. Restaurant, bar. Fitness room. Outdoor pool, whirlpool. **$**
🧍 🏊

★ ★ **EMBASSY SUITES.** *4800 S Tryon St, Charlotte (28217). Phone 704/527-8400; toll-free 800/ 362-2779; fax 704/527-7035. www.embassy-charlotte .com.* This all-suite hotel offers tons of fitness facilities, including a workout room, an indoor pool, Jacuzzi, and sauna. Each morning guests can enjoy a fully cooked-to-order complimentary breakfast before visiting the attractions in the area. 274 rooms, 8 story, all suites. Complimentary full breakfast. Check-in 3 pm, check-out noon. High-speed Internet access, wireless Internet access. Restaurant, bar. Fitness room. Indoor pool, whirlpool. Airport transportation available. Business center. **$**
✈ 🧍 🏊 🏃

★ **LA QUINTA INN AND SUITES CHARLOTTE COLISEUM.** *4900 S Tryon St, Charlotte (28217). Phone 704/523-5599; toll-free 800/687-6667; fax*

704/523-5156. 131 rooms. Check-in 3 pm, check-out 11 am. **$**

★ **RAMADA LIMITED.** *7900 Nations Ford Rd, Charlotte (28217). Phone 704/522-7110; toll-free 800/272-6232; fax 704/521-9778. www.ramada.com.* 110 rooms, 3 story. Pets accepted; fee. Complimentary continental breakfast. Check-in 3 pm, check-out noon. Restaurant, bar. Outdoor pool. **$**
🐾 🏊

★ **SUMMERFIELD SUITES.** *4920 S Tryon St, Charlotte (28217). Phone 704/525-2600; toll-free 800/ 833-4353; fax 704/521-9932. www.summerfieldsuites. com.* Centrally located just ten minutes from uptown Charlotte, this hotel is perfect for family vacations. With a relaxed atmosphere, it is well suited for relocation extended stays. 144 rooms, 5 story, all suites. Pets accepted, some restrictions; fee. Complimentary continental breakfast. Check-in 3 pm, check-out noon. High-speed Internet access. Fitness room. Outdoor pool, whirlpool. Airport transportation available. Business center. **$**
🐾 🧍 🏊 🏃

★ ★ **WYNDHAM GARDEN.** *2600 Yorkmont Rd, Charlotte (28208). Phone 704/357-9100; toll-free 800/ 996-3426; fax 704/357-9159. www.wyndham.com.* This 179-room property, across from the Charlotte Coliseum and 15 minutes from downtown, is great for business travelers. Rooms are comfortable with generous work space, a free daily newspaper, and complimentary transportation to the nearby airport. Relax amid the pool's gardenlike landscaping. 173 rooms, 3 story. Check-in 3 pm, check-out noon. High-speed Internet access. Restaurant, bar. Fitness room. Outdoor pool, whirlpool. Airport transportation available. **$**
✈ 🧍 🏊

Full-Service Hotels

★ ★ ★ **THE DUNHILL HOTEL.** *237 N Tryon St, Charlotte (28202). Phone 704/332-4141; toll-free 800/ 354-4141; fax 704/376-4117. www.dunhillhotel.com.* European-style hotel built in 1929; 18th-century furnishings, original artwork. 60 rooms, 10 story. Check-in 3 pm, check-out 11 am. High-speed Internet access, wireless Internet access. Restaurant, bar. **$$**

★ ★ ★ **HILTON CHARLOTTE CENTER CITY.** *222 E 3rd St, Charlotte (28202). Phone 704/377-1500; toll-free 800/445-8667; fax 704/377-4143. www.charlotte .hilton.com.* Perfect for business or pleasure, this hotel is in the financial district near the finest shops and restaurants in the area. Also nearby are beaches, golf courses, and the Carolina Mountains. This property also offers all amenities for guest comfort. 407 rooms, 22 story. Check-in 3 pm, check-out noon. High-speed Internet access. Restaurant, two bars. Business center. $$

★ ★ ★ **HILTON UNIVERSITY PLACE.** *8629 J. M. Keynes Dr, Charlotte (28262). Phone 704/547-7444; toll-free 925/210-8900; fax 704/548-1081. www.charlotteuniversity.hilton.com.* Guest rooms and suites that have great views of the university area, guests are sure to be pleased. Relax over dinner at the Lakeside Restaurant or in the Lakeside Lounge, enjoy the pool, or take advantage of the many nearby attractions. 393 rooms, 12 story. Check-in 3 pm, check-out noon. Wireless Internet access. Restaurant, bar. Fitness room. Outdoor pool. $$

★ ★ ★ **HYATT.** *5501 Carnegie Blvd, Charlotte (28209). Phone 704/554-1234; toll-free 800/233-1234; fax 704/554-8319. www.hyatt.com.* Found in the prestigious 90-acre South Park business district, this hotel is across from the South Park shopping mall and is near downtown Charlotte and the Charlotte/Douglas International Airport. 262 rooms, 7 story. Check-in 3 pm, check-out noon. Restaurant, bar. Fitness room. Indoor pool. Business center. $

★ ★ ★ **MARRIOTT CITY CENTER.** *100 W Trade St, Charlotte (28202). Phone 704/333-9000; toll-free 800/228-9290; fax 704/342-3419. www.marriottcitycenter.com.* Located in the central uptown business district, this hotel is only blocks from the New Charlotte Convention Center and Bank of America Stadium. 442 rooms, 19 story. Check-in 3 pm, check-out noon. High-speed Internet access. Four restaurants, three bars. Fitness room. Indoor pool, whirlpool. Business center. $$

★ ★ ★ **OMNI HOTEL.** *132 E Trade St, Charlotte (28202). Phone 704/377-0400; toll-free 800/843-6664; fax 704/347-0649. www.omnihotels.com.* This downtown hotel is located near a science center, performance and cultural center, and other attractions. 374 rooms, 15 story. Pets accepted; fee. Check-in 3 pm, check-out noon. High-speed Internet access, wireless Internet access. Restaurant, bar. Fitness room. Outdoor pool. Business center. $$

★ ★ ★ **THE PARK HOTEL.** *2200 Rexford Rd, Charlotte (28211). Phone 704/364-8220; toll-free 800/334-0331; fax 704/365-4712. www.theparkhotel.com.* Minutes from Charlotte's uptown business district, The Park Hotel enjoys a quiet location in the elegant enclave of South Park. While the convenient setting and modern amenities make this an obvious choice for business travelers, the nine-hole putting green, Charles Grayson Day Spa, and fitness center with pool are ideal for leisure visitors. Adjacent to the specialty shops of The Park at South Park, the hotel is also a perfect base for serious shoppers. The rooms and suites are tastefully appointed with rich colors and traditional furnishings, and the spacious bathrooms enhance the luxurious residential atmosphere. The specialty suites present an appealing alternative with their distinctive flair. The amiable staff provides intuitive service, adding to the seamless experience. Smoky's Grill has a cozy ambience, and its menu of universal favorites pleases all diners. 192 rooms, 6 story. Check-in 4 pm, check-out noon. High-speed Internet access, wireless Internet access. Restaurant, bar. Fitness room. Outdoor pool, whirlpool. Business center. $$

★ ★ ★ **RENAISSANCE SUITES.** *2800 Coliseum Center Dr, Charlotte (28216). Phone 704/357-1414; toll-free 800/468-3571; fax 704/357-1401. www.renaissancehotels.com.* Located just 15 minutes from downtown and next door to the Colliseum, this convention and conference hotel features comfortable, spacious rooms. 275 rooms, 9 story, all suites. Check-in 4 pm, check-out noon. High-speed Internet access. Restaurant, bar. Fitness room. Indoor/outdoor pool, whirlpool. Business center. $$

★ ★ ★ **THE WESTIN.** *601 S College St, Charlotte (28202). Phone 704/375-2600; toll-free 800/937-8461; fax 704/375-2623. www.westin.com/charlotte.* 700 rooms. Pets accepted, some restrictions. Check-in 3 pm, check-out noon. High-speed Internet access. Restaurant, bar. Fitness room. Indoor pool. Business center. $$

Full-Service Resort

★ ★ ★ **BALLANTYNE RESORT.** *10000 Ballantyne Commons Pkwy, Charlotte (28277). Phone 704/248-4000; fax 704/248-4005.* Golfers make a beeline for Charlotte's Ballantyne Resort. This elegant resort within the city limits is a paradise for golf enthusiasts, with one of the state's best 18-hole courses and the renowned Dana Rader Golf School. Guests who prefer to spend their time on the tennis courts will delight in the fantastic facility run by a leading pro, while spa-goers will be in bliss with more than 60 different treatments to soothe their troubles away. A continental flair dominates the guest rooms and suites, and lavish touches, such as marble entrances and bathrooms, leave a lasting impression. A natural choice for conferences, this resort is also ideal for quick breaks for couples or family vacations. 214 rooms. Check-in 4 pm, check-out noon. Restaurant, bar. Fitness room, spa. Indoor pool, whirlpool. Golf. Tennis. **$$**

Specialty Lodgings

The following lodging establishments are approved by Mobil Travel Guide, but due to their unique and individualized nature have not been given a traditional Mobil Star rating. Included in this listing you may find bed-and-breakfasts, limited-service inns, guest ranches, and other unique hotel properties.

THE DUKE MANSION. *400 Hermitage Rd, Charlotte (28207). Phone 704/714-4400; toll-free 888/202-1009; fax 704/714-4435. www.leeinstitute.org.* This gracious Southern estate is a lovely setting for a weekend getaway. The home was once owned by James Buchanan Duke, who is responsible for establishing both Duke Energy and Duke University. Today, acres of gardens surround the well-maintained home, which has treetop rooms as well as standard guest rooms, some with sleeping porches. The mansion also serves as a facility for meetings and retreats. 20 rooms. Check-in 3 pm, check-out noon. Fitness room. **$$**

THE MOREHEAD INN. *1122 Morehead St, Charlotte (28204). Phone 704/376-3357; fax 704/335-1110. www.moreheadinn.com.* 10 rooms. **$$**

VAN LANDINGHAM ESTATE. *2010 The Plaza, Charlotte (28205). Phone 704/334-8909; toll-free 888/524-2020. www.vanlandinghamestate.com.* 5 rooms. Check-in 3 pm, check-out noon. **$$**

THE VICTORIAN VILLA. *10925 Windy Grove Rd, Charlotte (28278). Phone 704/394-5545; fax 704/394-5525. www.victorianvillainn.com.* 5 rooms. Check-in 3 pm, check-out 11 am. **$$**

Restaurants

★ ★ ★ **BISTRO 100.** *100 N Tryon St, Charlotte (28202). Phone 704/344-0515; fax 704/344-4773. www.bistro100restaurant.com.* The rustic, homey atmosphere of this restaurant, set in an old restored barn, is what keeps diners coming back. A warm fireplace, quaint bushel-basket lights, and huge barrels of red delicious apples guard the entrance way, where diners wait to sit at tables set with old-fashioned red and white-checked tablecloths. French bistro menu. Lunch, dinner, Sun brunch. Bar. Children's menu. Business casual attire. Reservations recommended. Outdoor seating. **$$**

★ ★ ★ **BRAVO.** *555 S McDowell St, Charlotte (28204). Phone 704/372-5440; fax 704/348-4646.* Located in the Adams Mark hotel, this Italian restaurant features singing waiters and Italian décor throughout. Italian menu. Dinner. Bar. Children's menu. Valet parking. **$$**

★ ★ **FUSE BOX.** *227 W Trade St, Suite 1200, Charlotte (28202). Phone 704/376-8885; fax 704/376-8882.* Sushi, pan-Asian menu. Lunch, dinner. Closed Sun. Casual attire. **$$**

★ ★ **THE KABOB HOUSE.** *6432 E Independence Blvd, Charlotte (28212). Phone 704/531-2500.* Middle Eastern menu. Lunch, dinner. Closed Mon. Casual attire. Reservations recommended. **$$**

★ ★ ★ **LA BIBLIOTHEQUE.** *1901 Roxborough Rd, Charlotte (28211). Phone 704/365-5000; fax 704/365-3081.* If guests are looking for the full dining-out experience, this is the place. Included in this experience are the completely knowledgeable servers. Whatever diners order, they're guaranteed it will be served with the same professionalism every time. American, French menu. Lunch, dinner. Closed Sat-Mon; holidays. Bar. Jacket required. Outdoor seating. **$$$**

★ ★ ★ **LAVECCHIA'S SEAFOOD GRILLE.** *225 E 6th St, Charlotte (28202). Phone 704/370-6776. www.lavecchias.com.* Located in the heart of downtown Charlotte, LaVecchia's is a festive spot for lovers of sea-faring entrées like sea bass and seared yellowfin tuna. The fish is as fresh as you'll find in Charlotte, which must explain why the restaurant is a local favorite that's packed with a stylish crowd. To complement the oceanic menu—dishes like grilled swordfish, fried trout, and the signature lobster with citrus butter sauce (this one requires a bib)—the restaurant is decked out in a modern, urban, marine-themed design. Aquamarine is a prominent color, metal sculptures of sea creatures hang from the room's cavernous ceilings, and tropical fish-filled aquariums are tucked into the walls. Seafood menu. Dinner. Closed Sun. Bar. **$$$**

★ ★ **MCNINCH HOUSE.** *511 N Church St, Charlotte (28202). Phone 704/332-6159.* French menu. Dinner. Closed Mon-Sun; holidays. Bar. Jacket required. Reservations recommended. Valet parking. Outdoor seating. **$$$$**

★ **MERT'S HEART & SOUL.** *214 N College St, Charlotte (28202). Phone 704/342-4222; fax 704/342-4499. www.mertsuptown.com.* The super laid-back atmosphere of this neighborhood favorite is clear the moment you walk through the door—you're greeted by the smells of soul food simmering in the kitchen and eclectic décor in red, purple, and beige. Southern/Soul menu. Lunch, dinner, brunch. Casual attire. Outdoor seating. **$**

★ ★ ★ **PATOU BISTRO.** *2400 Park Rd, Suite M, Charlotte (28203). Phone 704/376-2233; fax 704/342-2381.* With outdoor dining and black-and-white photos displayed throughout, guests will enjoy the atmosphere of a true French bistro. French menu. Lunch, dinner. Closed Sun. Bar. Business casual attire. Reservations recommended. Outdoor seating. **$$**

★ **RAINBOW CAFE.** *201 S College St, Charlotte (28031). Phone 704/372-2256; fax 704/372-2257. www.rainbowcafeuptown.com.* The clean and simple décor of this second-floor eatery can be deceiving, as the lunch hour here is mobbed with hungry business people—sometimes the kitchen turns out up to 300 lunches a day. But don't be intimidated—the restaurant is popular for a reason and worth braving the crowds. American menu. Lunch, dinner, late-night. Closed Sat-Sun; holidays; also the week of July 4, and the week after Dec 25. Bar. Children's menu. Casual attire. **$**

★ **RANCH HOUSE.** *5614 Wilkinson Blvd, Charlotte (28208). Phone 704/399-5411. www.ranchhouseof charlotte.com.* Seafood, steak menu. Dinner. Closed Sun; holidays; also first two weeks in July. Bar. Children's menu. Casual attire. Reservations recommended. **$$**
🅳

★ ★ **RHEINLAND HAUS.** *2418 Park Rd, Charlotte (28203). Phone 704/376-3836; fax 704/333-0358. www.rheinlandhaus.com.* Charlotte's first and only

German restaurant is everything you could ask for in a traditional German establishment—fantastic dark wood paneling, traditional bands for their Oktoberfest celebration, and of course, famous apple strudel. The restaurant has been open since 1966, and the excellent European dishes prove why. German menu. Lunch, dinner. Closed Sun. Bar. Casual attire. Outdoor seating. **$$**

★ ★ ★ **SMOKY'S GRILL.** *2200 Rexford Rd, Charlotte (28211). Phone 704/364-1346; fax 704/442-9678. www.theparkhotel.com.* Located in the Park Hotel (see) on Rexford Road, this eatery has well-prepared and varied meals that are beautifully presented. Choose from a wide selection of entrées and relax and enjoy the tasty selections. Comfortable patio dining is available in good weather. American menu. Breakfast, lunch, dinner. Bar. Business casual attire. Reservations recommended. Valet parking. Outdoor seating. **$$**

★ ★ **TONY'S BOURBON STREET OYSTER BAR.** *201 S Tyron St, Charlotte (28202). Phone 704/343-2400. www.tonysbourbonstreet.com.* Cajun/Creole menu. Lunch, dinner. Closed Sun. Bar. Children's menu. Casual attire. **$$**

★ ★ ★ **UPSTREAM.** *6902 Phillips Place Ct, Charlotte (28210). Phone 704/556-7730.* Seafood menu. Lunch, dinner, brunch. Closed Mon. Bar. Business casual attire. Reservations recommended. Outdoor seating. **$$$$**

Cherokee (B-2)

See also Bryson City, Great Smoky Mountains National Park, Maggie Valley, Waynesville

Population 8,519
Elevation 1,991 ft
Area Code 828
Zip 28719
Information Cherokee Travel and Promotion, PO Box 460; phone 828/497-9195 or toll-free 800/438-1601
Web Site www.cherokee-nc.com

This is the capital of the Eastern Band of the Cherokee, who live on the Qualla Reservation at the edge of Great Smoky Mountains National Park (see) and the Blue Ridge Parkway. The reservation is the largest east of the Mississippi. These descendants of members of the tribe who avoided being driven to Oklahoma over the "Trail of Tears" are progressive in their ideas yet determined to maintain their ancient traditions.

What to See and Do

Cherokee Heritage Museum and Gallery. *Acquoni Rd, Cherokee. On Hwy 441 and Big Cove Rd. In Saunooke's Village. Phone 828/497-3211.* Interpretive center features Cherokee culture and history. Gift shop. (Daily; closed three weeks in late Dec-early Jan) **$$**

Museum of the Cherokee Indian. *589 Psali Blvd, Cherokee (28719). On Hwy 441 at Drama Rd. On Cherokee Reservation. Phone 828/497-3481.* Arts and crafts, audiovisual displays, portraits, prehistoric artifacts. (Daily; closed Jan 1, Thanksgiving, Dec 25) **$$$**

Oconaluftee Indian Village. *Hwy 441 N, Cherokee. 1/2 mile N on Hwy 441. Adjacent to Mountainside Theater. Phone 828/497-2111.* Replica of Native American village of more than 250 years ago. Includes seven-sided council house, herb garden, craft demonstrations, lectures. Guided tours (mid-May-late Oct, daily). **$$$**

Santa's Land. *Soco Rd, Cherokee. 3 miles E on Hwy 19 N. Phone 828/497-9191.* Christmas theme park featuring Santa Claus and helpers; rides; zoo; entertainment, including magic show; lake with pedal boats; primitive crafts; snack shops, picnic area, play areas; gardens. (Early May-late Oct, daily) **$$$$**

Special Event

Unto These Hills. *Mountainside Theater, Cherokee. On Hwy 441, 1/2 mile from jct Hwy 19. Phone 828/497-2111.* Kermit Hunter drama re-creating the history of the Cherokee Nation from 1540 to 1838; in a natural amphitheater. Mid-June-late Aug. Mon-Sat evenings.

Limited-Service Hotels

★ ★ **BEST WESTERN GREAT SMOKIES INN.** *441 N and Aquoni Rd, Cherokee (28719). Phone 828/497-2020; toll-free 800/937-8376; fax 828/497-3903. www.bestwestern.com.* 152 rooms, 2 story. Pets accepted; fee. Check-in 2 pm, check-out 11 am. Restaurant. Outdoor pool. **$**

★ **COMFORT INN.** *Hwy 19 S, Cherokee (28719). Phone 828/497-2411; toll-free 800/228-5150; fax 828/497-6555. www.comfortinn.com.* 87 rooms. Complimentary continental breakfast. Check-in 2 pm, check-out 11 am. Outdoor pool, whirlpool. **$**

★ ★ **HOLIDAY INN.** *Hwy 19 S, Cherokee (28719). Phone 828/497-9181; toll-free 800/465-4329; fax 828/*
497-5973. www.holiday-inn.com. 154 rooms, 2 story. Check-in 3 pm, check-out 11 am. Restaurant. Fitness room. Indoor pool, outdoor pool, whirlpool. **$**

Cherryville (B-4)

See also Gastonia, Shelby

Founded 1881
Population 5,361
Elevation 960 ft
Area Code 704
Zip 28021
Information Chamber of Commerce, 301 E Main St, PO Box 305; phone 704/435-3451 or 704/435-4200
Web Site www.gastontourism.com

Customs of Cherryville's original German settlers still live on in this town nestled in the rolling hills of the Piedmont.

Special Event

Shooting in the New Year. Old rite to bring fertility to fruit trees and for good luck in the coming year. Men chant blessings and fire black powder muzzleloaders as they go from home to home. Dec 31-Jan 1.

Concord (B-5)

See also Albemarle, Charlotte, Salisbury

Population 27,347
Elevation 704 ft
Area Code 704
Zip 28026
Information Chamber of Commerce, 23 Union St N, PO Box 1029; phone 704/782-4111
Web Site www.ci.concord.nc.us

Concord was founded by Scottish-Irish and German-Dutch settlers and received its name when the two factions settled a dispute regarding the location of the county seat. An early textile area in the South, Concord continues to lead in dyeing, finishing, and weaving of hosiery and knitted textiles.

What to See and Do

Concord Mills. *8111 Concord Mills Blvd, Concord (28027). Phone 704/979-3000. www.concordmills.com.*

This outlet mall has more than 200 stores, including factory outlets for popular chains such as Banana Republic and Saks Fifth Avenue. It draws more tourists on an annual basis than any other attraction in the Carolinas. It includes a movie theater. (Daily; closed holidays)

Concord Motorsport Park. *7940 Hwy 601 S, Concord (28025). Phone 704/782-4221. www.concordmotor sportpark.com.* The NASCAR Dodge Weekly Series runs Saturday nights from April through October at this 1/2-mile asphalt tri-oval 30 miles northeast of Charlotte, in the heart of NASCAR country. The grandstands seat 8,000, and there are spots for 28 RVs at Turn 3. **$$$$**

Dale Earnhardt Tribute. *Dale Earnhardt Plaza, Dale Earnhardt Blvd and Hwy 3, Kannapolis (28081). At Main and B sts. Phone toll-free 800/848-3740. www.cabarruscvb.com.* The people of Kannapolis have preserved the memory of their favorite son, Dale Earnhardt, in 900 pounds of bronze. The statue is near murals depicting Earnhardt's career.

NASCAR Silicon Motor Speedway. *Concord Mills, 8111 Concord Mills Blvd, Concord (28027). Phone 704/979-7223. www.smsonline.com.* Realitsic racing simulators that let visitors feel the sensation of racing at speeds of up to 200 miles per hour.

NASCAR Speedpark, Concord Mills. *8461-G1 Concord Mills Blvd, Concord (28027). Phone 704/979-6770. www.nascarspeedpark.com.* A 7-acre race-themed amusement park with five racetracks, a state-of-the-art interatctive arcade, one 18-hole miniature golf course, kiddie rides, Lazer Tag, and a snack bar. (Daily; closed Thanksgiving, Dec 25) **$$$$**

Race Shop Tours. *Phone 704/788-8802. www.raceshop tours.net.* Offers sightseeing tours of 23 race teams in eight stops in one seven-hour area tour. Most teams are based around Charlotte, and this is a way to check them out up close. Rates and itineraries vary, and special bookings may be made in advance. Private tours are also available for an additional charge. **$$$$**

Reed Gold Mine State Historic Site. *9621 Reed Mine Rd, Midland (28107). 10 miles SE on Hwy 601 and Hwy 200 to Georgeville, then 2 miles S on Hwy 1100. Phone 704/721-4653.* When you hear the phrase "There's gold in them thar hills," you probably think "California." But this coast has its own stockpile of the natural wonder. In fact, the Reed Gold Mine State Historic Site boasts the first documented discovery of gold in the United States way back in 1799, long before those California 'forty-niners hit the mines. Stop

and check out the underground mine tours, history trail, working machinery, demonstrations, exhibits, visitor center, and film, or enjoy the panning area and see what you find. Picnic areas are available for a pre- or post-tour meal. Panning area (Apr-Oct, daily; fee). (Tues-Sat; closed holidays) **FREE**

Richard Petty Driving Experience. *Lowe's Motor Speedway, 5555 Concord Pkwy S, Concord (28027). Phone toll-free 800/237-3889. www.1800bepetty.com.* Always wanted to rip a stock car around the curves at a NASCAR racetrack? This is the largest of the driving schools that takes fans right out onto the track at Lowe's Motor Speedway. For anywhere between $99 for a ride-along to almost $3,000 for an "advanced racing experience," you can live your dream. **$$$$**

Sam Bass Gallery. *6104 Performance Dr SW, Concord (28027). Phone 704/455-6915; toll-free 800/556-5464. www.sambass.com.* Sam Bass is the first officially licensed artist of NASCAR. His gallery sells NASCAR artwork and is down the road from Lowe's Motor Speedway. (Mon, Thurs-Fri 10 am-5 pm, Sat 10 am-4 pm) **FREE**

Cornelius (B-4)

See also Charlotte, Statesville

Founded 1893
Population 11,969
Elevation 831 ft
Area Code 704
Zip 28031
Information North Mecklenburg Chamber and Visitors Center, PO Box 760; phone 704/892-1922
Web Site www.lakenorman.org

A dispute between two cotton companies in Davidson during the late 1800s led to one of the firms relocating south of the city limits and establishing a new town. Originally called Liverpool, the community changed its name to Cornelius in honor of an investor.

What to See and Do

Lake Norman. *NW of town. Phone 704/443-5193.* Lake Norman is the state's largest freshwater lake, at 32,510 acres; it was created by the Cowans Ford Dam, a Duke Power project on the Catawba River. There are nine public access areas, with fishing areas and boating access.

Memory Lane Motorsports & Historic Automotive Museum. *769 River Hwy, Mooresville (28117). Phone*

704/662-3673. www.memorylaneautomuseum.com. One-of-a-kind vehicles from race cars to vintage cars and motorcycles are on display at the museum, in addition to toys, memorabilia, and more. (Mon-Sat 9 am-5 pm) **$$**

North Carolina Auto Racing Hall of Fame. *119 Knob Hill Rd, Mooresville (28117). I-77, exit 36. Phone 704/663-5331. www.ncarhof.com.* As Mooresville's official visitor's center, the museum offers a large display of more than 35 cars dedicated to all types of auto racing, and provides free race shop guides and maps to fans. Fans can savor racing's greatest moments at the Goodyear Mini-Theater, or marvel at the artistry of some of motorsport's top artists. The gift shop is also the official "Race City, USA" merchandise headquarters, and carries a wide selection of racing memorabilia. (Daily) **$**

Limited-Service Hotels

★ **BEST WESTERN LAKE NORMAN.** *19608 Liverpool Pkwy, Cornelius (28031). Phone 704/896-0660; toll-free 888/207-0666; fax 704/896-8633. www.bestwesternlakenorman.com.* Pets are welcome at this hotel located a short distance from both Lake Norman and Charlotte. A restaurant is adjacent, however, guests can also enjoy area dining and shopping as well. 80 rooms, 4 story. Pets accepted, some restrictions; fee. Complimentary continental breakfast. Check-in 3 pm, check-out 11 am. Fitness room. Outdoor pool, whirlpool. **$**
🐾 🕊 🕴 ⛵

★ **HAMPTON INN.** *19501 Statesville Rd, Cornelius (28031). Phone 704/892-9900; toll-free 800/426-7866; fax 704/896-7488. www.hamptoninn.com.* Located just off Interstate 77, this hotel features easy access to Lake Norman attractions and the excitement of the NASCAR races at Lowe's Motor Speedway. The surrounding area includes plenty of restaurant options for any taste. 116 rooms, 5 story. Complimentary continental breakfast. Check-in 3 pm, check-out noon. Fitness room. Outdoor pool. **$**
🕴 ⛵

★ ★ **HOLIDAY INN.** *19901 Holiday Ln, Cornelius (28031). Phone 704/892-9120; toll-free 800/465-4329; fax 704/892-3854. www.holiday-inn.com.* Conveniently set between Lake Norman and downtown Charlotte, this hotel features an on-site restaurant and bar, as well as a courtyard pool. Located near Davidson College, this is an ideal spot for visitors to the campus.

116 rooms, 2 story. Pets accepted; fee. Check-in 3 pm, check-out 11 am. Restaurant, bar. Fitness room. Outdoor pool. **$**
🐾 🕴 ⛵

Specialty Lodging

The following lodging establishment is approved by Mobil Travel Guide, but due to its unique and individualized nature has not been given a traditional Mobil Star rating. Included in this listing you may find bed-and-breakfasts, limited-service inns, guest ranches, and other unique hotel properties.

DAVIDSON VILLAGE INN. *117 Depot St, Davidson (28036). Phone 704/892-8044; toll-free 800/892-0796; fax 704/896-2184. www.davidsoninn.com.* 18 rooms, 3 story. Complimentary continental breakfast. Check-in 3 pm, check-out 11 am. **$**

Restaurant

★ ★ **KOBE JAPANESE HOUSE OF STEAK & SEAFOOD.** *20465 Chartwell Center Dr, Cornelius (28031). Phone 704/896-7778; fax 704/896-0579. www.kobelakenorman.com.* Japanese menu. Lunch, dinner. Closed Thanksgiving, Dec 25. Bar. Casual attire. Reservations recommended. **$$**

Dunn (B-7)

See also Fayetteville, Goldsboro, Smithfield

Population 9,196
Elevation 213 ft
Area Code 910
Zip 28334
Web Site www.dunnchamber.com

What to See and Do

Bentonville Battleground State Historic Site. *5466 Harper House Rd, Four Oaks. 15 miles E via Hwy 55 to Newton Grove, 3 miles N via Hwy 701 to Hwy 1008, then 3 miles E. Phone 910/594-0789.* Biggest battle on North Carolina soil, March 19-21, 1865. It was the last organized attempt to stop General William Tecumseh Sherman after he left Atlanta. A month later, the rebel cause was lost; Lee surrendered at Appomattox on April 9; Lincoln was shot on April 14; and Johnston surrendered on April 26. The restored Harper House was used as a hospital to treat the wounded of both sides. Reconstructed and original trenches. Picnic area. Visitor center, audiovisual show. (Hours vary; closed Jan 1, Thanksgiving, Dec 24-25) **FREE**

Limited-Service Hotel

★ **JAMESON INN.** *901 Jackson Rd, Dunn (28334). Phone 910/891-5758; toll-free 800/526-3766; fax 910/891-1290. www.jamesoninns.com.* 40 rooms. Pets accepted, some restrictions. Check-in 3 pm, check-out 11 am. Outdoor pool. **$**

Durham (A-6)

See also Chapel Hill, Raleigh

Founded 1853
Population 187,035
Elevation 406 ft
Area Code 919
Information Convention and Visitors Bureau, 101 E Morgan St, 27701; phone toll-free 800/772-2855
Web Site www.durham-nc.com

Durham's sparkle has brought it near-top national ranking in numerous livability studies. Known for excellence in medicine, education, research, and industry, Durham is also a recreational and cultural center in the rolling Piedmont region.

In 1924, an endowment from James B. Duke, head of the American Tobacco Company, helped establish Duke University as a leader among the nation's institutions of higher learning. North Carolina Central University makes its home here. In the 1950s, Durham County was chosen as the site of Research Triangle Park, a planned scientific research center that includes the Environmental Protection Agency, the National Institute for Environmental Health Sciences, IBM Corporation, the Glaxo Wellcome Company, and others. Duke University Medical Center, Durham Regional Hospital, and several other outstanding medical institutions here have earned Durham the title "City of Medicine, USA."

What to See and Do

Bennett Place State Historic Site. *4409 Bennett Memorial Rd, Durham (27705). Just SW of jct I-85 exit 173 and Hwy 70. Phone 919/383-4345.* Site of signing (Apr 26, 1865) of surrender of Confederate General Johnston to Union General Sherman, one of the last and most significant of the Confederate surrenders. Reconstructed Bennett homestead. Picnicking. Visitor center, exhibits, audiovisual show. (Mon-Fri; closed holidays) **FREE**

Duke Homestead State Historic Site. *2828 Duke Homestead Rd, Durham. 1/2 mile N of jct I-85, Guess Rd. Phone 919/477-5498.* (1852) Ancestral home of the Duke family; first Duke tobacco factory; curing barn; outbuildings; farm crops. Tobacco museum, exhibits, film; furnishings of period. Tours. (Tues-Sat; closed holidays) **FREE**

Duke University. *2138 Campus Dr, Durham (27706). Phone 919/684-3214.* (1838) (10,000 students) Situated on 8,000 acres. Includes original Trinity College. The West Campus, occupied since 1930, is the showplace of the university. On campus are

> **Duke Chapel.** *2138 Campus Dr, Durham (27706). Phone 919/681-1704.* Beautiful Gothic-style chapel with a carillon of 50 bells in its 210-foot tower; 5,000-pipe Flentrop organ. (Daily) Chapel Drive to main quadrangle.

> **Duke Libraries.** *2138 Campus Dr, Durham (27706). Phone 919/684-3009.* Most comprehensive in the South, with more than 4 million volumes and 7 million manuscripts. Large Confederate imprint collection; Walt Whitman manuscripts.

> **Duke Medical Center.** *Fulton and Elba sts, Durham (27710). Phone 919/684-8111.* Research and teaching complex. Treats more than 1/2 million patients annually.

> **Duke's Wallace Wade Stadium.** *Whitford and Science Dr, Durham (27708). Phone 919/681-2583.* (33,941 capacity) Home of the Duke Blue Devils. Also the 8,564-seat Cameron Indoor Stadium.

> **Museum of Art.** *N Buchanan Blvd and Trinity Ave, Durham. E Campus, off W Main St. Phone 919/684-5135.* (Tues-Sun; closed holidays) **FREE**

> **Sarah P. Duke Gardens.** *418 Anderson St, Durham (27705). Main entrance on Anderson St. Phone 919/684-3698.* 55 acres of landscaped gardens, pine forest. Continuous display. (Daily) **FREE**

Historic Stagville Center. *5825 Old Oxford Hwy, Bahama. 7 miles NE via Roxboro Rd and Old Oxford Hwy. Phone 919/620-0120.* State-owned historic property, once part of the Bennehan-Cameron plantation; several historic 18th- and 19th-century plantation buildings on 71 acres of land. (Mon-Fri; closed holidays) **FREE**

North Carolina Museum of Life and Science. *433 Murray Ave, Durham. Phone 919/220-5429.* North Carolina wildlife; hands-on science exhibits; aerospace, weather, and geology collections; train ride (fee); farmyard; science park; discovery rooms; Butterfly House. Picnic area. (Daily; closed Jan 1, Thanksgiving, Dec 25) **$$$**

West Point on the Eno. *5101 N Roxboro Rd, Durham (27704). I-85, Duke St, exit 3 1/2 miles N. Phone 919/471-1623.* A 371-acre park along the scenic Eno River; restored farmhouse (1850), working gristmill; museum of photography; blacksmith shop. Picnicking, hiking, fishing, boating; environmental programs (fee). Park (daily). Mar-Dec, Sat-Sun). **FREE**

Special Events

American Dance Festival. *715 Broad St, Durham (27705). Page Auditorium and Reynolds Industries Theater, Duke University, West Campus. Phone 919/684-6402.* Six weeks of performances by the finest of both major and emerging modern dance companies from the United States and abroad. June-July.

Bull Durham Blues Festival. *Historic Durham Athletic Park, 409 Blackwell St, Durham (27701). Phone 919/683-1709.* Celebrates the blues with performances held at the location where *Bull Durham* was filmed. Mid-Sept.

CenterFest. *Downtown, Durham. Phone 919/560-2722.* Two-day event with over 250 artists and craftsmen; musicians, jugglers, and clowns; continuous entertainment from three stages. Sept.

Limited-Service Hotels

★ **BEST WESTERN SKYLAND INN.** *5400 Hwy 70, Durham (27705). Phone 919/383-2508; toll-free 800/937-8376; fax 919/383-7316. www.bestwestern.com.* 31 rooms, 1 story. Pets accepted; fee. Complimentary continental breakfast. Check-in 2 pm, check-out noon. High-speed Internet access. Outdoor pool. **$**

★ **COURTYARD BY MARRIOTT.** *1815 Front St, Durham (27705). Phone 919/309-1500; toll-free 800/321-2211; fax 919/383-8189. www.courtyard.com.* 146 rooms, 4 story. Check-in 3 pm, check-out noon. High-speed Internet access. Fitness room. Outdoor pool, whirlpool. **$**

★ ★ **DOUBLETREE GUEST SUITES.** *2515 Meridian Pkwy, Durham (27709). Phone 919/361-4660; toll-free 800/365-9876; fax 919/361-2256. www.doubletree.com.* 203 rooms, 7 story. Check-in 3 pm, check-out noon. Restaurant, bar. Fitness room. Indoor pool, whirlpool. Tennis. Airport transportation available. Business center. **$**

★ **FAIRFIELD INN.** *3710 Hillsborough Rd, Durham (27705). Phone 919/382-3388; fax 919/382-9298.* 135 rooms, 3 story. Complimentary continental breakfast. Check-in 3 pm, check-out noon. Outdoor pool. **$**

Full-Service Hotels

★ ★ ★ **HILTON.** *3800 Hillsborough Rd, Durham (27705). Phone 919/383-8033; toll-free 800/445-8667; fax 919/383-0833. www.durham.hilton.com.* 194 rooms, 6 story. Check-in 3 pm, check-out noon. High-speed Internet access. Two restaurants, two bars. Fitness room. Outdoor pool. Business center. **$**

★ ★ ★ **MARRIOTT CIVIC CENTER.** *201 Foster St, Durham (27701). Phone 919/768-6000; fax 919/768-6037. www.marriott.com.* Located in downtown Durham, this beautifully renovated hotel has an elegant charm enhanced by fountains that flow through the lobby. Guests receive complimentary use of the nearby YMCA or can use the on site exercise facilities. 187 rooms, 10 story. Check-in 4 pm, check-out noon. High-speed Internet access. Restaurant, bar. Fitness room. Business center. **$**

★ ★ ★ **MARRIOTT RESEARCH TRIANGLE PARK.** *4700 Guardian Dr, Durham (27703). Phone 919/941-6200; toll-free 800/228-9290; fax 919/941-6229. www.marriott.com.* 225 rooms, 6 story. Check-in 4 pm, check-out noon. High-speed Internet access. Restaurant, bar. Fitness room. Indoor pool, whirlpool. Airport transportation available. Business center. **$$**

★ ★ ★ **MILLENNIUM HOTEL.** *2800 Campus Walk Ave, Durham (27705). Phone 919/383-8575; fax 919/383-8495. www.millennium-hotels.com.* Conveniently located near Duke University and Medical Center. Relax in the lounge, where mahogany bookshelves, overstuffed sofas, and wing-backed chairs provide the atmosphere of a private club. 315 rooms, 4 story. Check-in 3 pm, check-out noon.

Restaurant, bar. Fitness room, spa. Indoor pool, whirlpool. Airport transportation available. **$$**
🏃 🏊

★ ★ ★ **WASHINGTON DUKE INN & GOLF CLUB.** *3001 Cameron Blvd, Durham (27706). Phone 919/490-0999; toll-free 800/443-3853; fax 919/490-0999. www.washingtondukeinn.com.* Campus living never looked this elegant, yet the Washington Duke Inn & Golf Club calls 300 acres within the Duke University campus home. Tucked away within the forest and golf club, this elegant resort is Durham's leading hotel. Sophisticated and stylish, this inn has the amenities of a large resort with the charm and ambience of a country-house hotel. The rooms and suites reflect the English country influences, as does the daily afternoon tea. From the classic elegance of the lauded Fairview to the convivial spirit of the Bull Durham lounge, the dining choices here are terrific, and with a leading golf course just outside the door and privileges at the university's fitness facilities, guests are never at a loss for something to do. 171 rooms, 5 story. Check-in 3 pm, check-out noon. Restaurant, bar. Fitness room. Outdoor pool. Golf. Tennis. Airport transportation available. Business center. **$$**
🏃 🏊 🍴 🎿 🏃

Specialty Lodging

The following lodging establishment is approved by Mobil Travel Guide, but due to its unique and individualized nature has not been given a traditional Mobil Star rating. Included in this listing you may find bed-and-breakfasts, limited-service inns, guest ranches, and other unique hotel properties.

ARROWHEAD INN BED & BREAKFAST. *106 Mason Rd, Durham (27712). Phone 919/477-8430; toll-free 800/528-2207; fax 919/471-9538. www.arrowheadinn.com.* 9 rooms, 2 story. Complimentary full breakfast. Check-in 3 pm, check-out noon. **$**

Restaurants

★ ★ ★ **FAIRVIEW.** *3001 Cameron Blvd, Durham (27706). Phone 919/493-6699; fax 919/688-0105. www. washingtondukeinn.com.* Located in the Washington Duke Inn & Golf Club (see), this restaurant has been touted "the most elegant place to dine in the Research Triangle Park." Music from the baby grand piano only adds to the elegance and warmth that diners experience while enjoying a culinary delight. American

menu. Breakfast, lunch, dinner, Sun brunch. Bar. Jacket required. Reservations recommended. Valet parking. Outdoor seating. **$$$**

★ ★ ★ **MAGNOLIA GRILL.** *1002 9th St, Durham (27705). Phone 919/286-3609; fax 919/286-2691.* In Magnolia Grill, husband-and-wife chefs/owners Ben and Karen Barker mine an independent streak in Southern cooking. He handles the savories, taking Southern ingredients beyond regional confines in dishes like smoked trout with avocado and red pepper slaw, sea bass carpaccio with Thai crab vinaigrette, fennel-crusted grouper in lobster reduction, and roast pheasant with wild rice risotto. She creates the sweets that take Southern comforts upscale, including shaker pie and upside-down caramel banana cake with bourbon praline ice cream. Lodged in a former health food grocery, Magnolia Grill keeps the vibe casual with wooden floors and artwork on loan from local painters, encouraging neighborhood repeaters as well as special-occasion celebrants. American menu. Dinner. Closed Sun-Mon; also late July and late Dec. Bar. Business casual attire. Reservations recommended. **$$**

★ ★ **PAPA'S GRILL.** *1821 Hillandale Rd, Durham (27705). Phone 919/383-8502; fax 919/382-9529. www.papasgrill.citysearch.com.* Mediterranean menu. Lunch, dinner. Closed Sun; Easter, Dec 25. Bar. Casual attire. **$$**

★ ★ **PARIZADE.** *2200 W Main St, Durham (27705). Phone 919/286-9712; fax 919/416-9706. www.parizade.com.* Mediterranean menu. Lunch, dinner. Closed Dec 25. Bar. Outdoor seating. **$$**

Edenton (A-9)

Settled 1658
Population 5,394
Elevation 16 ft
Area Code 252
Zip 27932
Information Chamber of Commerce, 116 E King St, PO Box 245; phone 252/482-3400; or Historic Edenton, 108 N Broad St, PO Box 474, phone 252/482-2637
Web Site www.edenton.org

This is one of the oldest communities in North Carolina and was the capital of the colony for more than 22 years. The women of Edenton staged their own Revolutionary tea party on October 25, 1774, signing a resolution protesting British injustice. A bronze teapot, at the west side of the Courthouse Green, commemorates the event.

The seat of Chowan County, Edenton is now an important industrial town and marketing place. It is a charming town with the graciousness of the Old South and many houses and buildings that date back to the 1700s. Joseph Hewes, a signer of the Declaration of Independence, lived here.

What to See and Do

Historic Edenton. *108 N Broad St, Edenton (27932). Phone 252/482-2637.* Tour of historic properties, which may be seen individually or as a group; allow 2 1/2 to 3 hours for complete tour. (Mon-Sat; closed Jan 1, Dec 24-25) **$$$** Also here are

Chowan County Courthouse. *E King and Court sts, Edenton.* (1767) A fine example of Georgian architecture; in continuous use since it was built.

Cupola House. *W Water and S Broad sts, Edenton.* (1758) Considered an outstanding example of Jacobean architecture. Formal garden restored from 1769 map of Edenton.

Historic Edenton Visitor Center. *108 N Broad St, Edenton.* Audiovisual program (free), exhibits, visitor information, gift shop, tickets for guided tours of Historic Edenton.

James Iredell House. *108 N Broad St, Edenton (27932). Phone 252/482-2637.* (1800/1827). Home of early attorney general of North Carolina who was appointed by George Washington to first US Supreme Court.

St. Paul's Episcopal Church. *W Church and Broad sts, Edenton.* (1736). A charming church with many old gravestones in its yard; three colonial governors are buried here.

Merchant's Millpond State Park. *71 Hwy 158 E, Gatesville (27938). 25 miles N on Hwy 32, 5 miles N of Gatesville on Hwy 1403. Phone 252/357-1191.* This 2,900-acre swamp forest is dominated by massive gum and cypress trees. Pond fishing, canoeing (rentals). Nature trails. Picnicking. Developed and primitive camping. Interpretive program. Contact Superintendent, Rte 1, Box 141-A, Gatesville, 27938.

Newbold-White House. *151 Newbold White Rd, Hertford. 15 miles N on Hwy 17 Bypass to Hertford, SE on Hwy 1336. Phone 252/426-7567.* (1730) This brick structure was a meeting place for the proprietary government of North Carolina. (Mar-Dec, Mon-Sat) **$**

Other historic buildings. *71 Hwy 158 E, Gatesville (27938). Phone 252/482-2637.* Shown in a guidebook published by the Edenton Woman's Club and sold at the Historic Edenton Visitor Center ($). Since most houses are not open to the public, we suggest calling the Historic Edenton Visitor Center for further information.

Somerset Place State Historic Site. *2572 Lake Shore Rd, Creswell (27928). 18 miles SE via Hwy 32, Hwy 64 to Creswell, then 7 miles S. On Lake Phelps in Pettigrew State Park. Phone 252/797-4560.* Original plantation, one of the largest in North Carolina, encompassed more than 100,000 acres. First primary crop was rice, which gave way to corn and wheat. Mansion and outbuildings built (circa 1830). (Apr-Oct: daily; Nov-Mar: Tues-Sun) **FREE**

Specialty Lodgings

The following lodging establishments are approved by Mobil Travel Guide, but due to their unique and individualized nature have not been given a traditional Mobil Star rating. Included in this listing you may find bed-and-breakfasts, limited-service inns, guest ranches, and other unique hotel properties.

CAPTAIN'S QUARTERS INN. *202 W Queen St, Edenton (27932). Phone 252/482-8945; toll-free 800/482-8945. www.captainsquartersinn.com.* Built in 1907; antiques. 8 rooms, 2 story. Children over 8 years only. Complimentary full breakfast. Check-in 4-10 pm, check-out 11 am. **$**

LORDS PROPRIETORS INN. *300 N Broad St, Edenton (27932). Phone 252/482-3641; toll-free 800/348-8933; fax 252/482-2432. www.edentoninn.com.* This inn is actually three separate homes gracing 2 acres of what's known as the South's prettiest town. All 20 rooms are decorated with period antiques and reproductions. The New American dining room is for guests only and offers an impressive seasonal menu. 20 rooms, 2 story. Check-in 1 pm, check-out 11 am. **$$**

Elizabeth City (A-9)

Settled Circa 1665
Population 17,188
Elevation 18 ft
Area Code 252
Zip 27909
Information Elizabeth City Area Chamber of Commerce, 502 E Ehringhaus St, PO Box 426; phone 252/335-4365
Web Site www.elizcity.com

A town with a freshwater harbor on the Pasquotank River and accessible to the ocean, Elizabeth City has seen seafaring activity since the middle of the 17th century. In 1793, the town was chartered at the narrows of the river as Redding and, in 1801, was renamed Elizabeth City. The Dismal Swamp Canal, dug in 1793, provided a critical north-south transportation route and brought prosperity to Elizabeth City. Shipyards, warehouses, fisheries, tanneries, sawmills, and other industries flourished along with commission merchants, artisans, and navigators; trading occured with Norfolk, the West Indies, New England, New York, and Charleston.

Although captured in the Civil War, Elizabeth City sustained minor damage. Today, many antebellum homes still stand alongside the historic homes and commercial buildings of the late 19th and early 20th centuries, a testament to the vitality of the community. Wood, agriculture, small specialty industries, and the US Coast Guard contribute to the area's steady economic growth. The town also welcomes boating traffic from the Intracoastal Waterway and is a coveted location for sportfishing and hunting. It serves as a gateway to Nags Head and Cape Hatteras National Seashore (see).

What to See and Do

Dixieland Motorsports Complex. *1522 Northside Rd, Elizabeth City. Phone 252/771-5151.* The complex sponsors stock car, go-cart, and motorcycle races. Stock cars race on Fri, go-carts on Sat, and motorcycles on Sun. Apr-late Oct. **$$$**

Fun Junktion. *983 Simpson Ditch Rd, Elizabeth City. Phone 252/337-6600.* This 133-acre public park features lakes, nature trails, a swimming area, a children's playground, and picnic facilities.

Historic District. A 30-block area in the city center, that contains the largest number of antebellum commercial buildings in the state. Tour brochures are available at the Chamber of Commerce.

Museum of the Albemarle. *1115 Hwy 17 S, Elizabeth City. Phone 252/335-1453.* Regional historical displays; Native American exhibits; local artifacts, including decoys, fire engines; changing exhibits. (Tues-Sun; closed state holidays) **FREE**

Special Events

Albemarle Craftsman's Fair. *200 E Ward St, Elizabeth City (27909).* Late Oct.

Historic Ghostwalk. *Phone toll-free 888/936-7387.* Historic homes tour with skits. Late Oct.

Mistletoe Show. Crafts, wood carvings. Second weekend in Nov.

Limited-Service Hotels

★ **HAMPTON INN.** *402 Halstead Blvd, Elizabeth City (27909). Phone 252/333-1800; toll-free 800/426-7866; fax 252/333-1801. www.hamptoninn.com.* 100 rooms, 5 story. Complimentary continental breakfast. Check-in 3 pm, check-out 11 am. Outdoor pool, whirlpool. **$**

★ **HOLIDAY INN EXPRESS.** *306 S Hughes Blvd, Elizabeth City (27909). Phone 252/338-8900; toll-free 877/553-2964; fax 252/338-5120.* 80 rooms, 5 story. Complimentary continental breakfast. Check-out 11 am. Outdoor pool. **$**

Restaurant

★ **MARINA.** *Camden Causeway, Elizabeth City (27909). Phone 252/335-7307.* Seafood menu. Dinner. Closed Mon; Jan 1, Dec 25. Children's menu. Outdoor seating. **$$**

Fayetteville (C-6)

See also Dunn, Goldsboro

Founded 1739
Population 121,015
Elevation 102 ft
Area Code 910
Information Convention and Visitors Bureau, 245 Person St, 28301; phone 910/483-5311 or toll-free 800/255-8217
Web Site www.visitfayettevillenc.com

In 1783, the towns of Cross Creek and Campbellton merged and were renamed Fayetteville for the Marquis de Lafayette, becoming the first US city to honor him. It was the site of North Carolina's Constitutional Convention in 1787 and the capital of the state from 1789 to 1793. By 1831 it had become a busy commercial city.

Fayetteville is the state's farthest inland port, at the head of navigation on the Cape Fear River, with an 8-foot-deep channel connecting it to the Intracoastal Waterway. Fayetteville State University (1867) and Methodist College (1956) are located here. In 1985, Fayetteville received the All-America City Award. Today, it's a center for retail, manufacturing, and conventions, as well as the home of Fort Bragg and Pope Air Force Base.

Fayetteville Fun Fact

• In Fayetteville, Babe Ruth hit his first professional home run on March 17, 1914.

What to See and Do

Cape Fear Botanical Garden. *536 N Eastern Blvd, Fayetteville. Phone 910/486-0221.* On 85 acres overlooking Cross Creek and the Cape Fear River. Wildflowers, oaks, native plants. Nature trails. (Mid-Feb-mid-Dec: daily; rest of year: Mon-Sat; closed holidays) **$$**

First Presbyterian Church. *Bow and Ann sts, Fayetteville. Phone 910/483-0121.* Classic Southern colonial-style architecture and whale-oil chandeliers. Among contributors to the original building (destroyed by fire in 1831) were James Monroe and John Quincy Adams. Tours (by appointment only).

Fort Bragg and Pope AFB. *200 Maynard St, Pope AFB (28308). 10 miles NW on Hwy 24. Phone 910/394-4647.* Here are

82nd Airborne Division War Memorial Museum. *Gela and Ardennes sts, Fort Bragg. Phone 910/432-3443.* Weapons, relics of World War I and II, Vietnam, Korea, Desert Storm; history of 82nd airborne division; gift shop. (Tues-Sun; closed Jan 1, Dec 25) **FREE**

John F. Kennedy Special Warfare Museum. *Ardennes and Marion sts, Fort Bragg (28307). Phone 910/432-1533.* Guerrilla warfare weapons. (Tues-Sun; closed holidays) **FREE**

Parachute jumps. *Phone 910/396-6366 (schedule information).*

Museum of the Cape Fear. *801 Arsenal Ave, Fayetteville. Phone 910/486-1330.* Retraces the regional cultural history from prehistoric Indian artifacts through 20th century. A branch of the North Carolina Museum of History. (Tues-Sun; closed holidays) **FREE**

Special Events

Dogwood Festival. *301 Hay St, Fayetteville (28301). Phone 910/323-1934.* Late Apr.

Pope AFB/Fort Bragg Joint Open House and Air Show. *Phone 910/394-4183.* Aerial demonstrations, aircraft and equipment displays, military drill team performances. May.

Limited-Service Hotels

★ **COMFORT INN.** *1957 Cedar Creek Rd, Fayetteville (28301). Phone 910/323-8333; toll-free 800/621-6596; fax 910/323-3946. www.comfortinn.com.* 120 rooms, 2 story. Pets accepted; some restrictions. Complimentary continental breakfast. Check-in 3 pm, check-out noon. Fitness room. Outdoor pool. **$**

★ **FAIRFIELD INN.** *562 Cross Creek Mall, Fayetteville (28303). Phone 910/487-1400; toll-free 800/228-2800; fax 910/487-0081. www.fairfieldinn.com.* 135 rooms, 3 story. Complimentary continental breakfast. Check-in 3 pm, check-out noon. Outdoor pool. **$**

★ **HAMPTON INN.** *1922 Cedar Creek Rd, Fayetteville (28301). Phone 910/323-0011; fax 910/323-8764. www.hamptoninn.com.* 121 rooms, 2 story. Complimentary continental breakfast. Check-in 3 pm, check-out noon. Outdoor pool. **$**

★ ★ **HOLIDAY INN.** *1944 Cedar Creek Rd, Fayetteville (28301). Phone 910/323-1600; toll-free 800/465-4329; fax 910/323-0691. www.ichotelsgroup.com.* 198 rooms, 2 story. Pets accepted; fee. Check-in 3 pm, check-out noon. Restaurant, bar. Fitness room. Indoor pool. **$**

★ **HOLIDAY INN EXPRESS.** *1706 Skibo Rd, Fayetteville (28303). Phone 910/867-6777; toll-free 800/465-4329; fax 910/864-9541. www.hiexpress.com.* 84 rooms, 4 story. Complimentary continental breakfast. Check-in 2 pm, check-out 11 am. High-speed Internet access. Outdoor pool. **$**

★ ★ **QUALITY INN.** *I-95 Bus Route, Fayetteville (28306). Phone 910/485-8135; toll-free 800/828-2346; fax 910/485-8682. www.qualityinn.com.* 62 rooms. Pets accepted, some restrictions. Check-in noon, check-out noon. Restaurant. Outdoor pool. **$**

Restaurants

★ **CANTON STATION.** *301 N McPherson Church Rd, Fayetteville (28303). Phone 910/864-5555.* Lunch, dinner. Bar. Children's menu. Casual attire. **$**

★ ★ **TRIO CAFE.** *201 S McPherson Church Rd, Fayetteville (28303). Phone 910/868-2443; fax 910/868-1128.* Mediterranean menu. Dinner. Closed holidays. Bar. Outdoor seating. **$$**

Fontana Dam (B-1)

See also Bryson City, Great Smoky Mountains National Park

Founded 1947
Population 130
Elevation 2,900 ft
Area Code 704
Zip 28733
Web Site www.westernncattractions.com/fontana.htm

At the southwest corner of Great Smoky Mountains National Park, this village was originally built for the construction crew that worked on the Fontana Dam project. The 480-foot dam is crossed by the Appalachian Trail. The region is now a resort area, with swimming, fishing, boating, hiking, and horseback riding centering around Fontana Lake, 30 miles long.

Fort Raleigh National Historic Site (A-10)

See also Cape Hatteras National Seashore, Kill Devil Hills, Nags Head, Outer Banks

Web Site www.nps.gov/fora
Off Hwy 64, 3 miles N of Manteo.

The first English colony in America was attempted here on Roanoke Island in 1585. Virginia Dare, born here August 18, 1587, was the first child of English parents born in what is now the United States.

Governor John White left the island for England a few days after Virginia's birth, intending to return shortly with supplies. He was detained by the war with Spain and did not get back until August 1590. The colony had disappeared, leaving behind only the mysterious word "CROATOAN" cut into a tree or post.

What happened to the colonists is unknown, though some believe that the present-day Lumbee Indians of Robeson County descend from them. Fort Raleigh has been excavated, and the fort built by the colonists reconstructed. The Lindsay Warren Visitor Center has relics, an audiovisual program, and exhibits. Park and Visitor Center (daily; closed Dec 25). For further information, contact Fort Raleigh National Historic Site, Rte 1, Box 675, Manteo, 27954; phone 252/473-5772.

Special Event

***The Lost Colony* Outdoor Drama.** *Waterside Theater, Manteo. 3 miles NW of Manteo on Hwy 64/264. Phone toll-free 800/488-5012.* Outdoor drama by Pulitzer Prize winner Paul Green about the first English colony established in the New World, whose curious disappearance remains a mystery to this day. Mid-June-late Aug. Mon-Sat evenings. Reservations recommended. Contact 1409 Hwy 64, Manteo, 27954. **$$$$**

Franklin (B-2)

See also Bryson City, Cashiers, Highlands

Population 3,490
Elevation 2,133 ft
Area Code 828
Zip 28734
Information Chamber of Commerce, 425 Porter St; phone 828/524-3161 or toll-free 800/336-7829
Web Site www.franklin-chamber.com

Home of the Cowee Valley ruby mines, Franklin attracts rock hounds who often find interesting gems in surface mines. Franklin is surrounded by waterfalls, mountain lakes, and streams that offer excellent fishing for trout and bass, as well as boating, tubing, and swimming. Around the county are 420,000 acres of the Nantahala National Forest, which offers hiking trails, camping, and fishing. A Ranger District office is located here. The Appalachian Trail bisects the western part of the county through Standing Indian Wildlife Management area and over Wayah Bald Mountain.

What to See and Do

Franklin Gem and Mineral Museum. *25 Phillips St, Franklin. Phone 828/369-7831.* Gems and minerals; Native American artifacts, fossils; fluorescent mineral display. (May-Oct, Mon-Sat) **FREE**

Gem mines. There are more than a dozen mines in the area, most offering assistance and equipment for beginners. For a complete list of mines, contact the Chamber of Commerce.

Macon County Historical Museum. *6 W Main St, Franklin. Phone 828/524-9758.* Artifacts, documents depicting early history of Macon County; genealogical material. (Apr-Oct, Mon-Sat) **FREE**

Nantahala National Forest. *90 Sloan Rd, Franklin (28734). W of town. Phone 828/524-6441.* Nantahala, a Native American name meaning Land of the Noonday Sun, refers to Nantahala Gorge, so deep and narrow that the sun reaches the bottom only at noon. Scenic drives through the southern Appalachians; sparkling waterfalls, including the Whitewater Falls—a series of cascades dropping 411 feet within a distance of 500 feet—and the 17,013-acre Joyce Kilmer-Slickrock Wilderness (see ROBBINSVILLE), with more than 100 species of trees native to the region are part of this

518,560-acre forest. Hiking, camping (fee); swimming, boating, fishing for bass and trout; hunting for deer, wild boar, turkey, and ruffed grouse. For further information, contact the District Ranger, 100 Otis St, PO Box 2750, Asheville, 28802.

Perry's Water Garden. *136 Gibsons Aquantic Farms, Franklin (Macon Co) (28734). 8 miles NW on Hwy 28 to Cowee Creek Rd, then E 2 miles to Leatherman Gap Rd. Phone 828/524-3264.* Water park with 4 1/2-acre sunken garden, waterfall, hundreds of water lilies and other flowers, wishing well, trails, picnicking. (Mid-May-Labor Day, daily) **FREE**

Scottish Tartans Museum. *W. C. Burrell Building, 95 E Main St, Franklin. Phone 828/524-7472.* American extension of Scottish Tartans Society in Edinburgh, Scotland. Exhibits trace heritage of Scottish Tartan and traditional Scottish dress. Research library. Gift shop. (Daily; closed Jan 1, Easter, Dec 25) **$**

Special Events

Macon County Fair. Mid-Sept.

Macon County Gemboree. Jewelry and gem exhibits, ruby mining, field trips. Late July.

Limited-Service Hotel

★ **DAYS INN.** *1320 E Main St, Franklin (28734). Phone 828/524-6491; toll-free 800/329-7466; fax 828/369-9636. www.daysinn.com.* 41 rooms. Pets accepted, some restrictions; fee. Complimentary continental breakfast. Check-in 2 pm, check-out 11 am. Outdoor pool. Scenic view of mountains. **$**

Restaurants

★ ★ **FROG & OWL KITCHEN.** *46 E Main St, Franklin (28734). Phone 828/349-4112.* French menu. Lunch, dinner. Closed Sun-Mon; Thanksgiving, Dec 25. **$$**

★ **GAZEBO CAFE.** *44 Heritage Hollow, Franklin (28734). Phone 828/524-8783; fax 828/369-2725.* Deli menu. Lunch, dinner. Closed holidays; also late Oct-May. Children's menu. Entire restaurant is outdoors; three different patio levels for dining. **$**

Gastonia (B-4)

See also Charlotte, Cherryville, Shelby

Population 66,277
Elevation 816 ft
Area Code 704
Information Gaston County Department of Tourism, PO Box 2339, 2668; phone 704/867-2170 or toll-free 800/849-9994
Web Site www.gastontourism.com

This is an industrial town in the Piedmont, turning out textiles, textile machinery, and supplies. In addition, Gastonia produces chain saws, plastics, oil seals, lithium, automotive parts, trucks, and truck parts.

What to See and Do

Gaston County Museum of Art and History. *131 W Main St, Dallas. 6 miles N via Hwy 321, Dallas exit. Phone 704/922-7681.* Located in Hoffman Hotel (1852) and Dallas Depot (1901). Sculpture, paintings, Gaston County artifacts and documents, carriage and sleigh collection, textile history exhibit. 19th-century parlors. (Tues-Sun; closed holidays) **FREE**

Lake Wylie. *310 Blutcher Cir, Lake Wylie (29710). S on Hwy 274. Phone 803/831-2101.* An artificial lake formed by Duke Power Company development; fishing, swimming, water-skiing; marina.

Schiele Museum of Natural History and Planetarium. *1500 E Garrison Blvd, Gastonia (28052). Phone 704/866-6900. www.schielemuseum.org.* Habitat settings showcasing more than 75,000 mounted birds, mammals, reptiles, fish; rocks and minerals; Native American arts and crafts; forestry exhibits; and 28-acre nature park. Major exhibits on the Southeast and North Carolina, special exhibits and events, films, and a restored mid-1700s pioneer farm with living history programs. Hall of Natural History, Hall of Earth and Man. Also here is Catawba Indian Village, with recreated dwellings from 1500s to 1900s. Planetarium programs (fee). (Daily) **$**

Limited-Service Hotel

★ **HAMPTON INN.** *1859 Remount Rd, Gastonia (28054). Phone 704/866-9090; toll-free 800/426-7866; fax 704/866-7070. www.hamptoninn.com.* Conveniently situated, clean, and comfortable, this is an ideal lodging option for travelers visiting or passing through the Gastonia area. 108 rooms, 5 story. Complimentary continental breakfast. Check-in 3 pm, check-out noon. Outdoor pool. **$**

Goldsboro (B-7)

See also Dunn, Fayetteville, Smithfield

Established 1847
Population 39,043
Elevation 121 ft
Area Code 919
Information Wayne County Chamber of Commerce, 308 N William St, 27530; phone 919/734-2241
Web Site www.greatergoldsboro.com

Center of the bright-leaf tobacco belt, Goldsboro is also the seat of Wayne County and home of Seymour Johnson Air Force Base. Poultry production and tobacco warehousing and processing are important industries. There are also many food, wood product, and textile plants here.

What to See and Do

Cliffs of the Neuse State Park. *345 A Bark Entrance Rd, Seven Springs (28578). 14 miles SE, off Hwy 111. Phone 919/778-6234.* Over 700 acres on Neuse River. Swimming, bathhouse, fishing, boating (rowboat rentals). Nature trails. Picnicking. Tent and trailer sites (mid-Mar-Nov; fee). Museum, interpretive center.

Governor Charles B. Aycock Birthplace State Historic Site. *264 Governor Aycock Rd, Fremont (27830). 12 miles N, off Hwy 117 just S of Fremont. Phone 919/242-5581.* Mid-1800s farmhouse and outbuildings; audiovisual presentation in one-room school (1893); exhibits in visitor center portray life of the "educational governor." Picnicking. (Apr-Oct: daily; rest of year: Tues-Sun; closed holidays) **FREE**

Limited-Service Hotels

★ **HOLIDAY INN EXPRESS.** *909 N Spence Ave, Goldsboro (27534). Phone 919/751-1999; toll-free 800/465-4329; fax 919/751-1506. www.hiexpress.com/goldsboronc.* 122 rooms, 5 story. Pets accepted, some restrictions; fee. Complimentary continental breakfast. Check-in 3 pm, check-out noon. High-speed Internet access. Fitness room. Outdoor pool. Business center. **$**

★ ★ **QUALITY INN.** *708 Hwy 70, Goldsboro (27534). Phone 919/735-7901; fax 919/735-7901. www.qualityinn.com.* 125 rooms, 2 story. Pets accepted; fee. Complimentary continental breakfast. Check-in 3 pm, check-out noon. High-speed Internet access, wireless Internet access. Restaurant, bar. Fitness room. Outdoor pool. **$**

Great Smoky Mountains National Park (B-1)

See also Bryson City, Cherokee, Fontana Dam, Maggie Valley

Web Site www.nps.gov/grsm
50 miles W of Asheville off Hwy 19.

The Appalachian Mountains, product of a slow upthrusting of ancient sediments that took place more than 200 million years ago, stand tall and regal in this 800-square-mile area. Red spruce, basswood, eastern hemlock, yellow birch, white ash, cucumber trees, silverbells, Fraser fir, tulip poplar, red maple, and Fraser magnolias tower above hundreds of other species of flowering plants. Perhaps the most spectacular of these are the purple rhododendron, mountain laurel, and flame azalea, in bloom from early June to mid-July.

The moist climate has helped make this a rich wilderness. From early spring to late fall, the "coves" (as the open valleys surrounded by peaks are called) and forest floors are covered with a succession of flowers with colorful variety. Summer brings heavy showers, warm days (although 15° F to 20° F cooler than in the valleys below), and cool nights. Autumn is breathtaking as the deciduous trees change color. Winter brings snow, occasionally heavy, and fog over the mountains. Winter is a very good time to visit the park, but be aware of temporary road closures.

Half in North Carolina and half in Tennessee, with the Appalachian Trail following the state line along the ridge for 70 miles, this is a place to hike. In the lowlands are the cabins, barns, and mills of the mountain people whose ancestors came years ago from England and Scotland. It is also a place to see the descendants of the once mighty Cherokee Nation, whose ancestors hid in the mountains from the soldiers in the winter of 1838-1839 to avoid being driven over the Trail of Tears to Oklahoma. This is the tribe of Sequoyah, the brilliant chief who invented a written alphabet for the Cherokee people.

Stop first at one of the three visitor centers: Oconaluftee Center in North Carolina, 2 miles north of Cherokee on Newfound Gap Road, designated Hwy 441 outside the park (daily; closed Dec 25; phone 423/436-1200); Sugarlands in Tennessee, 2 miles southwest of Gatlinburg (daily; closed Dec 25; phone 423/436-1200); or Cades Cove in Tennessee, 10 miles southwest of Townsend (daily, closed Dec 25; phone 423/436-1200). All have exhibits and information about the park. There are hundreds of miles of foot trails and bridle paths. Camping is popular; ask at any visitor center for locations and regulations. There are developed campgrounds (fee). For reservations at Elkmont, Cades Cove, or Smokemont, phone toll-free 800/365-2267; reservations are not taken for other sites.

The views from Newfound Gap and the observation tower at Clingmans Dome (closed in winter) are spectacular. Cades Cove is an outdoor museum reflecting the life of the original mountain people, about 25 miles west of Sugarlands. It has log cabins and barns. Park naturalists conduct campfire programs and hikes during the summer. There are also self-guided nature trails. LeConte Lodge, reached only by foot or horseback, is an accommodation within the park. Phone 423/429-5704 (late Mar-mid-Nov).

Fishing is permitted with a Tennessee or North Carolina state fishing license. Obtain a list of regulations at the visitor centers and campgrounds. The park is a wildlife sanctuary; any disturbance of plant or animal life is forbidden. Dogs and cats are not permitted on trails but may be brought in if kept on a leash or other physical restrictive controls. Never feed, tease, or frighten bears; always give them a wide berth, as they can inflict serious injury. Watch bears from your car with the windows closed.

For the disabled, there is an all-access trail, the Sugarland Valley Nature Trail, equipped with special interpretive exhibits. Accessibility information is available at the visitor centers. **FREE**

For information, contact the Superintendent, Great Smoky Mountains National Park, 107 Park Headquarters Rd, Gatlinburg, TN 37738; phone 423/436-1200.

Greensboro (A-5)

See also Asheboro, Burlington, High Point, Winston-Salem

Founded 1808
Population 223,891
Elevation 841 ft
Area Code 336
Information Greensboro Area Convention and Visitors Bureau, 317 S Greene St, 27401; phone 336/274-2282 or toll-free 800/344-2282
Web Site www.greensboronc.org

William Sydney Porter (O. Henry) was born and raised near Greensboro, a diversified Piedmont industrial city whose products are typical of North Carolina: textiles, cigarettes, machinery, and electronic components. It was settled by Quakers, Germans, and the Scotch-Irish with a zeal for political, religious, and economic freedom. Men from this region fought in the Revolution and the War of 1812 and turned to the Confederacy in 1861. It was in Greensboro, the rebel supply depot, that Jefferson Davis met General Johnston after Richmond fell in 1865 and agreed on surrender terms. Today it is an educational, manufacturing, and distribution center.

What to See and Do

Charlotte Hawkins Brown Memorial State Historic Site. *6136 Burlington Rd, Sedalia. 10 miles E on I-85 to exit 135, then 1/2 mile W on Hwy 70. Phone 336/449-4846.* North Carolina's first state historic site, honoring the achievements of African-American education in the state. In 1902, C. H. Brown, granddaughter of former slaves, founded Palmer Memorial Institute, which became one of the finest preparatory schools for blacks in the nation. Guided tours of historic campus (several buildings being restored), visitor center, audiovisual program. Picnicking. (Apr-Oct: Tues-Sat; rest of year: Tues-Sun; closed holidays) **FREE**

⭐ **Chinqua-Penn Plantation.** *Reidsville, 2138 Wentworth St, Greensboro (27320). 20 miles N on Hwy 29, exit Hwy 14, 3 miles NW on Wentworth Rd. Phone 336/349-4567.* English-style country house, extensive formal and rose gardens; 27 rooms contain furnishings, art objects from around the world; no pets; picnic area. (Mar-Dec, Tues-Sat, also Sun afternoons; closed July 4, Thanksgiving, Dec 25) **$$$**

Greensboro Historical Museum. *130 Summit Ave, Greensboro (27401). Phone 336/373-2043. www.greensborohistory.org.* Housed in an 1892 building in the downtown area, the museum features displays on the Revolutionary War, First Lady Dolly Madison, and writer O. Henry, among others. (Tues-Sat 10 am-5 pm, Sun 2-5 pm; closed holidays) **FREE**

Guilford College. *5800 W Friendly Ave, Greensboro. 2 miles N of I-40. Phone 336/316-2000.* (1837) (1,300 students) Oldest coed college in the South. Beautiful wooded 340-acre campus with Georgian-style buildings and a unique solar energy fieldhouse. Quaker archives dating to 1680 (Tues-Fri, by appointment; closed holidays). Official home of Eastern Music Festival (June-Aug).

Guilford Courthouse National Military Park. *2332 New Garden Rd, Greensboro (27410). 6 miles NW and 1/4 mile E off Hwy 220 on New Garden Rd. Phone 336/288-1776.* On March 15, 1781, Lord Cornwallis won a costly victory that was one link in a series of events that led to his surrender at Yorktown in October of the same year. After destroying a quarter of the enemy troops, General Nathanael Greene (for whom the city is named) made a successful retreat and then severely hampered the British plan of subduing the Southern colonies. The 220-acre park, established in 1917, has monuments marking important locations and honoring those who fought here; two signers of the Declaration of Independence, John Penn and William Hooper, are also buried here. Self-guided auto tour; walking trails. The visitor center has a museum housing Revolutionary War weapons, other items; 20-minute film. (Daily; closed Jan 1, Dec 25) **FREE**

Hagan-Stone Park. *5920 Hagan Stone Park Rd, Pleasant Garden (27313). 6 miles S on Hwy 421, then 2 miles W on Hagan-Stone Park Rd. Phone 336/674-0472.* Swimming, fishing. Hiking. Picnicking, playground. Camping (hook-ups, dump station). Park (all year). Some fees. Pets on leash only.

Natural Science Center of Greensboro. *4301 Lawndale Dr, Greensboro (27455). Phone 336/288-3769. www.natsci.org.* Natural science museum with zoo and indoor exhibits including geology, paleontology, aquarium, herpetarium, and science and technology. Check out the 36-foot-tall Tyrannosaurus rex model.

Planetarium shows; inquire for schedule. (Mon-Sat 9 am-5 pm, Sun 12:30-5 pm) **$$**

University of North Carolina at Greensboro. *1000 Spring Garden St, Greensboro. Phone 336/334-5243 (Admissions).* (1891) (13,000 students)

> **Weatherspoon Art Museum.** *Spring Garden and Tate St, Greensboro (27402). Anne and Benjamin Cone Building. Phone 336/334-5770. www. weatherspoon.uncg.edu.* Permanent collection of over 4,000 contemporary paintings, graphic arts, sculpture. (Tues-Sun; closed school holidays) **FREE**

Special Event

Greater Greensboro Chrysler Classic Golf Tournament. *4600 Forest Oaks Dr, Greensboro (27406). Phone 336/ 379-1570.* Top golfers compete for more than $3 million on PGA circuit. Oct.

Limited-Service Hotels

★ **COMFORT INN.** *2001 Veasley St, Greensboro (27407). Phone 336/294-6220; toll-free 800/424-6423; fax 336/294-6220. www.choicehotels.com.* 122 rooms, 2 story. Complimentary continental breakfast. Check-in 2 pm, check-out noon. High-speed Internet access, wireless Internet access. Outdoor pool. **$**
⊠

★ ★ **EMBASSY SUITES.** *204 Centreport Dr, Greensboro (27409). Phone 336/668-4535; toll-free 800/ 362-2779; fax 336/668-3901. www.embassysuites greensboro.com.* Visitors can relax in this hotel's seven-story atrium filled with greenery and fountains and illuminated by the sun through skylights. The hotel is conveniently located near shopping, restaurants and other attractions. 219 rooms, 7 story, all suites. Complimentary full breakfast. Check-in 3 pm, check-out noon. Restaurant, bar. Fitness room. Indoor pool, whirlpool. Airport transportation available. Business center. **$$**
🏃 ⊠ 🏌

★ **HAMPTON INN.** *2004 Veasley St, Greensboro (27407). Phone 336/854-8600; toll-free 800/426-7866; fax 336/854-8741. www.hamptoninn.com.* 120 rooms, 2 story. Complimentary continental breakfast. Check-in 3 pm, check-out noon. Outdoor pool. **$**
⊠

★ **QUALITY INN.** *120 Seneca Rd, Greensboro (27406). Phone 336/275-9575; toll-free 800/424-6423;*

fax 336/275-9572. www.choicehotels.com. 115 rooms, 2 story. Complimentary full breakfast. Check-in 2 pm, check-out 11 am. Wireless Internet access. Outdoor pool, children's pool. **$**
⊠

Full-Service Hotels

★ ★ ★ **MARRIOTT GREENSBORO AIRPORT.** *1 Marriott Dr, Greensboro (27409). Phone 336/852-6450; toll-free 800/228-9290; fax 336/665-6522. www.marriott.com.* This hotel is located on the Piedmont Triad International Airport ground, but offers 17 acres of beautiful landscaped grounds with a lake. 299 rooms, 6 story. Check-in 3 pm, check-out noon. Two restaurants, bar. Fitness room. Indoor pool, outdoor pool, whirlpool. Airport transportation available. **$$**
🏃 ⊠

★ ★ ★ **MARRIOTT GREENSBORO DOWNTOWN.** *304 N Greene St, Greensboro (27401). Phone 336/379-8000; fax 336/275-2810. www.marriott.com.* Situated in the historic area of downtown Greensboro, this hotel is within walking distance of shopping, antique shops, water and city parks, fine and casual dining restaurants, and other attractions. 280 rooms, 11 story. Check-in 3 pm, check-out 11 am. Restaurant, bar. Children's activity center. Fitness room. Indoor pool, whirlpool. **$$**
🏃 ⊠

★ ★ ★ **O. HENRY HOTEL.** *624 Green Valley Rd, Greensboro (27408). Phone 336/854-2000; toll-free 800/ 965-8259; fax 336/854-2223. www.o.henryhotel.com.* 131 rooms. Complimentary full breakfast. Check-in 3 pm, check-out noon. High-speed Internet access. Restaurant, bar. Outdoor pool. Airport transportation available. Business center. **$$**
⊠ 🏌

Full-Service Resort

🌀 ★ ★ ★ **GRANDOVER RESORT AND CONFERENCE CENTER.** *1000 Club Rd, Greensboro (27407). Phone 336/294-1800; toll-free 800/472-6301; fax 336/856-9991. www.grandover.com.* The Grandover Resort and Conference Center simply can't be beaten for its exceptional, award-winning golf, fine dining, stylish accommodations, and good old southern hospitality. This contemporary resort is truly a golfer's dream, with 36 holes awaiting play, along with the Ken Venturi Golf School. A new spa has just been added to the property, perfect for those who need a post-game massage or for others who want to spend the entire day luxuriating at the sparkling facility. Four clay tennis courts and a state-of-the-art fitness center provide other diversions. The rooms and suites are spacious and inviting, with fantastic views over the emerald links, and personalized service adds to the experience. 247 rooms, 11 story. Check-in 4 pm, check-out noon. Restaurant, bar. Fitness room, spa. Indoor pool, outdoor pools, whirlpool. Golf, 36 holes. Tennis. **$$**

Restaurant

★ ★ **GATE CITY CHOP HOUSE.** *106 S Holden St, Greensboro (27407). Phone 336/294-9977; fax 336/294-1048. www.chophouserestaurants.com.* Enjoy a drink at the circular oak bar while waiting for seating in one of the five dining areas. American menu. Lunch, dinner. Closed Sun; July 4, Thanksgiving, Dec 24-25. Bar. Casual attire. Outdoor seating. **$$$**

Greenville (B-8)

See also Washington, Williamston

Founded 1786
Population 60,476
Elevation 55 ft
Area Code 252
Information Greenville-Pitt County Convention and Visitors Bureau, 525 S Evans St, PO Box 8027, 27835-8027; phone 252/752-8044 or toll-free 800/537-5564
Web Site www.visitgreenvillenc.com

An educational, cultural, commercial, and medical center, Greenville is one of the towns named for General Nathanael Greene, a hero of the American Revolutionary War.

What to See and Do

East Carolina University. *Medical Center campus, W side of town. Phone 252/328-6131.* (1907) (17,600 students) Jenkins Fine Arts Center, ECU Music School, and Gray Art Gallery offer many cultural events to the public.

East Carolina Village of Yesteryear. *117 W 5th St, Greenville (27858). 2 miles N via Hwy 264. Phone 252/758-6385.* Restoration and preservation of small-town life (1840-1940) within Pitt County and eastern North Carolina. The area contains a general store, railroad depot, museum, farmhouse, chicken house, and schoolhouse. (Weekends) **$**

Greenville Museum of Art. *802 Evans St, Greenville. Phone 252/758-1946.* Collections emphasize North Carolina contemporary fine arts and drawings, also paintings and prints of the period 1900-1945. (Tues-Fri, also Sun afternoons; closed holidays) **DONATION**

River Park North Science and Nature Center. *1000 Mumford Rd, Greenville (27834). 5 miles N on Mumford Rd. Phone 252/830-4561.* A 309-acre park with four lakes and 1.2 miles of Tar River water frontage. Science center near park entrance offers hands-on exhibits. Fishing, boating (ramp; no gas motors), pedal boats. Picnicking. (Tues-Sun; closed holidays) **$**

Limited-Service Hotels

★ **FAIRFIELD INN.** *821 S Memorial Dr, Greenville (27834). Phone 252/758-5544; fax 252/758-1416.* 114 rooms, 2 story. Complimentary continental breakfast. Outdoor pool. Airport transportation available. **$**

★ **HAMPTON INN.** *3439 S Memorial Dr, Greenville (27834). Phone 252/355-2521; toll-free 800/426-7866; fax 252/355-0262. www.hamptoninn.com.* 121 rooms, 2 story. Complimentary continental breakfast. Check-out noon. Outdoor pool. **$**

Full-Service Hotel

★ ★ **HILTON GREENVILLE.** *207 SW Greenville Blvd, Greenville (27834). Phone 919/355-5000; toll-free 800/774-1500; fax 919/355-5099. www.hilton.com.* This is a smaller hotel offering 141 guest rooms and more personal service. Recreational facilities include an outdoor pool, spa, and health club, plus guest will enjoy the restaurant and lobby piano bar. 141 rooms, 6 story. Check-out noon. Restaurant, bar. Outdoor pool, whirlpool. Airport transportation available. Business center. **$**

Restaurants

★ **BEEF BARN.** *400 St Andrews Dr, Greenville (27834). Phone 252/756-1161; fax 252/756-7655. www.beefbarn.net.* Steak, seafood menu. Lunch, dinner. Closed holidays. Bar. Children's menu. **$$**

★ **PARKER'S BAR-B-QUE.** *3109 Memorial Dr, Greenville (27834). Phone 252/756-2388; fax 252/756-6950.* Barbecue menu. Lunch, dinner. Closed Thanksgiving, Dec 25; also one week in mid-June. Children's menu. Outdoor seating. **$**

Hatteras (B-10)

See also Cape Hatteras National Seashore

Population 1,660
Elevation 2 ft
Area Code 252
Zip 27943
Web Site www.outerbanks.org

This Hatteras Island fishing village on the Outer Banks (see) was settled, it is said, by shipwrecked sailors from Devon, England. The Devon accent is indeed heard here and on the islands of Ocracoke and Manteo. There are ferries south to Ocracoke (see).

Henderson (A-7)

Founded 1840
Population 16,095
Elevation 509 ft
Area Code 252
Zip 27536
Information Vance County Tourism Department, 943K W Andrews Ave; phone 252/438-2222
Web Site www.kerrlake-nc.com

Tobacco has historically been the major crop in Vance County, of which Henderson is the seat. The manufacturing and processing of textiles, hosiery, furniture, food, tobacco, mobile homes, and glass containers are local industries. Tourism helps drive the economy.

What to See and Do

Kerr Reservoir. *6254 Satterwhite Point Rd, Henderson (27536). 6 miles N off I-85. Phone 252/438-7791.* Part of the development of the Roanoke River basin by the US Army Corps of Engineers. Approximately 800 miles of shoreline and 50,000 acres of water. Swimming, water-skiing, fishing, boating, several private marinas; picnicking, camping (fee). Seven state recreation areas around lake, some open only Apr-Oct. (Daily) State camping areas (water and electric hook-ups in all, except some sites in Bullocksville; standard fees).

Special Event

Parade of Lights on Water. *Kerr Lake, 269 Glass House Rd, Henderson (27356). Phone 252/438-7791.* Fireworks, entertainment. Labor Day weekend.

Hendersonville (B-3)

See also Asheville, Brevard, Tryon

Population 10,420
Elevation 2,146 ft
Area Code 828
Information Chamber of Commerce, 330 N King St, 28792; phone 828/692-1413
Web Site www.hendersonvillechamber.org

The county seat of Henderson County, Hendersonville is well-known as a summer resort colony and popular retirement community. Manufacturing, agriculture, and tourism help make up the county's balanced economy.

What to See and Do

✪ **Carl Sandburg Home National Historic Site.** *81 Carl Sandburg Ln, Flat Rock (28731). 3 miles S on Hwy 25. Phone 828/693-4178. www.nps.gov/carl.* The famous poet's 264-acre farm residence, Connemara, is maintained as it was when Sandburg and his family lived here from 1945 until his death in 1967. Tours lasting 30 minutes depart regularly throughout the day. On the grounds are a house and a historic barn for the three breeds of goats that Sandburg raised, as well as a visitor center. (Daily 9 am-5 pm; closed Dec 25) **$**

Holmes State Forest. *SW on Crab Creek Rd. Phone 828/692-0100.* This managed forest was designed to facilitate a better understanding of the value of forests in our lives. It features "talking trees" with recorded narration about the site and the forest's history. Picnicking (reservations required). Group camping (reservations required). For reservations or information, contact Rte 4, Box 308. (Mid-Mar-Nov, Tues-Sun) **FREE**

Jump-Off Rock. *5th Ave, 6 miles W.* Panoramic view from atop Jump-Off Mountain.

Special Events

Flat Rock Playhouse. *2661 Greenville Hwy, Flat Rock (28731). 3 1/2 miles S on Hwy 25. Phone 828/693-0731.* Outstanding professional theater since 1939;

State Theater of North Carolina since 1961. Vagabond Players offer ten Broadway and London productions in 15 weeks. Mid-May–mid-Dec. Wed-Sat evenings; Thurs, Sat, Sun matinees.

North Carolina Apple Festival. *401 N Main St, Hendersonville (28792). Phone 828/697-4557.* Labor Day weekend.

Limited-Service Hotels

★ **COMFORT INN.** *206 Mitchell Dr, Hendersonville (28792). Phone 828/693-8800; toll-free 800/424-6423; fax 828/693-8800. www.choicehotels.com.* 84 rooms, 2 story. Pets accepted; fee. Complimentary continental breakfast. Check-in 3 pm, check-out 11 am. Outdoor pool. **$**

★ **HAMPTON INN.** *155 Sugarloaf Rd, Hendersonville (28792). Phone 828/697-2333; toll-free 800/426-7866; fax 828/693-5280. www.hamptoninn.com/hi/hendersonville.* 118 rooms, 4 story. Complimentary continental breakfast. Check-in 2 pm, check-out noon. Outdoor pool. **$**

Full-Service Resort

★ ★ ★ **HIGHLAND LAKE INN.** *Highland Lake Rd, Flat Rock (28731). Phone 828/693-6812; toll-free 800/762-1376; fax 828/696-8951. www.hlinn.com.* 63 rooms, 3 story. Check-in 4 pm, check-out 11 am. High-speed Internet access. Restaurant, bar. Beach. Outdoor pool. Tennis. **$$**

Full-Service Inn

★ ★ **ECHO MOUNTAIN INN.** *2849 Laurel Park Hwy, Hendersonville (28739). Phone 828/693-9626; toll-free 800/324-6466; fax 828/697-2047. www.echoinn.com.* 45 rooms, 2 story. Complimentary continental breakfast. Check-in 2 pm, check-out 11 am. Outdoor pool. **$**

Specialty Lodgings

The following lodging establishments are approved by Mobil Travel Guide, but due to their unique and individualized nature have not been given a traditional Mobil Star rating. Included in this listing you may find bed-and-breakfasts, limited-service inns, guest ranches, and other unique hotel properties.

LAKE LURE INN. *Hwys 64 and 74A, Lake Lure (28746). Phone 828/625-2525; toll-free 800/277-5873; fax 828/625-9655.* 50 rooms, 3 story. Complimentary continental breakfast. Check-in 3 pm, check-out 11 am. Restaurant, bar. Outdoor pool. **$**

LODGE ON LAKE LURE BED & BREAKFAST. *361 Charlotte Dr, Lake Lure (28746). Phone 828/625-2789; toll-free 800/733-2785; fax 828/625-2421. www.lodgeonlakelure.com.* This inn promises a unique balance of the casual countryside with an elegant bed-and-breakfast. The innkeepers are family and welcome guests to their home for relaxed excursions. The beauty of the lake also adds a wonderful backdrop to this scenic property. 16 rooms, 2 story. Children over 8 years only. Complimentary full breakfast. Check-in 3-8 pm, check-out 11 am. **$$**

THE WAVERLY INN. *783 N Main St, Hendersonville (28792). Phone 828/693-9193; toll-free 800/537-8195; fax 828/692-1010. www.waverlyinn.com.* Restored guest house (1898); Victorian décor, upstairs sun porch. 15 rooms, 3 story. Complimentary full breakfast. Check-in 1 pm, check-out 11 am. **$**

WOODFIELD INN. *2905 Greenville Hwy, Flat Rock (28731). Phone 828/693-6016; toll-free 800/533-6016; fax 828/693-0437. www.woodfieldinn.com.* Built in 1852; antiques. 17 rooms, 3 story. Complimentary full breakfast. Check-in noon, check-out 11 am. Tennis. **$$**

Restaurants

★ ★ ★ **EXPRESSIONS.** *114 N Main St, Hendersonville (28792). Phone 828/693-8516; fax 828/696-8666.* This delightful restaurant has been a well-loved fixture of simple elegance on Main Street for more than a decade. The upscale cuisine, featuring seafood, beef, duck, quail, pork, and chicken is beautifully and innovatively presented. Guests can choose from a list of more than 200 fine domestic and French wines, and they also can enjoy a comfortable upstairs lounge that's perfect for unwinding after a busy day. American menu. Dinner. Closed Sun; holidays; also mid-Jan–mid-Feb. Bar. **$$$**

★ ★ **SINBAD.** *202 S Washington St, Hendersonville (28739). Phone 828/696-2039. www.sinbadrestaurant .com.* Choose between dining indoors overlooking the beautiful gardens or dining outdoors under the beautiful North Carolina skies. Mediterranean menu. Lunch, dinner. Closed Sun-Mon; also Jan 1, Thanksgiving, Dec 25. Bar. Outdoor seating. **$$**

Hickory (B-4)

See also Statesville

Population 37,222
Elevation 1,163 ft
Area Code 828
Information Catawba County Chamber of Commerce, 1055 Southgate Corporate Park SW, 28602; phone 828/328-6111
Web Site www.catawbachamber.org

Nationally known brands of furniture and hosiery are produced here, as are ceramics and electronic equipment.

What to See and Do

Arts Center of Catawba Valley. *243 3rd Ave NE, Hickory.* Here are

> **Catawba Science Center.** *243 3rd Ave NE, Hickory (28601). Phone 828/322-8169. www.catawbascience.org.* Interactive exhibits feature life, earth, medical, and physical sciences. Also changing exhibits. (Tues-Sun; closed holidays) **$$**

> **Hickory Museum of Art.** *234 3rd Ave, Hickory (28601). Phone 828/327-8576.* American realist 19th- and 20th-century art, including works by Gilbert Stuart; Hudson River School, Thos. Cole to Homer Martin; American impressionists; European, Oriental, and pre-Columbian pieces; changing exhibits quarterly. (Tues-Sun; closed Easter, Dec 25) **$**

Bunker Hill Covered Bridge. *On Hwy 70, approximately 10 miles E. Phone 828/465-0383.* One of only two remaining covered bridges in the state. Built in 1895, it spans Lyle's Creek. Nature trail, picnicking.

Catawba County Museum of History. *30 N College Ave, Newton (28658). 3 miles S, Courthouse Sq. Phone 828/465-0383.* Exhibits include a fire engine (1919), country doctor's office (1920), Waugh Cabin (1839), Barringer Cabin (1759), a blacksmith shop (1870), and an agriculture exhibit. (Tues-Fri, Sun; closed holidays) **FREE**

Lake Hickory. *4 miles N.* This 4,100-acre lake with a 105-mile shoreline was created by the Oxford Dam on the Catawba River. It offers boating, fishing, swimming, and marinas.

Lenoir-Rhyne College. *625 7th Ave and 8th St NE, Hickory (28601). Phone 828/328-1741.* (1891) (1,700 students) Observatory (Sept-Apr, evenings, weather permitting). Concerts, athletic contests, dramatic productions, art exhibits, convocation programs, and other special events throughout the academic year.

Murray's Mill. *1489 Murrays Mill Rd, Catawba (28609). 10 miles E via I-40. Phone 828/465-0383.* (1890) Overshot waterwheel, working machinery; milling museum and demonstrations. Country store (1890), folk art gallery (1880). (Thurs-Sun; closed holidays) **$**

Special Event

Auto racing. Hickory Motor Speedway. *3130 Hwy 70 SE, Newton. 4 miles E on Hwy 70. Phone 828/464-3655.* Stock car racing. Mid-Mar-early Oct.

Limited-Service Hotels

★ **COMFORT INN.** *1125 13th Dr SE, Hickory (28602). Phone 828/323-1211; fax 828/322-4395.* 116 rooms, 2 story. Complimentary full breakfast. Check-in 3 pm, check-out 11 am. Fitness room. Outdoor pool. **$**
🧍 ⛱

★ **HAMPTON INN.** *1520 13th Ave Dr SE, Hickory (28602). Phone 828/323-1150; toll-free 800/426-7866; fax 828/324-8979. www.hamptoninn.com.* 119 rooms, 2 story. Complimentary continental breakfast. Check-in 3 pm, check-out noon. Outdoor pool. **$**
⛱

★ ★ **HOLIDAY INN.** *1385 Lenoir Rhyne Blvd SE, Hickory (28602). Phone 828/323-1000; toll-free 800/366-5010; fax 828/322-4275. www.holiday-inn.com.* 200 rooms, 2 story. Complimentary continental breakfast. Check-in 3 pm, check-out noon. Restaurant, bar. Fitness room. Indoor pool, whirlpool. **$**
🧍 ⛱

Restaurants

★ ★ ★ **1859 CAFE.** *443 2nd Ave SW, Hickory (28602). Phone 828/322-1859; fax 828/322-5697. www.hickoryonline.com/1859cafe.* International/Fusion menu. Dinner. Closed Sun; Thanksgiving, Dec 24-25.

Bar. Casual attire. Reservations recommended. Outdoor seating. **$$$**

★ ★ ★ **VINTAGE HOUSE.** *271 3rd Ave NW, Hickory (28601). Phone 828/324-1210; fax 828/324-2218.* American menu. Dinner. Closed Sun; first week in June, first week in July. Bar. Casual attire. **$$**

High Point (A-5)

See also Asheboro, Burlington, Greensboro, Lexington, Winston-Salem

Founded 1859
Population 85,839
Elevation 939 ft
Area Code 336
Information Convention and Visitors Bureau, 300 S Main St, PO Box 2273, 27261; phone 336/884-5255 or toll-free 800/720-5255
Web Site www.highpoint.org

Furniture and hosiery are the products that make High Point prosperous. The city rests on the highest point along the North Carolina and Midland Railroad, which the state built in 1853. The plank road (finished in 1854), stretching 130 miles from Salem to Fayetteville, made it a center of trade; mileposts on this road had carved numbers instead of painted ones so travelers could feel their way at night.

What to See and Do

Furniture Discovery Center. *101 W Green Dr, High Point. Phone 336/887-3876.* Nation's only museum of modern-day furniture manufacturing. Hands-on displays; miniatures; hall of fame; special exhibits. (Apr-Oct: daily; rest of year: Tues-Sun; closed holidays) **$$**

Peterson Doll and Miniature Museum. *101 W Green Dr, High Point (27260). Phone 336/885-3655.* Collection of more than 2,000 dolls and related artifacts from around the world, some dating back to the 15th century. (Apr-Oct: daily; Nov-Mar: Tues-Sun; closed holidays) **$$**

World's Largest Chest of Drawers. *508 N Hamilton St, High Point. Phone 336/883-2016.* Building designed to look like a 19th-century dresser; symbolizes the city's position as a furniture center. Built in 1926. **FREE**

Special Events

Day in the Park. *City Lake Park, 602 W Main St, Jamestown (27282). Phone 336/889-2787.* Arts and crafts, rides, entertainment. Late Sept.

Gas Boat Drag Championships. *Oak Hollow Lake, High Point. Phone 336/883-2016.* One of several World Series Championship races. Fourth weekend in July.

North Carolina Shakespeare Festival. *High Point Theatre, 220 E Commerce Ave, High Point. Phone 336/841-2273.* Season includes three productions and *A Christmas Carol.* Aug-Oct and Dec.

Limited-Service Hotel

★ ★ **RADISSON HOTEL HIGH POINT.** *135 S Main St, High Point (27260). Phone 336/889-8888; toll-free 800/333-3333; fax 336/885-2737. www.radisson.com.* 252 rooms, 8 story. Pets accepted; fee. Check-in 3 pm, check-out noon. Restaurant, bar. Indoor pool. Airport transportation available. **$**
🐾 🏊

Specialty Lodging

The following lodging establishment is approved by Mobil Travel Guide, but due to its unique and individualized nature has not been given a traditional Mobil Star rating. Included in this listing you may find bed-and-breakfasts, limited-service inns, guest ranches, and other unique hotel properties.

BOULDIN HOUSE BED AND BREAKFAST. *4332 Archdale Rd, High Point (27263). Phone 336/431-4909; toll-free 800/739-1816; fax 336/431-4914. www.bouldinhouse.com.* 5 rooms. Children over 12 years only. Complimentary full breakfast. Check-in 5-7 pm, check-out 10:30 am. **$**
🅿

Restaurants

★ **CANCUN MEXICAN RESTAURANT.** *921 Eastchester Dr, High Point (27262). Phone 336/841-0983; fax 336/841-0983.* Mexican menu. Lunch, dinner. Bar. Casual attire. Outdoor seating. **$**

★ ★ ★ **J BASUL NOBLE'S.** *101 S Main St, High Point (27260). Phone 336/889-3354; fax 336/889-1424. www.noblesrestaurant.com.* Italian menu. Dinner. Closed Sun; holidays. Bar. Casual attire. Outdoor seating. **$$**

Highlands (C-2)

See also Cashiers, Franklin

Population 909
Elevation 3,835 ft
Area Code 828
Zip 28741
Information Chamber of Commerce, 396 Oak St, PO Box 404; phone 828/526-2112
Web Site www.highlandsinfo.com

Highlands is a summer resort near the Georgia state line. Many unusual plants are part of the primeval rain forest preserve. Completely encircled by Nantahala National Forest (see FRANKLIN), the area surrounding the town is called "land of the waterfalls." A Ranger District office is located here.

What to See and Do

Bridal Veil Falls, Dry Falls. *NW of town on Hwy 64, Hwy 28.* Behind Dry Falls the visitor may stand and look through to the Cullasaja River without getting wet. Also here is Lower Cullasaja Falls. The road here was cut from vertical cliffs and overlooks the river 250 feet below.

Highlands Nature Center. *Hwys 64 and 28, Highlands (28741). E Main St (Horse Cove Rd), 1/2 mile E of jct Hwy 64, Hwy 28. On the grounds of Highlands Biological Station.* Phone 828/526-2623. Cherokee artifacts, minerals of North Carolina; local flora and fauna, botanical garden; nature trail, hikes; lectures, movies. (Late May-Labor Day, Mon-Sat) **FREE**

Scaly Mountain Ski Area. *Dillard Rd, Scaly Mountain. 7 miles S on Hwy 106.* Phone 828/526-3737. www.scalymountain.com. Chair lift, rope tow; patrol, school, rentals; snowmaking; cafeteria. Longest run 600 feet; vertical drop 225 feet. (Mid-Dec-early Mar, daily) Half-day rates. **$$$$**

Limited-Service Hotel

★ **HIGHLANDS SUITE HOTEL.** *205 Main St, Highlands (28741).* Phone 828/526-4502; toll-free 800/221-5078; fax 828/526-4840. www.highlandssuitehotel .com. 28 rooms, 2 story, all suites. Complimentary continental breakfast. Check-in 4 pm, check-out noon. **$**

Full-Service Inn

★ ★ ★ **OLD EDWARDS INN AND SPA.** *445 Main St, Highlands (28741).* Phone 828/526-8008; toll-free 866/526-8008; fax 828/526-8301. www.oldedwardsinn.com. 18 rooms. Children over 11 only. Wireless Internet access. Complimentary continental breakfast. Check-in 4 pm, check-out noon. Spa. Restaurant, bar. **$$$$**

Specialty Lodging

The following lodging establishment is approved by Mobil Travel Guide, but due to its unique and individualized nature has not been given a traditional Mobil Star rating. Included in this listing you may find bed-and-breakfasts, limited-service inns, guest ranches, and other unique hotel properties.

HIGHLANDS INN. *4th and E Main sts, Highlands (28741).* Phone 828/526-9380; toll-free 800/964-6955; fax 828/526-8810. www.highlandsinn-nc.com. 29 rooms, 3 story. Closed Dec-Mar. Complimentary continental breakfast. Check-in 4 pm, check-out 11 am. **$**

Restaurants

★ ★ ★ **MADISON'S RESTAURANT AND WINE GARDEN.** *445 Main St, Highlands (28741).* Phone 828/526-5477; fax 828/526-8301. www.oldedwardsinn.com. American menu. Breakfast, lunch, dinner. Bar. Children's menu. Business causal. Outdoor seating. **$$$**

★ ★ **NICK'S.** *Hwy 28 at Satulah Rd, Highlands (28741).* Phone 828/526-2706; fax 828/526-2150. American menu. Lunch, dinner. Closed week of Dec 25-Feb. Children's menu. **$$**

★ ★ **ON THE VERANDAH.** *1536 Franklin Rd, Highlands (28741).* Phone 828/526-2338; fax 828/526-4132. www.ontheverandah.com. American menu. Dinner, Sun brunch. Closed Jan-Mar. **$$**

Jacksonville (C-8)

Population 66,715
Elevation 15 ft
Area Code 910
Web Site www.jacksonvillenc.net

This town is on the edge of the New River Marine Base (Camp Lejeune). There is excellent fishing nearby.

Limited-Service Hotels

★ **BEST WESTERN COURTYARD RESORT.**
603 N Marine Blvd, Jacksonville (28540). Phone 910/455-4100; fax 910/455-3023. www.bestwestern.com. 121 rooms. Complimentary continental breakfast. Check-in 3 pm, check-out noon. Wireless Internet access. Outdoor pool. Fitness room. **$**
🏋🚶🏊

★ **HAMPTON INN.** *474 Western Blvd, Jacksonville (28546). Phone 910/347-6500; toll-free 800/426-7866; fax 910/347-6858. www.hamptoninn.com.* 120 rooms, 2 story. Pets accepted, some restrictions; fee. Complimentary continental breakfast. Check-in 2 pm, check-out noon. Outdoor pool. **$**
🏋🐾🏊

★ **HOLIDAY INN EXPRESS.** *2115 Hwy 17 N, Jacksonville (28546). Phone 910/347-1900; toll-free 800/465-4329; fax 910/347-7593. www.holiday-inn.com.* 118 rooms, 4 story. Complimentary continental breakfast. Check-in 4 pm, check-out 11 am. High-speed Internet access, wireless Internet access. Outdoor pool. **$**
🏊

Jefferson (A-4)

See also Boone, Wilkesboro

Founded 1800
Population 1,422
Elevation 2,960 ft
Area Code 336
Zip 28640
Information Ashe County Chamber of Commerce, PO Box 31, 6 N Jefferson Ave, 28694; phone 336/246-9550
Web Site www.ashechamber.com

What to See and Do

Ashe County Cheese Factory. *106 E Main St, West Jefferson. 2 miles S on Hwy 194. Phone 336/246-2501; toll-free 800/445-1378.* North Carolina's only cheese factory. Viewing of cheese production; samples. (Mon-Sat; closed holidays; also Dec 26) **FREE**

Mount Jefferson State Park. *1 mile S off Hwy 221. At the summit of Mount Jefferson. Phone 336/246-9653.* A national natural landmark; excellent view of the Blue Ridge Mountains. Approximately 500 acres. Hiking, nature trails. Picnicking. No camping available.

Full-Service Inn

★★★ **GLENDALE SPRINGS INN.** *7414 Hwy 16, Glendale Springs (28629). Phone 336/982-2103; toll-free 800/287-1206; fax 336/982-2103. www.glendalespringsinn.com.* In a quaint community on the top of the Blue Ridge Mountains, this historic inn is as well known for its dining room as for its accommodations. The property was built in 1892. 9 rooms, 2 story. Complimentary full breakfast. Check-in 2 pm, check-out 11 am. Restaurant. **$**

Kill Devil Hills (A-10)

See also Cape Hatteras National Seashore, Fort Raleigh National Historic Site, Manteo, Nags Head

Population 5,897
Elevation 20 ft
Area Code 252
Zip 27948
Information Dare County Tourist Bureau, 704 US 64/264, PO Box 399, Manteo 27954; phone 252/473-2138 or toll-free 800/446-6262.
Web Site www.outerbanks.org

Although the name Kitty Hawk is usually associated with the Wright Brothers, their early flying experiments took place on and near these dunes on the Outer Banks (see).

What to See and Do

Wright Brothers National Memorial. *1401 National Park Dr, Kill Devil Hills (27954). Off Hwy 158, between mileposts 7 and 8. Phone 252/441-7430.* The field where the first powered flight took place on December 17, 1903, is marked showing the takeoff point and landing place. The living quarters and hangar buildings used by the Wrights during their experiments have been replicated. The visitor center has reproductions of a 1902 glider and a 1903 flyer, with exhibits on the story of their invention. Also 3,000-foot airstrip. (Daily; closed Dec 25) **$$**

Limited-Service Hotels

★ **BEST WESTERN OCEAN REEF SUITES.**
107 Virginia Dare Trail, Kill Devil Hills (27948). Phone 252/441-1611; toll-free 800/528-1234; fax 252/441-1482. www.bestwestern.com. 71 rooms, 5 story. Check-in 4 pm, check-out 11 am. Fitness room. Beach. Outdoor pool, whirlpool. **$$**
🚶🏊

★ **COMFORT INN.** *401 N Virginia Dare Trail, Kill Devil Hills (27948). Phone 252/480-2600; toll-free 800/424-6423; fax 252/480-2873. www.choicehotels.com.* 119 rooms, 3 story. Complimentary continental breakfast. Check-in 4 pm, check-out 11 am. Beach. Outdoor pool. **$**
🏊

★ **DAYS INN.** *101 N Virginia Dare Trail, Kill Devil Hills (27948). Phone 252/441-7211; toll-free 800/329-7466; fax 252/441-8080. www.daysinn.com.* 54 rooms. Complimentary continental breakfast. Check-in 4 pm, check-out 11 am. Beach. Outdoor pool. **$**
🐾 🏊

★ ★ **RAMADA INN.** *1701 S Virginia Dare Trail, Kill Devil Hills (27948). Phone 252/441-2151; toll-free 800/635-1824; fax 252/441-1830. www.ramadainnnagshead.com.* 171 rooms, 5 story. Pets accepted; fee. Check-out 11 am. High-speed Internet access. Restaurant, bar. Fitness room. Beach. Indoor pool, whirlpool. Business center. **$$**
🐾 🏃 🏊 ⛷

Full-Service Resort

🔍 ★ ★ ★ **THE SANDERLING.** *1461 Duck Rd, Duck (27949). Phone 252/261-4111; toll-free 800/701-4111; fax 252/261-1638. www.sanderlinginn.com.* Nestled on the northern reaches of North Carolina's ruggedly beautiful Outer Banks, The Sanderling is a resort for those who want to get away from it all without leaving comfort behind. From the low-rise cedar-shingled buildings to the Eco-Center, everything about this resort has been designed to complement the natural setting. Comprised of three inns and oceanside villas, The Sanderling offers a stylish, contemporary country atmosphere in its accommodations. Mornings begin with fresh-baked goods delivered to the rooms, and days are filled with a variety of adventures, including those that require little more than relaxing with a great massage. Miles of pristine beachfront beckon guests, and the seaside ambience extends to dining, where a highly intriguing restaurant is housed within a historic US lifesaving station. 88 rooms. Restaurant, bar. Fitness room. Indoor pool, whirlpool. Tennis. **$$**
🏃 🏊 🎿

Restaurants

★ ★ **FLYING FISH CAFE.** *2003 Croatan Hwy, Kill Devil Hills (27948). Phone 252/441-6894; fax 252/480-*
2073. www.flyingfishcafe.net. Seafood menu. Dinner. Bar. Children's menu. **$$**

★ **JOLLY ROGER.** *1836 N Virginia Dare Trail, Kill Devil Hills (27948). Phone 252/441-6530.* American menu. Breakfast, lunch, dinner. Bar. **$$**

★ ★ **PORT O' CALL.** *504 Virginia Dare Trail, Kill Devil Hills (27948). Phone 252/441-8001; fax 252/441-5725.* Seafood menu. Dinner, Sun brunch. Closed Jan-mid-Mar. Bar. Children's menu. **$$$**

Kinston (B-8)

See also New Bern

Population 23,688
Elevation 44 ft
Area Code 252
Zip 28501
Web Site www.visitkinston.com

What to See and Do

CSS *Neuse* State Historic Site. *2612 W Vernon Ave. Phone 252/522-2091.* Remains of Confederate ironclad gunboat sunk by her crew in 1865 and not raised until 1963. Visitor center relates story of the *Neuse* through an audio show, artifacts recovered from the gunboat, photographs; memorial has exhibits on life of Caswell, first elected governor of the state of North Carolina. Picnicking. (Apr-Sept: Tues-Sat; Oct-Mar: Mon-Fri; closed holidays)

Limited-Service Hotel

★ **HAMPTON INN.** *1382 Hwy 258 S, Kinston (28501). Phone 252/523-1400; toll-free 800/250-5370; fax 252/523-1326. www.hamptoninn.com.* 123 rooms, 4 story. Complimentary continental breakfast. Check-out noon. Outdoor pool. **$**
🏊

Laurinburg (C-6)

See also Pinehurst, Southern Pines

Settled (Circa 1700)
Population 15,874
Elevation 227 ft
Area Code 910
Information Laurinburg-Scotland County Area Chamber of Commerce, 606 Atkinson St, PO Box 1025, 28353; phone 910/276-7420
Web Site www.laurinburgchamber.org

Laurinburg is the seat of Scotland County, named for its early Scottish Highland settlers. Industrial development has expanded this agricultural center's economy.

What to See and Do

St. Andrews Presbyterian College. *S of city limits. Phone 910/277-5000.* (1958) (800 students) Contemporary-style buildings on an 800-acre campus around a 70-acre lake. Mosaic-tiled wall depicts story of humankind. On campus are

Science Center. *1700 Dogwood Mile, Laurinburg (28352).* Features interdisciplinary laboratory, guides. (Sept-May and summer session, Mon-Fri; other times by appointment) **FREE**

Vardell Art Gallery. *Vardell Building, 1700 Dogwood Mile, Laurinburg (28352). Phone 910/277-5000.* (Mid-Sept-May, Mon-Fri; closed school holidays) **FREE**

Limited-Service Hotel

★ ★ **COMFORT INN.** *1705 401 Bypass S, Laurinburg (28352). Phone 910/277-7788; toll-free 800/ 424-6423; fax 910/277-7229. www.choicehotels.com.* Set at the intersection of Highways 401 and 74, this award-winning hotel features cozy rooms and impeccable service. In-room amenities include down pillows and comforters. 80 rooms, 3 story. Complimentary continental breakfast. Check-in 3 pm, check-out noon. High-speed Internet access. Restaurant, bar. Fitness room. Outdoor pool. **$**
🏃 🏊

Lexington (B-5)

See also Asheboro, High Point, Salisbury, Winston-Salem

Settled 1750
Population 19,953
Elevation 809 ft
Area Code 336
Zip 27292
Information Chamber of Commerce, 16 E Center St, PO Box C, 27293; phone 336/248-5929
Web Site www.visitlexingtonnc.org

In 1775, settlers learned of the battle of Lexington in Massachusetts and decided to name this town for it. Local industry is diversified and includes furniture making, textiles and clothing, food processing, electronics, ceramics, machinery, and fiberglass. Native to the area is traditional pork barbecue, which can be found in many local restaurants.

What to See and Do

Davidson County Historical Museum. *2 S Main St, Lexington (27292). Center of city. Phone 336/242-2035.* (1858). Greek Revival building facing the town square; old courtroom houses museum of local history. (Tues-Sun; closed holidays) **FREE**

High Rock Lake. *10 miles SW on Hwy 70 or S on Hwy 8.* Its 300-mile shoreline is a center for water sports in the piedmont.

Linville (A-3)

See also Banner Elk, Blowing Rock, Boone, Little Switzerland

Population 244
Elevation 3,669 ft
Area Code 828
Zip 28646

Linville is in the heart of a ruggedly beautiful resort area. Several miles to the south, just off the Blue Ridge Parkway, is scenic Linville Falls, cascading down the steep Linville Gorge, designated a national wilderness. Visible from vantage points in this area are the mysterious Brown Mountain lights.

What to See and Do

⭐ **Grandfather Mountain.** *Linville (28646). 2 miles NE via Hwy 221, 1 mile S of jct Blue Ridge Pkwy and Hwy 221.* Phone 828/733-4337. www.grandfather.com. Highest peak of the Blue Ridge Mountains, with spectacular views, rugged rock formations, 1-mile-high swinging bridge; bald eagles, gold eagles, river otters, deer, cougars, black bears, bear cubs, and others in natural habitats. Hiking trails, picnic areas. Museum with exhibits on local animals, birds, flowers, geology; restaurant, gift shop. (Daily; winter, weather permitting; closed Thanksgiving, Dec 25) **$$$**

Special Events

Grandfather Mountain Highland Games. *Hwy 221 and Grandfather Mt, Linville. MacRae Meadows, on Hwy 221 at Grandfather Mountain.* Phone 828/733-2013. Gathering of members of more than 100 Scottish clans and societies to view or participate in traditional Scottish sports, track-and-field events, mountain marathon; highland dancing, piping, and drumming; ceremonies and pageantry. Mid-July.

Grandfather Mountain Nature Photography Weekend. *2050 Blowing Rock Hwy, Linville (28646). Grandfather Mountain.* Phone 828/733-2013. Nationally known photographers give illustrated lectures; nature photography contest; picnic dinner. Preregistration required. Late May-early June.

"Singing on the Mountain". *On the slopes of Grandfather Mountain.* All-day program of modern and traditional gospel music featuring top groups and nationally known speakers. Concessions or bring your own food. Fourth Sun in June.

Full-Service Resort

★ ★ ★ **THE ESEEOLA LODGE AT LINVILLE GOLF CLUB.** *175 Linville Ave, Linville (28646).* Phone 828/733-4311; toll-free 800/742-6717; fax 828/733-3227. www.eseeola.com. The Eseeola Lodge at Linville Golf Club appeals to the entire family with its array of activities, delicious dining, and comfortable accommodations. Avid golfers hit the historic links, designed by Donald Ross in 1924, and appreciate the services of the clubhouse and pro shop. Eight tennis courts keep tennis players busy; swimmers adore the pool; and the manicured croquet lawn inspires others to give this whimsical game a whirl. A well-equipped playground and day camp capture the attention of younger guests, while their parents enjoy the adult recreational opportunities. Antique and handmade quilts complete a captivating Americana décor in the rooms and suites, and modern amenities ensure comfort. The chef prepares his menu daily based on the freshest ingredients, and the four-course dinner of international dishes with a Southern bent is sure to please. 25 rooms, 2 story. Closed late Oct-mid-May. Complimentary full breakfast. Check-in 3:30 pm, check-out 11 am. Two restaurants, bar. Children's activity center. Fitness room. Outdoor pool. Golf, 18 holes. Tennis. Business center. **$$$**
🏋 🏖 🏌 🎾 🚶

Little Switzerland (B-3)

See also Burnsville, Linville, Marion, Morganton

Founded 1910
Population 200
Elevation 3,500 ft
Area Code 828
Zip 28749
Information Mitchell County Chamber of Commerce, Rte 1, Box 796, Spruce Pine 28777; phone 704/765-9483 or toll-free 800/227-3912
Web Site www.mitchell-county.com

A restful summer resort amid the high mountains of western North Carolina, Little Switzerland is bisected by the Blue Ridge Parkway.

What to See and Do

Emerald Village. *McKinney Mine Rd and Blue Ridge Pkwy, Little Switzerland.* Phone 828/765-6463. Historical area includes mines; North Carolina Mining Museum; Main Street 1920s Mining Community Museum; Gemstone Mine, where visitors can prospect for gems under shaded flumes (fee; equipment furnished); Mechanical Music Maker Museum; waterfall and scenic overlook; shops and deli. (Daily; closed holidays) **$$**

Mount Mitchell State Park. *20 miles S on Blue Ridge Pkwy, then N on Hwy 128. Adjacent to Pisgah National Forest, a natural national landmark.* Phone 828/675-4611. The road leads to the summit (6,684 feet; the highest point east of the Mississippi River) for incomparable views. Trails. Picnicking, restaurant, refreshment stands. Small-tent camping area. Observation tower, museum.

Museum of North Carolina Minerals. *79 Pkwy Maintenance Rd, Little Switzerland. At jct Blue Ridge Pkwy and Hwy 226.* Phone 828/765-2761. Mineral exhibits of the state. (May-Nov: daily; rest of year: Wed-Sun; closed Jan 1, Thanksgiving, Dec 24-26) **FREE**

Limited-Service Hotel

★ ★ **CHALET SWITZERLAND INN.** *226 A Blue Ridge Pkwy, Little Switzerland (28749). Phone 828/765-2153; toll-free 800/654-4026; fax 828/765-0049. www.switzerlandinn.com.* Named after its Swiss Alps-like view, this inn has welcomed guests since 1910 to a panoramic hideaway of misty mountains and lush valleys where accommodations fill four main buildings and several rustic, individual cottages. Dine inside or out on casual, American cuisine. 73 rooms, 2 story. Closed Nov-mid-Apr. Pets accepted. Complimentary full breakfast. Check-in 3 pm, check-out 11 am. Restaurant, bar. Outdoor pool. Tennis. **$**

Lumberton (C-6)

Founded 1787
Population 20,795
Elevation 137 ft
Area Code 910
Zip 28358
Information Visitors Bureau, 3431 Lackey St, 28358; phone 910/739-9999 or toll-free 800/359-6971
Web Site www.lumberton-nc.com

Lumberton is the county seat of Robeson County and the home of many industries, including one of the largest tobacco marketing centers in the state. Hunting for quail, duck, dove, and rabbit is excellent in the area. Pembroke, to the northwest, is the population center for some 30,000 Lumbee Native Americans, believed by some historians to include descendants of the "lost colonists" (see FORT RALEIGH NATIONAL HISTORIC SITE).

What to See and Do

Jones Lake State Park. *113 Joneslake Dr, Elizabethtown (28337). 25 miles E on Hwy 41 to Elizabethtown, then 4 miles N on Hwy 242.* Phone 910/588-4550. More than 2,200 acres with swimming, fishing, boating. Interpretive trails. Picnicking. Primitive camping (mid-Mar-Nov).

One-room schoolhouse. Restored early American furnished classroom. (Mon-Fri; closed holidays)

Special Event

Scottish Highland Games. *751 E 4th Ave, Red Springs (28377). Phone 910/843-5000.* Celebration of Scottish heritage with music, dancing, competitions, childrens events. First weekend in Oct.

Limited-Service Hotels

★ **COUNTRY INN & SUITES BY CARLSON.** *3010 Roberts Ave, Lumberton (28358). Phone 910/738-2481; toll-free 800/456-4000; fax 910/738-8260. www.countryinns.com/lumbertonnc.* Walking into this hotel is like walking into someone's home, with its high ceilings, fireplace, and cozy living area. And, just as at home, there is a desk in the common area with a computer and printer for guests' use. 53 rooms, 4 story. Complimentary continental breakfast. Check-in 3 pm, check-out noon. High-speed Internet access. Fitness room. Outdoor pool. **$**

★ ★ **HOLIDAY INN.** *101 Wintergreen Dr, Lumberton (28358). Phone 910/671-1166; toll-free 800/465-4329; fax 910/671-1166. www.holiday-inn.com.* In addition to the new carpeting, furniture, bedspreads, and drapes installed during a 2003 renovation, the rooms at this Holiday Inn feature just about everything a traveler could need, including high-speed Internet access, microwaves, refrigerators, a sofa bed, and coffee and tea makers. 107 rooms, 2 story. Check-in 3 pm, check-out noon. High-speed Internet access. Restaurant. Fitness room. Outdoor pool. **$**

Restaurant

★ ★ **JOHN'S.** *4880 Kahn Dr, Lumberton (28358). Phone 910/738-4709; fax 910/738-6060.* International/Fusion menu. Dinner. Closed Sun-Mon; holidays. Bar. Children's menu. Casual attire. **$$$**

Maggie Valley (B-2)

See also Asheville, Cherokee, Great Smoky Mountains National Park, Waynesville

Population 607
Elevation 3,020 ft

Area Code 828
Zip 28751
Information CVB Chamber of Commerce, 2487 Soco Rd, PO Box 87; phone 828/926-1686 or toll-free 800/785-8259
Web Site www.maggievalley.org

In 1909, Henry Setzer decided the expanding community of Plott needed a post office. He submitted the names of his three daughters to the postmaster general, who selected Maggie, then age 14. Lying in the shadow of the Great Smoky Mountains National Park (see), the town is 4 miles from the Soco Gap entrance to the Blue Ridge Parkway and has become a year-round resort area.

What to See and Do

Cataloochee Ski Area. *1080 Ski Lodge Rd, Maggie Valley (28751). 4 miles N via Hwy 19 to Fie Top Rd. Phone 828/926-0285; toll-free 800/768-0285. www.cataloochee.com.* Quad, two double chair lifts, T-bar, rope tow; patrol, school, rentals; snowmaking; half-day and twilight rates; cafeteria, bar. Longest run 3,800 feet, vertical drop 740 feet. (Dec-mid-Mar, daily) **$$$$**

Ghost Town in the Sky. *890 Soco Rd, Maggie Valley. On Hwy 19. Phone 828/926-1140; toll-free 800/446-7869.* Chair lift, incline railway or shuttle to top of mountain; shows, rides, gunfights, shops; food. (Early May-late Oct, daily) **$$$$**

Lindsey Miniature Village. *1110 Soco Rd, Maggie Valley. Phone 828/926-6277.* Over 120 miniature buildings, many historical, in garden setting. Doll shop. (Mid-Apr-early Jan, daily; limited hours after Labor Day) **$$$**

Soco Gardens Zoo. *3578 Soco Rd, Maggie Valley. Phone 828/926-1746.* A 2 1/2-acre zoo with more than 25 different species of animals, including exotic birds, alligators, bears, snow leopards, monkeys, jaguars, and wallabies. Reptile house, poisonous and non-poisonous snake shows. Guided tours. Gift shop. (May-Oct, daily) **$$**

Stompin Ground. *3116 Soco Rd, Maggie Valley. Phone 828/926-1288.* Bluegrass and country music; clogging; exhibition dancers; square dancing (audience participation). (May-Oct, nightly) **$$$**

Special Events

Clogging Hall of Fame. *71 Kyles Way, Maggie Valley (28751). Phone 828/926-1288.* World-class cloggers from all across the United States compete. Oct.

International Folk Festival. *282 N Haywood St, Waynesville (28786). Phone 828/452-2997.* Premier folk groups from over 10 countries demonstrate their cultural heritage through lively music and costumed dance. 11 days in late July.

Limited-Service Hotel

★ **COMFORT INN.** *3282 Soco Rd, Maggie Valley (28751). Phone 828/926-9106; toll-free 800/228-5150; fax 828/926-9106. www.comfortinn.com.* 68 rooms, 2 story. Complimentary continental breakfast. Check-in 2 pm, check-out 11 am. Outdoor pool. **$**

Specialty Lodging

The following lodging establishment is approved by Mobil Travel Guide, but due to its unique and individualized nature has not been given a traditional Mobil Star rating. Included in this listing you may find bed-and-breakfasts, limited-service inns, guest ranches, and other unique hotel properties.

CATALOOCHEE SKI AREA. *119 Ranch Dr, Maggie Valley (28751). Phone 828/926-0285; toll-free 800/868-1401; fax 828/926-0354. www.cataloochee.com.* This location offers awesome skiing for beginners and experts on exciting slopes and winding trails in the Great Smoky Mountains. Guests can relax in the lodge with a hot toddy and put their feet up around the crackling circular fireplace. Enjoy a hearty home-cooked meal or picnic on the sun-drenched deck overlooking the slopes. 26 rooms, 2 story. Check-in 3 pm, check-out 11 am. Children's activity center. Whirlpool. Tennis. **$**

Restaurant

★ ★ **J. ARTHUR'S.** *2843 Soco Rd, Maggie Valley (28751). Phone 828/926-1817; fax 828/926-0019. www.jarthurs.com.* Loft dining area. American menu. Dinner. Closed Thanksgiving, Dec 25. Bar. Children's menu. **$$**

Manteo (A-10)

See also Kill Devil Hills, Nags Head

Population 1,052
Elevation 5 ft
Area Code 252
Zip 27954
Information Dare County Tourist Bureau, 704 Hwy 64/264, PO Box 399; phone 252/473-2138 or toll-free 800/446-6262
Web Site www.outerbanks.org

Fishing in the waters off Manteo is excellent. A large sport fishing fleet is available for booking at Oregon Inlet as well as on Roanoke Island.

What to See and Do

Elizabethan Gardens. *1411 Hwy 4 and 264, Manteo (27954). 3 miles N on Hwy 64/264. On Roanoke Island. Phone 252/473-3234.* These 10 1/2 acres include Great Lawn, Sunken Garden, Queen's Rose Garden, an herb garden, a 16th-century gazebo with thatched roof, and an ancient garden statuary. Plants bloom all year: spring peak, mid-Apr; summer peak, mid-July; fall peak, mid-Oct; and winter peak, mid-Feb. Gate House Reception Center displays period furniture, English portraits, coat of arms. (Daily; closed Jan 1, Dec 25) **$$**

North Carolina Aquarium on Roanoke Island. *374 Airport Rd, Manteo (27954). 3 miles N via Hwy 64/264, Airport Rd exit. Phone 252/473-3493.* Aquarium and marine-oriented educational and research facility. Public aquaria and exhibits, films and educational programs. (Daily; closed Jan 1, Thanksgiving, Dec 25) **$$$**

Roanoke Island Festival Park. *Manteo waterfront, Manteo. Phone 252/475-1500.* Representative 16th-century sailing vessel similar to those that brought the first English colonists to the New World more than 400 years ago. Living history interpretation (summer). Visitor center with exhibits and audiovisual program. (Feb-Dec, daily; closed Thanksgiving, Dec 25) **$$$**

Full-Service Inn

★ ★ ★ **TRANQUIL HOUSE INN.** *405 Queen Elizabeth St, Manteo (27954). Phone 252/473-1404; toll-free 800/458-7069; fax 252/473-1526. www.tranquilinn.com.* Built in 1988 in the style of a 19th-century Outer Banks resort, this waterfront property offers continental breakfast and evening wine and cheese with each of its 25 rooms. Elegant dockside dining overlooking Shallowbag Bay can be found at 1587 Restaurant. 25 rooms, 3 story. Complimentary continental breakfast. Check-in 3 pm, check-out 11 am. Restaurant. **$$**

Restaurant

★ ★ **CLARA'S SEAFOOD GRILL.** *Queen Elizabeth Ave, Manteo (27954). Phone 252/473-1727; fax 252/473-1723.* American menu. Lunch, dinner. Closed Thanksgiving, Dec 25; also Jan-Feb. Bar. Children's menu. **$$**

Marion (B-3)

See also Little Switzerland, Morganton

Founded 1843
Population 4,943
Elevation 1,395 ft
Area Code 704
Zip 28752
Web Site www.marionnc.org

Permits for the Linville Gorge Wilderness of the Pisgah National Forest (see BREVARD) can be obtained at the Grandfather Ranger District Office (Rte 1, Box 110A; phone 704/652-2144) located here.

What to See and Do

Linville Caverns. *Hwy 221 N, Marion. Beneath Humpback Mountain. Phone toll-free 800/419-0540.* Half-hour guided tours. Gift shop. (Mar-Nov: daily; rest of year: weekends only) **$$**

Morehead City (C-9)

See also Beaufort

Founded 1857
Population 7,691
Elevation 16 ft
Area Code 252
Zip 28557
Information Crystal Coast Visitors Center, 3409 Arendell St, PO Box 1406; phone 252/726-8148 or toll-free 800/786-6962
Web Site www.sunnync.com

Just across the Intracoastal Waterway from Beaufort, Morehead City is the largest town in Carteret County and a year-round resort town. It is involved in both sport and commercial fishing. The port accommodates oceangoing vessels and charter boats.

What to See and Do

Carteret County Museum of History and Art. *1008 Arendell St, Morehead City. Phone 252/247-7533.* Paintings and artifacts from the 19th century. Includes genealogy research library. (Tues-Sat) **FREE**

Fishing. Onshore and offshore; charter boats available. Gulfstream fishing for marlin, amberjack, dolphin, mackerel, and bluefish.

Fort Macon State Park. *E Fort Macon Rd, Atlantic Beach. 2 miles E of town. On Bogue Banks. Phone 252/726-3775.* This restored fort, built in 1834, was originally used as a harbor defense. Beach (lifeguards in summer), bathhouse (fee); surf fishing; hiking, nature trails. Museum; interpretive program (summer); battle reenactments. Snack bar. **FREE**

Town of Atlantic Beach. *Across the bridge from Morehead.* Swimming, fishing, boating; boardwalk.

Special Events

Atlantic Beach King Mackerel Tournament. *125 W Fort Macon Rd, Atlantic Beach (28512). Phone 252/247-2334.* Mid-Sept.

Big Rock Blue Marlin Tournament. *209 N 35th St, Morehead City (28557). Phone 252/247-3575.* Largest tournament of its kind on the East Coast. Fishing for blue marlin, cash awards, registration required. Six days in early June.

North Carolina Seafood Festival. *404 A Evans St, Morehead City. Phone 252/726-6273.* Seafood, arts and crafts, music. First weekend in Oct.

Limited-Service Hotels

★ ★ **BEST WESTERN BUCCANEER INN.** *2806 Arendell St, Morehead City (28557). Phone 252/726-3115; toll-free 800/682-4982; fax 252/726-3864. www.bestwestern.com.* 91 rooms, 3 story. Complimentary full breakfast. Check-in 4 pm, check-out noon. Restaurant, bar. Outdoor pool. **$**

★ **HAMPTON INN.** *4035 Arendell St, Morehead City (28557). Phone 252/240-2300; toll-free 800/426-7866; fax 252/240-2311. www.hamptoninn.com.* 119 rooms, 4 story. Complimentary continental breakfast. Check-in 4 pm, check-out 11 am. Fitness room. Outdoor pool. **$**

Full-Service Hotel

★ ★ ★ **SHERATON ATLANTIC BEACH OCEANFRONT HOTEL.** *2717 Fort Macon Rd, Atlantic Beach (28512). Phone 252/240-1155; toll-free 800/624-8875; fax 252/240-1452. www.sheratonatlanticbeach.com.* This beachfront hotel features 200 rooms, each with a private balcony. It offers two restaurants, two lounges with entertainment, an indoor and outdoor pool, and more. Golf, tennis, and white-sand beaches are in the area. 200 rooms, 9 story. Pets accepted, some restrictions. Check-in 4 pm, check-out 11 am. Two restaurants, two bars. Fitness room. Beach. Indoor pool, outdoor pool, whirlpool. **$$**

Specialty Lodgings

The following lodging establishments are approved by Mobil Travel Guide, but due to their unique and individualized nature have not been given a traditional Mobil Star rating. Included in this listing you may find bed-and-breakfasts, limited-service inns, guest ranches, and other unique hotel properties.

EMERALD ISLE INN AND BED & BREAKFAST. *502 Ocean Dr, Emerald Isle (28594). Phone 252/354-3222; toll-free www.emeraldisleinn.com.* 4 rooms, 2 story. Complimentary full breakfast. Check-in 3 pm, check-out 11 am. On Bogue Banks. **$**

HARBOR LIGHT GUEST HOUSE. *332 Live Oak Dr, Cape Carteret (28584). Phone 252/393-6868; toll-free 800/624-8439; fax 252/393-6868.* 9 rooms, 3 story. Children over 16 years only. Complimentary full breakfast. Check-in 3 pm, check-out 11 am. Overlooks Bogue Sound. **$$**

Restaurants

★ ★ **ANCHOR INN.** *109 N 28th St, Morehead City (28557). Phone 252/726-2156; fax 252/726-3864. www.anchorinnrestaurant.com.* American menu. Breakfast, dinner. Closed Dec 24-25. Bar. Children's menu. **$$$**

★ **MRS. WILLIS.** *3114 Bridges St, Morehead City (28557). Phone 252/726-3741.* American menu. Lunch, dinner. Closed Dec 24-30. Bar. Children's menu. Three dining rooms. **$$**

★ **SANITARY FISH MARKET.** *501 Evans St, Morehead City (28557). Phone 252/247-3111; fax 252/247-5110. www.sanitaryfishmarket.com.* Seafood menu. Lunch, dinner. Closed Dec-Jan. Children's menu. **$$**

Morganton (B-3)

See also Little Switzerland, Marion

Population 17,310
Elevation 1,182 ft
Area Code 828
Zip 28655
Information Burke County Travel and Tourism, 102 E Union St, Courthouse Sq; phone 828/433-6793
Web Site www.ci.morganton.nc.us

This is the seat of Burke County and a manufacturing town producing furniture, textiles, shoes, chemicals, electronics, clothing, and other products. In 1893, the county became a haven for the Waldenses, a religious group from the French-Italian Alps that was seeking freedom and space to expand outside their alpine homeland.

What to See and Do

Boat tours. *9066 Hwy 126, New Bern (28761). Phone 828/584-0666.* Tours of Lake James on the 38-foot pontoon *Harbor Queen.* Departs Mountain Harbor Marina. **$$$**

Lake James. *8 miles W on Hwy 126.* **Lake Rhodhiss.** *10 miles E off Hwy 70.* Boating, fishing, and swimming.

Special Events

From This Day Forward. *Church St, Valdese. Phone toll-free 800/743-8398.* Outdoor historical drama depicting hardships of the Waldenses and their struggle for religious freedom. Thurs-Sun evenings. Mid-July–mid-Aug.

Historic Morganton Festival. *Downtown, 112 W Union St, Morganton (28655). Phone 828/438-5280.* Arts, crafts, ethnic foods, band concert. Mid-Sept.

Waldensian Celebration of the Glorious Return. *402 Main St W, Valdese (28690). Off I-40, exit 112. Phone 828/879-2129.* Commemoration of the end of persecution during the reign of Louis XIV; ethnic games, arts and crafts, dances, food. Mid-Aug.

Limited-Service Hotels

★ ★ **HOLIDAY INN MORGANTON.** *2400 S Sterling St, Morganton (28655). Phone 828/437-0171; toll-free 800/465-4329; fax 828/437-1639. www.holiday-inn.com.* 133 rooms, 2 story. Pets accepted; fee. Check-in 3 pm, check-out noon. Restaurant, bar. Fitness room. Outdoor pool. **$**
⛱ 🚶 ⛴

★ **SLEEP INN.** *2400 A S Sterling St, Morganton (28655). Phone 828/433-9000; toll-free 800/424-6423; fax 828/433-9000. www.choicehotels.com.* 61 rooms, 2 story. Pets accepted; fee. Complimentary continental breakfast. Check-in 3 pm, check-out 11 am. **$**
⛱

Nags Head (A-10)

See also Cape Hatteras National Seashore, Fort Raleigh National Historic Site, Kill Devil Hills, Manteo

Population 2,700
Elevation 10 ft
Area Code 252
Zip 27959
Information Dare County Tourist Bureau, 704 Hwy 64/264, PO Box 399, Manteo 27954; phone 252/473-2138 or toll-free 800/446-6262.
Web Site www.outerbanks.org

This is a year-round fishing and beachcombing town on the Outer Banks (see), just south of Kill Devil Hills (see). There are fishing piers and boats for rent. Swimming is good in summer. A museum is located at Jockey's Ridge State Park, which boasts one of the largest sand dunes on the East Coast.

The soft sand dunes and Atlantic breezes make this a popular area for hang gliding. Offshore, partly buried in the drifting sand, are many wrecks of both old sailing ships and more modern vessels.

Cape Hatteras National Seashore (see) is south of Nags Head.

Special Events

Hang Gliding Spectacular. *Jockeys Ridge State Park, Nags Head (27959). Phone 252/441-4124.* Hang gliding competition, novice through advanced. Spectacular flying and fun events. Second weekend in May.

Rogallo Kite Festival. *3941 S Croatan Hwy, Nags Head (27959). Phone 252/441-4124.* Competition for home-built kites; stunt kite performances, demonstrations; kite auction. Early July.

Limited-Service Hotels

★ **NAGS HEAD INN.** *4701 S Virginia Dare Trail, Nags Head (27959). Phone 252/441-0454; toll-free 800/ 327-8881; fax 252/441-0454. www.nagsheadinn.com.* 100 rooms, 5 story. Closed Sun after Thanksgiving-Dec 26. Check-in 4 pm, check-out 11 am. Beach. Indoor pool, whirlpool. **$**
☷

★ **SURF SIDE MOTEL.** *6701 S Virginia Dare Trail, Nags Head (27959). Phone 252/441-2105; toll-free 800/552-7873; fax 252/441-2456. www.surfsideobx.com.* 76 rooms, 5 story. Complimentary continental breakfast. Check-in 3 pm, check-out 11 am. Fitness room. Beach. Indoor pool, outdoor pool, whirlpool. **$**
🕴 ☷

Specialty Lodging

The following lodging establishment is approved by Mobil Travel Guide, but due to its unique and individualized nature has not been given a traditional Mobil Star rating. Included in this listing you may find bed-and-breakfasts, limited-service inns, guest ranches, and other unique hotel properties.

FIRST COLONY INN. *6720 S Virginia Dare Trail, Nags Head (27959). Phone 252/441-2343; toll-free 800/ 368-9390; fax 919/441-9234. www.firstcolonyinn.com.* This beach-style bed-and-breakfast has welcomed Outer Banks' visitors since 1932 and is on the National Register of Historic Places. Rooms are decorated in English antiques, and the shingled building is wrapped in wide, two-story verandas affording great sunset views. 26 rooms, 3 story. Complimentary full breakfast. Check-in 3 pm, check-out 11 am. Outdoor pool. **$**
☷

Restaurants

★ ★ **OWENS'.** *7114 S Virginia Dare Trail, Nags Head (27959). Phone 252/441-7309; fax 252/441-4670. www.owensrestaurant.com.* Historic artifacts of the US Lifesaving Service (forerunner of the US Coast Guard) on display; uniforms, log books, photographs. Seafood menu. Dinner. Closed Jan-mid-Mar. Bar. Children's menu. **$$**

★ ★ **PENGUIN ISLE.** *6708 S Croatan Hwy, Nags Head (27959). Phone 252/441-2637; fax 252/441-2562. www.penguinisle.com.* American menu. Dinner. Closed Dec 24-25. Bar. Children's menu. **$$$**

★ ★ **WINDMILL POINT.** *Hwy 158, Nags Head (27959). Phone 252/441-1535; fax 252/441-1569.* American menu. Dinner. Bar. Children's menu. **$$**

New Bern (B-8)

See also Kinston

Settled 1710
Population 23,128
Elevation 15 ft
Area Code 252
Information Visitor Information Center, 314 S Front St, PO Box 1413, 28560; phone 252/637-9400 or toll-free 800/437-5767
Web Site www.visitnewbern.com

The first settlers here, one of North Carolina's earliest towns, were Germans and Swiss seeking political and religious freedom in the New World. The name Bern came from the city in Switzerland. Many Georgian- and Federal-style buildings give New Bern an architectural ambience unique in North Carolina. Many of these homes can be visited during April and October.

Swimming, boating, and freshwater and saltwater fishing can be enjoyed on the Neuse and Trent rivers. A Ranger District Office of the Croatan National Forest is located here.

What to See and Do

Attmore-Oliver House. *510 Pollock St, New Bern. Phone 252/638-8558.* (Circa 1790) This house, headquarters for the New Bern Historical Society, exhibits 18th- and 19th-century furnishings and historical objects, including Civil War artifacts and a doll collection. (Early Apr-mid-Dec, Tues-Sat; also by appointment; closed July 4, Thanksgiving, Dec 25) **FREE**

Croatan National Forest. *160 Zillicoa St, Asheville. SE via Hwy 70. Phone 252/638-5628.* A unique coastal forest (157,724 acres), with many estuaries and waterways; northernmost habitat of the alligator. Pocosins (Native American for "swamp on a hill") have many unusual dwarf and insect-eating plants. Swimming, boating, and fishing in Neuse River; hunting for deer, bear, turkey, quail and migratory waterfowl; picnicking; camping (fee). For further information, contact the Forest Supervisor, 100 Otis St, PO Box 2750, Asheville 28802.

New Bern Firemen's Museum. *410 Hancock St, New Bern. Off Hwy 17, 70 Business. Phone 252/636-4087.* Antique fire-fighting equipment, relics, and pictures; 1927 double-size ladder trucks and engines, 1941 pumper. (Daily; closed Thanksgiving, Dec 25) **$**

⭐ **Tryon Palace Historic Sites and Gardens.** *610 Pollock St, New Bern. S end of George St, 1 block S of Hwy 17, 70 Business, Hwy 55. Phone toll-free 800/767-1560.* Built from 1767-1770 by Royal Governor, William Tryon, this "most beautiful building in the colonial Americas" burned by accident in 1798 and lay in ruins until being rebuilt between 1952-1959. It served as the colonial and first state capitol. Reconstruction, furnishings, and 18th-century English gardens are beautiful and authentic. Guided tours (Tues-Sat; closed Jan 1, Thanksgiving, Dec 24-26). Also self-guided garden tours. Combination ticket available. **$$$$** On grounds are

Dixon-Stevenson House. *610 Pollock St, New Bern (28560).* (Circa 1830) The early Federal architecture, including the interior woodwork and widow's walk, reflects maritime history of the area. Furnished in Federal and Empire antiques.

John Wright Stanly House. *307 George St, New Bern (28560).* (Circa 1780) Georgian-style house furnished with 18th-century American antiques. Elegant interior woodwork. Formal gardens typical of the period.

New Bern Academy. *500 New St, New Bern (28560). Phone 252/514-4874.* (Circa 1810) Four blocks from Tryon Palace complex, in the historic residential district. Major surviving landmark of an educational institution founded in the 1760s, the Academy is restored as a self-guided museum of New Bern Civil War history, early education, and local architecture.

Limited-Service Hotels

★ **COMFORT INN.** *218 E Front St, New Bern (28560). Phone 252/636-0022; fax 252/636-0051.* 100 rooms, 4 story. Complimentary continental breakfast. Check-in 3 pm, check-out 11 am. High-speed Internet access, wireless Internet access. Outdoor pool, whirlpool. **$**

★ **HAMPTON INN.** *200 Hotel Dr, New Bern (28562). Phone 252/637-2111; toll-free 800/448-8288; fax 252/637-2000. www.hamptoninn.com.* 101 rooms, 4 story. Complimentary continental breakfast. Check-in 3 pm, check-out 11 am. Fitness room. Outdoor pool, children's pool. **$**

Full-Service Hotel

★ ★ ★ **SHERATON NEW BERN HOTEL AND MARINA.** *100 Middle St, New Bern (28560). Phone 252/638-3585; toll-free 800/326-3745; fax 252/638-8112. www.newbernsheraton.com.* With a downtown waterfront location, this hotel offers all the amenities a visitor could want, with 171 rooms, 19 full suites, and 19 mini-suites. Historic paddlewheel rides. Golf, tennis, and beaches are nearby. 171 rooms, 5 story. Pets accepted, some restrictions; fee. Check-in 3 pm, check-out noon. High-speed Internet access. Restaurant, two bars. Fitness room. Outdoor pool. Business center. **$**

Specialty Lodgings

The following lodging establishments are approved by Mobil Travel Guide, but due to their unique and individualized nature have not been given a traditional Mobil Star rating. Included in this listing you may find bed-and-breakfasts, limited-service inns, guest ranches, and other unique hotel properties.

AERIE INN BED & BREAKFAST. *509 Pollock St, New Bern (28562). Phone 252/636-5553; toll-free 800/849-5553; fax 252/514-2157. www.aerieinn.com.* Victorian house built in 1880; antiques. One block east of Tryon Palace. 7 rooms, 2 story. Complimentary full breakfast. Check-in 3 pm, check-out 11 am. **$**

HARMONY HOUSE INN. *215 Pollock St, New Bern (28560). Phone 252/636-3810; toll-free 800/636-3113; fax 252/636-3810. www.harmonyhouseinn.com.*

Greek Revival house built in 1850. 10 rooms, 2 story. Complimentary full breakfast. Check-in 3 pm, check-out 11 am. Airport transportation available. **$**

MEADOWS INN. *212 Pollock St, New Bern (28560). Phone 252/634-1776; toll-free 800/551-1776; fax 252/634-1776. www.meadowsinn-nc.com.* In a restored house (circa 1848); antiques, canopied beds. 8 rooms, 3 story. Complimentary full breakfast. Check-in 3 pm, check-out 11 am. Airport transportation available. **$**

Restaurant

★ ★ ★ **HENDERSON HOUSE.** *216 Pollock St, New Bern (28560). Phone 252/637-4784; fax 252/637-6754.* Dinner in this restored historic New Bern home will be a time to remember. The interior features a collection of artwork and dining in private rooms. The menu includes dishes created with duck, lamb, veal, and pheasant. There is an extensive wine list, featuring French vintages and including wines from around the world. American menu. Dinner. Closed Sun-Mon. **$$**

Ocracoke (B-10)

See also Buxton, Cape Hatteras National Seashore

Population 769
Elevation 6 ft
Area Code 252
Zip 27960
Web Site www.ocracoke-nc.com

Settled in the 17th century, Ocracoke was, according to legend, once used as headquarters by the pirate Blackbeard. On the Outer Banks (see), Ocracoke offers excellent fishing and hunting for wildfowl. The lighthouse, built in 1823, is still in use.

One of the visitor centers for Cape Hatteras National Seashore (see) is here.

What to See and Do

Cedar Island to Ocracoke Ferry Service. *Hwy 12, Ocracoke. Phone 252/928-3841; toll-free 800/293-3779.* Winter and summer, daily. Swan Quarter to Ocracoke; all year, daily. Ferries are crowded; there may be a wait. Reservations are recommended; they may be made up to one year in advance.

Ocracoke to Hatteras Ferry. *N across Hatteras Inlet.*

Limited-Service Hotel

★ **ANCHORAGE INN.** *Hwy 12, Ocracoke (27960). Phone 252/928-1101; fax 252/928-6322. www.theanchorageinn.com.* 37 rooms, 4 story. Closed Dec-Feb. Pets accepted; fee. Complimentary continental breakfast. Check-in 3 pm, check-out 11 am. Outdoor pool. **$**

Specialty Lodgings

The following lodging establishments are approved by Mobil Travel Guide, but due to their unique and individualized nature have not been given a traditional Mobil Star rating. Included in this listing you may find bed-and-breakfasts, limited-service inns, guest ranches, and other unique hotel properties.

BERKLEY MANOR BED & BREAKFAST. *Hwy 12, Ocracoke (27960). Phone 252/928-5911; toll-free 800/832-1223.* 12 rooms, 2 story. Complimentary full breakfast. Check-in 2 pm, check-out 11 am. **$**

OCRACOKE ISLAND INN. *100 Lighthouse Rd, Ocracoke (27960). Phone 252/928-4351; toll-free 877/456-3466; fax 252/928-4352. www.ocracokeislandinn .com.* Built in 1901; antiques. 29 rooms, 3 story. Check-in 3 pm, check-out noon. Restaurant. Outdoor pool. **$$**

Restaurants

★ ★ **BACK PORCH.** *110 Back Rd, Ocracoke (27960). Phone 252/928-6401; fax 252/928-1043.* American menu. Dinner. Closed mid-Nov-mid-Mar. Children's menu. Outdoor seating. **$$**

★ **ISLAND INN.** *Hwy 12, Ocracoke (27960). Phone 252/928-7821; fax 252/928-4352. www.ocracokeisland inn.com.* American menu. Breakfast, dinner. Closed Dec-Feb. Children's menu. **$$**

Outer Banks (B-10)

See also Fort Raleigh National Historic Site

Web Site www.outer-banks.com

The Outer Banks are a chain of narrow, sandy islands stretching 175 miles from Cape Lookout to Back Bay, Virginia. Parts of the chain are 30 miles from the mainland. Cape Hatteras is about 75 miles from the southern end. The islands may be reached by bridge from Point Harbor and Manteo or by ferry from Cedar Island and Swan Quarter to Ocracoke (see).

The following Outer Banks areas are included in the Mobil Travel Guide. For information on any of them, see the individual alphabetical listing: Buxton, Cape Hatteras National Seashore, Hatteras, Kill Devil Hills, Nags Head, Ocracoke.

Pilot Mountain

Population 1,281
Elevation 1,152 ft
Area Code 336
Zip 27041

What to See and Do

Pilot Mountain State Park. *4 miles S on Hwy 52. Phone 336/325-2355.* More than 3,700 acres; hard-surfaced road up mountain to parking. Foot trail to base of rocky knob; extensive view. Canoeing on the Yadkin River. Nature and riding trails. Picnicking. Camping.

Pinehurst (B-6)

See also Laurinburg, Southern Pines

Founded 1895
Population 9,706
Elevation 529 ft
Area Code 910
Zip 28374
Information Convention and Visitors Bureau, PO Box 2270, Southern Pines 28388; phone 910/692-3330 or toll-free 800/346-5362
Web Site www.homeofgolf.com

A famous year-round resort village, Pinehurst preserves an era steeped both in tradition and golfing excellence. Its New England style was designed over 100 years ago by the firm of Frederick Law Olmsted, which also designed New York's Central Park and landscaped Asheville's Biltmore Estate. Handsome estates and other residences, mostly styled in Georgian Colonial, dot the village. The Pinehurst Resort and Country Club has eight 18-hole golf courses, a 200-acre lake, 24 tennis courts, and other recreational facilities that are open to members as well as to guests staying there.

What to See and Do

Sandhills Horticultural Gardens. *Sandhills Community College, 2200 Airport Rd, Pinehurst. Phone 910/695-3882.* The 25 acres include Ebersole Holly Garden; Rose Garden; Conifer Garden; Hillside Garden with bridges, waterfalls, and gazebo; Desmond Native Wetland Trail Garden, a nature conservancy, and bird sanctuary; and Sir Walter Raleigh Garden, a 1-acre formal English garden. Docent-guided group tours (by appointment only). (Daily) **FREE**

Limited-Service Hotel

★ **COMFORT INN.** *9801 Hwy 15-501, Pinehurst (28374). Phone 910/215-5500; toll-free 800/831-0541; fax 910/215-5535. www.comfortinn.com.* 77 rooms, 2 story. Complimentary continental breakfast. Check-in 3 pm, check-out noon. Bar. Fitness room. Outdoor pool. **$**

Full-Service Resort

★ ★ ★ ★ **THE CAROLINA HOTEL.** *Carolina Vista Dr, Pinehurst (28374). Phone 910/295-6811; toll-free 800/487-4653; fax 910/235-8466. www.pinehurst.com.* Pinehurst, in the southern Sandhills of North Carolina, is the ultimate destination for those who believe that emerald-green fairways are the paths to heaven. This place is a veritable Mecca for golfers, with eight 18-hole courses designed by the sport's leading names, including Fazio, Jones, Maples, and Ross. The 31 miles of golf contain 781 bunkers and the largest number of golf holes in the world at a single resort. It's no wonder that the finest players converge upon Pinehurst annually for internationally recognized championships; those needing to sharpen their skills head for the highly acclaimed Golf Advantage School. In the center of it all, The Carolina Hotel reigns as Pinehurst's finest lodging. This historic Victorian hotel set amid exquisitely manicured lawns provides guests with handsomely furnished accommodations and first-class service. A wraparound porch with hanging ferns and rocking chairs invites guests to relax and watch the world go by. Two of the resort's nine restaurants are located here, while the convenient setting places guests within walking distance of the luxurious spa, the fitness center, and a shopping village. Nongolfers are treated to a wide variety of activities, from tennis and sailing to swimming in the shimmering pool. Horse-and-carriage rides offer tours of the village, as does a complimentary shuttle. 474 rooms, 4 story. Check-in 4 pm, check-out noon. Restaurant, bar. Children's activity center. Fitness room, fitness classes available, spa. Beach. Indoor pool, outdoor pool, whirlpool. Golf, 144 holes. Tennis. Airport transportation available. Business center. **$$$**

Full-Service Inn

★ ★ ★ **HOLLY INN.** *Carolina Vista Dr, Pinehurst (28374). Phone 910/235-8467; toll-free 800/487-4653; fax 910/235-8736. www.pinehurst.com.* 80 rooms, 4 story. Check-in 4 pm, check-out noon. Restaurant, bar. Children's activity center. Fitness room, spa. Outdoor pool. Golf. Tennis. **$$$**

Specialty Lodging

The following lodging establishment is approved by Mobil Travel Guide, but due to its unique and individualized nature has not been given a traditional Mobil Star rating. Included in this listing you may find bed-and-breakfasts, limited-service inns, guest ranches, and other unique hotel properties.

MAGNOLIA. *65 Magnolia Rd, Pinehurst (28374). Phone 910/295-6900; toll-free 800/526-5562; fax 910/215-0858. www.themagnoliainn.com.* 11 rooms, 3 story. Complimentary full breakfast. Check-in 3 pm, check-out noon. Restaurant, bar. Outdoor pool. **$**

Spa

★ ★ ★ ★ **THE SPA AT PINEHURST.** *1 Carolina Vista Dr, Pinehurst (28374). Phone 910/235-8320. www.pinehurst.com.* Pinehurst is defined by its regal country club ambience, and the Spa at Pinehurst's design and spirit echo that feeling. Rich, dark woods are used throughout the facility to create a clubhouse of relaxation. Masculine, yet universally appealing, the spa is elegant and traditional. In addition to relaxation lounges and treatment rooms, the spa also offers salon

services with a traditional barber shop for men, and an exercise facility with fitness evaluations, consultations, and classes.

One step inside the spa and your concerns over your poor short game will quickly disappear. This spa relaxes with more than 40 different treatments inspired by nature and the resort's southern location. The body wraps are a celebration of the region, with magnolia mud and mint julep varieties available here. Pine-inspired treatments are also plentiful, from the pine salt body scrub to the exfoliating pine cream of the Pinehurst deluxe body treatment. Eight massage therapies are included on the menu, including a special massage designed for golfers. From soothing magnolia luxury facials to chemical peels, the facials and skin care treatments target dryness, fine lines, and wrinkles with botanical extracts and modern medicine. Nothing beats the relaxing effects of hydrotherapy, and the spa's baths and soaks menu features soothing water therapies.

Pittsboro

Founded 1771
Population 2,236
Area Code 919
Zip 27312
Information Chatham County Chamber of Commerce, 12 East St, PO Box 87, Pittsboro, 27312; phone 919/542-8200, or toll-free 800/468-6242
Web Site www.visitchathamcounty.com

Full-Service Inn

★ ★ ★ ★ **THE FEARRINGTON HOUSE COUNTRY INN.** *2000 Fearrington Village Center, Pittsboro (27312). Phone 919/542-2121; fax 919/542-4202. www.fearrington.com.* The Fearrington House offers just the right mix of country sensibilities and worldly sophistication. Eight miles south of Chapel Hill and part of a charming village of shops, this country house hotel is nestled on family farmland that dates from the 1700s. Its former incarnation as a dairy barn is evident today in the striped Galloway cows that still call the grounds their home. The rooms and suites feature a country theme sprinkled with eclectic items like ecclesiastical doors serving as headboards and pine floors rescued from a workhouse along the Thames. Canopied beds and original art lend a hand in creating a stylish look. Mornings are celebrated with hearty breakfasts, while English afternoon tea curbs midday hunger pangs. Aspiring chefs flock to the hotel's popular cooking school for an insider's look at the kitchen. The restaurant's artistry continues to dazzle diners and garner praise from top critics. 32 rooms, 2 story. Complimentary full breakfast. Check-in 3 pm, check-out noon. High-speed Internet access. Two restaurants, bar. Fitness room. Outdoor pool. Tennis. **$$$**

⚁ ⚄ ⚃

Restaurant

★ ★ ★ ★ THE FEARRINGTON HOUSE
RESTAURANT. *2000 Fearrington Village Center, Pittsboro (27312).* Phone 919/542-2121; toll-free 800/277-0130; fax 919/542-4202. www.fearrington.com. This charming Victorian-style country inn and restaurant is located near Chapel Hill, nestled into rolling green farmland dating to the 1700s. Settling in for dinner here is like stepping into a fairy tale. The property is covered with beautiful flower gardens and lush landscapes, and the restaurant is accented with elegant antique furnishings and little touches that may leave you questioning the need for modernity. Fearrington House is a restaurant for special occasions, especially those that call for a soft, intimate, and romantic setting. Dinner lives up to the lovely and serene surroundings. The upscale menu is American, with techniques borrowed from France and robust flavors taken from the local region. The thoughtful, seasonal menu is complemented by a deep international wine list that features close to 500 selections from the United States, France, and Australia, with a focus on Californian varietals. American menu. Breakfast, dinner. Bar. Jacket required. Reservations recommended. Valet parking. Outdoor seating. **$$$**

Raleigh (B-7)

See also Chapel Hill, Durham, Smithfield

Founded 1792
Population 276,093
Elevation 363 ft
Area Code 919
Information Greater Raleigh Convention and Visitors Bureau, 1 Hannover Sq, 421 Fayetteville St Mall, Suite 1505, PO Box 1879, 27602-1879; phone 919/834-5900 or toll-free 800/849-8499
Web Site www.raleighcvb.org

The capital of North Carolina, Raleigh is also known as a center of education and high-technology research. It still retains the flavor of a relaxed residential town with two centuries of history. Fine residences coexist with apartment houses and modern shopping centers; rural areas with meadows and plowed fields can be found within a few miles.

Named for Sir Walter Raleigh, the town was laid out in 1792, following a resolution by the North Carolina General Assembly that an "unalterable seat of government" should be established within 10 miles of Isaac Hunter's tavern. The founders were able to find a site just 4 miles from the tavern. The site was laid off in a square. Lots within and just outside the city were sold as residences, which helped finance the capitol building and the governor's residence. Both structures were subsequently destroyed (the capitol by fire in 1831, the governor's residence by Union troops during the Civil War). Their replacements remain standing today. Fortunately, many of the lovely homes and gardens of the antebellum period have survived.

Like much of North Carolina, Raleigh was sprinkled with Union sympathizers until Fort Sumter was fired upon. Lincoln's call for volunteers was regarded as an insult, and North Carolina joined the Confederacy. Raleigh surrendered quietly to General Sherman in April 1865. During Reconstruction, carpetbaggers and scalawags controlled the Assembly, voted themselves exorbitant salaries, set up a bar in the capitol, and left permanent nicks in the capitol steps from the whiskey barrels rolled up for the thirsty legislators.

Located within 15 miles of Raleigh is the Research Triangle Park, a 6,800-acre research and development center with more than 50 companies. Complementing these facilities are the resources of three major universities that form the triangle region—North Carolina State University, Duke University in Durham, and the University of North Carolina at Chapel Hill.

What to See and Do

Capital Area Visitor Center. *301 N Blount St, Raleigh.* Phone 919/733-3456. Information center, brochures. Tours may be scheduled to the State Capitol, the North Carolina Executive Mansion, the State Legislative Building, historic sites, and other attractions. (Daily; closed Jan 1, Thanksgiving, Dec 25-26) **FREE**

Carolina Hurricanes (NHL). *Raleigh Entertainment and Sports Arena, 1400 Edwards Mill Rd, Raleigh (27612). Phone 919/861-2300.*

Falls Lake State Recreation Area. *13304 Creedmoor Rd, Wake Forest (27587). 12 miles N via Hwy 50. Phone 919/676-1027.* This man-made lake was built as a reservoir and for flood control. Approximately 38,000 acres of land and water offer a swimming beach, water-skiing, fishing, and boating (ramps), as well as opportunities for hiking and picnicking (shelters). There are three state recreation areas in the vicinity. **$$**

J. C. Raulston Arboretum at North Carolina State University. *4301 Beryl Rd, Raleigh. Phone 919/515-3132.* Eight acres of gardens featuring more than 5,000 diverse trees and shrubs from around the world. (Daily)

Mordecai Historic Park. *1 Mimosa St, Raleigh (27604). Mimosa St and Wake Forest Rd. Phone 919/834-4844.* Preserved plantation home (1785 and 1826) with many original furnishings, noted for its neoclassical architecture; early Raleigh office building, St. Mark's chapel, Badger-Iredell Law Office, 1830s herb garden. Also house in which Andrew Johnson, 17th president of the United States, was born. Guided tours. (Mon-Fri) **$$**

North Carolina Museum of Art. *2110 Blue Ridge Rd, Raleigh. Phone 919/839-6262.* European and American paintings and sculptures; Egyptian, Greek, Roman, African, and pre-Columbian objects; Judaica collection; changing exhibits. Amphitheatre. Restaurant. (Tues-Sun; closed holidays) **FREE**

North Carolina Museum of History. *5 E Edenton St, Raleigh. Phone 919/715-0200.* Several innovative exhibits convey the state's history. Gift shop. Auditorium. (Tues-Sun) **FREE**

Pullen Park. *520 Ashe Ave, Raleigh. Phone 919/831-6468.* Scenic 72-acre park in the heart of downtown featuring 1911 carousel, train ride, paddleboats, indoor aquatic center, ball fields, tennis courts, playground, and picnic shelters. (Daily) **FREE**

State Capitol. *1 E Edenton St, Raleigh (27601). Capitol Sq. Phone 919/733-4994.* (1840) A simple, stately Greek Revival-style building. Statues of honored sons and daughters decorate the grounds. The old legislative chambers, in use until 1963, have been restored to their 1840s appearance, as have the old state library room and the state geologist's office. Self-guided tours. (Daily; closed Jan 1, Thanksgiving, late Dec) **FREE**

State Legislative Building. *16 W Jones St, Raleigh (27601). Salisbury and Jones sts. Phone 919/733-7928.* First building constructed to house a state general assembly (1963); designed by Edward Durell Stone in a blend of modern and classical styles. Tours of chambers may include view of legislators at work. (Daily; closed Jan 1, Thanksgiving, Dec 25) **FREE**

William B. Umstead State Park. *8801 Glenwood Ave, Raleigh (27617). Crabtree Creek Section. 10 miles NW on Hwy 70. Phone 919/571-4170 (Reedy Creek).* On 5,480 acres with a 55-acre lake. Fishing, boating. Hiking, riding. Picnicking. Camping (Mar-mid-Dec, Thurs-Sun). Nature study. Reedy Creek Section, 10 miles NW off I-40. Approximately 1,800 acres. Fishing. Hiking, riding. Picnicking. Nature study.

Special Events

Artsplosure Spring Arts Festival. *336 Fayetteville St Mall, Raleigh (27601). Moore Sq and City Market. Phone 919/832-8699.* Citywide celebration of the arts. Showcase for regional dance, music, theater performances by nationally known artists; outdoor arts and crafts show; children's activities. Mid-May.

North Carolina State Fair. *State Fairgrounds, 1025 Blue Ridge Blvd, Raleigh (27607). 5 miles W on Hwy 1, then 1 mile W on Hwy 54. Phone 919/733-2145. www.ncstatefair.org.* Midway, concerts, tractor pull, demolition derby, petting zoo. Mid-Oct.

Limited-Service Hotels

★ ★ **CLARION HOTEL.** *320 Hillsborough St, Raleigh (27603). Phone 919/832-0501; toll-free 800/424-6423; fax 919/833-1631. www.choicehotels.com.* 202 rooms, 19 story. Complimentary continental breakfast. Check-in 3 pm, check-out noon. Restaurant, bar. Outdoor pool. Business center. **$**
🏊 🏃

★ ★ **COURTYARD BY MARRIOTT.** *1041 Wake Towne Dr, Raleigh (27609). Phone 919/821-3400; toll-free 800/321-2211; fax 919/821-1209. www.courtyard.com.* 153 rooms, 3 story. Check-in 3 pm, check-out noon. High-speed Internet access. Restaurant. Fitness room. Outdoor pool, whirlpool. **$**
🏃 🏊

★ **DAYS INN.** *3901 S Wilmington St, Raleigh (27603). Phone 919/772-8900; fax 919/772-1536. www.daysinn.com.* 103 rooms, 3 story. Complimentary continental breakfast. Check-in 2 pm, check-out 11 am. Outdoor pool. **$**

★ ★ **EMBASSY SUITES.** *4700 Creedmoor Rd, Raleigh (27612). Phone 919/881-0000; toll-free 800/362-2779; fax 919/782-7225. www.embassysuites.com.* With a nine-story atrium for guests to relax in, plus a pool, Jacuzzi, and exercise room, this hotel is perfect for vacationers. The property is located near the Crabtree Valley Mall, where visitors will find great shopping and plenty of entertainment. 225 rooms, 9 story, all suites. Complimentary full breakfast. Check-in 3 pm, check-out noon. Restaurant, bar. Fitness room. Indoor pool, whirlpool. Airport transportation available. **$$**

★ **FAIRFIELD INN.** *2641 Appliance Court, Raleigh (27604). Phone 919/856-9800; fax 919/856-9898.* 132 rooms, 3 story. Complimentary continental breakfast. Check-in 3 pm, check-out noon. Outdoor pool. **$**

★ **HAMPTON INN.** *6209 Glenwood Ave, Raleigh (27612). Phone 919/782-1112; fax 919/782-9119. www.hamptoninn.com.* 141 rooms, 6 story. Complimentary continental breakfast. Check-in 3 pm, check-out noon. High-speed Internet access, wireless Internet access. Fitness room. Outdoor pool. Airport transportation available. **$**

★ ★ **HOLIDAY INN.** *1707 Hillsborough St, Raleigh (27605). Phone 919/828-0811; toll-free 800/331-7919; fax 919/834-0904. www.holiday-inn.com.* 188 rooms, 9 story. Check-in 3 pm, check-out noon. Restaurant, bar. Fitness room. Outdoor pool. Airport transportation available. **$**

Full-Service Hotels

★ ★ ★ **MARRIOTT RALEIGH CRABTREE VALLEY.** *4500 Marriott Dr, Raleigh (27612). Phone 919/781-7000; fax 919/781-3059. www.marriott.com.* Visitors will stay in one of 375 comfortable guest rooms and can enjoy the indoor and outdoor pools, health club, restaurant, and more. Located nearby are tennis facilities and museums of art, history, and natural science. 375 rooms, 6 story. Check-in 3 pm, check-out noon. Restaurant, bar. Fitness room. Indoor pool, outdoor pool, whirlpool. Airport transportation available. Business center. **$$**

★ ★ ★ **SHERATON RALEIGH CAPITAL CENTER HOTEL.** *421 S Salisbury St, Raleigh (27601). Phone 919/834-9900; toll-free 800/325-3535; fax 919/833-1217. www.sheratoncapital.com.* 355 rooms, 17 story. Check-in 3 pm, check-out noon. Restaurant, bar. Fitness room. Indoor pool, whirlpool. Airport transportation available. Business center. **$**

Restaurants

★ ★ **42 STREET OYSTER BAR & SEAFOOD.** *508 W Jones St, Raleigh (27603). Phone 919/831-2811; fax 919/831-2917.* Seafood menu. Lunch, dinner. Closed Jan 1, Thanksgiving, Dec 24-25. Bar. Casual attire. **$$$**

★ **ABYSSINIA ETHIOPIAN RESTAURANT.** *2109-146 Avent Ferry Rd, Raleigh (27606). Phone 919/664-8151. www.abyssiniarestaurantnc.com.* Ethiopian menu. Lunch, dinner. Bar. Casual attire. **$$**

★ ★ ★ **ANGUS BARN.** *9401 Glenwood Ave, Raleigh (27612). Phone 919/787-3505; toll-free 800/277-2270; fax 919/783-5568. www.angusbarn.com.* The name sort of gives it away, but just to make sure that you're paying attention, the Angus Barn is indeed a carnivore's carnival with a kitchen that specializes in—you guessed it— Angus beef. Filet mignon, strip steaks, porterhouses—any which way you slice it, it's prime Angus, and it's big, bold, and brilliant. The Angus Barn is not your average, run-of-the-mill steakhouse. This is one of the few restaurants in the country to age its own beef (it hangs around getting tender for 28 days) before it is hand-cut and then grilled to juicy, meaty perfection. This popular, cozy, barn-as-restaurant has been seducing meat lovers with its thick steaks since 1960, but it also wins bonus points for enormous lobster, fresh seafood, and cult steakhouse classics like oysters Rockefeller and Chateaubriand. The wine list is extensive and includes many gems to pair with the menu's offerings. The service is warm and friendly, ensuring that the evening is satisfying in most every way. Steak menu. Dinner. Bar. Children's menu. Business casual attire. Reservations recommended. Valet parking. **$$$**

★ ★ **CARVERS CREEK.** *2711 Capital, Raleigh (27604). Phone 919/872-2300; fax 919/850-0261. www.carverscreek.com.* American menu. Lunch, dinner. Children's menu. Casual attire. **$$**

★ ★ **CASA CARBONE RISTORANTE.** *6019-A Glenwood Ave, Raleigh (27612). Phone 919/781-8750;*

fax 919/781-8751. Italian menu. Dinner. Closed Mon; holidays; also Super Bowl Sun. Bar. Children's menu. Casual attire. **$$**

★ ★ **CHARTER ROOM.** *1505 Hillsborough St, Raleigh (27605). Phone 919/828-0333; toll-free 800/334-4372; fax 919/828-2656.* Set in a fine dining atmosphere in the Velvet Cloak Inn, guests will find their favorite meats prepared in traditional ways: smoked pork chops, barbecued chicken, and grilled fish. Every dinner entrée comes with vegetable, salad, and freshly baked dinner rolls. American menu. Breakfast, dinner, Sun brunch. Bar. Casual attire. **$$**

★ ★ **IRREGARDLESS CAFE.** *901 W Morgan, Raleigh (27603). Phone 919/833-8898; fax 919/833-2211. www.irregardless.com.* Seafood, vegetarian menu. Lunch, dinner, late-night, Sun brunch. Closed Mon. Bar. Children's menu. Casual attire. **$**

★ **LAS MARGARITAS.** *231 Timber Dr, Garner (27529). Phone 919/662-1030.* Mexican menu. Lunch, dinner. Closed holidays. Bar. Children's menu. Casual attire. **$$**

★ ★ **SIMPSON'S.** *5625 Creedmoor Rd, Raleigh (27612). Phone 919/783-8818; fax 919/783-9070. www.simpsonsrestaurant.com.* Guests can enjoy a warm and friendly atmosphere as they dine by candlelight with soft background music from the pianist. Seafood, steak menu. Dinner. Closed holidays. Bar. Children's menu. Casual attire. Reservations recommended. **$$**

★ **TIPPY'S MEXICAN RESTAURANT.** *808 Hodges St, Raleigh (27608). Phone 919/828-0797.* Tex-Mex menu. Lunch, dinner. Closed Sun. Children's menu. Casual attire. **$**

★ ★ **VINNIE'S STEAKHOUSE.** *7440 Six Forks Rd, Raleigh (27615). Phone 919/847-7319; fax 919/844-5665.* Italian menu. Lunch, dinner. Closed Jan 1, July 4, Dec 24-25. Bar. Casual attire. **$$**

★ ★ **WINSTON'S GRILLE.** *6401 Falls of Neuse Rd, Raleigh (27615). Phone 919/790-0700; fax 919/878-8710. www.winstons-grille.com.* American menu. Lunch, dinner. Closed Thanksgiving, Dec 25. Bar. Children's menu. Outdoor seating. **$$**

Roanoke Rapids (A-8)

Population 16,957
Elevation 170 ft
Area Code 252

Zip 27870
Information Halifax County Tourism Development Authority, PO Box 144; phone 252/535-1687 or toll-free 800/522-4282
Web Site www.visithalifax.com

What to See and Do

Historic Halifax State Historic Site. *25 Saint David, Halifax. 9 miles SE off Hwy 301 or S on I-95, exit 168. Phone 252/583-7191.* The Halifax Resolves, first formal sanction of American independence, were adopted here on April 12, 1776. Buildings include Owens House (1760), Burgess Law Office, Eagle Tavern (1790), Sally-Billy House, clerk's office, jail, Montfort Archaeology Exhibit Center. Other features are Magazine Spring, garden, and churchyard. Visitor center; audiovisual programs, exhibits. (Apr-Oct: daily; rest of year: Tues-Sun; closed holidays) Historical dramas presented in summer (fee). **FREE**

Lake Gaston. *10 miles W via Hwy 158 and Hwy 1214.* This 34-mile-long, 20,300-acre lake offers opportunities for fishing, boating (ramps), and picnicking.

Roanoke Rapids Lake. *NW edge of town.* Covers 5,000 acres. Launching facilities.

Limited-Service Hotel

★ **BEST WESTERN ROANOKE RAPIDS.** *I-95 N and Hwy 46, Roanoke Rapids (27870). Phone 252/537-1011; fax 252/537-9258.* 100 rooms, 2 story. Complimentary continental breakfast. Check-in 3 pm, check-out 11 am. Restaurant. Outdoor pool. **$**
⊠

Robbinsville (B-2)

See also Bryson City

Population 747
Elevation 2,064 ft
Area Code 828
Zip 28771

A Ranger District Office of the Nantahala National Forest (see FRANKLIN) is located here.

What to See and Do

Joyce Kilmer-Slickrock Wilderness. *13 miles NW via Hwy 129, Hwy 1116 and 1127. Inquire at District Ranger Office (mid-Apr-Oct, weekends and holidays), N* off *Hwy 129; Phone 828/479-6431.* A 17,013-acre area within Nantahala National Forest (see FRANKLIN). More than 100 species of trees native to region; trails through forest to view prime specimens. Located within the area is the Joyce Kilmer Memorial Forest, a 3,840-acre stand of virgin timber dedicated to the author of the poem *Trees*; and a National Recreation Trail. **FREE**

Rocky Mount (A-8)

See also Wilson

Settled 1840
Population 55,893
Elevation 120 ft
Area Code 252
Information Chamber of Commerce, 100 Coast Line St, 27802; phone 252/446-0323
Web Site www.rockymountchamber.org

This is one of the country's largest bright-leaf tobacco marts. Cotton products in the form of yarn, bolts of fabric, and ready-to-wear clothing flow from the mills. The factories produce fertilizer, furniture, chemicals, metal products, lumber, and pharmaceuticals. Rocky Mount is also the home of Hardee's Food Systems.

What to See and Do

Children's Museum. *225 Church St, Rocky Mount. Phone 252/972-1167.* Hands-on exhibits provide children with experiences of the latest technological advances. (Daily; closed Thanksgiving, Dec 25) **$**

Special Event

Tobacco auctions. Numerous warehouses. Inquire locally. Aug-mid-Nov.

Limited-Service Hotels

★ **HAMPTON INN.** *530 N Winstead Ave, Rocky Mount (27804). Phone 252/937-6333; toll-free 800/426-7866; fax 252/937-4333. www.hamptoninn.com.* 124 rooms, 4 story. Complimentary continental breakfast. Check-in 3 pm, check-out noon. Outdoor pool. **$**
⊠

★ ★ **HOLIDAY INN.** *651 Winstead Ave, Rocky Mount (27804). Phone 252/937-6888; toll-free 888/543-2255; fax 252/937-4788. www.holiday-inn.com.*

169 rooms, 4 story. Check-in 3 pm, check-out noon. Restaurant, bar. Fitness room. Outdoor pool. **$**
🏋 ⊠

Salisbury (B-5)

See also Concord, Lexington, Statesville

Founded 1753
Population 26,462
Elevation 746 ft
Area Code 704
Zip 28144
Information Rowan County Convention and Visitors Bureau, PO Box 4044, 28145; phone 704/638-3100 or toll-free 800/332-2343. Visit the visitor information center at 132 E Innes for brochures, maps, and audio tape tours.
Web Site www.visitsalisburync.com.

A trading, cultural, and judicial center since 1753, it is here that Daniel Boone spent his youth and Andrew Jackson studied law. Salisbury's wide, shady streets were twice taken over by military troops. The first time was by Lord Cornwallis during the Revolutionary War, and the Civil War brought General Stoneman. During the Civil War, Salisbury was the site of a Confederate prison for Union soldiers where 5,000 died; they are buried here in the National Cemetery. Among the dead was Robert Livingstone, Union soldier and son of African missionary David Livingstone. Livingstone College was named for the father. Catawba College and Rowan-Cabarrus Community College complete Salisbury's triad of higher learning.

What to See and Do

Dan Nicholas Park. *6800 Bringle Ferry Rd, Salisbury (28146). 2 miles N on I-85, to exit 79, then 6 miles SE. Phone 704/636-0154.* This 330-acre park has lake with fishing, paddleboats (fee). Hiking, nature trail; tennis, miniature golf (fee). Picnicking. Camping hook-ups (fee). Outdoor theater, two nature museums, petting zoo, carousel, and miniature train ride. Park (all year). **FREE**

Dr. Josephus Hall House. *226 S Jackson, Salisbury. Phone 704/636-0103.* (1820) Large antebellum house set amid giant oaks and century-old boxwoods; contains most of its original Federal and Victorian furnishings. House was used as Union commander's headquarters following Civil War. (Sat-Sun afternoons) **$$**

N. C. Transportation Museum. *411 S Salisbury Ave, Spencer. 2 miles NE via I-85.* Phone 704/636-2889. Once the steam locomotive repair facility for Southern Railway, now a transportation museum, railroad yards, and shops. Back shop and 37-stall Bob Julian Roundhouse (1924). Rolling stock includes six engines (steam and diesel); restored luxury private cars; freight cars, trolley, passenger coaches. Train ride (seasonal; fee). Visitor center, two exhibit buildings, audiovisual show. (Apr-Oct: daily; rest of year: Tues-Sun; closed Dec 25) **FREE**

Old Stone House. *Granite Quarry. 4 miles SE, off Hwy 52.* Phone 704/633-5946. (1766) Built of hand-laid granite with walls 2 feet thick. Restored (1966); authentically furnished; family burial ground opposite. (Weekends) **$$**

Poets and Dreamers Garden. *701 W Monroe St, Salisbury (28144). On campus of Livingstone College.* Formal, Biblical, and Shakespearean gardens; fountain, sundial. Tomb of founder Joseph Charles Price in garden.

Utzman-Chambers House. *116 S Jackson St, Salisbury. In Federal Town House Museum (1819).* Phone 704/633-5946. Period rooms, authentic regional furniture; 19th-century garden. (Thurs-Sun, afternoons; closed holidays, Dec 24) **$$**

Waterworks Visual Arts Center. *1 Water St, Salisbury.* Phone 704/636-1882. Adaptive restoration of former Salisbury Waterworks into arts center. Changing exhibits; studios, classes; courtyard; sensory garden. Guided tours. (Daily; closed holidays) **FREE**

Limited-Service Hotels

★ **HAMPTON INN.** *1001 Klumack Rd, Salisbury (28144).* Phone 704/637-8000; toll-free 800/426-7866; fax 704/639-9995. www.hamptoninn.com. The amenities at this business- and leisure-friendly hotel are really what make a stay here worthwhile. With new upgrades like high-speed Internet in the rooms, as well as special bed tables for laptops, and in-room microwaves and refrigerators, every traveler will feel at home here. 121 rooms, 4 story. Pets accepted. Complimentary continental breakfast. Check-in 3 pm, check-out noon. High-speed Internet access. Outdoor pool. **$**

★ ★ **HOLIDAY INN.** *530 Jake Alexander Blvd, Salisbury (28147).* Phone 704/637-3100; toll-free 800/ 465-4329; fax 704/637-9152. www.holiday-inn.com. With nearby shopping, dining, golfing, and a nightclub, this hotel is ideally located for the leisure traveler. The property also features a game room, open atrium, and a large pavilion area, which is perfect for group events. 181 rooms, 3 story. Pets accepted; fee. Check-in 2 pm, check-out noon. Wireless Internet access. Restaurant, bar. Fitness room. Indoor pool, outdoor pool, whirlpool. **$**

Sanford (B-6)

Population 23,220
Elevation 375 ft
Area Code 919
Zip 27330
Web Site www.sanfordnc.net

What to See and Do

House in the Horseshoe State Historic Site. *324 Alston House Rd, Sanford (27330). 12 miles W on Hwy 42 to Carbonton, then 5 miles S on Hwy 1644.* Phone 910/947-2051. House (circa 1770) was the residence of North Carolina governor Benjamin Williams; site of a Revolutionary War skirmish. (Apr-Oct: daily; rest of year: Tues-Sun; closed holidays) **FREE**

Raven Rock State Park. *3009 Raven Rock Rd, Lillington. 18 miles S on Hwy 421.* Phone 910/893-4888. A 2,990-acre park characterized by 152-foot outcrop of rock jutting over Cape Fear River. Fishing. Nature trails, interpretive programs. Picnicking. Primitive camping.

Limited-Service Hotel

★ **COMFORT INN.** *1403 N Horner Blvd, Sanford (27330).* Phone 919/774-6411; toll-free 877/424-6423; fax 919/774-7018. www.comfortinnsanfordnc.com. This motel is a great value for bargain seekers. In addition to amenities such as hair dryers, irons and ironing boards, data ports, cable TV, and a fitness center, a complimentary 30-item hot breakfast is offered to guests. 122 rooms, 2 story. Complimentary full breakfast. Check-in 2 pm, check-out noon. Bar. Fitness room. Outdoor pool. **$**

Shelby (B-4)

See also Cherryville, Gastonia

Population 19,477
Elevation 853 ft
Area Code 704
Information Cleveland County Economic Development, 311 E Marion St, PO Box 1210, 28151; phone 704/484-4999 or toll-free 800/480-8687
Web Site www.clevelandcounty.com/tourism

Seat of Cleveland County, this town in the Piedmont boasts of diversified industry and agriculture. It is named for Colonel Isaac Shelby, hero of the Battle of Kings Mountain in the Revolutionary War. The town celebrates its heritage and culture with special events, fairs, and historic preservation.

What to See and Do

Central Shelby Historic District Walking Tour. *101 N Washington St, Shelby (28150). Phone 704/481-1842.* Two-hour self-guided tour encompasses much of original area established in 1841. Features 38 architecturally significant structures circa the 1850s.

Smithfield (B-7)

See also Dunn, Goldsboro, Raleigh

Population 11,510
Elevation 153 ft
Area Code 919
Zip 27577
Web Site www.smithfield-nc.com

Limited-Service Hotels

★ **COMFORT INN.** *1705 Industrial Park Dr, Selma (27576). Phone 919/965-5200; toll-free 800/228-5150; fax 919/965-5200. www.comfortinn.com.* 80 rooms, 2 story. Complimentary continental breakfast. Check-in 2 pm, check-out 11 am. Fitness room. Outdoor pool.
$

South Brunswick Islands (D-8)

See also Southport

Web Site www.sbichamber.com

What to See and Do

South Brunswick Islands. *www.weblync.com/ sbi_chamber.* The South Brunswick Islands offer wide, gently sloping beaches and beautiful scenery. Located just 50 miles from the Gulf Stream, the region has a subtropical climate and mild temperatures. Resort activities are plentiful and include fishing, swimming, tennis, and golf. Shallotte is the hub of the area that includes Holden, Ocean Isle, and Sunset beaches. The islands are reached by bridges across the Intracoastal Waterway.

Special Events

A Day at the Docks. *Holden Beach, South Brunswick Islands. Phone 910/754-6644.* Arts and crafts, bobble race. Late Mar.

King Classic King Mackerel Tournament. *3238 Pompano St, Holden Beach (28462). Phone 910/754-6644.* Early Sept.

North Carolina Oyster Festival. *550 Whiteville Rd, South Brunswick Islands (28470). In Shallotte. Phone 910/754-6644.* Arts and crafts, music, sports, oyster-shucking contest. Third weekend in Oct.

Limited-Service Hotel

★ **THE WINDS INN AND SUITES.** *310 E 1st St, Ocean Isle Beach (28469). Phone 910/579-6275; toll-free 800/334-3581; fax 910/579-2884. www.thewinds.com.* 86 rooms, 4 story. Complimentary full breakfast. Check-in 4 pm, check-out 11 am. Restaurant, bar. Fitness room. Indoor pool, outdoor pool, whirlpool. Beach. **$**

Southern Pines (B-6)

See also Laurinburg, Pinehurst

Population 10,918
Elevation 512 ft
Area Code 910
Zip 28387
Information Convention and Visitors Bureau, PO Box 2270, 28388; phone 910/692-3330 or toll-free 800/346-5362
Web Site www.homeofgolf.com

The Sandhills, among fine longleaf and loblolly pines, are famed for golf and horses. Known as "sand country," it first gained popularity as a resort in the 1880s, but the enthusiasm for golf in the 1920s fueled Southern Pines' growth as a recreational and resort area. The area is still steeped in tradition and history, with golf and equestrian activities as popular as ever.

What to See and Do

Shaw House. *SW Broad St and Morganton Rd, Southern Pines. Phone 910/692-2051.* Antebellum house of simple and sturdy style is lightened by unusual mantels of carved cypress. Guided tours (Tues-Sat; closed holidays). Also on the premises are Britt Sanders Cabin and Garner House. **FREE**

Weymouth Woods-Sandhills Nature Preserve. *1024 N Fort Bragg Rd, Southern Pines (28387). 3 miles SE on Indiana Ave, then N on Fort Bragg Rd. Phone 910/692-2167.* Excellent examples of Sandhills ecology. Hiking trails along pine-covered "sandridges." Natural history museum. (Daily; closed Dec 25) **FREE**

Special Event

House and Garden Tour. Conducted by Southern Pines Garden Club. Mid-Apr.

Limited-Service Hotels

★ **HAMPTON INN.** *1675 Hwy 1 S, Southern Pines (28387). Phone 800/333-9266; toll-free 800/426-7866; fax 910/692-9298. www.hamptoninn.com.* 126 rooms, 2 story. Pets accepted, some restrictions; fee. Complimentary continental breakfast. Check-in 2 pm, check-out noon. High-speed Internet access. Outdoor pool. **$**

★ ★ **HOLIDAY INN.** *Hwy 1 and Morganton Rd, Southern Pines (28387). Phone 910/692-8585; toll-free 800/262-5737; fax 910/692-5213. www.holiday-inn.com.* 162 rooms, 2 story. Pets accepted; fee. Check-in 3 pm, check-out noon. Restaurant, bar. Fitness room. Outdoor pool. **$**

★ ★ ★ **MID PINES INN AND GOLF CLUB.** *1010 Midland Rd, Southern Pines (28387). Phone 910/692-2114; toll-free 800/747-7272; fax 910/692-4615. www.pineneedles-midpines.com.* Every hole remains where Donald Ross put it in 1921, when he designed the challenging golf course at this stately inn. The large main building houses a restaurant, lounge, and more than 100 nicely appointed rooms. 112 rooms, 3 story. Check-in 2 pm, check-out 11 am. Restaurant, bar. Outdoor pool. Golf, 18 holes. Tennis. **$**

Full-Service Resort

★ ★ ★ **PINE NEEDLES LODGE.** *1005 Midland Rd, Southern Pines (28388). Phone 910/692-7111; toll-free 800/747-7272; fax 910/692-5349. www.pineneedles-midpines.com.* Legendary golfer Peggy Kirk has been welcoming guests and players to Pine Needles for more than three generations. The course is designed by Donald Ross and has been host to two recent US Women's Opens. The rustic lodge and elegant restaurant make for a relaxing golf holiday. 78 rooms, 4 story. Check-in 3 pm, check-out 11 am. Restaurant, bar. Fitness room. Outdoor pool. Golf, 18 holes. Tennis. **$**

Restaurants

★ ★ **LA TERRACE.** *270 SW Broad St, Southern Pines (28387). Phone 910/692-5622; fax 910/692-4603.* French menu. Lunch, dinner. Closed Sun; Jan 1, Dec 25. Outdoor seating. **$$**

★ **SQUIRE'S PUB.** *1720 Hwy 1 S, Southern Pines (28387). Phone 910/695-1161; fax 910/695-3667.* Five dining areas. British menu. Lunch, dinner. Closed Sun; Thanksgiving, Dec 24-25. Bar. Children's menu. **$**

★ **VITO'S RISTORANTE.** *615 SE Broad St, Southern Pines (28387). Phone 910/692-7815.* Italian menu. Dinner. Closed Sun; holidays. **$$**

Southport (D-8)

See also South Brunswick Islands, Wilmington

Founded 1792
Population 2,351
Elevation 22 ft
Area Code 910
Zip 28461
Information Southport-Oak Island Area Chamber of Commerce, 4841 Long Beach Rd SE; phone 910/457-6964 or toll-free 800/457-6964
Web Site www.southport-oakisland.com

Saltwater and freshwater fishing are very good in the vicinity of Cape Fear. Deep-sea charter boats are available at Southport, Long Beach, and Shallotte Point. There is a good yacht harbor facility for small boats and yachts, a municipal pier, three ocean piers, as well as several beaches and golf courses nearby.

Fort Johnston (1764) was the first fort built in North Carolina. With Fort Fisher and Fort Caswell (1825), it guarded the mouth of the Cape Fear River during the Civil War, making it possible for blockade runners to reach Wilmington. Fort Johnston (restored) is the residence of the Commanding Officer of the Sunny Point Military Ocean Terminal.

What to See and Do

Brunswick Town-Fort Anderson State Historic Site. *8884 St Philips Road SE, Southport (28479). 14 miles N on Hwy 133, then 5 miles S on Plantation Rd. Phone 910/371-6613.* Brunswick, founded in 1726, thrived as a major port exporting tar and lumber. Fearing a British attack, its citizens fled when the Revolution began; in 1776 the town was burned by British sailors. Twenty-three foundations have been excavated. Built across part of the town are the Civil War earthworks of Fort Anderson, which held out for 30 days after the fall of Fort Fisher in 1865. Visitor center, exhibits, audiovisual show; marked historical trailside exhibits; nature trail, picnic area. (Apr-Oct: daily; rest of year: Tues-Sun; closed holidays) **FREE**

Carolina Power and Light Company Visitors Center. *8520 River Road, SE, Southport. 2 miles N on Hwy 87. Phone 910/457-6041.* Audiovisual presentations show history of energy and its use; nuclear reactor model. Picnic area. (Tues-Thurs) **FREE**

Ferry Service. *Southport to Fort Fisher, Hwy 211 and Ferry Rd, Southport. Phone 910/457-6942 (local service); toll-free 800/293-3779 (NC Department of Transportation).* Approximately 30-minute crossing.

Fort Fisher State Historic Site. *1610 Fort Fisher Blvd S, Kure Beach. 6 miles E via Hwy 421, ferry. Phone 910/458-5538.* The largest earthworks fort in the Confederacy; until the last few months of the Civil War, it kept Wilmington open to blockade runners. Some of the heaviest naval bombardment of land fortifications took place here on December 24-25, 1864, and on January 13-15, 1865. Tours. Visitor center has exhibits, audiovisual shows. Reconstructed gun emplacement. Picnic area. (Apr-Oct: daily; rest of year: Tues-Sun; closed holidays) **FREE**

Long Beach Scenic Walkway. *20th St SE and 19th Pl, Long Beach. Across Davis Canal. Phone 910/278-5518.* Crosses several important wetland communities; viewing of maritime forests, wetland birds, marsh animals, and seacoast fowl.

Maritime Museum. *116 N Howe St, Southport. Phone 910/457-0003.* Houses memorabilia pertaining to the history of the lower Cape Fear area. (Tues-Sat; closed holidays) **$**

Special Events

Robert Ruark Chili Cook-Off. *Franklin Square Park, Southport (28461). Corner of Howe and West sts. Phone 910/457-7927.* Easter weekend.

US Open King Mackerel Tournament. *606 W West St, Southport (28461).* First weekend in Oct.

Specialty Lodging

The following lodging establishment is approved by Mobil Travel Guide, but due to its unique and individualized nature has not been given a traditional Mobil Star rating. Included in this listing you may find bed-and-breakfasts, limited-service inns, guest ranches, and other unique hotel properties.

LOIS JANE'S RIVERVIEW INN. *106 W Bay St, Southport (28461). Phone 910/457-6701; fax 910/457-6701.* Built in 1892; antiques. 5 rooms. Complimentary full breakfast. Check-in 3 pm, check-out 10:30 am. **$**
🖪

Statesville (B-4)

See also Cornelius, Hickory, Salisbury

Founded 1789
Population 23,320
Elevation 923 ft
Area Code 704
Zip 28677
Information Greater Statesville Chamber of Commerce, 115 E Front St, PO Box 1064, 28687; phone 704/873-2892
Web Site www.statesvillechamber.org

Statesville is a community of many small, diversified industries, including furniture, apparel, metalworking, and textiles. Iredell County, of which Statesville is the seat, is known for its dairy and beef cattle.

What to See and Do

Fort Dobbs State Historic Site. *438 Fort Dobbs Rd, Statesville (28625). N via I-40, Hwy 21, State Rd 1930, then 1 1/2 miles W.* Phone 704/873-5866. Named for Royal Governor Arthur Dobbs, the now-vanished fort was built during the French and Indian War to protect settlers. Exhibits, nature trails, excavations. (Mon-Fri; closed holidays) **FREE**

Lake Norman State Park. *159 Inland Sea Dr, Troutman (28166). 10 miles S via I-77, Hwy 21.* Phone 704/528-6350. On Lake Norman (see CORNELIUS); 1,548 acres. Swimming, fishing, boating (ramp, canoes, paddle boats, rentals). Nature trails. Picnicking. Tent and trailer sites.

Special Events

Carolina Dogwood Festival. *Center St, Statesville (28687).* Apr.

Iredell County Fair. *I-40 and I-177, Statesville (28677).* Phone 704/872-4032. One week, beginning Labor Day.

National Balloon Rally. *115 E Front St, Statesville (28677).* Third weekend in Sept.

Tar Heel Classic Horse Show. Early May.

Limited-Service Hotels

★ **HAMPTON INN.** *715 Sullivan Rd, Statesville (28677).* Phone 704/878-2721; fax 704/873-6694. Families will love the outdoor pool and complimentary continental breakfast each morning at this comfortable, contemporary hotel, located right off Highway 40. 122 rooms, 2 story. Pets accepted. Complimentary continental breakfast. Check-in 3 pm, check-out 11 am. Outdoor pool. **$**
🐾 ⛱

★ ★ **HOLIDAY INN.** *1215 Gardner Bagnal Blvd, Statesville (28677).* Phone 704/878-9691; toll-free 800/465-4329; fax 704/873-6927. www.holiday-inn.com. Close to the beautiful Blue Mountain range and a few hours drive from the beach, this conveniently located hotel is just off Highway 77 and gives guests access to shopping and dining in the area. 134 rooms, 2 story. Check-in 3 pm, check-out noon. Restaurant, bar. Fitness room. Outdoor pool. **$**
🏃 ⛱

Specialty Lodging

The following lodging establishment is approved by Mobil Travel Guide, but due to its unique and individualized nature has not been given a traditional Mobil Star rating. Included in this listing you may find bed-and-breakfasts, limited-service inns, guest ranches, and other unique hotel properties.

HIDDEN CRYSTAL. *471 Sulphur Springs Rd, Hiddenite (28636).* Phone 828/632-0063; toll-free 800/439-1639; fax 828/632-3562. Hiddenite is known for its gem minerals, and guests at this inn will be pleased to find some samples on the premises. The inn is surrounded by gardens and is near museums and restaurants. 14 rooms, 2 story. Closed Dec 25. Complimentary full breakfast. Check-in 2 pm, check-out 11 am. Outdoor pool. **$**
⛱

Tryon (B-3)

See also Hendersonville

Population 1,760
Elevation 1,085 ft
Area Code 828
Zip 28782
Information Polk County Travel and Tourism, Visitor Information, 425 N Trade St; phone 828/859-8300 or toll-free 800/440-7848
Web Site www.nc-mountains.org

On the southern slope of the Blue Ridge Mountains in the "thermal belt," almost at the South Carolina border, Tryon was named for Royal Governor William Tryon, who held office during the Revolution. The Fine Arts Center is the focal point for much of the cultural life of the community.

What to See and Do

Foothills Equestrian Nature Center (FENCE). *500 Hunting Country Rd, Tryon. Phone 828/859-9021.* Nature preserve (300 acres) has 5 miles of riding and hiking trails; wildlife programs; bird and nature walks. Host to many equestrian events. (Daily) **FREE**

White Oak Mountain. Scenic drive around the mountain. Turn off onto Houston Rd at Columbus and take dirt road, which winds around mountain.

Special Events

Blue Ridge Barbecue. *2753 Lynn Rd, Tryon (28782). Phone 828/859-6236.* Music festival, arts and crafts. June.

Steeplechase Races. *1 Depot St, Tryon (28782). Phone toll-free 800/438-3681.* Apr.

Full-Service Inn

★ ★ ★ **PINE CREST INN.** *85 Pine Crest Ln, Tryon (28782). Phone 828/859-9135; toll-free 800/633-3001; fax 828/859-9135. www.pinecrestinn.com.* Located in the foothills of the Blue Ridge Mountains, near the Foothills Equestrian Nature Center, this lovely inn is meant to evoke an English country manor. The English innkeepers have restored the hardwood floors, stone fireplaces, and other historic fixtures of the buildings that comprise the inn. 39 rooms, 2 story. Complimentary full breakfast. Check-in 3 pm, check-out 11 am. Restaurant. **$$$**

Restaurant

★ ★ ★ **PINE CREST INN.** *85 Pine Crest Ln, Tryon (28782). Phone 828/859-9135. www.pinecrestinn.com.* Beamed ceilings, a stone fireplace, and heavy pine tables greet visitors at this restaurant with a colonial-style décor. American menu. Breakfast, dinner. Closed Sun. Bar. Outdoor seating. **$$**

Warsaw (C-7)

Population 3,051
Elevation 160 ft
Area Code 910
Zip 28398
Web Site www.townofwarsawnc.com

What to See and Do

Duplin Wine Cellars. *501 N Sycamore St, Rose Hill. 2 miles S via Hwy 117; off I-40 exit 380. Phone 910/289-3888.* Largest winery in state. Videotape, tour, wine tasting, retail outlet. (Mon-Sat; closed holidays) **FREE**

Washington (B-8)

See also Williamston; also see Greenville, SC

Founded 1776
Population 9,583
Elevation 14 ft
Area Code 252
Zip 27889
Information Chamber of Commerce, PO Box 665; phone 252/946-9168
Web Site ci.washington.nc.us

First American village named for the first president, Washington was rebuilt on the ashes left by evacuating Union troops in April 1864. The rebels lost the town in March 1862, and, because it was an important saltwater port, tried to retake it for two years. Evidence of the shelling and burning can be seen in the stone foundations on Water Street. Water sports, including sailing, yachting, fishing, and swimming, are popular.

What to See and Do

Bath State Historic Site. *207 Carteret St, Bath. 17 miles E on Hwy 264 and Hwy 92. Phone 252/923-3971.* Oldest incorporated town in state (1705). Buildings include Bonner House (circa 1820), Van Der Veer House (circa 1790) and Palmer-Marsh House (circa 1745). (Apr-Oct: daily; rest of year: Tues-Sun; closed holidays). Visitor center, film. Picnic area. **$**

Special Event

Washington Summer Festival. Beach music, street dance, ski show, arts and crafts, children's rides. Last full weekend in July.

Limited-Service Hotel

★ **COMFORT INN.** *1636 Carolina Ave, Washington (27889). Phone 252/946-4444; toll-free 800/424-6423;*

fax 252/946-2563. www.comfortinn.com. 56 rooms, 2 story. Complimentary continental breakfast. Check-in 2 pm, check-out noon. High-speed Internet access, wireless Internet access. Fitness room. Outdoor pool. **$**
🏃 🏊

Specialty Lodging

The following lodging establishment is approved by Mobil Travel Guide, but due to its unique and individualized nature has not been given a traditional Mobil Star rating. Included in this listing you may find bed-and-breakfasts, limited-service inns, guest ranches, and other unique hotel properties.

PAMLICO HOUSE BED & BREAKFAST. *400 E Main St, Washington (27889). Phone 252/946-7184; toll-free 800/948-8507; fax 252/946-9944. www.pamlicohouse.com.* 4 rooms, 2 story. Children over 6 years only. Complimentary full breakfast. Check-in 3 pm, check-out 11 am. **$**
📵

Waynesville (B-2)

See also Asheville, Bryson City, Cherokee, Maggie Valley

Population 9,232
Elevation 2,644 ft
Area Code 828
Zip 28786
Information Visitor and Lodging Information, 1233 N Main St, Suite 1-40; phone toll-free 800/334-9036
Web Site www.waynesville.com

Popular with tourists, this area offers mountain trails for riding and hiking, superb scenery, and golf and fishing in cool mountain streams. Waynesville is 26 miles from the Cherokee Indian Reservation (see CHEROKEE) and Great Smoky Mountains National Park (see). Maggie Valley (see), about 6 miles northwest, is in a particularly attractive area.

Full-Service Inns

★ ★ ★ **BALSAM MOUNTAIN INN.** *68 Seven Springs Dr, Balsam (28707). Phone 828/456-9498; toll-free 800/224-9498; fax 828/456-9298. www.balsaminn.com.* 50 rooms, 3 story. Pets accepted; fee. Complimentary full breakfast. Check-in 3 pm, check-out 11 am. Restaurant. **$**
🐾

⚲ ★ ★ ★ **THE SWAG COUNTRY INN.** *2300 Swag Rd, Waynesville (28785). Phone 828/926-0430; toll-free 800/789-7672; fax 828/926-2036. www.theswag.com.* The Swag Country Inn entices guests to get back to nature while in the lap of luxury. Situated atop a 5,000-foot mountain and nestled on 250 acres, with a private entrance to Great Smoky Mountain National Park, which is just a few steps away, this country inn enjoys majestic natural surroundings. Discreet and intimate, the inn wraps its guests in a cocoon of rustic elegance. The rooms and suites are distinguished by handcrafted interiors; handmade quilts, woven rugs, and original artwork speak to the mountaineer in all guests. Closed during the winter months, travelers reap the three-season rewards of this advantageous spot. Nature trails beckon adventuresome types, while others head for the redwood sauna and whirlpool. Gourmet comfort food is enjoyed throughout the day, from the picnic baskets and brown-bag lunches thoughtfully provided for day-trippers and hikers to delicious dinners, where the convivial spirit encourages many to forge new friendships. 15 rooms, 2 story. Closed mid-Nov.-Apr. Children over 7 only in main building. Complimentary full breakfast. Check-in 3 pm, check-out 11 am. Restaurant (public by reservation). Twenty-eight-person whirlpool. **$$$$**

Specialty Lodgings

The following lodging establishments are approved by Mobil Travel Guide, but due to their unique and individualized nature have not been given a traditional Mobil Star rating. Included in this listing you may find bed-and-breakfasts, limited-service inns, guest ranches, and other unique hotel properties.

WINDSONG: A MOUNTAIN INN. *459 Rockcliffe Ln, Clyde (28721). Phone 828/627-6111. www.windsongbb.com.* This hidden treasure in the Smoky Mountains cove offers a fantastic view and resortlike accommodations. Gourmet breakfasts, cozy rooms, and leisurely recreation are just a few of the amenities designed to pamper guests. 5 rooms, 3 story. Children over 12 years only. Complimentary full breakfast. Check-in 3-6 pm, check-out 11 am. Tennis. **$**
📵 🛏 🎿

YELLOW HOUSE ON PLOT CREEK ROAD. *89 Oakview Dr, Waynesville (28786). Phone 828/452-0991; toll-free 800/563-1236; fax 828/452-1140. www.theyellowhouse.com.* A place best described by its overwhelming beauty and serenity. With a collage of

gourmet breakfasts and springtime colors reminiscent of a French countryside, only closer. A fabulous yellow house tucked into the hills at a 3,000-foot elevation, the property has bedrooms that each complement the remarkable landscape. 6 rooms, 3 story. Children over 12 years only. Complimentary full breakfast. Check-in 2 pm, check-out 11 am. **$**
🅳

Wilkesboro (A-4)

See also Jefferson

Settled 1779
Population 3,159
Elevation 1,042 ft
Area Code 336
Zip 28697
Web Site www.north-wilkesboro.com

What to See and Do

Stone Mountain State Park. *3042 Frank Pkwy, Roaring Gap (28668). Phone 336/957-8185.* A 13,500-acre natural landmark with waterfalls and wooded areas. The mountain, in the center of the park, is a 600-foot dome-shaped granite mass measuring 6 miles in circumference. Three of the South's Civil War heroes—Robert E. Lee, Stonewall Jackson, and Jefferson Davis—are carved into its north face in the world's largest bas-relief sculpture. The park is popular for mountain climbing. There are 17 miles of designated trout streams. Extensive nature, hiking trails. Picnicking. Developed and primitive camping (dump station). Interpretive program in summer.

Williamston (B-8)

See also Greenville, Washington

Population 5,843
Elevation 80 ft
Area Code 252
Zip 27892
Web Site www.townofwilliamston.com

What to See and Do

Hope Plantation. *132 Hope House Rd, Williamston (27983). Hwy 13 to Windsor, then 4 miles W on Hwy 308. Phone 252/794-3140.* Two-hour guided tour of Georgian plantation house (circa 1800) built by

Governor David Stone. Period furnishings; outbuildings; gardens. (Mon-Sat, also Sun afternoons) **$$$** Included in admission is

King-Bazemore House. (1763) Tour of this unique Colonial-style house with gambrel roof, dormer windows, and solid brick ends. Period furnishings; outbuildings; gardens.

Limited-Service Hotels

★ **ECONO LODGE.** *100 East Blvd, Williamston (27892). Phone 252/792-8400; fax 252/809-4800.* 59 rooms, 2 story. Complimentary continental breakfast. Check-out noon. Fitness room. **$**
🏃

★ ★ **HOLIDAY INN.** *101 East Blvd, Williamston (27892). Phone 252/792-3184; toll-free 800/792-3101; fax 252/792-9003. www.holiday-inn.com.* 100 rooms, 2 story. Pets accepted. Check-out noon. Restaurant, bar. Outdoor pool. **$**
🐾 🌊

Wilmington (D-7)

See also Southport, Wrightsville Beach

Settled 1732
Population 75,838
Elevation 25 ft
Area Code 910
Information Cape Fear Coast Convention and Visitors Bureau, 24 N 3rd St, 28401; phone 910/341-4030 or toll-free 800/222-4757
Web Site www.cape-fear.nc.us

Chief port of North Carolina, Wilmington is the region's major trade and retail center. Manufacturing, tourism, and port-oriented business lead the area's growth.

Patriots who defied the Crown in the Revolution were led by William Hooper, a signer of the Declaration of Independence. In 1765, eight years before the Boston Tea Party, the citizens of Wilmington kept the British from unloading their stamps for the Stamp Act. In 1781, Cornwallis held the town as his main base of operation for almost a year. After the battle of Guilford Courthouse, the Lord General came back to Wilmington before heading for Yorktown and defeat.

During the Civil War, blockade runners brought fortunes in goods past Federal ships lying off Cape Fear, making Wilmington the Confederacy's chief port until January 1865, when it fell. Wilmington was North Carolina's biggest town until 1910, when railroad-fed industries of the inland Piedmont area outgrew the limited facilities of the harbor. The channel, harbor, and expanded port facilities bring goods from throughout the world to the area.

What to See and Do

Battleship *North Carolina*. *Battleship Rd, Wilmington (28401). Jct of Hwy 74/76, 17 and 421. Phone 910/251-5797.* World War II vessel moored on west bank of Cape Fear River. Tour of museum, gun turrets, galley, bridge, sick bay, engine room, wheelhouse. (Daily)

Bellamy Mansion Museum of History and Design Arts. *503 Market St, Wilmington. Phone 910/251-3700.* Restored 1859 landmark home has exhibits featuring history, restoration, Southern architecture, and regional design arts. Tours. (Tues-Sun) **$$$**

Burgwin-Wright House. *224 Market St, Wilmington. At 3rd St. Phone 910/762-0570.* (1770) Restored colonial town house built on foundation of abandoned town jail. British General Cornwallis had his headquarters here during April 1781. Eighteenth-century furnishings and garden. Tours. (Tues-Sat; closed holidays; also Jan and week of Dec 25) **$$$**

Cape Fear Museum. *814 Market St, Wilmington. Phone 910/341-7413.* Interprets social and natural history of Lower Cape Fear. Changing exhibits. (Tues-Sun; closed holidays) **$**

Captain J. N. Maffitt River Cruises. *Located at the foot of Market St. Phone 910/343-1611; toll-free 800/676-0162.* Five-mile narrated sightseeing cruise covering Wilmington's harbor life and points of interest. Also "river taxi" service (additional fee) from Battleship *North Carolina*. (May-Sept, daily)

Carolina Beach State Park. *1010 Masion Borro State Park Rd, Wilmington. 15 miles S off Hwy 421. Phone 910/458-8206.* This 700-acre park is a naturalist's delight; the rare Venus's flytrap, as well as five other species of insect-eating plants, grow here. Fishing, boating (ramps, marina). Picnicking, concession. Nature, hiking trails. Camping (dump station). Naturalist program.

Cotton Exchange. *321 N Front St, Wilmington. Phone 910/343-9896.* Specialty shops and restaurants in historic buildings on Cape Fear River. (Daily; closed holidays, some stores closed Sun)

Greenfield Gardens. *302 Willard St, Wilmington (28401). 2 1/2 miles S on Hwy 421. Phone 910/341-7855.* A 150-acre municipal park with 180-acre lake, 5-mile scenic drive; canoe and paddleboat rentals (Apr-Oct); bike path; fragrance garden; amphitheater; picnicking; nature trail. (Daily) **FREE**

Henrietta III Riverboat Cruises. *Downtown, Wilmington. At riverfront. Phone 910/343-1611; toll-free 800/676-0162.* Narrated sightseeing cruise (1 1/2 hours) down Cape Fear River to North Carolina State Port. (June-Aug, one cruise Tues-Sun; Apr-May, Sept-Oct, two cruises Tues-Sun) Dinner cruises (Apr-Dec, Fri-Sat).

Louise Wells Cameron Art Museum. *3201 S 17th St, Wilmington. Phone 910/395-5999.* Collection of Mary Cassatt prints; paintings and works on paper, Jugtown Pottery, sculpture. Changing exhibits; lectures; educational programs. (Tues-Sun; closed holidays)

Moores Creek National Battlefield. *40 Patriot Paul Dr, Currie. 17 miles N on Hwy 421, then 3 miles W on Hwy 210. Phone 910/283-5591.* In 1776, the loosely knit colonists took sides against each other—patriots versus loyalists. Colonels Moore, Lillington, and Caswell, with the blessing of the Continental Congress, broke up the loyalist forces, captured the leaders, and seized gold and quantities of weapons. The action defeated British hopes of an early invasion through the South and encouraged North Carolina to be the first colony to instruct its delegates to vote for independence in Philadelphia. The 86-acre park has a visitor center near its entrance to explain the battle. Picnic area. (Daily; closed Jan 1, Dec 25) **FREE**

North Carolina Aquarium/Fort Fisher. *2201 Fort Fisher Blvd S, Kure Beach. 21 miles S on Hwy 421. Phone 910/458-8257.* Fifteen aquariums of North Carolina native sea life; marine exhibits, films, workshops, programs; nature trails. (Daily; closed Jan 1, Thanksgiving, Dec 25) **$$$**

Orton Plantation Gardens. *9149 Orton Rd SE, Wilmington (28479). 18 miles S on Hwy 133. Phone 910/371-6851.* Formerly a rice plantation, now beautiful gardens (20 acres) with ancient oaks, magnolias, ornamental plants and lawn and water scenes; rice fields now a waterfowl refuge. Antebellum Orton House (not open), begun in 1730, can be seen from garden paths. Overlooks Cape Fear River. (Mar-Nov, daily) **$$$**

Poplar Grove Plantation. *10200 Hwy 17, Wilmington (28411). 8 miles NE on Hwy 17. Phone 910/686-9989.* (Circa 1850) Restored Greek Revival plantation; manor house, smokehouse, tenant house, blacksmith, loom weaver, basket weaver. Guided tours (daily; closed Easter, Thanksgiving, Dec 25; also the first Mon in Feb). **$$$**

Wilmington Railroad Museum. *501 Nutt St, Wilmington. Phone 910/763-2634.* Exhibits on railroading past and present, centering on the Atlantic Coast Line and other Southeastern rail lines. HO scale regional history exhibit on first and second floor; outside are ACL steam locomotive and caboose for on-board viewing. (Mid-Mar-Oct: daily; Nov-Feb: Mon-Sat; closed holidays) **$$**

Special Events

North Carolina Azalea Festival. *Phone 910/794-4650.* Garden and home tours, horse show, celebrity entertainers, pageants, parade, street fair. Early Apr.

Riverfest. *Phone 910/452-6862.* Arts and crafts, music, dancing, and entertainment; boat rides, raft regatta; street fair. First full weekend in Oct.

Limited-Service Hotels

★ ★ **COURTYARD BY MARRIOTT.** *151 Van Campen Blvd, Wilmington (28403). Phone 910/395-8224; toll-free 800/321-2211; fax 910/452-5569. www.marriott.com/ilmcy.* 128 rooms, 2 story. Check-in 3 pm, check-out noon. Fitness room. Outdoor pool, whirlpool. **$**

★ **HAMPTON INN.** *1989 Eastwood Rd, Wilmington (28403). Phone 910/256-9600; toll-free 877/256-9600; fax 910/256-1996. www.landfallparkhotel.com.* 120 rooms, 4 story. Complimentary continental breakfast. Check-in 3 pm, check-out 11 am. Bar. Outdoor pool. **$**

★ ★ **HOLIDAY INN.** *5032 Market St, Wilmington (28405). Phone 910/392-1101; toll-free 800/833-4721; fax 910/397-0698. www.holiday-inn.com.* Perfect for either a business trip or a family stay, this Holiday Inn is near the campus of the University of North Carolina-Wilmington, the Cape Fear Coast Convention Center, and the historic downtown area. 124 rooms, 5 story. Complimentary continental breakfast. Check-in 3 pm, check-out noon. Restaurant. Fitness room. Indoor pool, whirlpool. **$**

Full-Service Hotels

★ ★ ★ **HILTON WILMINGTON RIVERSIDE.** *301 N Water St, Wilmington (28401). Phone 910/763-5900; fax 910/763-0038. www.wilmingtonhilton.com.* This hotel is a short walk from shops, restaurants, cultural attractions, and the city's riverwalk. Guest rooms are comfortable and attractively decorated and offer magnificent views of Cape Fear River. 274 rooms, 9 story. Pets accepted, some restrictions; fee. Check-in 4 pm, check-out 11 am. Restaurant, bar. Fitness room. Outdoor pool. Airport transportation available. **$**

★ ★ ★ **THE WILMINGTONIAN.** *101 S 2nd St, Wilmington (28401). Phone 910/343-1800; toll-free 800/525-0909; fax 910/251-1149. www.thewilmingtonian.com.* Located in downtown Wilmington, just two blocks from Cape Fear River and a 40-minute drive to the beaches on the Atlantic Coast, this renovated inn caters to both leisure and business travelers. 40 rooms, 3 story. Pets accepted; fee. Complimentary full breakfast. Check-in 3 pm, check-out 11 am. Restaurant, bar. **$**

Specialty Lodgings

The following lodging establishments are approved by Mobil Travel Guide, but due to their unique and individualized nature have not been given a traditional Mobil Star rating. Included in this listing you may find bed-and-breakfasts, limited-service inns, guest ranches, and other unique hotel properties.

C. W. WORTH HOUSE. *412 S 3rd St, Wilmington (28401). Phone 910/762-8562; toll-free 800/340-8559; fax 910/763-2173. www.worthhouse.com.* 7 rooms, 3 story. Children over 8 years only. Complimentary full breakfast. Check-in 4-7 pm, check-out 11 am. **$**

CATHERINE'S INN. *410 S Front St, Wilmington (28401). Phone 910/251-0863; toll-free 800/476-0723; fax 910/763-5116. www.catherinesinn.com.* Built in 1883; antiques. 5 rooms, 2 story. Children over 10 years only. Complimentary full breakfast. Check-in 3-5 pm, check-out 10:30-11 am. **$**

DARLINGS BY THE SEA - OCEANFRONT WHIRLPOOL SUITES. *329 Atlantic Ave, Kure Beach (28449). Phone 910/458-8887; toll-free 800/383-8111; fax 910/458-6468. www.darlingsbythesea.com.* Best described as a quaint honeymooners cottage. Each whirlpool suite has a wonderful terrace overlooking the ocean. 5 rooms, 3 story, all suites. No children allowed. Complimentary continental breakfast. Check-in 2 pm, check-out 11 am. Fitness room. Beach. **$$**
⊠

FRONT STREET INN. *215 S Front St, Wilmington (28401). Phone 910/762-6442; toll-free 800/336-8184; fax 910/762-8991. www.frontstreetinn.com.* Brick building (1923) that once housed Salvation Army. 12 rooms, 2 story. Complimentary continental breakfast. Check-in 4 pm, check-out 11 am. Fitness room. **$$**
⊠ ⊠

THE GRAYSTONE INN. *100 S 3rd St, Wilmington (28401). Phone 910/763-2000; toll-free 888/763-4773; fax 910/763-5555. www.graystoneinn.com.* Experience true turn-of-the-century style in this historic, landmark bed-and-breakfast. The spacious, antique-filled public rooms include a music room with a grand piano, a mahogany-paneled library, and a chandelier-lit dining room. Rooms are decorated in period frunishings, some with claw-foot tubs. 7 rooms, 3 story. Children over 10 years only. Complimentary full breakfast. Check-in 4-7 pm, check-out 11 am. Fitness room. **$$**
⊠ ⊠

ROSEHILL INN. *114 S 3rd St, Wilmington (28401). Phone 910/815-0250; toll-free 800/815-0250; fax 910/815-0350. www.rosehill.com.* This elegant Victorian home was built in 1848 in the heart of the historic district in Wilmington. Enjoy the city's finest dining, shopping, and entertainment located only 3 blocks away. Each of the large, luxurious guest rooms has its own individual charm and is perfect for a romantic retreat. 7 rooms, 2 story. Children over 12 years only. Complimentary full breakfast. Check-in 4-6 pm, check-out noon. Business center. **$**
⊠ ⊠

THE VERANDAS. *202 Nun St, Wilmington (28401). Phone 910/251-2212; fax 910/251-1396. www.verandas.com.* This 8,500-square-foot, Victorian-Italianate mansion sits 2 blocks from Cape Fear River. The 1853 structure was almost entirely rebuilt and refurbished in 1996. Climb the spiral staircase to the enclosed cupola for a spectacular sunset view. 8 rooms, 3 story. Closed Jan. Children over 12 years only. Complimentary full breakfast. Check-in 4-8 pm, check-out 11 am. **$$**
⊠

Restaurants

★ **CAFE PHOENIX.** *9 S Front St, Wilmington (28401). Phone 910/343-1395; fax 910/251-8596. www.cafephoenix.com.* American menu. Lunch, dinner. Closed holidays. Bar. Children's menu. Outdoor seating. **$$**

★ **COTTAGE.** *1 N Lake Park Blvd, Carolina Beach (28428). Phone 910/458-4383. www.cottage.com.* Seafood menu. Lunch, dinner. Closed Sun; holidays; also Dec 26. Bar. Children's menu. Outdoor seating. **$$**

★ **DRAGON GARDEN.** *341-52 S College Rd, Wilmington (28403). Phone 910/452-0708; fax 910/452-4725.* Chinese menu. Lunch, dinner. Closed Thanksgiving, Dec 24-25. Bar. Reservations recommended. **$**

★ **EDDIE ROMANELLI'S.** *5400 Oleander Dr, Wilmington (28403). Phone 910/799-7000; fax 910/350-7862. www.atlanticquest.net.* Italian, American menu. Lunch, dinner. Closed Thanksgiving, Dec 25. Bar. Children's menu. **$$**

★ ★ **ELIJAH'S.** *2 Ann St, Wilmington (28401). Phone 910/343-1448; fax 910/251-7628. www.elijahs.com.* American menu. Lunch, dinner, Sun brunch. Closed Jan 1, Thanksgiving, Dec 25. Bar. Children's menu. Casual attire. Outdoor seating. **$$**

★ **FREDDIE'S.** *111 K Ave, Kure Beach (28449). Phone 910/458-5979; fax 910/458-7988.* Italian, American menu. Dinner. Closed Mon; Jan 1, Thanksgiving, Dec 25. Bar. Children's menu. **$**
⊠

★ ★ ★ **HARVEST MOON.** *5704 Oleander Dr, Wilmington (28403). Phone 910/792-0172; fax 910/792-1547.* American menu. Dinner. Closed Sun. Bar. Casual attire. **$$$**

★ ★ **HIERONYMUS SEAFOOD.** *5035 Market St, Wilmington (28405). Phone 910/392-6313; fax 910/392-6318. www.hieronymusseafood.com.* Seafood menu. Dinner. Closed Jan 1, Thanksgiving, Dec 24-25. Bar. Children's menu. Casual attire. Reservations recommended. Outdoor seating. **$$**

★ ★ **ITALIAN BISTRO.** *319 N Front St, Wilmington (28401). Phone 910/762-1222.* Italian menu. Lunch, dinner. Children's menu. Casual attire. Outdoor seating. **$**

★ ★ **MARKET STREET CASUAL DINING.** *6309 Market St, Wilmington (28405). Phone 910/395-2488.* American menu. Dinner. Closed Mon; Thanksgiving, Dec 25; also Super Bowl Sun. Bar. Children's menu. **$$**

★ ★ **PILOT HOUSE.** *2 Ann St, Wilmington (28401). Phone 910/343-0200; fax 910/343-0441. www.pilothouserest.com.* American menu. Lunch, dinner, Sun brunch. Closed Jan 1, Dec 24-25. Bar. Children's menu. Outdoor seating. **$$**

★ ★ ★ **PORT CITY CHOP HOUSE.** *1981 Eastwood Rd, Wilmington (28405). Phone 910/256-4955; fax 910/256-4926. www.portcitychophouse .com.* Seafood menu. Lunch, dinner. Closed Sun; Thanksgiving, Dec 25. Bar. Children's menu. Outdoor seating. **$$$**

★ ★ **ROY'S RIVERBOAT LANDING.** *2 Market St, Wilmington (28401). Phone 910/763-7227; fax 910/343-1038.* Southern regional menu. Lunch, dinner, Sun brunch. Bar. Children's menu. Casual attire. Outdoor seating. **$$**

★ **WATER STREET.** *5 S Water St, Wilmington (28401). Phone 910/343-0042; fax 910/762-6128.* Riverfront dining in old warehouse. American, Mediterranean menu. Lunch, dinner. Closed Thanksgiving, Dec 25. Bar. Children's menu. Reservations recommended. Outdoor seating. **$$**

Wilson (B-7)

See also Rocky Mount

Population 44,405
Elevation 145 ft
Area Code 252
Web Site www.wilson-nc.com

Located just off Interstate 95, midway between New York and Florida, Wilson is a convenient rest stop for road-weary travelers. It is one of the Southeast's leading antique markets and is said to have one of the nation's largest tobacco markets.

Limited-Service Hotels

★ **BEST WESTERN LA SAMMANA.** *817-A Ward Blvd, Wilson (27893). Phone 252/237-8700; toll-free 800/937-8376; fax 252/237-8092. www.bestwestern.com.* 83 rooms, 2 story. Pets accepted; fee. Complimentary continental breakfast. Check-in 2 pm, check-out 11 am. Outdoor pool. **$**
🐾 🌊

★ **COMFORT INN.** *4941 Hwy 264 W, Wilson (27893). Phone 252/291-6400; toll-free 800/424-6423; fax 252/291-7744. www.choicehotels.com.* 76 rooms, 2 story. Complimentary continental breakfast. Check-in 2 pm, check-out 11 am. Outdoor pool. **$**
🌊

★ **HAMPTON INN.** *1801 S Tarboro St, Wilson (27895). Phone 252/291-2323; fax 252/291-7696. www.hamptoninn.com.* 100 rooms, 2 story. Complimentary continental breakfast. Check-out 11 am. Outdoor pool. Business center. **$**
🌊 🏃

Winston-Salem (A-5)

See also Greensboro, High Point, Lexington

Founded Salem: 1766; Winston: 1849; combined as Winston-Salem: 1913
Population 185,776
Elevation 912 ft
Area Code 336
Information Convention and Visitors Bureau, 601 W 4th St, 27101; phone 336/728-4200 or toll-free 800/331-7018
Web Site www.wscvb.com

First in industry in the Carolinas and one of the South's chief cities, Winston-Salem is a combination of two communities. Salem, with the traditions of its Moravian founders, and Winston, an industrial center, matured together. Tobacco markets, large banks, and arts and crafts galleries contribute to this thriving community.

What to See and Do

Bowman Gray Stadium. *1250 S Martin Luther King Jr. Dr, Winston-Salem (27107). Phone 336/727-2900. www.bowmangrayracing.com.* Bowman Gray Stadium is a multi-use public arena that hosts Winston-Salem State Rams college football games, and features a 1/4-mile asphalt oval. Part of the city's Lawrence Joel

Veterans Memorial Coliseum Complex, Bowman Gray has been hosting races for more than 50 years, making it the longest operating NASCAR short track in the country. The stadium is about an hour away from Lowe's Motor Speedway and seats 17,000. **$$**

Hanging Rock State Park. *State Rd 1001, Danbury. 32 miles N, between Hwy 66 and 89 near Danbury.* Phone 336/593-8480. Approximately 6,200 acres in Sauratown Mountains. Lake swimming, bathhouse, fishing, boating (rentals). Nature trails. Picnicking, concession. Tent and trailer sites, six family cabins (Mar-Nov, by reservations only). Observation tower.

Historic Bethabara Park. *2147 Bethabara Rd, Winston-Salem.* Phone 336/924-8191. Site of first Moravian settlement in North Carolina (1753); restored buildings include Gemeinhaus (1788), Potter's House (1782), and Buttner House (1803); reconstructed palisade fort (1756-1763); stabilized archaeological foundations of original settlement and God's Acre (graveyard); reconstructed community gardens (1759). Visitor center, exhibits, slide show. Nature trails, 175-acre wildlife preserve with walking trails. Picnicking. (Apr-Nov, daily; walking tour all year) **$**

Historic Old Salem. *600 S Main St, Winston-Salem (27101). S of the business district on Old Salem Rd.* Phone 336/721-7300; toll-free 888/348-5420. (1766) Restoration of a planned community that Moravians, with their old-world skills, made the 18th-century trade and cultural center of North Carolina's Piedmont. Many of the sturdy structures built for practical living have been restored and furnished with original or period pieces. Early crafts are demonstrated throughout the town. Here also is an original Tannenberg organ in working condition. A number of houses are privately occupied. Nine houses plus outbuildings are open to the public. Tours (self-guided) start at the visitor center on Old Salem Rd. Special events are held during the year. (Daily; no tours Easter, Thanksgiving, Dec 24-25) **$$$$** In the old village are

> **Museum of Early Southern Decorative Arts.** *924 S Main St, Winston-Salem.* Phone 336/721-7300. Twenty-one period rooms and six galleries (1690-1820), with decorative arts of Maryland, Virginia, Georgia, Kentucky, Tennessee, and the Carolinas. (Daily; closed Thanksgiving, Dec 24-25) **$$$**

> **Salem Academy and College.** *601 S Church St, Winston-Salem (27101).* Phone 336/721-2600. (1772) (1,100 women) When founded by the

Moravians, it was the only school of its kind for women in the South. The Fine Arts Center offers art exhibits, lectures, films, concerts, and plays (mid-Sept-mid-May, daily; evenings during special events; some fees). Campus tours on request.

Reynolda House, Museum of American Art. *2250 Reynolda Rd, Winston-Salem. Approximately 2 miles N on University Pkwy, then 1/2 miles E on Coliseum Dr then N on Reynolda Rd.* Phone 336/725-5325. On estate of the late R. J. Reynolds of the tobacco dynasty. American paintings, original furniture, art objects, costume collection. Adjacent is Reynolda Gardens, 125 acres of open fields and naturalized woodlands; formal gardens, greenhouse. (Tues-Sat, also Sun afternoons; closed Jan 1, Thanksgiving, Dec 25) **$$$**

R. J. Reynolds Tobacco Company, Whitaker Park Cigarette Plant. *1100 Reynolds Blvd, Winston-Salem.* Phone 336/741-5718. (Mon-Fri; closed holidays) **FREE**

SciWorks. *400 W Hanes Mill Rd, Winston-Salem. At Hwy 52 N.* Phone 336/767-6730. www.sciworks.org. Hands-on exhibits of physical and natural sciences; planetarium; 31-acre outdoor environmental park and nature trails. (Mon-Sat; closed holidays) **$$$**

Southeastern Center for Contemporary Art. *750 Marguerite Dr, Winston-Salem.* Phone 336/725-1904. Exhibits by contemporary artists from across the country with accompanying educational programs. (Tues-Sun; closed holidays) **$$**

Tanglewood Park. *4061 Clemmons Rd, Clemmons (27012). 12 miles SW off I-40 (exit 182).* Phone 336/778-6300. Fishing, boating (paddleboats, canoes); horseback riding; golf, tennis; nature trail. Picnicking, playgrounds. Steeplechase (seasonal). (Daily) **$**

Wake Forest University. *1834 Wake Forest Rd, Winston-Salem.* Phone 336/758-5000. (1834) (5,600 students) On campus are Fine Arts Center, Museum of Anthropology; also Reynolda Village, a complex of shops, offices, and restaurants. Bowman Gray School of Medicine is on Medical Center Blvd.

Limited-Service Hotels

★ ★ **ADAM'S MARK PLAZA.** *425 N Cherry St, Winston-Salem (27101).* Phone 336/725-3500; fax 336/728-4020. www.adamsmark.com. 605 rooms, 17 story. Check-out 1 pm. Restaurant, bar. Fitness room. Indoor pool. **$**

★ **HAMPTON INN.** *5719 University Pkwy, Winston-Salem (27105). Phone 336/767-9009; toll-free 800/426-7866; fax 336/661-0448. www.hamptoninn.com.* 115 rooms, 2 story. Complimentary continental breakfast. Check-in 3 pm, check-out noon. Fitness room. Outdoor pool. **$**

★ ★ **HOLIDAY INN.** *5790 University Pkwy, Winston-Salem (27105). Phone 336/767-9595; toll-free 800/553-9595; fax 336/744-1888. www.holiday-inn.com.* 150 rooms, 6 story. Pets accepted; fee. Check-in 3 pm, check-out noon. Restaurant, bar. Fitness room. Outdoor pool. Business center. **$**

Specialty Lodgings

The following lodging establishments are approved by Mobil Travel Guide, but due to their unique and individualized nature have not been given a traditional Mobil Star rating. Included in this listing you may find bed-and-breakfasts, limited-service inns, guest ranches, and other unique hotel properties.

AUGUSTUS T ZEVELY. *803 S Main St, Winston-Salem (27101). Phone 336/748-9299; toll-free 800/928-9299; fax 336/721-2211. www.winston-salem-nc.com.* Built in 1844; restored to its mid-19th century appearance. Moravian ambience. 12 rooms, 3 story. Pets accepted, some restrictions; fee. Children over 12 years only. Complimentary continental breakfast. Check-in 3-9 pm, check-out 11:30 am. **$**

BROOKSTOWN INN. *200 Brookstown Ave, Winston-Salem (27101). Phone 336/725-1120; toll-free 800/845-4262; fax 336/773-0147. www.brookstowninn.com.* This historic inn was built in 1837 as a textile mill. The conversion preserved the original handmade brick and exposed beam construction. The romantic rooms include European-style breakfast. 71 rooms, 4 story. Complimentary continental breakfast. Check-in 3 pm, check-out noon. Fitness room. **$$**

COLONEL LUDLOW INN. *434 Summit and W 5th St, Winston-Salem (27101). Phone 336/777-1887; toll-free 800/301-1887; fax 336/777-0518. www.bbinn.com.* Victorian homes built in 1887 and 1895; restored and converted. 10 rooms, 2 story. Complimentary full breakfast. Check-in 3 pm, check-out 11:30 am. Restaurant. Fitness room. **$**

TANGLEWOOD PARK. *4061 Clemmons, Clemmons (27012). Phone 336/778-6300; fax 336/778-6379. www.tanglewoodpark.org.* Facilities of Tanglewood Park available. 28 rooms, 2 story. Complimentary continental breakfast. Check-in 2 pm, check-out noon. Golf. Tennis. **$**

Restaurants

★ ★ **RYAN'S RESTAURANT.** *719 Coliseum Dr, Winston-Salem (27106). Phone 336/724-6132; fax 336/724-5761. www.ryansrestaurant.com.* Wooded setting. American menu. Dinner. Closed Sun; Jan 1, Thanksgiving, Dec 24-25. Bar. Casual attire. **$$$**

★ ★ **VINEYARD.** *120 Reynolda Village, Winston-Salem (27106). Phone 336/748-0269; fax 336/723-5980.* American menu. Dinner. Closed Sun; holidays. Bar. **$$**

★ **ZEVELY HOUSE.** *901 W 4th St, Winston-Salem (27101). Phone 336/725-6666.* American menu. Dinner, Sun brunch. Closed Mon; holidays. Bar. Children's menu. Outdoor seating. **$$**

Wrightsville Beach (D-8)

See also Wilmington

Population 2,593
Elevation 7 ft
Area Code 910
Zip 28480
Web Site www.wrightsville.com

A very pleasant family-oriented resort town, Wrightsville Beach offers swimming, surfing, fishing, and boating. The public park has facilities for tennis, basketball, soccer, softball, volleyball, shuffleboard, and other sports.

Limited-Service Hotel

★ ★ **HOLIDAY INN SUNSPREE RESORT.** *1706 N Lumina Ave, Wrightsville Beach (28480). Phone 910/256-2231; toll-free 877/330-5050; fax 910/256-9208. www.holiday-inn.com.* 184 rooms. Check-in 3 pm, check-out noon. Three restaurants, bar. Indoor pool, outdoor pool. **$**

Restaurants

★ ★ **BRIDGE TENDER.** *1414 Airle Rd, Wrightsville Beach (28480). Phone 910/256-4519.* American menu. Lunch, dinner. Closed Sun; Jan 1, Thanksgiving, Dec 25. Bar. **$$**

★ **DOCKSIDE.** *1308 Airlie Rd, Wrightsville Beach (28403). Phone 910/256-2752; fax 910/256-3526.* American menu. Lunch, dinner. Closed Thanksgiving, Dec 24-25. Bar. Casual attire. Outdoor seating. **$$**

★ **KING NEPTUNE.** *11 N Lumina Ave, Wrightsville Beach (28480). Phone 910/256-2525. www.kingneptune restaurant.com.* Caribbean menu. Dinner. Closed Thanksgiving, Dec 25. Bar. Children's menu. **$$**

★ ★ **OCEAN TERRACE.** *275 Waynick Blvd, Wrightsville Beach (28480). Phone 910/256-2251; fax 910/256-5502. www.blockade-runner.com.* Seafood, American menu. Breakfast, lunch, dinner, Sun brunch. Closed week of Dec 25. Bar. Children's menu. Outdoor seating. **$$$**

★ ★ **OCEANIC.** *703 S Lumina Ave, Wrightsville Beach (28480). Phone 910/256-5551; fax 910/256-4527.* Seafood menu. Lunch, dinner, Sun brunch. Closed Jan 1, Thanksgiving, Dec 25. Bar. Children's menu. Outdoor seating. **$$**

★ ★ **RIALTO.** *530 Causeway Dr, Wrightsville Beach (28480). Phone 910/256-1099; fax 910/256-5975.* Italian menu. Dinner. Closed Jan 1, Thanksgiving, Dec 25. Bar. Children's menu. **$$**

You have many options for side trips from North Carolina. You can explore the beauty of Virginia—Hampton, Newport News, Norfolk, Richmond, and Virginia Beach, are all within a day's drive from Raleigh and offer much to see and do.

Hampton, VA

4 hours, 196 miles from Raleigh, NC

Settled 1610
Population 146,437
Elevation 12 ft
Area Code 757
Information Hampton Visitor Center, 710 Settlers Landing Rd, 23669; phone 757/727-1102 or toll-free 800/800-2202
Web Site www.hampton.va.us

Hampton is the oldest continuously English-speaking community in the United States (Jamestown, settled in 1607, is a national historical park, but not a town). The settlement began at a place then called Kecoughtan, with the building of Fort Algernourne as protection against the Spanish. In the late 1600s and early 1700s the area was harassed by pirates. Finally in 1718, the notorious brigand Blackbeard was killed by Lieutenant Robert Maynard and organized piracy came to an end here.

Hampton was shelled in the Revolutionary War, sacked by the British in the War of 1812, and burned in 1861 by retreating Confederates to prevent its occupation by Union forces. Only the gutted walls of St. John's Church survived the fire. The town was rebuilt after the Civil War by its citizens and soldiers. Computer technology, manufacturing, aerospace research, and commercial fishing are now big business here.

Langley Air Force Base, headquarters for the Air Combat Command, Fort Monroe, headquarters for the US Army's Training and Doctrine Command, and the NASA Langley Research Center are located here.

What to See and Do

Air Power Park and Aviation History Center. *413 W Mercury Blvd, Hampton (23666). Hwy 258. Phone 757/727-1163.* Over 50 indoor and outdoor exhibits feature real fighter aircraft, missiles, and rockets; local aviation history and model aircraft exhibits. Picnicking, playground. (Daily; closed Jan 1, Thanksgiving, Dec 25) **FREE**

Bluebird Gap Farm. *60 Pine Chapel Rd, Hampton (23666). Phone 757/727-6739.* This 60-acre farm includes barnyard zoo; indigenous wildlife such as deer and wolves; antique and modern farm equipment and farmhouse artifacts. Picnicking, playground. (Wed-Sun; closed holidays) **FREE**

Buckroe Beach. *22 Lincoln St, Hampton (23669). 4 miles E on Hwy 351, foot of E Pembroke Ave on Chesapeake Bay. Phone 757/727-6347.* Swimming; public park, concerts. Lifeguards (Memorial Day-Labor Day). **FREE**

Fort Monroe. *3 miles SE via Mercury Blvd, Ingalls Rd.* First fort here was a stockade called Fort Algernourne (1609); the second, Fort George, though built of brick, was destroyed by a hurricane in 1749; present fort was completed about 1834. **FREE** Here are

Casemate Museum. *20 Bernard Rd, Hampton (23651). Phone 757/788-3391.* Provides insight on heritage of the fort, Old Point Comfort, and the Army Coast Artillery Corps. Museum offers access to a series of casemates and a walking tour of the fort. Jefferson Davis casemate contains cell in which the Confederacy's president was confined on false charges of plotting against the life of Abraham Lincoln. Museum features Civil War exhibits, military uniforms, and assorted artwork, including three original Remington drawings, along with audiovisual programs. Scale models of coast artillery guns and dioramas represent the role of the coast artillery from 1901 to 1946. (Daily; closed Jan 1, Thanksgiving, Dec 25) **FREE**

Chapel of the Centurion. (1858) One of the oldest churches on the Virginia peninsula. Woodrow Wilson worshiped here occasionally.

Hampton Carousel. *602 Settlers Landing Rd, Hampton (23669). Downtown, on waterfront. Phone 757/727-6381.* (1920) Completely restored in 1991, antique carousel is housed in its own pavilion and features 48 hand-carved horses. (Apr-Sept: Mon-Sat, also Sun afternoons; Oct-Nov: daily, weather permitting; Dec 1-15: weekends only) **$**

Hampton University. *Cemetery Rd and Frissell Ave, Hampton (23669). E end of Queen St, 1/4 mile off I-64 exit 267. Phone 757/727-5253. www.hampton.edu.* (1868) (6,100 students) Founded by Union Brigadier General Samuel Chapman Armstrong, chief of the Freedman's Bureau, to prepare the youth of the South, regardless of color, for the work of organizing and instructing schools in the Southern states; many blacks and Native Americans came to be educated. Now Virginia's only coeducational, nondenominational, four-year private college. The Hampton choir is famous. It "sang up" a building, Virginia-Cleveland Hall, in 1870 on a trip through New England and Canada, raising close to $100,000 at concerts. On campus are

Emancipation Oak. The Emancipation Proclamation was read here.

Museum. *Huntington Building, Cemetery Rd and Frissell Ave, Hampton.* Collection of ethnic art; Native American and African artifacts; contemporary African-American works; paintings by renowned artists. (Daily; closed school holidays) **FREE**

Miss Hampton II Harbor Cruises. *764 Settlers Landing Rd, Hampton (23669). Phone 757/722-9102.* Narrated three-hour cruise includes a stop at Fort Wool, a Civil War island fortress. (Apr-Oct) **$$$$**

Settlers Landing Monument. *1/2 mile S, on grounds of the Veterans Affairs Medical Center between Hampton River and Mill Creek, off I-64 exit 268.* Marks approximate site of first settlers' landing near Strawberry Banks in 1607. Painting by Sidney King depicts visit to Kecoughtan by colonists en route to Jamestown. (Daily) **FREE**

St. John's Church and Parish Museum. *W Queens Way and Franklin St, Hampton. Phone 757/722-2567.* (1728) Fourth site of worship of Episcopal parish established in 1610. Bible dating from 1599; communion silver from 1618; Colonial Vestry Book; taped historical message. (Daily)

Virginia Air and Space Center and Hampton Roads History Center. *600 Settlers Landing Rd, Hampton (23669). Downtown, off I-64 exit 267. Phone 757/727-0900; toll-free 800/296-0800. www.vasc.org.* Exhibits show the historical link between Hampton Roads' sea-faring past and spacefaring future. Exhibits include 19 full-sized air- and spacecraft, the *Apollo 12* Command Module, a moon rock, and rare NASA artifacts. Films shown in 283-seat IMAX theater (daily). Gift shop. (daily; closed Thanksgiving, Dec 25) **$$$**

Special Events

Hampton Bay Days. *Phone 757/727-6122.* Arts and crafts, rides, science exhibits; entertainment. Mid-Sept.

Hampton Cup Regatta. *Phone toll-free 800/800-2202.* Inboard hydroplane races. Mid-Aug.

Hampton Jazz Festival. *Hampton Coliseum, 1000 Coliseum Dr, Hampton. Phone 757/838-4203 (box office).* Three days late June.

Limited-Service Hotels

★ **HAMPTON INN.** *1813 W Mercury Blvd, Hampton (23666). Phone 757/838-8484; toll-free 800/426-7866; fax 757/826-0725. www.hampton-inn.com/hi/hampton-newport.* 131 rooms, 6 story. Complimentary continental breakfast. Check-in 3 pm, check-out noon. High-speed Internet access. Fitness room. Airport transportation available. **$**
⊠

★ ★ **RADISSON HOTEL HAMPTON.** *700 Settlers Landing, Hampton (23669). Phone 757/727-9700; toll-free 800/333-3333; fax 757/722-4557. www.radisson.com/hamptonva.* Located on the waterfront in downtown Hampton, this hotel is conveniently located between Williamsburg and Virginia Beach and is close to business and leisure districts and military bases. 172 rooms, 9 story. Check-in 3 pm, check-out noon. 2 restaurants, bar. Fitness room. Outdoor pool, whirlpool. Airport transportation available. Business center. **$**
⊠ ⊠ ⊠

Restaurant

★ **SAMMY AND NICK'S.** *2718 W Mercury Blvd, Hampton (23666). Phone 757/838-9100; fax 757/838-9612.* Steak menu. Lunch, dinner. Closed Thanksgiving, Dec 25. Bar. Children's menu. Casual attire. **$$**

Newport News, VA

3 hours 40 minutes, 190 miles from Raleigh, NC

Settled 1619
Population 180,150
Elevation 25 ft
Area Code 757
Information Visitor Center, 13560 Jefferson Ave, 23603; phone 757/886-7777 or toll-free 888/493-7386
Web Site www.newport-news.org

One of the three cities that make up the Port of Hampton Roads, Newport News has the world's largest shipbuilding company, Newport News Shipbuilding. Fourteen miles long and 40 feet deep, Hampton Roads is one of the world's finest natural harbors, formed by the James, York, Elizabeth, and Nansemond rivers as they pass into Chesapeake Bay. The largest ships are accommodated at Newport News docks; huge tonnages of coal, ore, tobacco, and grain are shipped from the port annually. During the two World Wars it was a vitally important point of embarkation and supply. The area still has many important defense establishments.

Newport News is located on the historic Virginia Peninsula between Williamsburg and Virginia Beach. The peninsula contains Hampton, Yorktown, Jamestown, and Williamsburg. Some of the earliest landings in this country were here. The name of the town is said to derive from the good "news" of the arrival of Captain Christopher Newport, who brought supplies and additional colonists to the settlement at Jamestown.

What to See and Do

Fort Eustis. *213 Calhoun St, Newport News (23604). NW end of city on Mulberry Island, I-64 exit 250A. Phone 757/878-4920.* Headquarters of US Army Transportation Center. Self-guided auto tour available; brochures at Public Affairs Office (Building 213). **FREE** On grounds is

US Army Transportation Museum. *1387 Jackson Ave, Newport News (23604). Phone 757/878-1115.* Depicts development of Army transportation from 1776 to the present; "flying saucer," amphibious vehicles, trucks, helicopters. Gift shop. (Tues-Sun; closed holidays) **FREE**

Historic Hilton Village. *Warwick Blvd and Main St. I-64 exit 263 A.* Listed on the National Register of Historic Places, this village was built between 1918 and 1920 to provide wartime housing for workers at Newport News Shipbuilding. Architecturally significant neighborhood features 500 English cottage-style homes and antique and specialty shops. **FREE**

Mariners' Museum. *100 Museum Dr, Newport News (23606). Warwick and J. Clyde Morris blvds. From Williamsburg, take I-64 E to exit 258A. Travel 2 1/2 miles S on J. Clyde Morris Blvd; the museum entrance is straight ahead. Phone 757/596-2222. www.mariner.org.* Exhibits and displays represent international nautical history; ship models, figureheads, scrimshaw, paintings, decorative arts, and small craft. Age of Exploration Gallery chronicles advancements in shipbuilding, ocean navigation, and cartography that led to early transoceanic exploration. The Chesapeake Bay Gallery exhibits Native American artifacts, workboats, racing shells, multimedia exhibits, a working steam engine, and hundreds of artifacts and photos that tell the story of this body of water. The Crabtree Collection of Miniature Ships showcases 16 detailed miniatures that illustrate the evolution of the sailing ship. Small craft gallery showcases vessels from five continents. A short film, *Sea Power Beyond the Horizon,* shows the historic and modern importance of the sea. Historical interpreters; research library; museum shop. A 550-acre park on the James River features 5-mile Noland Trail with 14 pedestrian bridges; picnic area. Guided tours. (Daily; closed Thanksgiving, Dec 25) **$$$**

Newport News Park. *13560 Jefferson Ave, Newport News (23603). Hwys 105, 143, I-64 exit 250B. Phone 757/886-7912.* Facilities of this 8,065-acre park include freshwater fishing, canoes, paddleboats, boat rentals; history and nature trails, bicycle paths (rentals), archery, arboretum, discovery center, picnicking, Civil War earthworks, 188 campsites. (All year) Some fees. **$$$$**

Peninsula Fine Arts Center. *101 Museum Dr, Newport News (23606). I-64 exit 258A. Phone 757/596-8175. www.pfac-va.org.* Changing bimonthly exhibits ranging from national traveling exhibitions to regional artists; classes, workshops, and special events. Children's hands-on activity area; museum shop. (Daily; closed holidays) **$$**

Virginia Living Museum. *524 J. Clyde Morris Blvd, Newport News (23601). From Williamsburg take I-64 E to exit 258A and go S on J. Clyde Morris Blvd. Approximately 2 miles. Phone 757/595-1900. www.virginialivingmuseum.org.* Exhibits on natural science; wildlife, all native to Virginia, living in natural habitats; indoor and outdoor aviaries; aquariums;

wildflower gardens; planetarium with daily shows; observatory; children's hands-on Discovery Center. (Daily; closed holidays) **$$**

Virginia War Museum. *9285 Warwick Blvd, Newport News (23607). In Huntington Park, on Hwy 60, I-64 exit 263A. Phone 757/247-8523. www.warmuseum.org.* More than 60,000 artifacts, including weapons, uniforms, vehicles, posters, insignias, and accoutrements relating to every major US military involvement from the Revolutionary War to the Vietnam War. Military history library and film collection. Civil War tours and educational programs available. (Mon-Sat, also Sun afternoons; closed Jan 1, Thanksgiving, Dec 25). **$$**

Limited-Service Hotels

★ **COMFORT INN.** *12330 Jefferson Ave, Newport News (23602). Phone 757/249-0200; toll-free 800/368-2477; fax 757/249-4736. www.newportnewscomfort .com.* 124 rooms, 3 story. Pets accepted; fee. Complimentary full breakfast. Check-in 3 pm, check-out noon. Outdoor pool. Airport transportation available. Business center. **$**

★ **HAMPTON INN.** *12251 Jefferson Ave, Newport News (23602). Phone 757/249-0001; toll-free 800/426-7866; fax 757/249-3911. www.hamptoninn.com.* 120 rooms, 4 story. Complimentary full breakfast. Check-in 3 pm, check-out noon. High-speed Internet access, wireless Internet access. Fitness room. Outdoor pool. Airport transportation available. Business center. **$**

Full-Service Hotel

★ ★ ★ **OMNI NEWPORT NEWS HOTEL.** *1000 Omni Blvd, Newport News (23606). Phone 757/873-6664; toll-free 800/843-6664; fax 757/873-1732. www.omnihotels.com.* An upscale suburban hotel located in the Newport News central business district. 182 rooms, 9 story. Check-in 3 pm, check-out 11 am. High-speed Internet access. Restaurant, bar. Fitness room. Indoor pool, whirlpool. Business center. **$**

Restaurants

★ ★ **AL FRESCO.** *11710 Jefferson Ave, Newport News (23606). Phone 757/873-0644; fax 757/873-2355.* French, Vietnamese menu. Lunch, dinner. Closed Sun; holidays. Bar. **$$**

★ ★ **DAS WALDCAFE.** *12529 Warwick Blvd, Newport News (23606). Phone 757/930-1781.* German menu. Dinner. Closed Mon; holidays. Bar. **$$**

★ ★ **HERMAN'S HARBOR HOUSE.** *663 Deep Creek Rd, Newport News (23606). Phone 757/930-1000; fax 757/930-3831.* Seafood menu. Lunch, dinner. Closed Dec 25. Bar. Casual attire. **$$**

★ ★ **PORT ARTHUR.** *11137 Warwick Blvd, Newport News (23601). Phone 757/599-6474; fax 757/595-7599.* Chinese menu. Lunch, dinner. Closed Thanksgiving, Dec 25. Bar. Children's menu. Casual attire. **$$$**

Norfolk, VA

3 1/2 hours, 185 miles from Raleigh, NC

Founded 1682
Population 243,403
Elevation 12 ft
Area Code 757
Information Norfolk Convention and Visitors Bureau, 232 E Main St, 23510; phone 757/664-6620 or toll-free 800/368-3097
Web Site www.norfolkcvb.com

This city is part of the Port of Hampton Roads. It is a bustling trade center and has many historic, cultural, and resort areas nearby to attract the tourist. Harbor tours depart from Norfolk's downtown waterfront.

In 1682, the General Assembly bought from Nicholas Wise, a pioneer settler, 50 acres on the Elizabeth River for "ten thousand pounds of tobacco and caske." By 1736, the town that developed was the largest in Virginia. On January 1, 1776, Norfolk was shelled by the British and later burned by the colonists to prevent a British takeover. The battle between the *Merrimac* and the *Monitor* in Hampton Roads in March 1862 was followed by the fall of the city to Union forces in May of that year. In 1883, the first shipment of coal to the port by the Norfolk and Western Railway (now Norfolk Southern) began a new era of prosperity for the city.

Norfolk and Portsmouth are connected by bridge tunnels and a pedestrian ferry. Norfolk houses the largest naval facility in the world. It is also headquarters for the United States Navy's Atlantic Fleet and NATO's

Allied Command Atlantic. Norfolk has shipbuilding and ship repair companies, consumer and industrial equipment manufacturers, and food-processing plants. The city ships coal, tobacco, grain, seafood, and vegetables. It is also the region's cultural center, home to the Virginia Opera, Virginia Symphony, Virginia Waterfront International Arts Festival, and Virginia Stage Company.

Old Dominion University (1930), Virginia Wesleyan College (1967), Norfolk State University (1935), and Eastern Virginia Medical School (1973) are located here. This area is also the headquarters for year-round resort activities. Within a 50-mile radius are ocean, bay, river, and marsh fishing and hunting; nearby there are 25 miles of good beaches. The 17.6-mile-long Chesapeake Bay Bridge-Tunnel between Norfolk and the Delmarva Peninsula opened in 1964; toll for passenger cars is $10, including passengers.

Public Transportation

Airport. Information, phone 757/857-3351; lost and found, phone 757/857-3344; weather, phone 757/666-1212.

Buses (Tidewater Regional Transit), phone 757/640-6300.

What to See and Do

American Rover. *Waterside Marina, Waterside Dr exit off I-264. Phone 757/627-7245.* This 135-foot, three-masted topsail passenger schooner cruises the "smooth waters" of Hampton Roads historical harbor; spacious sun decks; below-deck lounges; concessions. Tour passes historic forts, merchant and US Navy ships. Some tours pass the naval base (inquire for tour schedule). (Apr-mid-Oct, two- and three-hour tours daily)

Carrie B Harbor Tours. *Departs from the Waterside. Phone 757/393-4735.* Replica of 19th-century riverboat takes narrated 90-minute tour of naval shipyard and inner harbor (Apr-Oct, daily); narrated 2 1/2-hour tour of naval base (Apr-Oct, daily); 2 1/2-hour sunset cruise to Hampton Roads and naval base (June-Labor Day, daily).

Chrysler Museum of Art. *245 W Olney Rd, Norfolk (23510). At Mowbray Arch. Phone 757/664-6200.* Art treasures representing nearly every important culture, civilization, and historical period of the past 4,000 years. Photography gallery; fine collection of Tiffany decorative arts and glass, includes the 8,000-piece Chrysler Institute of Glass. (Wed-Sun; closed holidays) **$$$**

General Douglas MacArthur Memorial. *City Hall Ave and Bank St, Norfolk (23510). Phone 757/441-2965.* Restored former city hall (1847) where MacArthur is buried. Nine galleries contain memorabilia of his life and military career. There are three other buildings on MacArthur Square: a theater where a film biography is shown, a gift shop, and the library/archives. (Mon-Sat 10 am-5 pm, Sun from 11 am; closed Jan 1, Thanksgiving, Dec 25) **DONATION**

Hermitage Foundation Museum. *7637 N Shore Rd, Norfolk (23505). Phone 757/423-2052.* Guided tours of fine arts museum in Tudor-style mansion. Collections of tapestries, Chinese bronzes and jade, ancient glass. (Daily; closed Jan 1, Thanksgiving, Dec 25) **$$**

Hunter House Victorian Museum. *240 W Freemason St, Norfolk (23510). Phone 757/623-9814.* Built in 1894 and rich in architectural details, the house contains the Hunter family's collection of Victorian furnishings and decorative pieces, including a Renaissance Revival bedchamber suite, a nursery with children's playthings, an inglenook, and stained-glass windows; lavish period reproduction floor and wall coverings, lighting fixtures, and drapery. Also exhibited is a collection of early-20th-century medical memorabilia. Tours begin every 30 minutes. (Apr-Dec, Wed-Sat, also Sun afternoons; closed Jan 1, Thanksgiving, Dec 25). **$$**

Moses Myers House. *331 Bank St, Norfolk (23510). Phone 757/333-6283.* (1792) Excellent example of Georgian architecture; many pieces of original furniture, silver and china. (Apr-Dec: Tues-Sun; rest of year: Tues-Sat; closed holidays) **$$**

Nauticus-The National Maritime Center. *1 Waterside Dr, Norfolk (23510). Phone 757/664-1000; toll-free 800/664-1080. www.nauticus.org.* Interprets aspects from marine biology and ecology to exploration, trade, and shipbuilding. Interactive computer exhibits allow visitors to navigate a simulated ocean voyage, design a model ship, pilot a virtual reality submarine, and view actual researchers at work in two working marine laboratories. Active US Navy ships and scientific research vessels periodically moor at Nauticus and open to visitors. Also 350-seat, 70mm wide-screen theater; shark petting tank. (Memorial Day-Labor Day: daily; rest of year: Tues-Sun; closed Jan 1, Thanksgiving, Dec 24 and 25). **$$$** Also here is

Hampton Roads Naval Museum. *1 Waterside Dr, Norfolk (23510). Phone 757/444-8971.* Interprets the extensive naval history of the Hampton Roads area; including detailed ship models, period photographs, archaeological artifacts, and a superior collection of naval prints and artwork. (Daily; closed Jan 1, Thanksgiving, Dec 25) **FREE**

Norfolk Botanical Garden. *6700 Azalea Garden Rd, Norfolk (23518). Adjacent Norfolk International Airport. Phone 757/441-5830. www.norfolkbotanical garden.org.* Azaleas, camellias, rhododendrons, roses (May-Oct), dogwoods, and hollies on 155 acres. Japanese, Colonial, perennial, and rose gardens; flowering arboretum; Hill of Nations; fragrance garden for the visually impaired; picnicking, restaurant, and gift shop; tropical pavilion. Flowering displays best from early Apr-Oct. Gardens (daily; closed special events). Information center (daily; closed Jan 1, Dec 25). Narrated boat ride (30 minutes) and tram tours (mid-Mar-Labor Day: daily; afterLabor day-Oct: weekends, trams only). **$$$**

Norfolk Naval Base and Norfolk Naval Air Station. *Hampton Blvd and I-564, Norfolk. Phone 757/444-7955.* The largest naval installation in the world. Ship visitors should check in at the Naval Base Pass Office on Hampton Blvd, opposite Gate 5. Naval base tours are also offered. Tour buses from Tour and Information Office, 9079 Hampton Blvd (Apr-Oct, daily). **$$**

Spirit of Norfolk. *Departs from the Waterside. Phone 757/625-1748.* Harbor cruise aboard 600-passenger cruise ship. Captain's narration highlights the harbor's famous landmarks, including Waterside Festival Marketplace, Portsmouth Naval Hospital, Old Fort Norfolk, Blackbeard's hiding place, Norfolk Naval Base, and downtown area's dynamic skyline. Luncheon cruise (Tues-Sun); evening dinner cruise (Tues-Sun); moonlight party cruise (Fri-Sat, in season).

St. Paul's Episcopal Church. *201 St. Paul's Blvd, Norfolk (23510). At City Hall Ave. Phone 757/627-4353.* (1739) Only building to survive burning of Norfolk in 1776. (Tues-Fri, also by appointment) **DONATION**

Virginia Zoological Park. *3500 Granby St, Norfolk (23504). Phone 757/441-5227. www.virginiazoo.com.* A combination zoo, park, and conservatory. Playground, tennis courts, basketball courts; picnic area, concession. (Daily 10 am-5 pm; closed Jan 1, Dec 25) **$$**

Waterside Festival Marketplace. *333 Waterside Dr, Norfolk (23510). www.watersidemarketplace.com.* A waterfront pavilion creating a lively marketplace with more than 90 shops, restaurants. (Mon-Sat 10 am-9 pm, Sun noon-6 pm; closed Thanksgiving, Dec 25) Bordering the Waterside are the city's marina and dock areas, where harbor tour vessels take on passengers. A brick promenade skirting the marina connects the Waterside to

Town Point Park. *120 W Main St, Norfolk (23510). Phone 757/441-2345.* Home to Norfolk Festevents, the park hosts more than 100 free outdoor concerts, parties, dances, movies, and festivals each year.

Willoughby-Baylor House. *601 E Freemason St, Norfolk (23510). Phone 757/664-6200.* (1794) Restored town house with period furnishings; herb and flower garden adjacent. (By appointment; inquire at Moses Myers House) **$$**

Special Events

Festival in the Park. *119 Park Ave, Norfolk (23510). Phone 757/625-1445.* Art exhibits, crafts, sports, food, parade, entertainment. Two weekends beginning the Fri before Memorial Day.

Harborfest. *Town Point Park, 120 W Main St, Norfolk (23510). Downtown waterfront on Wayside Dr. Phone 757/441-2149.* Sailboat and speedboat races, tall ships, ship tours, waterskiing, military demonstrations, entertainment, children's activities, fireworks, seafood. First full weekend in June.

International Azalea Festival. *Downtown and Norfolk Botanical Garden.* To honor NATO. Parade, coronation ceremony, air show (held at Norfolk Naval Air Station), events, concerts, fair, ball, entertainment. Late Apr.

Virginia Children's Festival. *Town Point Park, 120 W Main St, Norfolk (23510). Phone 757/441-2149.* More than 200 educational, creative, and interactive activities; entertainment. Early Oct.

Virginia Opera. *160 E Virginia Beach Blvd, Norfolk (23510). Harrison Opera House and other select locations. Phone 757/623-1223.* Statewide opera company; traditional and contemporary works. Features young American artists. Oct-Apr.

Virginia Symphony. *Chrysler Hall and other select locations. Phone 757/892-6366.* Five performance series. Sept-May.

Virginia Waterfront International Arts Festival. *Phone 757/664-6492.* Eighteen days of classical and contemporary music, dance, visual arts and theater performances. Late Apr-mid-May.

Limited-Service Hotels

★ **BEST WESTERN HOLIDAY SANDS INN & SUITES.** *1330 E Oceanview Ave, Norfolk (23503). Phone 757/583-2621; toll-free 800/525-5156; fax 757/587-7540.* 95 rooms, 5 story. Complimentary continental breakfast. Check-out 11 am. Fitness room. Outdoor pool. Airport transportation available. **$**

★ **COMFORT INN.** *8051 Hampton Blvd, Norfolk (23505). Phone 757/451-0000; toll-free 800/424-6423; fax 757/451-8394. www.comfortinnnavalbase.com.* 119 rooms, 2 story. Complimentary continental breakfast. Check-in 3 pm, check-out 11 am. Indoor pool, whirlpool. **$**

★ **HAMPTON INN.** *1450 N Military Hwy, Norfolk (23502). Phone 757/466-7474; fax 757/466-0117.* 130 rooms, 2 story. Complimentary full breakfast. Check-in 3 pm, check-out noon. Outdoor pool. Airport transportation available. **$**

Full-Service Hotels

★ ★ **BEST WESTERN CENTER INN.** *235 N Military Hwy, Norfolk (23502). Phone 757/461-6600; toll-free 800/237-5517; fax 757/466-9093. www.bestwestern.com.* 152 rooms, 2 story. Complimentary continental breakfast. Check-in 3 pm, check-out noon. Restaurant, bar. Fitness room. Indoor pool, outdoor pool, whirlpool. Airport transportation available. Business center. Near airport. **$**

★ ★ ★ **HILTON NORFOLK AIRPORT.** *1500 N Military Hwy, Norfolk (23502). Phone 804/466-8000; toll-free 800/445-8667; fax 804/466-7806. www.norfolk hilton.com.* Conveniently located 2 miles from Norfolk International Airport, this hotel is ideal for those visiting the business district or military installations. 254 rooms, 6 story. Check-in 3 pm, check-out 1 pm. High-speed Internet access, wireless Internet access. Three restaurants, two bars. Fitness room. Outdoor pool, whirlpool. Tennis. Airport transportation available. Business center. **$$**

★ ★ ★ **MARRIOTT NORFOLK WATERSIDE.** *235 E Main St, Norfolk (23510). Phone 804/627-4200; toll-free 800/228-9290; fax 804/628-6466. www.marriott.com.* 405 rooms, 24 story. Check-in 4 pm, check-out noon. High-speed Internet access, wireless Internet access. Two restaurants, two bars. Fitness room. Indoor pool, three whirlpools. Business center. **$$**

★ ★ ★ **SHERATON NORFOLK WATERSIDE HOTEL.** *777 Waterside Dr, Norfolk (23510). Phone 757/622-6664; toll-free 800/325-3535; fax 757/625-8271. www.sheraton.com.* Adjacent to Waterside Marketplace on the Elizabeth River, this landmark hotel affords great views of the harbor and downtown skyline. 445 rooms, 10 story. Pets accepted. Check-in 3 pm, check-out 11 am. High-speed Internet access. Restaurant, bar. Fitness room. Outdoor pool. Business center. **$**

Specialty Lodging

The following lodging establishment is approved by Mobil Travel Guide, but due to its unique and individualized nature has not been given a traditional Mobil Star rating. Included in this listing you may find bed-and-breakfasts, limited-service inns, guest ranches, and other unique hotel properties.

PAGE HOUSE. *323 Fairfax Ave, Norfolk (23507). Phone 757/625-5033; toll-free 800/599-7659; fax 757/623-9451. www.pagehouseinn.com.* This Georgian Revival mansion (1898), originally a family home and completely renovated in 1990, is located in the fashionable Ghent historic district. It offers distinctly decorated guest rooms. 7 rooms, 3 story. Children under 12 years only by reservations. Check-in 2-9 pm, check-out 11 am. Fitness room. **$$**

Restaurants

★ ★ **BAKER'S CRUST.** *330 W 21st St, Norfolk (23517). Phone 757/625-3600; fax 757/625-1855. www.bakerscrust.com.* Steak menu. Lunch, dinner. Bar. Children's menu. Casual attire. Outdoor seating. **$$**

★ **THE BANQUE.** *1849 E Little Creek Rd, Norfolk (23518). Phone 757/480-3600; fax 757/583-9622.* Western décor. Dinner. Closed Mon; Thanksgiving, Dec 24-25. Bar. **$$**

★ ★ **FREEMASON ABBEY.** *209 W Freemason St, Norfolk (23510). Phone 757/622-3966; fax 757/ 490-7678.* Renovated church (1873); many antiques. American, seafood menu. Lunch, dinner, Sun brunch. Bar. Children's menu. Casual attire. **$$**

★ ★ ★ **LA GALLERIA.** *120 College Pl, Norfolk (23510). Phone 757/623-3939; fax 757/623-9108.* Fine cuisine is the mainstay of this refreshingly cosmopolitan restaurant. All of the delectable desserts are made in-house. Italian menu. Lunch, dinner. Closed Sun; Thanksgiving, Dec 25. Bar. Children's menu. Valet parking. Outdoor seating. **$$**

★ ★ **MONASTERY.** *443 Granby St, Norfolk (23510). Phone 757/625-8193; fax 757/437-0513.* Czech, Eastern European menu. Lunch, dinner. Closed Mon; Easter, Thanksgiving, Dec 25; also July-Aug. Bar. Reservations recommended. **$$**

★ ★ ★ **SHIP'S CABIN.** *4110 E Ocean View Ave, Norfolk (23518). Phone 757/362-4659; fax 757/362-0627. www.shipscabin.com.* Only the freshest seafood is served, thanks to the proprietor's years in the boating business. A popular option is the "mix and match" menu: choose a tailored combination of fish, preparation method, and sauce to accompany. The atmosphere is casual, in keeping with its beach setting. Dinner. Bar. Outdoor seating. **$$**

★ **UNCLE LOUIE'S.** *132 E Little Creek Rd, Norfolk (23505). Phone 757/480-1225; fax 757/480-3540. www.unclelouies.com.* Breakfast, lunch, dinner. Closed Thanksgiving, Dec 25. Bar. Children's menu. **$**

Richmond, VA

3 hours, 157 miles from Raleigh, NC

Settled 1607
Population 197,790
Elevation 150 ft
Area Code 804
Information Convention and Visitors Bureau, 550 E Marshall St, 23219; phone 804/782-2777 or toll-free 800/370-9004
Web Site www.richmondva.org

Located at the falls of the James River, Richmond had to wait 170 years before becoming the state capital. Four hundred years later, with a history as old as Jamestown itself, the city blends its heritage with vibrant contemporary commerce and trade. Its location equidistant from the plantations of Tidewater Virginia and the Piedmont of central Virginia gives the city a unique mix of heritage, culture, and geography. It continues to be a city of contrasts and multiple perspectives that hosts the treasures of colonial times along with state-of-the-art contemporary offerings.

Richmond has served as the capital of Virginia and of the Confederate States of America. The heritage of these two dramatically different situations can be found in places like St. John's Church, site of Patrick Henry's famous speech ("Give me liberty or give me death"), and The Museum and White House of the Confederacy, the residence of Confederate President Jefferson Davis.

A gateway to the Virginia Piedmont and Tidewater, Richmond also serves as a gateway to Southside, the central, south-central part of Virginia that is less traveled and less explored. Travelers will find the rural communities, the pace, and the byways of Southside a welcome contrast to today's hectic times.

The Virginia Historical Society's Story of Virginia does a phenomenal job of laying out the complex history of the Richmond region. Beginning with "Becoming a Homeplace," illustrating its founding by John Smith, Richmond's story continues with "Becoming Virginians," followed by "Becoming Southerners," "Becoming Confederates," and "Becoming New Southerners," "Becoming Americans Again" and lastly "Becoming Equal." Supported with 10,000 artifacts, the story ultimately covers the gamut of American culture.

With all this heritage in one place, Richmond has something for everyone. Toss in a strong arts community, good restaurants, and Southern gentility, and you have a great place to visit and explore.

There have been few dull moments in Richmond's history. Native Americans and settlers fought over the ground on which it now stands. In 1775, Patrick Henry made his "liberty or death" speech in St. John's Church, and in 1780, the city was named capital of the state. At that time, Virginia extended all the way to the Mississippi. British soldiers plundered it brutally in the Revolutionary War. As the capital of the Confederacy from 1861 to 1865, it was constantly in danger. Finally, in 1865, the city was evacuated and retreating Confederate soldiers burned the government warehouse; a portion of the rest of the city also went up in flames.

However, Richmond did survive. As Virginia's capital, it proudly exemplifies the modern South. It is a city that is industrially aggressive yet culturally aware, respectful of its own historical background yet receptive to new trends in architecture and modes of living. Richmond esteems both the oldest monuments and the newest skyscrapers.

Tobacco and tobacco products, paper and paper products, aluminum, chemicals, textiles, printing and publishing, and machinery contribute to the city's economy. Richmond is also an educational center; Virginia Commonwealth University, Virginia Union University, and the University of Richmond are based here.

What to See and Do

6th Street Marketplace. *6th St, Richmond (23219). Downtown, between Coliseum and Grace St.* Restored area of shops, restaurants, and entertainment.

17th Street Farmers' Market. *17th and Main sts, Richmond (23219). Phone 804/646-0477. www.17thstreetfarmersmarket.com.* This farmers' market is built at the site of a Native American trading village and features seasonal produce in Shockoe Bottom. (Apr-Dec, Thurs and Sat-Sun)

Agecroft Hall. *4305 Sulgrave Rd, Richmond (23221). Cary St exit off I-195, turn onto N Thompson Ave, then right on Cary to Malvern, then left on Cantebury to Sulgrave Rd. Phone 804/353-4241. www.agecrofthall.com.* Half-timbered Tudor manor built in the late 15th century near Manchester, England. Disassembled, brought here, and rebuilt during the late 1920s in a spacious setting of formal gardens and grassy terraces overlooking the James River. English furnishings from 16th and 17th centuries. Audiovisual presentation explains the history of the house. (Tues-Sun; closed holidays) **$$**

Canal Club. *1545 E Cary St, Richmond (23219). Phone 804/643-2582. www.thecanalclub.com.* Catch live music, especially blues and rock, or shoot a game of pool in Shockoe Bottom. A bonus: the interesting menu at The Under the Stage Cafe. (Wed-Sat)

Canal Walk. *Enter at S 5th, 7th, 14th, 15th, or 17th sts.* The Canal Walk meanders 1 1/4 miles through downtown and features a pedestrian bridge to Brown's Island. Richmond Canal Cruisers (phone 804/649-2800) depart on the hour from noon to 7 pm on Fridays and Saturdays from the Turning Basin between 14th and Virginia streets.

★ **Capitol Square.** *9th and Grace sts, Richmond (23219). Bounded by Broad, Governor, Bank, and 9th sts, downtown. Phone 804/784-5736.* On Capitol Square are

Equestrian Statue of Washington. *9th and Grace sts, Richmond (23219).* By Thomas Crawford; cast in Munich over an 18-year period. Base features allegorical representations of six famous Revolutionary War figures from Virginia.

Governor's Mansion. *9th and Grace sts, Richmond (23219). E of State Capitol. Phone 804/371-2642.* (1813) This two-story Federal-style house was built after the capital was moved from Williamsburg. Oldest governor's mansion in the United States still in use as a governor's residence. Tours (by appointment). **FREE**

State Capitol. *9th and Grace sts, Richmond (23219). Capitol Sq. Phone 804/698-1788.* (1785-1788) Modeled after La Maison Carrée, an ancient Roman temple at Nímes, France, the Capitol was designed by Thomas Jefferson. In this building, where America's oldest continuous English-speaking legislative bodies still meet, is the famous Houdon statue of Washington. The rotunda features the first interior dome in the United States; here Aaron Burr was tried for treason, Virginia ratified the Articles of Secession, and Robert E. Lee accepted command of the forces of Virginia; the Confederate Congress also met in the building. (Mon-Sat, also Sun afternoons; closed Jan 1, Thanksgiving, Dec 25)

Virginia State Library and Archives. *800 E Broad St, Richmond (23219). Phone 804/692-3500. lva.lib.va.us.* Outstanding collection of books, maps, and manuscripts. (Mon-Sat; closed holidays) **FREE**

Carytown. *W Cary St, Richmond (23220). Between Boulevard St and Thompson St.* More than 250 shops and restaurants in this area include quirky clothing boutiques, antique shops, the city's best music store, and collectibles ranging from Christmas decorations to glass and dolls.

Church Hill Historic Area. *Main and 21st sts, Richmond (23223). Bounded by Broad, 29th, Main, and 21st sts, E of Capitol Sq.* Neighborhood of 19th-century houses, more than 70 of which predate Civil War.

Richmond's Historical Legacy

Richmond was the Civil War "Capital of the Confederacy," and this aspect of its past can easily be recalled on a two-hour, 2-mile walking tour of the city center. The city also enjoys other, less-troubling claims to historical fame, which will be pointed out along the way. Begin this walk at the Virginia State Capitol, designed in 1785 by Thomas Jefferson, himself a state governor, in the style of a classical temple. Surrounded by Capitol Square's expanse of well-tended lawn, it displays such majesty that it still commands the eye despite the modern-day structures that surround it. Step inside the Rotunda to see the famous life-size statue of George Washington, the only one executed of him from life. From Capitol Square, walk north (right) on 9th Street across Broad Street to the neighborhood once known as Court End, which now bustles with students and faculty of the Medical College of Virginia. At 818 East Marshall Street (intersecting 9th) stands the most important residence of Court End, the home of John Marshall, the distinguished chief justice of the US Supreme Court from 1801 to 1835. Built in 1790, the two-story brick house where he lived for 45 years is a museum dedicated

to his memory. Though it's a seven-block detour, head west on Marshall Street to 2nd Street and turn north (right) two blocks to 110 East Leigh Street, the Maggie Walker National Historic Site. A museum, the modest two-story brick home on a quiet residential street, honors a black woman of impressive ability. Despite physical handicaps, Walker became America's first female bank president, establishing the Penny Savings Bank in 1903 as a way of helping local blacks during the Jim Crow period. Double back via Marshall Street past the John Marshall House to the Valentine Museum at 1015 East Clay Street. A small, innovative museum with a contemporary outlook, it focuses on the people and history of Richmond. Conclude the tour a block down the street at 12th and East Clay at the adjacent Museum of the Confederacy and the White House of the Confederacy. Not surprisingly, the museum emphasizes Southern leaders, featuring mementos of General Robert E. Lee. The White House, a neoclassical mansion built in 1818, recounts the home life during the Civil War of Confederate President Jefferson Davis and his wife, Varina.

Some Church Hill houses are open during Historic Garden Week (see SPECIAL EVENTS). In the center of Church Hill is

Edgar Allan Poe Museum. *1914-1916 E Main St, Richmond (23223). Phone 804/648-5523. www.poemuseum.org.* Old Stone House portion is thought to be oldest structure in Richmond (1737). Three additional buildings house Poe mementos; James Carling illustrations of "The Raven"; scale model of the Richmond of Poe's time. Guided tours. (Tues-Sun; closed holidays). **$$**

St. John's Episcopal Church. *25th and Broad sts, Richmond (23223). Phone 804/648-5015.* (1741) Where Patrick Henry delivered his stirring "liberty or death" speech. Reenactment of the Second Virginia Convention (late May-early Sept, Sun). Guided tours. (Daily; closed holidays)

City Hall Observation Deck. *900 E Broad St, Richmond (23219). Phone 804/646-7000.* Eighteenth-floor observation deck offers a panoramic view of the city, including the Capitol grounds, James River, and

Revolutionary and Civil War-era buildings contrasted with modern skyscrapers. (Mon-Fri) **FREE**

Civil War Visitor Center. *470 Tredegar St, Richmond (23219). Phone 804/771-2145. www.nps.gov/rich.* Begin your exploration of Richmond's Civil War heritage at the National Park Service Center at the restored Tredegar Iron Works near the James River. On the bottom floor, a continuously running film orients you to the 12 battlefields in the area. Park Service guides explain to kids how to fire the kind of cannon that Tredgar Iron Works made for the war. (Daily 9 am-5 pm) **FREE**

⭐ **The Fan and Monument Avenue.** *Main and Belvidere sts, Richmond (23220). Bounded by Franklin St and Monument Ave, Boulevard, Main, and Belvidere sts. Phone 804/643-3589.* Named for the layout of streets that fan out from Monroe Park toward the western part of town. Historical neighborhood has restored antebellum and turn-of-the-century houses, museums, shops, restaurants, and famed Monument Avenue. The fashionable boulevard, between Lombard and Belmont streets, is dotted with imposing statues of Generals Lee, Stuart, and Jackson; of Jefferson Davis; and of Commodore Matthew Fontaine Maury, inventor of the electric torpedo. Within this area are

Children's Museum of Richmond. *2626 W Broad St, Richmond (23220). Phone 804/474-2667; toll-free 877/295-2667. www.c-mor.org.* A nice range of hands-on exhibits suitable for children ages 1-9, especially the interactive James River Waterplay, which explores the hydrology and history of the James River. (July-Aug: daily; Sept-June: Tues-Sun; closed holidays) **$$**

Science Museum of Virginia. *2500 W Broad St, Richmond (23220). N of Monument Ave. Phone 804/864-1400. www.smv.org.* Located in the historic Broad Street Station (train tracks are still on the ground floor), this is an engaging museum that will appeal to children ages 5-12 with exhibits about space, flight, electricity, physics, and the atom. Be sure to check out the laboratories and animal exhibits on the second floor. (Mon-Sat 9:30 am-5 pm, Sun 11:30 am-5 pm; closed Thanksgiving, Dec 25) **$$**

Virginia Historical Society. *428 N Boulevard St, Richmond (23220). Phone 804/358-4901. www.vahistorical.org.* The society has a comprehensive collection of Virginia history housed in its museum with permanent and changing exhibits, and the Library of Virginia History with historical and genealogical research facilities. Well worth an afternoon to explore the city's changing place in history. (Mon-Sat, museum also Sun afternoons; closed holidays) **$$**

Virginia Museum of Fine Arts. *2800 Grove Ave, Richmond (23221). At Boulevard St. Phone 804/340-1400. vmfa.state.va.us.* America's first state-supported museum of art. Collections of paintings, prints, and sculpture from major world cultures; Russian Imperial Easter eggs and jewels by Faberge; decorative arts of the Art Nouveau and Art Deco movements; sculpture garden; changing exhibits. Cafeteria. (Tues-Sun; closed holidays) **FREE**

Federal Reserve Money Museum. *701 E Byrd St, Richmond (23219). Downtown, on the first floor of the bank. Phone 804/697-8000. www.rich.frb.org/econed/museum/.* Exhibits of currency, include rare bills; gold and silver bars; money-related artifacts. (Mon-Fri 9:30 am-3:30 pm; closed holidays) **FREE**

Historic Richmond Tours. *707 E Franklin St, Richmond (23219). Phone 804/649-0711.* Offers guided van tours with pickup at Visitor Center and major hotels (daily); reservations required. Also guided walking tours (Apr-Oct, daily; fee). **$$$$**

Hollywood Cemetery. *412 S Cherry St, Richmond (23220). At Albemarle St. Phone 804/648-8501. www.hollywoodcemetery.org.* (1847) James Monroe, John Tyler, Jefferson Davis, other notables, and 18,000 Confederate soldiers are buried here; audiovisual program (Mon-Fri). (Daily 8 am-5 pm; walking tours Apr-Oct, Mon-Sat at 10 am) **FREE**

Jackson Ward. *Broad and Belvidere sts, Richmond (23218). Bounded by I-95, 7th, Broad, and Belvidere sts.* Historic downtown neighborhood that was home to many famous black Richmonders, including Bill "Bojangles" Robinson. The area has numerous 19th-century, Greek Revival, and Victorian buildings with ornamental ironwork that rivals the wrought iron of New Orleans. Within the ward are

Bill "Bojangles" Robinson Statue. *Leigh and Adams sts, Richmond (23218).* Memorial to the famous dancer who was born at 915 N 3rd St.

Black History Museum and Cultural Center. *00 Clay St, Richmond (23219). Phone 804/780-9093. www.blackhistorymuseum.org.* Limited editions, prints, art, photographs; African memorabilia; Sam Gilliam collection. (Tues-Sun 10 am-5 pm) **$$**

Maggie Walker National Historic Site. *110 1/2 E Leigh St, Richmond (23223). Phone 804/771-2017. www.nps.gov/malw.* Commemorates the life and career of Maggie L. Walker, daughter of former slaves, who overcame great hardships to become successful in banking and insurance; early advocate for women's rights and racial equality. Two-story, red brick house was home to her family from 1904 to 1934. (Mon-Sat; closed Jan 1, Thanksgiving, Dec 25) **FREE**

John Marshall House. *818 E Marshall St, Richmond (23219). Phone 804/648-7998.* (1790) Restored house of famous Supreme Court justice features original woodwork and paneling, family furnishings, and mementos. (Tues-Sun; closed holidays) Combination ticket available for Marshall House, Valentine Museum, Museum of the Confederacy, and White House of the Confederacy. **$**

Kanawha Canal Locks. *12th and Byrd sts, Richmond (23219). Downtown. Phone 804/780-0107 (walking tour).* Impressive stone locks were part of the nation's first canal system, planned by George Washington.

Narrated audiovisual presentation explains the workings of the locks and canal. Picnic grounds. (Mon-Sat) **FREE**

Meadow Farm Museum. *General Sheppard Crump Memorial Park, 8600 Dixon Powers Dr, Richmond (23228). Phone 804/501-5520. co.henrico.va.us/rec/mfarm.htm.* Living history farm museum depicting rural life in the 1860s. Orientation center, farmhouse, barn, outbuildings, crop demonstration fields, and 1860s doctor's office. Also a 150-acre park with picnic shelters, playground. (Mar-Dec, Tues-Sun) **$**

Monumental Church. *1224 E Broad St, Richmond (23219). N of Capitol Sq.* (1812) Located on the Medical College of Virginia campus of Virginia Commonwealth University. Octagonal domed building designed by Robert Mills, architect of the Washington Monument. Commemorative structure was built on the site where many prominent persons, including the governor, perished in a theater fire in 1811. Interior closed. Behind the church is the distinctive Egyptian Building (1845).

Museum of the Confederacy. *1201 E Clay St, Richmond (23219). Phone 804/649-1861. www.moc.org.* The museum features the world's largest collection of Confederate artifacts: uniforms, weapons, tattered flags, and daguerreotypes. Many of the exhibits feature artifacts from Confederate officers with descriptions of their demise. While it's comprehensive, the museum hasn't taken advantage of technology so you'll find yourself reading one typed description after another. (Mon-Sat 10 am-5 pm, Sun noon-5 pm; closed Jan 1, Thanksgiving, Dec 25) **$$**

Paddlewheeler *Annabel Lee. Departs from Intermediate Terminal. Broad St E to 21st St, turn right on 21st St to Dock St, turn left on Dock, follow until you reach the terminal. Phone 804/377-2020; toll-free 800/752-7093. www.spiritcitycruises.com/Richmond/onboard/.* Triple-decked, 350-passenger, 19th-century-style riverboat cruises the James River. Narrated tour; entertainment. Lunch, brunch, dinner, and plantation cruises. (Apr-Dec, at least one cruise Tues-Sun)

Parks. *Phone 804/780-5733.* For general information, contact the Department of Parks and Recreation.

Bryan. *Bellevue Ave and Hermitage Rd, Richmond (23227).* A 279-acre park, 20 acres of which are an azalea garden with more than 55,000 plants (best viewed late Apr-mid-May). Picnic facilities, tennis courts. **FREE**

James River. *W 22nd St and Riverside Dr, Richmond (23225).* The James River drops 105 feet over a 7-mile stretch that passes through downtown Richmond and produces Class IV whitewater rapids. When the river is high enough—generally April through October—you can whitewater raft practically in the shadows of the city's skyline. Check with Richmond Raft Co., phone toll-free 800/540-7238, www.richmondraft.com, or Adventure Challenge, phone 804/276-7600, www.adventure challenge.com/james.htm. **FREE**

Lewis Ginter Botanical Garden. *1800 Lakeside Ave, Lakeside (23228). Phone 804/262-9887. www.lewisginter.org.* Victorian-era estate features the Grace Arents Garden and the Henry M. Flagler Perennial Garden; seasonal floral displays; emphasis on daffodils, daylilies, azaleas, and rhododendrons. (Daily) **$$**

Maymont. *1700 Hampton St, Richmond (23220). At Pennsylvania Ave. Phone 804/358-7166.* Dooley mansion, late Victorian in style, houses an art collection and decorative arts exhibits (Tues-Sun; fee). Also here are formal Japanese and Italian gardens, an arboretum, a nature center with wildlife habitat for native species, an aviary, a children's farm, and a working carriage collection. (Daily) **FREE**

Pocahontas State Park. *10301 State Park Rd, Chesterfield (23832). S on Hwy 10, then W on Hwy 655. Phone 804/796-4255. www.dcr.state.va.us/parks/pocahont.htm.* More than 7,000 acres; Swift Creek Lake. Swimming, pool, bathhouse, fishing, boating (launch, rentals, electric motors only); hiking trails, bicycle path (rentals), picnicking, concession, tent and trailer sites (seasonal), group cabins. Nature center; evening interpretive programs (summer). (Daily)

William Byrd. *Boulevard St and Idlewood Ave, Richmond (23220).* Includes 287 acres of groves, artificial lakes, picnic areas. Tennis courts, softball fields, and a fitness course. Amphitheater (June-Aug). Virginia's World War I memorial, a 240-foot, pink brick carillon tower.

Plantation tours. *401 E Marshall St, Richmond (23220). Phone 804/783-7450.* The Richmond-Petersburg-Williamsburg area has many fine old mansions and estates. Some are open most of the year; others only during Historic Garden Week (see SPECIAL EVENTS). The Metro Richmond Visitors

Center has maps, information folders, and suggestions.

Regency Square. *1420 Parham Rd, Richmond (23229). Phone 804/740-7467. www.shopregencysqmall.com.* The largest department stores in the area, including JCPenney, Hecht's, and Sears, are located in this mall off exit 181A on Interstate 64. Among the specialty shops are American Eagle Outfitters, Champs Sports, and Spencer Gifts. (Mon-Sat 10 am-9 pm, Sun noon-6 pm)

Richmond Braves. *The Diamond, 3001 N Boulevard, Richmond (23230). Phone 804/359-4444; fax 804/359-0731. www.rbraves.com.* The Richmond Braves are the AAA farm team of the Atlanta Braves, playing their home games in a 12,134-seat stadium just off Interstate 95. While The Diamond, built in 1985, is beginning to show its age, it remains a good place to catch a game. **$**

Shockoe Slip. *11 S 12th St, Richmond (23219). E Cary St between 12th and 14th sts, downtown.* Restored area of historic buildings and gaslit cobblestone streets; shopping, restaurants, and galleries.

Southside Speedway. *12800 Genito Rd, Midlothian (23112). Phone 804/744-2700. www.southside-speedway.com.* If you need to see some short track action, this 1/3-mile asphalt oval is the ticket with Late Model Sportsman, Modified and Grand Stock racing on Friday nights. Heat races begin at 7 pm with the first feature at 8 pm. Closed on NASCAR race weekends. **$**

St. Paul's Church. *815 E Grace St, Richmond (23219). W of Capitol Sq. Phone 804/643-3589. www.stpauls-episcopal.org.* (Episcopal) Established in 1843, the church survived the Civil War intact. It was here that Jefferson Davis received news of Robert E. Lee's retreat from Petersburg to Appomattox. Beginning in 1890, the church added many fine stained-glass windows, including eight from the Tiffany studios. Sanctuary ceiling features decorative plasterwork interweaving Greek, Hebrew, and Christian motifs around a central panel. A Tiffany mosaic of da Vinci's *Last Supper* surmounts the altar. (Daily; closed holidays)

Valentine Museum. *1015 E Clay St, Richmond (23219). N of Capitol Sq. Phone 804/649-0711. www.valentinemuseum.com.* Traces the history of Richmond. Exhibits focus on city life, decorative arts, costumes and textiles, and industrial and social history; tour of restored 1812 Wickham House. Lunch is served in a walled garden (Apr-Oct). (Daily; closed holidays). **$$**

Virginia Aviation Museum. *5701 Huntsman Rd, Richmond (23250). At Richmond International Airport. Phone 804/236-3622. www.vam.smv.org.* Exhibits and artifacts on the history of aviation, with an emphasis on Virginia pioneers. (Daily; closed Thanksgiving, Dec 25) **$$**

Virginia House. *4301 Sulgrave Rd, Windsor Farms (23221). 1/2 mile off Hwy 147 (Cary St). Phone 804/353-4251. www.vahistorical.org.* A Tudor building constructed of materials from Warwick Priory (built in England in 1125 and rebuilt in 1565 as a residence); moved here in 1925. The west wing is modeled after Sulgrave Manor, at one time the home of Lawrence Washington. Furniture, tapestries, and paintings from the 15th to 20th centuries. Formal gardens. Tours by appointment only except during Historic Garden Week (see SPECIAL EVENTS). (Fri-Sat 10 am-4 pm, Sun 12:30-5 pm, otherwise by appointment; closed holidays) **$$**

Virginia War Memorial. *621 S Belvidere St, Richmond (23220). Downtown at N end of Robert E. Lee Bridge. Phone 804/786-2060. www.vawarmemorial.org.* Honors Virginians who died in World War II and the Korean and Vietnam wars. Mementos of battles; eternal flame; more than 12,000 names engraved on glass and marble walls. (Daily) **FREE**

White House of the Confederacy. *12th and Clay sts, Richmond (23219). N of Capitol Sq. Phone 804/649-1861. www.moc.org/exwhite.htm.* Next door to the Museum of the Confederacy downtown, this Classical Revival house (1818) was used by Jefferson Davis as his official residence during the period when Richmond was the capital of the Confederacy. Abraham Lincoln met with troops here during the Union occupation of the city. It has been restored to its pre-wartime appearance with many of its original furnishings. (Mon-Sat 10 am-5 pm, Sun noon-5 pm; closed Jan 1, Thanksgiving, Dec 25) **$$**

Wilton House Museum. *215 S Wilton Rd, Richmond (23226). Off Cary St, 8 miles W. Phone 804/282-5936. www.wiltonhousemuseum.org.* (1753) Georgian mansion built by William Randolph III. Fully paneled, authentic 18th-century furnishings. Headquarters of the National Society of Colonial Dames in Virginia. (Tues-Sun; closed holidays) Open during Historic Garden Week (see SPECIAL EVENTS). **$**

Special Events

Historic Garden Week in Virginia. *12 E Franklin St, Richmond (23219). Phone 804/644-7776. www.va gardenweek.org.* Many private houses and gardens of historic or artistic interest are opened for this event, which includes more than 200 houses and gardens throughout the state. Tours. Mid-late Apr.

June Jubilee. *Downtown, Richmond.* Performing and visual arts festival with ethnic foods, folk dances, music, and crafts. First weekend in June.

Richmond Newspapers Marathon. Last Sun in Oct.

Virginia State Fair. *600 E Laburnum Ave, Richmond (23222). Phone 804/228-3200. www.statefair.com.* Animal and 4-H contests, music, horse show, and carnival. Late Sept-early Oct.

Limited-Service Hotels

★ **DAYS INN.** *6910 Midlothian Tpke, Richmond (23225). Phone 804/745-7100; toll-free 800/329-7466; fax 804/276-6660. www.daysinn.com.* 130 rooms, 3 story. Pets accepted. Complimentary continental breakfast. Check-out noon. Outdoor pool. **$**

★ ★ **DOUBLETREE HOTEL.** *5501 Eubank Rd, Sandston (23150). Phone 804/226-6400; toll-free 800/222-8733; fax 804/226-1269. www.doubletree.com.* This hotel is just 40 minutes from Colonial Williamsburg and directly across from the Richmond International Airport. Area attractions include Kings Dominion, Busch Gardens, Richmond Coliseum, Aviation Museum, and the Museum of the Confederacy. 160 rooms, 5 story. Check-out noon. High-speed Internet access, wireless Internet access. Restaurant, bar. Fitness room. Outdoor pool, whirlpool. Airport transportation available. Business center. **$**

★ ★ **EMBASSY SUITES.** *2925 Emerywood Pkwy, Richmond (23294). Phone 804/672-8585; toll-free 800/362-2779; fax 804/672-3749. www.embassysuites.com.* Ideally located for the business traveler in Richmond's Commerce Center on the west end of the city, this hotel offers spacious accommodations and a complimentary full cooked-to-order breakfast, advantageous for families. Guest suites are all built around a large atrium that stretches the full eight floors of the building. 226 rooms, 8 story, all suites. Complimentary full breakfast. Check-in 3 pm, check-out noon. High-speed Internet access. Restaurant,

bar. Fitness room. Indoor pool, whirlpool. Airport transportation available. Business center. **$$**

★ ★ **LINDEN ROW INN.** *100 E Franklin St, Richmond (23219). Phone 804/783-7000; toll-free 800/348-7424; fax 804/648-7504. www.lindenrowinn.com.* With artwork from the Virginia Historical Society and many antiques throughout, guests can enjoy quiet Victorian surroundings at this elegant inn at the heart of downtown Richmond. The inn also features a secluded garden courtyard in a comfortable neighborhood setting and complimentary wine and cheese receptions in the evenings. 70 rooms, 4 story. Complimentary continental breakfast. Check-in 3 pm, check-out 11 am. High-speed Internet access. Restaurant (public by reservation). Bar. **$**

★ **QUALITY INN.** *8008 W Broad St, Richmond (23294). Phone 804/346-0000; toll-free 800/424-6423; fax 804/346-4547. www.qualityinn.com.* Within walking distance to many shopping and dining locations and offering convenient access to the highway, this comfortable motel is ideal for the business or leisure traveler on a budget. 191 rooms, 6 story. Pets accepted; fee. Complimentary continental breakfast. Check-in 3 pm, check-out 11 am. Fitness room. Outdoor pool. **$**

Full-Service Hotels

★ ★ ★ **THE BERKELEY HOTEL.** *1200 E Cary St, Richmond (23219). Phone 804/780-1300; toll-free 888/780-4422; fax 804/648-4728. www.berkeleyhotel.com.* This hotel opened in 1988 but appears to be a property of days gone by. It is located at the crossroads of the business district and Historic Shockoe Slip. Dark wood paneling adorns the lobby and dining room. Dramatic windows to the ceiling give it a European appearance, and diners at the hotel's restaurant get a view of the Slip's cobblestone and lamplights. 55 rooms, 6 story. Check-in 3 pm, check-out noon. Wireless Internet access. Restaurant, bar. Airport transportation available. Business center. **$$**

★ ★ **COURTYARD BY MARRIOTT.** *6400 W Broad St, Richmond (23230). Phone 804/282-1881; toll-free 800/321-2211; fax 804/288-2934. www.marriott.com.* Set on Richmond's west end, where business and shopping locations are abundant, this appealing hotel features a courtyard with a pool

and gazebo, loveseats in the comfortable guest rooms, and a restaurant with a courtyard view. 145 rooms, 3 story. Check-in 3 pm, check-out noon. High-speed Internet access. Restaurant, bar. Fitness room. Outdoor pool, whirlpool. Business center. **$**
🕇 ⛱ 🏃

★ ★ ★ **CROWNE PLAZA.** *555 E Canal St, Richmond (23219). Phone 804/788-0900; toll-free 800/ 227-6963; fax 804/788-7087. www.crowneplaza.com.* Just 9 miles from Richmond International Airport, this hotel is situated in the heart of the historic district and minutes from area attractions such as Shockoe Slip, Sixth Street Market Place, museums, theaters, and fine dining. The higher floors have a spectacular view of the James River. 299 rooms, 16 story. Check-in 3 pm, check-out noon. High-speed Internet access. Two restaurants, bar. Fitness room. Indoor pool, whirlpool. Business center. **$$**
🕇 ⛱ 🏃

★ ★ ★ ★ ★ **THE JEFFERSON HOTEL.** *101 W Franklin St, Richmond (23220). Phone 804/788-8000; fax 804/225-0334.* The Jefferson Hotel is an institution in the heart of Richmond. Imaginations run wild at this historic Beaux Arts landmark, dating to 1895. It's easy to conjure up the image of a beautifully dressed debutante gliding down the hotel's sweeping staircase, past a large statue of the hotel's namesake, or influential politicians having a heated debate under the impressive marble-style columns. The guest rooms are furnished in a traditional style defined by antique reproductions and fine art, while modern amenities and inimitable Southern hospitality ensure the comfort of all guests. Pedigreed residents take afternoon tea here. TJ's provides a casual setting for fine dining with local dishes like oyster chowder and peanut soup. The hotel's star restaurant is Lemaire (see), with its sparkling ambience and refined menu. Nearby are the city's financial district, museums, shopping, and the state capitol; complimentary car service transports guests to these and other destinations within a 3-mile radius. 264 rooms, 9 story. Pets accepted; fee. Check-in 3 pm, check-out noon. Wireless Internet access. Two restaurants, bar. Children's activity center. Fitness room, spa. Indoor pool, whirlpool. Airport transportation available. Business center. **$$**
🍴 🕇 ⛱ 🏃

★ ★ ★ **MARRIOTT RICHMOND.** *500 E Broad St, Richmond (23219). Phone 804/643-3400; toll-free 800/228-9290; fax 804/788-1230. www.marriott.com.* Attached to the Convention Center via sky-bridge,

this recently renovated high-rise hotel in the heart of the city is close to the Coliseum, and both the historic and River districts. Business travelers will appreciate a bilevel desk and high-speed Internet access in their rooms, while families will love the spacious rooms, indoor pool, and downtown location. 401 rooms, 17 story. Check-in 3 pm, check-out noon. High-speed Internet access. Two restaurants, bar. Fitness room. Indoor pool, whirlpool. Business center. **$$**
🕇 ⛱ 🏃

★ ★ ★ **OMNI RICHMOND HOTEL.** *100 S 12th St, Richmond (23219). Phone 804/344-7000; toll-free 800/843-6664; fax 804/648-6704. www.omnihotels.com.* This contemporary hotel is located in the center of the financial and historic districts and features scenic river views. It's across the street from the famous Tobacco Company restaurant and a great place to stay if you intend to explore Shockoe Slip and Shockoe Bottom. 361 rooms, 19 story. Pets accepted; fee. Check-in 3 pm, check-out noon. Wireless Internet access. Restaurant, bar. Fitness room, fitness classes available. Indoor pool. Airport transportation available. Business center. **$$**
🍴 🕇 ⛱ 🏃

★ ★ ★ **SHERATON RICHMOND WEST HOTEL.** *6624 W Broad St, Richmond (23230). Phone 804/285-2000; toll-free 800/325-3535; fax 804/288-3961. www.sheraton.com/richmond.* With luxurious furnishings such as chandeliers in the lobby area and plush pillows and duvets that sit upon "Sweet Sleeper" beds, this upscale hotel is located just off the highway in a richly landscaped business park. With oversize writing desks and in-room WiFi, the hotel is geared towards the business traveler but is also a great place for leisure travelers to Richmond as well. 372 rooms, 8 story. Pets accepted. Check-in 3 pm, check-out noon. High-speed Internet access, wireless Internet access. Two restaurants, two bars. Fitness room. Indoor pool, outdoor pool, whirlpool. Business center. **$**
🍴 🕇 ⛱ 🏃

Restaurants

★ ★ **ACACIA.** *3325 W Cary St, Richmond (23221). Phone 804/354-6060; fax 804/354-6062. www.acacia restaurant.com.* Chef Dale Reitzer was named one of America's best by *Food & Wine* magazine in 1999 so this is the place for a special dinner. Located in an old church building with a front porch that overlooks the sidewalks of Carytown, Acacia has a menu that changes daily to take advantage of the freshest ingredients of the season. American menu. Lunch, dinner. Closed Sun; July 4; also early Jan. Bar. Casual attire. Reservations recommended. Outdoor seating. **$$$**

★ ★ **AMICI.** *3343 W Cary St, Richmond (23221). Phone 804/353-4700; fax 804/278-6291. www.amiciristorante.net.* Italian menu. Lunch, dinner. Closed holidays. Bar. Casual attire. Reservations recommended. Outdoor seating. **$$$**
Ⓓ

★ ★ **BYRAM'S LOBSTER HOUSE.** *3215 W Broad St, Richmond (23230). Phone 804/355-9193. www.byrams.com.* American menu. Lunch, dinner. Closed holidays. Bar. Children's menu. Business casual attire. **$$**

★ ★ **CABO'S CORNER BISTRO.** *2053 W Broad St, Richmond (23220). Phone 804/355-1144. www.cabosbistro.com.* French bistro menu. Dinner. Closed Sun-Mon; holidays. Bar. Business casual attire. Reservations recommended. **$$$**

★ ★ **CAFE MANDOLIN.** *1309 W Main St, Richmond (23220). Phone 804/355-8558. www.cafemandolin.com.* International/Fusion menu. Lunch, dinner. Closed Sun-Mon; also one week in winter and one week in summer. Bar. Business casual attire. Reservations recommended. Outdoor seating. **$$**

★ ★ ★ **THE DINING ROOM AT THE BERKELEY HOTEL.** *1200 E Cary St, Richmond (23219). Phone 804/225-5105; toll-free 888/780-4422; fax 804/648-4728. www.berkleyhotel.com.* Located in a European-style hotel, this handsomely decorated dining room serves elegant, impeccably prepared meals in an atmosphere that is sophisticated and tranquil. Many fine Virginia products are served, and classical preparations prevail. American menu. Breakfast, lunch, dinner. Closed Dec 25. Bar. Children's menu. Business casual attire. Reservations recommended. Valet parking. **$$**

★ ★ **HALF WAY HOUSE.** *10301 Jefferson Davis Hwy, Richmond (23237). Phone 804/275-1760.* This antique-furnished manor house (1760) was a stop on the Petersburg stagecoach line until the late 19th century. It hosted Washington, Lafayette, Patrick Henry, and Jefferson, among others. It was also used as a Union headquarters during the 1864 siege of Richmond. American menu. Lunch, dinner. Business casual attire. Reservations recommended. **$$$**
Ⓓ

★ ★ **HELEN'S.** *2527 W Main St, Richmond (23220). Phone 804/358-4370; fax 804/358-4553.* Fusion menu. Dinner. Closed Mon. Bar. Casual attire. Reservations recommended. **$$**
Ⓓ

★ ★ **KABUTO JAPANESE HOUSE OF STEAK.** *8052 W Broad St, Richmond (23294). Phone 804/747-9573; fax 804/747-1563.* Japanese menu. Lunch, dinner. Bar. Business casual attire. Reservations recommended. **$$**

★ ★ **LA PETITE FRANCE.** *2108 Maywill St, Richmond (23230). Phone 804/353-8729; fax 804/353-4692. www.lapetitefrance.net.* French menu. Lunch, dinner. Closed Sun-Mon; holidays; also the last two weeks in Aug. Jacket required (dinner). Reservations recommended. **$$$**

★ ★ ★ **LEMAIRE.** *101 W Franklin, Richmond (23220). Phone 804/788-8000; fax 804/344-5162. www.jefferson-hotel.com.* Old-world fine dining comes to life at Lemaire, located in the historic Jefferson Hotel (see). The restaurant is named for Etienne Lemaire, who served as maitre d' to President Jefferson and was widely credited for introducing the fine art of cooking with wines to America. His love of food and wine is continued at Lemaire, where contemporary Southern cooking goes upscale with French accents, homegrown herbs, featherweight sauces, and seasonal ingredients. Professional and friendly service and quiet, intimate surroundings make dining at Lemaire a delight. American menu. Breakfast, lunch, dinner. Closed Memorial Day. Bar. Children's menu. Jacket required. Valet parking. **$$$**

★ ★ ★ **THE OLD ORIGINAL BOOKBINDER'S.** *2306 E Cary St, Richmond (23223). Phone 804/643-6900. www.oldoriginalbookbinders.com.* American menu. Dinner. Closed holidays. Bar. Children's menu. Business casual attire. Reservations recommended. Valet parking. Outdoor seating. **$$$**
Ⓓ

★ **O'TOOLES.** *4800 Forest Hill Ave, Richmond (23225). Phone 804/233-1781; fax 804/232-1737. www.mmmm-music.com/otooles.htm.* American menu. Lunch, dinner, late-night. Bar. Children's menu. Casual attire. **$$**

★ ★ ★ **RUTH'S CHRIS STEAK HOUSE.** *11500 Huguenot Rd, Richmond (23113). Phone 804/378-0600; fax 804/378-0776. www.sizzlingsteak.com.* Located in the historic Bellgrade Plantation House, this restaurant offers fine dining with elegant Southern hospitality. Dine on the patio or in a private room with period furnishings. Organist Tues-Sun. Steak menu. Dinner. Closed Thanksgiving, Dec 25. Bar. Business casual attire. Reservations recommended. Outdoor seating. **$$$**

★ ★ **SAM MILLER'S WAREHOUSE.** *1210 E Cary St, Richmond (23219). Phone 804/644-5465; fax 804/644-5470. www.sammillers.com.* This seafood restaurant is located in the historic district and features antique mirrors and a lobster tank. Seafood menu. Lunch, dinner, brunch. Bar. Business casual attire. Reservations recommended. **$$$**
🅳

★ ★ **SKILLIGALEE.** *5416 Glenside Dr, Richmond (23228). Phone 804/672-6200; fax 804/755-1312. www.skilligalee.com.* Seafood menu. Lunch, dinner. Bar. Children's menu. Business casual attire. Reservations recommended. **$$**

★ **STRAWBERRY STREET CAFE.** *421 N Strawberry St, Richmond (23220). Phone 804/353-6860; fax 804/358-3569. www.strawberrystreetcafe.com.* The old-fashioned bath tub that serves as the restaurant's salad bar earned its fame as a "Jeopardy!" question, but that's just part of the charm of a place filled with stained glass, rich woodwork, and a menu with a little something for every taste, from burgers to crab cakes. Located in the Fan neighborhood. American menu. Lunch, dinner, brunch. Closed Thanksgiving, Dec 25. Bar. Children's menu. Casual attire. Reservations recommended. Outdoor seating. **$$**
🅳

★ **TANGLEWOOD ORDINARY.** *2210 River Rd W, Maidens (23102). Phone 804/556-3284. www.ordinary.com.* Collection of *The Saturday Evening Post* dating to 1913. Traditional Southern menu. Dinner. Closed Mon-Tues; holidays. **$$**
🅳

★ ★ **TOBACCO COMPANY.** *1201 E Cary St, Richmond (23219). Phone 804/782-9555; fax 804/788-8913. www.thetobaccocompany.com.* The restaurant that helped pioneer the renaissance of Shockoe Slip is carved from a former tobacco warehouse. The centerpiece is a dramatic skylit atrium with an antique cage elevator servicing three floors of dining. The menu is extensive if not inventive: steaks, prime rib, lobster, veal, shrimp, scallops, salmon, rainbow trout, chicken, crab, Virginia ham, and pasta. Free buffet during happy hours, 5-7 pm, Wednesday through Friday. Cigars in the bar. American menu. Lunch, dinner, Sun brunch. Bar. Children's menu. Business casual attire. **$$**

★ **TRAK'S.** *9115 Quioccasin Rd, Richmond (23229). Phone 804/740-1700.* Greek, Italian menu. Lunch, dinner. Closed Sun; Thanksgiving, children's menu. Casual attire. Reservations recommended. **$$**

★ ★ **YEN CHING.** *6601 Midlothian Tpke, Richmond (23225). Phone 804/276-7430. www.yenchingdining.com.* Chinese menu. Lunch, dinner. **$$**

Virginia Beach, VA

4 hours, 202 miles from Raleigh, NC

Population 425,257
Elevation 12 ft
Area Code 757
Information Visitor Information Center, 2100 Parks Ave, 23451; phone 757/437-4882 or toll-free 800/446-8038
Web Site www.vbfun.com

As an Atlantic Coast vacation resort, Virginia Beach consistently ranks at the top. Strolling down the boardwalk, you can relive the pleasures of your youth and enjoy the buzz of exciting entertainment, good food, and people-watching at its finest.

The area's historical sites tie Virginia Beach to the first permanent English settlement of over 400 years ago. In fact, First Landing State Park is where John Smith alighted before he went on to Jamestown. They've got museums too, including the Virginia Marine Science Museum, voted on of the top ten marine science aquariums/museums in the United States.

If you think Virginia Beach is only beach, you're missing the boat. More than 106 square miles of wetlands and water, a 3,000-acre state park, and two wildlife refuges await. Amazingly, being this close to Virginia's largest city, the natural ecological areas surrounding Virginia Beach are among the most pristine and undiscovered ecological areas along the mid-Atlantic. Even on a rainy day (and there aren't many), the wildlife, including native birds, whales, and dolphins, are close enough for you to get a good look at them up close and personal.

What to See and Do

Adam Thoroughgood House. *1636 Parish Rd, Virginia Beach (23455). Phone 757/431-4000.* (Circa 1680) One of the oldest remaining brick houses in the United States; restored, furnished; restored gardens. (Apr-Dec: Tues-Sun; rest of year: Tues-Sat; closed holidays) **$$**

Association for Research and Enlightenment. *67th St and Atlantic Ave, Virginia Beach. Phone 757/428-3588. www.are-cayce.com.* Headquarters for study and research of work of psychic Edgar Cayce. Visitor Center has bookstore, library, displays, ESP-testing machine, movie, and daily lecture. (Daily; closed Thanksgiving, Dec 25) **FREE**

Contemporary Art Center of Virginia. *2200 Parks Ave, Virginia Beach (23451). Phone 757/425-0000. www.cacv.org.* This 32,000-square-foot facility is devoted to the presentation of 20th-century art through exhibitions, education, performing arts, and special events. (Mon-Sat, Sun afternoons; closed holidays) **$$**

First Landing/Seashore State Park. *2500 Shore, Virginia Beach (23451). 5 miles N on Hwy 60 at Cape Henry. Phone 757/412-2300.* More than 2,700 acres with lagoons, cypress trees, and sand dunes. Swimming at own risk, fishing, boating (ramp); hiking, bicycle, and self-guided nature trails; picnicking, tent and trailer sites (Mar-Nov; fee), 20 cabins (open all year round). Visitor center, interpretive programs. Access for disabled to nature trail. (Daily) **$$**

Fishing. *Linkhorn Bay and Rudee Inlet, Virginia Beach.* In the Lynnhaven and Rudee Inlets for channel bass, speckled trout, spots, croakers, flounder, and whiting in season; in the Back Bay area, 18 miles S on Hwy 615, for largemouth black bass, pickerel, and perch. Pier fishing and surf casting from piers jutting into the Atlantic and piers in the Chesapeake Bay. Reef, deep-sea, and Gulf Stream fishing from charter boats, for sea bass, weakfish, flounder, cobia, bonito, tuna, marlin, false albacore, blue, and dolphin. Lake and stream fishing at Lake Smith, Lake Christine, and the inland waterways of the Chesapeake and Albemarle Canal. Crabbing for blue crabs in Lynnhaven waters, Linkhorn Bay, and Rudee Inlet. (No license or closed season for saltwater fishing.)

Francis Land House Historic Site and Gardens. *3131 Virginia Beach Blvd, Virginia Beach (23452). On the S side of the boulevard, between Rosemont Rd and Lynnhoven Pwky. Phone 757/431-4000.* Late 18th-century plantation home features period rooms, special exhibits, gardens, and museum gift shop. (Tues-Sat, also Sun afternoons; closed holidays) **$$**

Lynnhaven House. *4405 Wishart Rd, Virginia Beach (23455). Phone 757/460-1688.* (Circa 1725). This stately story-and-a-half masonry structure is a well-preserved example of 18th-century architecture and decorative arts. (June-Sept: Tues-Sun; May and Oct: weekends only) **$$**

Motor World. *700 S Birdneck Rd, Virginia Beach (23451). Phone 757/422-6419.* Park includes go-carts, arcade. Also a 36-hole miniature Shipwreck Golf Course, batting cages, and large Children's Zone. (May-early Sept, daily)

Norwegian Lady Statue. *25th St and Boardwalk, Virginia Beach.* A gift to Virginia Beach from the people of Moss, Norway. The statue commemorates the tragic wreck of the Norwegian bark *Dictator* off the shores of Virginia Beach in 1891.

Ocean Breeze Water Park. *849 General Booth Blvd, Virginia Beach (23451). Phone 757/422-4444 (recording); toll-free 800/678-9453.* "Get wet, get wild" at this Caribbean paradise with slides, wave pool, rapids, and children's water amusements (mid-May-early Sept, daily). **$$$$**

Old Cape Henry Lighthouse and Memorial Park. *Virginia Beach. On Fort Story, an active army base. 6 miles N on Hwy 60.* First US-government-built lighthouse (circa 1791).

Old Coast Guard Station. *24th St and Atlantic Ave, Virginia Beach. Phone 757/422-1587. www.oldcoast guardstation.com.* Former Coast Guard Station (1903); visual exhibits of numerous shipwecks along the Virginia coastline tell of past bravery and disaster. "The War Years" exhibit relates United States Coast Guard efforts during World War I and World War II. Photographs, ship models, artifacts. Gift shop. (Memorial Day-Sept: daily; rest of year: Tues-Sun; closed holidays) **$$**

Virginia Marine Science Museum. *717 General Booth Blvd, Virginia Beach (23451). 2 miles S of resort area. Phone 757/425-3474. www.vmsm.com.* Live animals, interactive exhibits, six-story screen, 300-seat IMAX 3-D theater. Exhibits include ocean aquarium with sharks, large fish; sea turtle aquarium; seal and other habitats; aviary; salt marsh preserve; touch tank; river room; garden. (Daily; closed Thanksgiving, Dec 25) **$$$**

Special Events

Boardwalk Art Show. Works by more than 350 artists from United States and abroad. Mid-June.

East Coast Surfing Championship. *8437 Valley Pike, Middletown (22645). Phone 830/278-2016.* Fourth weekend in Aug.

Neptune Festival. *265 Kings Grant Rd, Virginia Beach (23452).* Last two weeks in Sept.

Pungo Strawberry Festival. *916 Princess Anne Rd, Virginia Beach (23457).* Sat and Sun of Memorial Day weekend.

Virginia Saltwater Fishing Tournament. *968 S Oriole Dr, Virginia Beach (23451). Phone 757/491-5160.* The Commonwealth of Virginia sponsors this annual program. No entry fee or registration requirements; open to everyone who fishes in tournament waters and complies with tournament rules. For information contact Virginia Saltwater Fishing Tournament at above address. Mar-Dec.

Winter whale-watching boat trips. *Phone 757/437-4882.* Mon, Wed, Fri-Sun. Jan-Mar.

Limited-Service Hotels

★ **COMFORT INN.** *2800 Pacific Ave, Virginia Beach (23451). Phone 757/428-2203; toll-free 800/441-0684; fax 757/422-6043. www.choicehotels.com.* 137 rooms, 7 story. Complimentary full breakfast. Check-in 3 pm, check-out 11 am. Fitness room. Beach. Indoor pool, outdoor pool, whirlpool. **$**

★ ★ **DOUBLETREE HOTEL.** *1900 Pavilion Dr, Virginia Beach (23451). Phone 757/422-8900; toll-free 800/222-8733; fax 757/428-6948. www.doubletree.com.* Adjacent to the Virginia Beach Pavilion Convention Center and only 6 blocks from the beach, this hotel offers amenities for both leisure and business travelers. 292 rooms, 12 story. Pets accepted; fee. Check-in 3 pm, check-out 11 am. High-speed Internet access. Restaurant, bar. Fitness room. Indoor pool. Tennis. Business center. **$$**

★ ★ **RAMADA PLAZA.** *5700 Atlantic Ave, Virginia Beach (23451). Phone 757/428-7025; toll-free 800/265-3032; fax 757/428-2921. www.ramada.com.* Located on the ocean in what locals refer to as the North End, this hotel provides guests with spectacular views. Explore the beach or rent a bike, boat, or jet ski. 216 rooms,

17 story. Check-out 11 am. Restaurant, bar. Children's activity center. Fitness room. Beach. Indoor pool, outdoor pool, whirlpool. Business center. **$$**

Full-Service Hotels

★ ★ ★ **CROWNE PLAZA HOTEL VIRGINIA BEACH.** *4453 Bonney Rd, Virginia Beach (23462). Phone 757/473-1700; fax 757/552-0477.* 149 rooms, 8 story. Check-in 3 pm, check-out 11 am. High-speed Internet access, wireless Internet access. Restaurant, bar. Fitness room. Indoor pool, whirlpool. Airport transportation available. Business center. **$$**

★ ★ ★ **FOUNDERS INN.** *5641 Indian River Rd, Virginia Beach (23464). Phone 757/424-5511; toll-free 800/926-4466; fax 757/366-0613. www.foundersinn.com.* Sitting on 26 manicured acres, this Georgian-style inn has a southern-colonial decor and a unique combination of intimate charm and extensive meeting space. 240 rooms. Check-in 4 pm, check-out noon. High-speed Internet access. Two restaurants, bar. Children's activity center. Fitness room, fitness classes available. Indoor pool, outdoor pool. Tennis. Airport transportation available. Business center. **$**

★ ★ **HOLIDAY INN.** *2607 Atlantic Ave, Virginia Beach (23451). Phone 757/491-6900; toll-free 800/810-2400; fax 757/491-2125. www.va-beach.com/surfside.* 143 rooms, 10 story. Check-in 4 pm, check-out 11 am. Restaurant, bar. Fitness room. Beach. Indoor pool, whirlpool. **$$**

Restaurants

★ ★ **ALDO'S.** *1860 Laskin Rd, Virginia Beach (23454). Phone 757/491-1111; fax 757/491-0597. www.gohamptonroad.com.* Italian menu. Lunch, dinner. Closed Thanksgiving, Dec 25. Bar. Outdoor seating. **$$**

★ ★ **BLUE PETE'S SEAFOOD AND STEAK.** *1400 N Muddy Creek Rd, Virginia Beach (23456). Phone 757/426-2005; fax 757/721-3792.* Seafood menu. Dinner. Closed Mon. Bar. Children's menu. Outdoor seating. **$$$**

★ ★ **COASTAL GRILL.** *1427 N Great Neck Rd, Virginia Beach (23454). Phone 757/496-3348.*

www.coastalgrill.com. Dinner. Closed holidays. Bar. Children's menu. **$$**

★ **CUISINE AND COMPANY.** *3004 Pacific Ave, Virginia Beach (23451). Phone 757/428-6700; fax 757/428-0138. www.cuisineandcompany.com.* California menu. Breakfast, lunch, dinner. Closed Jan 1, Thanksgiving, Dec 25. **$**

★ ★ **DUCK-IN RESTAURANT AND GAZEBO.** *3324 Shore Dr, Virginia Beach (23451). Phone 757/481-0201; fax 757/481-9780. www.duck-in.com.* Where can you find the best place in Virginia Beach to eat and drink simply and cheaply and then kick back? Try this eatery. For beachcombers looking for a watering hole on the shore, this is the top pick. Try the fried popcorn shrimp and other seafood entrées, made simple and fresh. Seafood menu. Lunch, dinner. Children's menu. **$$**

★ ★ **IL GIARDINO.** *910 Atlantic Ave, Virginia Beach (23451). Phone 757/422-6464; fax 757/422-1175. www.ilgiardino.com.* Italian menu. Dinner. Closed Thanksgiving, Dec 25. Bar. Children's menu. Valet parking. Outdoor seating. **$$**

★ ★ **INLET.** *3319 Shore Dr, Virginia Beach (23451). Phone 757/481-7300; fax 757/481-0625. www.theinletrestaurant.com.* On Lynnhaven Inlet; 2-story saltwater aquarium in dining area. Seafood menu. Lunch, dinner, Sun brunch. Bar. Children's menu. Valet parking. Outdoor seating. Lobster tank. **$$**

★ ★ **THE LIGHTHOUSE.** *1st St and Atlantic Ave, Virginia Beach (23451). Phone 757/428-7974; fax 757/422-9914. www.thelighthouseva.com.* Seafood menu. Lunch, dinner, brunch. Bar. Children's menu. **$$**

★ ★ **LUCKY STAR.** *1608 Pleasure House Rd, Virginia Beach (23455). Phone 757/363-8410; fax 757/460-4714.* Dinner. Closed Sun; holidays. Bar. Reservations recommended. **$$**

★ ★ **LYNNHAVEN FISH HOUSE.** *2350 Starfish Rd, Virginia Beach (23451). Phone 757/481-0003; fax 757/481-3474. www.lynnhavenfishhouse.net.* Lobster tank. On the Lynnhaven fishing pier. Seafood menu. Lunch, dinner. Closed Thanksgiving, Dec 25. Bar. Children's menu. Valet parking. **$$**

★ **PUNGO GRILL.** *1785 Princess Anne Rd, Virginia Beach (23456). Phone 757/426-6655.* Dining room on enclosed porch of 1919 Aladdin house. American menu. Lunch, dinner. Closed Mon; Thanksgiving, Dec 24-25; also Jan-Feb. Bar. Children's menu. Outdoor seating. **$$**

★ ★ **RUDEE'S.** *227 Mediterranean Ave, Virginia Beach (23451). Phone 757/425-1777; fax 757/425-5107. www.rudees.com.* On inlet; transient slips available for boats. Seafood, steak menu. Lunch, dinner, Sun brunch. Closed Thanksgiving, Dec 25. Bar. Children's menu. Valet parking. Outdoor seating. **$$$**

South Carolina

In South Carolina, the modern age has neither masked the romance of the Old South nor overshadowed the powerful events of colonial and Confederate times. This state's turbulent and romantic history tells a story that remains deeply ingrained in the history of the United States.

Spanish explorers made the first attempt to settle in present-day South Carolina in 1526, less than 35 years after the Europeans discovered America. A severe winter, hostile natives, and disease proved too much for the Spanish to overcome, and the settlement was abandoned. In 1562, a group of French Huguenots, led by Jean Ribaut, landed near the site of present-day Parris Island Marine Corps Base. The French colony might have been a success, had Ribaut's return to the colony from business in France not been delayed. The remaining colonists, fearing they had been abandoned, built a craft and sailed for home. Light winds stranded their boat at sea, and they faced the danger of starvation until a passing English ship rescued them.

The task of settlement fell to the English, whose challenge to Spanish control of the New World eventually met with success. A land grant from England's King Charles II gave the Carolinas to eight English noblemen (still known today as the "Lords Proprietors"). In 1670, the English arrived at Albemarle Point and established Charles Towne, the first successful European settlement in the Carolinas.

During the American Revolution, almost 200 battles and skirmishes were fought in South Carolina. The first overt act of revolution occurred at Fort Charlotte on July 12, 1775; this was the first British property seized by American Revolutionary

Population: 3,497,800

Area: 30,207 square miles

Elevation: 0-3,560 feet

Peak: Sassafras Mountain (Pickens County)

Entered Union: Eighth of original 13 states (May 23, 1788)

Capital: Columbia

Motto: Prepared in Mind and Resources; While I Breathe, I Hope

Nickname: Palmetto State

Flower: Carolina Yellow Jessamine

Bird: Carolina Wren

Tree: Palmetto

Fair: October in Columbia

Time Zone: Eastern

Web Site: www.travelsc.com

forces. On December 20, 1860, South Carolina became the first state to secede from the Union. The initial clash of the Civil War also occurred on South Carolina soil; the bombardment of Fort Sumter in 1861 resulted in its seizure by Confederate forces, who maintained possession until the evacuation of Charleston in 1865. Bloodied, impoverished, and blackened by the fires of General Sherman's "March to the Sea," South Carolina emerged from the difficult Reconstruction days and was readmitted to the Union in 1868.

For most of the period since the Civil War, South Carolina has had economic problems, but in recent years these difficulties have eased as industry has been attracted by hospitable communities and favorable tax rates. From town to town throughout the state, diversified industries have brought greater prosperity with them. South Carolina is a major producer of tabacco, cotton, pine lumber, corn, oats, sweet potatoes, soybeans, peanuts, peaches, melons, beef cattle, and hogs. Power projects have been created by damming the Santee, Saluda,

Calendar Highlights

MARCH

Triple Crown *(Aiken). For more information, contact the Aiken Chamber of Commerce, Phone 803/641-1111. Three events: trials (Aiken Training Track), steeplechase (Clark Field), harness race (Aiken Mile Track).*

APRIL

Family Circle Magazine Cup Tennis Tournament *(Hilton Head Island). Sea Pines Racquet Club. Phone 843/534-2400 or toll-free 800/677-2293.*

MAY

Freedom Weekend Aloft *(Greenville). Phone 864/232-3700. More than 200 balloonists compete.*

Spoleto Festival USA *(Charleston). Phone 843/722-2764. Internationally acclaimed counterpart to the arts festival in Spoleto, Italy, founded by Gian Carlo Menotti; includes opera, ballet, dance, visual arts, theater, chamber music, jazz, symphonic, and choral performances and much more. Piccolo Spoleto, running concurrent with the main festival, has performances by local and regional artists.*

JUNE

Sun Fun Festival *(Myrtle Beach). Contact the Chamber of Commerce, phone 843/626-7444 or toll-free 800/356-3016. More than 60 seaside entertainment events, including parades.*

SEPTEMBER

Hilton Head Island Celebrity Golf Tournament *(Hilton Head Island). Palmetto Hall, Indigo Run, and Sea Pines Plantation. Phone 843/842-7711.*

Southern 500 *(Darlington). Darlington Raceway. For tickets, phone 843/395-8499. 500-mile stock car classic; beauty pageant; "Southern 500" Festival parade; golf tournament. Preceded by two days of trials.*

OCTOBER

Colonial Cup International Steeplechase *(Camden). Springdale Race Course. Phone 803/432-6513.*

Fall Tour of Homes and Gardens *(Beaufort). Contact the Historic Beaufort Foundation, phone 843/524-3163 or toll-free 800/638-3525.*

South Carolina State Fair *(Columbia). Fairgrounds. Phone 803/799-3387. Agricultural, floral, home, craft, livestock, and commercial exhibits. Entertainment, shows, carnival.*

Savannah, and other rivers. Four atomic energy plants provide commercial energy. Tourism, the state's second-largest industry, continues to grow.

When to Go/Climate

South Carolina enjoys a moderate climate, making it an attractive all-year resort. The cool upland western area merges into a subtropical seacoast. Summers, however, especially in the low country and along the coast, can be uncomfortably hot and humid. The barrier islands and up-country elevations provide summer havens from the blistering heat. Early spring and late fall are good times to visit, with comfortable temperatures and moderate rainfall.

AVERAGE HIGH/LOW TEMPERATURES (° F)

Charleston

Jan 56/41	**May** 80/66	**Sept** 83/71
Feb 59/43	**June** 85/72	**Oct** 75/61
Mar 65/50	**July** 88/75	**Nov** 67/52
Apr 73/58	**Aug** 87/75	**Dec** 60/45

Greenville

Jan 50/30	**May** 80/56	**Sept** 81/61
Feb 54/32	**June** 86/64	**Oct** 72/49
Mar 64/40	**July** 88/68	**Nov** 63/41
Apr 72/48	**Aug** 87/67	**Dec** 53/33

TRAVELING THE LOW COUNTRY

South Carolina's Atlantic coastline stretches from developed beaches at the North Carolina border to the "low country" at the Georgia border, a region of remote marshlands and subtropical barrier islands of palmetto, live oak, and Spanish moss. The 100 miles between Charleston and Savannah form the heart of the low country.

Head west from Charleston along Highway 17 south, the old Atlantic Coast Highway, a well-used local route. Take every opportunity to detour east to remote islands for a close look at the distinct coastal ecology. The first side trip takes you 24 miles south from Highway 17 along Highway 174 to Edisto Beach. This island is developed as a low-key beach town with vacation homes, restaurants, and lodgings. Stay at the beachfront campground or at cozy state park cabins a short drive from the wide white-sand beach. Return to Highway 17 and continue south 22 miles to the Highway 21 turnoff to Beaufort, 18 miles east. A modest, quiet village, Beaufort serves as the unofficial capital of the low country. Downtown, tidy Victorian homes and a small set of storefronts overlook a beautiful marshland landscape. Several restaurants and a shoreline path give visitors a chance to enjoy the view.

Cross the marsh on the Highway 21 bridge east to St. Helena Island. Less than 10 miles in, a central village of sorts holds a restaurant, gas station, and the Penn Center, which tells the story of the island's history. In 1861, federal troops took St. Helena Island, freeing the 10,000 slaves who worked local cotton plantations. The next year, women religious leaders from Philadelphia started the Penn Center as one of the first schools for African Americans in the nation. The museum contains exhibits about the teachers, students, and the Sea Islander community.

Continue beyond St. Helena Island to Hunting Island. Stop at the impeccable white-sand beaches of Hunting Island State Park to swim, sunbathe, fish, or go crabbing. The beachfront campground is a great place to spend the night.

Retrace your path to return to Beaufort, but instead of heading back to Highway 17, take Highway 170 southeast from Beaufort through Chelsea to Highway 278 south. This route juts east to Hilton Head Island, named after English sea captain William Hilton, who explored the island in 1664. Before the Civil War, the island was rich in Sea Island cotton, rice, and indigo. Now it's rich with vacationers looking for recreation for the whole family: not only sand and surf, but also two dozen golf courses, hundreds of tennis courts, horseback riding, and all kinds of water sports. From the southern tip of Hilton Head Island, a passenger ferry makes the trip over to neighboring Daufuskie Island, accessible only by boat. Daufuskie is the home of Gullah community, descended from African Americans so isolated on these islands that they were able to maintain many more African traditions than more assimilated mainlanders.

Return west on Highway 278 to Highway 170 to connect back up with Highway 17, the old Atlantic Coast Highway, which crosses the state line at the Savannah River. Proceed into Savannah to visit a historic district that rivals Charleston's. You'll have a wonderful selection of places to eat and stay overnight. When you're ready to return to Charleston, you may prefer to head up I-95 north as a speedy alternative, or you can retrace your steps through the low country. **(Approximately 100 miles)**

Parks and Recreation

Water-related activities, hiking, various other sports, picnicking, and visitor centers, as well as camping, are available in many of South Carolina's state parks. Cabins are located at Barnwell, Cheraw, Devils Fork, Dreher Island, Edisto Beach, Givhans Ferry, Hickory Knob Resort, Hunting Island, Keowee-Toxaway, Myrtle Beach, Oconee, Poinsett, Santee, and Table Rock. No pets are allowed in cabins. Cabin res-ervations can be made at individual parks. Camping: 14-day maximum; reservations accepted only at Calhoun Falls, Devils Fork, Dreher Island, Edisto Beach, Hunting Island, Huntington Beach, Lake Hartwell, Myrtle Beach, Oconee, Santee, and Table Rock; $10-$23/night; pets on leash only. Not all state parks are open every day; hours of operation also vary. Contact the Columbia office or the individual park before making your final trip plans. Fees subject to change. For cabin rates and further information, contact the

Department of Parks, Recreation, and Tourism, Edgar A. Brown Building, 1205 Pendleton St, Columbia 29201; phone 803/734-0156 or toll-free 888/887-2757.

FISHING AND HUNTING

There is no closed fishing season; well-stocked lakes and rivers are close at hand in all parts of the state. Surf casting and deep-sea fishing can be enjoyed all along the Atlantic shore. Mountain streams offer trout fishing. Nonresident freshwater license: $35; seven-day nonresident license: $11. Saltwater stamp: $5.50. No license or permit is required for children under 16. Fees are subject to change.

Quail, dove, wild turkey, white-tailed deer, rabbit, squirrel, and fox are all legal quarry. Nonresident annual license: $100; 10-day (consecutive) license: $50; three-day (consecutive) license: $25; wildlife management area permit: $76. Nonresident big game permit for deer, turkey, and bear: $89. State duck stamp: $5.50. Fees are subject to change. For further hunting and fishing information, contact the South Carolina Department of Natural Resources, PO Box 167, Columbia 29202; phone 803/734-3888 (general information) or 803/734-3886 (wildlife and freshwater fisheries).

Driving Information

Safety belts are mandatory for all persons anywhere in a vehicle. Children must be in approved safety seats or wear safety belts. For more information phone 803/737-8340.

INTERSTATE HIGHWAY SYSTEM

The following alphabetical listing of South Carolina towns listed in this book shows that these cities are within 10 miles of the indicated interstate highways. Check a highway map for the nearest exit.

Highway Number	Cities/Towns within 10 Miles
Interstate 20	Aiken, Camden, Columbia, Darlington, Florence.
Interstate 26	Charleston, Clinton, Columbia, Newberry, Orangeburg, Spartanburg.
Interstate 77	Columbia, Rock Hill.
Interstate 85	Anderson, Clemson, Gaffney, Greenville, Spartanburg.
Interstate 95	Darlington, Dillon, Florence, Hardeeville, Santee, Walterboro.

Additional Visitor Information

For additional information about South Carolina, contact the Department of Parks, Recreation, and Tourism, 1205 Pendleton St, Columbia 29201; phone 803/734-0122 or toll-free 888/727-6453.

There are 10 travel information centers in South Carolina; visitors will find the information provided at these stops useful for planning travel and making lodging reservations in the state. Their locations are at the eastern end of the state, on I-95 on the SC/NC border; in the eastern coastal region on Hwy 17 on the SC/NC border; in the southern section on Hwy 301 on the SC/GA border and on I-95 on the SC/GA border; midstate on the southbound side of I-95 near Santee; on the southwestern side on I-20 on the SC/GA border; in the western part of the state on I-85 on the SC/GA border; in the northwestern part of the state, centers are located on I-85 on the SC/NC border and on I-26 on the SC/NC border; in the northern part of the state on I-77 on the SC/NC border and at the State House Tour and Information Center located in Columbia.

Aiken (D-3)

See also Allendale, Orangeburg

Founded 1834
Population 25,337
Elevation 476 ft
Area Code 803
Information Chamber of Commerce, 121 Richland Ave E, PO Box 892, 29802; phone 803/641-1111
Web Site www.goaiken.com

Aiken is a popular social and sports center in the winter months, providing flat-racing training, steeplechase and harness racing, polo, fox hunts, drag hunts, tennis, and golf. The University of South Carolina-Aiken is located here.

What to See and Do

Aiken County Historical Museum. *433 Newberry St SW, Aiken. Phone 803/642-2015.* Period room settings and displays in late-1800s home. Log cabin (1808) and one-room schoolhouse (1890) on grounds. Special features include an archaeology exhibit and a 1950s drug store. Museum store. (Tues-Fri, also Sat-Sun afternoons; closed holidays) **DONATION**

Aiken State Park. *1145 State Park Rd, Aiken (29856). 16 miles E on unnumbered road between Hwy 78 and Hwy 4. Phone 803/649-2857.* Approximately 1,000 acres on the South Edisto River. Swimming, fishing, boating (rentals). Nature trail. Picnicking (shelters), playground. Camping (hook-ups, dump station).

Hopeland Gardens. *Whiskey Rd and Dupree Pl, Aiken. Phone 803/642-7630.* A 14-acre public garden on a former estate; terraces, reflecting pools, continuous blooms; sculptures. Garden trail for the visually impaired. Summer concert series (May-Aug, Mon evenings). (Daily) **FREE** Also here is

> **Thoroughbred Racing Hall of Fame.** *Whiskey Rd and Dupree Pl, Aiken. Phone 803/642-7630.* Enshrinement of champion horses trained and wintered in Aiken. (Oct-May, Tues-Sun) **FREE**

Redcliffe. *181 Redcliffe Rd, Beech Island (29842). 15 miles SE off Hwy 278, near Beech Island. Phone 803/827-1473.* On 350 acres. Built in the 1850s by James Henry Hammond. Greek Revival mansion furnished with family pieces, Southern antiques, art collection, historic documents, and books. Picnic area. (Thurs-Mon) **$**

Special Events

Lobster Race. *Phone 803/648-4981.* Aiken restaurants provide seafood fare. Festivities include lobster races, beach music, and other activities. May.

Polo games. *Whitney Field, Aiken.* Guest are invited to the wide-open spaces (10-football fields worth), fresh air, and the beauty and excitement of a polo match; and they mingle in the clubhouse while stomping divots at halftime. Sun afternoons. Feb-July and Sept-Nov.

Triple Crown. Three events: trials (Aiken Training Track), steeplechase (Clark Field), harness race (Aiken Mile Track). Three consecutive Sat in Mar.

Full-Service Hotel

★ ★ ★ **THE WILLCOX.** *100 Colleton Ave SE, Aiken (29801). Phone 803/648-1898; fax 803/648-6664.* The Willcox perfectly captures the romance and refinement of the South. This distinguished mansion set on 2,000 acres of the Hitchcock Woods shares the best of South Carolina's horse country with lucky guests. From the rocking chairs on the large porch to the afternoon tea, everything about The Willcox oozes laid-back sophistication. Warm and welcoming, the guest rooms and suites are gloriously decorated with antiques, Oriental rugs, and four-poster beds, and most accommodations have working fireplaces. Dining is equally exceptional here, where great Southern breakfasts signal the arrival of morning and evenings are spent savoring the elegant riffs on Southern favorites. If the gentle pace and small-town charm haven't calmed frayed nerves, the European-style spa certainly will. 22 rooms, 3 story. Pets accepted, some restrictions; fee. Complimentary full breakfast. Check-in 3 pm, check-out noon. Restaurant. Fitness room, spa. **$$$**

Restaurant

★ ★ ★ **SEEGER'S AT THE WILLCOX.** *100 Colleton Ave, Aiken (29801). Phone 803/648-1898. www.thewillcox.com.* Chef Guenter Seeger of Seeger's in Atlanta brings his highly acclaimed cooking to the Willcox, a new luxury resort in rural Aiken, South Carolina, 20 miles east of Georgia's golf-centric Augusta and home to high society and the horse-and-hound set for a century. The German-born, French-trained Seeger marries continental culinary skills to regional foodstuffs, resulting in dishes such as Carolina trout with apples and horseradish cream, sweet potato gnocchi served with shaved pecans, and pecan pie paired with ginger ice cream. Rooms at the refined hotel, which start at $1,000, include dinner in the elegant, candlelit restaurant. Fortunately for the unendowed, the kitchen also serves the public at a considerable savings. American menu. Lunch, dinner. Bar. Business casual attire. Reservations recommended. Valet parking. **$$$**

Allendale (E-4)

See also Aiken, Orangeburg, Walterboro

Population 4,052
Elevation 191 ft
Area Code 803
Zip 29810
Information Chamber of Commerce, PO Box 517; phone 803/584-0082
Web Site www.allendalecounty.com

Having moved 6 miles in 1872 to its present site to be on the old Port Royal Railroad line, Allendale is an agricultural town with access to the lush hunting and fishing areas of the Savannah River Valley. More than 130 commercial farms with an average size in excess of 1,000 acres—the largest in the state—surround the town.

What to See and Do

Barnwell State Park. *223 State Park Rd, Blackville. 17 miles N on Hwy 278 to Barnwell, then 7 miles N on Hwy 3. Phone 803/284-2212.* Approximately 300 acres preserved in their natural state with an abundance of trees and flowers. Boating (rentals); fishing. Nature trails. Picnicking (shelters), barbecue pit, playground. Camping, cabins.

Rivers Bridge State Historic Site. *15 miles E off Hwy 641. Phone 803/267-3675.* Approximately 400 acres on the site of a Civil War skirmish. River fishing. Nature trails. Picnicking (shelter), recreation building (rentals). Camping (hook-ups, dump station).

Anderson (C-2)

See also Clemson, Greenville, Greenwood

Founded 1826
Population 25,514
Elevation 770 ft
Area Code 864
Information Anderson Area Chamber of Commerce, 706 E Greenville St, PO Box 1568, 29622; phone 864/226-3454
Web Site www.andersonscchamber.com

Textile mills and fiberglass plants lead an array of diversified industries that team with the products of the surrounding farmland to make Anderson a lively

business center. The town was created as the seat of Anderson County; both were named for General Robert Anderson, who fought in the Revolutionary War.

What to See and Do

Agricultural Museum. *History Ln and Hwy 76, Anderson (29670). Phone 864/646-3782.* Antique farming equipment, tools, pre-Eli Whitney cotton gin. (By appointment) **FREE**

Hartwell Dam and Lake. *5625 Anderson Hwy, Hartwell (30643). W and S of town via Hwy 29. Phone 706/376-4788; toll-free 888/893-0678.* This 56,000-acre reservoir with a 962-mile shoreline was created by a dam on the Savannah River. Swimming, water-skiing, boating (81 ramps, five marinas), fishing. Picnicking (shelters). Camping (Mar-Nov; some all year; hook-ups, dump station). Fee for some activities. On the lake are

  Lake Hartwell State Park. *19138 A S Hwy 11, Anderson (29643). S on I-85 exit 1. Phone 864/972-3352.* Located on 680 acres along Lake Hartwell. Swimming, fishing, boating (ramps). Nature trail. Picnicking (shelter), playground, store. Camping (hook-ups, dump station), laundry. (Daily)

  Sadlers Creek State Park. *940 Sadlers Creek Park Rd, Anderson (29626). 13 miles SW off I-85 and Hwy 187. Phone 864/226-8950.* On 395 acres. Lake fishing, boating (ramps). Nature trails. Picnicking (shelters), playground. Camping (hook-ups, dump station). (Daily)

"The Old Reformer." *Main and Whitner sts, Anderson. In front of the courthouse.* Cannon used by both British and Americans during the Revolution; was fired in 1860, when the Ordinance of Secession was signed.

Pendleton Historic District and Tourism. *7 miles NW of I-85 off Hwy 76. Phone 846/646-3782 (tour information).* Settled in 1790, this town was the seat of what is now Anderson, Oconee, and Pickens counties. There are self-guided tours (free), 2 1/2-hour guided group tours (by appointment, fee) or auto/walking tape tours (cassette, also in French; fee) of 45 historic homes and buildings. For information, contact the Pendleton District Historical and Recreational Commission, 125 E Queen St, PO Box 565. (Mon-Fri; closed holidays). Research library, Hunter's Store (circa 1850) across from village green; arts and crafts shop; visitor center (Mon-Fri; closed holidays). On Pendleton Town Square are

Historic homes. *Phone 864/646-3782.* Two of the many beautiful homes in the area are Ashtabula and Woodburn. (Apr-Oct, Sun; also by appointment) **$$**

Pendleton Farmers' Society Building. (1826) Begun as the courthouse, bought and completed by the Farmers' Society. Believed to be the oldest Farmers' Society building in America in continuous use.

Special Event

Anderson County Fair. *431 Williamston Rd, Anderson (29621). www.andersoncountyfair.com.* Circus, car derby, entertainment, and carnival rides are some of the activities found at this county fair. Mid-Oct.

Beaufort (F-4)

See also Charleston, Hardeeville, Hilton Head Island, Kiawah Island, Walterboro

Founded 1710
Population 12,950
Elevation 11 ft
Area Code 843
Zip 29902
Information Greater Beaufort Chamber of Commerce, 1106 Carteret St, PO Box 910, 29901-0910; phone 843/524-3163
Web Site www.beaufortsc.org

The atmosphere of antebellum days is preserved in this old town's gracious houses and churches. Second oldest town in the state, Beaufort (BEW-fort) looks to the sea from Port Royal Island, one of 64 islands that comprise the county. Tourism and the military are major sources of income in this community.

Spanish explorers first noted the harbor in 1514-1515. In 1526, colonists from Spain made an unsuccessful attempt to settle the area. In 1562, a group of Frenchmen established the first Protestant colony on the continent, which also failed. English and Scottish attempts followed, with success finally coming when the present city was laid out and named for the Duke of Beaufort. The town was almost completely destroyed by Native Americans in 1715, captured by the British in the Revolution, and menaced by British cannons in 1812. Nearly the entire population evacuated Beaufort when it was captured by Northern troops during the Civil War.

What to See and Do

Beaufort Museum. *703 Craven St, Beaufort.* In the Beaufort Arsenal 1795. Collections of antique guns, fossils, paintings, arrowheads, and Civil War relics. (Mon-Tues, Thurs-Sat; closed holidays) **$**

Hunting Island State Park. *2555 Sea Island Pkwy, Beaufort (29920).* 16 miles SE on Hwy 21. Phone 843/838-2011. A 5,000-acre barrier island in a semi-tropical setting; beaches, forest, marshes; lighthouse. Swimming, ocean fishing. Nature trails. Picnicking (shelters), playground, boardwalk; concession. Camping (hook-ups, dump station), cabins. Recreation and nature programs. **$**

John Mark Verdier House Museum. *801 Bay St, Beaufort.* Phone 843/524-6334. (Circa 1790) Federal period house once known as the Lafayette Building; the Marquis de Lafayette is said to have spoken here from the piazza in 1825. (Tues-Sat; closed Thanksgiving, Dec 25)

Marine Corps Air Station. *Boundary St, Beaufort.* Phone 843/522-7201. Home of Marine Aircraft Groups MACS-5, MWSS-273, MALS-31, and CSSD-23. Windshield tours available.

National Cemetery. *Boundary St, Beaufort.* (1863) More than 11,000 interments, including Confederate and Union soldiers.

Parris Island. *10 miles S.* Phone 843/525-3650. Famous US Marine Corps Recruit Depot. Visitor center in Building 283; museum in War Memorial Building. Ribaut Monument is a memorial to Jean Ribaut, French Huguenot founder of Charlesfort (1562); Iwo Jima monument; monument to Spanish settlement of Santa Elena (1521).

St. Helena's Episcopal Church. *507 Newcastle St, Beaufort.* At North St. Phone 843/522-1712. (1712) Still in use; tombstones from surrounding burial ground became operating tables when the church was used as a hospital during the Civil War. Silver Communion set in church was donated in 1734 by Captain John Bull in memory of his wife, who was captured by Native Americans. (Mon-Sat)

US Naval Hospital. *4 miles S on Hwy 802, between Beaufort and Port Royal, an early French settlement.* On the grounds are ruins of Fort Frederick (1731), one of the largest "tabby" (cement and oyster shell) forts in the United States.

Special Events

Beaufort Shrimp Festival. *1106 Carteret St, Beaufort. Phone 843/524-3163.* Waterfront. Bridge Run, shrimp recipe tastings, frogmore stew contest, Bless'en de Fleet. Mid-Oct.

Beaufort Water Festival. *912 8th St, Beaufort. Along the waterfront at the harbor. Phone 843/524-0600.* Parade, water show, boat races, concerts, dance. Mid-July.

Fall Tour of Homes and Gardens. *208 Scott St, Beaufort. Phone 843/524-6334.* Owners of historic mansions and plantations graciously welcome visitors on tours. Late Oct.

Limited-Service Hotel

★ **BEST WESTERN SEA ISLAND INN.** *1015 Bay St, Beaufort (29902). Phone 843/522-2090; fax 843/521-4858. www.bestwestern.com.* 43 rooms, 2 story. Complimentary continental breakfast. Check-in 3 pm, check-out 11 am. Fitness room. Outdoor pool. **$**

Full-Service Inns

★ ★ **BEAUFORT INN.** *809 Port Republic St, Beaufort (29902). Phone 843/521-9000; fax 843/521-9500. www.beaufortinn.com.* Built in 1897, this romantic low country inn offers rooms; suites; and a private, two-bedroom cottage, all including a full breakfast and afternoon tea. The dining room offers seasonal, plantation-style cuisine and an extensive wine list. 21 rooms, 3 story. Children over 8 years in the inn only. Complimentary full breakfast. Check-in 3 pm, check-out 11 am. Restaurant. **$$$**

★ ★ ★ **THE RHETT HOUSE INN.** *1009 Craven St, Beaufort (29902). Phone 843/524-9030; toll-free 888/480-9530; fax 843/524-1310. www.rhetthouseinn.com.* Travelers take a step back in time while visiting Beaufort, where stately homes and massive oaks draped in Spanish moss capture the essence of the Old South. One block from the Intracoastal Waterway, The Rhett House Inn is Beaufort's best lodging. With its gracious manner and country charm, this plantation home, which dates back to 1820, opens its arms to visitors. The guest rooms have a distinctive allure, with floral fabrics, fireplaces,

four-poster beds, and antiques. Oriental rugs grace the hardwood floors in this quintessentially low country home. Breakfast convinces guests to rise early for pancakes, French toast, and traditional Southern grits. Visitors succumb to the region's unhurried rhythms on the verandah, where afternoons are spent sipping tea and nibbling freshly baked cookies or brownies, and cool evenings are spent relaxing in the wicker chairs and enjoying cocktails and hors d'oeuvres. 17 rooms, 3 story. Children over 5 years only. Complimentary continental breakfast. Check-in 3 pm, check-out 11 am. **$$**

Restaurants

★ ★ **THE BANK GRILL & BAR.** *926 Bay St, Beaufort (29902). Phone 843/522-8831.* Seafood, steak menu. Lunch, dinner. Closed Thanksgiving, Dec 25; also Super Bowl Sun. Bar. Children's menu. Casual attire. Outdoor seating. **$$**

★ ★ **BEAUFORT INN.** *809 Port Republic St, Beaufort (29902). Phone 843/521-9000; fax 843/521-9500. www.beaufortinn.com.* The elegant décor of this restaurant makes for a wonderful dining experience. Southern menu. Breakfast, dinner, Sun brunch. Closed Dec 25. Bar. Casual attire. Outdoor seating. **$$$**

★ ★ **BISTRO 205.** *205 W St, Beaufort (29902). Phone 843/524-4994.* French menu. Dinner. Closed Sun; Memorial Day, Labor Day, Dec 24-25. Bar. Casual attire. Outdoor seating. **$$**

★ ★ **BRITISH OPEN PUB OF BEAUFORT.** *8 Waveland Cat Island, Beaufort (29920). Phone 843/524-4653.* American menu. Lunch, dinner. Closed Mon; Dec 25. Bar. Casual attire. Outdoor seating. **$$**

★ ★ **PLUMS.** *904 1/2 Bay St, Beaufort (29402). Phone 843/525-1946.* American menu. Lunch, dinner. Closed Jan 1, Thanksgiving, Dec 25. Bar. Children's menu. Casual attire. Outdoor seating. **$$**

Bennettsville (C-6)

See also Cheraw, Darlington, Dillon, Florence, Hartsville

Founded 1819
Population 9,425
Elevation 150 ft
Area Code 803
Zip 29512
Information Marlboro County Chamber of

Commerce, 300 W Main St, PO Box 458; phone 803/479-3941
Web Site www.marlborocountysc.org

Near the geographic center of the Carolinas, Bennettsville radiates highway spokes in every direction. Founded by Welsh settlers, and now the seat of Marlboro County, it has diversified industry including paper and electrical products, textiles, and farm equipment. Agriculture is still important; cotton is the leading crop.

What to See and Do

Jennings-Brown House Restoration. *119 S Marlboro St, Bennettsville.* (1826) Served as headquarters for Union troops when Bennettsville was captured in 1865. The restored house is furnished with antiques predating 1860. (Mon-Fri, also by appointment; closed holidays) **$**

Lake Wallace. *At N edge of city, off Country Club Dr.* A 500-acre lake with separate sections for swimming (June-Labor Day), water-skiing, fishing, and boating. Waterfowl refuge.

Camden (D-5)

See also Cheraw, Columbia, Hartsville, Sumter

Settled 1732
Population 6,682
Elevation 213 ft
Area Code 803
Zip 29020
Information Kershaw County Chamber of Commerce and Visitor Center, 724 S Broad St, PO Box 605; phone 803/432-2525 or toll-free 800/968-4037
Web Site www.camden-sc.org

The oldest inland town in the state, Camden was named after Lord Camden, defender of colonial rights. During the Revolution, General Cornwallis occupied Camden and made it the principal British garrison in the state and the interior command post for the South. Although several battles were fought in and near the town, including the Battle of Camden, the town was never recaptured by the Americans. Instead, it was evacuated and burned by the British in 1781. Camden contributed six generals to the Confederate cause and served as a storehouse, a hospital for the wounded, and a haven of refuge until captured by General Sherman in 1865.

Today, Camden is famous for its history and equestrian sports—horseback riding, horse shows, hunt meets, polo, and steeplechase races. There are 200 miles of bridle paths in the area and three race tracks; Springdale Course is an extremely difficult and exciting steeplechase run.

What to See and Do

Bethesda Presbyterian Church. *502 DeKalb St, Camden. On Hwy 1.* (1820) Called House of Five Porches; steeple in rear. Designed by the architect of the Washington Monument, Robert Mills; the church is considered a masterpiece. (Mon-Sat) In front of the church is

> **DeKalb Monument.** German-born hero of Battle of Camden is buried here; the monument consists of modest shaft with a base of 24 granite blocks, one for each state in the Union at that time. General Lafayette laid the cornerstone on March 9, 1825.

Camden Antique District. *King, DeKalb, Campbell, and Fair sts, 724 Broad St, Camden. Phone 803/432-2525.* Offers all varieties of antiques in 13 stores, some housing over 35 dealers. (Daily; closed holidays)

Historic Camden Revolutionary War Site. *(Hwy 521 S), 222 S Broad St, Camden (29020). Phone 803/432-9841. www.camden-sc.org.* Archaeological site of South Carolina's oldest inland town. Visitor area includes two early 19th-century log cabins and a restored 18th-century townhouse. Trails lead to the reconstructed foundation of a pre-Revolutionary War powder magazine, Kershaw-Cornwallis House, and two reconstructed British fortifications. Picnicking, nature trail, historical film. The site of the Battle of Camden, a National Historic Landmark, lies 5 miles north of town. Self-guided and guided tours (Tues-Sun). (See SPECIAL EVENTS) (Daily; closed holidays) **$**

Lake Wateree State Recreation Area. *881 State Park Rd, Camden (29810). S on Hwy 1, E on Hwy 34, then N on Hwy 21 to Hwy 41, continue W. Phone 803/482-6401.* Approximately 200 acres. Fishing, boating (ramp), bait shop. Nature trail. Picnicking, store. Camping (hook-ups, dump station).

N. R. Goodale State Park. *650 Park Rd, Camden (29020). 2 miles NW off Hwy 1 on Old Wire Rd. Phone 803/432-2772.* Approximately 763 acres. Lake swimming, boating (rentals), fishing. Nine-hole golf course. Picnicking (shelters), recreation building.

Quaker Cemetery. *Broad and Meeting sts, SW edge of town.* Buried here are Richard Kirkland, who gained fame in the Battle of Marye's Hill by risking death to take water to dying Union troops; two of the three residents of the county who won Congressional Medals of Honor prior to World War II; and Dr. George Todd, brother-in-law of Abraham Lincoln.

Rectory Square. *Chesnut and Lyttleton sts, Camden.* Pantheon; six columns serve as a memorial to Camden's six generals of the Confederacy.

Special Events

Carolina Cup Steeplechase. *Springdale Race Course, 200 Knights Hill Rd, Camden. Phone 803/432-6513.* The annual 'rites of spring' draws over 70,000 fans to enjoy the sport of steeplechase horse racing amid a flurry of spring fashions and elaborate tailgate parties. Early Apr.

Carolina Downhome Blues Festival and Fine Arts Center. *Center of Kershaw County, 810 Lyttleton St, Camden. Phone 803/425-7676.* The annual Carolina Downhome Blues Festival is a blues 'club crawl' with performances in the cozy theatre of the Fine Arts Center of Kershaw County. Most venues are in walking distance of each other. Early Oct.

Colonial Cup International Steeplechase. *Springdale Race Course, 200 Knights Hill Rd, Camden. Phone 803/432-6513.* Known as 'Where Champions are Crowned' the Colonial Cup draws over 15,000 fans and horsemen from around the world. The Colonial Cup provides the seasons grand finale—often deciding all the national titles including jockey of the year, trainer of the year, and horse of the year. Mid-Nov.

Revolutionary War Field Days. *Historic Camden Revolutionary War Site, 222 Broad St, Camden. Phone 803/432-9841.* Two-day American Revolution encampment, festivities, battle reenactments. First full weekend in Nov.

Specialty Lodging

The following lodging establishment is approved by Mobil Travel Guide, but due to its unique and individualized nature has not been given a traditional Mobil Star rating. Included in this listing you may find bed-and-breakfasts, limited-service inns, guest ranches, and other unique hotel properties.

GREENLEAF INN. *1308 Broad St, Camden (29020). Phone 803/425-1806; toll-free 800/437-5874;* fax 803/425-5853. www.greenleafinnofcamden.com. The Greenleaf Inn is located in the historic district. Its guesthouses were built in 1805 and 1890 and are decorated in Victorian style. 10 rooms, 2 story. Complimentary full breakfast. Check-in 3 pm, check-out 11 am. Wireless Internet access. Restaurant. **$**

Restaurant

★ ★ **LUCY'S.** *1043 Broad St, Camden (29020). Phone 803/432-9096; fax 803/432-9099.* This is a gourmet restaurant located in a historic building. The signature dish is lightly breaded veal sautéed with mushrooms. Other dishes include salmon and grits with dill saffron sauce, or shrimp and grits with tasso gravy. American menu. Lunch, dinner. Closed Sun-Tues; Jan 1, Thanksgiving, Dec 25; also week of July 4. Bar. Business casual attire. Reservations recommended. **$$**

Charleston (E-5)

See also Beaufort, Kiawah Island, Summerville, Walterboro

Founded 1670
Population 96,650
Elevation 9 ft
Area Code 843
Information Visitor Reception and Transportation Center, 375 Meeting St, PO Box 975, 29402; phone 843/853-8000 or toll-free 800/868-8118
Web Site www.charlestoncvb.com

This aristocratic and storied American city lives up to its reputation for cultivated manners. Charleston's homes, historic shrines, old churches, lovely gardens, winding streets, and intricate iron-laced gateways exude charm and dignity.

Charleston enjoys international and coastal commerce in the fine harbor formed, according to local opinion, where the "Ashley and Cooper rivers unite to form the Atlantic Ocean." The strategic harbor, inlets, and sea islands provide recreational retreats.

The Charleston of today is the survivor of siege, flood, hurricane, and epidemic. Capital of the province until 1786, its history and that of South Carolina are almost the same. Charleston received colonists from the Old World and sent them into the wilderness. The city

Exploring the Historic District

Named for King Charles II, Charles Towne was founded by British settlers in 1670. Today, the beautiful city retains outstanding architecture in its large historic district downtown, with a rich mix of styles from early Colonial, Georgian, Federal, Greek Revival, and Italianate to Victorian. It is a wonderful place to explore on foot.

The Old City Market, (Market St at Church), is the classic starting point. Here, on a site where vendors have swapped their wares for centuries, such favorite Charleston souvenirs as handmade sweetgrass baskets and fresh pralines can be found. Horse-drawn carriage tours depart from here.

A walk three blocks down Church Street from the Old City Market passes the old power magazine built in 1713, the oldest building in the city, which now houses exhibits from 18th-century Charleston. The 1772 Heyward-Washington House (87 Church St at Broad; phone 843/772-0354), where George Washington slept during a 1791 visit, is now a house museum. Jog west 1 block to Meeting Street and proceed south to the Nathaniel Russell House (51 Meeting St at Water). Built in 1808, the house is considered one of the finest examples of Federal-style architecture and is also the home of the

Historic Charleston Foundation. Continue south through the stunning residential district here to White Point Gardens, a wide shady park of tall oaks and palmettos at the waterfront with a panoramic view of Charleston Harbor. Lining the shore is the Battery, where cannons remain posed to protect the harbor. When the first shots of the Civil War were fired at Fort Sumter in the center of the harbor, Charlestonians gathered here to watch.

Follow the Battery north around to East Bay Street. Here the cobblestone lanes hold many shops, cafés, and restaurants, such as Magnolia's (185 East Bay St, phone 843/722-9200), which serves nouveau Southern cuisine. On the water side, a walk-through fountain attracts children—and some adults—to jump in and cool off. Behind the fountain, a wide pier has swinging benches that are ideal spots for unwinding after a long day of sightseeing.

East Bay Street leads back to the Old City Market where you started. But part of the greatest fun of a visit to Charleston is simply to wander the streets at random for a glimpse of a back garden through a set of ornamental gates that may be as lovely an image to take home with you as that of the most revered restoration.

served as the personification of Europe's luxury and culture in the New World.

The first permanent settlement in the Carolinas, Charles Towne, as it was first called, was established as a tiny colony, westward across the Ashley River, by Anthony Ashley Cooper, Earl of Shaftesbury. At the same time, he established the only American nobility in history, with barons, landgraves (dukes), and caciques (earls), each owning great plantations.

This nobility lasted less than 50 years, but it was the foundation for an aristocratic tradition that still exists, even though the rice and indigo that made the early Charleston people rich are gone. Colonists from Barbados, England, and Ireland came to enlarge the settlement in 1670, and by 1680, the colony moved across the river to become a city-state. Although many of the colonists went on to the Carolina low country and established grand plantations, every year on the traditional date of May 10, the planters and

their families moved back to Charleston to escape the mosquitoes and malarial heat. From spring to frost, these planters created a season of dancing, sport, musicales, theater, and socials. Commerce and plantations provided the prosperity on which the city's cosmopolitan graces were based. Charleston founded the first playhouse designed solely for presentation of drama, the first museum, the first public school in the colony, the first municipal college in America, and the first fire insurance company on the continent. (It was a victim the next year of a fire that destroyed half the city.) The city became famous throughout the world as "a flourishing capital of wealth and ease."

The First Provincial Congress of South Carolina met in Charleston in 1775 and prepared the city to repulse a British attack on June 28, 1776. But in 1780, the city was captured and occupied by the enemy for two and a half years. Charleston was almost the last point in the state to be cleared of British troops. With peace came great prosperity, but rivalry between the small farmers of the interior and the merchants and plantation owners of the lowlands resulted in removal of the capital to Columbia.

The convention that authored the Ordinance of Secession came to Charleston to pass that declaration; the Civil War then began with the bombardment of Fort Sumter by Fort Johnson. A long siege followed, including the gallant defense of Fort Sumter (1863-1865), blockade running, the first submarine warfare, evacuation after Sherman had demolished Columbia, and, finally, bombardment of the city by the Union Army.

Additional Visitor Information

Forever Charleston, a multimedia presentation about the city, is shown every half hour at the visitor center.

The Charleston Visitor Reception and Transportation Center, 375 Meeting Street, has information on other points of interest, tours, campsites, fishing trips, cultural events, special events, maps, and self-guided walking tour of the city. (Daily; closed Jan 1, Thanksgiving, Dec 25) Contact PO Box 975, 29402; phone 843/853-8000. For city bus service information, phone SCE & G at 843/747-0922; for DASH, Downtown Area Shuttle, phone 803/577-6970, ext 500.

What to See and Do

Aiken-Rhett House. *48 Elizabeth St, Charleston (29403). Corner of Judith St. Phone 843/724-8481. www. historiccharleston.org.* Built around 1818, this palatial residence was enlarged and redecorated by Governor and Mrs. William Aiken Jr. in the mid-1800s. After traveling in Europe, they returned home with crystal and bronze chandeliers, paintings, and classical sculptures. Many treasures are still in the rooms for which they were purchased. This home, which remained in the family until 1975, is on the National Register of Historic Places. (Daily; closed Thanksgiving, Dec 24-25) **$$**

Beth Elohim Synagogue. *90 Hasell St, Charleston (29401). Between King and Meeting sts. Phone 843/723-1090.* Attracted by civil and religious freedoms and economic opportunities, the first Jews came to the Charleston area shortly after 1670. By 1749, enough Jewish settlers were present to organize a congrega-

tion. The current synagogue, a Greek Revival structure dating to 1840, is the second oldest in the United States and the oldest in continuous use. A previous synagogue was built in 1794 but was destroyed by fire in 1838. In 1824, the first Reform Jewish congregation in the United States was born here. (Mon-Fri) **FREE**

⭐ **Boone Hall Plantation.** *1235 Long Point Rd, Mount Pleasant (29464). Phone 843/884-4371. www.boone hallplantation.com.* This 738-acre estate encompasses a 1935 Georgian-style house similar to the original plantation house that fell into ruin, as well as an avenue of Spanish moss-draped oak trees, a cotton gin house, a pecan grove, and gardens of antique roses. Several rooms on the first floor of the house may be visited. Nine original slave cabins, haunting in their emptiness, were constructed of brick made on-site. If the property, originally a cotton plantation, somehow seems familiar to visitors, it's probably because *The North and the South,* a TV miniseries, and other productions were filmed here. Battle reenactments are held during the summer and draw Civil War buffs. (Apr-Labor Day: Mon-Sat 8:30 am-6:30 pm, Sun 1-5 pm; Labor Day-Mar: Mon-Sat 9 am-5 pm, Sun 1-4 pm; closed Thanksgiving, Dec 25) **$$$**

Chamber of Commerce. *81 Mary St, Charleston. Phone 843/577-2510.* (Organized in 1773) Building was once the South Carolina Railway Warehouse, home of one of the nation's first steam locomotives. This is one of the oldest city commercial organizations in the country.

Charles Towne Landing. *1500 Old Town Rd, Charleston (29407). On Hwy 171, W of the Ashley River. Phone 843/852-4200. www.discoversouthcarolina .com/stateparks.* It's back to the beginning at this 664-acre park. In 1670, colonists established the first permanent English settlement in the Carolinas in this location. Today, visitors find archaeological investigations, reconstructed fortifications, an experimental garden of 1670s crops, and formal gardens, as well as nature trails, a colonial village, and a replica of *Adventure,* a 17th-century trading ketch. Tram tours are available, and there also is a natural habitat zoo of indigenous animals on-site. (Daily) **$**

⭐ **Charleston Museum.** *360 Meeting St, Charleston (29403). Across the street from the Charleston Visitor Center. Phone 843/722-2996. www.charlestonmuseum .org.* Founded in 1773 and first opened to the public in 1824, the Charleston Museum claims status as America's oldest museum. The institution has a rich and eclectic collection of all things Charlestonian but interprets them in such a way as to make visitors—even Yankees—feel engaged and interested. Key components in the natural and cultural history of Charleston and the South Carolina low country include an impressive early silver display (George Washington's christening cup is among the pieces), an Egyptian mummy, South Carolina ceramics, a skeleton of a primitive toothed whale, South Carolina ornithology, the chairs that delegates sat in to sign South Carolina's Ordinance of Secession, and firearms used in the ensuing Civil War (or, as Southerners prefer to say, the War between the States). Children will especially enjoy the museum's hands-on exhibits. (Mon-Sat 9 am-5 pm, Sun 1-5 pm; closed holidays) **$$**

Charleston Water Tours. *196 Concord St, Charleston (29402). Foot of Market St. Phone 843/722-1112.* Tours (approximately two hours) of harbor, US Naval Base, view of forts, other points of interest. Contact PO Box 861, 29402-0861. **$$$$**

The Citadel, Military College of South Carolina. *171 Moultrie St, Charleston (29409). Phone 843/953-5006. www.citadel.com.* The Citadel is one of those storied institutions that inspires pride in the hearts of South Carolinians, especially those who live in Charleston. Established in 1842 by an act of the South Carolina General Assembly, the Citadel originally was located on Marion Square in downtown Charleston near the Revolutionary War rampart. In 1922, the college was moved to a picturesque setting on the bank of the Ashley River. Nearly 2,000 students are enrolled in 19 degree programs. The site is home to 24 major buildings, including Sumerall Chapel, a shrine of patriotism and remembrance, as well as a popular place for weddings. A full athletic schedule includes football, baseball, basketball, and other events. Citadel parades on Friday afternoons are said to be "the best free show in Charleston." Visitors may take self-guided campus tours. Cadet-led tours for groups of eight or more are available through the Public Affairs Office, at phone 843/953-6779. (Mon-Fri; closed Sat-Sun) On campus is

Citadel Archives Museum. *171 Moultrie St, Charleston (29409). Phone 843/953-6846. www.citadel.com.* In a city (and region) that reveres the past, it would be hard to over-exaggerate the importance of the history of the Citadel. The Museum presents the history of the Military College of South Carolina from its beginning to the present day, with exhibits featuring military, academic, athletic, and social aspects of cadet life. Here are photographs, memorabilia from special events, biographical sketches of college presidents,

cadet uniforms and arms. Citadel rings from 1895 to the present are displayed in the museum's foyer. Self-guided and group tours of the museum are available. The Archives contain more than 300 collections that relate to the history of the Citadel itself or have military significance. Among the noteworthy documents are military papers and photographs of World War II General Mark W. Clark. (Daily; archives Mon-Fri; closed holidays) **FREE**

City Hall Art Gallery. *80 Broad St, Charleston (29401). At Meeting St. Phone 843/724-3799.* On the site of a colonial marketplace, this handsomely proportioned 1801 building first housed the Bank of the United States and then became Charleston's City Hall in 1818. A gallery in the Council Chamber on the second floor grew out of a custom of commissioning artists to paint famous visitors. The gallery includes a portrait of George Washington by John Trumbull (considered one of the best of the general in his later years) and also a portrait of President James Monroe by Samuel F. B. Morse. A guide is available to answer questions. (Mon-Fri) **FREE**

Cypress Gardens. *3030 Cypress Garden Rd, Moncks Corner (29461). 24 miles N off Hwy 52, between Goose Creek and Moncks Corner.* Giant cypresses, a blackwater swamp, and a butterfly house share 163 acres with luxuriant dogwoods, azaleas, camellias, and daffodils. Visitors can wander along 4 miles of walking trails, paddle a flat-bottomed boat through a cypress swamp, and explore a freshwater aquarium and reptile house, whose residents include crocodiles, snakes, and turtles. (Daily; closed Thanksgiving, Dec 25) **$$**

Dock Street Theatre. *135 Church St, Charleston (29401). SW corner of Church and Queen sts. Phone 843/720-3968. www.charlestonstage.com.* In 1736, a building on this site opened as the very first in America constructed specifically for theatrical productions. Later, the street name changed to Queen, but the Dock Street Theatre name stuck. Today's theater is on the site of the original and presents numerous productions of the Charleston Stage Company during the spring and fall. Dock Street Theatre also is a performance venue for Charleston's Spoleto Festival USA (see SPECIAL EVENTS).

Drayton Hall. *3380 Ashley River Rd, Charleston (29414). 9 miles NW via Hwy 6. Phone 843/766-0188.* One of the oldest surviving pre-American Revolution plantation houses (1738) in the area, this Georgian Palladian house is surrounded by live oaks and is located on the Ashley River. Held in the Drayton family for seven generations, the mansion has been maintained in virtually its original condition. A National Trust for Historic Preservation property. Tours (hourly). (Daily; closed Jan 1, Thanksgiving, Dec 25) **$$$$**

Edisto Beach State Park. *8377 State Cabin Rd, Edisto Island (29438). 21 miles W on Hwy 17, then 29 miles S on Hwy 174. Phone 843/869-2756.* The 1,255-acre park on this remote sea island makes for a nice day trip out of Charleston. Fortunately, vacation cabins and a campground are available for those who can't bear to leave the live oak forest, extensive sea marsh, and towering palmetto trees so soon. A 4-mile nature trail winds along, with views to write home about. Surf and marsh fishing, boating, swimming, picnicking, and searching the beach for shells are among the options here. Rich in Native American history, this beachfront park was initially developed by the Civilian Conservation Corps in the 1930s. (Standard time, daily 8 am-6 pm; daylight savings time, daily 6 am-10 pm) **$**

Edmondston-Alston House. *21 E Battery, Charleston. Phone 843/722-7171.* (Circa 1825) Built by a wealthy merchant and wharf owner, remodeled by the next owner, an important rice planter, beginning in 1838; Greek Revival style. Uninterrupted view across the harbor. Documents, engravings, portraits, original furnishings, elaborate woodwork. Guided tours (daily; closed first full week in Feb, Thanksgiving, Dec 25).

Folly Beach County Park. *1010 W Ashley Ave, Charleston (29439). S via Hwy 171 on W end of Folly Island. Phone 843/588-2426.* Located on the 6-mile-long barrier island of the same name, this is the beach that's closest to the historic heart of Charleston. With some 4,000 feet of ocean frontage, 2,000 feet of river frontage, a 600-foot swimming beach, and a 1,045-foot fishing pier, it is an easy-to-get-to place to get away from it all. (May-Aug: daily 9 am-7 pm; Apr and Sept-Oct: daily 10 am-6 pm; Nov-Mar: daily 10 am-5 pm) **$**

Fort Sumter Tours. *Liberty Square at Aquarium Wharf, Charleston. Phone 843/881-7337; toll-free 800/789-3678. www.spiritlinecruises.com.* A trip to Fort Sumter National Monument (see also), located on a small manmade island in Charleston Harbor, is a unique opportunity to cruise back in time to the morning hours of April 12, 1861, when South Carolina troops of the Confederacy fired upon the Union-occupied fort in what became the opening engagement of the Civil War. Visitors can learn more about the fort and the war at a museum and from National Park service rangers on site. The tour also includes narration describing Charleston Harbor and a good look at many of the historic homes nestled among the trees that line the Battery (the tip of the peninsula) and other points of interest. The tour takes about two hours and 15 minutes. In addition to Liberty Square, you can purchase tickets on the Cooper River in downtown Charleston, in Mount Pleasant, and at Patriots Point Maritime Museum (40 Patriot Point Dr, Mount Pleasant). **$$$**

Francis Marion National Forest. *2421 Witherbee Rd, Cordesville (29434). NE via Hwy 17 and 17 A, Hwy 41. Phone 843/335-3248.* Francis Marion grew up in the wilds of South Carolina's backcountry and became well versed in unconventional warfare at an early age. He put these skills to good use during the Revolutionary War and frustrated the British by slipping away into the backwoods swamps, where tracking was impossible. This magnificent 250,000-acre forest, named for the "Swamp Fox," lies along the Intracoastal Waterway some 40 miles north of Charleston. Camping, hiking, fishing, hunting, horseback riding, biking, boating, canoeing, nature study, bird watching, photography, and picnicking are excellent reasons for coming here. Bald eagles are among the 250 species of birds in the forest. Other residents include beavers, bobcats, black bears, and otters. The best time to visit is from late fall through early spring. Summers can be very hot and humid.

French Huguenot Church. *136 Church St, Charleston (29401). Phone 843/722-4385.* As early as 1687, French Huguenots were worshipping in a church on this site, having fled France to avoid religious persecution. The current church, the third, is a National Historic Landmark. Completed in 1845, it was the first Gothic Revival building in Charleston. Constructed of brick covered with stucco, the church features distinctive windows, buttresses, and unusual ironwork. Even the clear glass windows are original. The first church, while not destroyed *by* fire, was destroyed *because* of fire. In 1796, the building was detonated to create a fire break for a fire that raced through the neighborhood. A second church was completed in 1800, but was torn down to make way for the current building. In early days, services were timed with the tides. Over the years, the church has been closed at times because of declining membership. Reestablished most recently in 1983, this is the only French Calvinist congregation in the United States. Sunday services are held at

10:30 am, with a French liturgy service held every spring.

⭐ **Gibbes Museum of Art.** *135 Meeting St, Charleston (29401). Phone 843/722-2706. www.gibbesmuseum.org.* This museum, which will be 100 years old in 2005, has an eclectic collection that includes Japanese woodblock prints, as well as miniature rooms depicting traditional American and French architecture, decorative arts, and design. This museum is also known for its portraits of notable South Carolinians by notable artists, including Thomas Sully, Benjamin West, and Rembrandt Peale, and one of the oldest and finest miniature portrait collections in the country. Don't miss the Charleston Renaissance Gallery, which showcases works by Charleston artists who were responsible for the city's cultural renaissance in the 1920s and 1930s. Special exhibitions and other events are scheduled throughout the year. Docents give an overview of the museum's exhibitions at 2:30 pm every Tues and Sat. Tours at 5 pm on the second Tues of every month are part of the museum's Art After Dark program. (Tues-Sat 10 am-5 pm, Sun 1-5 pm) **$$**

Gray Line bus tours. *14 Hayne St, Charleston. Phone 843/722-4444.* For information or reservations, contact PO Box 219, 29402-0219.

Hampton Park. *Rutledge Ave and Cleveland St, Charleston. Phone 843/724-7321.* Historic park with camellias and azaleas in spring, roses in summer; 1-mile nature trail; Charleston's mounted horse patrol stables. **FREE**

⭐ **Heyward-Washington House.** *87 Church St, Charleston (29403). Phone 843/722-0354. www.charlestonmuseum.org/heyward.asp.* Located in the heart of Charleston's historic district, within the area of the original city walls, this brick double house was built in 1772 during the Revolutionary era. Rice planter Daniel Heyward gave the house, which is noteworthy for its handsome collection of Charleston-made furniture, to his son Thomas Heyward Jr., a signer of the Declaration of Independence. George Washington stayed here during his weeklong visit to the city in 1791. Outdoors are a carriage shed, a 1740s kitchen building, and a formal garden with plants that would have been familiar to late-18th-century Charlestonians. Years later, Dubose Heyward used the evocative neighborhood in which the house stands as the setting for *Porgy and Bess.* (Daily; closed holidays) **$$**

Joseph Manigault House. *350 Meeting St, Charleston (29403). Across from the Charleston Museum. Phone 843/722-2996. www.charlestonmuseum.org/manigault.* Another house that rice built, this home was designed by Gabriel Manigault for his brother, Joseph. The brothers were descendants of a French Huguenot family who left Europe and came to the United States to avoid persecution. (Gabriel also is said to have designed the Charleston City Hall and the South Carolina Society Hall.) This elegant neoclassical three-story brick town house, a National Historic Landmark, reflects the wealthy lifestyle of the Manigault family, as well as living conditions of the slaves who worked there. A dramatic, sweeping staircase connects restored rooms on the first and second floors. The home has been furnished with outstanding examples of early 19th-century American, English, and French pieces. Outdoors are the kitchen, slave quarters, stable, and privy. (Daily; closed holidays) **$$$**

⭐ **Magnolia Plantation and Gardens.** *3550 Ashley River Rd, Charleston (29414). 10 miles NW on Hwy 61. Phone 843/571-1266; toll-free 800/367-3517. www. magnoliaplantation.com.* These internationally famous gardens are America's oldest (circa 1676); they now cover 50 acres with camellias, azaleas, magnolias, and hundreds of other flowering species. Azaleas are best from mid-Mar-Apr; camellias put on their best show from mid-Nov-Mar. Also on the grounds are a 125-acre waterfowl refuge, a trilevel observation tower, a 16th-century maze, an 18th-century herb garden, biblical gardens, a topiary garden, nature trails, and a petting zoo. Canoe and bicycle rentals are available, and there are designated areas for picnicking. Gift shop, snack shop; orientation theater. Plantation home and local art gallery (additional fee). (Mar-Oct: 8 am-dusk; Nov-Feb: call for hours) **$$$** Through Magnolia Plantation, enter

Audubon Swamp Garden. *3550 Ashley River Rd, Charleston (29414). Phone 843/571-1266; toll-free 800/367-3517. www.magnoliaplantation.com.* Boardwalks, bridges, and dikes make this 60-acre blackwater cypress and tupelo swamp accessible to visitors. Home to all local species of wildlife, including alligators, this colorful area is planted with hundreds of varieties of local and exotic flowering shrubs. (Mar-Oct: daily 8 am-dusk; Nov-Feb: call for hours) **$**

Medical University of South Carolina. *171 Ashley Ave, Charleston. Phone 843/792-3621. www.musc.edu.*

(1824) (2,200 students) The oldest medical school in the South. On campus is

Waring Historical Medical Library & Macaulay Museum of Dental History. *175 Ashley Ave, Charleston (29425). Phone 843/792-2288. waring.library.musc.edu.* (Mon-Fri; closed holidays) **FREE**

Middleton Place Plantation. *4300 Ashley River Rd, Charleston (29414). 14 miles NW on Hwy 61. Phone 843/556-6020; toll-free 800/782-3608. www.middletonplace.org.* Once the home of Arthur Middleton, a signer of the Declaration of Independence, Middleton Place encompasses America's oldest landscaped gardens, the Plantation Stableyards, and the restored House Museum. The gardens, laid out in 1741, highlight ornamental butterfly lakes, sweeping terraces, and a wide variety of flora and fauna. The Stableyards feature numerous craftspeople demonstrating skills necessary for a self-sufficient 18th-century plantation. House (additional fee). Guided tours (additional fee). Special events include Starlight Pops (May), Spoleto Finale (mid-June), Plantation Days (Nov), and Plantation Christmas (Dec). (Daily from 9 am) **$$$$**

Moo Roo Handbags. *316 King St, Charleston (29401). Phone 843/724-1081; toll-free 866/666-7661. www.mooroo.com.* For the woman who has everything and needs a chic bag to carry it around in, this Charleston upstart on busy King Street may be just the place to look. Sharon Stone, Andie MacDowell, and other glitterati are fans and customers. Locals like the creatively fashioned bags, too—think satin, leather, and wool tweed, with semi-precious stones, flowers, or other embellishments. (Mon-Sat) **FREE**

⭐ **Nathaniel Russell House.** *51 Meeting St, Charleston (29401). Phone 843/724-8481. www.historiccharleston .org.* Regarded as Charleston's grandest neoclassical house museum, this beauty (circa 1808) features graceful interiors, lavish plasterwork, oval drawing rooms, and a magnificent "free-flying" staircase. Period antiques and works of art furnish the home, set among formal gardens. This mansion interprets the lives of both the Russells and their slaves. (Daily; closed Thanksgiving, Dec 24-25) **$$**

⭐ **Old Exchange and Provost Dungeon.** *122 E Bay St, Charleston (29401). Phone 843/727-2165. www.oldexchange.com.* The history of the Royal Exchange and Custom House is more colorful and turbulent than the stately Georgian-style building would suggest. Completed by in 1771, this structure is one of the most historically significant buildings of Colonial and Revolutionary America. Designed primarily to accommodate heavy export-import trade and as a place to conduct business on upper levels, the lower level confined common prisoners, pirates, and suspected rebels, also known as American Patriots. Among the latter were three signers of the Declaration of Independence (Arthur Middleton, Thomas Heyward Jr., and Edward Rutledge). In 1776, South Carolina declared independence from Great Britain on the Exchange steps, and in 1788, South Carolina delegates gathered in the building to ratify the US Constitution. George Washington was a guest of honor here at a grand ball in 1791. Nearly 200 years later, restored and remodeled, the Old Exchange was reopened to the public. (Daily) **$$**

Old Powder Magazine. *79 Cumberland St, Charleston (29401). Phone 843/805-6730. www.historiccharleston .org/museum/powder.html.* The oldest public building in the Carolinas, the Powder Magazine dates back to the Lords Proprietors, a group of English nobles who owned and ruled the joint province. The building was authorized in 1703 and constructed about ten years later. Crucial for the storage of powder in defense of the city, the magazine was still in use during the Revolutionary era, although a "new" powder magazine had been built in 1748. Now a National Historic Landmark, this gabled brick structure houses an exhibit on colonial Charleston. (Mid-Mar-Oct, daily) **FREE**

Old South Carriage Company. *14 Hayne St, Charleston (29401). Phone 843/577-0042.* Offers narrated, horse-drawn carriage tours of Old Charleston (One hour). Free shuttle service from visitor center. (Daily; closed Thanksgiving, Dec 25)

Palmetto Carriage Tours. *40 N Market St, Charleston. Phone 843/723-8145.* One-hour tour through Old Charleston by horse- and mule-drawn carriages. Tours originate at Rainbow Market. (Daily; closed Dec 25). **$$$$**

Palmetto Islands County Park. *444 Needlerush Pkwy, Charleston (29464). N on Hwy 17, 1/2 mile past Snee Farm, then left on Long Point Rd. Phone 843/884-0832.* Nature-oriented park in tropical setting. Bicycle paths, marsh boardwalks, picnicking, and grills throughout park. Pond. Canoe trails. Pedal boat, canoe, and bicycle rentals. BigToy Playground. 50-foot observation tower with play area. Interpretive trails. Splash Island Water Park. Fishing supplies; concession. (Daily; closed Jan 1, Thanksgiving, Dec 24-25) **$**

Rainbow Row. *79-107 E Bay St, Charleston (29401).* Many of Charleston's sights are simply free for the looking. One of the most delightful spots to take a look at the city's past is Rainbow Row, a series of private homes numbering from 79 to 107 on East Bay Street. These town houses, constructed in the mid-1700s, are painted whatever color—pink, pale blue, yellow—that the current owners favor. Originally, these buildings were owned by merchants who lived on the upper floors and used the ground floors for counting rooms and shops.

⭐ **South Carolina Aquarium.** *100 Aquarium Wharf, Charleston (29401). On Charleston Harbor at the end of Calhoun St. Phone 843/720-1990. www.scaquarium.org.* Charleston's most-visited attraction is making a big splash, with more than 10,000 fish, river otters, snakes, loggerhead turtles, sharks, jellyfish, alligators, birds, and other animals. Since the aquarium's opening in 2002, exhibits have focused on the Appalachian Watershed—the mountains, piedmont, coastal plain, coast, and ocean. Interpretive programs encourage interaction and enhance the aquarium experience for all ages. Expansive views of Charleston Harbor and refreshing breezes are an added bonus. (Opens daily at 9 am; closing times vary by season; closed Thanksgiving, Dec 25) **$$$**

St. John's Lutheran Church. *5 Clifford St, Charleston (29401). Archdale and Clifford sts. Phone 843/723-2426.* Completed in 1818, this church displays both Federal and Baroque elements and is home to Charleston's oldest Lutheran congregation. The Italianate steeple, added in 1859, was built by David Lopez, who was the contractor for Kadal Kadosh Beth Elohim Synagogue. The first Lutheran congregation was organized by 1752, and dedicated a wooden church located behind the site of the current building. Two pastors stand out: Rev. John Nicholas Martin was expelled from the city by the British during the American Revolution because he refused to pray for the king of England, and Dr. John Bachman, pastor during the Civil War, collaborated with John James Audubon on the famous books *Birds of America* and *The Quadrupeds of North America.* (Mon-Fri; also Sun worship)

⭐ **St. Mary's Church.** *89 Hassell St, Charleston (29401). Phone 843/722-7696.* This is the mother church for the Catholic diocese of the Carolinas and Georgia. The congregation was organized in 1789 and first worshiped in a rundown Methodist meeting house on the present site. A new church built in 1801 was destroyed by fire in 1838. The present building, completed in 1839, is a wonderful example of the Classical Revival style, featuring galleries on three sides of the sanctuary. Among the paintings in the church is an 1814 work that was salvaged from the 1838 fire and restored by the original artist, John S. Cogdell. Other paintings, copies of Old Masters, were done in Rome and installed in St. Mary's in 1896. Newer elements include a series of stained-glass windows. In the churchyard, many of the tombstones are in French. Parish records were kept in that language until 1822. (Mon-Fri)

⭐ **St. Michael's Episcopal Church.** *14 St. Michael's Alley, Charleston (29401). SE corner of Meeting and Broad sts. Phone 843/723-0603. www.stmichaelschurch .net.* On Sunday mornings in Charleston, church bells ring in loud and joyful cacophony to awaken residents and visitors alike. Among the city's handsome and historic houses of worship, St. Michael's, with its 186-foot-tall white steeple, stands out. Completed in 1761, with bells dating to 1764, the building of St. Michael's Church is the oldest in the city. Many other houses of worship were destroyed by fire, which periodically ravaged Charleston. George Washington worshiped here when he visited Charleston in 1791, and Robert E. Lee's name also is on a pew. **FREE**

St. Philip's Episcopal Church. *146 Church St, Charleston (29401). Phone 843/722-7734.* Established in 1670, this is the oldest congregation in Charleston and the first Episcopal church in the Carolinas. The first church building stood at the corner of Meeting and Broad sts, where St. Michael's Church now stands. Fire destroyed earlier buildings on the present site. Today's building was completed in 1838. During the Civil War, its bells were removed and converted into cannons for the Confederacy. New bells were placed in the steeple on July 4, 1976. Among the notables buried in the churchyard are John C. Calhoun, Charles Pinckney, John Rutledge, and Dubose Heyward.

⭐ **Sword Gates.** *32 Legare St, Charleston (29402).* Practical, graceful, durable, and sometimes downright fanciful, wrought iron was, and still is, a highly prized art form in Charleston. One of handsomest examples around is a set of gates that features two horizontal swords joining at the center of a broadsword to form a cross. Beyond the gates stands a masonry and frame home, which date to the early 1800s. The famed gates were forged around 1838 by Christopher Werner, an important Charleston ironsmith. They were designed for the City Guard House, which explains the design, and placed here about 10 years later. Wrought-iron fences and gates served as more than mere decoration. Although they ensured a certain degree of privacy for owners, they also hindered escape by slaves.

⭐ **Unitarian Church.** *8 Archdale St, Charleston (29401). Phone 843/723-4617.* A National Historic Landmark, this is the oldest Unitarian church in the South and the second oldest church in Charleston. Its history threads back to 1772, when the Independent Church on Meeting Street was growing so rapidly that it needed to construct a second church building on Archdale Street. Construction was interrupted by British occupation during the Revolutionary War. The building was completed in 1787 and chartered as the Second Independent Church, with a Unitarian minister presiding. As the American Unitarian Association was not organized until 1825, it was 1839 by the time this congregation was recharted as Unitarian. The building was remodeled in the mid-1800s with a crenelated tower, arched windows, pseudo-buttresses, and Tudor arch entrance. The interior vaulting was modeled on that of the Henry VII chapel at Westminster Abbey in London. Repairs were made after the church suffered damage in the earthquake of 1886 and Hurricane Hugo in 1989. (Mon-Fri)

White Point Gardens. *Murray Blvd and E Bay St, Charleston (29401).* After a day of traipsing through historic homes, museums, and shops, visitors tend to drift toward the tip of the peninsula that the city of Charleston graces. They come here to admire the gardens, rest under the live oaks and palmettos, and marvel at the magnificent antebellum homes. They also come to take in the refreshing ocean breezes. This is, after all, where the Ashley and Coopers rivers come together to form the Atlantic Ocean. Old cannons are mounted here, too, as a reminder of battles past and of strong-willed Charlestonians. Out in the harbor lie Fort Moultrie and Fort Sumter. This park was an excellent vantage point for the opening chapter of the Civil War as Confederate forces at Fort Moultrie fired upon Fort Sumter. Early settlers named this area White Pointe because of the discarded oyster shells left here by Indians. The area was first used as a public garden in 1837.

Special Events

Fall House and Garden Candlelight Tours. *147 King St, Charleston (29401). Phone 843/722-4630; toll-free 800/968-8175. www.preservationsociety.org.* The traditional allure of Charleston presents itself during the annual Candlelight Tours of Homes and Gardens. Visitors are welcomed into significant residential architecture of the 18th, 19th, and 20th centuries in historic districts that are listed on the National Register of Historic Places. Tours are self-paced and self-guided (although there are volunteer guides at each site) and include eight to ten stops per tour, rain or shine. For comfort and safety, wear walking shoes—no high-heeled shoes allowed—and bring a flashlight. The Preservation Society of Charleston sponsors these tours, in keeping with its goal "to transmit the city not less, but greater and more beautiful than it was." Founded in 1920, the Society is the oldest community-based organization of its kind in the country. Late Sept-late Oct.

Festival of Houses and Gardens. *40 E Bay St, Charleston (29402). Phone 843/722-3405. www.historic charleston.org.* Sponsored by the Historic Charleston Foundation, this award-winning series of tours and special events enables visitors to experience the real Charleston—past and present—as they explore the interiors and stroll through the private gardens of some of Charleston's grandest homes. The welcome mats are out at 150 historic private homes in 11 colonial and antebellum neighborhoods, and spring blossoms are at their peak. Also available are additional excursions, lectures, luncheons featuring low country foods and beverages, afternoon teas, wine tastings, and book signings. Charleston's homes and gardens are widely admired, so early reservations are an absolute must. Most events sell out well in advance. Mid-Mar-mid-Apr. **$$$$**

Piccolo Spoleto Festival. *Phone 843/724-7305. www.piccolospoleto.com.* This 17-day arts event in late May and early June is a companion piece to the larger Spoleto Festival USA, reaching out to children as well as adults. Events are held in 40 various venues throughout the city, including the Customs House, theaters, churches, parks, storefronts, and on the streets—wherever people might gather to watch, listen, sing, and dance. Performances showcase young artists and performers from South Carolina and elsewhere in the Southeast. Late May-early June.

Southeastern Wildlife Exposition. *211 Meeting St, Charleston. Phone 843/723-1748. www.sewe.com.* The largest event of its kind in the nation, this three-day celebration kicks off the spring season in Charleston, attracting more than 500 exhibitors (including some 150 artists), plus some 40,000 visitors interested in wildlife art, environmental education, and conservation. Paintings, sculptures, crafts, and outdoor sporting goods are for sale, and a variety of demonstrations are held. The exposition takes place at various locations in and around Charleston and includes grand parties and oyster roasts. Mid-Feb.

⭐ **Spoleto Festival USA.** *Gaillard Municipal Auditorium, 77 Calhoun St, Charleston. Phone 843/579-3100. www.spoletousa.org.* One of the best, and best-known, arts festivals in the country, Spoleto USA is a counterpart to the arts festival held in Spoleto, Italy, that was founded by composer Gian Carlo Menotti. The Charleston festival encompasses a cornucopia of offerings in opera, dance, chamber music, theater, symphonic music, jazz, solo voice, choral performance, visual arts, and varied special events, including conversations with various artists—more than 120 offerings in total. Venues include the Gaillard Auditorium and historic Dock Street Theatre in Charleston, as well as less-conventional locales such as Middleton Place and Mapkin Abbey Monastery. Late May-early June. **$$$$**

Limited-Service Hotels

⭐ **BEST WESTERN KING CHARLES INN.** *237 Meeting St, Charleston (29401). Phone 843/723-7451; toll-free 866/546-4700; fax 843/723-2041. www.kingcharlesinn.com.* 93 rooms, 4 story. Check-in 4 pm, check-out noon. Restaurant. Outdoor pool. **$**
🛏️

⭐ **BEST WESTERN SWEETGRASS INN.** *1540 Savannah Hwy, Charleston (29407). Phone 843/571-6100; toll-free 800/937-8376; fax 843/766-6261. www.bestwestern.com.* 87 rooms. Pets accepted, some restrictions; fee. Complimentary continental breakfast. Check-in 3 pm, check-out noon. Outdoor pool. **$**
🐾 🛏️

⭐ ⭐ **DOUBLETREE HOTEL.** *181 Church St, Charleston (29401). Phone 843/577-2644; toll-free 877/408-8733; fax 843/577-2697. www.doubletree.com.* This Hilton chain includes a full, Southern-breakfast buffet and signature chocolate-chip cookies. The elegant lobby, with its traditional Southern touches, is in the historic district near City Market, theaters, shops, and restaurants. 182 rooms, 5 story, all suites. Complimentary full breakfast. Check-out noon. Fitness room. Whirlpool. **$$**
🧍

⭐ **HAMPTON INN.** *11 Ashley Pointe Dr, Charleston (29407). Phone 843/556-5200; toll-free 800/426-7866; fax 843/571-5499. www.hamptoninn.com.* 175 rooms, 4 story. Complimentary continental breakfast. Check-in 4 pm, check-out noon. Outdoor pool. **$**
🛏️

⭐ **HAMPTON INN.** *345 Meeting St, Charleston (29403). Phone 843/723-4000; toll-free 888/759-4001; fax 843/722-3725. www.charleston-hotels.net.* 171 rooms, 5 story. Complimentary continental breakfast. Check-in 4 pm, check-out noon. Outdoor pool. **$**
🛏️

⭐ **THE INN AT MIDDLETON PLACE.** *4290 Ashley River Rd, Charleston (29414). Phone 843/556-0500; toll-free 800/543-4774; fax 843/556-5673. www.middletonplace.org.* 52 rooms, 3 story. Complimentary full breakfast. Check-in 4 pm, check-out noon. Restaurant, bar. Children's activity center. Outdoor pool. Business center. **$$**
🛏️ 🧍

Full-Service Hotels

⭐ ⭐ ⭐ **CHARLESTON PLACE.** *205 Meeting St, Charleston (29401). Phone 843/722-4900; fax 843/722-0728.* A sweeping staircase topped off by a huge Venetian glass chandelier sets the tone at Charleston Place, where luxury and Southern hospitality blend to create a memorable experience. Located on Meeting Street in the heart of the historic district, the hotel puts antebellum mansions, luscious gardens, shopping temptations, and colonial markets within an easy stroll. The guest rooms are traditional and attractively appointed with Early American-style furnishings. A fitness center, pool with retractable roof, and shops such as Godiva and Gucci make this a perfect base for travelers who relish modern comforts. This well-rounded hotel features three restaurants with varied settings. Lazy afternoons are best spent at Palmetto Grill, and the Lobby Lounge is a local favorite for its afternoon tea. Charleston Grill, acclaimed for its sassy interpretation of Southern classics, is a surefire hit, especially when accompanied by the mellow sounds of the Frank Duvall Jazz Trio. 441 rooms, 8 story. Check-in 4 pm, check-out noon. High-speed Internet access. Two restaurants, two bars. Fitness room, fitness classes available, spa. Indoor pool, outdoor pool, children's pool, whirlpool. Tennis. Business center. **$$$**
🧍 🛏️ 🏊 🧍

⭐ ⭐ ⭐ **FRANCIS MARION HOTEL.** *387 King St, Charleston (29403). Phone 843/722-0600; toll-free 877/756-2121; fax 843/723-4633. www.francismarion charleston.com.* Originally opened in 1924, as the largest and grandest hotel in the Carolinas, this European-style hotel was named for the "Swamp Fox" of the American Revolution. This property, with its expansive lobby, has been carefully restored. It now boasts over 14,000 square feet of meeting and banquet space and offers all the traditional services of a grand hotel and an excellent restaurant. While the rooms are cozy and even cramped, the amenities of this hotel and its prompt, courteous service make for a comfortable stay. 259 rooms, 12 story. Check-in 4 pm, check-out noon. Restaurant, two bars. Fitness room. Business center. **$$**

★ ★ ★ **MARKET PAVILION HOTEL.** *225 E Bay St, Charleston (29401). Phone 843/723-0500; toll-free 877/440-2250; fax 843/723-4320. www.marketpavilion.com.* 66 rooms. Complimentary continental breakfast. Check-in 3 pm, check-out noon. High-speed Internet access. Two restaurants, two bars. Fitness room. Outdoor pool. **$$$**

★ ★ ★ **RENAISSANCE CHARLESTON HOTEL HISTORIC DISTRICT.** *68 Wentworth St, Charleston (29401). Phone 843/534-0300; fax 843/534-0700. www.renaissancehotels.com.* 166 rooms, 4 story. Check-in 3 pm, check-out noon. High-speed Internet access, wireless Internet access. Restaurant, bar. Fitness room. Outdoor pool. Business center. **$$**

Full-Service Resort

★ ★ ★ **HILTON CHARLESTON HARBOR RESORT AND MARINA.** *20 Patriot's Pl, Mount Pleasant (29464). Phone 843/856-0028; toll-free 888/856-0028; fax 843/856-8333. www.charlestonharborresort.com.* This luxurious resort sits on an 18-hole private championship golf course, private beach, and 450-slip marina. Spectacular sunsets across the Charleston Harbor and historic skyline, with many antebellum buildings and churches, are visible from most rooms. All types of water sports are available, from charter fishing to parasailing. 129 rooms, 4 story. Pets accepted; fee. Check-in 4 pm, check-out 11 am. High-speed Internet access. Two restaurants, bar. Outdoor pool, whirlpool. Business center. **$$**

Full-Service Inns

★ ★ ★ **ANCHORAGE INN.** *26 Vendue Range, Charleston (29401). Phone 843/723-8300; toll-free 800/421-2952; fax 843/723-9543. www.anchoragencharleston.com.* Afternoon tea, English toiletries, and period furnishings make for a sophisticated stay at this inn in the downtown historic district. 21 rooms, 2 story. Complimentary continental breakfast. Check-in 3 pm, check-out 11 am. **$**

★ ★ ★ **CHARLESTON'S VENDUE INN.** *19 Vendue Range, Charleston (29401). Phone 800/845-7900; toll-free 800/845-7900; fax 843/577-2913. www.vendueinn.com.* With its polished pine floors, Oriental rugs, period furniture, and other historic accents, this romantic inn affords a perfect Charleston stay. Many of the individually decorated rooms overlook the Charleston Harbor and Waterfront Park. 69 rooms, 3 story. Complimentary full breakfast. Check-in 3 pm, check-out noon. Restaurant, bar. Fitness room. **$**

★ ★ ★ **HARBOUR VIEW INN.** *2 Vendue Range, Charleston (29401). Phone 843/853-8439; toll-free 888/853-8439; fax 843/853-4034. www.harbourviewcharleston.com.* Spectacular vistas of Charleston's East Harbor, opposite beautiful Waterfront Park, await the discerning traveler who demands both a choice location and luxurious accommodations. This modern, architectural award-winning inn sits amid some of the city's best restaurants, placing Charleston's renowned cuisine within easy walking distance. Complimentary wine and cheese and late-night snack. Comfortable rooms and suites, many with great views from large windows. 57 rooms, 4 story. Check-in 3 pm, check-out noon. **$$**

★ ★ ★ **PLANTERS INN.** *112 N Market St, Charleston (29401). Phone 843/722-2345; toll-free 800/845-7082; fax 843/577-2125. www.plantersinn.com.* Historic Charleston is at the doorstep of the Planters Inn. This delightful inn, located right on the Market, carefully blends historic references with modern amenities. Grace and charm are the hallmark of this special place. White glove service cossets guests who luxuriate in the spacious and elegant rooms and suites. Period furnishings reflect the city's signature style, while whirlpool baths, fireplaces, or piazzas overlooking the courtyard add to the modern-day traveler's experience. This hotel's dedication to excellence extends to its award-winning restaurant, the Peninsula Grill (see), where the chef wins kudos from locals and guests alike for his artfully presented and palate-pleasing culinary creations. 68 rooms, 4 story. Complimentary continental breakfast. Check-in 4 pm, check-out noon. Restaurant. **$$**

★ ★ ★ **WENTWORTH MANSION.** *149 Wentworth St, Charleston (29401). Phone 843/ 853-1886; toll-free 888/466-1886; fax 843/720-5290. www.wentworthmansion.com.* Steeped in tradition, the Wentworth Mansion offers guests a glimpse of Charleston's Gilded Age. Once a private home, this stunning mansion in the city's historic center has visitors swooning over its exquisite details. Hand-carved marble fireplaces, ornate plasterwork, Tiffany stained-glass windows, and tile floors reflect the elegance of a bygone era. The guest rooms offer a taste of the good life, with patrician furnishings, gas fireplaces, and charming views. The public rooms are glorious, and guests often roam from room to room enjoying the resplendent settings. The sun porch hosts a bountiful European breakfast each morning, and the Rodgers Library calls for a good read or a snifter of brandy. Visitors in the know are sure to book a table at the inn's restaurant (circa 1886). Nestled in the gardens behind the mansion, this white glove establishment tantalizes the palate with its sensational creations and dazzles the eye with its refined setting. 21 rooms, 4 story. Pets accepted. Complimentary full breakfast. Check-in 4 pm, check-out noon. Restaurant. Business center. **$$$**

Specialty Lodgings

The following lodging establishments are approved by Mobil Travel Guide, but due to their unique and individualized nature have not been given a traditional Mobil Star rating. Included in this listing you may find bed-and-breakfasts, limited-service inns, guest ranches, and other unique hotel properties.

ANSONBOROUGH INN. *21 Hasell St, Charleston (29401). Phone 843/723-1655; toll-free 800/522-2073; fax 843/577-6888. www.ansonboroughinn.com.* 37 rooms, all suites. Complimentary continental breakfast. Check-in 3 pm, check-out noon. Bar. Business center. **$$**

BARKSDALE HOUSE INN. *27 George St, Charleston (29401). Phone 843/577-4800; toll-free 888/ 577-4980; fax 843/853-0482. www.barksdalehouse.com.* Built as a town home in 1778 by a wealthy Charlestonian, George Barksdale, this stately bed-and-breakfast is filled with period furnishings and modern conveniences. It is located in the historic district. 14 rooms, 3 story. Children over 10 years only. Complimentary continental breakfast. Check-in 3 pm, check-out 11 am. **$**

BATTERY CARRIAGE HOUSE INN. *20 S Battery St, Charleston (29401). Phone 843/727-3100; toll-free 800/775-5575; fax 843/727-3130. www.batterycarriage house.com.* Hidden within the flowering gardens of the Steven-Lathers Mansion, an exquisite private home, this 1843 bed and breakfast offers private entrances and romantic décor. The location overlooking Charleston Harbor can't be beat. 12 rooms, 2 story. Children over 12 years only. Complimentary continental breakfast. Check-in 3 pm, check-out noon. **$**

THE GOVERNOR'S HOUSE INN. *117 Broad St, Charleston (29401). Phone 843/720-2070; toll-free 800/720-9812. www.governorshouse.com.* 11 rooms. Check-in 3 pm, check-out 11 am. **$$$**

INDIGO INN. *1 Maiden Ln, Charleston (29401). Phone 843/577-5900; toll-free 800/845-7639; fax 843/577-0378. www.indigoinn.com.* Housed in an 1850 warehouse once used to store indigo for dying textiles, this colorful inn is located in the middle of the historic district, justone block from City Market. Each of the rooms is color coordinated. 40 rooms, 3 story. Pets accepted, some restrictions; fee. Complimentary continental breakfast. Check-in 3 pm, check-out noon. **$**

JOHN RUTLEDGE HOUSE INN. *116 Broad St, Charleston (29401). Phone 843/723-7999; fax 843/720-2615.* This genteel inn not only sends you back to an earlier era, but puts you in the midst of historic living. Arrive late in the afternoon and take tea in the salon. Enjoy the luxuriously appointed rooms with great views of the city's spires. 19 rooms, 1 story. Complimentary continental breakfast. Check-in 4 pm, check-out noon. **$$**

KINGS COURTYARD INN. *198 King St, Charleston (29401). Phone 843/723-7000; fax 843/720-2608.* This three-story, antebellum, Greek Revival structure was built in 1854 and remains one of the gems of Charleston's historic district. 44 rooms, 3 story. Complimentary continental breakfast. Check-in 3 pm, check-out noon. Restaurant, bar. **$**

MAISON DU PRE. *317 E Bay St, Charleston (29401). Phone 843/723-8691; toll-free 800/844-4667; fax 843/723-3722. www.maisondupre.com.* The main house dates from 1804, as does the charm of the welcome. Located in historic downtown, adjacent to the Gaillard Auditorium, this inn is decorated in period furniture and art made by the family that runs it. 15 rooms, 3 story. Complimentary continental breakfast. Check-in 2 pm, check-out noon. **$**
🔒

MEETING STREET INN. *173 Meeting St, Charleston (29401). Phone 843/723-1882; toll-free 800/842-8022; fax 843/577-0851. www.meetingstreetinn.com.* Each room in this classic, Charleston-style single-house inn opens onto the piazza and courtyard. The rooms are individually decorated with period furniture. The inn is conveniently located opposite the City Market in historic downtown. 56 rooms, 4 story. Complimentary continental breakfast. Check-in 3 pm, check-out noon. Bar. **$**

VICTORIA HOUSE INN. *208 King St, Charleston (29401). Phone 843/720-2944; toll-free 800/933-5464; fax 843/720-2930.* Built in the late 1880s, this Romanesque-style Victorian house now serves as a lovely inn. Located in the downtown historic district, the inn offers genteel amenities, such as a bedside champagne breakfast. 22 rooms, 3 story. Complimentary continental breakfast. Check-in 3 pm, check-out noon. **$**
🔒

Restaurants

★ ★ **82 QUEEN.** *82 Queen St, Charleston (29401). Phone 843/723-7591; toll-free 800/849-0082; fax 843/577-7463. www.82queen.com.* Low country menu. Lunch, dinner, Sun brunch. Bar. Children's menu. Casual attire. Outdoor seating. **$$**

★ ★ **ANSON.** *12 Anson St, Charleston (29401). Phone 843/577-0551; fax 843/720-1955. www.ansonrestaurant.com.* Low country menu. Dinner. Children's menu. Casual attire. Outdoor seating. Bilevel dining. **$$$**

★ ★ **BLOSSOM CAFE.** *171 E Bay St, Charleston (29401). Phone 843/722-9200; fax 843/722-0035. www.magnolias-blossom-cypress.com.* Italian menu. Lunch, dinner. Closed Thanksgiving, Dec 25. Bar. Children's menu. Casual attire. Outdoor seating. **$$**

★ ★ **CAROLINA'S.** *10 Exchange St, Charleston (29401). Phone 843/724-3800; toll-free 888/486-7673;* *fax 843/722-9493. www.cardinasrest.com.* Dinner. Closed Dec 25. Bar. Casual attire. **$$**

★ ★ ★ **CHARLESTON GRILL.** *224 King St, Charleston (29401). Phone 843/577-4522; fax 843/724-8405. www.charlestongrill.com.* The Charleston Grill is a posh, clubby spot located in the Charleston Place hotel. Stained-glass French doors, dark wood-paneled walls, marble floors, and vases filled with impressive floral arrangements come together to create a classy, old-world atmosphere. Menu appearances by such dishes as Maine lobster tempura with lemon grits and fried mini green tomatoes and baked country crepinette of local rabbit loin with seared foie gras and Vidalia onions in a sausage sawmill gravy should give you a good idea of the delicious sort of low country fare served at this sophisticated, ever-popular destination restaurant. Live jazz and terrific classic cocktails make this a hotspot for a young crowd of music lovers as well as a mature audience of discerning foodies. American menu. Dinner. Bar. Children's menu. Business casual attire. Reservations recommended. Valet parking. Outdoor seating. **$$$$**

★ ★ ★ **CIRCA 1886.** *149 Wentworth St, Charleston (29401). Phone 843/853-7828; fax 843/720-5292. www.wentworthmansion.com.* American menu. Lunch, dinner. Bar. Business casual attire. Reservations recommended. Valet parking. **$$$**
🔒

★ ★ ★ **CYPRESS.** *167 E Bay St, Charleston (29401). Phone 843/727-0111.* American menu. Dinner. Closed Thanksgiving, Dec 25; also Super Bowl Sun. Bar. Children's menu. Business casual attire. **$$**

★ ★ ★ **CYPRESS A LOWCOUNTRY GRILLE.** *167 E Bay Street, Charleston (29401). Phone 843/727-0111; fax 843/937-4027. www.magnolias-blossoms-cypress.com.* American menu. Dinner. Bar. Children's menu. Business casual attire. Reservations recommended. **$$$**

★ ★ **FULTON FIVE.** *5 Fulton St, Charleston (29401). Phone 843/853-5555; fax 843/853-6212.* This restaurant, with its Euopean décor and intimate atmosphere, does all of its own baking on-site. Italian menu. Dinner. Closed Sun; holidays; also late Aug-first week in Sept. Bar. Casual attire. **$$$**

★ ★ **GAULART & MALICLET FRENCH CAFE.** *98 Broad St, Charleston (29401). Phone 843/577-9797.* French menu. Breakfast, lunch, dinner. Closed Sun. Casual attire. **$$**

★ ★ **HANK'S SEAFOOD RESTAURANT.** *10 Hayne St, Charleston (29401). Phone 843/723-3474.* Seafood menu. Dinner. Bar. Children's menu. Casual attire. **$$**

★ ★ **HIGH COTTON.** *199 E Bay St, Charleston (29401). Phone 843/724-3815.* American menu. Dinner. Closed Dec 25; Super Bowl Sun. Bar. Children's menu. Business casual attire. **$$**

★ ★ **HOMINY GRILL.** *207 Rutledge Ave, Charleston (29401). Phone 843/937-0930. www.hominygrill.com.* Low country Southern menu. Breakfast, lunch, dinner. Closed Thanksgiving; late Dec. Casual attire. Outdoor seating. **$$**

★ ★ ★ **MAGNOLIAS.** *185 E Bay St, Charleston (29401). Phone 843/577-7771; fax 843/722-0035. www.magnolias-blossom-cypress.com.* This smart, uptown restaurant specializes in updated Southern food. Chef Barickman uses Southern ingredients in mouth-watering combinations. He constantly focuses on the quality of prime ingredients, freshness, and the use of local products. American menu. Lunch, dinner. Closed Dec 25. Bar. **$$**

★ ★ ★ **MCCRADY'S.** *2 Unity Alley, Charleston (29401). Phone 843/577-0025; fax 843/577-3681. www.mccradysrestaurant.com.* Housed in a beautifully restored former tavern that was built in 1778, McCrady's is a one-of-a-kind restaurant. As you enter the long, sexy, dark-wood bar and take a seat amid the swanky cocktail crowd, you know you are somewhere special. The experience gets even better when you move to the clubby dining room, with original hardwood floors and brickwork, vaulted wood-beamed ceilings, soaring skylights, magnificent floor-to-ceiling windows, and lavish tufted leather seating. The service is warm and knowledgeable and specializes in little details like offering black linen napkins to guests who don't wish to leave with white lint coating their dark trousers. But the food really takes the cake. Chef-partner Michael Kramer wows his savvy guests with his bold brand of flashy, progressive American fare. Plates arrive in a hush of envy from other tables and return to the kitchen empty, making easy work for the dishwashers. Coffee-rubbed filet mignon is a signature and will have you saving coffee grinds to reinvent this dish at home. Eclectic/International menu. Dinner. Closed Jan 1, Thanksgiving, Dec 25. Bar. Business casual attire. Reservations recommended. **$$$**

★ ★ **MERITAGE.** *235 E Bay St, Charleston (29401). Phone 843/723-8181.* Eclectic menu. Dinner. Closed Dec 24-25; second Sun in June. Bar. Children's menu. Casual attire. Outdoor seating. **$**

★ ★ ★ ★ **PENINSULA GRILL.** *112 N Market St, Charleston (29401). Phone 843/723-0700; fax 843/577-2125. www.peninsulagrill.com.* Located in the Planter's Inn, Peninsula Grill is a place where the words *fun* and *Four-Star dining* can easily be used in the same sentence. The comfortably elegant restaurant is richly styled with crushed velvet walls, polished dark woods, and local cypress crown moldings. It has the sophisticated feel of an urban eatery without losing sight of its Southern charm and hospitality. The menu is inventive and exciting, offering boldly flavored dishes spiced up with low-country accents like collards, hushpuppies, grits, and black-eyed peas. A perfect way to start any meal is with a glass of champagne, and at Peninsula Grill, you have five champagnes and sparkling wines by the glass to choose from. There's also a fun "Champagne Bar Menu" of decadent little treats like oysters, lobster, foie gras, caviar, and duck pâté to match up with your glass(es) of bubbly. Prepare your toasts in advance. The staff at Peninsula Grill will guide you effortlessly through an evening that is both delicious and entertaining. Before you know it, many hours and many glasses of wine will have passed, and you'll want to do it all over again. American menu. Dinner. Bar. Business casual attire. Reservations recommended. Outdoor seating. **$$$**

★ ★ **SERMET'S CORNER.** *276 King St, Charleston (29401). Phone 843/853-7775; fax 843/853-7770.* Mediterranean menu. Lunch, dinner. Closed Thanksgiving, Dec 25. Bar. Children's menu. **$$**

★ ★ **SLIGHTLY NORTH OF BROAD.** *192 E Bay St, Charleston (29401). Phone 843/723-3424; fax 843/724-3811. www.slightlynorthofbroad.net.* Low country menu. Lunch, dinner. Closed July 4, Dec 25. Bar. Children's menu. Casual attire. **$$**

★ ★ **VINTAGE.** *14 N Market St, Charleston (29401). Phone 843/577-0090.* American menu. Dinner. Closed Jan 1, Thanksgiving, Dec 25. Bar. Casual attire. **$$**

Cheraw (C-5)

See also Bennettsville, Camden, Darlington, Florence, Hartsville

Settled 1740
Population 5,524
Elevation 150 ft
Area Code 843
Zip 29520

Information Chamber of Commerce, 221 Market St; phone 843/537-8425 or 843/537-7681
Web Site www.cheraw.com

Profiting in commerce from both Carolinas, Cheraw grew rapidly when the Pee Dee River was opened for traffic. It is said that the town owes its many trees to an ordinance that required every person seen intoxicated in public to go out into the woods and fetch a tree for planting within the town.

What to See and Do

Carolina Sandhills National Wildlife Refuge. *On Hwy 1, 4 miles NE of McBee; approximately 20 miles SW on Hwy 1. Phone 843/335-8401.* Approximately 46,000 acres house almost 300 species of birds, mammals, reptiles, and amphibians. Auto tour route, hiking trails, and observation towers available. Fishing, hunting permitted. Interpretive displays available at headquarters. (Mon-Fri, dawn-dusk) **FREE**

★ **Cheraw Historical District.** *221 N Market St, Cheraw (29520). Phone 843/537-8425. www.cheraw.com.* Cheraw showcases a 213-acre historic district with several recommended walking routes. The town's roots date back to before the Revolutionary War, and Cheraw has a deep Civil War history as well. The town green (circa 1768) is the site of the small Cheraw Lyceum Museum (circa 1820). Other notable buildings are Town Hall (circa 1858), Market Hall (circa 1837), and the Inglis-McIver Law Office (circa 1830). Victorian and Revival homes dot the walking trail through the heavily wooded town. Limit your drinking: local lore has it that in the past, anyone found drunk in public in Cheraw had to plant a tree in the town limits. **FREE**

Cheraw State Park. *100 State Park Rd, Cheraw (29520). 4 miles SW on Hwy 52. Phone 843/537-9656; toll-free 800/868-9630.* Located on 7,361 acres of gently rolling green sandhills, the park offers lake swimming, boat rentals, fishing, nature trails, an 18-hole golf course, picnic shelters, a playground, and a recreation building. You'll also find camping and cabins. Unusually cool in hot-weather periods. **$**

Old St. David's Episcopal Church. *221 Market St, Cheraw. Phone 843/537-7681.* (1768) Restored to the 1820s period; last Anglican parish established in the state prior to the American Revolution. Used as a hospital by British during Revolution, later by Union Army during Civil War; about 50 British soldiers are buried in the churchyard. Tours (by appointment); for self-tours, pick up keys at Chamber of Commerce.

Special Event

Spring Festival. *200 Powe St, Cheraw. Phone 843/537-8420.* Family Fun Run; tours; arts and crafts shows; Confederate reenactments; entertainment, trolley rides, car show. Early Apr.

Chester (C-4)

See also Rock Hill

Settled 1755
Population 6,476
Elevation 485 ft
Area Code 803
Zip 29706
Information Chester County Chamber of Commerce, 109 Gadsden St, PO Box 489; phone 803/581-4142
Web Site www.chestersc.org

Seat of Chester County, this town was named by settlers from Pennsylvania. Aaron Burr, guarded here in 1807 while under arrest for treason, broke away and climbed a high rock. After haranguing a surprised crowd, he was recaptured.

What to See and Do

Chester State Park. *759 State Park Dr, Chester (29706). 3 miles SW on Hwy 72. Phone 803/385-2680.* Approximately 500 acres. Lake fishing, boating. Nature trail. Picnicking (shelters), recreation building. Camping (hook-ups, dump station). Equestrian show ring. **$**

Clemson (C-2)

See also Anderson, Greenville

Founded 1889
Population 11,939
Elevation 850 ft
Area Code 864
Zip 29631
Information Clemson Area Chamber of Commerce, PO Box 1622, 29633; phone 864/654-1200 or toll-free 800/542-0746
Web Site www.clemsonchamber.org

Home of Clemson University, this community also hosts vacationers attracted to the huge lake that the Hartwell Dam has formed on the Savannah River.

What to See and Do

Clemson University. *11 miles NW of I-85 at jct Hwy 76, Hwy 93. Phone 864/656-3311.* (1889) (17,000 students) Named for Thomas G. Clemson, son-in-law of John C. Calhoun, who bequeathed the bulk of his estate, Fort Hill, for establishment of a scientific college. On this 1,400-acre campus are

Fort Hill. *Phone 864/656-2475.* (1803) Mansion on 1,100 acres acquired by Calhoun during his first term as vice president. House has many original furnishings belonging to Calhoun, Clemson. (Daily; closed holidays) **FREE**

Hanover House. *102 Garden Trail, Clemson (29634). Phone 864/656-2475.* (1716) This French Huguenot house was moved here from its original site in Berkeley County to prevent submersion by Lake Moultrie. (Mon-Sat, also Sun afternoons). **FREE**

State Botanical Gardens. *102 Garden Trail, Clemson (29634). E side of campus. Phone 864/656-3405.* This 250-acre area includes azalea and camelia trails, ornamental plantings, large collection of shrubs; dwarf conifer flower and turf display gardens; wildflower pioneer and bog garden labeled in Braille. (Daily) **FREE**

Oconee State Park. *624 State Park Rd, Mountain Rest (29664). 20 miles NW of town, 12 miles NW of Walhalla on Hwy 107. Phone 864/638-5353.* Approximately 1,100 acres of park nestled in the foothills of the Blue Ridge and surrounded by Sumter National Forest (see GREENWOOD). Lake swimming, lifeguard (summer), boating (rentals), fishing. Nature, hiking trails; recreation building; recreation and nature programs (summer); carpet golf. Picnicking (shelters), playground, concession, restaurant. Camping (hook-ups, dump station), cabins. **$**

Raft trips. *1251 Academy Rd, Long Creek (29658). 34 miles NW on Hwy 76. Phone toll-free 800/451-9972.* Guided whitewater rafting trips on the Chattooga National Wild and Scenic River. Reservations required. Also canoe and kayak clinics and overnight trips. (Daily, Mar-Oct)

World of Energy. *7812 Rochester Hwy, Seneca (29672). 12 miles NW on Hwys 130, 123. Phone 864/885-4600; toll-free 800/777-1004. www.dukepower.com.* Three-dimensional displays on the "Story of Energy," with exhibits on hydro, coal, and nuclear production of electricity; also displays on radiation and supplemental energy sources. Computer games; films. Overlooks Lake Keowee and one of the world's largest nuclear generating plants. Picnic area and boat dock adjacent. (Mon-Fri 9 am-5 pm, Sat-Sun noon-5 pm; closed Jan 1, Thanksgiving, Dec 24-25) **FREE**

Special Event

Clemson Fest. *133 E Queen St, Clemson. Phone 864/654-1200.* Entertainment, arts and crafts, children's activities. Boat parade and contest precedes fireworks display. July 3.

Limited-Service Hotel

★ **COMFORT INN.** *1305 Tiger Blvd, Clemson (29631). Phone 864/653-3600; toll-free 800/252-7466; fax 864/654-3123. www.comfortinn.com.* 122 rooms, 4 story. Pets accepted, some restrictions. Complimentary continental breakfast. Check-in 4 pm, check-out noon. Outdoor pool, whirlpool. **$**

Specialty Lodging

The following lodging establishment is approved by Mobil Travel Guide, but due to its unique and individualized nature has not been given a traditional Mobil Star rating. Included in this listing you may find bed-and-breakfasts, limited-service inns, guest ranches, and other unique hotel properties.

SUNRISE FARM BED & BREAKFAST INN. *325 Sunrise Dr, Salem (29676). Phone 864/944-0121; toll-free 888/991-0121; fax 864/944-6195.* Built in 1890; Victorian country farmhouse. 8 rooms, 2 story. Complimentary full breakfast. Check-in 3-6 pm, check-out 11 am. **$**

Clinton (C-3)

See also Greenville, Greenwood, Newberry, Spartanburg

Population 8,091
Elevation 680 ft
Area Code 864
Zip 29325
Information Laurens County Chamber of Commerce, PO Box 248, Laurens 29360; phone 864/833-2716

Web Site www.laurenscounty.org

In 1865, Clinton was "a mudhole surrounded by barrooms," according to the young Rev William Jacobs, who not only rid the town of barrooms, but founded a library, orphanage, high school, and Presbyterian College (1880). A young attorney by the name of Henry Clinton Young was hired by the townspeople to help lay out the streets, hence the town came to be named for his middle name.

What to See and Do

Rose Hill Plantation State Historic Site. *2677 Sardis Rd, Union (29379). 15 miles E on Hwy 72, 2 miles N on Hwy 176, then W on Sardis Rd. Phone 864/427-5966.* (Circa 1825) Forty-four acres. Located in Rose Hill State Park, this restored cotton plantation was the home of William H. Gist, known as South Carolina's secession governor. The Federal-style house with 1860 furnishings sits on a gently rising knoll amid boxwoods and roses. House (Thurs-Mon 1-4 pm; tour, $). Grounds (Thurs-Mon 9 am-6 pm). Picnic area, nature trail. **FREE**

Columbia (D-4)

See also Camden, Newberry, Orangeburg, Sumter

Founded 1786
Population 116,278
Elevation 213 ft
Area Code 803
Information Columbia Metropolitan Visitors Center, PO Box 15, 29202; phone 803/254-0479 or toll-free 800/264-4884
Web Site www.columbiachamber.com

The broad-boulevarded capital of South Carolina is not only the state's political and governmental capital, but also its wholesale and retail trade center. Located within 3 miles of the geographic center of the state, Columbia was laid out as the capital as a compromise between the contending up country and low country farmers. The city rarely departs from a checkerboard pattern; the streets are sometimes 150 feet wide, planned that way originally to discourage malaria.

The General Assembly met for the first time in the State House in Columbia on January 4, 1790. George Washington was a guest here during his Southern tour the next year. On December 17, 1860, a convention assembled in Columbia's First Baptist Church and drew up the Ordinance of Secession, setting off a chain of events that terminated, for the city, on February 17, 1865, when General William T. Sherman's troops occupied Columbia and reduced it to ashes. An area of 84 blocks and 1,386 buildings was destroyed; on Main Street only the unfinished new statehouse and the home of the French consul were spared. From these ashes, a city of stately buildings has risen.

The economy of the city is based on trade, industry, finance, and government.

Since 1801, when the South Carolina College, now the University of South Carolina, was established here, the city has been an educational center; today it is the site of nine schools of higher education.

Columbia is the headquarters for the Francis Marion National Forest (see CHARLESTON) and the Sumter National Forest (see GREENWOOD).

What to See and Do

Columbia Museum of Art. *Main and Hampton sts, Columbia. Phone 803/799-2810.* Galleries house Renaissance paintings from the collection of Samuel H. Kress; 19th- and 20th-century American, emphasizing the Southeast, and European paintings; changing exhibitions drawn from permanent collection and objects on loan. Concerts, films, lectures, and special events accenting exhibitions. (Tues-Sat, also Sun afternoons; closed holidays) **$$**

Confederate Relic Room and Museum. *301 Gervais St, Columbia. Phone 803/737-8095.* Relic collection from the Colonial period through the space age with special emphasis on South Carolina's Confederate period. (Call for hours and fees)

Congaree National Park. *100 National Park Rd, Hopkins (29061). 20 miles SE off Hwy 48. Phone 803/776-4396. www.nps.gov/cosw/.* Congaree is South Carolina's only and the nation's newest national park. The lush enclave has a Jurassic-era feel. Roughly 22,000 acres of old-growth forest spill across wetlands rich with wildlife. There are 20 miles of hiking trails, fishing, canoeing, and boardwalks. Primitive camping is allowed by permit. (Daily; closed Dec 25) **FREE**

First Baptist Church. *1306 Hampton St, Columbia. Phone 803/256-4251.* (1859) First Secession Convention, which marked the beginning of the Civil

War, met here on Dec 17, 1860. (Mon-Fri, Sun; closed holidays)

First Presbyterian Church. *1324 Marion St, Columbia. At Lady St. Phone 803/799-9062.* (1853) First congregation organized in Columbia (1795); President Woodrow Wilson's parents are buried in churchyard. (Daily)

Fort Jackson. *442 Jackson Blvd, Columbia (29634). E edge of city, between I-20 and Hwy 76. Phone 803/751-7419.* The most active initial entry training center for the US Army, with 16,000 soldiers assigned. Museum on Jackson Blvd has displays on the history of the fort and today's army. (Tues-Fri; closed holidays) **FREE**

Governor's Mansion. *800 Richland St, Columbia. Phone 803/737-1710.* (1855) Built as officers' quarters for Arsenal Academy. Tours (Tues-Thurs). Reservations required. **FREE**

Hampton-Preston Mansion. *1615 Blanding St, Columbia. Phone 803/252-1770.* (1818) Purchased by Wade Hampton I; occupied by the Hamptons and the family of his daughter, Mrs. John Preston. In Feb 1865, it served as headquarters for Union General J. A. Logan. Many Hampton family furnishings and decorative arts of the antebellum period. (Tues-Sun; closed holidays) **$$**

Hampton Park. *1117 Brandon Ave, Columbia (29209). Lyttleton St near Hwy 1.* Named for a Confederate general who later became governor. Flagstones used in crosswalks were once part of the sidewalks of old Camden and are said to have been brought over as ballast in British ships.

Lake Murray. *2184 N Lake Dr, Columbia. 15 miles NW via I-26, Irmo exit. Phone 803/749-1554.* The lake is 41 miles long, with a 520-mile shoreline; it's impounded by the Saluda Dam for hydroelectric purposes. Swimming, water-skiing, boating, fishing; picnicking, camping (fee). Lighthouse Marina is 17 miles NW.

Lexington County Museum Complex. *231 Fox St, Lexington. 10 miles W via Hwy 378 at Fox St. Phone 803/359-8369.* A historic restoration from the mid-1700s; depicts the life of area farmers. Period country furnishings, textiles, decorative arts. Spinning and weaving tours. (Tues-Sat 10 am-4 pm, Sun 1-4 pm; closed holidays)

Riverbanks Zoo and Garden. *500 Wildlife Pkwy, Columbia (29210). Phone 803/779-8717. www.riverbanks.org.* Exhibits of animals in nonrestrictive natural habitat areas; aquarium-reptile complex with diving demonstrations; demonstrations at Riverbanks Farm; penguin and sea lion feedings. (Daily 9 am-5 pm; closed Thanksgiving, Dec 25) **$$**

Robert Mills Historic House and Park. *1616 Blanding St, Columbia. Phone 803/252-1770.* (1823) One of a few residences designed by Robert Mills, Federal architect and designer of the Washington Monument; mantels, art, furnishings of Regency period. (Tues-Sun; closed holidays) **$$**

Sesquicentennial State Park. *9564 Two Notch Rd, Columbia (29223). 13 miles NE on Hwy 1. Phone 803/788-2706.* On 1,445 acres. Log house (1756). Interpretive center. Lake swimming, bathhouse, boating (rentals), fishing. Nature, biking, exercise trails. Picnicking (five shelters), playground. Recreation building. Camping (hook-ups, dump station). Swimming and boating (Memorial Day-Labor Day). (Daily 8 am-6 pm) **$**

South Carolina Archives Building. *8301 Parklane Rd, Columbia. Phone 803/896-6100.* Historical and genealogical research facility with documents dating from 1671; changing exhibits. Research room (Mon-Fri; closed holidays). Tours (by appointment). **FREE**

South Carolina State Museum. *301 Gervais St, Columbia (29201). Phone 803/898-4921. www.museum.state.sc.us.* Located in the world's first fully electric textile mill (1894); exhibits on art, natural history, cultural history, and science and technology with an emphasis on contributions by South Carolinians; numerous hands-on exhibits; dioramas. Included is a center dedicated to Nobel Prize winner Charles Townes, who helped develop the laser. Gift shop. (Tues-Sat 10 am-5 pm, Sun 1-5 pm; closed holidays) **$**

Town Theatre. *1012 Sumter St, Columbia. Phone 803/799-2510.* One of the oldest (since 1919) community theater groups in the United States. Broadway plays and musicals. Tours (by appointment). Performances (late Sept-late May; also summer show).

Trinity Cathedral. *1100 Sumter St, Columbia. At Senate St, opposite Statehouse. Phone 803/771-7300.* (1846) Reproduction of Yorkminster, England; the oldest church building in Columbia and one of the largest Episcopal congregations in the United States. Hiram Powers baptismal font, box pews, English stained glass. Three Wade Hamptons (a politically prominent South Carolina family) are buried in the churchyard; graves of seven governors and six bishops are also here. In 1977, it became the Cathedral Parish of the

Episcopal Diocese of Upper South Carolina. (Daily) **FREE**

University of South Carolina. *Pendleton and Assembly sts, Columbia. Phone 803/777-0169 (exc SC); toll-free 800/922-9755.* (1801) (26,000 students) Located downtown. For campus tour information, stop at the University of South Carolina Visitor Center. (Mon-Sat) Points of interest include

Carolina Coliseum. *Assembly and Blossom sts, Columbia.* Houses Gamecock basketball games and other sports events, concerts, exhibitions, trade shows, circuses, and other entertainment.

The Horseshoe. *Off Sumter St. Original campus area.* Ten of the 11 buildings on the quadrangle date back to the 19th century and are listed in the National Register of Historic Places. Monument erected in 1827 was designed by Robert Mills.

Koger Center for the Arts. *Assembly and Greene sts, Columbia.* Contemporary structure houses center for the performing arts. Diverse musical, theatrical, and dance programs.

McKissick Museum. *Bull and Pendleton sts, Columbia (29201). At the head of the Horseshoe. Phone 803/777-7251. www.cla.sc.edu/mcks.* Houses Bernard M. Baruch Silver Gallery with antique European silver, J. Harry Howard gemstone collection, Laurence L. Smith Mineral Library, Catawba Native American pottery collection, Southern folk art, historical collections, art gallery, education museum, broadcasting archives. (Tues-Fri 9 am-4 pm, Sun 1-5 pm; closed holidays) **FREE**

Woodrow Wilson Boyhood Home. *1705 Hampton St, Columbia. Phone 803/252-1770.* (1872) The house was built by Wilson's father and contains items associated with Wilson's family and career. (Tues-Sun; closed holidays) **$$**

Special Event

South Carolina State Fair. *Fairgrounds, 1200 Rosewood Dr, Columbia. Phone 803/799-3387.* Agricultural, floral, home, craft, livestock, and commercial exhibits. Entertainment, shows, carnival. Mid-Oct.

Limited-Service Hotels

★ ★ **EMBASSY SUITES.** *200 Stoneridge Dr, Columbia (29210). Phone 803/252-8700; toll-free 800/362-2779; fax 803/256-8749. www.embassysuites.com.* Near the city's main attractions, this hotel offers spacious suites and a seven-story atrium. Its location places it near shopping malls, the state capitol, the university, and the airport. 214 rooms, 7 story, all suites. Complimentary full breakfast. Check-in 3 pm, check-out noon. Restaurant, bar. Fitness room. Indoor pool, whirlpool. Airport transportation available. **$**

★ **HAMPTON INN-DOWNTOWN HISTORIC DISTRICT.** *822 Gervais St, Columbia (29201). Phone 803/231-2000; fax 803/231-2868. www.hamptoninncolumbia.com.* 122 rooms. Complimentary continental breakfast. Check-in 3 pm, check-out noon. High-speed Internet access, wireless Internet access. Fitness room. Outdoor pool. Business center. **$**

★ ★ **HOLIDAY INN.** *7510 Two Notch Rd, Columbia (29223). Phone 803/736-3000; toll-free 800/465-4329; fax 803/736-6399. www.holiday-inn.com.* 253 rooms, 2 story. Pets accepted, some restrictions; fee. Complimentary continental breakfast. Check-in 4 pm, check-out noon. Restaurant, bar. Children's activity center. Fitness room. Indoor pool, outdoor pool, whirlpool. **$**

★ ★ **RAMADA PLAZA.** *8105 Two Notch Rd, Columbia (29223). Phone 803/736-5600; fax 803/736-1241. www.ramada.com.* 186 rooms, 6 story. Pets accepted; fee. Check-in 3 pm, check-out noon. Restaurant, bar. Fitness room. Outdoor pool. **$**

Specialty Lodging

The following lodging establishments is approved by Mobil Travel Guide, but due to its unique and individualized nature has not been given a traditional Mobil Star rating. Included in this listing you may find bed-and-breakfasts, limited-service inns, guest ranches, and other unique hotel properties.

CLAUSSENS INN. *2003 Greene St, Columbia (29205). Phone 803/765-0440; toll-free 800/622-3382; fax 803/799-7924. www.claussensinn.com.* Located in the Five Points neighborhood, about 1 mile from downtown, this inn features four-poster beds and other country-inn charms. The building is a renovated bakery (1928). 29 rooms, 2 story. Complimentary continental breakfast. Check-in 3 pm, check-out noon. Whirlpool. **$$**

Restaurants

★ ★ **HAMPTON STREET VINEYARD.** *1207 Hampton St, Columbia (29201). Phone 803/252-0850; fax 803/929-0604. www.hamptonstreetvineyard.com.* American menu. Lunch, dinner. Closed Sun; also week of July 4. Bar. Casual attire. Reservations recommended. Valet parking. Outdoor seating. **$$**
🅓

★ ★ **HENNESSY'S.** *1649 Main St, Columbia (29201). Phone 803/799-8280; fax 803/254-6276. www.hennessyssc.com.* International menu. Lunch, dinner. Closed Sun. Bar. Converted hardware store. Business casual attire. Reservations recommended. **$$**

★ ★ **RISTORANTE DIVINO.** *803 Gervais St, Columbia (29201). Phone 803/799-4550.* Italian menu. Dinner. Closed Sun-Mon; Jan 1, Dec 25. **$$**

Darlington (D-5)

See also Bennettsville, Cheraw, Dillon, Florence, Hartsville

Founded 1798
Population 6,720
Elevation 157 ft
Area Code 843
Zip 29532
Information Greater Darlington Chamber of Commerce, PO Box 274; phone 843/393-2641
Web Site www.visitdarlingtoncounty.org

Darlington is situated in one of the most fertile sections of the state. Along with its agricultural economy, the area has diversified industry. Darlington was a pioneer in the culture and marketing of tobacco as a cash crop and has a large tobacco market. It is the home of what is said to be the nation's largest automobile auction market and is a stock car racing center.

What to See and Do

Joe Weatherly Stock Car Museum and National Motorsports Press Association Stock Car Hall of Fame. *1301 Harry Byrd Hwy, Darlington (29532). 1 mile W on Hwy 34 at Darlington Raceway, the oldest super-speedway in the country. Phone 843/395-8499. www.darlingtonraceway.com.* Explore Darlington's storied history with NASCAR. The Hall of Fame features everyone from David Pearson and Dale Earnhardt to NASCAR's first champion, Red Byron.

Several rooms are filled with stock cars that once sped across the raceway, including the blue Plymouth that Richard Petty drove to victory in ten races back in 1967; a 1991 Chevy driven by Darrell Waltrip that rolled eight times during a race; and a 1971 Mercury driven by Pearson, the all-time winner at Darlington. It adjoins a small gift shop. (Daily 9 am-5 pm; closed Thanksgiving, Dec 25) **$**

Liberty Lane Walk of Fame. *100 Pearl St, Darlington (29532). 100 block of Pearl St. Phone toll-free 888/ 427-8720.* Stroll down the Walk of Fame, which honors NASCAR stock car drivers who have won at Darlington Raceway. Compare your hands with the cement prints of NASCAR greats like Neil Bonnett, Dale Earnhardt, Bill Elliott, Harry Gant, and Richard Petty. **FREE**

Special Events

Southern 500. *Darlington Raceway, 1301 Harry Byrd Hwy, Darlington.* 500-mile stock car classic; beauty pageant; "Southern 500" Festival parade; golf tournament. Preceded by two days of trials. Labor Day weekend.

Sweet Potato Festival. *505 Anderson Dr, Darlington (29532). Phone 843/395-2940.* Entertainment, food, clowns and the famous spud are just some of the activities found at this event. Early Oct.

TranSouth Financial 400. *Darlington Raceway, 1301 Harry Byrd Hwy, Darlington.* Late-model stock car race. Late Mar.

Dillon (C-6)

See also Bennettsville, Darlington, Florence

Settled 1887
Population 6,316
Elevation 115 ft
Area Code 843
Zip 29536

Industrial growth and diversification characterize this town, which is the county seat. Dillon also serves as a shipping center for farm produce.

What to See and Do

Little Pee Dee State Park. *1298 State Park Rd (Hwy 22), Dillon (29536). 11 miles SE between Hwys 9 and 57, near I-95. Phone 843/774-8872. www.discoversouth*

carolina.com/stateparks. Along the Little Pee Dee River and convenient to Interstate 95, this 835-acre park offers a tranquil setting for picnicking, fishing in the 54-acre Lake Norton, camping, or just relaxing. Roam through the small river swamp and dry sandy areas and explore the variety of flora and fauna. (Daily 9 am-6 pm) **$**

Full-Service Inn

★ ★ ★ **ABINGDON MANOR.** *307 Church St, Latta (29565). Phone 843/752-5090; toll-free 888/752-5090; fax 843/752-6034. www.abingdonmanor.com.* Located midway between New York and Miami, this Greek Revival mansion has been beautifully restored in the style of an English manor. Because of its exquisite service and luxurious accommodations, it provides the attention of a small hotel with the comfort and seclusion of a grand home. Gourmet dining is a specialty, and the manor features seasonal menus to reflect the local produce. 7 rooms, 2 story. Children over 12 years only. Complimentary full breakfast. Check-in 3 pm, check-out 11 am. Restaurant. **$**
🅳

Florence (D-5)

See also Bennettsville, Cheraw, Darlington, Dillon, Hartsville

Settled 1890
Population 30,248
Elevation 149 ft
Area Code 843
Information Greater Florence Chamber of Commerce, 610 W Palmetto St, PO Box 948, 29503; phone 843/665-0515
Web Site www.florencesccvb.com

Since extensive railroad shops and yards were established here by the Atlantic coastline, this community has grown from a sparsely settled crossroads into a major retail and wholesale distribution center. The economy is no longer dependent on agriculture; a balance of farm and industry has been attained. Florence is also the home of Francis Marion College and Florence-Darlington Technical College.

What to See and Do

Beauty Trail. 12-mile trail within city featuring beautiful gardens (usually best in Apr). **FREE**

Florence Museum of Art, Science, and History. *558 Spruce St, Florence (29501). At Graham St. Phone 843/662-3351. www.florenceweb.com/museum.htm.* This interesting local museum showcases rotating art exhibits; historic objects from the Florence and Pee Dee area; Southwestern pueblo pottery; African and Asian artifacts; and a Civil War collection donated by Francis A. Lord, the author of a five-volume encyclopedia about Civil War collectibles. The museum also has an outpost Railroad Museum nearby, which allows visitors to stroll through a vintage caboose and box car filled with railroad memorabilia from Florence's days as a railroad town (June-Aug: Sat-Sun 3-5 pm). (Tues-Sat 10 am-5 pm, Sun 2-5 pm; closed holidays) **$**

Florence National Cemetery. *803 E National Cemetery Rd, Florence (29501). S on Hwy 52/301 to Cherokee Rd. Phone 843/669-8783.* This is the smaller of South Carolina's Civil War cemeteries, after the better-known Beaufort Union captives who died at the neighboring stockade are buried here. Researchers have identified many of the dead, who were originally buried as unknown soldiers. Lists are available from the cemetery. **FREE**

Florence Stockade. *Stockade and National Cemetery rds, Florence (29506). Off National Cemetery Rd, near Hwy 95.* The stockade was a Civil War prison that housed Union soldiers transferred from the notorious Andersonville prison. Roughly 2,800 soldiers died there over about six months of operation, including Florena Budwin, who Friends of the Florence Stockade say is the only female Civil War prisoner to die in captivity. She is buried in the adjoining cemetery. The site is a Civil War Heritage Site, and the society has put a marker along the south wall to commemorate the soldiers who died. A 1947 marker put up by the United Daughters of the Confederacy of Florence memorializes "the Confederate soldiers and the citizens of the community who in the line of duty guarded these prisoners." **FREE**

Jeffries Creek Nature Park. *Deberry Blvd, Florence.* Fishing. Nature trails. Picnicking, playground. **FREE**

Lucas Park. *Santee Dr and Azalea Ln, Florence.* Picnicking, playground; tennis courts. Rose gardens, camellias, azaleas, rhododendrons; lighted fountain. **FREE**

Lynches River State Park. *902 Spine Rd, Florence (29530). 15 miles S off Hwy 52. Phone 843/389-2785.* Approximately 650 acres. Located on old stagecoach route. Swimming pool (fee), fishing. Nature trail, bird-watching. Picnicking, playground, community building. Primitive camping.

McLeod Park. *Santiago Dr, Florence.* Swimming pool (fee), fishing pond. Lighted tennis; basketball courts, ball fields. Picnicking, playground.

Mister Mark's Fun Park. *1331 N Cashua Dr, Florence (29501). Phone 843/669-7373. www.mistermarksfun park.com.* This entertainment complex has a restaurant, an 18-hole miniature golf course ($), an oval sprint car track and go-cart road course ($$$$), and a 10,000-square-foot arcade. (Hours vary by season)

Pee Dee Golfing. *3290 W Radio Dr, Florence (29501). Phone 843/669-0950; toll-free 800/325-9005.* Pee Dee Golfing arranges packages including accommodations, breakfast, 18-hole greens fees, and cart fees. It can book times at a variety of local courses.

Pee Dee Pride Minor League Hockey Team. *Florence City-County Civic Center, 3300 W Radio Rd, Florence (29501). Phone 843/669-7825. www.peedeepride.com.* In addition to hockey games, the arena also has a full schedule of other events and some public skating hours. Updated schedules and prices on the civic center Web site at www.florenceciviccenter.com.

Pee Dee State Farmers' Market. *2513 W Lucas St (Hwy 52), Florence (29501). Between Florence and Darlington. Phone 843/665-5154.* The Pee Dee State Farmers' Market draws farmers from around the state and fills table after table with fresh produce and local cheese and honey. This is a great place for campers to find fresh food, or for racegoers to catch a break from restaurants. It's also the first stop for picnickers or hikers on their way to the region's parks. Open year-round.

Timrod Park. *Timrod Park Dr and S Coit St, Florence. Phone 843/665-3253.* One-room schoolhouse in which Henry Timrod, Poet Laureate of the Confederacy, taught. Playgrounds, picnic areas, barbecue pits; lighted tennis courts. Azalea display in spring. Test rose gardens. Nature trails; fitness station, jogging trail. Special fitness court for the disabled. (Daily) **FREE**

War Between the States Museum. *107 S Guerry St, Florence (29501). Phone 843/669-1266. www.florenceweb.com/warmuseum.htm.* Explore artifacts, pictures, and stories that bring you back to the Civil War. (Wed, Sat 10 am-5 pm) **$**

Woods Bay State Natural Area. *Olanta. 24 miles SW, off Hwy 301 and I-95. Phone 843/659-4445.* Approximately 1,500 acres of unique natural area with an abundance of wildlife, including alligators and more than 150 species of birds, in a "Carolina Bay" (an elliptical, swampy depression mostly underwater). Lake fishing, canoe trail (rentals). Picnic area (shelter). Boardwalk for nature and wildlife observation. (Thurs-Mon 9 am-6 pm) **$**

Special Event

Arts Alive. *Francis Marion University, Florence. Phone 843/661-1225.* Arts, crafts, music, dance, theater, demonstrations, exhibits. Apr.

Fort Sumter National Monument (E-5)

See also Charleston, Kiawah Island

Web Site www.nps.gov/fosu

On an island in Charleston Harbor. Accessible by private boat or by Fort Sumter tour boat, leaving from the City Marina, Lockwood Dr, Charleston; and from Patriots Point Naval Museum, Mount Pleasant.

The national monument includes Fort Sumter, located 3 miles southeast of Charleston at the harbor entrance, and Fort Moultrie, located 1 mile east of Fort Sumter on Sullivan's Island. Fort Moultrie is reached via Hwy 17 to Hwy 703; turn right and follow the signs. Fort Moultrie was originally built in 1776, of sand and palmetto logs. Colonel William Moultrie's forces drove British ships from Charleston Harbor at Fort Moultrie in June 1776. The present Fort Moultrie was completed in 1809 and was garrisoned by Union forces in late 1860, when these forces were moved to Fort Sumter.

South Carolina, the first state to secede, passed its Ordinance of Secession on December 20, 1860. Surrender of Fort Sumter was demanded on April 11, 1861. This demand was refused by Major Robert Anderson, in command of Union forces at the fort. At 4:30 am on April 12, Confederate firing began, and the fort was surrendered after 34 hours of intense bombardment. This attack compelled President Lincoln to call for 75,000 volunteers to put down the rebellion, thus beginning the Civil War. Fort Sumter and Fort Moultrie have been modified through the years. Both were active through World War II.

Fort Moultrie has been restored by the National Park Service; visitor center has an audiovisual program depicting the evolution of seacoast defense. Self-guided tour. (Daily; closed Dec 25) **$**

Fort Sumter's ruins have been partially excavated, and a museum has been established. (Daily; closed Dec 25) Contact the Superintendent, 1214 Middle St, Sullivan's Island 29482; phone 843/883-3123 or 843-883-3124. Daily tour boat (fee). **$**

Gaffney (C-3)

See also Charlotte, Rock Hill, Spartanburg

Settled 1803
Population 12,968
Elevation 779 ft
Area Code 864
Zip 29340
Information Cherokee County Chamber of Commerce, 225 S Limestone St; phone 864/489-5721
Web Site www.cherokeechamber.org

Once a prosperous resort town where plantation owners sought to cure malaria attacks with the supposedly therapeutic waters of the limestone springs, Gaffney is now a textile and metalworking center and the home of a variety of other industries and agricultural products, particularly peaches. On I-85, just outside of town, stands the Gaffney Peachoid (1981), an elevated tank that resembles a gigantic peach and holds a million-gallon water supply.

> ### Gaffney Fun Fact
>
> • The Peachoid water tank in Gaffney is the only water tank of its kind in the world; it holds 1 million gallons of water.

What to See and Do

Carolina Factory Shops. *1 Factory Shops Blvd, Gaffney. At exit 90 off I-85.* Phone 864/902-0096. An open-air, village-style manufacturers' outlet. Contains 235,000 square feet of space, featuring 65 outlet shops. (Daily)

Cowpens National Battlefield. *4001 Chesnee Hwy, Gaffney (29341). 11 miles NW on Hwy 11, 1/2 mile from jct Hwy 110.* Phone 864/461-2828. www.nps.gov/cowp. This was the scene of the victory of General Daniel Morgan's American Army over superior British forces on Jan 17, 1781. The British suffered 110 men killed, 200 wounded, and 550 captured, while American losses were minimal. This victory was followed by the Battle of Guilford Courthouse, and then the forces moved on to Yorktown, where Cornwallis was forced to surrender. An 843-acre tract with exhibits, an information and visitor center, a self-guided tour road, and a walking trail with audio stations and a restored 1830 historic house. Slide program (fee). Picnicking (shelters). (Daily 9 am-5 pm; closed Jan 1, Thanksgiving, Dec 25) **FREE**

Kings Mountain National Military Park. *20 miles NE of Gaffney off I-85, near Grover, NC.* On these 3,950 rugged acres, a fierce attack by Carolina, Georgia, and Virginia frontiersmen in October 1780 broke up Britain's southern campaign. The mountain men and other patriots were faced with the invasion of their homes by advancing Tories. After traveling more than 200 miles, the Americans surrounded and attacked Cornwallis's left wing, which was encamped atop Kings Mountain spur and under the command of Major Patrick Ferguson. Although untrained in formal warfare, American patriots killed, wounded, or captured Ferguson's entire force of 1,104 Tories. Twenty-eight patriots were killed, and 62 were wounded. The battle led to renewed American resistance and American victory at Yorktown. Near the center of the park is the battlefield ridge, with several monuments, including the Centennial Monument, dedicated in 1880, and the US Monument, erected in 1909. The visitor center has exhibits and a film. Self-guided trail leads to main features of battlefield. (Daily; closed Jan 1, Thanksgiving, Dec 25) Contact Superintendent, PO Box 40, Kings Mountain, NC 28086. Phone 864/936-7921. **FREE**

Special Event

South Carolina Peach Festival. Arts and crafts, sports events, entertainment. Mid-July.

Georgetown (E-6)

See also Myrtle Beach

Founded 1729
Population 8,950
Area Code 843

Zip 29440
Information Georgetown County Chamber of Commerce, 1001 Front St, PO Box 1776, 29442; phone 843/546-8436 or toll-free 800/777-7705
Web Site www.georgetownchamber.com

A seaport throughout its long history, Georgetown enjoyed a resurgence of ship traffic following the deepening of the channel and the building of a new cargo dock. The shore of Winyah Bay, on which Georgetown is situated, was the site of the first European settlement on the North American mainland outside of Mexico. In 1526, a group of Spaniards settled here, only to be driven out within a year by disease and Native American attacks. Rice and indigo plantations were established along nearby rivers around 1700. Georgetown was founded by Rev Elisha Screven, son of the first Baptists in the South; the city was finally laid out to honor King George II of England. It became increasingly important as an export center with quantities of lumber and naval stores, rice, and indigo. Lafayette landed near here to join the American cause in the Revolution. The city was later occupied by British troops. Known as a sawmill city during the first three decades of this century, Georgetown currently boasts several manufacturing industries as well as a thriving tourist economy.

What to See and Do

Brookgreen Gardens. *1931 Brookgreen Dr, Murrells Inlet (29576). 18 miles N on Hwy 17, 3 miles S of Murrells Inlet. Phone 803/235-6000; toll-free 800/849-1931. www.brookgreen.org.* On the site of former rice and indigo plantations, these gardens contain more than 500 pieces of American sculpture; boxwood, massive moss-hung oaks, and native plants; and a wildlife park with native animals. Creek and all-terrain vehicle excursions take visitors through forests, creeks, old plantation homes, and old rice fields that are now inhabited by alligators, snakes, and other creatures. Picnicking. (Daily 9:30 am-5 pm, until 9 pm Wed-Fri in summer; closed Mon in winter; also closed Dec 25) **$$$**

Captain Sandy's Plantation Tours. *Phone 803/527-4106.* Leaves from Harborwalk Seaport. **$$$$**

Fishing. Charter boats from docks. Channel fishing for bass or deep-sea fishing for barracuda, amberjack, albacore, bonito, mackerel. (Apr-Nov)

Hampton Plantation State Park. *1950 Rutledge Rd, McClellanville. 20 miles S off Hwy 17. Phone 803/546-9361.* Restored 18th-century mansion was centerpiece of large rice plantation; ancestral home of Rutledge family. Guided tours, special programs. (Thurs-Mon) **$**

Harold Kaminski House. *1003 Front St, Georgetown. Phone 803/546-7706.* (Circa 1760) Pre-Revolutionary house furnished with antiques. Tours. (Daily; closed holidays) **$$**

Hopsewee Plantation. *494 Hopsewee Rd, Georgetown (29440). 12 miles S on Hwy 17. Phone 803/546-7891.* (Circa 1740) Preserved rice plantation house on the North Santee River. Birthplace of Thomas Lynch Jr., a signer of the Declaration of Independence. Grounds (daily). House (Mar-Nov: Tues-Fri; rest of year: by appointment). **$$**

Huntington Beach State Park. *16148 Ocean Hwy, Georgetown (29576). 17 miles N on Hwy 17, 3 miles S of Murrells Inlet. Phone 803/237-4440.* Approximately 2,500 acres. Ocean swimming, surf fishing. Hiking, nature trails; marsh boardwalk. Picnicking (shelters); playground; concession. Camping. **$$** Also here is

Atalaya. Former home and studio of the sculptor Anna Hyatt Huntington. (June-Labor Day; daily) Art festival (mid-late Sept). **$**

Prince George Winyah Church. *Broad and Highmarket sts, Georgetown. Phone 803/546-4358.* (Circa 1750) The English stained-glass window behind the altar was originally a part of St. Mary's Chapel for Negroes at Hagley Plantation on Waccamaw. The church has been in continuous use since its founding, except during the American Revolution and the Civil War. Tours are available. (Mar-Oct, Mon-Fri) **FREE**

Town Clock Building. *633 Front St, Georgetown.* (Rebuilt 1842) Tablet marks landing of Lafayette at North Island in 1777; Federal troops came ashore on the dock, at the rear of building, in an attempt to capture the town. Inside is

Rice Museum. *633 Front St, Georgetown. Phone 803/546-7423.* Maps, dioramas, film, artifacts, and exhibits depict development and production of crop that was once the basis of Georgetown's economy. (Mon-Sat; closed holidays) **$**

Limited-Service Hotel

★ **CAROLINIAN INN.** *706 Church St, Georgetown (29440). Phone 843/546-5191; toll-free 800/722-4667; fax 843/546-1514.* 89 rooms, 2 story. Pets accepted. Complimentary continental breakfast. Check-in

11 am, check-out 11 am. Outdoor pool. **$**

Specialty Lodging

The following lodging establishment is approved by Mobil Travel Guide, but due to its unique and individualized nature has not been given a traditional Mobil Star rating. Included in this listing you may find bed-and-breakfasts, limited-service inns, guest ranches, and other unique hotel properties.

SEAVIEW INN. *414 Myrtle Ave, Pawleys Island (29585). Phone 843/237-4253; fax 843/237-7909. www.seaviewinn.net.* 20 rooms, 2 story. Closed Nov-mid-Apr. Children over 3 years only. Check-in noon, check-out 11 am. Beach. **$$**

Restaurants

★ ★ **RICE PADDY.** *732 Front St, Georgetown (29440). Phone 843/546-2021; fax 843/546-0211.* American menu. Lunch, dinner. Closed Sun; holidays. Bar. Children's menu. Casual attire. **$$**

★ ★ **RIVER ROOM.** *801 Front St, Georgetown (29440). Phone 843/527-4110; fax 843/546-0706.* Seafood menu. Lunch, dinner. Closed Sun; Thanksgiving, Dec 24-25. Bar. Children's menu. **$$**

Greenville (C-3)

See also Anderson, Clemson, Clinton, Spartanburg; also see Washington, NC

Founded 1797
Population 56,002
Elevation 966 ft
Area Code 864
Information Convention and Visitors Bureau, 206 S Main St, City Hall Building, PO Box 10527, 29603; phone 864/233-0461 or toll-free 800/717-0023
Web Site www.greatergreenville.com

Greenville has several hundred manufacturing plants producing clothing, nylon, chemicals, plastic film, and machinery. It is best known for its numerous textile plants. Yet the town is also well named—beautiful trees line the streets, and there are many forested parks in the area. The Reedy River, passing over falls in the heart of Greenville, originally provided the city's power. Pleasant streets now border the twisting Sylvan Stream.

What to See and Do

Bob Jones University. *1700 Wade Hampton Blvd, Greenville (29614). At jct Hwys 29, 291. Phone 864/242-5100.* (1927) (5,000 students) During the academic year, the university offers vesper concerts (twice/month, Sun). Multimedia presentation (daily; closed holidays). Tours. On campus are

Bob Jones University Collection of Religious Art. *1700 Wade Hampton Blvd, Greenville (29609). Phone 864/242-5100.* Houses collection of rare biblical material and collection of sacred art, including works by Botticelli, Veronese, Rembrandt, Rubens. Children under 6 years not permitted. (Tues-Sun; closed holidays) **$$**

Mack Memorial Library. Contains Archives Room and Jerusalem Chamber, display area for the university's collection of rare Bibles.

Caesars Head State Park. *8155 Geer Hwy, Cleveland (29635). 30 miles NW via Hwy 276. Phone 864/836-6115.* Approximately 7,000 acres. At 3,208 feet above sea level, the park overlooks a valley of almost impenetrable brush and dense forest. One side of the mountain resembles Caesar's head. Raven Cliff Falls. Scenic overlook. Hiking trails. Picnicking (shelter). Trailside camping, store, special programs. **$**

Greenville County Museum. *420 College St, Greenville. Phone 864/271-7570.* Permanent collection of American art, featuring historical and contemporary works. Changing exhibits include painting, sculpture, photography. Lectures, tours. (Tues-Sun; closed holidays) **FREE**

Greenville Zoo. *150 Cleveland Park Dr, Greenville. Phone 864/467-4300.* Wildlife from around the world are displayed in natural, open-air exhibits. Picnicking, concessions. Lighted tennis courts, ball field; nature, jogging, hiking, and bicycle trails; park. (Daily; closed Jan 1, Thanksgiving, Dec 25) Children under 13 must be accompanied by an adult. **$$**

Paris Mountain State Park. *2401 State Park Rd, Greenville (29609). 6 miles N off Hwys 276 and 253. Phone 864/244-5565.* Approximately 1,300 acres with three lakes. Thick forest setting with swiftly flowing streams. Lake swimming, fishing, pedal boats (rentals); nature, hiking trail, picnicking, playground, camping (hook-ups, dump station). (Daily 9 am-6 pm) **$**

Table Rock State Park. *158 E Ellison Ln, Pickens (29671). 16 miles N on Hwy 25, then 15 miles W on Hwy 11. Phone 864/878-9813.* Approximately 3,000 acres. Extends over Table Rock Mountain (elevation 3,124 feet) and valleys. Lake swimming; fishing; boating, canoeing (rentals). Hiking trail; carpet golf. Picnicking, restaurant, store. Camping (hook-ups, dump station), cabins; recreation building. Nature center; nature and recreation programs. (Daily 7 am-9 pm) **$**

Special Event

Freedom Weekend Aloft. *Phone 864/232-3700.* More than 100 balloonists compete. Memorial Day.

Limited-Service Hotels

★ ★ **COURTYARD BY MARRIOTT.** *70 Orchard Park Dr, Greenville (29615). Phone 864/234-0300; fax 864/234-0296. www.courtyard.com.* 146 rooms, 3 story. Check-in 3 pm, check-out noon. Fitness room. Outdoor pool, whirlpool. **$**

★ ★ **EMBASSY SUITES.** *670 Verdae Blvd, Greenville (29607). Phone 864/676-9090; toll-free 800/362-2779; fax 864/676-0669. www.embassysuites.com.* Located in the foothills of the Blue Ridge Mountains, this golf resort/conference center will please visitors. Guests will enjoy the many lakes and whitewater rivers and other attractions including shopping and dining locations. 268 rooms, 9 story, all suites. Complimentary full breakfast. Restaurant, bar. Fitness room. Indoor pool, outdoor pool, whirlpool. Golf. Tennis. Airport transportation available. Business center. **$**

★ **FAIRFIELD INN.** *60 Roper Mountain Rd, Greenville (29607). Phone 864/297-9996; fax 864/297-9965.* 132 rooms, 3 story. Complimentary continental breakfast. Check-in 3 pm, check-out noon. Outdoor pool. **$**

★ **HAMPTON INN.** *246 Congaree Rd, Greenville (29607). Phone 864/288-1200; fax 864/288-5667. www.hamptoninn.com.* 123 rooms, 4 story. Complimentary continental breakfast. Check-in 3 pm, check-out noon. Outdoor pool. **$**

Full-Service Hotel

★ ★ ★ **HILTON GREENVILLE AND TOWERS.** *45 W Orchard Park Dr, Greenville (29615). Phone 864/232-4747; fax 864/235-6248. www.greenvillesc.hilton.com.* This hotel is surrounded by landscaped gardens in Greenville's business district. 256 rooms, 9 story. Pets accepted. Check-in 3 pm, check-out noon. Restaurant, bar. Fitness room. Indoor pool, whirlpool. Airport transportation available. Business center. **$**

★ ★ ★ **HYATT REGENCY GREENVILLE.** *220 N Main St, Greenville (29601). Phone 864/235-1234; fax 864/232-7584. www.hyatt.com.* This hotel is located in Greenville's business and entertainment district with many attractions found within a short walking distance. 330 rooms, 8 story. Check-in 2 pm, check-out noon. Restaurant, bar. Children's activity center. Fitness room. Outdoor pool. Airport transportation available. Business center. **$**

★ ★ ★ **MARRIOTT GREENVILLE SPARTANBURG AIRPORT.** *1 Parkway E, Greenville (29615). Phone 803/297-0300; toll-free 800/833-2221; fax 803/281-0801. www.marriott.com.* Located only 3 1/2 miles from the Greenville/Spartanburg International Airport. 204 rooms, 7 story. Pets accepted. Check-in 3 pm, check-out noon. Restaurant. Fitness room. Indoor pool, outdoor pool, whirlpool. Airport transportation available. Business center. **$**

★ ★ ★ **THE WESTIN POINSETT.** *120 Main St, Greenville (29601). Phone 864/421-9700; fax 864/421-0460. www.westin.com.* 200 rooms, 11 story. Check-in 3 pm, check-out 11 am. Restaurant, bar. Airport transportation available. Business center. **$**

Restaurant

★ ★ ★ **STAX'S PEPPERMILL.** *30 Orchard Park Dr, Greenville (29615). Phone 864/288-9320; fax 864/288-7202. www.staxs.com.* Considered one of the best dining establishments in town, this restaurant delivers the best of traditional American cuisine with friendly service. The lovely terrace is a great place to enjoy the long summer nights in this emerald, Southern city. International/Fusion menu. Dinner. Closed Sun; holidays. Bar. Outdoor seating. **$$$**

Greenwood (D-3)

See also Anderson, Clinton, Newberry

Settled 1830
Population 22,071
Elevation 665 ft
Area Code 864
Information Chamber of Commerce, 110 Phoenix St, 29648; phone 864/223-8431
Web Site www.greenwoodscchamber.org

At the junction of highways and railways, Greenwood was originally the plantation of Green Wood; it later became known as the community of Woodville and finally adopted its present name. Greenwood's Main Street is one of the widest (316 feet) in the nation. The town enjoys diversified industry.

Greenwood Fun Fact

- Greenwood, South Carolina, has the widest Main Street in the world.

What to See and Do

Baker Creek State Park. *McCormick. 28 miles SW via Hwy 221, Hwy 378 W. Phone 864/443-2457.* Approximately 1,300 acres. Lake swimming, bathhouse; lake fishing; boating (ramps). Nature, bridle trails; carpet golf. Picnicking, playground. Camping (dump station). **$**

Hickory Knob Resort. *McCormick. 32 miles SW via Hwy 221, Hwy 378 W. Phone toll-free 800/491-1764.* On 1,091 acres. Water-skiing; lake fishing, supplies, boating (ramps, rentals). Nature trails; 18-hole golf course, putting green, field archery course, skeet range, field trial area. Playground, restaurant. Camping (hook-ups, dump station), lodge, cabins. Recreation and nature programs. Convention facilities.

J. Strom Thurmond Lake. *McCormick. 30 miles SW via Hwy 221, 378. Phone 864/333-2476.* Formed by the damming of the Savannah River. Fishing, boating (ramps). Picnicking (shelters). Campgrounds (fees). (Daily) **FREE**

Lake Greenwood. *302 State Park Rd, Greenwood (29666). 13 miles E on Hwy 34, then N on Hwy 702. Phone 864/543-3535.* On 914 acres bordering Greenwood Lake, which is 20 miles long and 2 miles wide. Water-skiing, fishing, bait shop, boating (ramps). Nature trails. Picnicking (shelters), store. Camping (hook-ups, dump station). Recreation building.

The Museum. *106 Main St, Greenwood. Phone 864/229-7093.* Features a nostalgic "street" lined with houses, shops. Displays of minerals, mounted animal heads, Native American artifacts, ethnographic materials. Art gallery with regional art, traveling exhibits. (Wed-Fri, also Sat-Sun afternoons; closed holidays) **$**

Ninety Six National Historic Site. *1103 Hwy 248 S, Ninety Six. 9 miles E on Hwy 34 to present town of Ninety Six, then 2 miles S on Hwy 248. Phone 864/543-4068.* Site of old Ninety Six, an early village in South Carolina backcountry, so named because of its distance of 96 miles from the Cherokee Village of Keowee on the Cherokee Path. Site of the South's first land battle of the American Revolution in 1775 and of the 28-day siege of Ninety Six in 1781. The earthworks of the British-built Star Fort remain, along with reconstructed siegeworks and other fortifications of the period. Visitor center; museum, video presentation. Also here are subsurface remains of two village complexes, a trading post/plantation complex, and a network of 18th-century roads. (Daily; closed Jan 1, Dec 25) **FREE**

Sumter National Forest. *In three sections: SW via Hwy 221; NW via Hwy 28; and NE via Hwy 72. Phone 864/561-4000.* Approximately 353,000 acres in the Piedmont Plateau and the Blue Ridge Mountains. Miles of trails through pine and hardwood forest; canoeing, whitewater trips, swimming, trout fishing; hunting for deer, turkey, quail; picnicking, camping. Fees may be charged at recreation sites.

Special Event

South Carolina Festival of Flowers. *Phone 864/223-8411.* Arts and crafts, photography display, musical groups, golf and tennis tournaments, theater, water show, Railroad Historical Exhibit, flower shows, Park Seed Flower Day. Third weekend in June.

Specialty Lodging

The following lodging establishment is approved by Mobil Travel Guide, but due to its unique and individualized nature has not been given a traditional

Mobil Star rating. Included in this listing you may find bed-and-breakfasts, limited-service inns, guest ranches, and other unique hotel properties.

BELMONT INN. *104 E Pickens St, Abbeville (29620). Phone 864/459-9625; toll-free 877/459-8118; fax 864/459-9625. www.belmontinn.net.* Historic building (1903); restored. Period reproduction; antique furnishings. 25 rooms, 3 story. Complimentary continental breakfast. Check-in 3 pm, check-out noon. Restaurant, bar. **$**

Hardeeville (F-4)

See also Beaufort, Hilton Head Island

Population 1,793
Elevation 80 ft
Area Code 843
Zip 29927
Web Site www.cityofhardeeville.com

What to See and Do

Savannah National Wildlife Refuge. *1000 Business Center Dr, Suite 10, Hardeeville (31405). 17 miles S via Hwy 17. Phone 912/652-4415.* Approximately 25,600 acres. More than half the acreage consists of bottomland hardwoods reminiscent of the great cypress/tupelo swamps that once extended along the Carolina and Georgia low country. Argent Swamp can only be reached by boat; wild azaleas, iris, spider lilies, and other flowers bloom in succession, beginning in spring. Laurel Hill Wildlife Dr, open to cars, allows viewing of wildlife, especially waterfowl (Dec-Feb). Migrating songbirds are abundant in spring and fall. Tupelo-Swamp Walk (mid-Mar-Sept) is best for bird-watchers and photographers. (Daily; some areas closed Oct-Nov for hunting; impoundments N of Hwy 17 closed Nov-mid-Mar; Laurel Hill Dr hours posted at gate) **FREE**

Limited-Service Hotel

★ **HOLIDAY INN EXPRESS.** *Hwy 17 and I-95, Hardeeville (29927). Phone 843/784-2221; fax 843/784-6102.* 100 rooms, 2 story. Check-out 11 am. Outdoor pool. **$**

Hartsville (C-5)

See also Bennettsville, Camden, Cheraw, Darlington, Florence

Settled 1760
Population 7,556
Elevation 200 ft
Area Code 843
Zip 29550
Information Chamber of Commerce, 214 N 5th St, PO Box 578, 29551; phone 843/332-6401
Web Site www.hartsvillesc.com

From a crossroads store, Hartsville has become a vigorous trading center, raising crops of cotton, soybeans, tobacco, and oats, and boasts 15 major manufacturers—including makers of consumer packaging, plastic bags, fertilizer, roller bearings, boats, brass, textiles, and paper. The town developed from what was once the Hart plantation and the pioneer store established by Major James Lide Coker, a Harvard graduate who founded a series of businesses here and built a railroad to the town.

What to See and Do

Hartsville Museum. *222 N Fifth St, Hartsville (29550). Phone 843/383-3005. www.hartsvillemuseum.org.* Founded in 1980, this local history museum is housed in a 1930s post office building. The galleries depict history, arts, and present-day events, and include Native American art and an ancient spinning wheel. After perusing the museum, head outside to wander through the sculpture courtyard. (Mon-Fri 10 am-5 pm, Sat 10 am-2 pm) **FREE**

Kalmia Gardens of Coker College. *1624 W Carolina Ave, Hartsville (29550). Approximately 2 1/2 miles W on Carolina Ave. Phone 843/383-8145. www.coker.edu/kalmia.* A 30-acre botanical garden with walking trails through blackwater swamp; mountain laurel thickets; uplands of pine, oak, and holly; and a beech bluff. Plantings of azaleas, camellias, and other ornamentals complement the native plants. (Daily) **FREE**

Lee State Park. *487 Loop Rd, Bishopville (29010). 16 miles SW via Hwy 15, 3 miles S on Hwy 341, then 2 miles E off I-20, exit 123. Phone 803/428-3833.* Approximately 2,500 acres on Lynches River. Lake swimming; river fishing, boating (pedal boat rentals). Nature trails; horse trails, show ring, stable (no rentals). Picnicking (shelters), playground. Camping (hook-ups, dump station). Recreation building. **$**

Restaurant

★ **STEAMERS SEAFOOD COMPANY.** *28 Coligny Plz, Hilton Head (29928). Phone 843/785-2070.* Seafood menu. Lunch, dinner. Closed Dec 24-25. Bar. Children's menu. Casual attire. Outdoor seating. **$$**

Hilton Head Island (F-4)

See also Beaufort, Hardeeville

Population 33,862
Elevation 15 ft
Area Code 843
Information Chamber of Commerce, PO Box 5647, 29938; phone 843/785-3673
Web Site www.hiltonheadisland.org

This year-round resort island, the development of which began in 1956, is reached by a bridge on Highway 278. The island is bordered by one of the few remaining unpolluted marine estuaries on the East Coast and is the largest sea island between New Jersey and Florida. Its growth was rapid; there are 12 miles of beaches, and the climate is delightful. Activities include numerous golf courses and tennis courts; swimming; miles of bicycle paths; horseback riding; four nature preserves; and deep-sea, sound, and dockside fishing. The facilities also include nine marinas and a paved 3,700-foot airstrip with parallel taxiway. There are more than 3,000 hotel and motel rooms, more than 6,000 homes/villas/condos on the rental market, more than 200 restaurants, and 28 shopping centers. For the less athletic, there are many art galleries and numerous sporting and cultural events.

What to See and Do

Daufuskie Island Resort golf. *421 Squire Pope Rd, Hilton Head (29926). Phone 843/842-2000. www.daufuskieresort.com.* In terms of getting more golf for your money, Daufuskie is a good bet. Rates for both resort guests and day players are relatively low for the great course they get to play on in return for their greens fee. There are two 18-hole courses on the property, the Melrose (designed by Jack Nicklaus) and the Bloody Point (designed by Tom Weiskopf and

Jay Morrish), both of which offer challenging holes and great views of the Atlantic Ocean, which abuts the courses at several points. **$$$$**

Harbour Town Golf Links. *Sea Pines Resort, 32 Greenwood Dr, Hilton Head Island (29928). Phone toll-free 888/807-6873. www.seapines.com.* Perhaps the most famous course in South Carolina, Pete Dye-designed Harbour Town features its signature red-and-white-striped lighthouse, which serves as a backgroup for the course's 18th hole. The par-71 layout is less than 7,000 yards from the back tees, but the fairways can be narrow and the greens small, making for a good target golf experience. There are plenty of deep bunkers to make you think twice about challenging the greens, which can play fast and unaccepting to approach shots that are not hit well. Two other courses at the resort, Ocean and Sea Pines, add 36 more holes to the offerings. **$$$$**

Special Events

Hilton Head Island Celebrity Golf Tournament. *Phone 843/842-7711.* This golf event matches amateurs and celebrities to raise funds for 19 children's charities on 3 of the world's finest courses: The Golf Club at Indigo Run, The Robert Trent Jones Course in Palmetto Dunes, & The Harbour Town Golf Links in Sea Pines. Labor Day weekend.

MCI Heritage Classic. *71 Lighthouse Rd # 414, Hilton Head Island. Phone 843/671-2448.* Harbour Town Golf Links. Top PGA golfers. Mid-Apr.

Springfest. *Phone 843/686-4944.* Food, wine, and seafood festivals. Sports events. Concerts, shows, and house tours. Mar.

St. Luke's Tour of Homes. *Phone 843/785-4099.* Tour of distinctive contemporary houses. Oct.

Limited-Service Hotels

★ **FAIRFIELD INN.** *9 Marina Side Dr, Hilton Head Island (29928). Phone 843/842-4800; toll-free 800/228-2880; fax 843/842-5388. www.fairfieldinn.com.* 119 rooms, 3 story. Complimentary continental breakfast. Check-in 3 pm, check-out 11 am. Outdoor pool. **$**
🛏

★ **HAMPTON INN.** *1 Dillon Rd, Hilton Head Island (29926). Phone 843/681-7900; toll-free 800/426-7866; fax 843/681-4330. www.hamptoninn.com.* 125 rooms, 2 story. Complimentary continental breakfast. Check-in 4 pm, check-out noon. Outdoor pool. **$**
🛏

Full-Service Hotel

★ ★ ★ **CROWNE PLAZA.** *130 Shipyard Dr, Hilton Head Island (29928). Phone 843/842-2400; toll-free 800/227-6963; fax 843/785-8463. www.cphiltonhead.com.* Located in Shipyard Plantation, this 11-acre resort is paradise for golfers and tennis players. Of course, there are also miles of sandy oceanfront. 340 rooms, 5 story. Check-in 4 pm, check-out noon. Three restaurants, one bar. Children's activity center. Fitness room. Beach. Indoor pool, outdoor pool, children's pool, whirlpool. Tennis. Business center. **$$**

Full-Service Resorts

★ ★ ★ **DAUFUSKIE ISLAND RESORT AND BREATHE SPA.** *421 Squire Pope Rd, Hilton Head Island (29926). Phone 843/842-2000; toll-free 800/648-6778; fax 843/341-8524. www.daufuskieresort.com.* Part of the Daufuskie Island Resort, which also includes vacation cottages and villas. 192 rooms. Pets accepted, some restrictions; fee. Check-in 4 pm, check-out 2 pm. Three restaurants, four bars. Children's activity center. Fitness room, spa. Beach. Outdoor pool, children's pool, whirlpool. Golf, 36 holes. Tennis. Business center. **$$**

★ ★ ★ **HILTON HEAD MARRIOTT BEACH AND GOLF RESORT.** *1 Hotel Cir at Palmetto Dunes, Hilton Head Island (29928). Phone 843/686-8400; toll-free 800/228-9290; fax 843/686-8412. www.hiltonheadmarriott.com.* The hotel is located at Palmetto Dunes, within walking distance from the Shelter Cove Marina shops and attractions. 512 rooms, 10 story. Check-in 4 pm, check-out 11 am. Three restaurants, two bars. Children's activity center. Fitness room, fitness classes available. Beach. One indoor pool, two outdoor pools, three whirlpools, children's pool. Business center. **$**

★ ★ ★ **HILTON OCEANFRONT RESORT HILTON HEAD ISLAND.** *23 Ocean Ln, Hilton Head Island (29928). Phone 803/341-8000; toll-free 800/845-8001; fax 803/341-8033. www.hiltonheadhilton.com.* Enjoy the widest beach on the island at this lush, self-contained resort. Manicured gardens and lagoons adorn the property, part of the 2,000-acre private Palmetto Dunes development. 324 rooms, 5 story. Check-in 4 pm, check-out 11 am. Three restaurants, two bars. Children's activity center. Fitness room, fitness classes available. Beach. Two outdoor pools, children's pool, two whirlpools. Golf. Tennis. Business center. **$$$**

★ ★ ★ ★ **THE INN AT PALMETTO BLUFF.** *476 Mount Pilla Rd, Bluffton (29910). Phone 843/706-6500; toll-free 866/706-6565; fax 843/706-6550. www.palmettobluffresort.com.* 50 rooms, all suites. Check-in 3 pm, check-out 11 am. Restaurant, bar. Fitness Room. Golf. **$$$$**

★ ★ ★ **THE WESTIN RESORT, HILTON HEAD ISLAND.** *2 A Grasslawn Ave, Hilton Head Island (29928). Phone 843/681-4000; fax 843/681-1096.* Situated on 24 acres of oceanfront property, this self-contained resort boasts everything from golf and water recreation to state-of-the-art business to first-rate dining facilities. Rooms have balconies overlooking either the ocean or the island. 412 rooms, 5 story. Pets accepted, some restrictions; fee. Check-in 3 pm, check-out noon. High-speed Internet access. Three restaurants, bar. Children's activity center. Fitness room, fitness classes available. Beach. Indoor pool, two outdoor pools, whirlpool. Airport transportation available. Business center. **$$**

Full-Service Inn

★ ★ ★ **MAIN STREET INN.** *2200 Main St, Hilton Head Island (29926). Phone 843/681-3001; toll-free 800/471-3001; fax 843/681-5541. www.mainstreetinn.com.* The Main Street Inn is a beacon of sophistication on South Carolina's renowned Hilton Head Island. The heady scents of jasmine and gardenia fill the air and invite repose in the lovely Charleston-style gardens at this endearing hotel. The inn, with its sumptuous décor and personalized service, is the antithesis of the impersonal mega-resort. The 32 rooms are individually designed, yet all feature luxurious velvet and silk linens, unique artwork, and distinctive furnishings. A bountiful breakfast buffet is served daily in the elegant breakfast room, and afternoon tea is a daily tradition here, making it a challenge to venture beyond the inn's doors to explore the island's celebrated golf courses and beaches. 32 rooms, 3 story. Children over 12 years only. Complimentary full breakfast. Check-in 3 pm, check-out noon. Outdoor pool, whirlpool. **$**

Restaurants

★ ★ **ALEXANDER'S.** *76 Queens Folly Rd, Hilton Head Island (29928). Phone 843/785-4999; fax 843/785-2117.* American, seafood menu. Dinner. Closed Thanksgiving, Dec 24-25. Bar. Children's menu. Casual attire. **$$**

★ ★ **CAFE EUROPA.** *160 Lighthouse Rd, Hilton Head Island (29928). Phone 843/671-3399; fax 843/671-6655.* Seafood menu. Breakfast, lunch, dinner. Closed Nov-mid-Feb. Children's menu. **$$**

★ ★ **CHARLIE'S L'ETOILE VERTE.** *8 New Orleans Rd, Hilton Head Island (29928). Phone 843/785-9277.* Eclectic décor with French artwork and fresh flowers give this restaurant a feel of France. French menu. Lunch, dinner. Closed Sun-Mon; holidays. Bar. Casual attire. Reservations recommended. **$$**

★ ★ ★ **GASLIGHT 2000.** *29 Park Plaza, Hilton Head Island (29928). Phone 843/785-5814; fax 843/363-2263. www.hiltonhead.com.* Guests will find this restaurant in a strip mall, but should not let that deter their visit. French menu. Dinner. Closed Sun; Jan 1, Dec 25. Bar. Casual attire. **$$**

★ ★ **HARBOURMASTER'S.** *Shelter Cove Harbour, Hilton Head Island (29938). Phone 843/785-3030; fax 843/842-2252.* This is waterfront dining at its finest. Located on the waterway entrance to Shelter Cove Harbour, it offers the finest in creative cuisine. Exceptional service, unmatched ambience, and dramatic views offer the dining guest the finest the island has to offer. American, seafood menu. Dinner. Closed Sun; Thanksgiving, Dec 25; also Jan. Bar. Children's menu. Casual attire. Outdoor seating. **$$$**

★ ★ **HOFBRAUHAUS.** *Pope Ave and Executive Park, Hilton Head Island (29928). Phone 843/785-3663; fax 843/342-3529.* Festive German décor; stained-glass windows, stein and mug collection. German, American menu. Dinner. Closed the first two weeks in Dec. Bar. Children's menu. Casual attire. **$$**

★ ★ **IRON WOLF CHOP HOUSE.** *Hwy 278, Building B, Hilton Head Island (29928). Phone 843/341-2467; fax 843/341-6775.* Steak menu. Dinner, brunch. Bar. Children's menu. Casual attire. Reservations recommended. **$$**

★ ★ **LITTLE VENICE.** *Shelter Cove, Hilton Head Island (29928). Phone 843/785-3300.* Italian menu. Lunch, dinner. Bar. Children's menu. Casual attire. Outdoor seating. **$$**

★ ★ **NENO IL TOSCANO.** *105 Festival Center, Hilton Head Island (29928). Phone 843/342-2400; fax 843/342-2871.* Italian menu. Dinner. Closed Sun; holidays. Bar. Children's menu. Casual attire. **$$$**

★ ★ **OLD OYSTER FACTORY.** *101 Marshland Rd, Hilton Head Island (29928). Phone 843/681-6040. www.oldoysterfactory.com.* Seafood menu. Dinner. Closed Thanksgiving, Dec 25. Bar. Children's menu. Outdoor seating. **$$**

★ ★ **RED FISH.** *8 Anchor Rd, Hilton Head Island (29928). Phone 843/686-3388.* Cuban menu. Lunch, dinner. Closed Thanksgiving, Dec 25. Bar. Children's menu. Casual attire. Outdoor seating. **$$$**

★ **SCOTT'S FISH MARKET.** *Shelter Cove Harbour, Hilton Head Island (29928). Phone 843/785-7575. www.scottsfishmarket.com.* American, seafood menu. Dinner. Closed Sun; holidays; also Jan. Bar. Children's menu. Casual attire. Outdoor seating. **$$**

Isle of Palms (E-5)

Population 4,583
Area Code 843
Web Site www.isle-of-palms.sc.us

Full-Service Resort

★ ★ ★ **BOARDWALK INN AT WILD DUNES RESORT.** *5757 Palm Blvd, Isle of Palms (29451). Phone 843/886-6000; toll-free 800/845-8880; fax 843/886-2916. www.wilddunes.com.* Only 20 minutes from downtown, Isle of Palms is where Charlestonians have been coming to relax for decades. This breezy barrier island blends sophistication with seaside ease, especially at its top resort, Wild Dunes. The Boardwalk Inn, in the heart of the resort's old-fashioned walking village, is the shining star of this resort complex. Beachy elegance defines the atmosphere at this top-notch property. Two 18-hole Tom Fazio-designed golf courses, a 17-court tennis center, a marina, and a fitness center are among the many recreational opportunities available here, and the resort's plentiful restaurants make dining a memorable event. The resort's signature friendly spirit makes it a perfect choice for families, while its cosmopolitan attitude appeals to couples. 93 rooms, 5 story. Check-in 4 pm, check-out 11 am. High-speed Internet access. Two restaurants, two bars. Children's activity center. Fitness room, fitness classes available. Outdoor pool, children's pool. Golf, 36 holes. Tennis. **$$**

Restaurant

★ ★ THE BOATHOUSE RESTAURANT. *10 Palm Blvd, Isle of Palms (29451). Phone 843/886-8000.* Seafood menu. Dinner. Closed Dec 24-25. Bar. Children's menu. Casual attire. Outdoor seating. **$$$**

Kiawah Island (F-5)

See also Beaufort, Charleston, Fort Sumter National Monument

Population 1,163
Area Code 843
Information Visitor Center, 22 Beachwalker Dr, 29455; phone 843/768-5116 or 843/768-5117
Web Site www.charlestoncvb.com

Kiawah Island (pronounced KEE-a-wah) is one of the richest natural environments in the Middle Atlantic states. The island is a model for maintaining the ecological balance while allowing human habitation. Named for the Native Americans who once hunted and fished here, the island is separated from the mainland by the Kiawah River and a mile-wide salt marsh.

Extensive environmental study has helped preserve nature while also providing for human needs. Separate resort areas and private residential neighborhoods have been planned to provide a minimum of automobile traffic and leave much of the island untouched. The Kiawah Island Resort offers activities like golf, tennis, and nature programs that take advantage of the island's natural beauty.

Full-Service Resorts

★ ★ ★ KIAWAH ISLAND INN. *12 Kiawah Beach Dr, Kiawah Island (29455). Phone 843/768-2121; toll-free 800/654-2924; fax 843/768-2736. www.kiawahresort.com.* Warm, gentle breezes bathe Kiawah Island, where 10 miles of unspoiled beaches, meandering rivers, and scenic marshland seduce visitors. The great beauty of this place is matched only by its notable golf, experienced at the island's premier Kiawah Island Inn. Five courses, including the notable Ocean Course which has hosted several professional championships, leave golfers breathless, and with a state-of-the-art instructional facility, this resort truly celebrates the sport. From oceanfront homes and golf villas to a charming inn and pampering oceanfront resort, the accommodations feature something for everyone. Golf may be the favorite pastime here, but it's not the only activity, with tennis, nature activities, shopping, fine dining, and children's programming among the many offerings. 610 rooms, 3 story. Pets accepted, some restrictions; fee. Check-in 4 pm, check-out 11 am. Restaurants, bar. Children's activity center. Fitness room. Seven outdoor pools, children's pool. Golf. Tennis. Business center. **$$**

★ ★ ★ ★ THE SANCTUARY AT KIAWAH ISLAND. *1 Sanctuary Beach Dr, Kiawah Island (29455). Phone 843/768-6000; fax 843/768-5150.* With five championship courses just outside its door, The Sanctuary at Kiawah Island is a natural choice for golfers, yet this serenely elegant resort appeals to a wide range of travelers with its fine dining, first-class spa, and beautiful setting. Just 30 minutes from downtown Charleston, this resort retains the sophistication and Southern hospitality associated with that city while celebrating its slow pace and rugged natural beauty. The accommodations blend traditional Early American-style furnishings with a crisp coastal ambience, and all rooms showcase ocean views from spacious balconies. Inspired by the beachfront setting, the nature-themed spa entices guests with its luscious treatments incorporating mineral-rich mud, seaweed, and botanical extracts, while the three restaurants also borrow from the locale with seafood-heavy menus and striking views of the water. 255 rooms. Check-in 4 pm, check-out noon. High-speed Internet access, wireless Internet access. Three restaurants, three bars. Children's activity center. Fitness room, fitness classes available, spa. Beach. Indoor pool, two outdoor pools, children's pool, whirlpool. Golf, 90 holes. Tennis. Airport transportation available. Business center. **$$$$**

Restaurant

★ OLD POST OFFICE RESTAURANT. *1442 Hwy 174, Edisto Island (29438). Phone 843/869-2339; fax 843/869-2372.* Childhood friends Philip Bardin and David Gressette revamped this community building into a Southern low-country restaurant in 1988. Guests will enjoy dining at this charming white-clapboard cottage. American menu. Dinner. Closed Sun-Mon; holidays; also one week in Jan. Bar. Casual attire. **$$**

Mount Pleasant

Founded 1680
Population 47,609
Information Mount Pleasant/Isle of Palms Visitor Center, 311 Johnnie Dodds Blvd (Bridge Way Village); phone 843/884-8517
Web Site www.townofmountpleasant.com

What to See and Do

Patriots Point Naval and Maritime Museum. *40 Patriots Point Rd, Mount Pleasant (29464). Phone 843/ 884-2727. www.state.sc.us/patpt.* This is an amazing assemblage of naval equipment and lore, appropriately located in Charleston Harbor. There's plenty of detail for adult visitors and ample space for kids to roam. The undisputed star of the show is the famed World War II aircraft carrier, the USS *Yorktown.* A film, *The Fighting Lady,* depicts life aboard the carrier. Onboard the *Yorktown* are numerous displays, including the Congressional Medal of Honor Society's museum and headquarters, the World War II Fast Carrier exhibit, the Battle of Midway Torpedo Squadrons memorial, and a World War II cruiser room. Other vessels include the *Savannah,* the world's first nuclear-powered merchant ship; the *Laffey,* a World War II destroyer; the *Clamagore,* a World War II submarine; and the *Ingham,* a Coast Guard cutter. (Apr-Sept: 9 am- 7:30 pm; Oct-Mar: 9 am-6:30 pm; closed Dec 25) **$$$**

Restaurant

★ **THE WRECK.** *106 Haddrell St, Mount Pleasant (29464). Phone 843/884-0052.* Seafood menu. Dinner. Jacket required. Outdoor seating. No credit cards accepted. **$**
🅳

Myrtle Beach (D-6)

See also Georgetown

Population 22,759
Elevation 30 ft
Area Code 843
Information Myrtle Beach Area Chamber of Commerce, 1200 N Oak St, PO Box 2115, 29578; phone 843/626-7444 or toll-free 800/356-3016
Web Site www.myrtlebeachlive.com

With the Gulf Stream only a few miles offshore and dunes to shelter miles of white sand, Myrtle Beach is one of the most popular seaside resorts on the Atlantic Coast. Swimming, fishing, golf, tennis, and boardwalk amusements combine to lure millions of vacationers each summer. The many myrtle trees in the area give this resort its name.

What to See and Do

Barefoot Landing. *4898 Hwy 17 S, Myrtle Beach (29582). Phone 803/272-8349; toll-free 800/272-2320. www.bflanding.com.* With a mixture of specialty shops and factory stores, Barefoot Landing appeals to a variety of shoppers, from Birkenstock wearers to beer enthusiasts. There are also more than a dozen eateries and a variety of entertainment options, including the House of Blues for live music and a video arcade. (Daily, hours vary by season; closed Dec 25, Dec 31)

Barefoot Resort. *4980 Barefoot Resort Bridge Rd, North Myrtle Beach (29582). Phone 843/390-7999. www.bfresort.com.* Maybe the best place in Myrtle Beach to play golf, Barefoot Resort features four stunning courses designed by some of the sport's biggest names. Davis Love III, Tom Fazio, Greg Norman, and Pete Dye all took a piece of the land and crafted courses boasting their signature touches. The courses take the best of both British and American golf and bring them together in one spectacular place. **$$$$**

Broadway at the Beach. *1325 Celebrity Cir, Myrtle Beach (29577). Phone 843/444-3200; toll-free 800/386- 4662. www.broadwayatthebeach.com.* This sprawling 350-acre complex, billed as the largest venue of its kind in South Carolina, brings together shops, dining, nightclubs, and a wide variety of entertainment. Shops run the gamut from Build-A-Bear Workshop to Gap to Harley Davidson, with many options for picking up souvenirs and beach items. When you get hungry, stop in at one of the center's many restaurants, which include standards like Joe's Crab Shack, Hard Rock Cafe, and NASCAR Cafe. Several of them stay open late, joining several nightclubs to offer dancing and libations. Also on-site are a 16-screen movie theater, an IMAX theater, a NASCAR SpeedPark, a miniature golf course, a water park, and an aquarium. Broadway at the Beach is home to the Myrtle Beach Pelicans, a Class A affiliate of the Atlanta Braves, too. (Daily, hours vary by season; closed Dec 25)

⭐ **"The Grand Stand."** Sixty miles of beach from the North Carolina border south to Georgetown. Camping, fishing, golf, tennis, amusement parks.

Myrtle Beach State Park. *4401 S Kings Hwy, Myrtle Beach (29575). 3 miles S on Hwy 17 Business. Phone 843/238-5325.* Approximately 300 acres. Ocean and pool swimming; surf fishing (supplies available). Nature trail. Picnicking (shelters), playground, stores. Camping, cabins. Interpretive center. **$**

NASCAR Speedpark. *1820 21st Ave N, Myrtle Beach (29577). Phone 843/918-8725. www.nascarspeedpark.com.* Enjoy racing fun with tracks you can drive, miniature golf courses, kiddie rides, an indoor climbing wall, bumper boats, an arcade, and NASCAR souvenirs.

Special Event

Sun Fun Festival. *1200 Oak St, Myrtle Beach.* More than 60 seaside entertainment events, including parades. First weekend in June.

Limited-Service Hotels

★ ★ **BEACH COVE RESORT.** *4800 S Ocean Blvd, North Myrtle Beach (29582). Phone 843/918-9000; toll-free 800/331-6533; fax 843/918-8399. www.beachcove.com.* 320 rooms, 16 story, all suites. Check-in 3 pm, check-out 11 am. Restaurant, two bars. Children's activity center. Fitness room. Beach. Indoor pool, three outdoor pools, children's pool, four whirlpools. **$**

★ ★ **THE BREAKERS RESORT.** *2006 N Ocean Blvd, Myrtle Beach (29578). Phone 843/444-4444; toll-free 800/845-0688; fax 843/626-5001.* 550 rooms, 18 story. Check-in 3 pm, check-out 11 am. Restaurant, bar. Children's activity center. Fitness room. Beach. Indoor pool, outdoor pool, children's pool, whirlpool. Airport transportation available. **$**

★ ★ **COURTYARD BY MARRIOTT MYRTLE BEACH-BAREFOOT LANDING.** *1000 Commons Blvd (Hwy 17), Myrtle Beach (29572). Phone 843/361-1730; toll-free 877/502-4653; fax 843/361-1729. www.courtyard.com.* 157 rooms. Check-in 3 pm, check-out noon. Restaurant. Indoor pool, whirlpool. **$**

★ **FAIRFIELD INN.** *1350 Paradise Cir, Myrtle Beach (29577). Phone 843/444-8097; toll-free 800/228-2800; fax 843/444-8394. www.fairfieldinn.com/myrfb.* 111 rooms, 4 story. Complimentary continental break-fast. Check-in 3 pm, check-out noon. Outdoor pool, whirlpool. **$**

★ **HAMPTON INN & SUITES OCEANFRONT.** *1803 S Ocean Blvd, Myrtle Beach (29577). Phone 843/946-6400; toll-free 877/946-6400; fax 843/946-0031. www.hamptoninnoceanfront.com.* 116 rooms. Complimentary continental breakfast. Check-in 3 pm, check-out 11 am. High-speed Internet access. Fitness room. Beach. Indoor pool, outdoor pool, children's pool, whirlpool. Airport transportation available. Business center. **$$**

★ **HAMPTON INN.** *1140 Celebrity Cir, Myrtle Beach (29577). Phone 843/916-0600; toll-free 888/916-2001; fax 843/946-6308. www.hamptoninnbroadwayatthebeach.com.* 141 rooms, 8 story. Complimentary continental breakfast. Check-in 3 pm, check-out 11 am. High-speed Internet access. Bar. Children's activity center. Fitness room. Indoor pool, outdoor pool, whirlpool. Airport transportation available. Business center. **$**

★ **LA QUINTA INN.** *1561 21st Ave N, Myrtle Beach (29577). Phone 843/916-8801; toll-free 800/687-6667; fax 843/916-8701. www.laquinta.com.* 128 rooms, 4 story. Complimentary continental breakfast. Check-in 3 pm, check-out noon. Fitness room. Outdoor pool, whirlpool. **$**

★ ★ ★ **RADISSON PLAZA HOTEL.** *2101 N Oak St, Myrtle Beach (29577). Phone 843/918-5000; toll-free 800/333-3333; fax 843/918-5004. www.radisson.com.* 402 rooms. Check-in 3 pm, check-out noon. High-speed Internet access. Restaurant, bar. Fitness room. Indoor pool, whirlpool. Airport transportation available. Business center. **$$**

★ ★ **SEA ISLAND INN ON THE BEACH.** *6000 N Ocean Blvd, Myrtle Beach (29577). Phone 843/449-6406; toll-free 800/548-0767; fax 843/449-4102. www.seaislandinn.com.* 113 rooms, 5 story. Check-in 2 pm, check-out 11 am. Restaurant. Children's activity center. Swimming beach. Outdoor pool, children's pool. Airport transportation available. **$**

Full-Service Hotel

★ ★ ★ HILTON MYRTLE BEACH RESORT.

10000 Beach Club Dr, Myrtle Beach (29572). Phone 843/449-5000; toll-free 877/887-9549; fax 843/497-0168. www.hilton.com. 385 rooms, 15 story. Check-in 4 pm, check-out noon. High-speed Internet access. Three restaurants, two bars. Fitness room. Beach. Indoor pool, outdoor pool, children's pool, whirlpool. Golf, 18 holes. Tennis. **$$**

Full-Service Resorts

★ ★ COMPASS COVE OCEANFRONT RESORT.

2311 S Ocean Blvd, Myrtle Beach (29577). Phone 843/448-8373; toll-free 800/228-9894; fax 843/448-5444. www.compasscove.com. 532 rooms, 16 story, all suites. Pets accepted. Check-in 3 pm, check-out 11 am. Two restaurants, bar. Children's activity center. Fitness room. Beach. Two indoor pools, sixteen outdoor pools, three children's pools, whirlpool. Airport transportation available. **$**

★ ★ ★ EMBASSY SUITES.

9800 Queensway Blvd, Myrtle Beach (29572). Phone 843/449-0006; toll-free 800/876-0010; fax 843/497-7910. www.kingstonplantation.com. All suites offer either a lakefront, or a woodside, tennis court, or poolside view. This hotel has it all. Located on a white-sand beach, visitors can enjoy swimming, sailing, or just relaxing by the water. Shopping and downtown are nearby. 255 rooms, 20 story. Complimentary full breakfast. Check-in 4 pm, check-out noon. Restaurant, bar. Children's activity center. Fitness room. One indoor pool, six outdoor pools, children's pool, whirlpool. Golf. Tennis. Business center. **$$**

★ ★ ★ LITCHFIELD PLANTATION.

King's River Rd, Pawleys Island (29585). Phone 843/237-9121; toll-free 800/869-1410; fax 843/237-1688. www.litchfield plantation.com. 35 rooms, 2 story. Complimentary full breakfast. Check-in 3 pm, check-out 11 am. Restaurant, bar. Outdoor pool. Tennis. Business center. **$$**

★ ★ OCEAN CREEK RESORT.

10600 N Kings Hwy, Myrtle Beach (29572). Phone 843/272-7724. 410 rooms. Check-in 4 pm, check-out 11 am. Restaurant, bar. Children's activity center. Fitness room. Beach. Outdoor pool. Tennis. **$$$**

Specialty Lodgings

The following lodging establishments are approved by Mobil Travel Guide, but due to their unique and individualized nature have not been given a traditional Mobil Star rating. Included in this listing you may find bed-and-breakfasts, limited-service inns, guest ranches, and other unique hotel properties.

THE CYPRESS INN.

16 Elm St, Conway (29528). Phone 843/248-8199; toll-free 800/575-5307; fax 843/248-0329. www.acypressinn.com. Relax in this graceful 12-room bed-and-breakfast located in the quiet town of Conway. Guests can enjoy bicycle riding or surrender their worries to a massage therapist. Tucked away in a quaint marina, guests have the options to take on deep-sea fishing or simply walk the beautiful stretches of South Carolina beaches, located only 15 minutes away. 12 rooms, 3 story. Complimentary full breakfast. Check-in 4 pm, check-out 11 am. **$**

SERENDIPITY, AN INN.

407 71st Avenue N, Myrtle Beach (29572). Phone 800/762-3229; toll-free 800/762-3229; fax 843/449-3998. www.serendipityinn.com. 15 rooms, 2 story. Complimentary continental breakfast. Check-in 2 pm, check-out 11 am. Outdoor pool, whirlpool. **$**

Restaurants

★ ★ BARONS STEAKS & CHOPS.

9650 N Kings Hwy, Myrtle Beach (29572). Phone 843/497-8970. American menu. Dinner. Closed Sun; Labor Day, Thanksgiving, Dec 24-25. Bar. Children's menu. Casual attire. Outdoor seating. **$$**

★ ★ BLUE WATER BISTRO.

503 61st Ave, Myrtle Beach (29577). Phone 843/692-2202; fax 843/692-2221. International/Fusion menu. Lunch, dinner. Bar. Business casual attire. Reservations recommended. Outdoor seating. **$$**

★ CAGNEY'S OLD PLACE.

9911 N Kings Hwy, Myrtle Beach (29577). Phone 843/449-3824; fax 843/692-9407. American menu. Dinner. Closed Sun; also Jan and Dec. Bar. Children's menu. Casual attire. Reservations recommended. **$$**

★ ★ CAPTAIN DAVE'S DOCKSIDE.

Hwy 17 Business, Murrell's Inlet, Myrtle Beach (29576). Phone 843/651-5850; fax 843/651-8915. www.captaindaves dockside.com. Seafood, steak menu. Lunch, dinner. Closed Jan 1, Thanksgiving, Dec 24-25; also two weeks in Jan. Bar. Children's menu. Casual attire. Outdoor seating. **$$**

★ **CAPTAIN GEORGE'S SEAFOOD.** *1401 29th Ave Ext, Myrtle Beach (29577). Phone 843/916-2278.* Seafood menu. Dinner. Closed Dec 25. Bar. Children's menu. Casual attire. **$$**

★ ★ **CHESTNUT HILL RESTAURANT.** *9922 Hwy 17 N, Myrtle Beach (29572). Phone 843/449-3984.* American menu. Dinner. Closed Thanksgiving, Dec 24-25; also Super Bowl Sun. Bar. Children's menu. Casual attire. **$$**

★ ★ **COLLECTORS CAFE.** *7726 N Kings Hwy, Myrtle Beach (29572). Phone 843/449-9370; fax 843/449-6129. www.collectorscafeandgallery.com.* Mediterranean menu. Dinner. Closed Sun; also two weeks in Jan. Bar. Casual attire. Reservations recommended. **$$$**

★ **DIRTY DON'S OYSTER BAR & GRILL.** *408 21st Ave N, Myrtle Beach (29577). Phone 843/448-4881.* American, seafood menu. Lunch, dinner, late-night. Bar. Children's menu. Casual attire. Outdoor seating. **$$**

★ ★ **GARCIA'S.** *9676 N Kings Hwy, Myrtle Beach (29572). Phone 843/449-4435.* Mexican menu. Lunch, dinner. Closed Thanksgiving, Dec 24-25. Bar. Children's menu. Casual attire. **$$**

★ ★ **JOE'S BAR AND GRILL.** *810 Conway Ave, North Myrtle Beach (29582). Phone 843/272-4666; fax 843/272-3691. www.dinejoes.com.* American menu. Lunch, dinner. Closed Dec 25. Bar. Children's menu. Casual attire. Outdoor seating. **$$**

★ ★ **MARINA RAW BAR.** *1203 Hwy 17, North Myrtle Beach (29582). Phone 843/249-3972.* Seafood menu. Lunch, dinner. Closed Thanksgiving, Dec 25. Bar. Casual attire. Outdoor seating. **$$**

★ ★ **SEA CAPTAIN'S HOUSE.** *3000 N Ocean Blvd, Myrtle Beach (29577). Phone 843/448-8082; fax 843/626-6960.* Sea captain's house design; flowering shrubs. Seafood menu. Breakfast, lunch, dinner. Closed Thanksgiving, Dec 24-27; also day after Labor Day. Bar. Children's menu. Casual attire. **$$**

★ **SHUCKERS RAW BAR.** *300 N Kings Hwy, Myrtle Beach (29577). Phone 843/448-6162.* Seafood menu. Lunch, dinner, late-night. Bar. Casual attire. Outdoor seating. **$$**

★ ★ **SUGAMI.** *9711 N Kings Hwy, Myrtle Beach (29572). Phone 843/449-7271.* Japanese menu. Dinner.

Closed Memorial Day weekend. Bar. Casual attire. Reservations recommended. Outdoor seating. **$$**

★ **TONY'S.** *1407 Hwy 17, North Myrtle Beach (29582). Phone 843/249-1314; fax 843/281-9081.* Italian menu. Dinner. Closed Sun; early Dec-early Feb. Bar. Children's menu. **$$**

Newberry (D-3)

See also Clinton, Columbia, Greenwood

Population 10,580
Elevation 500 ft
Area Code 803
Zip 29108
Web Site www.cityofnewberry.com

What to See and Do

Dreher Island State Park. *3677 State Park Rd, Newberry (29127). 20 miles SE via Hwy 76 to Chapin, then 9 miles SW via unnumbered road. Phone 803/364-4152.* Approximately 340 acres. Three islands with 12-mile shoreline. Lake swimming, fishing (supplies), boating (ramps, rental slips). Nature trail. Picnicking (shelters), playground, recreation building, store. Camping (hook-ups, dump station; higher fees for lakefront campsites in summer).

Sumter National Forest. *N via Hwy 121, Hwy 176.* (See GREENWOOD)

Orangeburg (E-4)

See also Aiken, Allendale, Columbia, Santee

Settled 1730s
Population 12,765
Elevation 245 ft
Area Code 803
Zip 29115
Information Orangeburg County Chamber of Commerce, 1570 John C. Calhoun Dr, Box 328, 29116-0328; phone 803/534-6821
Web Site www.orangeburgsc.net

Named for the Prince of Orange, this community is the seat of Orangeburg County, one of the most prosperous farm areas in the state. Manufacturing plants for wood products, ball bearings, textiles, textile equipment, chemicals, hand tools, and lawn mowers are all located within the county.

What to See and Do

Edisto Memorial Gardens. *367 Green St, Orangeburg. S on Hwy 301, within city limits, alongside N Edisto River.* Phone 803/533-6020. City-owned 110-acre site. Seasonal flowers bloom all year; more than 3,200 rose bushes, camellias, azaleas; also many flowering trees. Gardens (daily). Wetlands boardwalk park. Tennis courts, disc-golf, mountain brook, picnic areas, shelters nearby, playground. **FREE**

South Carolina State University. *300 College St NE, Orangeburg.* Phone 803/536-7000. (1896) (5,000 students) On campus is

I. P. Stanback Museum and Planetarium. *300 College St NE, Orangeburg (29115).* Phone 803/536-7174 *(for show reservations).* Museum has changing exhibits (Sept-May, Mon-Fri; closed holidays). Planetarium Christmas shows (First and second Sun in Dec, by reservation). **FREE**

Special Event

Orangeburg County Fair. *Pawleys Island Fairgrounds, Orangeburg.* 4-H shows, tractor pulls, entertainment, and carnival rides are some of the activities found at this county fair. Late Sept-early Oct.

Restaurant

★ ★ ★ **LOUIS'S AT PAWLEYS & THE FISH CAMP BAR.** *10880 Ocean Hwy, Hwy 17, Pawleys Island (29585).* Phone 843/237-8757. Low country menu. Lunch, dinner. Closed Dec 25; also Super Bowl Sun. Bar. Children's menu. Casual attire. Reservations recommended. Outdoor seating. **$$**

Ridgeway (D-4)

Restaurant

★ ★ **BOYKIN'S AT THE MILL POND.** *83 Boykin Mill Rd, Rembert (29128).* Phone 803/425-8825. Some of the area's best high-end dining, Southern-style, is offered at this restaurant about ten minutes from Camden. The menu includes staples like grits and fried green tomatoes. American menu. Dinner. Closed Sun-Mon; Jan 1, Dec 25; also the first week in July. Bar. Casual attire. Reservations recommended. **$$$**

Rock Hill (C-4)

See also Chester, Gaffney

Founded 1852
Population 49,765
Elevation 667 ft
Area Code 803
Information York County Convention & Visitors Bureau, 201 E Main St, PO Box 11377, 29731; phone 803/329-5200 or toll-free 800/866-5200
Web Site www.yccvb.com

Both a college and an industrial town, Rock Hill takes its name from the flint rock that had to be cut through when a railroad was being built through town.

What to See and Do

Andrew Jackson State Park. *196 Andrew Jackson Park Rd, Lancaster (29720). 9 miles N on Hwy 521.* Phone 803/285-3344. Approximately 360 acres. Lake fishing, boating (rentals). Nature trail. Picnicking (shelters). Camping. Recreation building, outdoor amphitheater. Log house museum contains documents, exhibits of Jackson lore. One-room school with exhibits. **$**

Catawba Cultural Center. *1536 Tom Steven Rd, Rock Hill.* Phone 803/328-2427. Located on the Catawba Indian Reservation, this center strives to preserve the heritage of the Catawba's culture. Tours and programs demonstrating the Catawba's culture and heritage are available (by appointment; fee). Gift shop. (Mon-Sat; closed holidays) **FREE**

Glencairn Garden. *725 Crest St, Rock Hill.* Phone 803/329-5620. Municipally owned 6 acres of colorful azaleas, dogwood, redbud, crepe myrtle, boxwood; pool, fountain. (Daily) **FREE**

Historic Brattonsville. *1444 Brattonsville Rd, Rock Hill. SW via Hwy 322, near McConnells.* Phone 803/684-2327. Learn about local history in this restored village of over two dozen structures, including Backwoodsman Cabin, Colonel Bratton Home (circa 1780), Homestead House (circa 1823), and Brick Kitchen. Gift shop. Guided tours (by appointment). Self-guided audio tour. (Mar-Nov, Tues-Sat, also Sun afternoons; closed holidays) **$$**

Lake Wylie. *N on Hwy 274.* Phone 704/382-8587. Created by Duke Power Company Dam on the Catawba River. 12,455 acres. Freshwater fishing, boating, waterskiing, swimming.

Landsford Canal State Park. *2051 Park Dr, Catawba. 15 miles S off Hwy 21.* Phone *803/789-5800.* Approximately 250 acres. Site of a canal built in the 1820s; locks, stone bridges. Trail parallels canals. Picnicking (shelter), community building. (Thurs-Mon) **$**

Museum of York County. *4621 Mount Gallant Rd, Rock Hill (29732). 7 miles NW, off I-77 exit 82 A.* Phone *803/329-2121.* Contains a large collection of mounted African hoofed mammals; large African artifacts collection. Hall of Western Hemisphere contains mounted animals from North and South America. Art galleries and planetarium. Catawba pottery sold here. Nature trail, picnic area. (Daily; closed Jan 1, Thanksgiving, Dec 24-25) **$$**

Winthrop University. *701 Oakland Ave, Rock Hill (29733).* Phone *803/323-2236.* (1886) (5,000 students) Coeducational; 100 undergraduate and graduate programs. Concerts, lectures, sports, plays, art galleries. Large lake and recreational area.

Special Event

"Come-See-Me." Art shows, tour of houses, entertainment, road race, concerts. Ten days early Apr.

Limited-Service Hotels

★ **HAMPTON INN.** *2111 Tabor Dr, Rock Hill (29730).* Phone *803/325-1100; toll-free 800/426-7866; fax 803/325-7814. www.hampton-inn.com.* 162 rooms, 5 story. Complimentary continental breakfast. Check-in 2 pm, check-out 11 am. High-speed Internet access, wireless Internet access. Fitness room. Outdoor pool. Business center. **$**
⛹ 🏊 🏋

★ **MICROTEL INN AND SUITES.** *1047 Riverview Rd, Rock Hill (29732).* Phone *803/817-7700; toll-free 888/771-7179; fax 803/817-7700. www.microtelinn.com.* 77 rooms. Check-in 3 pm, check-out 11 am. Complimentary continental breakfast. Wireless Internet access. **$**

Specialty Lodging

The following lodging establishment is approved by Mobil Travel Guide, but due to its unique and individualized nature has not been given a traditional Mobil Star rating. Included in this listing you may find bed-and-breakfasts, limited-service inns, guest ranches, and other unique hotel properties.

EAST MAIN GUEST HOUSE. *600 E Main St, Rock Hill (29730).* Phone *803/366-1161; fax 803/366-1210. www.eastmainsc.com.* Built in 1910. 3 rooms, 2 story. Children over 12 years only. Complimentary full breakfast. Check-in 3 pm, check-out noon. **$**
🄳

Restaurant

★ **TAM'S TAVERN.** *1027 Oakland Ave, Rock Hill (29732).* Phone *803/329-2226. www.tamstavern.com.* California menu. Lunch, dinner. Closed Sun; also week of July 4. Bar. Children's menu. Casual attire. **$$**

Santee (E-5)

See also Orangeburg

Population 740
Elevation 250 ft
Area Code 803
Zip 29142
Information Santee-Cooper Country, PO Drawer 40; phone 803/854-2131 or toll-free 800/227-8510 outside SC
Web Site www.santeecoopercountry.org

This community serves as the gateway to the Santee-Cooper lakes recreation area, created by the Pinopolis and Santee dams on the Santee and Cooper rivers. There are numerous marinas and campgrounds on the Santee-Cooper lakes.

What to See and Do

Eutaw Springs Battlefield Site. *12 miles SE off Hwy 6.* Site where ragged colonials fought the British on Sept 8, 1781, in what is considered to be the last major engagement in South Carolina; both sides claimed victory. Three acres maintained by state. No facilities. **FREE**

Fort Watson Battle Site and Indian Mound. *4 miles N, 1 mile off Hwy 15/301. On Lake Marion.* A 48-foot-high mound; site of American Revolution battle Apr 15-23, 1781, during which General Francis Marion attacked and captured a British fortification, its garrison, supplies, and ammunition. Three acres maintained by state. No facilities. Observation point has view of Santee-Cooper waters. **FREE**

Santee National Wildlife Refuge. *Secondary State Rd 803 and Hwy 301/15, Summerton (29148). 4 miles N* on Hwy 15/301 or exit 102 from I-95. Phone 803/478-2217. Attracts many geese and ducks during winter. Observation tower, self-guided nature trail; visitor information center with exhibits (Mon-Fri; closed holidays). Seasonal hunting and fishing, wildlife observation, and photography. **FREE**

Santee State Park. *251 State Park Rd, Santee (29152). 3 miles NW off Hwy 6.* On shores of Lake Marion. *Phone 803/854-2408.* Approximately 2,500 acres. Lake swimming, fishing (supplies available), boating (ramp, rentals, dock). Scenic lake tours. Nature trails; tennis. Picnicking (shelters), playground, restaurant, groceries. Camping, cabins (higher fees for lakefront sites), primitive camping. Interpretive center, recreation building. **$**

Limited-Service Hotel

★ ★ **BEST WESTERN.** *Hwy 6, Santee (29142). Phone 803/854-3089; fax 803/854-3093. www.bestwestern.com.* 108 rooms. Complimentary continental breakfast. Check-in 2 pm, check-out 11 am. Restaurant. Outdoor pool, whirlpool. **$** 🛏

Spartanburg (C-3)

See also Clinton, Gaffney, Greenville

Founded 1785
Population 39,673
Elevation 816 ft
Area Code 864
Information Convention and Visitors Bureau, 298 Magnolia St, PO Box 1636, 29306; phone 864/594-5050
Web Site www.visitspartanburg.com

An array of highways and railroads feeds agricultural products into, and moves manufactured products out of, heavily industrialized Spartanburg. Textiles and peaches are the leading products. The Spartan Regiment of South Carolina militia, heroes of the Battle at Cowpens, gave both the county and its seat their names.

What to See and Do

Arts Council of Spartanburg. *385 S Spring St, Spartanburg. Phone 864/583-2776.* Permanent and changing exhibits; classes in visual and performing arts. (Daily; closed holidays) **FREE**

Croft State Park. *450 Croft State Park Rd, Spartanburg (29302). 3 miles SE on Hwy 56. Phone 864/585-1283.* On part of old Camp Croft military area. Approximately 7,000 acres. Swimming pool (fee), lake fishing. Nature, exercise trails, bridle trail (no rentals); stable, show ring; tennis. Picnicking (shelters), playground. Camping (hook-ups, dump station). **$**

Regional Museum. *100 E Main St, Spartanburg. Phone 864/596-3501.* Exhibits depict up-country history of state; Pardo Stone (1567), doll collections, Native American artifacts. (Tues-Sat; closed holidays) **$**

Walnut Grove Plantation. *1200 Otts Shoals Rd, Roebuck (29376). 8 miles SE near jct I-26, Hwy 221. Phone 864/576-6546.* (1765). Restored girlhood home of Kate Moore Barry, Revolutionary heroine; period furniture; schoolhouse, kitchen, doctor's office, other buildings; family cemetery; herb gardens with "dipping well." (Apr-Oct: Tues-Sun; rest of year: Sun only; closed holidays) **$$**

Special Event

Piedmont Interstate Fair. *275 Bishop St, Spartanburg. Phone 864/582-7042.* Art exhibit, livestock and flower shows, needlecraft and food displays; auto race. Second full week in Oct.

Limited-Service Hotel

★ **DAYS INN.** *1000 Hearon Cir, Spartanburg (29303). Phone 864/503-9048; fax 864/503-0576. www.daysinn.com.* 56 rooms, 3 story. Pets accepted. Complimentary continental breakfast. Check-in 3 pm, check-out noon. Fitness room. **$** 🐾 🚶

Summerville (E-5)

See also Charleston

Population 27,752
Information Summerville-Dorchester County Chamber of Commerce and Visitor Center, 402 N Main St, 29483; phone 843/873-2931
Web Site www.summervilletourism.com

What to See and Do

✪ **Francis Beidler Forest.** *336 Sanctuary Rd, Summerville (29483). From Charleston, 40 miles NW via I-26 W to exit 187, then S on Hwy 27 to Hwy 78, then W to Hwy 178 and follow the signs. Phone*

843/462-2150. www.audubon.org/local/sanctuary/ beidler. Located in the heart of the low country, this 11,000-acre site in Four Holes Swamp encompasses the largest remaining virgin stand of bald cypress and tupelo gum trees in the world. Oak, ash, and black-gum also grow here, as do 300 varieties of wildlife and numerous flowers, ferns, vines, and other plants. The swamp is fed by springs and runoff from surrounding areas (probably carved by tides and wind when the Atlantic Ocean covered more of the coastal plain than it does now) and joins the Edisto River, from which it exits into the ocean. A National Audubon Society sanctuary, the forest is named for a lumberman who championed conservation on both public and private lands. A 6,500-foot boardwalk into the swamp leads out from and back to the visitor center. Guided walks and canoe trips are available. (Tues-Sun 9 am-5 pm; closed holidays) **$$**

Old Dorchester State Historic Site. *300 State Park Rd, Summerville (29485). 19 miles NW on Hwy 642. Phone 843/873-1740.* This 325-acre park is on the site of a colonial village founded in 1697 by a group repre-senting the Congregational Church of Dorchester, Massachusetts. The town prospered, but it was seized by the British during the American Revolution. By the time the war was over, the town had been abandoned. Overlooking the Ashley River, the site today includes remnants of a fort, a cemetery, and the bell tower of St. George's Parish Church. Archaeological excava-tions are ongoing. Kiosks describe the history of the area and what life was like on the upper Ashley River. Fishing, hiking, boating, and picnic areas are available. (Thurs-Mon 9 am-6 pm) **$**

Full-Service Resort

★ ★ ★ ★ WOODLANDS RESORT & INN.
125 Parsons Rd, Summerville (29483). Phone 843/ 875-2600; toll-free 800/774-9999; fax 843/875-2603. www.woodlandsinn.com. The Woodlands Resort & Inn expertly blends the essence of the English countryside with the inimitable flavor of the South. This country estate, set on 42 acres, is a lovely retreat just down the road from some of the low country's most famous plantations. The 1906 Greek Revival Main House has casual, refined, and lavishly appointed guest rooms designed by interior decorator David Eskell-Briggs. Individually characterized, the accommodations share a common theme of English floral patterns and Early American reproductions. Guests dip their toes in the pool, volley on the two clay tennis courts, play croquet matches on the lawn, and ride bikes to the nearby

town of Summerville. Sandalwoods Day Spa features Aveda products in all of its treatments. The Dining Room (see) turns out delicious meals and is a sight to be seen with its 14-foot coffered ceilings of blue sky and white clouds. 19 rooms, 3 story. Closed two weeks in Jan. Pets accepted. Check-in 3 pm, check-out noon. Restaurant, bar. Children's activity center. Outdoor pool. Tennis. Airport transportation available. Business center. **$$$**

🔖 🏊 ⛷ 🏃

Restaurant

★ ★ ★ ★ ★ THE DINING ROOM AT THE WOODLANDS.
125 Parsons Rd, Summerville (29483). Phone 843/875-2600; toll-free 800/774-9999; fax 843/875-2603. www.woodlandsinn.com. Inside the Woodlands Resort & Inn (see), a charming 1906 country home turned resort just a short distance from Charleston, you'll discover The Dining Room, an elegant European-styled restaurant that is accented with fresh roses, cherry wood furnishings, cream-colored walls, a marble fireplace, and white linen tables topped with fine crystal and floral-print china. Perfecting the atmo-sphere of Southern charm in a post-plantation setting, The Dining Room offers gracious service and a daily changing menu of flavorful, regional American dishes that play with colorful accents from the Mediterranean, Asia, and the American South. The kitchen showers loving attention on ingredients from the region, often mentioning local farmers by name. This practice adds a nice sense of place to the menu and enhances your experience on an educational level. The trouble with an evening at The Dining Room at the Woodlands is that, as with most good things, it must come to an end. But with desserts like white chocolate beignets, it is a sweet ending indeed. American menu. Breakfast, lunch, din-ner, brunch. Bar. Jacket required (dinner). Reservations recommended. Valet parking. Outdoor seating. **$$$$**

Sumter (D-5)

See also Camden, Columbia

Settled 1785
Population 39,643
Elevation 173 ft
Area Code 803
Information Convention and Visitors Bureau, 32 E Calhoun St, PO Box 1449, 29150; phone 803/778-5434 or toll-free 800/688-4748
Web Site www.sumter-sc-tourism.com

Long the center of a prosperous agricultural area, Sumter has, in recent years, become an industrial center. Both the city and county are named for General Thomas Sumter, the "fighting gamecock" of the American Revolution. As a tourism spot, Sumter offers a unique contrast of antebellum mansions and modern facilities. Shaw Air Force Base, headquarters of the 9th Air Force and the 363rd Tactical Fighter Wing, is nearby.

What to See and Do

Church of the Holy Cross. *335 N Kings Hwy, Stateburg (29154). 10 miles W via Hwy 76, exit at Hwy 261. Phone 803/494-8101.* (1850) Built of *pise de terre* (rammed earth); unusual architectural design and construction. Also noted for stained-glass windows set to catch the rays of the rising sun. Many notable South Carolinians from the 1700s are buried in the old church cemetery, including Joel R. Poinsett.

Opera House. *21 N Main St, Sumter (29150). Phone 803/436-2500; toll-free 800/688-4748.* Today the 1893 Opera House stands not only as a symbol of the past but also as an active sign of the ongoing progressive spirit of the people of Sumter. The 600-seat auditorium is used for concerts, school events, and other local happenings. Fees vary for booked activities; many performances are free. (By appointment only; closed holidays) **FREE**

Poinsett State Park. *6660 Poinsett Park Rd, Wedgefield (29168). 18 miles SW via Hwy 763, 261. Phone 803/494-8177.* Approximately 1,000 acres of mountains, swamps. Named for Joel R. Poinsett, who introduced the poinsettia (which originated in Mexico) to the United States. Spanish moss, mountain laurel, rhododendron. Fishing, boating (rentals). Hiking, nature trails. Picnicking (shelters). Primitive and improved camping (dump station), cabins. Nature center. **$**

Sumter County Museum. *122 N Washington St, Sumter. Phone 803/775-0908.* Two-story Edwardian house depicting Victorian lifestyle; period rooms, historical exhibits, war memorabilia, economic and cultural artifacts, artwork, and archives (genealogical research). Museum is surrounded by formal gardens designed by Robert Marvin; several outdoor exhibits of farm implements, rural life; carriage house. (Tues-Sun; closed holidays) **DONATION**

Sumter Gallery of Art. *421 N Main St, Sumter. Phone 803/775-0543.* Located in the historic Elizabeth White house, regional artwork features paintings, drawings, sculpture, photography, and pottery; permanent collection of touchable works for the blind and changing exhibits. (Tues-Sun afternoons; closed holidays and July) **FREE**

Swan Lake Iris Gardens. *W Liberty St, Sumter.* Covers 150 acres. Kaempferi and Japanese iris; seasonal plantings, nature trails; ancient cypress, oak, and pine trees; 45-acre lake with all eight species of swan. Picnicking, playground. (Daily) Home to the Iris Festival held every May. (See SPECIAL EVENTS) **FREE**

Special Events

Fall Fiesta of Arts. *Swan Lake Gardens, 10 Mood Ave, Sumter. Phone 803/436-2258.* Features visual and performing arts, concerts, and choral groups. Third weekend in Oct.

Sumter Iris Festival. Fireworks display, parade, art show, golf and tennis tournaments, barbecue cook-off, local talent exhibition, square dance, iris gardens display. Late May.

Limited-Service Hotel

★ **FAIRFIELD INN.** *2390 Broad St, Sumter (29150). Phone 803/469-9001; toll-free 800/228-2800; fax 803/469-9070. www.fairfieldinn.com.* Close to a number of area universities and colleges, as well as the Swan Lake Iris Gardens and the Sumter Opera House, this well-appointed hotel is sure to please guests. 124 rooms, 2 story. Complimentary continental breakfast. Check-in 3 pm, check-out noon. Fitness room. Outdoor pool. Business center. **$**

🧍 🏊 🏋️

Walterboro (E-4)

See also Allendale, Beaufort, Charleston

Settled 1784
Population 5,153
Area Code 843
Zip 29488
Information Walterboro-Colleton Chamber of Commerce, 109-C Benson St, PO Box 426; phone 843/549-9595
Web Site www.walterboro.org

Settled in 1784 by Charleston plantation owners as a summer resort area, Walterboro has retained its charm of yesterday despite its growth. The town boasts a casual pace and rural lifestyle where people can enjoy fishing and hunting, early-19th-century architectural designs, plantations, and beach and recreational facilities.

What to See and Do

Colleton County Courthouse. *31 Klein St, Walterboro. Hampton St and Jefferies Blvd.* Building designed by Robert Mills; the first public nullification meeting in the state was held in 1828.

Colleton State Park. *147 Way 5 Ln, Canadys (29433). 11 miles N on Hwy 15. Phone 843/538-8206.* On 35 acres; tree-shaded area on banks of Edisto River. Canoeing (dock), river fishing. Nature trails. Picnicking (shelters). Camping (hook-ups, dump station). **$**

Old Colleton County Jail. *239 N Jefferies Blvd, Walterboro (29488). Phone 843/549-2303.* (1855) Neo-Gothic structure resembles a castle and is home to the Colleton Museum and the Chamber of Commerce. Served as Walterboro jail until 1937.

South Carolina Artisans Center. *334 Wichman St, Walterboro. In Hickory Valley Historic District. Phone 843/549-0011.* Features handcrafted art and gifts by regional artists. Craftspeople demonstrate their skills. Educational programs and special events also offered. (Daily; closed holidays) **FREE**

Special Events

Edisto Riverfest. *Colleton State Park, 1205 Pendleton St, Canadys. Phone 803/734-0156.* Canoe and kayak trips, river rafting, music, displays, and workshops. June.

Rice Festival. *Phone 803/549-1079.* Entertainment, parade, arts and crafts, street dances, soapbox derby. Last full weekend in Apr.

Limited-Service Hotel

★ ★ **COMFORT INN & SUITES.** *97 Downs Ln, Walterboro (29488). Phone 843/538-5911; toll-free 800/ 424-6423; fax 843/538-3673. www.comfortinn.com.* 96 rooms, 2 story. Complimentary continental breakfast. Check-in 2 pm, check-out 11 am. High-speed Internet access. Restaurant. Fitness room. Outdoor pool. Business center. **$**

Index

Quality Inn Merry Acres (Albany, GA), *6*

Quality Inn on the Lake (Birmingham, AL), *85*

Quality Inn West End (Richmond, VA), *194*

R

R. J. Reynolds Tobacco Company, Whitaker Park Cigarette Plant (Winston-Salem, NC), *178*

Race Shop Tours (Concord, NC), *127*

Radisson Hotel Birmingham (Birmingham, AL), *85*

Radisson Hotel Hampton (Hampton, VA), *182*

Radisson Hotel High Point (High Point, NC), *145*

Radisson Hotel Tallahassee (Tallahassee, FL), *98*

Radisson Plaza Hotel (Myrtle Beach, SC), *243*

Radisson Riverfront Hotel Augusta (Augusta, GA), *29*

Radisson Riverwalk Hotel (Jacksonville, FL), *94*

Raft trips (Long Creek, SC), *225*

Raft trips. Southeastern Expeditions (Atlanta, GA), *38*

Rainbow Cafe (Charlotte, NC), *125*

Rainbow Row (Charleston, SC), *217*

Ramada Inn (Kill Devil Hills, NC), *148*

Ramada Inn (Montgomery, AL), *88*

Ramada Inn (Montgomery, AL), *89*

Ramada Inn Mandarin (Jacksonville, FL), *94*

Ramada Inn, Albany,GA (Albany, GA), *6*

Ramada Limited (Charlotte, NC), *122*

Ramada Plaza (Virginia Beach, VA), *199*

Ramada Plaza (Columbia, SC), *228*

Ranch House (Charlotte, NC), *125*

Raven Rock State Park (Lillington, NC), *166*

Ray's Killer Creek Chop House (Alpharetta, GA), *7*

Ray's on the River (Atlanta, GA), *25*

Rectory Square (Camden, SC), *210*

Red Bluff Cottage Bed (Montgomery, AL), *89*

Red Fish (Hilton Head Island, SC), *240*

Red Top Mountain State Lodge Park (Cartersville, GA), *36*

Redcliffe (Beech Island, SC), *205*

Reed Bingham State Park (Adel, GA), *5*

Reed Gold Mine State Historic Site (Midland, NC), *127*

Regency Inn - Albany (Albany, GA), *6*

Regency Square (Richmond, VA), *193*

Regional Museum (Spartanburg, SC), *248*

Regional Ogeechee Fair (Statesboro, GA), *74*

Renaissance Asheville Hotel (Asheville, NC), *106*

Renaissance Charleston Hotel Historic District (Charleston, SC), *220*

Renaissance Pineisle Resort And Golf Club (Buford, GA), *33*

Renaissance Suites (Charlotte, NC), *123*

Resaca Confederate Cemetery (Calhoun, GA), *34*

Restaurant Eugene (Atlanta, GA), *25*

Revolutionary War Field Days (Camden, SC), *210*

Reynolda House, Museum of American Art (Winston-Salem, NC), *178*

Rheinland Haus (Charlotte, NC), *125*

Rhett House Inn (Beaufort, SC), *208*

Rialto (Wrightsville Beach, NC), *180*

Rice Festival (Walterboro, SC), *251*

Rice Museum (Georgetown, SC), *233*

Rice Paddy (Georgetown, SC), *234*

Richard B. Russell Scenic Highway (Helen, GA), *50*

Richard Petty Driving Experience (Concord, NC), *127*

Richmond Braves (Richmond, VA), *193*

Richmond Hill Inn (Asheville, NC), *107*

Richmond Newspapers Marathon (Richmond, VA), *194*

Rickwood Caverns State Park (Warrior, AL), *83*

Ristorante Divino (Columbia, SC), *229*

Ritz-Carlton Lodge, Reynolds Plantation (Greensboro, GA), *49*

Ritz-Carlton, Amelia Island (Amelia Island, FL), *89*

Ritz-Carlton, Atlanta (Atlanta, GA), *18*

Ritz-Carlton, Buckhead (Atlanta, GA), *18*

Rivendell Bed and Breakfast (Watkinsville, GA), *10*

River Forest Manor (Belhaven, NC), *110*

River Forest Manor (Belhaven, NC), *111*

River House (Savannah, GA), *71*

River Park North Science and Nature Center (Greenville, NC), *141*

River Room (Atlanta, GA), *25*

River Room (Georgetown, SC), *234*

River Street Inn (Savannah, GA), *70*

Riverbanks Zoo and Garden (Columbia, SC), *227*

Riverfest (Wilmington, NC), *175*

Riverfest Weekend (Columbus, GA), *39*

Rivers Bridge State Historic Site (Allendale, SC), *206*

Riverside Art Festival (Jacksonville, FL), *93*

Riverside Arts Festival (Bainbridge, GA), *30*

Riverwalk (Augusta, GA), *29*

Road Atlanta (Gainesville, GA), *48*

Roanoke Island Festival Park (Manteo, NC), *153*

Roanoke Rapids Lake (Roanoke Rapids, NC), *164*

Robert Mills Historic House and Park (Columbia, SC), *227*

Robert Ruark Chili Cook Off (Southport, NC), *169*

Robert Toombs House State Historic Site (Washington, GA), *79*

Robert W. Woodruff Arts Center (Atlanta, GA), *14*

Rock Bottom (Atlanta, GA), *26*

Rock Eagle Effigy (Eatonton, GA), *45*

Rogallo Kite Festival (Nags Head, NC), *156*

Rome-Days Inn Downtown (Rome, GA), *65*

Rooney's (St. Simons Island, GA), *74*

Rose Festival (Thomasville, GA), *75*

Rose Hill Plantation State Historic Site (Union, SC), *226*

Rosehill Inn (Wilmington, NC), *176*

Roy's Riverboat Landing (Wilmington, NC), *177*

Rudee's (Virginia Beach, VA), *200*

Rudolph's (Gainesville, GA), *49*

Ruffner Mountain Nature Center (Birmingham, AL), *83*

Ruth's Chris Steak House (Atlanta, GA), *26*

Ruth's Chris Steak House (Richmond, VA), *196*

Ryan's Restaurant (Winston-Salem, NC), *179*

S

Sadlers Creek State Park (Anderson, SC), *206*

Salem Academy and College (Winston-Salem, NC), *178*

Sam Bass Gallery (Concord, NC), *127*

Sam Miller's Warehouse (Richmond, VA), *197*

Samford University (Birmingham, AL), *83*

Notes

Notes

Notes

Notes

Notes

Notes

Notes

Notes

Notes

Notes

Notes

Notes